third edition

Measurement for Evaluation
in Physical Education and Exercise Science

Ted A. Baumgartner
University of Georgia

Andrew S. Jackson
University of Houston

wcb
Wm. C. Brown Publishers
Dubuque, Iowa

Book Team

Editor *Brenda Flemming Roesch*
Assistant Editor *Raphael Kadushin*
Production Editor *Kay J. Brimeyer*
Designer *Kay Dolby*
Permissions Editor *Carla D. Arnold*
Photo Research Editor *Carol Smith*
Product Manager *Marcia Stout*

wcb group

Wm. C. Brown *Chairman of the Board*
Mark C. Falb *President and Chief Executive Officer*

wcb

Wm. C. Brown Publishers, College Division

G. Franklin Lewis *Executive Vice-President, General Manager*
E. F. Jogerst *Vice-President, Cost Analyst*
George Wm. Bergquist *Editor in Chief*
Beverly Kolz *Director of Production*
Chris C. Guzzardo *Vice-President, Director of Sales and Marketing*
Bob McLaughlin *National Sales Manager*
Julie A. Kennedy *Production Editorial Manager*
Marilyn A. Phelps *Manager of Design*
Faye M. Schilling *Photo Research Manager*

GV436 B33 1987

Contents

Preface to the third edition

One skill that physical education teachers and exercise specialists must possess is the ability to measure and evaluate the participants in their program. Our philosophy, reflected in this book, is that tests need to be used in a sound manner. The understanding of essential statistical techniques, relevant measurement theory, and available tests enables creative professionals to develop valid methods of evaluation.

As we prepared this third edition we made several major changes. All material we believe should not be taught in an undergraduate or masters level measurement course was eliminated. Several chapters in the second edition were altered considerably. The chapters devoted to reliability and validity, and to physical fitness in the second edition were each divided into two chapters. Also, the chapters on general motor ability and measurement in the psychomotor domain were combined, and the chapter dealing with evaluating student achievement was moved from the eleventh to the fifth chapter. Finally, considerably more emphasis was placed on measurement techniques for the students seeking a career other than in teaching, and the application of microcomputers in measurement was vastly expanded.

The tests we included in the third edition are those that physical educators and exercise specialists can use in their day-to-day programs. Space did not permit us to include all the tests they might use. However, we provided appropriate references so that you may consult additional sources to find needed tests.

Since the publication of the second edition, new issues relevant to measurement and evaluation have been published. We revised the third edition in light of those new findings. In particular, two factors are responsible for the major revisions. These are: (1) Expansion of nonteaching careers for physical education teachers and exercise specialists. (2) Expanded availability and use of microcomputers.

Numerous career opportunities exist for physical education teachers and exercise specialists in nonteaching settings like adult fitness, corporate fitness, and physical performance testing. Many of the measurement techniques and tests used by teachers are useful to the nonteacher. However, there are some measurement procedures unique to nonteaching situations and these techniques have been included in this third edition, most notably in the chapter on adult fitness testing.

Microcomputers are abundant in the schools, businesses, industries, and homes. They are so powerful that they can do most of the things that were once restricted to big mainframe computers. Specialized training is required to write computer programs. However, for many applications, well-designed computer programs exist. We have found that undergraduate students can learn, without difficulty, how to use standard computer programs for data analysis and other applications. Thus we have revised the third edition to include more computer applications. These appear in several chapters.

We have tried to present measurement in physical education from a sound theoretical standpoint. We feel that physical educators and exercise specialists will be better able to apply the theory of measurement and evaluation if they first understand it. We hope that this book prepares students to cope with any problems of measurement and evaluation that they may encounter once they are on the job.

We would like to express our gratitude to the many people who reviewed the second edition of the book or the third edition manuscript and offered excellent suggestions for improvements. They include Professor Andrew Proctor (California Polytechnic State University), Professor Stephen Langendorfer (Kent State University), Professor Dale Mood (University of Colorado–Boulder), Professor Antoinette Tiburzi (SUNY at Cortland), Professor George McGlynn (University of San Francisco), Professor Harry Duvall (University of Georgia–Athens).

We would also like to thank our wives for their patience and consideration during the preparation of the manuscript. Finally, we would like to express our thanks to former teachers, who contributed to our knowledge of measurement techniques, as well as our former students, who forced us to bridge the gap between theory and practice.

T. A. B.
A. S. J.

To the student

The major goal of this text is to help you apply the principles of measurement and evaluation to your job. Often evaluation is viewed as a necessary evil, not directly related to the real purpose of the job. This text was designed to help you learn how to use evaluation as an essential part of the total process.

We developed the text with two purposes in mind. First, we want to help you master the essential content, principles, and concepts needed to become an effective evaluator. We tried to provide the practical aspects, the "how" and the "why" of evaluation. We want this text to help you build a foundation based on theoretical concepts, so that you can then apply these concepts in developing, using, and evaluating various tests.

Second, we designed the text to provide the practical skills and materials that you will need. We provide a wide assortment of tests, administrative instructions, and norms. We selected the tests, which provide the "how" of evaluation, either for their application to the job setting or for their value for teaching basic concepts discussed in the text.

A practical tool for you to use now and later is the computer. Practical computer applications are provided by example with a standard program, SPSS, available at most college and university computer centers, and several microcomputer programs. Learn to use the computer as a student while help is available and it will be easy to use whatever computer support is available on the job.

The approach we use in the text follows a teaching method that has influenced recent educational thought. It is basically an outgrowth of Benjamin Bloom's ideas on "mastery learning." The method stresses letting the student know what is to be learned; providing the material to accomplish the learning; and furnishing evaluation procedures to determine whether the learning has been achieved.

This approach, formative evaluation, is an essential feature of mastery learning. Psychologists maintain that feedback is one of the most important factors in learning. Formative evaluation is designed to provide that feedback. It enables you to diagnose weaknesses. It lets you know the content you have mastered, so that you can put more effort into problem areas.

Instructional objectives at the beginning of each chapter enable you to focus your attention on the concepts to be learned. The **text**—supplemented with class lectures, discussions, projects, and laboratory experiments—provides the information you need to help you achieve the objectives. **Test questions** at the end of each chapter help you determine whether you have mastered the skills set forth.

The formative evaluation in this text offers two types of questions. The first, in **question/answer format,** is most appropriate for testing yourself on the statistics content. If you cannot calculate a statistic, you have not mastered the technique. The second type of question requires you to define, summarize, analyze, apply, or synthesize content. This is typical of an **essay-type question,** and is more appropriate for testing yourself on basic content, principles, and concepts.

A common complaint of students is that they dislike learning by rote. We hope that the techniques of instructional objectives and formative evaluation will help you to avoid that approach. The objectives and evaluation questions identify the key points in a given chapter. Once you have read the chapter itself, you should be familiar with these points. Finally we hope that by using this approach you will master important content rather than just isolated facts.

We are aware that each student studies differently. However, you may find that the following suggestions will help you achieve mastery learning.

1. Before reading a chapter, review the instructional objectives and formative evaluation questions for the chapter. This gives you an overview and directs your attention to the important content areas.

2. Read the chapter, underlining important content. Also underline material that you do not fully understand. After reading the entire chapter, return to the underlined parts to reinforce the important content and to try to grasp the material you do not fully understand.

3. Without referring to the text, answer the formative evaluation questions. After you have written your answers, go back to the material in the text and check your answers. Spend additional time on the questions that you did not answer correctly. If you do not feel comfortable with your answers to some questions, spend more time on these as well.

4. Practical learning activities are provided at the end of each chapter. Try them. We have found that these exercises help students gain further insight into the statistical or theoretical concepts being stressed. (Many of these suggested activities are enjoyable as well as helpful.)

5. When studying for summative exams, use the formative evaluation questions and your corrected answer as the basis for final review of the instructional objectives of each chapter. Examine the list of key words at the end of each chapter. They are a second means for formative evaluation. If you find that you cannot think of a precise definition of a term, go back over the chapter until you find the term's definition.

We wish you good luck with your evaluating techniques.

T. A. B.
A. S. J.

Introduction

Part I

Measurement and Evaluation for a Changing Profession

1

Contents

Key Words

Criterion-Referenced Standard
Evaluation
Formative Evaluation
Health-Related Fitness
Mainframe Computer
Measurement
Norm-Referenced Standard
Norms
Objective
Subjective
SPSS
Summative Evaluation

Objectives

The dynamic nature of physical education is altering the type of measurement and evaluation skills needed by physical education teachers and exercise specialists. Graduates of physical education programs are not only becoming teachers and coaches, but also exercise specialists, physical and occupational therapists, sport psychologists, and consultants. This chapter should help you understand the nature of these changes and how measurement and evaluation are affected.

After reading chapter 1 you should be able to:

1. Differentiate between measurement and evaluation.
2. Define and differentiate between criterion- and norm-referenced standards.
3. Define and differentiate between formative and summative methods of evaluation.
4. Cite the evidence supporting the growth of health-related fitness.
5. Identify the impact of equal opportunity on physical testing.
6. Be knowledgeable of the changes in computer technology and list its impact on physical education teachers and exercise specialists.

INTRODUCTION

Americans tend to regard test results as a valid basis for decision making. Certainly they govern such crucial matters as student promotions and college acceptances. Unfortunately, we give too little attention to the quality of test results and judgments involved in such decision-making processes.

The terms measurement and evaluation are widely used, but often with little regard for their meanings. **Measurement** is the collection of information on which a decision is based; **evaluation** is the use of measurements in making decisions. This chapter should clarify these concepts within the changing context of physical education and exercise science and introduce the procedures that have evolved to meet the challenges they offer.

MEASUREMENT AND EVALUATION

Measurement and evaluation are interdependent concepts. Evaluation is a process that uses measurements and the purpose of measurement is to collect information. Tests are used for this purpose. In the evaluation process, information is interpreted according to established standards so that decisions can be made. Clearly, the success of evaluation depends on the quality of the data collected. If test results are not consistent (or reliable) and truthful (or valid), accurate evaluation is impossible. The measurement process is the first step in evaluation; improved measurement leads to accurate evaluation.

People are different. They vary in body size, shape, speed, strength, and in many other respects. Measurement determines the degree to which an individual possesses a defined characteristic. It involves first defining the characteristic to be measured and then selecting the instrument with which to measure it (Ebel 1973). Stopwatches, tape measures, written tests, attitude scales, skinfold calipers, treadmills, and bicycle ergometers are common instruments used by physical education teachers and exercise specialists to obtain measurements.

Test scores vary between being objective or subjective. A test is **objective** when two or more people score the same test and assign similar scores. Tests that are most objective are those that have a defined scoring system and are administered by trained testers. A multiple-choice written test, stopwatch, skinfold calipers, and ECG heart rate tracing all have a defined scoring system. Testers need to be trained to secure objective measurements. For example, if percent body fat is to be measured by the skinfold method, the tester needs to be trained in the proper method of measuring a skinfold with a caliper. A **subjective** test lacks a standardized scoring system, which introduces a source of measurement error. We use objective measurements whenever possible because they are more reliable than subjective measurements.

Evaluation is a dynamic decision-making process focusing on changes that have been made. This process involves (1) collecting suitable data (measurement); (2) judging the value of these data according to some standard; and (3) making decisions based on these data. The function of evaluation is to facilitate rational decisions. For the teacher, this can be to facilitate student learning and for the exercise specialist, this could mean helping someone establish scientifically-sound weight reduction goals.

Figure 1.1 A systematic model for evaluation.

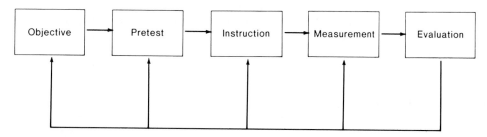

A Systematic Model of Evaluation

Figure 1.1 is a model that can be used for evaluation. It shows the relationship of objectives, instruction, testing, and evaluation procedures. The model is equally valid for the public school physical education teacher and the adult fitness specialist.

Objectives.   Preparation of objectives is the first step in the evaluation process because objectives determine what we will seek to achieve. It gives direction to the instructional or training program.

Pretest.   With some type of pretest, one can answer three questions: (1) How much has already been learned or achieved? (2) What are the individual's current status and capabilities? (3) What type of activity should be prescribed to help achieve the objectives? Pretesting does not necessarily involve administering the same test that will be given after instruction; it can include any form of measurement that helps to answer these questions. For example, a simple health risk appraisal might be used prior to the start of a fitness class to assess the cardiovascular risk of the participants.

Instruction.   Sound instructional and training methods are needed to achieve the agreed-on objectives. Different instructional procedures may be needed to meet students' individual needs. A key to a successful adult fitness program is an individualized program that meets the participant's needs, interests, and capabilities.

Measurement.   This involves the selection or development of a test to gauge the achievement of the objectives. It is crucial that the test be designed to measure the behavior specified in the objectives. Often, teachers will need to develop their own tests because standardized tests are not consistent with instructional objectives. The type of tests used in an adult fitness program may vary for several reasons. For example, if the program is medically supervised, a maximal stress test may be used to measure changes in aerobic fitness, but if not medically supervised, a submaximal fitness test is the better choice.

Evaluation.   Once the instructional or training phase has been completed and achievement has been measured, test results are judged (i.e., evaluated) to determine whether the desired changes were made to achieve the stated objective. At this stage, you may discover the objectives are not appropriate and may need to be altered.

Functions of Measurement and Evaluation

Too often tests are administered with no definite purpose in mind. The ultimate purpose of testing is to enhance the decision-making process so that instruction is improved. Beyond this, however, six general purposes that facilitate the instructional process are widely accepted:

Placement.   Tests can be used to place students in classes or groups according to their abilities. Adult fitness tests are used to determine current status so an individualized program can be prescribed.

Diagnosis.   Tests can be used to diagnose weaknesses, so that individual remedial work can be given. Whereas placement usually involves the status of the individual relative to others, diagnosis is used to isolate specific deficiencies that make for low status.

Evaluation of Achievement.   The goal of testing is to determine whether important objectives have been reached. Placement, diagnosis, and the evaluation of achievement together form the basis of individualized instruction.

Prediction.   Test results can be used to predict one's level of achievement in future activities. Prediction is like placement in that it seeks, from a measure of present status, information on future achievement; it differs from placement in helping students to select the activities they are most likely to master. For example, a student's performance in a physical education program may suggest a high probability of success in interschool athletics. An adult found to have a high aerobic capacity may decide to engage in road racing or become a triathlete.

Program Evaluation.   Test results of participants can be used as one bit of evidence to evaluate the program. To illustrate, fitness scores of school-aged children are falling (see chapter 9). By plotting the results of a school district against national norms or comparing the yearly changes made within a school district, general comparisons can be made.

Motivation.   Test scores can be motivating. Successful achievement of important standards can encourage one to achieve higher levels of performance.

Standards for Evaluation

Evaluation is the process of giving meaning to a measurement by judging it against some standard. The two most widely used types of standards are criterion- and norm-referenced. Glaser (1963) explains that scores on testing instruments can provide two kinds of information. One concerns the degree to which the student has attained a particular level of skill, determined by criterion-referenced standards. Developing **criterion-referenced standards** requires explicit definition of the task to be achieved. Often expert judgment must be used to determine a criterion-referenced standard. For example, a criterion-referenced standard for an adult fitness course could be the ability to jog continuously for 30 minutes. This standard would be in keeping with the recommendation of the American College of Sports Medicine (1978). In contrast, **norm-referenced standards** involve the hierarchical ordering of individuals. Statistical procedures are used to develop norm-referenced standards, often simply called **norms.**

Norm-referenced standards are used to judge an individual's performance in relation to the performances of other members of a well-defined group, for example, 11-year-old boys. Percentile norms are most commonly used. This type of norm reflects the percentage of the group that can be expected to score below a given value. For example, a mile run time of 11:31 for a boy 11 years of age is at the 25th percentile; only 25% ran slower, while 75% of the 11-year-old boys could be expected to exceed this time. Percentile norms are used at the Cooper Medical Clinic, Dallas, Texas, to communicate fitness and health status to patients. Pollock, Wilmore and Fox (1984) have published the Cooper percentile norms. Fitness and motor performance test percentile norms are provided in chapters 7 through 9 of this text.

In many instances, normative data are used to develop criterion-referenced standards. For example, the AAHPERD Health-Related Fitness Test (1980) furnishes both norm- and criterion-referenced standards. Several measurement and fitness experts studied the normative data and then logically developed the criterion-referenced standards. There are very few instances where a criterion-referenced standard can be explicitly defined; one example would be a body temperature of 98.6 degrees. The percent body fat criterion often used to define adult obesity is 22% for men and 32% for women (Jackson and Pollock 1985; Lohman 1982). These levels were derived from examining normative data, but it is not presently possible to determine with precision the percent body fat level where someone would become more prone to obesity-related diseases. The percent body fat levels represent a realistic level defined through logical judgment and an understanding of normative data.

Both types of standards can be used to judge performance. The selection is governed by the type of decision to be made. Assume, for example, that a test for a unit on physical fitness measures the distance a student can run and that a distance of 1.5 miles in 12 minutes is the criterion-referenced standard. Further assume a student runs 1.75 miles in the 12-minute period. The student has achieved an acceptable level of physical fitness by our criterion and the norm-referenced standard would compare the distance the student ran to that run by other students of the same sex and age, tested under the same conditions. Using the norm-referenced standard, the teacher could say that the student's performance is at the 99th percentile—1.75 miles is longer than the distances covered by 99% of students of the same age and sex.

Criterion-referenced standards are useful for setting performance standards for all students. Norm-referenced standards are valuable for comparisons among individuals when the situation requires a degree of selectivity. Using the criterion-referenced standards, the teacher would determine simply that the student who ran 1.75 miles in 12 minutes had achieved an acceptable level of fitness. But using the norm-referenced standard, the teacher could decide that the student had good prospects of excelling as a distance runner. On the basis of this judgment, the student could be encouraged to become involved in distance running.

Formative and Summative Evaluation

Typically, **summative evaluation** involves the administration of tests at the conclusion of an instructional unit or training period. Motor-learning research indicates that feedback is one of the most powerful variables in learning and testing during instruction, while formative evaluation enhances learning. Bloom et al. (1971) postulate that to achieve mastery, evaluation needs to be continuous.

Formative evaluation was developed initially for use in classroom settings. **Formative evaluation** begins during the early stages and continues throughout instruction. It involves dividing instruction into smaller units of learning, and evaluating the student's mastery of these subunits during instruction. Its main purpose is "to determine the degree of mastery of a given learning task and to pinpoint the part of the task not mastered" (Bloom et al. 1971, p. 61). The strength of formative evaluation is that it provides feedback.

In contrast, summative evaluation takes place at the end of instruction. It is used to determine whether broad objectives have been achieved. Summative evaluation is also useful in areas of learning when goals cannot be explicitly defined. The similarities and differences between formative and summative evaluation identified by Bloom et al. (1971) are summarized in table 1.1.

Formative and summative evaluation and master learning (Bloom et al. 1971) were developed for use by classroom teachers. However, the logic of the system can be applied to adult fitness programs. Helping adults set realistic fitness goals and using periodic testing to determine current status can be used to provide feedback facilitating achievement. A key element of a successful self-supervised fitness program for NASA executives was periodic fitness testing (Owen, Beard and Jackson 1980). Measuring body weight daily is a behavioral strategy used for weight loss programs (deBakey et al. 1984). The fitness training program can become a major source of information for formative evaluation. To illustrate, increasing the intensity and/or duration of aerobic exercise is not only a sound instructional method of improving fitness, but it can provide formative evaluation. At the end of this chapter is an example of a computer generated exercise prescription (see figure 1.13). Over the six-step prescription, exercise intensity has been increased from 65% to 75% of maximal aerobic capacity and duration from 25–45 minutes. The increase in caloric expenditure can serve as a means for formative evaluation; it communicates to the participant that improvements in fitness are being achieved. A fitness test at the end of training can serve as a summative evaluation. This is shown in chapter 8.

You are encouraged to use the formative evaluation provided at the end of each chapter. After you have read the chapter, attempt to answer the questions. If you cannot answer a question or if you feel unsure of your answer, this is an indication you need additional work. The key element of formative evaluation is the feedback it provides; it communicates to the participant what yet needs to be achieved. For this course, your instructor will likely administer several major tests that will evaluate your ability to integrate and apply the readings. This would be an example of summative evaluation.

Table 1.1

Similarities and Differences between Formative and Summative Evaluation.

	FORMATIVE	SUMMATIVE
Purpose	Feedback to student and teacher on student progress throughout an instructional unit	Certification or grading at the end of a unit, semester, or course
Time	During instruction	At the end of a unit, semester, or course
Emphasis in evaluation	Explicitly defined behaviors	Broader categories of behaviors or combinations of several specific behaviors
Standard	Criterion-referenced	Norm-referenced but can be criterion-referenced

A CHANGING PROFESSION

Our profession is changing. When we published the first edition of this text in 1975, professional physical education curricula were designed to produce teachers and coaches. This has changed. Most colleges and universities still have large teacher education programs, but the professional preparation curriculum has been expanded with more emphasis on exercise science. Many physical education graduates are now being employed in the health and fitness industry. This shift can be traced to several different reasons, but declining public school enrollments, advances in exercise science, and public interest in adult health and fitness are major reasons.

Health and fitness has become big industry. Americans are seeking ways to become physically active. Corporations are starting health promotion programs in an effort to keep employee morale at a high level and cut health care costs. Fitness programs are often the key element for the health promotion program. Medically supervised exercise programs are being prescribed for patients with a high risk of a heart attack and for cardiac patients. It is now common practice to have coronary bypass patients on a treadmill three days after cardiac surgery. Private fitness and athletic clubs are opening to help meet the increased demands of American adults for physical activity. This interest in adult fitness has increased the need for trained exercise specialists.

The process of measurement and evaluations used by the teacher and coach in the public school and by the exercise specialist is essentially the same. The measurement concepts of reliability (accuracy of data) and validity (truthfulness of data) are equally important for both environments. The statistical procedures used to establish test reliability and validity and norms are identical. The testing environment is different. The teacher will be in the gymnasium or classroom and use fitness and motor-skill tests that are feasible for mass testing. In contrast, the exercise specialist will likely test one person at a time in a laboratory and will use specialized equipment (see figure 1.2).

Figure 1.2 Graded exercise stress test conducted at NASA is administered on a treadmill with heart rate measured by an electrocardiogram.

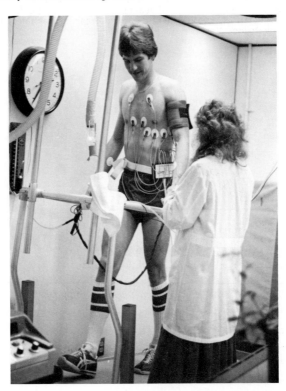

Important changes in education and society will inevitably affect the process of measurement and evaluation. Three current factors especially influencing the process of contemporary physical education measurement and evaluation are: (1) the increased evidence supporting the therapeutic value of aerobic exercise has placed more emphasis on health-related fitness testing; (2) the American value of equal opportunity has placed more emphasis on physical testing of female athletes and women seeking employment in physically demanding occupations; and (3) the dramatic advances in computer technology have changed the measurement and evaluation methods. New methods are being introduced daily.

HEALTH-RELATED PHYSICAL FITNESS

Physical educators have long believed that exercise is important to maintain good health. Today, degenerative diseases (cancer, heart disease, strokes) have replaced communicable diseases (tuberculosis, pneumonia) as leading causes of death in Americans (see figure 1.3). Cardiovascular disease is the number one public health hazard in the

Figure 1.3 Changes in the major cause of death for the years 1900 to 1980. The graph shows the number of deaths per 100,000. Cardiovascular diseases (CVD) surpassed pneumonia and influenza in about 1910 as the major cause of death of Americans and the CVD rate continued to grow until 1960, when it started to drop. The rate is still dropping. (Graph developed by MacASJ from data published by Pollock, Wilmore and Fox, 1984, p. 25.)

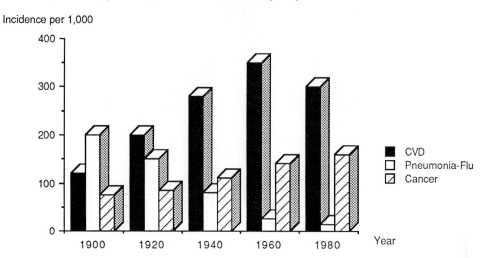

United States and other highly industrialized countries (see figure 1.4). In 1980, cardiovascular diseases, particularly coronary heart disease and strokes, were the leading cause of death in Americans. Figures published by the American Heart Association reveal that about 1.5 million Americans will have a heart attack this year, and only 50% will survive. Of all American males between the ages of 40 and 60 years, 10% will develop symptoms of heart disease. In over half of these men, the first indication will be an unexpected heart attack. Medical researchers have shown that poor aerobic fitness, obesity, and lack of development of certain types of muscular strength and flexibility are related to certain diseases. **Health-related fitness** is defined by these components.

There was an epidemic rise in the cardiovascular disease mortality rate from the early 1900s to the mid-1960s, then the trend turned downward and declined 37% between 1963 and 1982 (Kannel and Thom 1984). This translates into about 500,000 fewer cardiovascular disease deaths per year. It is not possible to determine the exact reason for this change, but many believe it can be traced to a healthier life-style that includes a sound diet, exercise, and weight control.

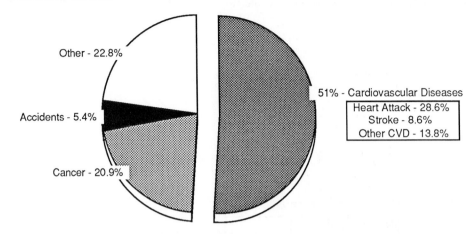

Figure 1.4 Leading causes of death in the United States, 1980. Data from the National Center for Health Statistics, U.S. Public Health Service, Department of Health and Human Services. (Graphics by MacASJ)

Medical scientists have sought to identify factors related to cardiovascular diseases. These are known as risk factors. The American Heart Association has identified several risk factors that are associated with increased chances of developing heart disease in later life. The most potent risk factors include hypertension (high blood pressure), high levels of blood cholesterol, and habitual cigarette smoking. These major risk factors cause a person to have a greater than average chance of experiencing a major cardiovascular event such as a heart attack or stroke.

Medical scientists have studied the role of exercise on cardiovascular disease risk. Recent research by prominent medical researchers have documented that caloric expenditure and body weight are also important cardiovascular disease risk factors.

Caloric Expenditure as a Risk Factor

Occupational physical activity has been shown to be related to heart disease. Individuals employed in physically demanding jobs have a lower incidence of heart disease (Morris 1953; Taylor 1960). Paffenbarger and his associates (1977; 1978; 1984) have been able to go one step further and show that high levels of caloric[1] expenditure ($\geq$2,000 kcal/week) from both recreation and occupational exercise, provide a level of protection from heart attacks. They first studied longshoremen (1977) and quantified the energy expended at work. They were able to show that the workers who expended the fewest calories at work had a heart attack risk over eight times higher than the longshoremen who had the higher energy expenditure jobs. The combination of low-energy output, heavy smoking, and higher blood pressure increased the longshoremen's risk by over 20-fold and it was estimated that if these adverse influences were

---

1. The scientific term used to define energy expenditure is kilocalorie, often simply referred to as calorie. One kilocalorie *represents the heat required* to raise the temperature of 1 kilogram of water 1° C.

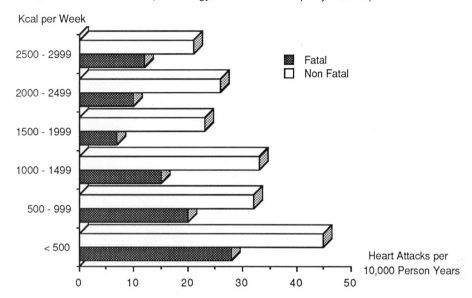

Figure 1.5 Age-adjusted first heart attack rates, by physical activity index in a 6–10 year follow-up of Harvard male alumni. (Graph compiled from data published by Paffenbarger, R. S., Jr., A. L. Wing, and R. T. Hyde, 1978. "Physical Activity as an Index of Heart Attack Risk in College Alumni," *American Journal of Epidemiology,* 108:161–175. Graph by MacASJ)

controlled, the longshoremen could have had an 88% reduction in their fatal heart attack rate during the 22 years they were studied.

In a second study (Paffenbarger et al. 1978; 1984), the exercise habits of Harvard alumni were studied. These data were assessed by a survey, and standard methods were used to convert their self-report exercise into caloric expenditure. It was found that a threshold of energy expenditure was related to the risk of heart attacks. These data are presented in figure 1.5.

The Paffenbarger data clearly show a steady decrease in both fatal and nonfatal heart attacks for energy expenditure rates ranging from 500 to 2,000 kcal/week. After the 2,000 kcal/week level is reached, the trend levels off. The energy expenditure of the alumni included exercise from both recreational activities such as playing vigorous sports and daily tasks like walking and climbing stairs.

Many mistakenly believe that athletic participation promotes health and fitness. Certainly, the vigorous exercise required during training develops an athlete's fitness, but what about the long-term benefits of college athletics? Paffenbarger and his associates examined the Harvard alumni who were college athletes and compared them with nonathletes. This comparison is provided in figure 1.6. Being a college athlete does not provide protection from a heart attack. Athletes were like nonathletes, those who exercised at the 2,000 kcal/week level had fewer heart attacks than their more sedentary counterparts. In fact, the greatest difference was found for the alumni who expended fewer than 500 kcal/week. Sedentary athletes had more heart attacks than the sedentary nonathletes.

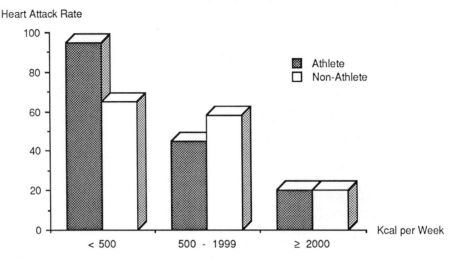

Figure 1.6 Age-adjusted heart attack rates among Harvard male alumni athletes and nonathletes in a 6–10 year follow-up. The heart attack rate is expressed as the number of heart attacks per 10,000 people-years of observation. Graph developed by MacASJ based on data from R. S. Paffenbarger, Jr., A. L. Wing and R. T. Hyde, "Physical Activity as an Index of Heart Attack Risk in College Alumni" in *American Journal of Epidemiology, 108,* 161–175, 1978.

Paffenbarger and his associates have been able to show with both their longshoremen and Harvard alumni data that exercise was an independent cardiovascular disease risk factor. Provided in figure 1.7 is the effect of sedentary living in combination with other major risk factors on alumni heart attack risk. The addition of sedentary living (SD) to the established risk factors of hypertension (BP) and cigarette smoking (CS) substantially increased heart disease risk. Being hypertensive, a cigarette smoker, and inactive increases the risk of heart attack by over seven times. This demonstrates that a sedentary life-style is a risk factor independent of hypertension and smoking. High levels of caloric expenditure are achieved with aerobic exercise of a suitable intensity (i.e., 50% to 85% of maximal aerobic capacity), for a suitable duration and frequency. Increasing aerobic fitness enhances one's caloric expenditure capacity and these data support the validity of aerobic fitness as a major component of health.

Obesity as a Risk Factor

Data from insurance companies have consistently demonstrated that people who were overweight had a higher incidence of many degenerative diseases including hypertension, heart disease, strokes, and diabetes. Data recently published from the Framingham heart study (Hubert et al. 1983) conclusively showed that adults who were obese for an extended period of time (i.e., at least 8 years) were at a higher cardiovascular disease risk than average, and changes in body weight altered the risk odds. These trends are shown in figures 1.8 and 1.9.

Figure 1.7 Age-adjusted relative risk of first heart attack among Harvard male alumni in a 6–10 year follow-up by specific combinations of cardiovascular risk factors, including BP, history of high blood pressure; CS, cigarette-smoking habit; and SD, physical activity index < 2,000 kcal/ week. A value of 1 is used to represent the absence of all three risk factors; thus the relative risk can be interpreted as the number of times the presence of the factor increases the risk of a heart attack. (Graph developed from data published by Paffenbarger et al., [1978]. Graph by MacASJ)

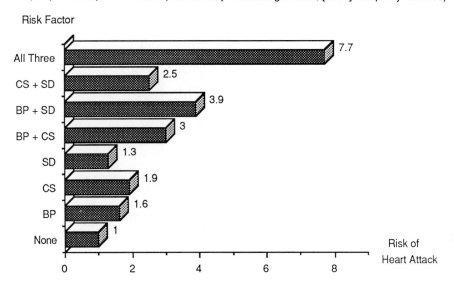

Figure 1.8 Twenty-six year incidence of cardiovascular disease by Metropolitan Relative Weight at entry for men and women in the Framingham heart study. The subjects were under 50 years of age and free of major risk factors. (Graph was compiled from data published by Hubert, H. B. et al., 1983. "Obesity as an Independent Risk Factor for Cardiovascular Disease: A 26-Year Follow-Up of Participants in the Framingham Heart Study." *Circulation.* 67:968–977. Graph by MacASJ)

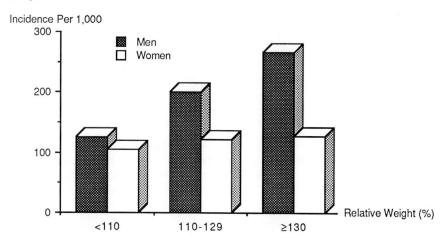

Figure 1.9 The relative odds of developing cardiovascular disease (CVD) corresponding to degrees of change in Metropolitan Relative Weight from age 25 to the date entered in the study. A relative odds of "1" is with no change in weight. These data show that losing weight decreases the risk of CVD while gaining weight increases the risk of CVD. (Graph was developed from data published by Hubert, H. B. et al., 1983. "Obesity as an Independent Risk Factor for Cardiovascular Disease: A 26-Year Follow-Up of Participants in the Framingham Heart Study." *Circulation.* 67: 968–977. Graph by MacASJ)

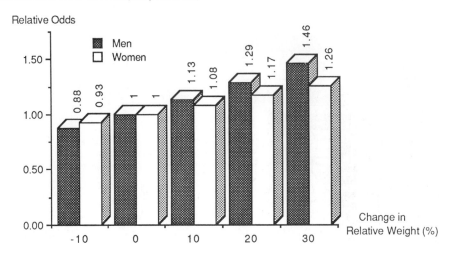

The Metropolitan Relative Weight is body weight for a given height. The data in figure 1.8 show that those individuals who were more overweight were at a higher cardiovascular disease risk. Obesity was independent of other major risk factors. The trend was especially strong for men.

The Framingham data showed that the cardiovascular disease risk was related to the number of years one was overweight, and that changes in relative weight altered the odds (see figure 1.9). For both men and women, changes in weight were directly related to cardiovascular disease risk. Adult obesity has its roots in childhood and about 85% of obese youngsters become obese adults (Pollock, Wilmore and Fox 1984). These data underscore the need to teach sound principles of weight control and support the validity of including body composition as a component of health-related fitness.

Effect of Exercise on Mortality

Aerobic exercise is not only helpful for reducing cardiovascular disease risk factors, but there is also evidence that strongly supports the conclusion that individuals who expend a sufficient number of calories through exercise have higher survival rates.

Paffenbarger and his associates (1986) showed that Harvard alumni who consistently exercised during their lifetime have a lower mortality rate than their sedentary classmates. It was discovered that alumni who walked regularly or played either light or vigorous sports (see figure 1.10) enjoyed a lower mortality rate than those who were

Figure 1.10 The graphs show the relationship between exercise and mortality rates. Mild forms of aerobic exercise such as playing light sports and walking promote health. (The graph was developed from data published by Paffenbarger, R. S. et al., 1986. ''Physical Activity, All-Cause Mortality, and Longevity of College Alumni.'' *New England Journal of Medicine.* 314:605–613. Graphs by MacASJ)

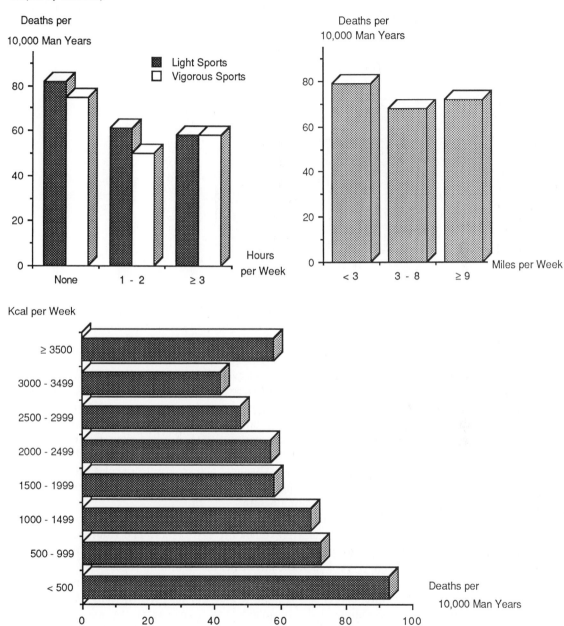

Figure 1.11 The graph shows the years added to life to age 80 from an active lifestyle. These data show the value of starting an exercise program early in life and keeping with it. The life expectancy values were adjusted for difference in blood pressure status, cigarette smoking, gain in body weight, and age of parental death; thus the added years reflect the benefit of just regular, vigorous exercise on longevity. (The graph was created from data published by Paffenbarger, R. S. et al., 1986. "Physical Activity, All-Cause Mortality, and Longevity of College Alumni." *New England Journal of Medicine*. 314:605–613. Graph by MacASJ)

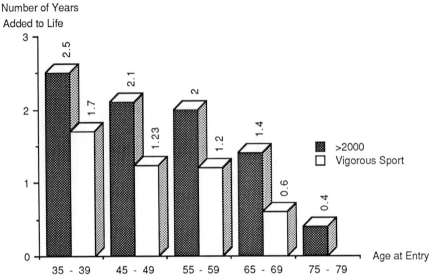

Source: Graph developed by MacASJ based on data from Pollock, M. L., J. H. Wilmore, and S. M. Fox, *Health and Fitness Through Physical Activity*. John Wiley & Sons, 1984, p. 25.

sedentary. The medical investigators discovered that the total amount of energy expended through exercise was most highly related to mortality rates. Total caloric expenditure was computed from light and vigorous sports, jogging, walking, and less strenuous daily tasks such as climbing stairs, walking to work, and working in the yard. As total caloric expenditure went up, mortality rates become progressively lower. The group who expended less than 500 kilocalories/week had the highest death rates, while the alumni who expended between 3,000 and 3,500 kcal/week enjoyed the lowest mortality rate. The data provided in figure 1.10 show that many different types of aerobic exercise can be used for promoting health.

Some dramatic data have been published from the Harvard Alumni study (see figure 1.11). Exercising regularly extends life expectancy. The data provided in the figure compare the alumni who expended 2,000 kcal/week or greater with those who were very sedentary. At age 35, the physically active alumni could be expected to live about 2.5 years longer than their sedentary classmates. This may not sound like much. However, Dr. Paffenbarger has made a rather startling comparison.[2] If all forms of cancer deaths were eliminated (i.e., nobody died from cancer), the average increase in

2. Personal communication between Andrew S. Jackson and Dr. R. Paffenbarger at the 1985 Texas Chapter Meeting of the American College of Sports Medicine, Houston, Texas.

longevity would also be just slightly over 2 years. Routine exercise is equally beneficial to cancer prevention. The data presented in figure 1.11 provide strong scientific evidence supporting the role of regular, vigorous exercise for promoting health and the value of exercising during one's entire lifetime.

Position Statements

The research showing the relationship between caloric expenditure, body fat, and cardiovascular diseases has led to the endorsement of regular, vigorous exercise for preventive medical purposes by the American Heart Association and the American Medical Association, among others. Part of the American Heart Association's position statement is quoted next.

> Evidence suggests that regular, moderate or vigorous occupational or leisure-time physical activity may protect against coronary heart disease and may improve the chances of survival from a heart attack.

In 1978, the American College of Sports Medicine (ACSM) published a position paper that provides the physiological basis for contemporary physical fitness programs. The guidelines emphasize the need for caloric expenditure sufficient to develop fitness and control body weight. The minimum energy expenditure recommended for a 70 kilogram person is 300 kilocalories per session and 900 kilocalories per week. This is less than the 2,000 kilocalorie threshold defined by Paffenbarger et al. (1978), but the ACSM guideline considers just the exercise program and not daily living tasks. A brief summary of the ACSM position is:

> Based on the existing evidence concerning exercise prescription for healthy adults and the need for guidelines, the American College of Sports Medicine makes the following recommendations for the quantity and quality of training for developing and maintaining cardiorespiratory fitness and body composition in the healthy adult:
> 1. Frequency of training. 3 to 5 days per week
> 2. Intensity of training. 60% to 90% of maximum heart rate reserve, or 50% to 85% of maximum oxygen uptake ($\dot{V}O_2$ Max)
> 3. Duration of training. 15 to 60 minutes of continuous aerobic activity. Duration is dependent on the intensity of the activity, thus lower intensity activity should be conducted over a longer period of time. Because of the importance of the "total fitness" effect and the fact that it is more readily attained in longer duration programs, and because of the potential hazards and compliance problems associated with high intensity activity, lower to moderate intensity activity of longer duration is recommended for the nonathletic adult.
> 4. Mode of activity. Any activity that uses large muscle groups, that can be maintained continuously, and is rhythmical and aerobic in nature, e.g., running-jogging, walking-hiking, swimming, skating, bicycling, rowing, cross-country skiing, rope skipping, and various endurance game activities.

Health-Related Fitness Tests

With this changing view of the value of exercise has come a changing philosophy of physical fitness testing. Evaluating aerobic fitness and body composition is now recommended for adult and youth fitness programs. These test batteries are provided in chapters 8 and 9.

The newer, health-related fitness tests can be used, not only to evaluate physical fitness, but also to provide a means of integrating the cognitive aspects of health into physical education. Topics covering heart disease, obesity, nutrition, and exercise physiology can be integrated into the curriculum. For example, measuring a student's body composition provides an excellent opportunity to teach students the role of diet and exercise in the maintenance of proper body weight, and the effect of obesity on disease. Although many cognitive courses are taught at college level, most students do not attend college; and with heart disease the number one killer of Americans, the need for such courses in public schools becomes more apparent. There are several excellent sources (Falls et al. 1980; Getchell 1979; Jackson and Ross 1986; Pollock, Wilmore and Fox 1984) that target on the health-related aspects of exercise.

EQUAL OPPORTUNITY

Equality of opportunity in education and employment is protected by federal statute. Title IX has increased coeducational physical education programs and athletic participation of women. Title VI of the 1966 Civil Rights Act (Arvey 1979) has created job opportunities for women in what has been traditional male-dominated occupations.

Title IX

The effects of Title IX have been felt by public school physical educators and coaches in the increased number of coeducational classes and, more dramatically, in girls' interscholastic athletics. Between 1971 and 1977, one survey showed a 460% increase in girls participating in interscholastic athletics sponsored by public schools (Hogan 1977).

Title IX not only has changed athletics in America, it has helped initiate scientific programs for conditioning female athletes. Reviewing the literature on the physiological differences between men and women, Drinkwater (1973) reported a lack of basic data on females. This lack, and the rise in women's athletics, have led to increased research on conditioning women. For example, Wilmore (1974) showed that weight training, once reserved for men, strengthened women and altered their body composition without developing the muscle-bound appearance feared by critics of women's strength-development programs. Strength-development programs are now accepted methods for training female athletes.

Wells and Plowman (1983) provide an excellent summary of the physiological differences between males and females and speculate on how these differences affect athletic performance. A question that remains to be answered, however, is the extent to which these differences are truly biological and not cultural. This can raise major issues in establishing norm-referenced standards (Safrit, Baumgartner, Jackson and Stamm 1980).

Employment Equality

Women are applying for and being hired for jobs traditionally reserved for males. For example, women are police officers, prison guards, firefighters, underground coal miners, and "roustabouts" on oil production rigs. Title IV of the civil rights legislation has made it illegal to hire on the basis of minority status. To insure objectivity in hiring, many governmental agencies and private sector employers have developed job-related physical tests that are used to make objective hiring decisions.

The summary of male and female physiological differences (Wells and Plowman 1983) shows that the typical woman will have a higher percentage of body fat and less absolute lean weight than the average male. Because of this, women will have less absolute strength than men and the difference is considerable for upper body strength. This has been confirmed with West Point cadets (Hoffman, Stouffer and Jackson 1979). Much of the work in physically demanding jobs involves upper body strength and data published by Keyserling et al. (1980) showed that injuries are related to a worker's strength level. Therefore, preemployment tests are being developed to identify potentially safe productive workers.

COMPUTER INTENSIVE ENVIRONMENT

The advances in computer technology are coming so fast that by the time this book is published, this section will likely be outdated. Statistical procedures are essential to measurement and evaluation, yet few have used the statistical procedures taught in basic measurement courses, perhaps because statistical analysis without the aid of computers takes a considerable amount of time and effort. However, it is quite likely that most of you will have access to a high-powered computer, either a mainframe or microcomputer. Many, if not most, of you will own a computer in the near future. The trend is clear, we will be living in a computer intensive environment.

Most universities, governmental agencies, and large businesses have a mainframe computer. A **mainframe computer** has enormous capacity, allowing for storage of data bases, and conducts complex data analyses. At first, punch cards were mostly used to enter data and run programs. That has all changed. Now terminals are used and almost everything is done electronically. Several standard statistical packages are available and can be used by the nonsophisticated computer user. In various sections of the text, we have provided illustrations of a common statistical package, **SPSS** (1983). If you have access to a mainframe computer, the chances are excellent that SPSS will be available for your use. You will, however, need to learn how to interact with the mainframe computer. It is not possible to provide the commands needed to interact with the mainframe because all are different. Most major computer centers will have a *help desk* where someone will help you work with the computer.

The major change in computer usage has been with microcomputers, available in most schools and businesses. Personal computers, or **microcomputers,** have advanced from disc drive systems where data and programs were stored on *floppy discs,* to hard disc systems with enormous storage capacities. At the University of Houston, we use a hard disc Compaq computer to store fitness assessments, log exercise, and conduct nutritional analyses (the computer output is shown in a later section of this chapter).

Computers can help students learn basic exercise principles.

(Photo courtesy of Apple Computer, Inc.).

The system will store data on thousands of subjects. Many of the programs developed for the mainframe can now be run on hard disc microcomputers. For example, a version of SPSS is available for a hard disc microcomputer. The outlook for the future is to move much of the computer work from the mainframe to the microcomputer. Computers are extremely helpful, but they are not without problems. Once you start using them you will know what we mean. Many of you will be able to write programs, but this is very expensive in terms of time and money. At the time this chapter was being written, the Apple computers were very popular for use in public schools, and IBM compatible computers (e.g., Compaq) were the leading brands used in a research and industrial setting. Programs written for the Apple will not run on the IBM. In fact, many computer companies claim they are compatible with IBM or Apple, but you may find this is not always the case. Microcomputers are unique; you must find programs that will run on your equipment and meet your specific needs. Many excellent programs are available for the leading microcomputers. Programs for IBM and Apple computers have been written to perform some calculations presented in this text (e.g., calculated percent body fat and $\dot{V}O_2$ Max, chapter 8), and in addition, commercial versions that run on these two microcomputer systems are illustrated.

Figure 1.12 Maximal oxygen uptake can be easily measured with a computerized metabolic system. (Photo from Gould Equipment Company.)

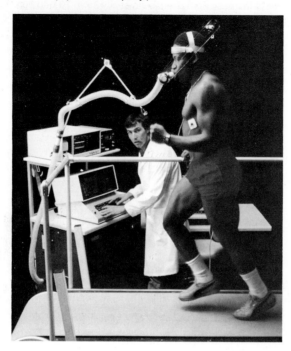

Microcomputers have at least two direct applications to the area of exercise science. First, computers are now being interfaced with various types of research equipment to automate data collection. Maximal oxygen uptake ($\dot{V}O_2$ Max) is an important fitness variable. $\dot{V}O_2$ Max is the maximal amount of oxygen one can utilize during exhausting exercise and is fully discussed in chapter 8. Prior to the computer era, $\dot{V}O_2$ Max was very time consuming to measure because expired gases were collected in a bag for analysis. Now this can be done quickly and accurately with a computer (see figure 1.12).

Dr. Kenneth Cooper (1970) developed a system for the quantification of exercise with aerobic points. When Tenneco developed their health and fitness programs, a computerized system (Baun and Baun 1984) was developed to quantify exercise by caloric expenditure. The Tenneco program was designed to run on the company's mainframe. Now commercially developed computer programs[3] are available for use on a personal computer. The programs are designed to assess fitness, prescribe an individualized exercise program based on the fitness assessment, and log the energy expended during exercise. Sample output for assessing fitness is shown in chapter 8. Sample output for the exercise prescription and logging programs are furnished in figures 1.13 and 1.14.

3. Computer programs developed by Cardio Stress Incorporated (CSI), 15425 North Freeway, Suite 180, Houston, Texas 77090. Programs are fully compatible with IBM, Compaq, Wang, Altos, and other computers that use PC.DOS and compatible MS.DOS operating systems.

Figure 1.13 Exercise prescription written by the CSI GENERAL FITNESS ASSESSMENT® program for a walk-jog exercise program. The $\dot{V}O_2$ Max of the person was 51 mlkg^{-1}min^{-1}. The prescription was written to increase both exercise intensity (from 70% to 80% $\dot{V}O_2$ Max) duration for 20 to 35 minutes over the 7-step program. (From the CSI GENERAL FITNESS ASSESSMENT.® Sample computer output used with the permission of Cardio-Stress, Inc., Houston, Texas. Taken from: Jackson, A. S. and R. M. Ross. *Understanding Exercise for Health and Fitness.* MacJ-R Publishing Co., Houston, Texas, 1986.)

EXERCISE PROGRAM

FOR

FREDDY FIT

Date: 05-13-86

WARM UP

Smoothly perform 4-5 repetitions for each flexibility exercise.
Attempt to hold stretch for 5-10 seconds.

AEROBICS: (15-20 min)

This is the HEART of your conditioning program. Once you reach your
Maintenance Level, perform your aerobic exercise in your training
heart rate zone (THRZ).

The TRAINING LEVELS (Distance and Time) in the Maintenance Program
should be used only as a guide. Modify them appropriately, according
to your actual pulse rate (THRZ) or your perceived exertion level. As
you improve, you will go further or perform more work at the same
training heart rate.

WALK-JOG PROGRAM

Build up to the appropriate pace gradually over 2-3 min.
Exercise at the prescribed pace at least 3 sessions/week.

Conditioning Program - Start here if out of shape.

STEP	METS	MILES	LAPS	PACE (min/mi)	CAL/WEEK	TIME/SESSION
1	9	1.89	7.6	10:36	846	20: 0
2	10	2.24	9.0	10: 2	1005	22:30
3	10	2.62	10.5	9:32	1175	25: 0
4	11	3.03	12.1	9: 5	1357	27:30
5	12	3.46	13.8	8:40	1551	30: 0
6	12	3.92	15.7	8:17	1757	32:30

Maintenance Program - THRZ: 164 - 174

| 7+ | 13 | 4.41 | 17.6 | 7:57 | 1974 | 35: 0 |

** 1 mile = 4 laps

APPROACH TO YOUR EXERCISE PROGRAM

Attempt to perform your exercise program three to four times per
week. Log your exercise activities to document improvement.

Figure 1.14 Sample output of the CSI EXERCISE LOGGING® program. (Credit: Sample computer output used with the permission of Cardio-Stress, Inc., Houston, Texas. Taken from: Jackson, A. S. and R. M. Ross. *Understanding Exercise for Health and Fitness*. MacJ-R Publishing Co., Houston, Texas, 1986.)

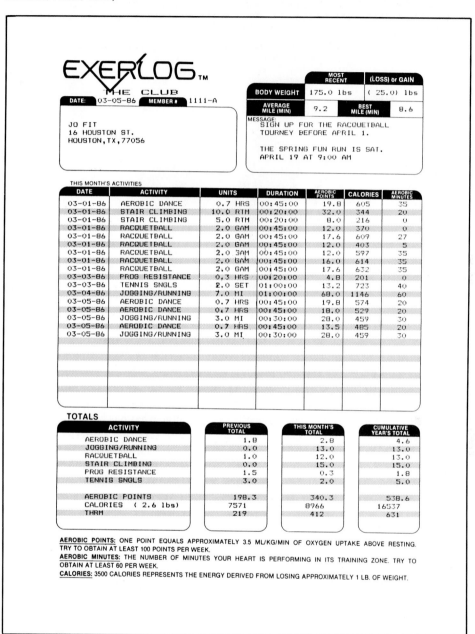

Employees in the Tenneco Health and Fitness program (Houston, Texas) monitor their exercise on a computer.

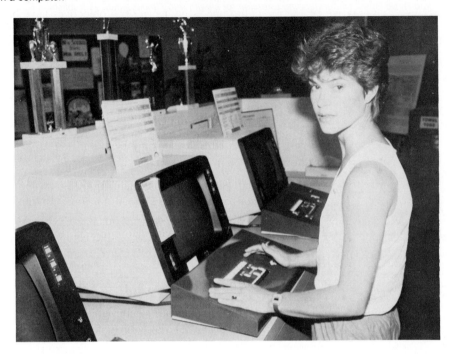

Computers are not only useful for data storage and analysis, but also for education. For example, one of the most popular aspects of the highly successful Tenneco Health and Fitness Program has been their computer logging program.[4] The computer provides the employee with instant feedback on the calories expended during the exercise session. This allows the employee to objectively determine what has been accomplished and make intelligent exercise choices. An adult fitness text that integrates exercise science principles with the CSI computer programs has been published (Jackson and Ross 1986). This allows the computer to not only serve as a tool for data analysis and data management, but also provide laboratory experiences that reinforce exercise science concepts that are presented in the text. The educational impact of the computer explosion has just started to be realized.

SUMMARY

Measurement uses reliable and valid tests to secure the data essential to the evaluation process. Evaluation is a decision-making process with a goal for improved instruction. Tests can be used in six ways: (1) placing students in homogeneous groups to facilitate instruction; (2) diagnosing weaknesses; (3) determining whether important objectives have been reached; (4) predicting performance levels in future activities; (5) comparing a program with others like it; and (6) motivating participants.

4. Personal communication with William Baun, Director of Health and Fitness, Tenneco, Houston, Texas.

Evaluation is a means not only of determining whether objectives are being reached, but also for facilitating achievement. Formative evaluation clarifies what remains to be achieved; summative evaluation determines whether general objectives have been reached. Evaluation, then, is the feedback system by which the quality of the instructional or training process is monitored. Criterion-referenced standards specify the level of performance necessary to achieve specific instructional objectives; norm-referenced standards identify a level of achievement within a group of individuals.

Recent legislative activity and health-related research have changed the nature of physical education and physical testing. The research showing that energy expenditure and obesity are independent cardiovascular disease risk factors has increased the popularity of health-related fitness testing and enhanced the validity of aerobic fitness and body composition as fitness components. Girls and women are increasing their participation in athletic programs and women are now being employed in physically demanding jobs previously reserved for men. This has created a new emphasis in physiological research and physical testing of women.

Computers have changed the way physical education teachers and exercise specialists practice. Not only are computers used for data storage and complicated data analyses, but now special programs are being developed for use in exercise science.

FORMATIVE EVALUATION OF OBJECTIVES

Objective 1 Differentiate between measurement and evaluation.

1. The terms measurement and evaluation often are used interchangeably. Define each term.
2. What are the key differences between measurement and evaluation?
3. Although measurement and evaluation are distinct functions, explain how they are related.

Objective 2 Define and differentiate between criterion- and norm-referenced standards.

1. What are the key differences between criterion- and norm-referenced standards?
2. Explain how a physical education teacher or exercise specialist could use both types of standards.

Objective 3 Define and differentiate between formative and summative methods of evaluation.

1. Many believe that greater achievement is possible if both formative and summative evaluation are used. Briefly describe formative and summative evaluation.
2. What are the key differences between formative and summative evaluation?
3. Why could you expect to stimulate greater achievement by using both formative and summative evaluation?

Objective 4 Cite the evidence relating the growth of health-related fitness.

1. What is the scientific evidence supporting caloric expenditure on heart attack?
2. Is obesity an independent cardiovascular disease risk factor?
3. How much exercise is needed to develop or maintain physical fitness?

Objective 5 Identify the impact of equal opportunity on physical testing.

1. Describe the conditions that will increase the use of physical testing of men and women.

Objective 6 Be knowledgeable of the changes in computer technology and list their impact on physical education teachers and exercise specialists.

1. What is the difference between a mainframe and microcomputer?
2. What types of computer programs are available for use in physical education and exercise science? You will gain a better understanding by skimming the chapters of the book.

ADDITIONAL LEARNING ACTIVITIES

1. Develop a unit of instruction showing how you could use both formative and summative evaluation procedures.
2. For the same unit of instruction, develop criterion-referenced standards for the tests. Are there any norm-referenced standards that you may want to use?
3. Read a research article that evaluates the physical capabilities of girls or women. Compare these capabilities with data published on boys and men.
4. Visit a facility that conducts an adult fitness program. Identify the types of tests that are administered.
5. Visit a microcomputer store and have various computers and programs demonstrated. In most stores they will encourage you to try a computer.

BIBLIOGRAPHY

AAHPER. 1976. *Youth Fitness Test Manual.* Washington D.C.

AAHPERD. 1980. *Health Related Physical Fitness Manual.* Washington, D.C.

American College of Sports Medicine. 1978. "Position Statement on the Recommended Quantity and Quality of Exercise for Developing and Maintaining Fitness in Healthy Adults." *Medicine and Science in Sports* 10:vii.

Arvey, R. D. 1979. *Fairness in Selecting Employees.* Reading: Addison-Wesley Publishing Co.

Baun, W. B., and M. Baun. 1984. "A Corporate Health and Fitness Program Motivation and Management by Computers." *JOPERD* 55-43-45.

Bloom, B. S., J. T. Hastings, and G. F. Madaus. 1971. *Handbook on Formative and Summative Evaluation of Student Learning.* New York: McGraw-Hill.

Cooper, K. H. 1970. *The New Aerobics*. New York: Bantam Books.

deBakey, M. F., A. M. Gotto Jr., L. W. Scott, and J. Foreyt. 1984. *The Living Heart Diet*. New York: Simon and Schuster.

Drinkwater, B. L. 1973. "Physiological Responses of Women to Exercise." *Exercise and Sport Sciences Reviews,* vol. 1. J. H. Wilmore, (ed.) New York: Academic.

Ebel, R. L. 1973. *Measuring Educational Achievement*. Englewood Cliffs, N.J.: Prentice-Hall.

Falls, H. B., A. M. Baylor, and R. K. Dishman. 1980. *Essentials of Fitness*. Philadelphia, Pa.: W. B. Saunders.

Getchell, L. 1979. *Physical Fitness: A Way of Life*. New York: Wiley.

Glaser, R. 1963. "Instructional Technology and the Measurement of Learning Outcomes: Some Questions." *American Psychologist* 27:519–21.

Golding, L. A., C. R. Meyers, and W. E. Sinning. 1982. *The Y's Way to Physical Fitness*. 2d ed. Chicago, Ill.: National Board of YMCA.

Hoffman, T.; R. Stouffer; and A. S. Jackson. 1979. "Sex Differences in Strength." *American Journal of Sports Medicine* 7:265–67.

Hogan, D. L. 1977. "From Here to Equality: Title IX." *Women's Sports* 4:16–26, 60.

Hubert, H. B. et al. 1983. "Obesity as an Independent Risk Factor for Cardiovascular Disease: a 26-Year Follow-up of Participants in the Framingham Heart Study." *Circulation* 67:968–77.

Jackson, A. S., and M. L. Pollock. 1985. "Practical Assessment of Body Composition." *The Physician and Sportsmedicine* 13:76–90.

Jackson, A. S., and R. M. Ross. 1986. *Understanding Exercise for Health and Fitness*. Houston, Tx.: Mac J-R Publishing Company.

Kannel, W. B., and T. J. Thom. 1984. "Declining Cardiovascular Mortality." *Circulation* 70:331–36.

Kannel, W. B., and P. Sorlie. 1979. "Some Health Benefits of Physical Activity: The Framingham Study." *Archives of Internal Medicine* 139:857–61.

Keyserling, W. M. et al. 1980. "Isometric Strength Testing as a Means of Controlling Medical Incidents on Strenuous Jobs." *Journal of Occupational Medicine* 22:332–36.

Lohman, T. G. 1982. "Body Composition Methodology in Sports Medicine." *The Physician and Sportsmedicine* 10:46–58.

Morris, J. N. et al. 1953. "Coronary Heart Disease and Physical Activity or Work." *Lancet* 2:1053–63.

Owen, C. A., E. F. Beard, and A. S. Jackson. 1980. "Longitudinal Evaluation of an Exercise Prescription Intervention Program with Periodic Ergometric Testing: A Ten-Year Appraisal." *Journal of Occupational Medicine* 22:235–40.

Paffenbarger, R. S. et al. 1986. "Physical Activity, All-Cause Mortality, and Longevity of College Alumni." *New England Journal of Medicine* 314:605–13.

Paffenbarger, R. S. et al. 1984. "A Natural History of Athleticism and Cardiovascular Health." *Journal of American Medical Association* 252:491–95.

Paffenbarger, R. S. et al. 1978. "Physical Activity as an Index of Heart Attack Risk in College Alumni." *American Journal of Epidemiology* 108:161–75.

Paffenbarger, R. S., Jr. et al. 1977. "Work-Energy Level, Personal Characteristics, and Fatal Heart Attack: A Birth-Cohort Effect." *American Journal of Epidemiology* 105:200–13.

Pollock, M. L., J. H. Wilmore, and S. M. Fox. 1984. *Exercise in Health and Disease*. Philadelphia, Pa.: W. B. Saunders.

Safrit, M. J., T. A. Baumgartner, A. S. Jackson, and C. L. Stamm. 1980. "Issues in Setting Motor Performance Standards." *Quest* 32:152–63.

SPSS User's Guide. 1983. New York: McGraw-Hill.

Taylor, H. L. 1960. "Chapter 3: The Mortality and Morbidity of Coronary Heart Disease of Men in Sedentary and Physically Active Occupations." *Exercise and Fitness.* The Athletic Institute: Chicago, Ill.: 20–39.

Wells, C. L., and S. A. Plowman. 1983. "Sexual Differences in Athletic Performance: Biological or Behavioral?" *The Physician and Sportsmedicine* 11:52–63.

Wilmore, J. H. 1974. "Alterations in Strength, Body Composition and Anthropometric Measurements Consequent to a 10-Week Weight Training Program." *Medicine and Science in Sports* 6:133–38.

Quantitative Aspects of Measurement

Part 2

Statistical Tools in Evaluation

2

Contents

Key Words

Bell-Shaped Curve
Central Tendency
Continuous Scores
Correlation
Correlation Coefficient
Curvilinear Relationship
Data
Discrete Scores
Frequency Polygon
Interval Scores
Linear Relationship
Mean
Median
Mode
Nominal Scores
Normal Curve
Ordinal Scores
Percentile
Percentile Rank
Prediction
Range
Ratio Scores
Simple Frequency Distribution
Simple Prediction (Regression)
Skewed Curve
Standard Deviation
Standard Error of Prediction
Standard Error of the Mean
Standard Score
T-score
Variability
z-score

Objectives

This chapter presents statistical techniques that can be applied to evaluate a set of scores. Not all techniques are used on every set of scores, but you should be familiar with all of them in order to select the appropriate one for a given situation.

After reading chapter 2 you should be able to:

1. Select the statistical technique that is correct for a given situation.
2. Calculate accurately with the formulas presented.
3. Interpret the statistical value selected or calculated.
4. Make decisions based on all available information about a given situation.

INTRODUCTION

Once test scores have been collected, they must be analyzed. You can use the techniques presented here to summarize the performance of a group and to interpret the scores of individuals within that group. Many of these techniques are used and discussed in later chapters.

You may find a good elementary statistics book such as Bloomers and Lindquist (1960), Bloomers and Forsyth (1977), Ferguson (1981), Glass and Stanley (1970), or Roscoe (1975) helpful when studying the material in this chapter. Many other good books are also available.

ELEMENTS OF SCORE ANALYSIS

There are many reasons why we analyze sets of test scores. For a large group, a simple list of scores has no meaning. Only by condensing the information and applying to it descriptive terms can we interpret the overall performance of a group; its improvement from year-to-year or since the beginning of a teaching or training unit, or its performance in comparison to other groups of like background.

Score analysis is also used to evaluate individual achievement. Once information on the overall performance of a group has been obtained, an individual's achievement can be evaluated in relation to it. Analysis also helps the teacher develop performance standards, either for evaluative purposes or simply to let students know how they are doing.

Types of Scores

Scores can be classified as either continuous or discrete. **Continuous scores,** as most are in physical education and exercise science, have a potentially infinite number of values because they can be measured with varying degrees of accuracy. Between any two values of a continuous score exist countless other values that may be expressed as fractions. For example, 100-yard-dash scores are usually recorded to the nearest tenth of a second; but they could be recorded in hundredths or thousandths of a second if accurate timing equipment were available. The amount of weight a person can lift might be recorded in 5-, 1-, or ½-pound scores, depending on how precise a score is desired. **Discrete scores** are limited to a specific number of values and usually are not expressed as fractions. Scores on a throw or shot at a target numbered 5-4-3-2-1-0 are discrete because one can receive a score of only 5, 4, 3, 2, 1, or 0. A score of 4.5 or 1.67 is impossible.

Most continuous scores are rounded off to the nearest unit of measurement when they are recorded. For example, the score of a student who runs the 100-yard dash in 10.57 seconds is recorded as 10.6 because 10.57 is closer to 10.6 than to 10.5. Usually when a number is rounded off to the nearest unit of measurement, it is increased only when the number being dropped is 5 or more. Thus 11.45 is rounded off to 11.5, while 11.44 is recorded as 11.4. A less common method is to round off to the last unit of measure, awarding the next higher score only when that score is actually accomplished. For example, an individual who does 8 pull-ups but cannot complete the 9th receives a score of 8.

We can also classify scores as ratio, interval, ordinal, or nominal (Ferguson 1981). How scores are classified influences what calculations may be done on them. **Ratio scores** have a common unit of measurement between each score and a true zero point so that statements about equality of ratios can be made. Length and weight are examples, since 1 measurement may be called 2 or 3 times another. **Interval scores** have a common unit of measurement between each score but do not have a true zero point. (A score of 0 as a measure of distance is a true zero, indicating no distance. However, a score of 0 on a knowledge test is not a true zero because it does not indicate a total lack of knowledge; it simply means that the respondent answered none of the questions correctly.) In physical education most scores are either ratio or interval. **Ordinal scores** do not have a common unit of measurement between each score, but there is an order in the scores that makes it possible to characterize one score as higher than another. Class ranks, for example, are ordinal: if 3 students receive push-up scores of 16, 10, and 8 respectively, the first is ranked 1, the next 2, and the last 3. Notice that the number of push-ups necessary to change the class ranks of the second and third students differs. Thus there is not a common unit of measurement between consecutive scores. **Nominal scores** cannot be hierarchically ordered. For example, individuals can be classified by sport preference, but we cannot say that one sport is better than another.

Common Unit Measure

Many scores are recorded in feet and inches or in minutes and seconds. To analyze scores, they must be recorded in a single unit of measurement, usually the smaller one. Thus distances and heights are recorded in inches rather than feet and inches, and times are recorded in seconds rather than minutes and seconds. Recording scores in the smaller unit of measure as they are collected is less time consuming than translating them into that form later.

Calculators and Computers

Score analysis should be accurate and quick. Particularly when a set of scores is large, say 50 or more, calculators and computers should be used to ensure both accuracy and speed. Today calculators are available in desktop and pocket forms, and pocket calculators especially are inexpensive. A pocket calculator that will serve you well as a student and later on the job should cost under $20. Your calculator should have the four basic mathematical operations, square root and squaring keys, and a memory.

Calculators work well to a point, but when the number of scores is very large, the use of a calculator is time consuming and the user tends to make more errors. Computers are very fast and accurate. As discussed in chapter 1, computers are increasingly available in school districts and universities, agencies, and businesses.

ORGANIZING AND GRAPHING TEST SCORES

Simple Frequency Distribution

The 50 scores in table 2.1 are not very useful in their present form. They become more meaningful if we know how many students received each score when we order the scores. To do this, we first find the lowest and highest scores in the table. Now we find the number of students who received each score between the lowest (46) and the highest (90) by making up a tally like the one in figure 2.1.

Notice that all possible scores between 40 and 99 appear on the chart. The first score in table 2.1 is 66, so we make a mark in row 60 under column 6 (60 + 6 = 66). This mark indicates that 1 score of 66 has been tabulated. We continue through the table, making a mark in the appropriate row and column for each score.

Once the scores are ordered, it is easy to make up a simple frequency distribution of the results, as shown in table 2.2. We list the scores in descending order, the best score first. In most cases, the higher scores are better scores, but this is not true of running events, golf scores, numbers of errors, etc. A **simple frequency distribution** of a running event would list the lower scores first.

Table 2.1
Standing Long Jump Scores for 50 Junior High-School Boys.

66*	67	54	63	90
56	56	65	71	82
68	68	76	55	78
47	58	68	78	76
46	68	68	90	62
58	49	62	84	75
75	65	66	72	73
71	75	83	83	64
60	76	65	79	56
68	70	48	77	59

*66 inches

From a simple frequency distribution we can determine the range of scores at a glance, as well as the most frequently received score and the number of students receiving each score. For example, from table 2.2 we can see that the scores ranged from 90 down to 46, that the most frequently received score was 68, and that with one exception all scores had a frequency of 3 or less.

With a large number of scores, forming a simple frequency distribution is time consuming without a computer. The computer allows you to enter the scores into the computer and to analyze them using any one of a number of programs, among them the FREQUENCIES program (see figure 2.5) in the SPSS package (Nie et al. 1975), which is available on most university campuses, and in many agencies and industries. The SPSS package and the FREQUENCIES program are discussed in detail in the last section of this chapter. Many other packages of statistical programs for mainframe and microcomputers have a frequency count program. FREQUENCIES in the *Statistics with Finesse* package (Bolding 1985) is one such microcomputer package.

Figure 2.1 Ordering a set of scores.

	0	1	2	3	4	5	6	7	8	9
40							/	/	/	/
50					/	/	///		//	/
60	/		//	/	/	///	//	/	ℳ	
70	/	//	/	/		///	///	/	//	/
80				/	//	/				
90	//									

Table 2.2
Simple Frequency Distribution of Standing Long Jump Scores of 50 Junior High-School Boys.

x	f	x	f	x	f
90*	2	72	1	60	1
84	1	71	2	59	1
83	2	70	1	58	2
82	1	68	6	56	3
79	1	67	1	55	1
78	2	66	2	54	1
77	1	65	3	49	1
76	3	64	1	48	1
75	3	63	1	47	1
73	1	62	2	46	1

*90 inches

Grouping Scores for Graphing

We could present the information in table 2.2 in the form of a graph. A graph shows the general shape of a score distribution, with like scores grouped together. In grouping a set of scores, we try to form 10 to 20 groupings with 15 usually the ideal, using the following steps:

Step 1
Divide the difference between the largest and smallest scores by 15, rounding off the result to the nearest whole number if necessary.

$$\text{Interval size} = \frac{\text{largest score} - \text{smallest score}}{15}$$

This number, the interval size, tells us how many scores to group together. Ideally, the interval size is an odd number.

Step 2
Design the first grouping to contain the best score. If the interval size is even, the smallest score of this first grouping should be a multiple of the interval size. If the interval size is odd, the midpoint of this first grouping should be a multiple of the interval size.

Problem 2.1 Group the 50 standing long jump scores listed in table 2.2.

Solution Before we can determine the actual groupings, we must determine the interval size.

Step 1
From the table we see that the largest score is 90 and the smallest is 46, giving us an interval size of 3:

$$\text{Interval size} = \frac{90 - 46}{15} = \frac{44}{15} = 2.9 = 3$$

Step 2
The first grouping must contain 3 possible scores, including the score 90 (the best score; and because the interval size is odd, its midpoint must be a multiple of 3). Although both 90-92 and 88-90 include the largest score, neither grouping meets the midpoint requirement: 91 and 89 are not multiples of 3. Our first grouping, then, must be 89-91, which meets both the high-score inclusion and midpoint requirements.

Once the first grouping is established, it is easy to work up the rest:

Grouping	Tally	Frequency
89–91	//	2
86–88		0
83–85	///	3
80–82	/	1
77–79	////	4
74–76	//// /	6
71–73	////	4
68–70	//// //	7
65–67	//// /	6
62–64	////	4
59–61	//	2
56–58	////	5
53–55	//	2
50–52		0
47–49	///	3
44–46	/	1

Figure 2.2 is a graph of the 50 scores. Test scores, in intervals of 3 (only midpoints are plotted), are listed along the horizontal axis with low scores on the left to high scores on the right. The frequency is listed on the vertical axis starting with 0 and increasing upward. We place a dot above each score to indicate its frequency. For example, the dot above score 66 is opposite the frequency value 6, indicating that 6 students received scores in the grouping 65–67. By connecting the dots with straight lines, we complete the graph, forming an angled figure called a **frequency polygon.**

By smoothing out the frequency polygon, we create a curve that, by its shape, tells us the nature of the distribution. In figure 2.2 the smoothing out is indicated by the broken line. If that line resembles the curve in figure 2.3, the graph is called a **normal** or **bell-shaped curve.** The normal curve is discussed in detail later in the chapter.

When a smoothed graph has a long, low tail on the left, indicating that few students received low scores, it is called a **negatively skewed curve.** When the tail of the curve is on the right, the curve is called **positively skewed.** A curve is called **leptokurtic** when it is more sharply peaked than a normal curve, and **platykurtic** when it is less sharply peaked (see figure 2.4). Leptokurtic curves are characteristic of extremely homogeneous groups. Platykurtic curves are characteristic of heterogeneous groups.

Figure 2.2 A graph of standing long jump scores recorded in inches.

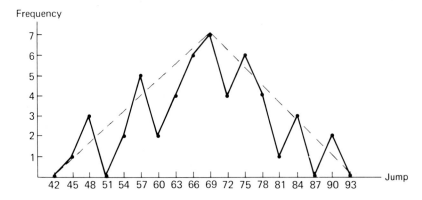

Figure 2.3 A normal curve.

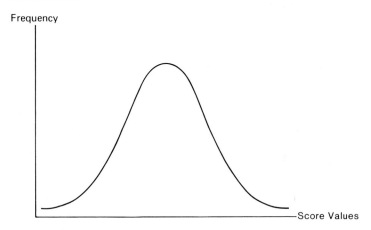

DESCRIPTIVE VALUES

Once a large set of scores has been collected, certain descriptive values can be calculated—values that summarize or condense the set of scores, giving it meaning. Descriptive values are used, not only to evaluate individual performance by the physical educator or exercise specialist who administered the test, but also to describe the group's performance or compare its performance with that of another group.

Figure 2.4 Negatively skewed, positively skewed, leptokuritic, and platycurtic curves.

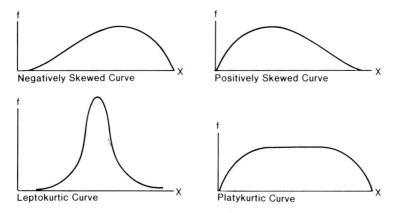

Negatively Skewed Curve

Positively Skewed Curve

Leptokurtic Curve

Platykurtic Curve

Measures of Central Tendency

One type of descriptive value is the measure of **central tendency,** that indicates those points at which scores tend to be concentrated. There are three measures of central tendency: the mode, the median, and the mean.

Mode
The **mode** is the score most frequently received. It is used with nominal data. In table 2.2 the mode is 68: more students received a score of 68 than any other one score in the set. It is possible to have several modes if several scores tie for most frequent. The mode is not a stable measure because the addition or deletion of a single score can change its value considerably. Unless the data is nominal or the most frequent score is desired, other measures of central tendency are more appropriate.

Median
The **median** is the middle score; half the scores fall above the median and half below. It cannot be calculated unless the scores are listed in order from best to worst. Where n is the number of scores in the set, we can calculate the position of the approximate median using the following formula:

$$\text{Position of approximate median} = \frac{n + 1}{2}$$

Notice that the formula calculates the median's position, or rank, in the listing— not the median itself. The approximate value, always a whole or half number, is that score in the position determined by the equation.

Problem 2.2   Find the approximate median score for the 9 numbers 4, 3, 1, 4, 10, 7, 7, 8, and 6.

Solution   The approximate median score is the 5th score in the ordered listing, or the score 6.

$$\text{Position of approximate median} = \frac{9 + 1}{2} = \frac{10}{2}$$
$$= 5, \text{ or the 5th score}$$

1, 3, 4, 4, 6, 7, 7, 8, 10
    ↳————Median

Problem 2.3   Find the approximate median score for the 6 numbers 1, 3, 4, 5, 6, and 10.

Solution   The approximate median score is that score that falls halfway between the 3rd and 4th scores in the ordered listing, or the score 4.5

$$\text{Position of approximate median} = \frac{6 + 1}{2} = \frac{7}{2}$$
$$= 3.5, \text{ or the 3.5th score}$$

1, 3, 4, 5, 6, 10
   ↳————Median

The approximate value of the median is often used by teachers, exercise specialists, and other practitioners in preference to the exact value, which is harder to obtain and unnecessarily precise. Notice that the value of the median is affected only by the position, not the value, of each score. If in Problem 2.2 the scores were 0, 1, 2, 3, 6, 6, 7, 8, and 10, the approximate median would still be 6. This characteristic of the median is sometimes a limitation.

When scores are listed in a simple frequency distribution, we can obtain either an approximate or an exact value of the median. The approximate value of the median for the scores in table 2.2 falls halfway between the 25th and 26th scores, at a median score of 68. Notice that we count up the frequency column from the lowest score to the 25th and 26th scores received; we do not work in the score column until we have reached the approximate median value.

Researchers are likely to need an exact value of the median. When scores in a simple frequency distribution are listed from best to worst, we can calculate the exact value of the median.

The calculation of the median is a 3-step process:

Step 1
Order the scores in a simple frequency distribution, listing the best score first (see table 2.2).

Step 2
Make a cumulative frequency (cf) column by adding the frequencies, starting with the worst score and working upward to the best.

Step 3

Calculate the median using the following formula:

$$\text{Median} = \text{lrl} + \left(\frac{.5n - \text{cfb}}{\text{fw}}\right)(\text{UM})$$

where X is the score that contains the median score (the score below which half of the frequencies lie), lrl is the lower real limit (X − .5UM), n is the number of scores (the sum of the frequency column), cfb is the cumulative frequency below (the number of scores below X), fw is the frequency within (the frequency for X), and UM is the unit of measurement in which the scores are expressed.

Problem 2.4 Find the exact median for the scores listed in table 2.2.

Solution Because the scores in table 2.2 are presented in a simple frequency distribution, Step 1 has been done.

Step 2

To make the cumulative frequency column (cf), we begin adding the frequencies from the worst score (46) up to the best score (90). Thus the starting values are 1, 2(1 + 1), and 3(2 + 1) as seen in the chart below:

X	f	cf	X	f	cf
90	2	50	60	1	13
—	—	—	59	1	12
70	1	30	58	2	11
68	6	29	56	3	9
67	1	23	55	1	6
66	2	22	54	1	5
65	3	20	49	1	4
64	1	17	48	1	3
63	1	16	47	1	2
62	2	15	46	1	1

Step 3

Where X is 68, lrl is 67.5 (68 − .5), n is 50, cfb is 23, and UM is 1 (because the scores are in inches, UM is 1), the exact median score is 67.83:

$$\text{Median} = 67.5 + \left(\frac{25 - 23}{6}\right)(1)$$

$$= 67.5 + \left(\frac{2}{6}\right)(1) = 67.5 + .33 = 67.83$$

Notice how close this is to the approximate median score, 68.

When the scores in a simple frequency distribution are listed from lowest to highest, as they would be in a running event, we use a different formula to calculate the exact median score:

$$\text{Median} = \text{url} + \left(\frac{\text{cfb} - .5n}{\text{fw}} \right)(\text{UM})$$

where url is the upper real limit $(X + .5\text{UM})$.

Problem 2.5 Find the exact median score of the 100-yard-dash times listed in the frequency distribution below.

X	f	cf
10.0	1	36
10.1	2	35
10.2	4	33
10.3	7	29
10.4	8	22
10.5	9	14
10.7	4	5
11.0	1	1

Solution Where X is 10.4, url is 10.45 (10.4 + .05), n is 36, cfb is 14, fw is 8, and UM is .1 (because the scores are in tenths of a second, UM is .1), the exact median score is 10.4:

$$\text{Median} = 10.45 + \left(\frac{14 - 18}{8} \right)(.1)$$

$$= 10.45 + \left(\frac{-4}{8} \right)(.1) = 10.45 + (-.5)(.1)$$

$$= 10.45 + (-.05) = 10.45 - .05 = 10.4$$

Mean
The mean is ordinarily the most appropriate measure of central tendency with interval or ratio data. It is affected by both the value and the position of each score. The **mean** is the sum of the scores divided by the number of scores:

$$\overline{X} = \frac{\Sigma X}{n}$$

where $\overline{X}$ is the mean, ΣX is the sum of the scores, and n is the number of scores.

Problem 2.6 Calculate the mean of the following scores: 2, 3, 6, 7, 1, 5, and 10.

Solution Where ΣX is 34 and n is 7, the mean is 4.86: ·

$$\overline{X} = \frac{34}{7} = 4.857 = 4.86$$

Notice that the scores need not be ordered hierarchically to calculate the mean. For example, the mean for the scores in table 2.1 is 67.78, the sum of the randomly ordered scores divided by 50.

When the graph of the scores is a normal curve, the mode, median, and mean are equal. When the graph is positively skewed, the mean is larger than the median; when it is negatively skewed, the mean is less than the median. For example, the graph for the scores 2, 3, 1, 4, 1, 8, and 10 is positively skewed with mean 4.14 and median 3.

The mean is the most common measure of central tendency. But when scores are quite skewed or lack a common interval between consecutive scores (as do ordinal scores), the median is the best measure of central tendency. The mode is used only when the mean and median cannot be calculated (for instance, with nominal scores) or when the only information wanted is the most frequent score (for instance, most common uniform size, most frequent error).

Measures of Variability

A second type of descriptive value is the measure of **variability,** which describes the set of scores in terms of their spread or heterogeneity. For example, consider these pull-up scores for 2 groups:

Group 1	Group 2
9	5
1	6
5	4

For both groups the mean and median are 5. If you simply report that the mean and median for both groups are identical without showing the scores, another person could conclude that the 2 groups have equal or similar ability. This is not true: group 2 is more homogeneous in performance than is group 1. A measure of variability is the descriptive term that indicates this difference in the spread, or heterogeneity of a set of scores. There are two such measures: the range, and the standard deviation.

Range
The range is the easiest measure of variability to obtain and the one that is used when the measure of central tendency is the mode or median. The **range** is the difference between the highest and lowest scores. For example, the range for the scores in table 2.2 is 44 (90 − 46). The range is neither a precise nor stable measure because it depends on only 2 scores and is affected by a change in either of them. For example, the range of scores in table 2.2 would have been 38 (84 − 46) if the students who scored 90 had been absent.

Standard Deviation

The **standard deviation** is the measure of variability used with the mean. It originally was intended to indicate the average amount that all the scores differ or deviate from the mean. Because the sum of the deviations from the mean is always 0, we define the standard deviation as follows (some books, calculators, and computer programs use the term $n - 1$ in the denominator, which usually has little effect on s):

$$s = \sqrt{\frac{\Sigma(X - \overline{X})^2}{n}} \text{ (definitional formula)}$$

where s is the standard deviation, X is the scores, $\overline{X}$ is the mean, and n is the number of scores.

This formula is seldom used to calculate the standard deviation, because it is cumbersome when the mean is a fraction. Instead, we use the following formula to calculate s:

$$s = \sqrt{\frac{\Sigma X^2}{n} - \frac{(\Sigma X)^2}{n^2}} \text{ (calculational formula)}$$

where ΣX^2 is the sum of the squared scores, ΣX is the sum of the scores, and n is the number of scores.

Problem 2.7 Compute the standard deviation of the following set of scores: 7, 2, 7, 6, 5, 6, 2.

Solution The process is 3 steps: calculate ΣX, calculate ΣX^2, and determine s. We can combine the first 2 steps by creating a table, working first across the rows and then totaling the columns:

X	X^2
7	49
2	4
7	49
6	36
5	25
6	36
2	4
35	203

When ΣX is 35, ΣX^2 is 203, and n is 7, the standard deviation is 2:

$$s = \sqrt{\frac{203}{7} - \frac{35^2}{7^2}} = \sqrt{\frac{203}{7} - \frac{1225}{49}} = \sqrt{29 - 25} = \sqrt{4} = 2$$

Notice that with this formula the scores are listed in a column and the square of each score is listed in a second column. The sums of these 2 columns are needed to calculate the standard deviation.

Remember that the standard deviation indicates the variability of a set of scores around the mean. The larger the standard deviation, the more heterogeneous the scores. The minimum value of s is 0.

The calculations in Problem 2.7 are easy because the number of scores is small and the number for which we needed the square root (4) is a perfect square. Unhappily you usually will be working with between 50 and 300 scores and a number that is not a perfect square. You can speed up the calculations using a calculator. In fact, there are calculators that compute the mean and the standard deviation once the data are entered, just by pushing the appropriate key.

There are desktop calculators (and one may be available at your university or where you work) that can accumulate ΣX and ΣX^2, making it unnecessary to list the square of each score when calculating a standard deviation. These calculators almost always have a square root key as well, another timesaving factor. To obtain ΣX and ΣX^2, enter each score in turn and then square it. You can then display the 2 sums by pressing the appropriate keys. (The Instructor's Manual to this text, describes a technique that can be used with a simple calculator to square each score and accumulate ΣX and ΣX^2 as the scores are being squared.) Remember, though, that if the number of scores is very large you may find a computer more accurate and faster than a calculator. Mainframe and microcomputer programs that calculate means and standard deviations are very common and easy to use.

MEASURING GROUP POSITION

Percentile Ranks

After a test session, most individuals want to know how their performance compares with those of others in the group. Ranks can be calculated by assigning the individual who earned the best score the rank of 1, the individual who earned the next best score the rank of 2, and so on. But rank has little meaning unless the number of individuals in the group is known. A rank of 35 is quite good when there are 250 individuals in the group; it is very poor when there are 37. **Percentile ranks** that indicate the relative position of an individual in a group are easily understood even without knowing group size. They indicate the percentage of the group that scored below a given score.

The calculation of percentile ranks is a 3-step process:

Step 1
Order the scores in a simple frequency distribution, listing the best score first (see table 2.2).

Step 2
Make a cumulative frequency (cf) column, by adding the frequencies, starting with the worst score and working upward to the best.

Step 3
Calculate the percentile rank of a given score using the following formula:

$$PR_x = \left(cfb + \frac{fw}{2}\right)\left(\frac{100}{n}\right)$$

where PR_x is the percentile rank of score X, cfb is the number of scores below X (the entry in the cf column one level below X), fw is the frequency of X, and n is the number of scores (the sum of the frequency column).

Problem 2.8 Given the following scores and frequencies, determine the percentile rank for a score of 6:

X	f
10	1
6	4
5	10
4	6
3	3
0	1

Solution Because the scores are presented in a simple frequency distribution, Step 1 has been done.

> **Step 2**
> To make the cumulative frequency column, we begin adding the frequencies from the worst score (here, 0) up to the best score (10). Thus the entry in the cf column opposite score 3 would be 4 ($1 + 3 = 4$); and the entry opposite score 4 would be 10 ($4 + 6 = 10$). The final chart would look like this:

X	f	cf
10	1	25
6	4	24
5	10	20
4	6	10
3	3	4
0	1	1

> **Step 3**
> The percentile rank of score 6 where cfb is 20, fw is 4, and n is 25 is 88:

$$PR_6 = \left(20 + \frac{4}{2}\right)\left(\frac{100}{25}\right)$$
$$= (20 + 2)(4) = (22)(4) = 88$$

Of the scores received, 88% are below 6.

In the percentile rank formula, the term $cfb + \dfrac{fw}{2}$ is the number of scores in theory below the score (x). This is based on the assumption that half the individuals who have received a given score actually scored below that score before rounding off.

That is, when four people receive a score of 10, we assume that two of them originally had scores between 9.5 and 10.0.

Usually the percentile rank for each score in a set is calculated. Because the value of $\frac{100}{n}$ in the formula is seldom a whole number, computing PRs can be tedious without a calculator. Using a calculator, carry $\frac{100}{n}$ out to three digits to the right of the decimal point (thousandths), rounding off the PR to a whole number only after multiplying the cfb $+ \frac{fw}{2}$ value by $\frac{100}{n}$. For example, if n in our set of scores in Problem 2.8 had been 26 rather than 25, the value of $\frac{100}{n}$ would have been 3.846 $\left(\frac{100}{26} = 3.846\right)$ and the PR for score 6 would have been 85:

$$PR_6 = (22)(3.846) = 84.612 = 85$$

Disadvantages

Percentile ranks are ordinal scores. There is no common unit of measurement between consecutive percentile rank values because they are position measures, totally depending on the scores of the group. We can see this clearly in the PR column below, the percentile ranks for the complete set of scores with which we have been working.

X	f	cf	PR
10	1	25	98
6	4	24	88
5	10	20	60
4	6	10	28
3	3	4	10
0	1	1	2

As the scores go up from 4 to 5 and from 5 to 6, notice that the percentile ranks rise at different rates: 32 and 28 respectively. For this reason Bloomers and Lindquist (1960) and Downie and Heath (1965) maintain that it is inappropriate to add, subtract, multiply, or divide percentile rank values.

Another disadvantage is that a small change in actual performance near the mean results in a disproportionate change in percentile rank; the opposite is true of changes at the extremes. We can see this in the columns above, where a change of 1 from X = 4 to X = 5 is a PR change of 32, while a score change of 4 from 6 to 10 is a PR change of only 10.

Percentiles

We often express test standards, or norms, in percentile ranks that are multiples of 5 (5, 10, 15, and so on). To develop these norms we must first determine the test score, or **percentile,** that corresponds to each rank. Previously we were given a score from which to calculate a percentile rank. Here we have a percentile rank from which to calculate a test score (percentile). When the larger score is the better score, we use the following formula to calculate the test score that corresponds to a particular rank:

$$P = lrl + \left[\frac{\frac{(PR)(n)}{100} - cfb}{fw} \right] (UM)$$

where P is the test score (percentile) that corresponds to the percentile rank, X is the score that contains the percentile (the score below which the wanted percentage of frequencies fall), lrl is the lower real limit $(X - .5UM)$, PR is the percentile rank, n is the number of scores (sum of the frequency column), cfb is the number of scores below X, fw is the frequency for X, and UM is the unit of measurement in which the test scores are expressed.

Note: When the smaller score is the better score, the formula becomes

$$P = url + \left[\frac{cfb - \frac{(PR)(n)}{100}}{fw} \right] (UM)$$

where url is the upper real limit $(X + .5UM)$. Note that the formulas for calculating the median are a special case of these formulas.

Problem 2.9   Given the scores and frequency distribution in table 2.3, determine which score has a percentile rank of 45. (What is P for a PR of 45?)

Table 2.3
Sample Scores and Frequency Distribution.

x	f	cf
21	2	52
18	3	50
15	3	47
14	4	44
13	4	40
11	10	36
10	7	26
9	4	19
8	6	15
7	5	9
6	2	4
5	1	2
1	1	1

Solution   Before we can solve the formula for P, we must determine the value of X that gives us terms lrl, cfb, and fw:

$$\frac{(PR)(n)}{100} = \frac{(45)(52)}{100} = \frac{2340}{100} = 23.4$$

So X is the 23.4th score from the bottom. Looking at the cf column in table 2.3, we see that score 10 contains the 23.4th score. Now we can solve for P. Where lrl is 9.5 $(10 - .5)$, PR is 45, n is 52, cfb is 19, fw is 7, and UM is 1, P is 10:

$$P = 9.5 + \left[\frac{\frac{(45)(52)}{100} - 19}{7} \right] (1)$$

$$= 9.5 + \left[\frac{\frac{2340}{100} - 19}{7} \right] (1) = 9.5 + \frac{23.4 - 19}{7}$$

$$= 9.5 + \frac{4.4}{7} = 9.5 + .63 = 10.13 = 10$$

The score below which 45% of the scores fall is 10; it has a percentile rank of 45.

Using the Mean and Standard Deviation to Calculate P

Norms should be developed on the basis of a large number of scores. When the graph of these scores resembles the normal curve (figure 2.3), we can identify percentiles using the mean and standard deviation of the set of scores. Table 2.4 can be used to develop norms in percentile ranks that are multiples of 5. This table assumes that the larger score is the better score. When the smaller score is the better score, reverse the sign on the amount being added to or subtracted from the mean. For example, when

PR_x is 80, use $\overline{X} - .84s$ for a speed event.

Problem 2.10   The mean and standard deviation for a bent-knee sit-up test are 45 and 8 respectively. Determine the score that corresponds to a PR_x of 60.

Solution   Where $\overline{X}$ is 45 and s is 8, from table 2.4 we see that P for a PR of 60 must equal 47:

$$P = 45 + (.25)(8) = 45 + 2 = 47$$

Using the Computer

Percentiles, percentile ranks, and the other statistics discussed to this point can be obtained from a computer. The data in table 2.3 were analyzed using the FREQUEN-CIES program in the SPSS package (Nie et al. 1975). The information in figure 2.5 is the output from the FREQUENCIES program.

Table 2.4

Calculating Selected Percentiles Using the Mean ($\overline{X}$) and Standard Deviation (s).

PR	PERCENTILE	PR	PERCENTILE
99.9	$\overline{X} + 3.00s$	45.0	$\overline{X} - .13s$
95.0	$\overline{X} + 1.64s$	40.0	$\overline{X} - .25s$
90.0	$\overline{X} + 1.28s$	35.0	$\overline{X} - .39s$
85.0	$\overline{X} + 1.04s$	30.0	$\overline{X} - .52s$
80.0	$\overline{X} + .84s$	25.0	$\overline{X} - .67s$
75.0	$\overline{X} + .67s$	20.0	$\overline{X} - .84s$
70.0	$\overline{X} + .52s$	15.0	$\overline{X} - 1.04s$
65.0	$\overline{X} + .39s$	10.0	$\overline{X} - 1.28s$
60.0	$\overline{X} + .25s$	5.0	$\overline{X} - 1.64s$
55.0	$\overline{X} + .13s$	0.1	$\overline{X} - 3.00s$
50.0	$\overline{X} + .00s$		

Figure 2.5 Output from FREQUENCIES program, using the data in Table 2.3.

CODE	ABSOLUTE FREQUENCY	RELATIVE FREQUENCY (%)	ADJUSTED FREQUENCY (%)	CUMULATIVE FREQUENCY (%)
21	2	3.8	3.8	99.9
18	3	5.8	5.8	96.1
15	3	5.8	5.8	90.3
14	4	7.7	7.7	84.5
13	4	7.7	7.7	76.8
11	10	19.2	19.2	69.1
10	7	13.5	13.5	49.9
9	4	7.7	7.7	36.4
8	6	11.5	11.5	28.7
7	5	9.6	9.6	17.2
6	2	3.8	3.8	7.6
5	1	1.9	1.9	3.8
1	1	1.9	1.9	1.9
	52	100.0	100.0	

MEAN	10.885	STD DEV	3.896*	RANGE	20.000
MODE	11.000	MINIMUM	1.000ʳ	SUM	566.000
MEDIAN	10.500	MAXIMUM	21.000		

*SPSS uses $n - 1$ rather than n in the denominator; either is correct.

ʳThis represents the minimum score.

In figure 2.5 the first two columns are the scores and frequencies for the scores. The third column indicates what percentage of the students received each score. For example, for code (score) 21, 2 of the 52 students, or 3.8% $\left(\dfrac{2}{52}\right)$ received that score.

If all 52 students did not have a score, each absolute frequency would be divided only by the number who had a score, and the percentages in the fourth column would differ from the values in the third. The last column is basically the percentile ranks, in that the values indicate the total percentage of scores at and below a particular score. For example, 69.1% of the scores are 11 or less.

We could use this last column in the figure to develop percentile norms expressed in multiples of 5. Usually this would not be done with as few scores (52) as listed in figure 2.5 because percentile ranks can change so fast that all wanted values cannot be identified. (The dashes represent these unidentifiable values in the list below.) The identifiable percentile norms developed from figure 2.5 are as follows:

PR	X	PR	X	PR	X
100	21	65	—	30	—
95	18	60	—	25	—
90	15	55	—	20	—
85	14	50	10	15	7
80	—	45	—	10	6
75	13	40	—	5	5
70	11	35	9	0	1

Similar information can be obtained using a microcomputer. FREQUENCIES and PERCENTILES in the *Statistics with Finesse* package (Bolding 1985) provide these statistics.

STANDARD SCORES

Standard scores are used frequently to evaluate students at the end of a semester or to determine class ranks based on all the tests administered over a period of time. When each student has scores, for example, on sit-ups, a dash, and a standing long jump, how does the teacher determine which student's overall performance is best? A physical educator working in a health club or corporate fitness program could face the same problem. The three scores cannot be added together because the unit of measurement differs from test to test (executions, seconds, inches). We eliminate this problem by translating each test score into a standard score, and summing the standard scores for each student or participant. The individual with the largest sum is the best overall.

z-Scores

A **z-score** indicates how many standard deviations above or below the mean a test score lies. We calculate z-scores with the following formula:

$$z = \frac{X - \overline{X}}{s}$$

A person who scores at the mean receives a z-score of 0; a person who scores $\frac{1}{2}$ standard deviation below the mean receives a z-score of $-.5$. Thus the mean z-score is 0, and the standard deviation for a distribution of z-scores is 1.

T-Scores

Because z-scores are usually fractional and can be negative, physical educators are more likely to use **T-scores** to combine different tests together. T-scores are usually rounded off to the nearest whole number and are rarely negative. The mean T-score is 50, and the standard deviation for a distribution of T-scores is 10. The formula for calculating T-scores is as follows:

$$T = \frac{10(X - \overline{X})}{s} + 50$$

Note that the term $\frac{(X - \overline{X})}{s}$ in the T-score formula is the equation for determining the z-score. We could restate the T-score formula, then, as follows:

$$T = 10z + 50$$

Problem 2.11   Given a mean of 87 and a standard deviation of 2.35, determine the T-score for a score of 90.

Solution   Where X is 90, $\overline{X}$ is 87, and s is 2.35, T is 63:

$$T = \frac{(10)(90 - 87)}{2.35} + 50 = \frac{(10)(3)}{2.35} + 50$$

$$= \frac{30}{2.35} + 50 = 12.76 + 50 = 62.76 = 63$$

Notice that T-scores rise as performances rise above the mean. When smaller scores are better, T-scores must rise as performances fall below the mean. Thus, for speed events, we use the following formula to calculate T-scores:

$$T = \frac{10(\overline{X} - X)}{s} + 50$$

The relationship among test scores, z-scores, and T-scores for a hypothetical test with mean 75 and standard deviation 8 is shown in table 2.5. From the table we can see that a T-score of 50 is equivalent to a z-score of 0, or a test score equal to the test mean. Also a test score 2 standard deviations above the mean equals a T-score of 70.

Table 2.5

Relationship Among Test Scores (Mean 75, Standard Deviation 8), z-Scores, and T-Scores.

	$\bar{X} - 3s$	$\bar{X} - 2s$	$\bar{X} - s$	$\bar{X}$	$\bar{X} + s$	$\bar{X} + 2s$	$\bar{X} + 3s$
				SCORE POSITION			
Hypothetical test scores	51	59	67	75	83	91	99
z-scores	−3	−2	−1	0	1	2	3
T-scores	20	30	40	50	60	70	80

Table 2.6

T-Scores Calculated by Formula and Rounded to Whole Numbers.

STUDENT	PULL-UPS*	LONG JUMP†	50-YARD DASH‡	PULL-UPS T	JUMP T	DASH T	SUM T
1	11	63	7.9	70	42	50	162
2	7	72	8.0	58	54	48	160
3	4	84	7.1	48	69	63	180
4	3	69	8.0	45	50	48	143
5	4	60	8.6	48	39	38	125
6	0	51	9.7	36	27	20	83
7	6	75	7.7	55	58	53	166
8	6	69	8.0	55	50	48	153
9	1	63	8.2	39	42	45	126
10	0	69	7.6	36	50	55	141
11	3	66	7.9	45	46	50	141
12	2	69	8.1	42	50	46	138
13	9	81	6.9	64	65	66	195
14	4	66	8.2	48	46	45	139
15	6	78	7.0	55	62	65	182
16	7	81	7.3	58	65	60	183
17	0	63	8.3	36	42	43	121
18	10	66	7.7	67	46	53	166
19	6	63	7.5	55	42	56	153
20	1	72	7.8	39	54	51	144

*Mean 4.50; standard deviation 3.25.
†Mean 69; standard deviation 7.82.
‡Mean 7.88; standard deviation 0.6.

T-scores are easy to interpret if we remember the mean T-score of 50 and the standard deviation for T-scores is 10. For example, a T-score of 65 is 1.5 standard deviations above the mean, a T-score of 40 is 1 standard deviation below the mean, and a T-score of 78 is 2.8 standard deviations above the mean.

The T-scores for 20 students with 3 test scores are listed in table 2.6. Student 13 is the best overall student because the sum of that student's scores (195) is the largest.

Methods for Determining T-Scores

Obviously, translating test scores to T-scores takes time and effort. Few physical education teachers or exercise specialists, given 5 to 15 scores for each of a hundred or more individuals, have the time to calculate T-scores by hand. However, it would be unfortunate to bypass a good, easy technique for lack of time. There are two methods that allow us to obtain T-scores quickly: calculated conversion tables, and computer analysis.

Calculated Conversion Tables.   For most tests, each score will be obtained by several people. For example, we can see in table 2.6 that 3 students did no pull-ups, 2 students did 1 pull-up, and so on. Once the T-score for a test score is determined, it is not necessary to recalculate the T-score every time that test score is repeated. Instead, we develop a test score–T-score conversion table. The method of development is either calculation by hand or the addition and subtraction method, depending on the number of different scores.

When the number of different scores is small, we can construct the test score–T-score conversion table by hand, calculating the T-score for each existing test score and expressing the T-score as a whole number. For example, from the pull-up scores in table 2.6 we can develop this conversion table:

X	0	1	2	3	4	5	6	7	9	10	11
T	36	39	42	45	48	52	55	58	64	67	70

When the number of different test scores is large or when the T-score for all possible (not actual) test scores is needed, the addition and subtraction method works better than calculation. Remember that the mean test score equals a T-score of 50 and that the standard deviation of T-scores is 10. When we divide the test score standard deviation by the T-score standard deviation, 10, we are left with a constant amount, $\frac{s}{10}$, that we can use to obtain all possible T-scores. For example, a T-score of 51 equals $\overline{X} + \frac{s}{10}$; by adding the constant amount to that sum we calculate the test score equivalent to a T-score of 52. For scores below the mean, we subtract the constant amount. The steps to follow are:

1. List the T-scores from 20 to 80 on the left side of a piece of paper.
2. Next to T-score 50, record the test score mean.
3. Either by hand or using a calculator, add the constant amount, $\frac{s}{10}$, to the test score mean. Record this amount opposite T-score 51.
4. Continue to add the constant amount to the previous sum to find test scores for all T-scores above 50.
5. Subtract the constant amount from the test score mean to find the test score that corresponds to T-score 49.
6. Continue to subtract the constant amount from the previous result to find test scores for all T-scores below 50.

7. Round off the test scores.
8. Use the T-score that corresponds to the highest of equivalent test scores (after rounding) in developing the test score–T-score conversion table.

For example, to apply the addition and subtraction method to the pull-up scores in table 2.6, we would first determine $\frac{s}{10}$. Where the standard deviation is 3.25, $\frac{s}{10}$ is .325, or .33. With the constant amount in hand, we begin adding to the mean (4.50) for scores above it, and subtracting from the mean for scores below it. Our worksheet section around the mean would look like this:

T	X	
.		
.		
.		
53	5.49	5.16 + .33
52	5.16	4.83 + .33
51	4.83	4.50 + .33
50	4.50	
49	4.17	4.50 − .33
48	3.84	4.17 − .33
47	3.51	3.84 − .33
.		
.		
.		

The worksheet would continue above 53 to T-score 80 and below 47 to T-score 20.

Because pull-up results are reported in whole numbers, we would round the corresponding test scores to the nearest whole number. The 4.83 pull-ups that correspond to T-score 51 should be rounded off to 5, as should the 5.16 and 5.49 pull-up scores. Taking the highest equivalent score, we would use a T-score of 53 to correspond to 5 pull-ups in our conversion table. The complete test score–T-score conversion table for the pull-up scores in table 2.6 looks like this:

X	0	1	2	3	4	5	6	7	8	9	10	11	12	13	14
T	36	40	43	46	49	53	56	59	62	65	68	71	74	77	80

Notice that by rounding off the test scores to whole numbers we have arrived at slightly different values than those that appear in table 2.6. The T-scores in the table were calculated for each test score and were themselves rounded off to whole numbers.

Computer Analysis. The fastest and easiest way to calculate T-scores is through computer analysis. In fact, with a large amount of data, it may be the only feasible method. A computer program (TSCORE (Prusaczuk and Baumgartner 1986)) is discussed in the last section of this chapter.

THE NORMAL CURVE

Earlier in this chapter we discussed the normal curve as a model for the graph of a set of scores. In chapter 5 the normal curve is used as a method of evaluating student achievement. Here we discuss the normal curve and its role in making probability statements.

Characteristics

The **normal curve** is a mathematically defined, smooth, bilaterally symmetrical curve, centered around a point that is simultaneously the mode, median, and mean. Because the center point is both mode and median, it is the most frequent score and that score below which half the scores fall. The normal curve, by mathematical definition, has a mean of 0 and a standard deviation of 1. Thus the normal curve is the graph of an infinite number of z-scores.

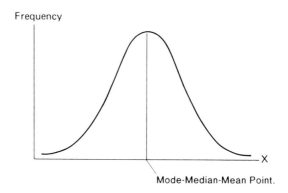

Mode-Median-Mean Point.

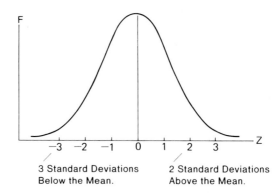

3 Standard Deviations Below the Mean.

2 Standard Deviations Above the Mean.

Probability

When you flip a coin, the probability of it coming up heads is $\frac{1}{2}$: there are 2 possible outcomes, and heads represents only 1 of those outcomes—the event or outcome desired. The statement is written $P(H) = \frac{1}{2}$. In general, the probability of an event is the number of possible outcomes that satisfy the event divided by the total number of possible outcomes.

For example, when you flip 2 coins, what is the probability of their both coming up tails (TT)? You have 4 possible outcomes: both heads (HH), both tails (TT), the first coin heads and the second tails (HT), and vice versa (TH). The wanted outcome, event TT, is 1 of the 4 possible outcomes, so the probability of TT occurring is $\frac{1}{4}$:

$$P(TT) = \frac{1}{4}$$

To use the normal curve to make probability statements, think of the area under the curve as 100 equal portions. If there are 100 possible outcomes under the normal curve, then 50 of these outcomes lie on each side of the mean. Because the curve is symmetrical, the number of outcomes between 0 and -1 equals the number of outcomes between 0 and 1.

Problem 2.12   What is the probability of a z equal to or greater than ($\geq$) 0?

Solution   To begin, we must determine the percentage of the area under the curve that lies to the right of 0. From our definition we know that half the possible outcomes lie to each side of 0 (the midpoint). Any of the 50 outcomes that lie to the right of 0 would satisfy $z \geq 0$. Thus, the probability of $z \geq 0$ is $\frac{1}{2}$:

$$P(z \geq 0) = \frac{50}{100} = \frac{1}{2}$$

This problem is simple because we have the answers to it by definition. To answer most probability statements about the normal curve, we have to use a special table, which appears here as table 2.7. The table allows us to determine the percentage of a given area under the curve, and thus the basis for determining the probability of z falling within that area. The values along the left side and top of the table are z values, or standard deviation distances from the mean. The values in the body of the table indicate the percentage of the area under the curve between a given z-score and the mean z-score, 0.

Table 2.7

Percentage of Total Area under the Normal Curve between the Mean and Ordinate Points at Any Given Standard Deviation Distance from the Mean.

z	.00	.01	.02	.03	.04	.05	.06	.07	.08	.09
0.0	00.00	00.40	00.80	01.20	01.60	01.99	02.39	02.79	03.19	03.59
0.1	03.98	04.38	04.78	05.17	05.57	05.96	06.36	06.75	07.14	07.53
0.2	07.93	08.32	08.71	09.10	09.48	09.87	10.26	10.64	11.03	11.41
0.3	11.79	12.17	12.55	12.95	13.31	13.68	14.06	14.43	14.80	15.17
0.4	15.54	15.91	16.28	16.64	17.00	17.36	17.72	18.08	18.44	18.79
0.5	19.15	19.50	19.85	20.19	20.54	20.88	21.23	21.57	21.90	22.24
0.6	22.57	22.91	23.24	23.57	23.89	24.22	24.54	24.86	25.17	25.49
0.7	25.80	26.11	26.42	26.73	27.04	27.34	27.64	27.94	28.23	28.52
0.8	28.81	29.10	29.39	29.67	29.95	30.23	30.51	30.78	31.06	31.33
0.9	31.59	31.86	32.12	32.38	32.64	32.90	33.15	33.40	33.65	33.89
1.0	34.13	34.38	34.61	34.85	35.08	35.31	35.54	35.77	35.99	36.21
1.1	36.43	36.65	36.86	37.08	37.29	37.49	37.70	37.90	38.10	38.30
1.2	38.49	38.69	38.88	39.07	39.25	39.44	39.62	39.80	39.97	40.15
1.3	40.32	40.49	40.66	40.82	40.99	41.15	41.31	41.47	41.62	41.77
1.4	41.92	42.07	42.22	42.36	42.51	42.65	42.79	42.92	43.06	43.19
1.5	43.32	43.45	43.57	43.70	43.83	43.94	44.06	44.18	44.29	44.41
1.6	44.52	44.63	44.74	44.84	44.95	45.05	45.15	45.25	45.35	45.45
1.7	45.54	45.64	45.73	45.82	45.91	45.99	46.08	46.16	46.25	46.33
1.8	46.41	46.49	46.56	46.64	46.71	46.78	46.86	46.93	46.99	47.06
1.9	47.13	47.19	47.26	47.32	47.38	47.44	47.50	47.56	47.61	47.67
2.0	47.72	47.78	47.83	47.88	47.93	47.98	48.03	48.08	48.12	48.17
2.1	48.21	48.26	48.30	48.34	48.38	48.42	48.46	48.50	48.54	48.57
2.2	48.61	48.64	48.68	48.71	48.75	48.78	48.81	48.84	48.87	48.90
2.3	48.93	48.96	48.98	49.01	49.04	49.06	49.09	49.11	49.13	49.16
2.4	49.18	49.20	49.22	49.25	49.27	49.29	49.31	49.32	49.34	49.36
2.5	49.38	49.40	49.41	49.43	49.45	49.46	49.48	49.49	49.51	49.52
2.6	49.53	49.55	49.56	49.57	49.59	49.60	49.61	49.62	49.63	49.64
2.7	49.65	49.66	49.67	49.68	49.69	49.70	49.71	49.72	49.73	49.74
2.8	49.74	49.75	49.76	49.77	49.77	49.78	49.79	49.79	49.80	49.81
2.9	49.81	49.82	49.82	49.83	49.84	49.84	49.85	49.85	49.86	49.86
3.0	49.87									
3.5	49.98									
4.0	49.997									
5.0	49.99997									

From Lindquist, E. F., *A First Course in Statistics* (Boston: Houghton Mifflin, 1942), p. 242. By permission.

Problem 2.13   What percentage of the area under the normal curve lies between $0(z = 0)$ and $1.36(z = 1.36)$?

Solution   Because

$$1.36 = 1.30 + .06$$

we read down the left side of the table to 1.3 and across the row to column .06. The value listed there, 41.31, is that percentage of the area under the normal curve that lies between 0 and 1.36.

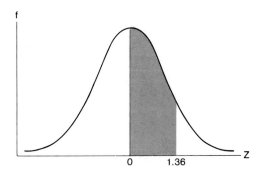

Once we know the possible outcomes that satisfy an event, we can determine the probability of that event happening. The probability that z falls between 0 and 1.36 on the normal curve is the satisfactory outcomes (41.31) divided by the possible outcomes (100), or 41%:

$$P(z \text{ between 0 and } 1.36) = \frac{41.31}{100} = .4131 = .41$$

Because the normal curve is symmetrical, the values in table 2.7 hold true for equivalent distances from the mean to the left of it. That is, the percentage of the area under the normal curve between 0 and -1.36 is still 41.31, and the probability that z falls somewhere between 0 and -1.36 is still 41%.

Although the table lists percentages only from the mean, we can extrapolate from it, remembering that 50% of all possible outcomes lie to each side of the mean.

Problem 2.14   What is the probability that z is equal to or greater than 1.03?

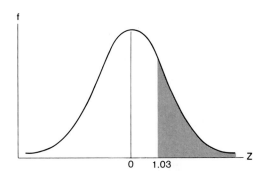

Solution   First we determine the overall area between 0 and 1.03. Reading down the left side of table 2.7 to 1.0 and across to column .03, we see that 34.85% of the total area to the right of the mean lies between 0 and 1.03. Because we know that the possible outcomes to the right (or left for that matter) of 0 represent $\frac{50}{100}$, we can subtract the amount we know, $\frac{34.85}{100}$, from $\frac{50}{100}$. The result is our answer. The probability that z is equal to or greater than 1.03 is 15%.

$$P(z \geq 1.03) = \frac{50}{100} - \frac{34.85}{100}$$
$$= .50 - .3485 = .1515 = .15$$

Often the probability statement requires a translation from test score X to the equivalent Z, or vice versa, as we can see in the following problems.

Problem 2.15   A teacher always administers 100-point tests and always gives A's to scores of 93 and above. On the last test the mean was 72 and the standard deviation was 9. Assuming test scores are normally distributed, what was the probability of receiving an A on that test?

Solution   This is the same as asking what percentage of the class probably received A's: what is the probability that a score X was greater than or equal to 93? Before we can solve the probability statement, then, we must change score 93 to a z-score. Where X is greater than or equal to 93, $\overline{X}$ is 72, and s is 9, the z-score must be greater than or equal to 2.33:

$$z \geq \frac{93 - 72}{9} \geq \frac{21}{9} \geq 2.33$$

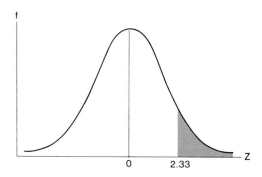

Now, using table 2.7, it is easy to determine the probability. At the intersection of z row 2.3 and column .03, we see that the percentage under the normal curve between 0 and 2.33 is 49.01. By subtracting that amount from the percentage of possible outcomes, we see that the probability that z is greater than or equal to 2.33 is 1%:

$$P(z \geq 2.33) = \frac{50}{100} - \frac{49.01}{100} = \frac{.99}{100} = .0099 = .01$$

Problem 2.16   To develop some performance standards, a teacher decides to use the normal curve to determine that score above which 7% of the scores should fall. That is, what is the z-score above which 7% of the area under the normal curve falls?

$$P(z \geq ?) = \frac{7}{100}$$

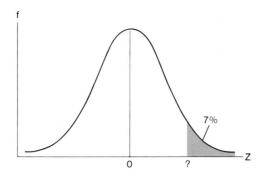

Solution   We know that 43% of the area under the curve lies between 0 and the unknown z-score. If we scan table 2.7, we see that percentage 43.06 is closest to 43%.
Because 43.06 is at the intersection of z row 1.4 and column .08, the unknown z-score
(the z-score above which 7% of the area falls) is 1.48. Thus the teacher would use the
following formula to calculate X:

$$X = \overline{X} + z(s)$$
$$X = \overline{X} + 1.48(s)$$

and if $\overline{X} = 31.25$, s = 5.0 then

$$X = 31.25 + 1.48(5.0) = 31.25 + 7.4 = 38.65$$

DETERMINING RELATIONSHIPS BETWEEN SCORES

There are many situations in which the physical education teacher and exercise specialist would like to know the relationship between scores on 2 different tests. For example, if speed and the performance of a sport skill were found to be related, the physical
education teacher might try to improve the speed of poor performers. Or, if weight and
high-jump ability were found to be related, the instructor might want to use a different
evaluation standard for each weight classification. Knowing the relationship between
scores also can lead to greater efficiency in a measurement program. For example, if
there are 7 tests in a physical fitness battery and 2 of them are highly related, the
battery could be reduced to 6 tests with no loss of information. We use two different
techniques to determine score relationships: a graphing technique and a mathematical
technique called correlation.

The Graphing Technique

The graphing technique is quicker than the mathematical technique, but not as precise.
It requires that each individual have a score on each of the two measures. To graph a
relationship, we develop a coordinate system according to those values of the measure
listed along the horizontal axis and those of the other measure, listed along the vertical
axis. We plot a point for each individual above his score on the horizontal axis and
opposite his score on the vertical axis, as shown in figure 2.6.

Figure 2.6 Graph of a positive relationship.

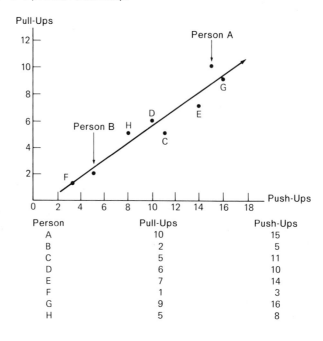

Person	Pull-Ups	Push-Ups
A	10	15
B	2	5
C	5	11
D	6	10
E	7	14
F	1	3
G	9	16
H	5	8

Figure 2.7 Graph of a negative relationship.

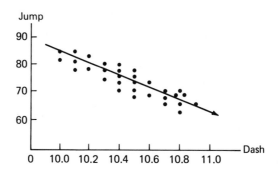

The point plotted for Person A is at the intersection of push-up score 15 and pull-up score 10, the scores the person received on the 2 tests. The straight line—the **line of best fit** or the **regression line**—represents the trend in the data, in this case that individuals with large push-up scores have large pull-up scores, and vice versa. When large scores on one measure are associated with large scores on the other measure, the relationship is **positive**. When large scores on one measure are associated with small scores on the other measure, as shown in figure 2.7, the relationship is **negative**.

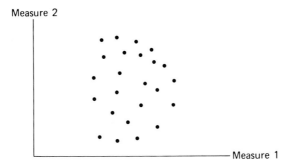

Measure 2

Measure 1

The closer all the plotted points are to the trend line, the higher or larger the relationship. The maximum relationship occurs when all plotted points are on the trend line. When the plotted points resemble a circle, making it impossible to draw a trend line, there is no linear relationship between the two measures being graphed. We can see this in the above graph.

The Correlation Technique

Correlation is a mathematical technique for determining the relationship between 2 sets of scores. The formula was developed by Karl Pearson to determine the degree of relationship between 2 sets of measures (called X measures and Y measures):

$$r = \frac{n\Sigma XY - (\Sigma X)(\Sigma Y)}{\sqrt{[n\Sigma X^2 - (\Sigma X)^2][n\Sigma Y^2 - (\Sigma Y)^2]}}$$

where r is the Pearson product-moment correlation coefficient, n is the number of individuals, ΣXY is the sum of each individual's X times Y value, ΣX is the sum of the scores for one set of measures, ΣY is the sum of the scores for the other set of measures, ΣX^2 is the sum of the squared X scores, and ΣY^2 is the sum of the squared Y scores.

Problem 2.17   Using the figures in table 2.8, determine the correlation between the pull-up scores (X) and the push-up scores (Y).

Table 2.8
Student Scores for Correlation Calculation.

Individual	Pull-ups (X)	Push-ups (Y)	XY	X²	Y²
A	10	15	150	100	225
B	2	5	10	4	25
C	5	11	55	25	121
D	6	10	60	36	100
E	7	14	98	49	196
F	1	3	3	1	9
G	9	16	144	81	256
H	5	8	40	25	64
n = 8	$\Sigma X = 45$	$\Sigma Y = 82$	$\Sigma XY = 560$	$\Sigma X^2 = 321$	$\Sigma Y^2 = 996$

Solution   Where n is 8 (the number of individuals), ΣXY is 560 (the sum of column XY), ΣX is 45 (the sum of column X), ΣY is 82 (the sum of column Y), ΣX^2 is 321 (the sum of column X^2), and ΣY^2 is 996 (the sum of column Y^2), the correlation coefficient r is 0.96:

$$r = \frac{(8)(560) - (45)(82)}{\sqrt{[(8)(321) - 45^2][(8)(996) - 82^2]}}$$

$$= \frac{4480 - 3690}{\sqrt{(2568 - 2025)(7968 - 6724)}} = \frac{790}{\sqrt{(543)(1244)}}$$

$$= \frac{790}{\sqrt{675492}} = \frac{790}{821.88} = .96$$

Correlation coefficients have two characteristics, direction and strength. Direction of the relationship is indicated by whether the correlation coefficient is positive or negative, as indicated under the graphing technique. Strength of the relationship is indicated by how close the r is to 1, the maximum value possible. A correlation of 1 (r = 1) shows a perfect positive relationship, indicating that an increase in scores on one measure is accompanied by an increase in scores on the second measure. A perfect negative relationship (r = -1) indicates that an increase in scores on one measure is accompanied by a decrease in scores on the second. (Notice that a correlation of -1 is just as strong as a correlation of 1.) Perfect relationships are rare, but any such relationship that does exist is exactly described by mathematical formula. An example of a perfect positive and a perfect negative relationship is shown in table 2.9. When the correlation coefficient is 0 (r = 0), there is no relationship between the two sets of scores.

Because the relationship between two sets of scores is seldom perfect, the majority of correlation coefficients are fractions (.93, -.85, and the like). The closer the correlation coefficient is to 1 or -1, the stronger the relationship. When the relationship is not perfect, the scores on one measure only tend to change with the scores on the other measure. Look, for example, at table 2.10. The correlation between height and weight is not perfect: Individual C, whose height is 75 inches, is not heavier than Individual E, whose height is only 70 inches.

Table 2.9
Examples of Perfect Relationships.

Individual	Height	Weight	Individual	100-Yard Dash	Pull-Ups
A	60	130	A	10.6	14
B	52	122	B	10.6	14
C	75	145	C	11.2	8
D	66	136	D	11.7	3
E	70	140	E	10.5	15
	r = 1			r = −1	
	Exact formula: weight = height + 70			Exact formula: dash = 12 − .1 (pull-ups)	

When the scores for the 2 sets of scores are ranks, a correlation coefficient called **rho** or **Spearman's rho** or the **rank order correlation coefficient** may be calculated. The formula is just a simplification of the Pearson correlation formula. Since the same value will be obtained by applying the Pearson correlation formula to the 2 sets of ranks, the formula is not presented.

Interpreting the Correlation Coefficient

A high correlation between two measures does not usually indicate a cause and effect relationship. The perfect height and weight relationship in table 2.9, for example, does not indicate that an increase in weight causes an increase in height. Also, the degree of relationship between two sets of measures does not increase at the same rate as does the correlation coefficient. The true indicator of the degree of relationship is the **coefficient of determination**—the amount of variability in one measure that is explained by the other measure. The coefficient of determination is the square of the correlation coefficient (r^2). For example, the square of the correlation coefficient in table 2.10 is .83 ($.91^2$), which means that 83% of the variability in height scores is due to the individuals having different weight scores.

Thus when one correlation coefficient is twice as large as another, the larger coefficient really explains four times the amount of variation that the smaller coefficient explains. For example, when the r between agility and balance is .80 and the r between strength and power is .40, the r^2 for agility and balance is $.80^2$, or 64%; and the r^2 for strength and power is $.40^2$, or 16%.

Remember, when you interpret a correlation coefficient that there are no absolute standards for labeling a given r "good" or "poor"; only the relationship you want or expect determines the quality of a given r. For example, if you or others had obtained a correlation coefficient of .67 between leg strength and standing long jump scores for males, you might expect a similar correlation coefficient in comparing leg strength and long jump scores for females. If the relationship between the females' scores were only .45, you might label that correlation coefficient "poor" because you expected it to be as high as that of the males.

There are two reasons why correlation coefficients can be negative: (1) opposite scoring scales and (2) true negative relationships. When a measure on which a small score is a better score is correlated with a measure on which a larger score is a better score, the correlation coefficient probably will be negative. Consider, for example, the relationship between scores on a speed event like the 50-yard dash and a nonspeed

Table 2.10
Example of an Imperfect Correlation.

INDIVIDUAL	HEIGHT (INCHES)	WEIGHT (POUNDS)
A	60	130
B	52	125
C	75	145
D	66	136
E	70	150
	r = .91	

event like the standing long jump. Usually the best jumpers are the best runners, but the correlation is negative because the scoring scales are reversed. Two measures can be negatively related as well. We would expect, for example, a negative correlation between body weight and measures involving support or motion of the body (pull-ups, dips).

The Question of Accuracy

In calculating r we assume that the relationship between the 2 sets of scores is basically linear. A **linear relationship** is shown graphically by a straight line, as is the trend line in figure 2.6. However, a relationship between 2 sets of scores can be represented by a curved line, as shown in the following **curvilinear relationship.** A curvilinear relationship between two measures is best described by a curved line. Learning curves and fatigue curves, where X is trials or time and Y is mean performance of a group, are examples of curvilinear relationships. If a relationship is truly curvilinear, the correlation coefficient will underestimate the relationship. For example, r could equal 0 even when a definite curvilinear relationship exists.

Although we need not assume when calculating r that the graph of each of the 2 sets of scores is a normal curve, we do assume that the 2 graphs resemble each other. If they are dissimilar, the correlation coefficient will underestimate the relationship between the scores. Considerable differences in the 2 graphs are occasionally found, usually when the number of people tested is small. For this reason, the correlation coefficient ideally should be calculated with the scores of several hundred people.

Other factors also affect the correlation coefficient. One is the reliability of the scores; low reliability reduces the correlation coefficient (see chapter 3). Another factor is the range in the scores; the correlation coefficient will be smaller for a homogeneous group than for a heterogeneous group. Ferguson (1981) suggests that generally the range in scores increases as the size of the group tested increases. Certainly small groups exhibit a greater tendency than large groups to be either more homogeneous or more heterogeneous than is typical for the group measured and the test administered. This is another reason to calculate the correlation coefficient only when the group tested is large. Ferguson (1981) and Walker and Lev (1969) cover this subject in greater detail.

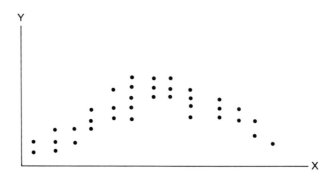

When the test group is large or when the physical education teacher and exercise specialist want the correlation between all possible pairings of more than 2 tests (pull-ups and sit-ups, pull-ups and 50-yard dash, sit-ups and 50-yard dash), using a computer is the most efficient way to obtain the correlation coefficients. Computer programs that calculate correlation coefficients are commonly found in computer centers, the SPSS package (Nie et al. 1975) for example and in packages of statistical programs for microcomputers. Computer programs are discussed in greater detail in the last section of this chapter.

PREDICTION

Teachers, coaches, exercise specialists, and researchers have long been interested in predicting scores that are either difficult or impossible to obtain at a given moment. Prediction is estimating a person's score on one measure based on the person's score on one or more other measures. Although prediction is often imprecise, it is occasionally useful to develop a prediction formula.

Simple Prediction

Simple predictions predict an unknown score Y′ for an individual by using that person's performance X on a known measure. To develop a **simple prediction,** or regression formula, a large number of subjects must be measured and a score on the predictor variable X and the predicted variable Y obtained for each.

$$Y' = \left[r\left(\frac{s_y}{s_x}\right) \right] (X - \overline{X}) + \overline{Y}$$

where Y′ is the predicted Y score for an individual, r is the correlation between X and Y scores, s_y is the standard deviation for the Y scores, s_x is the standard deviation for the X scores, X is the individual's known score on measure X, $\overline{X}$ is the mean for the X scores, and $\overline{Y}$ is the mean for the Y scores. Once the formula is developed for any given relationship, only the predictor variable X is needed to predict the performance of an individual on measure Y. One index of the accuracy of a simple prediction equation is r.

Problem 2.18   A coach found the correlation coefficient between physical fitness and athletic ability to be .65. The mean of the physical fitness test is 330; its standard deviation is 50. The mean of the athletic ability test is 9; its standard deviation is 2. What is the predicted athletic ability score for an athlete with a physical fitness score of 350?

Solution   Where r is .65, s_y is 2, s_x is 50, X is 350, $\overline{X}$ is 330, and $\overline{Y}$ is 9, the athlete's predicted athletic ability score, Y′, is 9.52:

$$Y' = \left[(.65)\left(\frac{2}{50}\right) \right] (350 - 330) + 9$$
$$= (.026)(20) + 9 = .52 + 9 = 9.52$$

The Standard Error of Prediction

An individual's predicted score, Y', will not equal the actual score Y unless the correlation coefficient used in the formula is perfect—a rare event. Thus for each individual there is an error of prediction. We find the standard deviation of this error, the **standard error of prediction,** using the following formula:

$$s_{y \cdot x} = s_y \sqrt{1 - r^2}$$

where $s_{y \cdot x}$ is the standard error of score Y predicted from score X, s_y is the standard deviation for the Y scores, and r^2 is the square of the correlation coefficient (the coefficient of determination) for the X and Y scores. (Notice that the larger the coefficient, the smaller the standard error.) We can expect to find an individual's actual score Y in the boundaries $Y' \pm s_{y \cdot x}$ 68% of the time. The standard error of prediction is another index of the accuracy of a simple prediction equation.

Problem 2.19 What is the standard error of prediction for predicted score Y' in Problem 2.18?

Solution Where s_y is 2 and r^2 is .42 (.65^2), the standard error for predicted score Y' is 1.52:

$$s_{y \cdot x} = 2\sqrt{1 - .42} = 2\sqrt{.58} = 2(.76) = 1.52$$

The probability is 68% that an athlete with X score of 350 will receive an actual score Y between 8 (9.52 − 1.52) and 11.04 (9.52 + 1.52).

If the prediction formula and standard error seem acceptable, the physical education teacher or exercise specialist should try to prove the prediction formula on a second group of individuals similar to the first. This process is called **cross-validation.** If the formula works satisfactorily for the second group, it can be used with confidence to predict score Y for any individual who resembles the individuals used to form and cross-validate the equation. If the formula does not work well for the second group, it is unique to the group used to form the equation and has little value in predicting performance.

Multiple Prediction

A prediction formula using a single measure X is usually not very accurate for predicting a person's score on measure Y. **Multiple correlation-regression** techniques allow us to predict score Y using several X scores. For example, a **multiple prediction** formula has been developed to predict arm strength in pounds (Y') using both the number of pull-ups (X_1) and pounds of body weight (X_2):

$$Y' = 3.42(X_1) + 1.77(X_2) - 46$$

Although more than 2 X scores can be used as predictors, it is very difficult to develop that complex an equation by hand.

The **multiple correlation coefficient** R is one index of the accuracy of a multiple prediction equation. The minimum and maximum values of R are 0 and 1 respectively. The percentage of variance in the Y scores explained by the multiple prediction equation is R^2. A second index of the accuracy of a multiple prediction equation is the standard error of prediction. Multiple prediction formulas and multiple correlation are presented in later chapters of this book (see chapter 8, Body Composition). More comprehensive coverage of multiple regression can be found in Cohen and Cohen (1975), Ferguson (1981), Kerlinger and Pedhazur (1973), and the SPSS manual (Nie et al. 1975).

Using the Computer

The simple prediction and multiple prediction equations are both time consuming and complicated, especially when the number of people being tested is large. (It is suggested that prediction equations be developed using the scores of several hundred people.) Computer programs that do either simple or multiple prediction are commonly available for both the mainframe and microcomputer. For example, the REGRESSION program in the SPSS package can be used to obtain either a simple or multiple prediction equation.

RELIABILITY OF THE MEAN

Throughout this chapter we have placed considerable emphasis on the usefulness of the mean in describing the performance of a group. The mean is not constant: it can vary from day to day among the same individuals in a retest or from year to year if a new but similar group of individuals is tested. The performance of a group of individuals changes from day to day, even if ability has not changed, simply because people have good days and bad days. And the mean performances of different groups of individuals are seldom identical, even when the subjects are apparently equal in ability. If we can expect little variation in the mean, it is a highly reliable indicator of group ability; if we can expect considerable variation, it is not very reliable. We call the estimated variability of the mean the **standard error of the mean.** It is found using the following formula:

$$s_{\bar{x}} = \frac{s}{\sqrt{n - 1}}$$

where $s_{\bar{x}}$ is the standard error of the mean, s is the standard deviation for the scores, and n is the number of individuals in the group.

Statistics books show that when many groups—all members of the same larger group, or population—are tested, the graph of the means is normal, centered around the population mean. The standard error is the standard deviation of the group means. The standard error can be used with the normal curve in the same manner as can the standard deviation; that is, 68% of the group means will be within 1 standard error of the population mean.

Problem 2.20   The mean for an agility test performed by 82 senior citizens is 12.5; the standard deviation is .81. Determine the standard error of the mean.

Solution   Where s is .81 and n is 82, the standard error of mean 12.5 is .09:

$$s_{\bar{x}} = \frac{.81}{\sqrt{82 - 1}} = \frac{.81}{\sqrt{81}} = \frac{.81}{9} = .09$$

If 12.5 is the population mean, 68% of the means for groups belonging to this population (senior citizens) will fall between 12.41 (12.5 − .09) and 12.59 (12.5 + .09). Thus any senior citizens' groups with agility test means between 12.41 and 12.59 are probably similar in ability. In fact, if the group with mean 12.5 is tested on another day, the probability is 68% that its mean performance will fall between 12.41 and 12.59.

ADDITIONAL STATISTICAL TECHNIQUES

The statistical techniques in this chapter are those commonly used in measurement situations. There are many other statistical techniques that are not discussed in this chapter. Researchers commonly use t-tests (not to be confused with T-scores) and Analysis of Variance (ANOVA) to determine if there is a large enough difference between two or more groups in mean performance to conclude that the groups are not equal in mean performance. A few professors present t-tests and ANOVA in the graduate level measurement course and there may be some occasions where you want to use these two techniques. However, presentation of t-tests and ANOVA in sufficient details to do justice to the topic is past the scope of this book.

If you wish to learn about t-tests and ANOVA, the two topics are discussed in nonmathematical terms in most research technique books like Thomas and Nelson (1985). A more complete coverage of t-tests and ANOVA can be found in any introductory level statistics book. The presentations by Roscoe (1975) and Ferguson (1981) are easy to follow. Other books like Bloomers and Lindquist (1960), Downie and Heath (1965), Glass and Stanley (1970), and Walker and Lev (1969) are good sources. Numerous computer packages of statistical programs include t-test and ANOVA (Bolding 1985; Nie et al. 1975; SPSS 1983).

ANOVA is presented in chapter 3 of this book, but with an application to measurement rather than research. However, the calculations are similar or the same with both applications.

COMPUTERS IN EVALUATION

The evaluation of individuals' achievement is time consuming. Yet the more information—scores and analysis of scores—teachers and exercise specialists can gather on each person, the better job they can do in evaluating and counseling the individual.

Despite the increasing availability of computers, many physical educators are not using them for data analysis, often because they feel computers are too complicated. However, it is not necessary for the ultimate user to instruct the computer. Sets of instructions, called **programs,** for the calculation of means, standard deviations, percentile ranks, standard scores, and the like are available for nearly all computers. Often these programs are part of a nationally distributed package of programs, like SPSS (Nie et al. 1975), which is available on most campuses for use on mainframe computers. Programs for microcomputers are plentiful but often specific to the make and model. Each program comes with directions, which specify the calculations or information the program will provide and the information the user must provide for the program to function correctly.

Computer programs may be classified as either **"instruction"** or **"friendly"** type. Mainframe computer programs tend to be instruction type while microcomputer programs are almost always friendly type. With instruction-type programs the computer user must read the directions accompanying the program to determine the order that information must be entered into the computer and what columns on the terminal screen must be used to enter the information. This information is usually (1) the statistical technique to use, (2) the number of people tested, (3) the number of scores per person, and (4) the columns on the terminal screen that contain the data. The computer user follows these directions to the best of his/her ability and enters the required information into the computer. If the information is entered correctly, the computer analyzes the data. If the information is not entered correctly, the computer prints an **"error message"** and does not analyze the data. It is then the responsibility of the computer user, maybe with the assistance of a computer consultant, to correct the mistake and try again to have the computer analyze the data.

With friendly-type computer programs the computer asks the computer user a series of questions, or prompts the user to do something and after each question or prompt the user provides some information. This question and answer procedure is always conducted on the screen (display) of a computer terminal or microcomputer. Basically, the same information that was entered with an instruction-type program will be entered with a friendly program. The big advantage of friendly-type programs over instruction-type programs is that the computer asks for information in the order that it wants it, generally it is not concerned about what columns on the screen of the terminal or microcomputer were used to enter information, and if the question or prompt was misinterpreted and the wrong information was provided it asks the question again. Wrong in this case does not mean incorrect. Entering numbers when the computer expected alphabetic letters or vice versa is wrong, but entering 63 as the number of people tested when you meant 36 is incorrect and the computer will not detect this until you are entering the data or the computer tries to analyze your data.

With mainframe computers you will never be asked to operate the computer. A trained operator is available who may also answer questions. In most computer centers, there are consultants who answer the majority of computer user's questions. All you have to do as a computer user is enter the information the computer needs to analyze a set of data, although in some situations there are even students or employees to do this.

With microcomputers you will probably have to operate the computer. However, in many schools and agencies there are microcomputer operators who are students learning computer techniques or people hired as operators. In these cases you will not have to enter any information into the computer.

Computers may be intimidating at first. It is much like learning a new physical skill. At first you do not feel confident and make many mistakes. But, with time and practice you become more proficient. While you are learning, do not be afraid to ask for help. On the following pages is a brief discussion and presentation of some computer programs referenced in this chapter. Based on this information we hope you will start using computers to assist you in data analysis.

Mainframe Computer

Mainframe computers are the big, expensive computers, that have been used by universities, agencies, businesses, and the government for many years. Most likely, the computer program is written on magnetic tape and stored in the computer center. Also, the program is probably a direction type. The directions for the program can be obtained from computer center personnel or purchased in a bookstore if the program is one of a package of computer programs. The directions for the program specify the order that information must be entered into the computer. This arrangement is fairly standard from program to program, as shown in table 2.11.

The **system information** consists of identifying the user (so that use of computer time can be charged accordingly) and the wanted program on magnetic tape. Although system information may vary among computers, it seldom varies in a computer from program to program. The **control information** is what is specified in the computer program directions such as the number of people tested, the number of scores per person, and wanted options. This information does not vary among computers but does change from program to program. The **data** are the scores to be analyzed. Using a computer terminal, the data are typed on the terminal, one line per person.

Many schools and agencies share a computer with other schools, agencies, or industries. Some schools and agencies use several installations to hook up to a mainframe computer of their own. In either case, each school, agency, or installation is connected to the computer by a terminal. Information, then, is entered into the computer through the terminal.

When all information is entered into the computer, the computer executes the analysis or computations specified in the computer program. The results of this analysis may be listed on the computer terminal screen, but more commonly are printed out on paper. Occasionally, the results of the analysis are incorrect due to an error in entering information. In computer centers, computer operators and consultants are very helpful in showing you how to correct mistakes.

Throughout chapter 2 we have referenced the SPSS package of computer programs (Nie et al. 1975). These programs are instruction type for mainframe computers. The same basic control information (see table 2.11) is used for all programs in the package. As an example of this control information, the statements entered into the computer to analyze the data in table 2.3 with the FREQUENCIES program are presented in figure 2.8. (Users of SPSS version 10 or later versions will use different statements.) The output from this program has already been presented in figure 2.5.

Table 2.11
General Order of Information Entered into the Computer.

1. System information
2. Control information
3. Data

Figure 2.8 Input statements for FREQUENCIES program, using the data in Table 2.3.

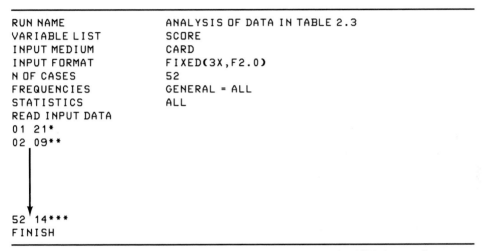

```
RUN NAME             ANALYSIS OF DATA IN TABLE 2.3
VARIABLE LIST        SCORE
INPUT MEDIUM         CARD
INPUT FORMAT         FIXED(3X,F2.0)
N OF CASES           52
FREQUENCIES          GENERAL = ALL
STATISTICS           ALL
READ INPUT DATA
01 21*
02 09**



52 14***
FINISH
```

*This was the first data line; 01 is the identification number of the first person tested and 21 is the person's score.
**This was the second data line; the second person tested was one of the four people in table 2.3 with a score of 9.
***This was the last data line; the 52nd person tested had a score of 14.

SPSS requires that each statement has a name, which is specified by the directions and goes in columns 1–15 of the statement line. Columns 16–80 are used to provide information unique to the set of data to be analyzed. The purpose of the RUN NAME statement is to provide a title that will be on the top of each page of printout. In figure 2.8 we used the title ANALYSIS OF DATA IN TABLE 2.3. The VARIABLE LIST statement is used to give each set of scores a name. Since each person had 1 score we called it SCORE. The INPUT MEDIUM statement tells the computer where to find the data. By saying CARD, the computer expects the data to be after the READ INPUT DATA statement rather than on DISK, the other option. The FIXED(3X,F2.0) after INPUT FORMAT indicates that the columns used to enter the data will be the same (fixed) for each line (row) of data and that the computer should skip over (not read) columns 1–3 (the 3X) but read the value in columns 4–5 as a whole number (the F2.0). N OF CASES indicates to the computer how many people have a score or scores. The FREQUENCIES ____ GENERAL = ALL tells the computer to use the FREQUEN-CIES program, one of the many programs in the SPSS package. If we had wanted to use a different program we would have inserted its name at this point. The ALL after STATISTICS says that all statistics this program can provide are desired. The READ INPUT DATA with nothing after it always comes just before the data. In figure 2.8 there would be 52 lines of data. Finally, the FINISH says there is no more data analysis desired.

If a person wished to obtain frequency counts and all possible correlation coefficients for the 3 scores per student in table 2.6 using SPSS, the input statements would be similar to those in figure 2.9.

Notice on the VARIABLE LIST each test was given a name that was used thereafter when telling the computer which test scores to analyze. The INPUT FORMAT indicates that in reading each data line the computer should skip columns 1–3, read a whole number in columns 4–5, skip column 6, read a whole number in columns 7–8, skip column 9, and read a fractional number in columns 10 and 11 with the digit in column 11 considered to the right of the decimal point. Entering the data in specific columns and having to provide the computer an input format statement is called *fixed field* or *variable field* format. Notice the dash score was always entered without the decimal point because the position of the decimal point can be specified on the INPUT FORMAT. Also, notice that after the last data line, we specified the PEARSON CORR (correlation) program should also be applied to the data. In this statement every test on the left side of the WITH will be correlated with every test on the right side of the WITH.

Figure 2.9 Input statements for obtaining frequencies and correlations, using the data in Table 2.6.

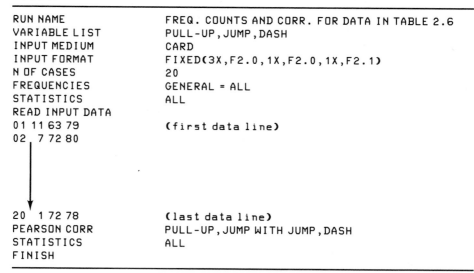

```
RUN NAME              FREQ. COUNTS AND CORR. FOR DATA IN TABLE 2.6
VARIABLE LIST         PULL-UP,JUMP,DASH
INPUT MEDIUM          CARD
INPUT FORMAT          FIXED(3X,F2.0,1X,F2.0,1X,F2.1)
N OF CASES            20
FREQUENCIES           GENERAL = ALL
STATISTICS            ALL
READ INPUT DATA
01 11 63 79           (first data line)
02  7 72 80




20  1 72 78           (last data line)
PEARSON CORR          PULL-UP,JUMP WITH JUMP,DASH
STATISTICS            ALL
FINISH
```

Figure 2.10 Input statements for SPSS Version 10, comparable to those in Figure 2.8.

```
TITLE                    ''ANALYSIS OF TABLE 2.3 DATA USING SPSS VERSION
                         10''
DATA LIST                FILE = INLINE   FIXED RECORDS = 1/   Score 4-5
FREQUENCIES              GENERAL = ALL/
                         STATISTICS = ALL

BEGIN DATA
01 21*
02 09
```

```
52 14*
END DATA
FINISH
```

*First and last data lines respectively.

The SPSS examples presented so far have been for versions 7 through 9 of the SPSS package. Each program in these versions of the SPSS package is explained in the SPSS manual (Nie et al. 1975). Version 10 of the SPSS package uses a different sequence of control information (see table 2.11) and has a different manual (SPSS 1983) than earlier versions. The SPSS version 10 statements comparable to those in figure 2.8 are presented in figure 2.10. The version 10 does not require the use of columns 1–15 for statement names and 16–80 for information. Other SPSS version 10 examples are presented in chapter 7.

SPSS is not the only package of statistical programs nationally distributed, but it is one of the most commonly used. Other packages, if available, will be equally good.

Microcomputer

Microcomputers are the small, desktop, inexpensive computers that have become popular for use in the home, school, and business since the mid 1970s. Microcomputers by Apple, Commodore, IBM, Radio Shack, etc., seem to be everywhere. A program for a microcomputer is undoubtedly a friendly type, stored on a floppy disk, and in your possession. A word of warning; a program on disk for a certain computer (Apple II for example) will not run in another computer (IBM, Radio Shack, etc.) or even in another model (Apple Macintosh). The directions for the program are more of an explanation of what the program does than actual directions. The floppy disk is put into the disk drive of the microcomputer and read by the computer after turning the computer on or pressing the reset button. If there are several programs on the disk, the microcomputer will list them in a menu and ask you which one you want to use. If there is only 1 program on the disk, the microcomputer will ask you a question or prompt you about the data you want to analyze (for instance, how many people have data).

After you have answered all the questions or prompts from the microcomputer and entered your data, the microcomputer will probably ask if you would like the data displayed on the microcomputer screen so you can check and/or correct it before it is analyzed. Usually, the results of the data analysis can be displayed on the computer screen, printed on paper, or both.

Microcomputers accept numbers in a free field format rather than the fixed field format usually required by mainframe computers. In free field format, numbers can go in any columns but they must be separated by one or more blank spaces. So, an input format statement is not required for input of data. However, when inputting data, remember that a blank cannot be used to represent a zero score or missing score, the decimal point must be entered as part of a fractional number, and all numbers entered into the computer will be analyzed.

In the section on standard scores, a computer program called TSCORE was referenced. Originally TSCORE (Prusaczuk and Baumgartner 1986) was an instruction-type mainframe program but now a version is available for several types of microcomputers. The microcomputer version is entirely user friendly, menu driven, full of prompts, able to output to screen or printer, and able to run on a microcomputer with 1 disk drive. When TSCORE starts up, a menu is displayed with several options: (1) create a new data file, (2) add a subject to a file, (3) edit an existing file, (4) print an existing file, (5) compute T-scores, and (6) compute percentile ranks. The typical user will select option 1, inputting the data to be analyzed and saving it on disk, followed by option 5.

This program allows up to 8 variables and 500 subjects. Missing data are allowed (but not desirable), so all subjects do not have to take all tests. The mean and standard deviation are calculated for each test. In the 5th procedure, T-scores and the sum of the weighted T-scores are calculated for each subject, but missing data are not used in the calculations. The mean and standard deviations are calculated for the sum of the weighted T-scores using the data of subjects who had no missing scores. In the 6th procedure, percentile ranks are calculated for each T-score and sum of the weighted T-scores.

Table 2.12 lists the scores of 40 students on the AAHPER Youth Fitness Test (1976). After selecting option 1 from the TSCORE menu, a person who types 30 words per minute entered these scores onto the computer in 30 minutes. Then options 5 and 6 were selected and the scores were analyzed using the TSCORE program. The output of that program is shown in figure 2.11.

From the figure we can see each subject's (pupil) T-scores listed for each test and the sum of each subject's T-scores is listed as well. For example, the sum of subject 1's T-scores is 385.86. Mean and standard deviation are provided for each test. The printout also shows that for the 39 subjects who were measured on all 7 tests (subject 18 did not take all the tests), the mean and standard deviation for the sum of the T-scores were 350.13 and 54.89 respectively. Finally, at the bottom of the figure are percentile ranks for each test score, as well as a percentile rank for the sum of each subject's T-scores. For example, subject 1 had a percentile rank of 66 on the sit-up test and an overall percentile rank of 73.

Table 2.12
Scores of 40 Students on the AAHPER Fitness Test.

PUPIL	SIT-UPS	PULL-UPS	SHUTTLE RUN	LONG JUMP	BALL THROW	600-YARD RUN	50-YARD DASH
1	100	11	10.5	63	132	120	7.9
2	100	7	11.0	72	150	114	8.0
3	100	4	10.2	84	153	112	7.1
4	100	3	11.0	69	106	129	8.0
5	100	4	11.4	60	111	156	8.6
6	70	0	12.2	51	90	138	9.7
7	100	6	10.4	75	145	102	7.7
8	100	6	10.3	69	123	120	8.0
9	100	1	11.5	63	108	146	8.2
10	50	0	10.8	69	138	112	7.6
11	100	3	10.5	66	135	127	7.9
12	100	2	11.9	69	145	115	8.1
13	100	9	10.5	81	163	95	6.9
14	100	4	11.4	66	93	132	8.2
15	100	6	10.1	78	138	101	7.0
16	100	7	11.1	81	170	98	7.3
17	52	0	11.1	63	144	132	8.3
18	100		11.3		135	128	8.6
19	100	10	11.2	66	129	110	7.7
20	100	6	11.5	63	114	111	7.5
21	100	1	10.7	72	168	110	7.8
22	100	4	11.9	63	115	128	8.2
23	100	0	10.8	75	93	113	8.3
24	100	11	10.6	66	135	108	7.5
25	100	4	10.6	69	110	108	7.6
26	70	3	11.0	66	109	120	8.3
27	30	1	12.4	48	63	151	10.3
28	100	0	12.4	48	86	124	8.6
29	100	4	11.2	66	118	114	8.4
30	22	3	11.8	66	104	146	8.5
31	50	3	11.2	63	133	116	7.3
32	60	1	9.7	69	110	107	7.6
33	40	1	11.1	63	95	114	8.3
34	100	1	10.5	72	125	112	8.0
35	25	0	11.7	51	118	133	8.4
36	100	16	10.8	81	141	96	6.8
37	32	1	11.3	54	97	140	9.1
38	50	2	10.4	66	126	107	7.6
39	100	2	10.5	78	148	105	7.5
40	75	3	11.4	60	54	124	8.3

Numerous statistical programs for microcomputers exist. For all commonly used microcomputers, several packages of statistical programs exist. By shopping around, programs and packages of programs can often be obtained quite reasonably. Thomas and Nelson (1985) have 10 Apple II programs listed in their research book. AAHPERD published a software directory (Cicciarella 1985) that is helpful. Information about the TSCORE program can be addressed to Wm. C. Brown.

Figure 2.11 Sample computer printout of data in Table 2.12.

T-SCORES:

Subj #	SC 1	SC 2	SC 3	SC 4	SC 5	SC 6	SC 7	Sum
1	56.44	69.72	58.80	45.67	53.96	49.56	51.71	385.86
2	56.44	58.69	50.76	55.99	60.93	53.57	50.25	386.63
3	56.44	50.42	63.63	69.76	62.09	54.91	63.42	420.67
4	56.44	47.66	50.76	52.55	43.90	43.55	50.25	345.11
5	56.44	50.42	44.32	42.23	45.83	25.50	41.47	306.21
6	44.96	39.39	31.46	31.91	37.71	37.53	25.37	248.33
7	56.44	55.93	60.41	59.43	58.99	61.59	54.64	407.43
8	56.44	55.93	62.02	52.55	50.48	49.56	50.25	377.23
9	56.44	42.15	42.72	45.67	44.67	32.18	47.32	311.15
10	37.31	39.39	53.98	52.55	56.28	54.91	56.10	350.52
11	56.44	47.66	58.80	49.11	55.12	44.88	51.71	363.72
12	56.44	44.91	36.28	52.55	58.99	52.90	48.79	350.86
13	56.44	64.20	58.80	66.32	65.96	66.27	66.35	444.34
14	56.44	50.42	44.32	49.11	38.87	41.54	47.32	328.02
15	56.44	55.93	65.24	62.88	56.28	62.26	64.89	423.92
16	56.44	58.69	49.15	66.32	68.67	64.26	60.50	424.03
17	38.07	39.39	49.15	45.67	58.61	41.54	45.86	318.29
18	56.44	–*–	45.93	–*–	55.12	44.21	41.47	–*–
19	56.44	66.96	47.54	49.11	52.80	56.24	54.64	383.73
20	56.44	55.93	42.72	45.67	47.00	55.58	57.57	360.91
21	56.44	42.15	55.58	55.99	67.90	56.24	53.18	387.48
22	56.44	50.42	36.28	45.67	47.38	44.21	47.32	327.72
23	56.44	39.39	53.98	59.43	38.87	54.24	45.86	348.21
24	56.44	69.72	57.19	49.11	55.12	57.58	57.57	402.73
25	56.44	50.42	57.19	52.55	45.45	57.58	56.10	375.73
26	44.96	47.66	50.76	49.11	45.06	49.56	45.86	332.97
27	29.65	42.15	28.24	28.47	27.25	28.84	16.59	201.19
28	56.44	39.39	28.24	28.47	36.16	46.89	41.47	277.06
29	56.44	50.42	47.54	49.11	48.54	53.57	44.40	350.02
30	26.59	47.66	37.89	49.11	43.12	32.18	42.93	279.48
31	37.31	47.66	47.54	45.67	54.35	52.23	60.50	345.26
32	41.13	42.15	71.67	52.55	45.45	58.25	56.10	367.30
33	33.48	42.15	49.15	45.67	39.64	53.57	45.86	309.52
34	56.44	42.15	58.80	55.99	51.25	54.91	50.25	369.79
35	27.74	39.39	39.50	31.91	48.54	40.87	44.40	272.35
36	56.44	83.50	53.98	66.32	57.45	65.60	67.81	451.10
37	30.42	42.15	45.93	35.35	40.41	36.19	34.15	264.60
38	37.31	44.91	60.41	49.11	51.64	58.25	56.10	357.73
39	56.44	44.91	58.80	62.88	60.16	59.59	57.57	400.35
40	46.88	47.66	44.32	42.23	23.77	46.89	45.86	297.61

-*- Indicates missing data

RAW SCORE SUMMARY:

Score	Mean	Std Dev	Missing
Sit-ups	83.15	26.12	0
Pull-ups	3.84	3.62	1
S. Run	11.04	.62	0
L. Jump	66.76	8.71	1
B. Throw	121.75	25.83	0
600-run	119.34	14.96	0
50-dash	8.01	.68	0

Sum of Weighted T-Scores:

Mean   : 350.13
Std dev : 54.89
Missing : 1

Score Table:

1. Sit-ups
2. Pull-ups
3. S. run
4. L. jump
5. B. throw
6. 600-run
7. 50-dash

PERCENTILE RANKS:

Subj #	SC 1	SC 2	SC 3	SC 4	SC 5	SC 6	SC 7	Sum
1	66	95	79	27	59	41	58	73
2	66	85	54	76	89	54	50	76
3	66	64	94	99	91	64	91	88
4	66	49	54	64	24	24	50	37
5	66	64	26	15	36	1	11	19
6	28	8	6	8	9	14	4	4
7	66	77	88	82	83	89	65	86
8	66	77	91	64	49	41	50	68
9	66	24	20	27	26	8	39	24
10	16	8	61	64	73	64	73	47
11	66	49	79	46	66	31	58	58
12	66	37	10	64	83	49	44	50
13	66	88	79	94	94	99	96	96
14	66	64	26	46	13	20	39	32
15	66	77	96	87	73	91	94	91
16	66	85	46	94	99	94	88	94
17	21	8	46	27	79	20	29	27
18	66	–*–	33	–*–	66	28	11	–*–
19	66	91	39	46	56	73	65	71
20	66	77	20	27	39	69	81	55
21	66	24	66	76	96	73	61	78
22	66	64	10	27	41	28	39	29

PERCENTILE RANKS:

Subj #	SC 1	SC 2	SC 3	SC 4	SC 5	SC 6	SC 7	Sum
23	66	8	61	82	13	59	29	42
24	66	95	70	46	66	78	81	83
25	66	64	70	64	33	78	73	65
26	28	49	54	46	29	41	29	35
27	6	24	3	3	4	4	1	1
28	66	8	3	3	6	35	11	12
29	66	64	39	46	45	54	20	45
30	1	49	14	46	21	8	16	14
31	16	49	39	27	61	46	88	40
32	24	24	99	64	33	83	73	60
33	11	24	46	27	16	54	29	22
34	66	24	79	76	51	64	50	63
35	4	8	16	8	45	16	20	9
36	66	99	61	94	76	96	99	99
37	9	24	33	12	19	11	6	6
38	16	37	88	46	54	83	73	53
39	66	37	79	87	86	86	81	81
40	31	49	26	15	1	35	29	17

−*−Indicates missing data

Score Table:
1. Sit-ups
2. Pull-ups
3. S. run
4. L. jump
5. B. throw
6. 600-run
7. 50-dash

On several occasions in chapter 2, we have referenced microcomputer programs from the *Statistics with Finesse* package (Bolding 1985). These programs run on either the Apple II or IBM-PC. The programs are on disks titled "Descriptive Statistics," "t-Tests and ANOVA," "Nonparametric Statistics," "Multivariate," and "Test Analysis." Each disk comes with a file management system for creating and modifying a disk file. The programs have all the nice features desired—user friendly, menu, good prompts, and user's manual. Further, the disks of programs are very reasonably priced and the complete set of disks should satisfy the statistical needs of any teacher, exercise specialist, or researcher. Output from FREQUENCIES on the "Descriptive Statistics" disk is presented in figure 2.12.

SUMMARY

You should be sufficiently familiar with each of the techniques presented in this chapter to determine when it should be used, to calculate its value, and to interpret the results. Among the techniques discussed, means and standard deviations are used most widely.

Figure 2.12 Sample output from a microcomputer program.

FILE NAME: DATA1
VARIABLE: PULL-UP SCORE

Score	Freq.	Cum. f	Percent	Cum. %
20	1	32	3.13	100.00
19	2	31	6.25	96.88
18	2	29	6.25	90.63
17	2	27	6.25	84.38
16	5	25	15.63	78.13
15	3	20	9.38	62.50
14	4	17	12.50	53.13
13	3	13	9.38	40.63
12	5	10	15.63	31.25
11	3	5	9.38	15.63
10	2	2	6.25	6.25

T-scores, a very useful measure, are being used more frequently every year. The concept of correlation is crucial to the determination of reliability and validity, as will be discussed in chapters 3 and 4. Also, you will find that percentile-rank norms accompany most physical performance tests.

FORMATIVE EVALUATION OF OBJECTIVES

Objective 1   Select the statistical technique that is correct for a given situation.

1. The situations listed below are common to most physical education teachers and exercise specialists. In each case, determine what statistical value(s) is(are) needed.
   a. Determining the typical group performance.
   b. Determining which of 2 groups is the more heterogeneous in performance.
   c. Determining whether a group has improved in performance during a 6-week training unit.
   d. Determining what percentage of the class scores fall below 70 on a 100-point knowledge test.
   e. Determining on which of four fitness tests an individual performed best in reference to the mean performance of his or her peers.
   f. Determining whether a certain test discriminates against heavy individuals.
   g. Determining whether a performance standard for a test is realistic in regard to the mean and standard deviation of the test.
   h. Determining the typical group performance if the scores are ordinal or the distribution of scores is skewed.
2. One reason for calculating various statistical values is to help in describing group performance. What statistics must be calculated to adequately describe the performance of a group?

Objective 2   Calculate accurately with the formulas presented.

1. The ability to calculate accurately using the formulas presented in the text is vital. To check your ability to work with the formulas, use the following scores to calculate
   a. The three measures of central tendency and the standard deviation for the 50 scores.
   b. The mean and standard deviation for each column of scores.
   c. The percentile rank for scores 66 and 82.

84	82	95	92	83
80	58	82	81	60
79	87	71	90	69
82	75	70	89	85
69	79	80	74	69
84	81	71	90	87
66	79	52	92	72
70	86	87	77	87
90	89	69	68	83
85	92	76	74	89

2. There are many reasons why physical education teachers and exercise specialists use T-scores. You should not only realize when T-scores are needed, but also be able to calculate them.
   a. Determine the T-score when X is 60 for a 2-minute sit-up test with mean 42 and standard deviation 8.
   b. Determine the T-score when X is 11.3 for a 100-yard dash with mean 11.6 and standard deviation .55.
   c. Use the information below to determine which individual did best overall when both tests are considered.

	100-yard dash	*600-yard run*
Tom	10.50	2 minutes
Bill	11.10	1 minute, 35 seconds
Mean	10.74	2 minutes
Standard Deviation	1.12	20 seconds

3. It is possible to solve probability statements using the normal curve, and there are several advantages to doing so. Consider the following probability statements, and solve them using the normal curve.
   a. $P(0 < z < 1.5)$
   b. $P(-.78 < z < 0)$
   c. $P(z < -1.34)$
   d. $P(X > \overline{X} + 2s)$
   e. $P(.5 < z < 1.5)$
   f. $P(z < .53)$
   g. $P(X > 15$, if $\overline{X} = 11$ and $s = 2.5)$
   h. $P(z < ?) = (10/100)$

4. The median is sometimes used instead of the mean. Use the counting method to determine the median for each set of following scores.
   a. 1,13,12,1,8,4,5,10,2,5,6,8
   b. 7,13,2,1,1,9,12,5,6,11,4,10
   c. 5,1,4,8,14,7,1,2,5
5. Correlation coefficients have many uses in physical education, as you will see in the next chapter. A correlation coefficient should be calculated using the scores of a large number of people, but to give you practice, the scores of only a few people are listed below. Calculate the correlation coefficient for the two sets of scores.

Person	Long jump	Dash
A	67	5.2
B	68	5.4
C	57	6.1
D	60	5.5
E	71	5.1

Objective 3 Interpret the statistical value selected or calculated.

1. In addition to being able to calculate with the formulas presented in the chapter, you should be able to interpret the statistical values you have selected or calculated. For each situation below, indicate how you might explain or describe the statistical value to a group with which you typically work.
   a. Mean 11.67 and standard deviation 2.39 for a pull-up test
   b. Percentile rank 83 for a 100-yard dash score of 11.9
   c. T-score 61 for the test described in part a
2. In the next chapter, correlation coefficients are used and referenced extensively. It is essential, then, that you understand both the term and its interpretation. In your own words, summarize what a correlation coefficient is and how to interpret either a positive or negative value.

Objective 4 Make decisions based on all available information about a given situation.

1. The text presents several methods for calculating T-scores for the entire class. Identify which formulas you would use if an adding machine or desk calculator were available.

ADDITIONAL LEARNING ACTIVITIES

1. Using the techniques presented for finding T-scores for the entire class, determine the T-score for each score in a set of scores.
2. Select three units you would teach during a semester and decide which tests you would administer after each unit. Now decide which statistical techniques you would apply to the scores collected during the semester.

BIBLIOGRAPHY

AAHPER. 1976. *Youth Fitness Test Manual.* Washington, D.C.

Bloomers, P., and E. F. Lindquist. 1960. *Elementary Statistical Methods.* Boston, Mass.: Houghton Mifflin.

Bloomers, P. J., and R. A. Forsyth. 1977. *Elementary Statistical Methods.* 2d ed. Boston, Mass.: Houghton Mifflin.

Bolding, J. 1985. *Statistics with Finesse.* Fayetteville, Ark.: Publisher.

Cicciarella, C. F. (ed.). 1985. *Directory of Computer Software with Application to Sport Science, Health, and Dance.* Reston, Va.: AAHPERD.

Cohen, J., and P. Cohen. 1975. *Applied Multiple Regression/Correlation Analysis for the Behavioral Sciences.* New York: Wiley.

Downie, N. M., and R. W. Heath. 1965. *Basic Statistical Methods.* 2d ed. New York: Harper & Row.

Ferguson, G. A. 1981. *Statistical Analysis in Psychology and Education.* 5th ed. New York: McGraw-Hill.

Glass, G. V., and J. C. Stanley. 1970. *Statistical Methods in Education and Psychology.* Englewood Cliffs, N.J.: Prentice-Hall.

Kerlinger, F. N., and E. J. Pedhazur. 1973. *Multiple Regression in Behavioral Research.* New York: Holt, Rinehart and Winston.

Nie, N. H. et al. 1975. *Statistical Package for the Social Sciences.* 2d ed. New York: McGraw-Hill.

Prusaczuk, K., and T. Baumgartner. 1986. TSCORE. Dubuque, Ia.: Wm. C. Brown.

Roscoe, J. T. 1975. *Fundamental Research Statistics for the Behavioral Sciences.* 2d ed. New York: Holt, Rinehart and Winston.

SPSS Inc. 1983. *SPSSX User's Guide.* New York: McGraw-Hill.

Thomas, J. R., and J. K. Nelson. 1985. *Introduction to Research in Health, Physical Education, Recreation, and Dance.* Champaign, Ill.: Human Kinetics Publishers.

Walker, H. M., and J. Lev. 1969. *Elementary Statistical Methods.* 3d ed. Chicago, Ill.: Holt, Rinehart and Winston.

Reliability and Objectivity

Contents

Key Words

Analysis of Variance
Change Score
Criterion Score
Difference Score
Improvement Score
Internal-Consistency Reliability Coefficient
Intraclass Reliability Coefficient
Objectivity
Reliability
Split-Half Method
Stability Reliability Coefficient
Standard Error of Measurement
Test-Retest Method

Objectives

This chapter discusses the methods used to estimate reliability and objectivity, and the factors that influence both of these values.

Many physical performance tests can be given several times in the same day. When there are multiple trials of a test, the physical education teacher and exercise specialist must decide how many to administer and what trial(s) to use as the criterion score.

After reading chapter 3 you should be able to:

1. Define and differentiate between reliability and objectivity, and outline the methods used to estimate these values.
2. Identify those factors that influence reliability and objectivity.

INTRODUCTION

There are certain characteristics essential to a measurement; without them, little faith can be put in the measurement and little use made of it. Measurement theory, the discussion of these characteristics, is covered in detail in this chapter, and is referred to throughout the book.

One important quality of a measurement is **reliability.** A reliable test or instrument measures whatever it measures consistently. That is, if an individual whose ability has not changed is measured twice with a perfectly reliable measuring device, the 2 scores will be identical.

A second important characteristic is validity. A test or measuring instrument is valid if it measures what it is supposed to measure. Validity is discussed in greater detail in chapter 4.

A third important characteristic of a measurement is objectivity. **Objectivity** is sometimes called rater reliability because it is defined in terms of the agreement of competent judges about the value of a measurement. Thus, if 2 judges scoring the same individual on the same test cannot agree on a score, the test lacks objectivity and neither score is really reliable nor valid. A lack of objectivity, then, reduces both reliability and validity.

RELIABILITY

Reliability may be discussed in terms of norm-referenced or criterion-referenced tests. Since Safrit (1981) has an excellent discussion of reliability for criterion-referenced tests and reliability is usually discussed in terms of norm-referenced tests, we will limit our discussion to reliability of norm-referenced tests.

Theory

We can better understand reliability if we understand the mathematical theory underlying it. Feldt and McKee (1958), Ferguson (1981), and Safrit et al. (1974) explain reliability in terms of "observed scores," "true scores," and "error scores." Reliability theory assumes that any measurement on a continuous scale contains an inherent component of error, the measurement error. Any one or more of the following factors can be a source of measurement error: (1) lack of agreement among scorers, (2) lack of consistent performance by the individual tested, (3) failure of an instrument to measure consistently, and (4) failure of the tester to follow standardized testing procedures.

Assume that we are about to measure the heights of 5 boys, all 68 inches tall. If we report any scores other than 68, an error of measurement has occurred. Thus the variance for the reported heights is a good indicator of the amount of measurement error. The variance is the square of the standard deviation and is symbolized as σ^2 for the variance of a population or s^2 as the variance of a sample. A population is all the people who have a specified set of characteristics; a sample is a subgroup of a population. If all reported scores are 68, or very close to 68, the measurement error is not serious and the variance is small. However, if the 5 boys are not all the same height, the variance for the reported heights may be due either to a true difference in height or to an error of measurement. In either case, the variance cannot be used as an indicator of measurement error.

In theory, the observed (recorded) score X is the sum of the true score t and an error of measurement score e:

$$X = t + e$$

For example, if an individual who is 70.25 inches tall (t) has a recorded height of 70.5 (X), the error of measurement (e) is .25:

$$70.5 = 70.25 + .25$$

If that individual is measured again and the recorded score is 69.5, the error of measurement equals $-.75$:

$$69.5 = 70.25 + -.75$$

The variance for a set of observed scores equals the variance of the true scores plus the variance of the error scores:

$$\sigma_x^2 = \sigma_t^2 + \sigma_e^2$$

where σ_x^2 is the variance of the observed scores, σ_t^2 is the variance of the true scores, and σ_e^2 is the variance of the error scores.

Reliability, then, is the ratio of the true-score variance to the observed-score variance:

$$\text{Reliability} = \frac{\sigma_t^2}{\sigma_x^2} = \frac{\sigma_x^2 - \sigma_e^2}{\sigma_x^2} = 1 - \frac{\sigma_e^2}{\sigma_x^2}$$

We can see from this formula that, when no measurement error exists—that is, when σ_e^2 equals 0—the reliability is 1. As measurement error increases, σ_x^2 increases and reliability decreases. Thus reliability is an indicator of the amount of measurement error in a set of scores.

Reliability depends on two basic factors: (1) reducing the variation attributable to measurement error and (2) detecting individual differences (that is, variation of the true scores) within the group measured. The reliability of an instrument, then, must be viewed in terms of its measurement error (error variance) and its power to discriminate among different levels of ability within the group measured (true-score variance).

Issues

The reliability of physical performance measures has traditionally been estimated by one of two methods. However, there are many methods for estimating reliability, several of which we discuss here. Because each yields a different reliability coefficient, it is important to use the most appropriate method for a given measuring instrument. It is also important to notice the methods others have used to calculate their reliability coefficients. Remember too that a test may be reliable for one group of individuals and not for another. For example, a test that is highly reliable for college students may be only moderately reliable for high school students or participants in a fitness program. Because there are several methods of calculating the reliability coefficient for an instrument and because reliability is not constant, we call the reliability coefficient an estimate of reliability.

There are two issues involved in the calculation of a reliability coefficient. One is whether the reliability coefficient should indicate stability or internal consistency. The other is whether an interclass or intraclass correlation coefficient should be used as the reliability coefficient.

Stability Reliability

When individual scores change little from one day to the next, they are stable. When scores remain stable, we consider them reliable. We use the test-retest method to obtain the **stability reliability coefficient,** which is an estimate of a measuring instrument's reliability. Each person is measured with the same test or instrument on several (usually 2) different days (day 1, day 2, and so on). The correlation between the two sets of scores is the stability reliability coefficient. The closer this coefficient is to positive one ($+1$), the more stable and reliable the scores. Traditionally, the stability reliability coefficient has been a Pearson product-moment correlation coefficient, which, as is discussed later, may well be inappropriate.

Three factors can contribute to poor score stability (a low stability reliability coefficient): (1) the people tested may perform differently, (2) the measuring instrument may operate or be applied differently, and (3) the person administering the measurement may change. Lack of sleep, minor injuries, and anxiety all tend to lower one's level of performance. Also, if the instrument is not consistent from day to day—for example, if a stopwatch slows down or a measuring tape is bent—or if the procedures used to collect the measures change, stability reliability decreases. Finally, if the way in which the administrator scores the people tested or perceives their performances changes, reliability decreases.

As a rule of thumb, test-retest scores are collected 1 to 3 days apart. (We found fatiguing tests to be an exception. The collection of day-2 scores 2 days after day-1 scores was too soon for a modified pull-up test because students were still sore. For a maximum-effort test, we advise retesting 7 days later.) If the interval between measurement is too long, scores may change because of increased maturation or practice, factors that are generally not considered sources of measurement error.

Some physical education teachers and exercise specialists object to the **test-retest method** because of the time required to administer a measuring instrument at least twice. Also, only the day-1 scores are used as performance measures; subsequent scores are used solely to determine reliability. Yet the method is probably the most appropriate of the procedures for determining the reliability of physical performance measures. Without test-retest consistency, we lack a true indicator, not only of each person's ability, but of the faith we can place in the measure.

To save time, it is acceptable to calculate the test-retest reliability coefficient by retesting only part of the individuals tested. The typical procedure is to administer the test to all people on day 1, and then to pick 30 to 60 people at random to be retested. (Draw names from a hat or use any procedure that gives all people an equal chance of being selected.) The test-retest reliability is then calculated using the scores of the randomly selected people.

Most physical measures are stable from day to day, exhibiting test-retest reliability coefficients between .80 and .95. There are others, however, among them resting heart rate, that are not particularly stable from day to day. Baumgartner (1969b) found that scores may not be stable if subjects have not had prior experience and/or practice with the test prior to being measured. Of course, the reliability of a test or instrument depends on the type of measure, the age and gender of the subjects, the abilities of the administrator, and other factors, making it impossible to specify a universal minimum acceptable reliability. Each physical education teacher and exercise specialist must base his or her minimum acceptable reliability on the degree of reliability necessary and that which other people have obtained with similar individuals.

Internal-Consistency Reliability

Many physical education teachers and exercise specialists use an internal-consistency coefficient as an estimate of the reliability of their measures. The advantage of this coefficient is that all measures are collected in a single day. Internal consistency refers to a consistent rate of scoring by the individuals being tested throughout a test or, when multiple trials are administered, from trial to trial.

To obtain an **internal-consistency reliability coefficient,** the evaluator must give at least 2 trials of the test within a single day. Change in the scores of the people being tested from trial to trial indicates lack of test reliability. Obviously this technique should not be used with a maximum-performance test (the 12-minute run, for example), when fatigue would certainly affect the second trial scores.

Traditionally, the **split-half method** has been used to estimate internal-consistency reliability, which, as we discuss below, is inappropriate. With this method, an even number of trials is administered. The criterion, or performance measure, for each person is the sum of all trials or the mean of the trial scores. Thus, the "whole test" is the combination of all the trials. To estimate the reliability of the whole test, it is divided into 2 equal parts and a score is calculated for each person on each part. The test may simply be split in half, although it is more common to divide it by treating the odd-numbered trials as one half and the even-numbered trials as the other half. Each person, then, receives 2 scores: the sum of the odd-numbered test trials and the sum of the even-numbered test trials. The correlation between these 2 sums is the internal-consistency reliability for half the whole test. To estimate the internal-consistency reliability for the whole test (the sum or mean of all trials), we apply the Spearman-Brown prophecy formula (discussed on page 97). The reliability coefficient for the whole test, then, is the correlation coefficient that would be obtained if the whole test were correlated with itself or with another whole test composed of the same number of trials.

Stability versus Internal Consistency

The internal-consistency reliability coefficient is not comparable to the **stability reliability coefficient.** The former is not affected by day-to-day changes in performance, a major source of measurement error in the latter. An internal-consistency coefficient is almost always higher than its corresponding stability reliability coefficient. In fact, internal-consistency coefficients between .85 and .99 are not uncommon for motor-performance tests.

Education, psychology, and other disciplines that rely heavily on paper-and-pencil tests seldom, if ever, use the test-retest method, using instead the split-half technique. Remember that the stability coefficient assumes true ability has not changed from one day to the next, an assumption often unjustifiable with paper-and-pencil tests because cognitive learning usually does occur between administrations. Psychomotor learning is less apt to vary in a 1- or 2-day span, making the stability coefficient a better indicator of the reliability of data collected in physical education.

Interclass versus Intraclass Coefficients

Both the test-retest and split-half methods use a correlation coefficient to estimate reliability. Traditionally, this correlation coefficient has been the Pearson product-moment coefficient discussed in chapter 2. This coefficient is no longer considered an appropriate reliability coefficient. It is an interclass coefficient, limited to situations where there are 2 scores per person. Where there are more than 2 scores per person, the scores must be combined to form 2 scores, as we saw in the summing of the odd- and even-numbered trials in the split-half method. Finally, the Pearson product-moment coefficient basically compares change in group position from one set of measures to next, not absolute change in the scores between the 2 sets of measures.

The intraclass correlation coefficient appears to be the better method for estimating reliability, whether scores are collected on 1 day or several days. It allows more than 2 scores per person. Further, it is sensitive to more sources of measurement error (lack of reliability), and thus gives a truer picture of test reliability. The intraclass method is also the only method that considers changes in the mean and standard deviation from one set of measures to the next (say from day 1 to day 2 with the stability method) to be measurement error (Kroll 1962).

The product-moment coefficient was designed to determine the relationship between 2 sets of scores, each from a different test. The distribution of these 2 sets of scores is referred to in statistics texts as "bivariate." But the repeated measurement of individuals on the same test, as is done to determine reliability, is a univariate, not a bivariate, situation—it is the distribution of a single variable. It makes sense, then, to use a univariate statistic, like the intraclass correlation coefficient, in a univariate situation. For additional discussion on this subject see Kroll (1962, 1967) and Safrit (1974, 1981).

Intraclass Correlation Coefficient

As we have noted, theoretically an observed score X is composed of a true score t and an error score e. Furthermore, the variance of the observed scores σ_x^2 equals the variance of the true scores σ_t^2 plus the variance of the error scores σ_e^2; reliability equals the true-score variance divided by the observed-score variance. Just as observed-score variance can be divided into several parts, the total variability s^2 for a set of scores can be divided into several parts. To divide, or petition the variance we use the technique of **analysis of variance** (ANOVA). We can then use these parts of the total variance to calculate an intraclass reliability coefficient.

One-Way Analysis of Variance

To calculate an intraclass correlation coefficient R as an estimate of reliability, each subject or person, tested in a physical education class, activity or fitness program, or research setting must have at least two scores. Here we replace the reliability formula

$$\text{Reliability} = \frac{\sigma_t^2}{\sigma_x^2}$$

with

$$R = \frac{MS_a - MS_w}{MS_a}$$

where R is the **intraclass correlation coefficient** (the reliability of the mean test score for each subject), MS_a is the mean square among subjects, and MS_w is the mean square within subjects. In other words, the term $MS_a - MS_w$ is an estimate of σ_t^2; and the term MS_a is an estimate of σ_x^2. A mean square value is a variance just like the variance s^2 discussed in chapter 2.

To calculate MS_a and MS_w, we must first define 6 values from the sets of scores: (1) the sum of squares total, SS_T, and the degrees of freedom total, df_T, which are used to check our calculations; and (2) the sum of squares among subjects SS_a, the sum of squares within subjects, SS_w, the degrees of freedom among subjects, df_a, and the degrees of freedom within subjects, df_w, all of which are used to determine MS_a and MS_w

$$SS_T = \Sigma X^2 - \frac{(\Sigma X)^2}{nk} \quad SS_a = \frac{\Sigma T_i^2}{k} - \frac{(\Sigma X)^2}{nk} \quad SS_w = \Sigma X^2 - \frac{\Sigma T_i^2}{k}$$
$$df_T = (n)(k) - 1 \quad df_a = n - 1 \quad df_w = n(k - 1)$$

where ΣX^2 is the sum of the squared scores, ΣX is the sum of the scores of all subjects; n is the number of subjects; k is the number of scores for each subject, and T_i is the sum of the scores for subject i. With these values in hand, it is a simple matter to calculate the mean square among subjects,

$$MS_a = \frac{SS_a}{df_a} = \frac{SS_a}{n - 1}$$

and the mean square within subjects,

$$MS_w = \frac{SS_w}{df_w} = \frac{SS_w}{n(k - 1)}$$

Problem 3.1 Using one-way analysis of variance, calculate R for the data in table 3.1.

Table 3.1
One-Way ANOVA Data.

STUDENT	DAY 1	DAY 2
A	9	9
B	1	2
C	8	7

Solution   To solve for R, we use a 9-step procedure:

Step 1
Obtain the sum of the scores, T, for each person:

Subject	Day 1	Day 2	T
A	9	9	18
B	1	2	3
C	8	7	15

Step 2
Obtain the sum of the scores, ΣX, and the sum of the squared scores, ΣX^2:

$$\Sigma X = 9 + 9 + 1 + 2 + 8 + 7* = 36$$
$$\Sigma X^2 = 9^2 + 9^2 + 1^2 + 2^2 + 8^2 + 7^2$$
$$= 81 + 81 + 1 + 4 + 64 + 49 = 280$$

*You could total the T column for this value as well: $(18 + 3 + 15 = 36)$.

Step 3
Calculate the 3 sum-of-squares values:

$$SS_T = \Sigma X^2 - \frac{(\Sigma X)^2}{nk} = 280 - \frac{36^2}{(3)(2)}$$
$$= 280 - \frac{1296}{6} = 280 - 216 = 64$$

$$SS_a = \frac{\Sigma T_i^2}{k} - \frac{(\Sigma X)^2}{nk} = \frac{18^2 + 3^2 + 15^2}{2} - \frac{36^2}{(3)(2)}$$
$$= \frac{324 + 9 + 225}{2} - \frac{1296}{6} = \frac{558}{2} - 216 = 279 - 216 = 63$$

$$SS_w = \Sigma X^2 - \frac{\Sigma T_i^2}{k} = 280 - \frac{18^2 + 3^2 + 15^2}{2}$$
$$= 280 - \frac{324 + 9 + 225}{2} = 280 - \frac{558}{2} = 280 - 279 = 1$$

Step 4
Check your calculations. The sum of squares among subjects (SS_a) plus the sum of squares within subjects (SS_w) should equal the sum of squares total (SS_T):

$$63 + 1 = 64$$

(If your figures here were incorrect, you would go back and recalculate.)

Step 5
Calculate the 3 degrees of freedom values:

$$df_T = (n)(k) - 1 = (3)(2) - 1 = 5$$
$$df_a = n - 1 = 3 - 1 = 2$$
$$df_w = n(k - 1) = 3(2 - 1) = 3$$

Step 6

Check your calculations. The degrees of freedom among people (df_a) plus the degrees of freedom within people (df_w) should equal the degrees of freedom total (df_T):

$$2 + 3 = 5$$

Step 7

Calculate MS_a and MS_w. Where SS_a is 63, n is 3, SS_w is 1, and k is 2, the mean square among subjects, MS_a, is 31.50 and the mean square within subjects, MS_w, is .33:

$$MS_a = \frac{63}{3-1} = \frac{63}{2} = 31.50$$

$$MS_w = \frac{1}{(3)(2-1)} = \frac{1}{3} = .33$$

Step 8

Place all your values in an ANOVA summary table to make sure nothing has been left out and everything is correct.

Source	df	SS	MS
Among people	df_a	SS_a	MS_a
Within people	df_w	SS_w	MS_w
Total	df_T		

Source	df	SS	MS
Among people	2	63	31.50
Within people	3	1	.33
Total	5	64	

Step 9

Now we can calculate R. Where MS_a is 31.50 and MS_w is .33, the intraclass reliability coefficient R is .99:

$$R = \frac{31.50 - .33}{31.50} = \frac{31.17}{31.50} = .99$$

R indicates the reliability of the mean test score for each person. When R equals 0 there is no reliability; when R equals 1 there is maximum reliability. Whenever multiple trials are administered on 1 day or a test is administered on at least 2 days, we can use R to estimate the reliability of the mean score. If the person's scores change from trial to trial or from day to day, R will be lower.

Although the calculation of an intraclass R may seem difficult and time consuming, it is no more difficult or time consuming than the calculation of the Pearson correlation coefficient, which has been used for years. And, with the availability of calculators and computers, the calculation of R is easier and faster than ever before.

A simple, or one-way analysis-of-variance computer program provides the mean squares needed to calculate R. These computer programs are easily found for any mainframe or microcomputer. If a computer program is used, notice that each subject is treated as a group.

This reliability coefficient is only one of many intraclass reliability coefficients. It is the simplest to determine because it requires the least calculation and decision making. Slightly more advanced procedures may yield a more precise criterion score. Some of these more advanced procedures are presented at the end of this chapter under Advanced Procedures. Baumgartner (1969a) describes a selection procedure that yields a criterion score minimally influenced by learning or fatigue, and the intraclass reliability for that score. Feldt and McKee (1958) present a way to estimate reliability using the intraclass method when multiple trials are administered on each of several days. Safrit (1974, 1981) discusses intraclass reliability and related topics in detail.

Single Score

The formula for calculating the intraclass reliability coefficient has been for the average or sum of all trials or days. Once in a while, it is necessary to estimate the reliability of a single trial or day. In this case, we calculate R with the following equation:

$$R = \frac{MS_a - MS_w}{MS_a + (k - 1)(MS_w)}$$

where R is the reliability of a single trial or day score, and k is the number of trial or day scores for each subject.

We can see this easily in a test-retest situation, for example, if people were tested on each of 2 days and the physical education teacher or exercise specialist wants to estimate the reliability of a score collected on one of those days. In this case, the formula for R is:

$$R = \frac{MS_a - MS_w}{MS_a + MS_w}$$

Problem 3.2   Calculating R for a single score, using the data in table 3.1.

Step 1
From Step 5 in Problem 3.1, $MS_a = 31.5$ and $MS_w = .33$.

Step 2
Calculate R.

$$R = \frac{31.5 - .33}{31.5 + .33} = \frac{31.17}{31.83} = .98$$

R indicates the reliability of a test score collected on 1 day.

Several authors, including Safrit (1981), present formulas for estimating or predicting what R would be if the number of trials was increased or decreased. This formula is:

$$\text{Estimated R} = \frac{MS_a - MS_w}{MS_a + (k/k' - 1)(MS_w)}$$

where k is the number of trials administered and k' is the number of trials for which R is estimated.

Intraclass R in Summary

Occasionally, an intraclass correlation coefficient will be lower than wanted even though the test seemed reliable (individual scores changed little from trial to trial or day to day). This happens when the sum of squares among subjects is small, indicating a group homogeneous in ability. In a situation like this one thing to do is to realize why the coefficient is low. The better thing to do is to try to increase test sensitivity or ability to discriminate among individuals in terms of ability. Remember though that you cannot accept something as reliable if the reliability coefficient is low.

Interval data are assumed in calculating an intraclass R. When the data are ranks, consider instead the Rho, Tau, or Concordance coefficients (Stamm 1976; Stamm and Safrit 1977) that are presented in many statistics books like Ferguson (1981). When the data are ordinal (we consider data from a rating scale [Likert, for example] to be ordinal), the coefficient alpha can be used to determine reliability (Ferguson 1981; Nunnally 1967).

Spearman-Brown Prophecy Formula

This equation is used to estimate the reliability of a test when its length is increased. It assumes that the additional length (or new trial), although as difficult as the original, is neither mentally nor physically tiring.

$$r_{k,k} = \frac{k(r_{1,1})}{1 + (k - 1)(r_{1,1})}$$

where $r_{k,k}$ is the estimated reliability of a test increased in length k times, k is the number of times the test is increased in length, and $r_{1,1}$ is the reliability of the present test.

Traditionally, the reliability of the present tests $r_{1,1}$, has been calculated using the Pearson product-moment correlation coefficient. Numerous sources, among them Winer (1962), show that an intraclass R can be used as $r_{1,1}$.

Problem 3.3   The reliability of a 6-trial test was found to be .94. Determine the reliability if 18 trials were administered.

Solution   Where k is 3 and $r_{1,1}$, is .94, the estimated reliability of a criterion score based on 18 trials is .98:

$$r_{k,k} = \frac{(3)(.94)}{1 + (3 - 1)(.94)} = \frac{2.82}{1 + (2)(.94)}$$
$$= \frac{2.82}{1 + 1.88} = \frac{2.82}{2.88} = .979 = .98$$

Baumgartner (1968) investigated the accuracy with which the Spearman-Brown prophecy formula predicts reliability. He compared the predicted reliability coefficients to the reliability coefficients actually obtained when the number of trials of a test was increased. He found that the formula's accuracy increased as the value of k in the formula decreased, concluding, then, that the reliability coefficient predicted by the Spearman-Brown formula is the maximum reliability that can be expected.

Standard Error of Measurement

It is sometimes useful to be able to estimate the measurement error in each test score. The average amount of measurement error in test scores is estimated by calculating the standard error of measurement by the following formula:

$$s_e = s_x \sqrt{1 - r_{x,x}}$$

where s_e is the standard error of measurement, s_x is the standard deviation for the test scores, and $r_{x,x}$ is the reliability coefficient for the test scores.

Since the variance of all measurements contains some measurement error, the **standard error of measurement** of a test score reflects the degree one may expect a test score to vary due to measurement error.

Problem 3.4   A written test has a standard deviation of 5 and a reliability coefficient of .91. Determine the standard error of measurement for the test.

Solution   Where s_x is 5 and $r_{x,x}$ is .91, the standard error of measurement s_e is 1.5:

$$s_e = 5\sqrt{1 - .91} = 5\sqrt{.09} = (5)(.3) = 1.5$$

The standard error acts like a test score's standard deviation, and can be interpreted in much the same way using the normal curve. From the normal curve table (table 2.7, page 60), we know that approximately 68% of the scores lie within 1 standard deviation of the mean, which in this case is the test score. If a person who scored 73 on the test in Problem 3.4 were to take the test 100 times and his or her ability did not change, we would expect the person's scores to fall between 71.5 (73 − 1.5) and 74.5 (73 + 1.5) 68 times out of 100. The standard error, then, specifies the limits within which we can expect scores to vary due to measurement error. In fact, there is a growing tendency to report a confidence band—the score plus and minus the standard error—with test scores. For more lengthy discussion, see Ferguson (1981) or any other statistics text that includes a chapter on measurement theory.

Factors Affecting Reliability

Many factors can affect test reliability. Among them are scoring accuracy, the number of test trials, test difficulty, instructions, the testing environment, as well as the subject's familiarity with the test and present performance level. The range of talent and the use of a reliability coefficient also can affect reliability (Remmers et al. 1969). Ebel (1979) notes that the reliability coefficient is larger for scores from a long test than those from a short one, and for a group with a broad range of abilities than for one with a narrow range of abilities.

Table 3.2 shows a categorization proposed by Zuidema (1969) of the factors that influence test reliability. We can expect an acceptable degree of reliability when (1) the subjects are heterogeneous in ability, motivated to do well, ready to be tested, and informed about the nature of the test; (2) the test discriminates among ability groups, and is long enough or repeated sufficiently for each subject to show his or her best performance; (3) the testing environment and organization are favorable to good performance; (4) the person administering the test is competent. The reliability coefficient should be calculated using the scores of a large group (at least 100 people), since with a small group it is relatively easy to obtain extremely high or low correlation coefficients.

Table 3.2

Factors Influencing Test Reliability.

CATEGORY OF FACTORS	ILLUSTRATIVE SOURCES OF IMPERFECT RELIABILITY
Characteristics of the performers	Range of talent; motivation; good day vs. bad day; learning; forgetting; fatigue
Characteristics of the test	Length; difficulty; discriminative power; trial homogeneity; number of performers
Characteristics of the testing situation	Instructions; environment; class organization; class management; warm-up opportunity
Characteristics of the measurement process	Nature of measurement instrument; selection of scoring unit; precision; errors in measurement; number of trials; recording errors
Characteristics of the evaluator(s)	Competences; confidence in test; concentration on task; familiarity with instrument; motivation; number of evaluators
Characteristics of the mode of statistical estimation	Breakdown of observed score variance into true score and error score variance, with retest design: error source is variation within individuals between days. Does not include within-day variance. With split-trial design: variation within individuals between trials. Does not include between-day variance or variance between grouped trials.

Difference Scores

Difference scores, also called **change scores** or **improvement scores,** are used to determine the degree to which a subject's scores have changed over time—from the beginning to the end of a teaching or training unit, for example. The use of difference scores raises two problems. First, individuals who perform well at the outset do not have the same opportunity to achieve as large difference scores as do individuals who begin poorly. For example, the 9.3 sprinter has less chance for improvement than does the 12.5 sprinter. Second, difference scores are not very reliable (Ferguson 1981). Highly reliable measures between which the correlation is low are necessary if the difference scores are going to be reliable. It would seem impossible, then, to expect reliability in difference scores that are usually calculated from 2 sets of scores (one at the beginning and one at the end of a teaching or training unit) whose correlation is normally .70 or higher.

Physical education teachers and exercise specialists have used difference scores as a way of allowing for the fact that all individuals do not start out a teaching or training unit equal and to allow for gender or body-type differences in performance levels. Based on the discussion above, it would seem that the use of difference scores for this purpose should cease. However, the physical education teacher and exercise specialist who needs some alternative to difference scores might look at the use of residual scores and exponential improvement scores (Henry 1956; Glass and Stanley 1970; Hale and Hale 1972; East 1979). The computations in these techniques are so demanding that computer support is almost mandatory.

OBJECTIVITY

Objectivity, or rater reliability, is an important characteristic of a test or measuring instrument. We can define objectivity as the close agreement between the scores assigned to each subject by 2 or more judges. Judges in this case could be judges in gymnastics or timers in a 100-yard dash.

Estimation

To determine the degree of objectivity in a physical performance test, two or more judges score each subject as he is tested. Then we calculate an intraclass correlation coefficient on the basis of judges' scores of each person.

To calculate the objectivity coefficient, we think of the judges as trials, inserting their individual scores into the trial terms of our reliability formulas. If all judges are supposed to be using the same standards, we would consider a difference among judges to be measurement error and would calculate objectivity using the one-way ANOVA formula:

$$R = \frac{MS_a - MS_w}{MS_a}$$

If all judges are not expected to use the same standards, we would calculate objectivity using either the alpha coefficient or the appropriate intraclass R formula (see Formula 3 under Advanced Topics at the end of this chapter). Very seldom, if ever, would we discard the data of judges as was suggested by Baumgartner (1969a) with multiple trials.

Factors Affecting Objectivity

Objectivity depends on two related factors: (1) the clarity of the scoring system and (2) the degree to which the judge can assign scores accurately. Certain tests have clearly defined methods of scoring: a 50-yard dash is scored with a stopwatch; a long jump, with a tape measure. In a test of this sort the rater can easily determine the subject's scores. In contrast, an essay test or a dance performance does not offer a well-defined scoring system, relying on the rater's judgment in the assignment of points.

The second factor is more obvious. If a judge does not know how to assign a score, he or she cannot do it accurately. For example, a scorer who is unfamiliar with stopwatches will probably not assign an accurate score on a timed speed event. Of course, it is a simple matter to train a scorer in the use of scoring equipment and scoring procedures.

A high degree of objectivity is essential when 2 or more people are administering a test. For example, say that a group of 50 people is divided into 2 groups and each group is tested by a different person. If a high degree of objectivity is lacking because the 2 scorers of the test use different administrative procedures and/or scoring standards, a subject's score is dependent on the identity of the scorer. If 1 scorer is more lenient than the other, the subjects tested by that scorer have an advantage.

A high degree of objectivity is also needed when 1 person scores on several occasions. For example, a scorer may measure one-third of a group on each of 3 days, or the entire group at the beginning and end of a teaching or training unit. Certainly in the first case it is essential that the same administrative procedures and scoring standards be used each day. This is true in the second case as well, where any variation in a subject's scores should represent changed performance, not changed procedures or standards.

ADVANCED TOPICS

Intraclass R from Two-Way ANOVA

As a brief review, earlier in this chapter we applied a one-way analysis of variance (ANOVA) to the k scores of n subjects in order to calculate an intraclass correlation coefficient (R). This R was used as an estimate of test reliability. From the one-way

ANOVA we obtained the values necessary to calculate R. The ANOVA values and R formula are presented below:

Sum of squares among subjects—SS_A
Sum of squares within subjects—SS_W
Sum of squares total—SS_T
Mean square among subjects—MS_A
Mean square within subjects—MS_W

$$R = \frac{MS_A - MS_W}{MS_A} \qquad (1)$$

Now another way of analyzing the data and calculating an intraclass correlation coefficient will be presented.

Suppose that k scores were collected for each of n subjects. These scores could have been collected over k trials or k days. For discussion purposes, we will refer to the k scores as trials. If a two-way analysis of variance were applied to the k scores of these n subjects, a summary table could be developed as shown in table 3.3.

For two-way ANOVA, the following formulas are used to calculate the various sums of squares:

Sum of squares total $(SS_T) = \Sigma X^2 - \dfrac{(\Sigma X)^2}{nk}$

Sum of squares among subjects $(SS_S) = \dfrac{\Sigma(T_i)^2}{k} - \dfrac{(\Sigma X)^2}{nk}$

Sum of squares among trials $(SS_t) = \dfrac{\Sigma(T_j)^2}{n} - \dfrac{(\Sigma X)^2}{nk}$

Sum of squares interaction $(SS_I) = \Sigma X^2 + \dfrac{(\Sigma X)^2}{nk} - \dfrac{\Sigma(T_i)^2}{k} - \dfrac{\Sigma(T_j)^2}{n}$

where ΣX^2 is the sum of the squared scores, ΣX is the sum of the scores of all subjects, n is the number of subjects, k is the number of scores for each subject, T_i is the sum of the scores for Subject i, and T_j is the sum of the scores for Trial j.

Problem 3.5 Using the two-way analysis of variance formulas, develop a summary table of the data in table 3.4.

Table 3.3
Sample ANOVA Summary Table for n Subjects and k Trials.

SOURCE	df	SS	MS
Among subjects	n − 1	SS_S	MS_S
Among trials	k − 1	SS_t	MS_t
Interaction	(n − 1)(k − 1)	SS_I	MS_I
Total	nk − 1	SS_T	

Quantitative aspects of measurement

Table 3.4

Two-Way ANOVA Data for 3-Trial Test Administered on 1 Day.

SUBJECT	TRIAL 1	TRIAL 2	TRIAL 3
A	5	6	7
B	3	3	4
C	4	4	5
D	7	6	6
E	6	7	5

Solution   The first 4 steps in the procedure are similar to those used in one-way ANOVA.

Step 1

Set up a table to calculate the sum of scores for each subject (T_i) and for each trial (T_j):

Subject	Trial 1	Trial 2	Trial 3	T_i
A	5	6	7	18
B	3	3	4	10
C	4	4	5	13
D	7	6	6	19
E	6	7	5	18
T_j	25	26	27	

Step 2

Calculate the values needed to determine the sums of squares: ΣX^2, ΣX, $\dfrac{\Sigma(T_i)^2}{k}$, and $\dfrac{\Sigma(T_j)^2}{n}$.

$$\Sigma X^2 = 5^2 + 6^2 + 7^2 + \cdots + 6^2 + 7^2 + 5^2$$
$$= 25 + 36 + 49 + \cdots + 36 + 49 + 25 = 432$$
$$\Sigma X = 5 + 6 + 7 + \cdots + 6 + 7 + 5^* = 78$$

*Here too the sum of the T_i column could be used.

$$\frac{\Sigma(T_i)^2}{k} = \frac{18^2 + 10^2 + 13^2 + 19^2 + 18^2}{3}$$
$$= \frac{324 + 100 + 169 + 361 + 324}{3}$$
$$= \frac{1278}{3} = 426$$

$$\frac{\Sigma(T_j)^2}{n} = \frac{25^2 + 26^2 + 27^2}{5} = \frac{625 + 676 + 729}{5} = \frac{2030}{5} = 406$$

Step 3

Where ΣX^2 is 432, ΣX is 78, n is 5, k is 3, $\dfrac{\Sigma(T_i)^2}{k}$ is 426, and $\dfrac{\Sigma(T_j)^2}{n}$ is 406, SS_T,

SS_A, SS_t, and SS_I are as follows:

$$SS_T = 432 - \frac{78^2}{(5)(3)} = 432 - \frac{6084}{15} = 432 - 405.6 = 26.4$$

$SS_S = 426 - 405.6 = 20.4$

$SS_t = 406 - 405.6 = .4$

$SS_I = 432 + 405.6 - 426 - 406 = 837.6 - 832 = 5.6$

Step 4

Check your calculations. The sum of the sum of squares among the sum of subjects, the sum of squares among trials, and the sum of squares interaction should equal the sum of squares total:

$$20.4 + .4 + 5.6 = 26.4$$

Step 5

Following the procedure in table 3.3, the summary table for the data in table 3.4 would look like this:

Source	df	SS	MS
Among subjects	4	20.4	5.10
Among trials	2	.4	.20
Interaction	8	5.6	.70
Total	14	26.4	

The F-Test Once the summary table has been developed, we can determine whether the trial means differ significantly using the F-test formula:

$$F = \frac{MS_t}{MS_I}$$

For example, the F from the summary table in Problem 3.5 is .29:

$$F = \frac{.20}{.70} = .29$$

If the F is significant, there is a real, or true, difference among the trial means. If the F is nonsignificant, the difference among trial means is not considered a true difference, but rather a chance one. To determine whether an F is significant, look in table 3.5. As closely as possible find the degrees of freedom for the among-trials source across the top of the table and the degrees of freedom for the interaction source down the left side of the table. Notice that not all possible values of df_t and df_I appear in table 3.5. If the degrees of freedom happened to be 13 and 73, you would read down column 12 and across row 70, for an F of 1.87 at the .05 level. Coming down from df_t and across from df_I, the point of interaction is the F needed for significance at the .05 level (light type) and .01 level (bold type). Most people use the .05 value.

Table 3.5

Critical Values of F
.05 Level (Light Type) and .01 Level (Bold Type) Points for the Distribution of F.

DEGREES OF FREEDOM FOR NUMERATOR

df (denom)	1	2	3	4	5	6	7	8	9	10	11	12	14	16	20	24	30	40	50	75	100	200	500	∞
1	101	200	216	225	230	234	237	239	241	242	243	244	245	246	248	249	250	251	252	253	253	254	254	254
	4052	**4999**	**5403**	**5625**	**5764**	**5859**	**5928**	**5981**	**6022**	**6056**	**6082**	**6106**	**6142**	**6169**	**6208**	**6234**	**6258**	**6286**	**6302**	**6323**	**6334**	**6352**	**6361**	**6366**
2	18.51	19.00	19.16	19.25	19.30	19.33	19.36	19.37	19.38	19.39	19.40	19.41	19.42	19.43	19.44	19.45	19.46	19.47	19.47	19.48	19.49	19.49	19.50	19.50
	98.49	**99.01**	**99.17**	**99.25**	**99.30**	**99.33**	**99.34**	**99.36**	**99.38**	**99.40**	**99.41**	**99.42**	**99.43**	**99.44**	**99.45**	**99.46**	**99.47**	**99.48**	**99.48**	**99.49**	**99.49**	**99.49**	**99.50**	**99.50**
3	10.13	9.55	9.28	9.12	9.01	8.94	8.88	8.84	8.81	8.78	8.76	8.74	8.71	8.69	8.66	8.64	8.62	8.60	8.58	8.57	8.56	8.54	8.54	8.53
	34.12	**30.81**	**29.46**	**28.71**	**28.24**	**27.91**	**27.67**	**27.49**	**27.34**	**27.23**	**27.13**	**27.05**	**26.92**	**26.83**	**26.69**	**26.60**	**26.50**	**26.41**	**26.35**	**26.27**	**26.23**	**26.18**	**26.14**	**26.12**
4	7.71	6.94	6.59	6.39	6.26	6.16	6.09	6.04	6.00	5.96	5.93	5.91	5.87	5.84	5.80	5.77	5.74	5.71	5.70	5.68	5.66	5.65	5.64	5.63
	21.20	**18.00**	**16.69**	**15.98**	**15.52**	**15.21**	**14.98**	**14.80**	**14.66**	**14.54**	**14.45**	**14.37**	**14.24**	**14.15**	**14.02**	**13.93**	**13.83**	**13.74**	**13.69**	**13.61**	**13.57**	**13.52**	**13.48**	**13.46**
5	6.61	5.79	5.41	5.19	5.05	4.95	4.88	4.82	4.78	4.74	4.70	4.68	4.64	4.60	4.56	4.53	4.50	4.46	4.44	4.42	4.40	4.38	4.37	4.36
	16.26	**13.27**	**12.06**	**11.39**	**10.97**	**10.67**	**10.45**	**10.27**	**10.15**	**10.05**	**9.96**	**9.89**	**9.77**	**9.68**	**9.55**	**9.47**	**9.38**	**9.29**	**9.24**	**9.17**	**9.13**	**9.07**	**9.04**	**9.02**
6	5.99	5.14	4.76	4.53	4.39	4.28	4.21	4.15	4.10	4.06	4.03	4.00	3.96	3.92	3.87	3.84	3.81	3.77	3.75	3.72	3.71	3.69	3.68	3.67
	13.74	**10.92**	**9.78**	**9.15**	**8.75**	**8.47**	**8.26**	**8.10**	**7.98**	**7.87**	**7.79**	**7.72**	**7.60**	**7.52**	**7.39**	**7.31**	**7.23**	**7.14**	**7.09**	**7.02**	**6.99**	**6.94**	**6.90**	**6.88**
7	5.59	4.74	4.35	4.12	3.97	3.87	3.79	3.73	3.68	3.63	3.60	3.57	3.52	3.49	3.44	3.41	3.38	3.34	3.32	3.29	3.28	3.25	3.24	3.23
	12.25	**9.55**	**8.45**	**7.85**	**7.46**	**7.19**	**7.00**	**6.84**	**6.71**	**6.62**	**6.54**	**6.47**	**6.35**	**6.27**	**6.15**	**6.07**	**5.98**	**5.90**	**5.85**	**5.78**	**5.75**	**5.70**	**5.67**	**5.65**
8	5.32	4.46	4.07	3.84	3.69	3.58	3.50	3.44	3.39	3.34	3.31	3.28	3.23	3.20	3.15	3.12	3.08	3.05	3.03	3.00	2.98	2.96	2.94	2.93
	11.26	**8.65**	**7.59**	**7.01**	**6.63**	**6.37**	**6.19**	**6.03**	**5.91**	**5.82**	**5.74**	**5.67**	**5.56**	**5.48**	**5.36**	**5.28**	**5.20**	**5.11**	**5.06**	**5.00**	**4.96**	**4.91**	**4.88**	**4.86**
9	5.12	4.26	3.86	3.63	3.48	3.37	3.29	3.23	3.18	3.13	3.10	3.07	3.02	2.98	2.93	2.90	2.86	2.82	2.80	2.77	2.76	2.73	2.72	2.71
	10.56	**8.02**	**6.99**	**6.42**	**6.06**	**5.80**	**5.62**	**5.47**	**5.35**	**5.26**	**5.18**	**5.11**	**5.00**	**4.92**	**4.80**	**4.73**	**4.64**	**4.56**	**4.51**	**4.48**	**4.41**	**4.36**	**4.33**	**4.31**
10	4.96	4.10	3.71	3.48	3.33	3.22	3.14	3.07	3.02	2.97	2.94	2.91	2.86	2.82	2.77	2.74	2.70	2.67	2.64	2.61	2.59	2.56	2.55	2.54
	10.04	**7.56**	**6.55**	**5.99**	**5.64**	**5.39**	**5.21**	**5.06**	**4.95**	**4.85**	**4.78**	**4.71**	**4.60**	**4.52**	**4.41**	**4.33**	**4.25**	**4.17**	**4.12**	**4.05**	**4.01**	**3.96**	**3.93**	**3.91**
11	4.84	3.98	3.59	3.36	3.20	3.09	3.01	2.95	2.90	2.86	2.82	2.79	2.74	2.70	2.65	2.61	2.57	2.53	2.50	2.47	2.45	2.42	2.41	2.40
	9.65	**7.20**	**6.22**	**5.67**	**5.32**	**5.07**	**4.88**	**4.74**	**4.63**	**4.54**	**4.46**	**4.40**	**4.29**	**4.21**	**4.10**	**4.02**	**3.94**	**3.86**	**3.80**	**3.74**	**3.70**	**3.66**	**3.62**	**3.60**
12	4.75	3.88	3.49	3.26	3.11	3.00	2.92	2.85	2.80	2.76	2.72	2.69	2.64	2.60	2.54	2.50	2.46	2.42	2.40	2.36	2.35	2.32	2.31	2.30
	9.33	**6.93**	**5.95**	**5.41**	**5.06**	**4.82**	**4.65**	**4.50**	**4.39**	**4.30**	**4.22**	**4.16**	**4.05**	**3.98**	**3.86**	**3.78**	**3.70**	**3.61**	**3.56**	**3.49**	**3.46**	**3.41**	**3.38**	**3.36**

DEGREES OF FREEDOM FOR DENOMINATOR

Reprinted by permission from STATISTICAL METHODS, Seventh Edition, by G. W. Snedecor and W. G. Cochran, © 1980 by the Iowa State University Press, Ames, Iowa, 50010.

Table 3.5 Continued

DEGREES OF FREEDOM FOR NUMERATOR

DEGREES OF FREEDOM FOR DENOMINATOR	1	2	3	4	5	6	7	8	9	10	11	12	14	16	20	24	30	40	50	75	100	200	500	∞
13	4.67	3.80	3.41	3.18	3.02	2.92	2.84	2.77	2.72	2.67	2.63	2.60	2.55	2.51	2.46	2.42	2.38	2.34	2.32	2.28	2.26	2.24	2.22	2.21
	9.07	**6.70**	**5.74**	**5.20**	**4.86**	**4.62**	**4.44**	**4.30**	**4.19**	**4.10**	**4.02**	**3.96**	**3.85**	**3.78**	**3.67**	**3.59**	**3.51**	**3.42**	**3.37**	**3.30**	**3.27**	**3.21**	**3.18**	**3.16**
14	4.60	3.74	3.34	3.11	2.96	2.85	2.77	2.70	2.65	2.60	2.56	2.53	2.48	2.44	2.39	2.35	2.31	2.27	2.24	2.21	2.19	2.16	2.14	2.13
	8.86	**6.51**	**5.56**	**5.03**	**4.69**	**4.46**	**4.28**	**4.14**	**4.03**	**3.94**	**3.86**	**3.80**	**3.70**	**3.62**	**3.51**	**3.43**	**3.34**	**3.26**	**3.21**	**3.14**	**3.11**	**3.06**	**3.02**	**3.00**
15	4.54	3.68	3.29	3.06	2.90	2.79	2.70	2.64	2.59	2.55	2.51	2.48	2.43	2.39	2.33	2.29	2.25	2.21	2.18	2.15	2.12	2.10	2.08	2.07
	8.68	**6.36**	**5.42**	**4.89**	**4.56**	**4.32**	**4.14**	**4.00**	**3.89**	**3.80**	**3.73**	**3.67**	**3.56**	**3.48**	**3.36**	**3.29**	**3.20**	**3.12**	**3.07**	**3.00**	**2.97**	**2.92**	**2.89**	**2.87**
16	4.49	3.63	3.24	3.01	2.85	2.74	2.66	2.59	2.54	2.49	2.45	2.42	2.37	2.33	2.28	2.24	2.20	2.16	2.13	2.09	2.07	2.04	2.02	2.01
	8.53	**6.23**	**5.29**	**4.77**	**4.44**	**4.20**	**4.03**	**3.89**	**3.78**	**3.69**	**3.61**	**3.55**	**3.45**	**3.37**	**3.25**	**3.18**	**3.10**	**3.01**	**2.96**	**2.89**	**2.86**	**2.80**	**2.77**	**2.75**
17	4.45	3.59	3.20	2.96	2.81	2.70	2.62	2.55	2.50	2.45	2.41	2.38	2.33	2.29	2.23	2.19	2.15	2.11	2.08	2.04	2.02	1.99	1.97	1.96
	8.40	**6.11**	**5.18**	**4.67**	**4.34**	**4.10**	**3.93**	**3.79**	**3.68**	**3.59**	**3.52**	**3.45**	**3.35**	**3.27**	**3.16**	**3.08**	**3.00**	**2.92**	**2.86**	**2.79**	**2.76**	**2.70**	**2.67**	**2.65**
18	4.41	3.55	3.16	2.93	2.77	2.66	2.58	2.51	2.46	2.41	2.37	2.34	2.29	2.25	2.19	2.15	2.11	2.07	2.04	2.00	1.98	1.95	1.93	1.92
	8.28	**6.01**	**5.09**	**4.58**	**4.25**	**4.01**	**3.85**	**3.71**	**3.60**	**3.51**	**3.44**	**3.37**	**3.27**	**3.19**	**3.07**	**3.00**	**2.91**	**2.83**	**2.78**	**2.71**	**2.68**	**2.62**	**2.59**	**2.57**
19	4.38	3.52	3.13	2.90	2.74	2.63	2.55	2.48	2.43	2.38	2.34	2.31	2.26	2.21	2.15	2.11	2.07	2.02	2.00	1.96	1.94	1.91	1.90	1.88
	8.18	**5.93**	**5.01**	**4.50**	**4.17**	**3.94**	**3.77**	**3.63**	**3.52**	**3.43**	**3.36**	**3.30**	**3.19**	**3.12**	**3.00**	**2.92**	**2.84**	**2.76**	**2.70**	**2.63**	**2.60**	**2.54**	**2.51**	**2.49**
20	4.35	3.49	3.10	2.87	2.71	2.60	2.52	2.45	2.40	2.35	2.31	2.28	2.23	2.18	2.12	2.08	2.04	1.99	1.96	1.92	1.90	1.87	1.85	1.84
	8.10	**5.85**	**4.94**	**4.43**	**4.10**	**3.87**	**3.71**	**3.56**	**3.45**	**3.37**	**3.30**	**3.23**	**3.13**	**3.05**	**2.94**	**2.86**	**2.77**	**2.69**	**2.63**	**2.56**	**2.53**	**2.47**	**2.44**	**2.42**
21	4.32	3.47	3.07	2.84	2.68	2.57	2.49	2.42	2.37	2.32	2.28	2.25	2.20	2.15	2.09	2.05	2.00	1.96	1.93	1.89	1.87	1.84	1.82	1.81
	8.02	**5.78**	**4.87**	**4.37**	**4.04**	**3.81**	**3.65**	**3.51**	**3.40**	**3.31**	**3.24**	**3.17**	**3.07**	**2.99**	**2.88**	**2.80**	**2.72**	**2.63**	**2.58**	**2.51**	**2.47**	**2.42**	**2.38**	**2.36**
22	4.30	3.44	3.05	2.82	2.66	2.55	2.47	2.40	2.35	2.30	2.26	2.23	2.18	2.13	2.07	2.03	1.98	1.93	1.91	1.87	1.84	1.81	1.80	1.78
	7.94	**5.72**	**4.82**	**4.31**	**3.99**	**3.76**	**3.59**	**3.45**	**3.35**	**3.26**	**3.18**	**3.12**	**3.02**	**2.94**	**2.83**	**2.75**	**2.67**	**2.58**	**2.53**	**2.46**	**2.42**	**2.37**	**2.33**	**2.31**
23	4.28	3.42	3.03	2.80	2.64	2.53	2.45	2.38	2.32	2.28	2.24	2.20	2.14	2.10	2.04	2.00	1.96	1.91	1.88	1.84	1.82	1.79	1.77	1.76
	7.88	**5.66**	**4.76**	**4.26**	**3.94**	**3.71**	**3.54**	**3.41**	**3.30**	**3.21**	**3.14**	**3.07**	**2.97**	**2.89**	**2.78**	**2.70**	**2.62**	**2.53**	**2.48**	**2.41**	**2.37**	**2.32**	**2.28**	**2.26**
24	4.26	3.40	3.01	2.78	2.62	2.51	2.43	2.36	2.30	2.26	2.22	2.18	2.13	2.09	2.02	1.98	1.94	1.89	1.86	1.82	1.80	1.76	1.74	1.73
	7.82	**5.61**	**4.72**	**4.22**	**3.90**	**3.67**	**3.50**	**3.36**	**3.25**	**3.17**	**3.09**	**3.03**	**2.93**	**2.85**	**2.74**	**2.66**	**2.58**	**2.49**	**2.44**	**2.36**	**2.33**	**2.27**	**2.23**	**2.21**
25	4.24	3.38	2.99	2.76	2.60	2.49	2.41	2.34	2.28	2.24	2.20	2.16	2.11	2.06	2.00	1.96	1.92	1.87	1.84	1.80	1.77	1.74	1.72	1.71
	7.77	**5.57**	**4.68**	**4.18**	**3.86**	**3.63**	**3.46**	**3.32**	**3.21**	**3.13**	**3.05**	**2.99**	**2.89**	**2.81**	**2.70**	**2.62**	**2.54**	**2.45**	**2.40**	**2.32**	**2.29**	**2.25**	**2.19**	**2.17**

Table 3.5 Continued

DEGREES OF FREEDOM FOR NUMERATOR

DEGREES OF FREEDOM FOR DENOMINATOR	1	2	3	4	5	6	7	8	9	10	11	12	14	16	20	24	30	40	50	75	100	200	500	∞
26	4.22	3.37	2.98	2.74	2.59	2.47	2.39	2.32	2.27	2.22	2.18	2.15	2.10	2.05	1.99	1.95	1.90	1.85	1.82	1.78	1.76	1.72	1.70	1.69
	7.72	5.53	4.64	4.14	3.82	3.59	3.42	3.29	3.17	3.09	3.02	2.96	2.86	2.77	2.66	2.53	2.50	2.41	2.36	2.28	2.25	2.19	2.15	2.13
27	4.21	3.35	2.96	2.73	2.57	2.46	2.37	2.30	2.25	2.20	2.16	2.13	2.08	2.03	1.97	1.93	1.88	1.84	1.80	1.76	1.74	1.71	1.68	1.67
	7.68	5.49	4.60	4.11	3.79	3.56	3.39	3.26	3.14	3.06	2.98	2.93	2.83	2.74	2.63	2.55	2.47	2.38	2.33	2.25	2.21	2.16	2.12	2.10
28	4.20	3.34	2.95	2.71	2.56	2.44	2.36	2.29	2.24	2.19	2.15	2.12	2.06	2.02	1.96	1.91	1.87	1.81	1.78	1.75	1.72	1.69	1.67	1.65
	7.64	5.45	4.57	4.07	3.76	3.53	3.36	3.23	3.11	3.03	2.95	2.90	2.80	2.71	2.60	2.52	2.44	2.35	2.30	2.22	2.18	2.13	2.09	2.06
29	4.18	3.33	2.93	2.70	2.54	2.43	2.35	2.28	2.22	2.18	2.14	2.10	2.05	2.00	1.94	1.90	1.85	1.80	1.77	1.73	1.71	1.68	1.65	1.64
	7.60	5.42	4.54	4.04	3.73	3.50	3.33	3.20	3.08	3.00	2.92	2.87	2.77	2.68	2.57	2.49	2.41	2.32	2.27	2.19	2.15	2.10	2.06	2.03
30	4.17	3.32	2.92	2.69	2.53	2.42	2.34	2.27	2.21	2.16	2.12	2.09	2.04	1.99	1.93	1.89	1.84	1.79	1.76	1.72	1.69	1.66	1.64	1.62
	7.56	5.39	4.51	4.02	3.70	3.47	3.30	3.17	3.06	2.98	2.90	2.84	2.74	2.66	2.55	2.47	2.38	2.29	2.24	2.16	2.13	2.07	2.03	2.01
32	4.15	3.30	2.90	2.67	2.51	2.40	2.32	2.25	2.19	2.14	2.10	2.07	2.02	1.97	1.91	1.86	1.82	1.76	1.74	1.69	1.67	1.64	1.61	1.59
	7.50	5.34	4.46	3.97	3.66	3.42	3.25	3.12	3.01	2.94	2.86	2.80	2.70	2.62	2.51	2.42	2.34	2.25	2.20	2.12	2.08	2.02	1.98	1.96
34	4.13	3.28	2.88	2.65	2.49	2.38	2.30	2.23	2.17	2.12	2.08	2.05	2.00	1.95	1.89	1.84	1.80	1.74	1.71	1.67	1.64	1.61	1.59	1.57
	7.44	5.29	4.42	3.93	3.61	3.38	3.21	3.08	2.97	2.89	2.82	2.76	2.66	2.58	2.47	2.38	2.30	2.21	2.15	2.03	2.04	1.98	1.94	1.91
36	4.11	3.26	2.86	2.63	2.48	2.36	2.28	2.21	2.15	2.10	2.06	2.03	1.98	1.93	1.87	1.82	1.78	1.72	1.69	1.65	1.62	1.59	1.56	1.55
	7.39	5.25	4.38	3.89	3.58	3.35	3.18	3.04	2.94	2.86	2.78	2.72	2.62	2.54	2.43	2.35	2.26	2.17	2.12	2.04	2.00	1.94	1.90	1.87
38	4.10	3.25	2.85	2.62	2.46	2.35	2.26	2.19	2.14	2.09	2.05	2.02	1.96	1.92	1.85	1.80	1.76	1.71	1.67	1.63	1.60	1.57	1.54	1.53
	7.35	5.21	4.34	3.86	3.54	3.32	3.15	3.02	2.91	2.82	2.75	2.69	2.59	2.51	2.40	2.32	2.22	2.14	2.08	2.00	1.97	1.90	1.86	1.84
40	4.08	3.23	2.84	2.61	2.45	2.34	2.25	2.18	2.12	2.07	2.04	2.00	1.95	1.90	1.84	1.79	1.74	1.69	1.66	1.61	1.59	1.55	1.53	1.51
	7.31	5.18	4.31	3.83	3.51	3.29	3.12	2.99	2.88	2.80	2.73	2.66	2.56	2.49	2.37	2.29	2.20	2.11	2.05	1.97	1.94	1.88	1.84	1.81
42	4.07	3.22	2.83	2.59	2.44	2.32	2.24	2.17	2.11	2.06	2.02	1.99	1.94	1.89	1.82	1.78	1.73	1.68	1.64	1.60	1.57	1.54	1.51	1.49
	7.27	5.15	4.29	3.80	3.49	3.26	3.10	2.96	2.86	2.77	2.70	2.64	2.54	2.46	2.35	2.26	2.17	2.08	2.02	1.94	1.91	1.85	1.80	1.78
44	4.06	3.21	.282	2.58	2.43	2.31	2.23	2.16	2.10	2.05	2.01	1.98	1.92	1.88	1.81	1.76	1.72	1.66	1.63	1.58	1.56	1.52	1.50	1.48
	7.24	5.12	4.26	3.78	3.46	3.24	3.07	2.94	2.84	2.75	2.68	2.62	2.52	2.44	2.32	2.24	2.15	2.06	2.00	1.92	1.88	1.82	1.78	1.75
46	4.05	3.20	2.81	2.57	2.42	2.30	2.22	2.14	2.09	2.04	2.00	1.97	1.91	1.87	1.80	1.75	1.71	1.65	1.62	1.57	1.54	1.51	1.48	1.46
	7.21	5.10	4.24	3.76	3.44	3.22	3.05	2.92	2.82	2.73	2.66	2.60	2.50	2.42	2.30	2.22	2.13	20.4	1.98	1.90	1.86	1.80	1.76	1.72

Table 3.5 *Continued*

DEGREES OF FREEDOM FOR NUMERATOR

DEGREES OF FREEDOM FOR DENOMINATOR	1	2	3	4	5	6	7	8	9	10	11	12	14	16	20	24	30	40	50	75	100	200	500	∞
48	4.04	3.19	2.80	2.56	2.41	2.30	2.21	2.14	2.08	2.03	1.99	1.96	1.90	1.86	1.79	1.74	1.70	1.64	1.61	1.56	1.53	1.50	1.47	1.45
	7.19	5.08	4.22	3.74	3.42	3.20	3.04	2.90	2.80	2.71	2.64	2.58	2.48	2.40	2.28	2.20	2.11	2.02	1.96	1.88	1.84	1.78	1.73	1.70
50	4.03	3.18	2.79	2.56	2.40	2.29	2.20	2.13	2.07	2.02	1.98	1.95	1.90	1.85	1.78	1.74	1.69	1.63	1.60	1.55	1.52	1.48	1.46	1.44
	7.17	5.06	4.20	3.72	3.41	3.18	3.02	2.88	2.78	2.70	2.62	2.56	2.46	2.39	2.26	2.18	2.10	2.00	1.94	1.86	1.82	1.76	1.71	1.68
55	4.02	3.17	2.78	2.54	2.38	2.27	2.18	2.11	2.05	2.00	1.97	1.93	1.88	1.83	1.76	1.72	1.67	1.61	1.58	1.52	1.50	1.46	1.43	1.41
	7.12	5.01	4.16	3.68	3.37	3.15	2.98	2.85	2.75	2.66	2.59	2.53	2.43	2.35	2.23	2.15	2.06	1.96	1.90	1.82	1.78	1.71	1.66	1.64
60	4.00	3.15	2.76	2.52	2.37	2.25	2.17	2.10	2.04	1.99	1.95	1.92	1.86	1.81	1.75	1.70	1.65	1.59	1.56	1.50	1.48	1.44	1.41	1.39
	7.08	4.98	4.13	3.65	3.34	3.12	2.95	2.82	2.72	2.63	2.58	2.50	2.40	2.32	2.20	2.12	2.03	1.93	1.87	1.79	1.74	1.68	1.63	1.60
65	3.99	3.14	2.75	2.51	2.36	2.24	2.15	2.08	2.02	1.98	1.94	1.90	1.85	1.80	1.73	1.68	1.63	1.57	1.54	1.49	1.46	1.42	1.39	1.37
	7.04	4.95	4.10	3.62	3.31	3.09	2.93	2.79	2.70	2.61	2.54	2.47	2.37	2.30	2.18	2.09	2.00	1.90	1.84	1.76	1.71	1.64	1.60	1.56
70	3.98	3.13	2.74	2.50	2.35	2.23	2.14	2.07	2.01	1.97	1.93	1.89	1.84	1.79	1.72	1.67	1.62	1.56	1.53	1.47	1.45	1.40	1.37	1.35
	7.01	4.92	4.08	3.60	3.29	3.07	2.91	2.77	2.67	2.59	2.51	2.45	2.35	2.28	2.15	2.07	1.98	1.88	1.82	1.74	1.69	1.62	1.56	1.53
80	3.96	3.11	2.72	2.48	2.33	2.21	2.12	2.05	1.99	1.95	1.91	1.88	1.82	1.77	1.70	1.65	1.60	1.54	1.51	1.45	1.42	1.38	1.35	1.32
	6.96	4.88	4.04	3.56	3.25	3.04	2.87	2.74	2.64	2.55	2.48	2.41	2.32	2.24	2.11	2.03	1.94	1.84	1.78	1.70	1.65	1.57	1.52	1.49
100	3.94	3.09	2.70	2.46	2.30	2.19	2.10	2.03	1.97	1.92	1.88	1.85	1.79	1.75	1.68	1.63	1.57	1.51	1.48	1.42	1.39	1.34	1.30	1.28
	6.90	4.82	3.98	3.51	3.20	2.99	2.82	2.69	2.59	2.51	2.43	2.36	2.26	2.19	2.06	1.98	1.89	1.79	1.73	1.64	1.59	1.51	1.46	1.43
125	3.92	3.07	2.68	2.44	2.29	2.17	2.08	2.01	1.95	1.90	1.86	1.83	1.77	1.72	1.65	1.60	1.55	1.49	1.45	1.39	1.36	1.31	1.27	1.25
	6.84	4.78	3.94	3.47	3.17	2.95	2.79	2.65	2.56	2.47	2.40	2.33	2.23	2.15	2.03	1.94	1.85	1.76	1.68	1.59	1.54	1.46	1.40	1.37
150	3.91	3.06	2.67	2.43	2.27	2.16	2.07	2.00	1.94	1.89	1.85	1.82	1.76	1.71	1.64	1.59	1.54	1.47	1.44	1.37	1.34	1.29	1.25	1.22
	6.81	4.75	3.91	3.44	3.14	2.92	2.76	2.62	2.53	2.44	2.37	2.30	2.20	2.12	2.00	1.91	1.83	1.72	1.66	1.56	1.51	1.43	1.37	1.33
200	3.89	3.04	2.65	2.41	2.26	2.14	2.05	1.98	1.92	1.87	1.83	1.80	1.74	1.69	1.62	1.57	1.52	1.45	1.42	1.35	1.32	1.26	1.22	1.19
	6.76	4.71	3.88	3.41	3.11	2.90	2.73	2.60	2.50	2.41	2.34	2.28	2.17	2.09	1.97	1.88	1.79	1.69	1.62	1.53	1.48	1.39	1.33	1.28
400	3.86	3.02	2.62	2.39	2.23	2.12	2.03	1.96	1.90	1.85	1.81	1.78	1.72	1.67	1.60	1.54	1.49	1.42	1.38	1.32	1.28	1.22	1.16	1.13
	6.70	4.66	3.83	3.36	3.06	2.85	2.69	2.55	2.46	2.37	2.29	2.23	2.12	2.04	1.92	1.84	1.74	1.64	1.57	1.47	1.42	1.32	1.24	1.19
1000	3.85	3.00	2.61	2.38	2.22	2.10	2.02	1.95	1.89	1.84	1.80	1.76	1.70	1.65	1.58	1.53	1.47	1.41	1.36	1.30	1.26	1.19	1.13	1.08
	6.66	4.62	3.80	3.34	3.04	2.82	2.66	2.53	2.43	2.34	2.26	2.20	2.09	2.01	1.89	1.81	1.71	1.61	1.54	1.44	1.38	1.28	1.19	1.11
∞	3.84	2.99	2.60	2.37	2.21	2.09	2.01	1.94	1.88	1.83	1.79	1.75	1.69	1.64	1.57	1.52	1.46	1.40	1.35	1.28	1.24	1.17	1.11	1.00
	6.64	4.60	3.78	3.32	3.02	2.80	2.64	2.51	2.41	2.32	2.24	2.18	2.07	1.99	1.87	1.79	1.69	1.59	1.52	1.41	1.36	1.25	1.15	1.00

Figure 3.1 Two-way ANOVA decision process.

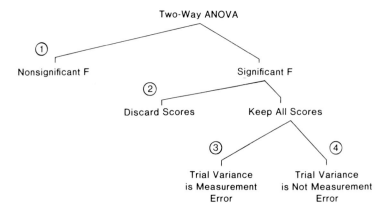

For example, using the summary table in Problem 3.5, at the intersection of df_t 2 and df_I 8, F is 4.46 at the .05 level and 8.65 at the .01 level. Because the calculated F for the data in the problem is .29, the difference among trial means is nonsignificant.

After the F-test, there are four potential ways the analysis can progress, as shown in figure 3.1.

Nonsignificant F If there is a nonsignificant F, indicating no difference among the trial means, the reliability of the criterion score, which is the sum or mean of a subject's trial scores, is as follows:

$$R = \frac{MS_S - MS_W}{MS_S} \qquad (2)$$

where

$$MS_W = \frac{SS_t + SS_I}{df_t + df_I}$$

Using the data in Problem 3.5, where MS_W is $.6 \left[\frac{(.4 + 5.6)}{(2 + 8)} \right]$, R is .88:

$$R = \frac{5.10 - .6}{5.10} = \frac{4.50}{5.10} = .882$$

Notice that formulas 1 and 2 are the same as the formula for R presented with a one-way ANOVA since SS_S in a two-way ANOVA is the same as SS_A in a one-way ANOVA. Applying the one-way ANOVA formulas to the data in table 3.4 we obtain the following:

$$\Sigma X = 78 \qquad\qquad n = 5$$
$$\Sigma X^2 = 432 \qquad\qquad k = 3$$

Σ of the trial scores for students are 18, 10, 13, 19, 18 respectively.

$$SS_T = 432 - \frac{78^2}{(5)(3)} = 432 - 405.6 = 26.4$$

$$SS_A = \frac{18^2 + 10^2 + 13^2 + 19^2 + 18^2}{3} - \frac{78^2}{(5)(3)} = 426 - 405.6 = 20.4$$

$$SS_W = 432 - \frac{18^2 + 10^2 + 13^2 + 19^2 + 18^2}{3}$$

$$= 432 - 426 = 6$$

$$MS_A = \frac{20.4}{5 - 1} = 5.1$$

$$MS_W = \frac{6}{(5)(3 - 1)} = .6$$

$$R = \frac{5.1 - .6}{5.1} = .88$$

Significant F   The other alternative ways for the analysis to go are possible when the F is significant, indicating a difference among the trial means. With the first technique (number 2 in figure 3.1) (Baumgartner 1969a), which can be used when each subject is tested several times in 1 day or on several days, the scores from trials whose means are lower than or not approximately equal to the means of the other trials are discarded. A second two-way analysis of variance is then conducted on the retained scores, and another F-test is calculated. If the recalculated F is nonsignificant, Formula 2 is used to estimate the reliability of the **criterion score,** representing the sum or mean of all the subject's retained trial scores. For example, suppose the data for a 6-trial test were as follows:

			Trial			
	1	2	3	4	5	6
Mean	48	53	57	58	58.3	49

Trials 1, 2, and 6 would be discarded, and another two-way ANOVA would be conducted using the scores from Trials 3, 4, and 5.

The purpose of this technique is to find a measurement schedule free of trial differences and yielding the largest possible criterion score for most subjects. This criterion score is usually very reliable. Baumgartner and Jackson (1970) used this technique. Trial-to-trial variance is random after finding a nonsignificant F, so it is considered a measurement error in Formula 2. Interaction is also considered a measurement error.

Another alternative (number 3 in figure 3.1), again assuming significant difference among trial means, is to apply Formula 2 immediately, without discarding any scores, in which case it would have been easier to follow the procedures of a one-way analysis of variance, using Formula 1. The decision not to discard data even when there is a difference among trial means is made when that difference is considered a measurement error. For example, subject scores on multiple trials or on each of several days are supposed to be consistent from trial to trial or day to day; when they are inconsistent, measurement error has occurred.

The last alternative (number 4 in figure 3.1) does not consider a trial-to-trial variance as measurement error. This technique is often used when it is known that subjects will improve from trial to trial. Also, this technique is often used when estimating objectivity (judges replace trials) and all judges are not expected to use the same standards. The formula for estimating the reliability of the criterion score (the sum or mean of all trials) is as follows:

$$R = \frac{MS_S - MS_I}{MS_S} \tag{3}$$

For the data in Problem 3.5, using Formula 3, R is .86:

$$R = \frac{5.10 - .70}{5.10} = \frac{4.40}{5.10} = .86$$

Measurement error is supposed to be random. Significant difference among the trial means indicates a lack of randomness. Thus, when significant difference is found, one could argue that the variance for trials should not be combined with the sum of squares interaction to form the mean square within of Formulas 1 and 2. Statistically this position is defensible. However, one could counter that every source of variance not attributable to students is error-score variance. In keeping with this philosophy, you can either conduct a one-way analysis of variance with the test scores and use Formula 1 or, as Baumgartner (1969a) advocates, discard scores until no significant difference among trial means is found in the data.

Most researchers are using the computer to apply a two-way ANOVA to their data. Two-way ANOVA computer programs, that will handle repeated measures on each subject, are very common on both mainframe and microcomputers. Unless the amount of data is small, all physical educators and exercise specialists should use the computer to do a two-way ANOVA on their data. The advantage of a two-way ANOVA over a one-way ANOVA is that the computer will give you the mean for each trial, a significance test for difference among trial means is possible, and the R can still be calculated as if a one-way ANOVA was used (Formula 2) or by Formula 3 that requires a two-way ANOVA.

Of the four potential data analyses shown in figure 3.1, it seems that most people are using alternatives 2 and 4. Only when people must do the data analysis by hand or believe that alternative 3 is appropriate is a one-way ANOVA initially applied to the data.

All the formulas for calculating the intraclass reliability coefficient thus far have been for the average or sum of all trials or days. Sometimes it is necessary to estimate the reliability of a single trial or day. Two formulas are used to calculate the reliability of a single score when there are k trials or days; the decision which to use rests on the analysis procedure. If the procedures leading to Formula 2 were used, we calculate R with the following equation:

$$R = \frac{MS_S - MS_w}{MS_S + (k - 1)(MS_w)}$$

If the procedures leading to Formula 3 were used, we use this formula instead:

$$R = \frac{MS_S - MS_I}{MS_S + (k - 1)(MS_I)}$$

Several authors, including Safrit (1981), present formulas for estimating or predicting what R would be if the number of trials was increased or decreased. Depending on whether the procedures leading to Formula 2 or Formula 3 were used, this formula is either

$$\text{Estimated } R = \frac{MS_S - MS_w}{MS_S + (k/k' - 1)(MS_w)}$$

or

$$\text{Estimated } R = \frac{MS_S - MS_I}{MS_S + (k/k' - 1)(MS_I)}$$

where k is the number of trials administered and k' is the number of trials for which R is estimated.

Coefficient Alpha

When the data are ordinal, we use the coefficient alpha to determine reliability (Ferguson 1981; Nunnally 1967). In fact, with internal data the coefficient alpha is the same as the intraclass R $\left[R = \frac{(MS_S - MS_I)}{MS_S} \right]$ just discussed. Coefficient alpha is an estimate of the reliability of a criterion score that is the sum of the trial scores in 1 day. There is no reason why the coefficient could not be applied to multiple-day or multiple-judge data to estimate stability reliability or objectivity, although some modification in the formula is necessary if the criterion score is to be other than the sum of the scores for all days or all judges. We determine coefficient alpha using the following formula:

$$r_\alpha = \left(\frac{k}{k - 1} \right) \frac{s_x^2 - \Sigma s_j^2}{s_x^2} \tag{4}$$

where r_α is coefficient alpha, k is the number of trials, s_x^2 is the variance for the criterion score, and Σs_j^2 is the sum of the variances for the trials.

Problem 3.6   Calculate coefficient alpha for the data in table 3.4.

Solution   Here too the procedure is a multistep one.

Step 1

For our calculations we must determine the sum of the scores for each trial (ΣX), the sum of the squared scores for each trial (ΣX^2), the sum of the scores for each subject (T), and the sum of those scores (ΣT). The simplest way to do this is to set up a table like the one below:

Subject	Trial 1		Trial 2		Trial 3		T
	X_1	$(X_1)^2$	X_2	$(X_2)^2$	X_3	$(X_3)^2$	
A	5	25	6	36	7	49	18
B	3	9	3	9	4	16	10
C	4	16	4	16	5	25	13
D	7	49	6	36	6	36	19
E	6	36	7	49	5	25	18
	25	135	26	146	27	151	78

Step 2

Using the formula

$$s^2 = \frac{\Sigma X^2}{n} - \frac{(\Sigma X)^2}{n^2}$$

calculate the variance for each trial:

$$s_1^2 = \frac{135}{5} - \frac{25^2}{5^2} = 27 - \frac{625}{25} = 27 - 25 = 2$$

$$s_2^2 = \frac{146}{5} - \frac{26^2}{5^2} = 29.2 - \frac{676}{25} = 29.2 - 27.04 = 2.16$$

$$s_3^2 = \frac{151}{5} - \frac{27^2}{5^2} = 30.2 - \frac{729}{25} = 30.2 - 29.16 = 1.04$$

Step 3

Using the formula

$$s^2 = \frac{\Sigma T^2}{n} - \frac{(\Sigma T)^2}{n^2}$$

Where T is the sum of the scores for each subject, we can calculate the variance for the criterion score:

$$s_x^2 = \frac{18^2 + 10^2 + 13^2 + 19^2 + 18^2}{5} - \frac{78^2}{5^2}$$

$$= \frac{324 + 100 + 169 + 361 + 324}{5} - \frac{6084}{25}$$

$$= \frac{1278}{5} - 243.36 = 255.6 - 243.36 = 12.24$$

Step 4

Now we can calculate r_α. Where k is 3, s_x^2 is 12.24, and Σs_j^2 is 5.2 (the sum of s_1^2, s_2^2, and s_3^2: $2 + 2.16 + 1.04$), the coefficient alpha r_α is .86:

$$r_\alpha = \left(\frac{3}{3-1}\right)\frac{12.24 - 5.2}{12.24} = \left(\frac{3}{2}\right)\frac{7.04}{12.24} = \frac{21.12}{24.48} = .86$$

Notice R = .86 with Formula 3.

Computer analysis, especially to calculate the variances for each trial and the criterion score, speeds up the procedure for obtaining r_α. The computer can also provide the correlations for the trial scores with the sum of the trial scores, which could be useful in deciding which trials to sum as the criterion score. Only trials that correlate positively at a reasonably high value with the sum of the trial scores should be retained. Normally, with motor performance tests, each trial is correlated with the sum of all trials. Version 7 of the SPSS package (Nie et al. 1975) and later versions offer the RELIABILITY program, which provides both the intraclass and alpha correlation coefficients. The program's standard output includes the correlation between each trial and the sum of all trials, and the reliability when the trial is eliminated.

If the data is ordinal and a sum of the scores for each subject can legitimately be obtained, Formula 4 and the procedures in Problem 3.6 could be used to determine reliability. An example might be a rating scale where, on each item of the scale, a person was rated on a 5-point scale with excellent = 5, above average = 4, average = 3, below average = 2, and terrible = 1. Some people maintain that ordinal scores cannot legitimately be summed because the numbers assigned to the ratings are just codes and not measured values (for example, excellent = 5 could just as well be excellent = 10). However, many people handle ratings as if they are interval data and sum the ratings.

SUMMARY

There are three characteristics essential to a sound measuring instrument: reliability, objectivity, and validity. Reliability and objectivity were discussed in this chapter. A test has reliability when it consistently measures what it is supposed to measure. There are two types of reliability: stability and internal consistency. The procedures that traditionally have been used to determine these measures of reliability (test-retest method and split-half method) have used the Pearson product-moment correlation coefficient, an interclass coefficient that limits the correlation to 2 scores per person. Today an intraclass coefficient, developed through analysis of variance, is rapidly gaining popularity in physical education and sports science measurement and research programs. One other aspect of reliability coefficients is very important to physical education teachers and exercise specialists: difference scores. You should be aware of the inherent unfairness and lack of reliability in this too-common form of evaluation.

Objectivity, the second vital characteristic of a sound instrument, is the degree to which different judges agree in their scoring of each individual in a group. A fair test is one in which qualified judges rate individuals similarly and/or offer the same conditions of testing to all individuals equally.

FORMATIVE EVALUATION OF OBJECTIVES

Objective 1   Define and differentiate between reliability and objectivity, and outline the methods used to estimate these values.

1. Two important characteristics of all measurements are that they be reliable and objective. Describe the basic nature of each of these characteristics.
2. In theory, reliability is the ratio of the true-score variance to the observed-score variance. Observed-score variance consists of both error-score variance and true-score variance. Describe these basic sources of variance and the combination that yields the highest estimate of reliability.
3. Two basic methods are used to estimate the reliability of a measuring instrument: stability reliability and internal-consistency reliability. Briefly describe each method and the procedure it uses to estimate reliability.
4. The standard error of measurement is an estimate of the amount of measurement error in the test score. List the formula for the standard error of measurement and describe the characteristics of the statistic.
5. Objectivity, or rater reliability, is achieved when the scores of 2 or more different judges closely agree. The correlation between the scores is an objectivity coefficient. Summarize the procedures that yield high objectivity.

Objective 2   Identify those factors that influence reliability and objectivity.

1. Acceptable reliability is essential for all measurements. Many factors affect the reliability of a measurement and some of these are listed below. Identify the conditions under which the highest reliability can be expected for the following factors:
   a. Subjects tested   c. Testing environment
   b. Test length   d. Test administrator
2. According to measurement theory, if a test is lengthened, its reliability is increased. If the reliability of a standing long-jump test composed of 2 jumps is found to be .82, how reliable might the test be if 6 jumps were scored?
3. If a physical education teacher or exercise specialist wants to evaluate subjects on improvement, usually a test is given at the beginning and end of a teaching or training unit and the difference between the 2 scores is used as the measure of improvement. Evaluate this procedure in terms of reliability.
4. A physical education teacher or exercise specialist can improve test objectivity in several ways. Summarize them.

ADDITIONAL LEARNING ACTIVITIES

1. Many tests suggest 2 or 3 trials within a day. The number may have been arbitrarily selected so that the test can be given quickly. Administer a multiple-trial test with more trials than recommended. By looking at the trial means, determine when the performance of the group reaches its maximum and becomes consistent.

2. There are many tests commonly used in testing programs (runs, jumps, maximum effort). Administer one of these tests and determine the reliability of it.

3. Construct a new physical performance test. Administer the test and decide how to calculate its reliability and objectivity.

BIBLIOGRAPHY

Baumgartner, T. A. 1968. "The Application of the Spearman-Brown Prophecy Formula When Applied to Physical Performance Tests." *Research Quarterly* 39:847–56.

————. 1969a. "Estimating Reliability When All Test Trials Are Administered on the Same Day." *Research Quarterly* 40:222–25.

————. 1969b. "Stability of Physical Performance Test Scores." *Research Quarterly* 40:257–61.

————. 1974. "Criterion Score for Multiple Trial Measures." *Research Quarterly* 45:193–98.

Baumgartner, T. A., and A. S. Jackson. 1970. "Measurement Schedules for Tests of Motor Performance." *Research Quarterly* 41:10–17.

East, W. B. 1979. "Mathematical Techniques for Estimating Motor Performance Improvement." Ed.D. dissertation, University of Georgia.

Ebel, R. L. 1979. *Essentials of Educational Measurement.* 3d ed. Englewood Cliffs, N.J.: Prentice-Hall.

Feldt, L. S., and M. E. McKee. 1958. "Estimating the Reliability of Skill Tests." *Research Quarterly* 29:279–93.

Ferguson, G. A. 1981. *Statistical Analysis in Psychology and Education.* 5th ed. New York: McGraw-Hill.

Glass, G. V., and J. C. Stanley. 1970. *Statistical Methods in Education and Psychology.* Englewood Cliffs, N.J.: Prentice-Hall.

Hale, P. W., and R. M. Hale. 1972. "Comparison of Student Improvement by Exponential Modification of Test-Retest Scores." *Research Quarterly* 43:113–20.

Henry, F. M. 1956. "Evaluation of Motor Learning When Performance Levels Are Heterogeneous." *Research Quarterly* 27:176–81.

Kroll, W. 1962. "A Note on the Coefficient of Intraclass Correlation as an Estimate of Reliability." *Research Quarterly* 33:313–16.

————. 1967. "Reliability Theory and Research Decision in Selection of a Criterion Score." *Research Quarterly* 38:412–19.

Nie, N. H. et al. 1975. *Statistical Package for the Social Sciences,* 2d ed. New York: McGraw-Hill.

Nunnally, J. C. 1967. *Psychometric Theory.* New York: McGraw-Hill.

Remmers, H. H., N. L. Gage, and J. F. Rummel. 1969. *A Practical Introduction to Measurement and Evaluation.* New York: Harper & Row.

Safrit, M. J. 1981. *Evaluation in Physical Education,* 2d ed. Englewood Cliffs, N.J.: Prentice-Hall.

———. et al. 1974. *Reliability Theory Appropriate for Motor Performance Measures.* New York: AAHPER.

Stamm, C. L. 1976. "An Alternative Method for Estimating Reliability." *JOPERD* 47:66–67.

Stamm, C. L., and M. J. Safrit. 1977. "Comparisons of Two Nonparametric Methods for Estimating the Reliability of Motor Performance Tests." *Research Quarterly* 48:169–76.

Winer, B. J. 1962. *Statistical Principles in Experimental Design.* New York: McGraw-Hill.

Zuidema, M. A. 1969. "A Brief on Reliability Theory: Theoretical Concepts, Influencing Factors, and Empirical Estimates of the Reliability of Measurements Especially Applied to Physical Performance Tests." Mimeographed. University of Indiana, Bloomington, Ind.

Validity

4

Contents

Key Words

Concurrent Validity
Construct Validity
Content Validity
Criterion Score
Face Validity
Predictive Validity
Validity

Objectives

This chapter discusses the methods used to estimate validity, the relationship between reliability and validity, and the factors that influence validity.

Many physical performance tests can be given several times in the same day. When there are multiple trials of a test, the teacher must decide how many to administer and what trial(s) to use as the criterion score.

After reading chapter 4 you should be able to:

1. Define validity, and outline the methods used to estimate it.
2. Describe the influence of test reliability on test validity.
3. Identify those factors that influence validity.
4. Select a reliable, valid criterion score based on sound measurement theory.

INTRODUCTION

There are certain characteristics essential to a measurement; without them, little faith can be put in the measurement and little use made of it. Two of these characteristics, reliability and objectivity, were discussed in chapter 3. A third important characteristic of a measurement is validity.

A test or measuring instrument is valid if it measures what it is supposed to measure. For example, chin-ups are a valid measure of arm strength and endurance because biceps strength and endurance are necessary to do a chin-up; but chin-ups are not a valid measure of arm speed because the number of chin-ups one can execute is not influenced by arm speed. For a measure to be valid it must be reliable, but a reliable test may not be valid. Obviously for a test or instrument to measure what it is supposed to measure, it must first measure consistently. For example, the 50-yard dash test is reliable and is a valid measure of running speed; however, it is not a valid measure of flexibility.

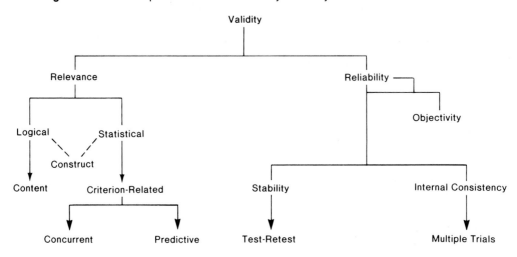

Figure 4.1 Relationship of relevance and reliability to validity.

VALIDITY

When a test measures what it purports to measure, it is a valid test. To have **validity,** then, a test must be both relevant and reliable—relevant to the material being tested and reliable as a measurement of that material. Figure 4.1 shows the interrelationship among validity, relevance, and reliability.

In figure 4.1 it can be seen that validity has two major components, relevance and reliability, with objectivity (sometimes called rater reliability) a component of reliability. As we found in chapter 3, there are two basic types of reliability, stability estimated by the test-retest method and internal consistency estimated by the multiple-trials-within-a-day method. As we will find in this chapter, there are two basic types of relevance with definite estimation methods leading to what is called content validity, construct validity, concurrent validity, and predictive validity.

Types and Estimation

A test's degree of validity should indicate to the user the degree to which that test is capable of achieving certain aims (American Psychological Association et al. 1966). These aims and the four types of validity that parallel these aims are content validity, concurrent validity, predictive validity, and construct validity.

That a measuring instrument be valid is crucial to measurement procedures. Validity can be estimated either logically or statistically. Recently the trend in education and psychology has been away from the statistical approach. This does not necessarily mean that physical education and sports science should follow suit. Education and psychology work predominantly with paper-and-pencil tests, while physical education and sports science work predominantly with physical performance tests. The test method for estimating validity must be chosen in terms of the situation, not the trend.

Content Validity

A measuring instrument has **content validity** to the extent that it measures the capacities about which conclusions are to be drawn. Content, or **face, validity** is established logically by examining the capacities to be measured and determining whether the instrument, in fact, is measuring them. For example, the 50-yard dash and 100-yard dash are obviously valid tests of running speed because they measure the speed at which a person can run. A written test has content validity when its questions are reliable and measure the stated educational objectives. For a complicated, multicomponent skill, such as team sports or physical fitness, clearly defined objectives provide the only means of determining the degree of content validity.

Content validity, then, rests solely on subjective decision making, which has led to criticism of this type of validity. However, this type of validity is not the only one to rest on subjective decision: concurrent validity is often determined by using the subjective decisions of an expert judge or judges.

Concurrent Validity

Concurrent validity is a measure of a test's correlation to some specified criterion. This is a traditional procedure for establishing the validity of a test. It involves calculating the Pearson product-moment correlation coefficient or some other similar type of correlation between scores on the test and those achieved on a criterion measure. The resulting correlation coefficient—the validity coefficient—is an estimate of the validity of the test. When the validity coefficient is close to 1, the instrument is measuring similarly to the criterion measure and is valid; when the coefficient is close to 0, the instrument has little validity.

A crucial step in establishing the concurrent validity of a test is the choice of a suitable criterion measure. Expert ratings, tournament standings, and predetermined criteria are all common criterion measures.

Expert Ratings. One criterion measure is the subjective rating of one or more experts. Because one judge may overlook certain factors in a person's performance or may have certain biases that affect his or her ratings, the use of a criterion score, the sum of several qualified judges' ratings, is a more reliable criterion measure. Obviously, high objectivity among judges is vital.

Subjective ratings usually take the form of either class ranks or a point scale. Using class ranks, the subjects are ordered from best to worst on the basis of performance. Using a point scale, the subjects are scored individually on a numbered point scale, as they would be in a gymnastics meet. Class ranks become unworkable as the size of the group increases. Further, a point scale system is preferable, since it does not require that one person be ranked best and another worst. One usually obtains higher validity with a scoring system than with class ranks provided the scoring system is well defined so that high objectivity is possible.

Expert ratings are commonly used to estimate the validity of skill tests. A skill test has certain advantages over tests that must be judged by experts. Judges' evaluations are fine measures, of course, providing the judges are qualified. And theoretically it should be possible to bring in expert judges for every skill test. But in practice it is hard to find even one expert, let alone several, who have the time to subjectively evaluate a class of students. Then, too, skill tests are usually easier to administer and less time consuming than are subjective evaluations.

Tournament Standings.   A second method of estimating the validity of an instrument is to correlate the scores from the instrument (using the Pearson product-moment correlation coefficient or some other appropriate correlation coefficient) with the tournament standings of the students being measured. The method assumes that tournament standing is a good indicator of overall ability in the tested skill, usually an individual or dual activity like tennis or badminton. Many teachers are eager to find an instrument that is a valid indicator of skill. Such an instrument makes it unnecessary to conduct round-robin tournaments to evaluate the skill level of the students.

Predetermined Criteria.   The final method uses a known valid, accepted instrument, which yields a quantitative score as the criterion measure. The validity of a test is then estimated by determining the Pearson product-moment correlation coefficient between scores from the test and scores from the accepted instrument. The method is usually used in developing a test that is quicker and/or easier to administer than is the accepted instrument. For example, this procedure has been used to validate the use of skinfolds to measure body composition (see chapter 8). A valid, accepted measure of percentage body fat can be obtained by weighing a subject under water: a person with a high percentage body fat weighs less under water because fat tissue is less dense than muscle and bone. Skinfold measurements are easy to obtain and correlate highly (r at least .80) with the percentage of fat determined by the more complicated underwater-weighing method. By obtaining selected skinfold measurements, we can predict the subject's percentage body fat using a regression equation. In fact, multiple correlation and regression equations (see chapter 2) are often used to establish concurrent validity.

Predictive Validity

Predictive validity, like concurrent validity, is determined by using a criterion measure. Any of the three criterion measures previously discussed can be used to establish predictive validity. **Predictive validity** represents the value of a measure for predicting performance on another measure (criterion) at some future date.

Consider, for example, the question of predicting success in graduate programs. A student's performance on a standardized test such as the Graduate Record Exam, administered before graduate school, is correlated with a criterion measure of success in the graduate program, usually the student's graduate grade point average. The correlation between the two instruments indicates the predictive validity of the test.

Predictive validity can be difficult to establish. Often it is impossible to determine a suitable criterion measure. We could question, for example, whether graduate grade point averages are a truthful index of success in graduate school.

A criterion measure that represents a composite of several tests is almost always preferred to one based on a single measure. The sum of the T-scores for several tests is the most common composite criterion measure.

For example, let us go back to the problem of predicting student success in graduate programs. The criterion measure—the measure of success—could be a composite of a student's graduate grade point average in required courses, his or her grade point average in nonrequired courses, and a subjective rating by the faculty. To determine the predictive validity of the Graduate Record Exam, then, we would take the following steps:

Step 1
Collect the Graduate Record Exam scores, the two grade point averages, and the faculty's subjective ratings for each student.

Step 2
Calculate the T-scores for each of the three components of the criterion measure and the sum of the T-scores for each student.

Step 3
Determine the correlation—the predictive validity coefficient—between Graduate Record Exam scores and the sum of the T-scores.

Construct Validity

Content validity, concurrent validity, and predictive validity are established methods for examining test validity; construct validity is a comparatively new and more complex validation procedure. It was first introduced in 1954 by the American Psychological Association, and has been used extensively in psychological testing since then. Today the method is being used more and more in physical education testing as well (Safrit 1975).

Construct validity is used with abstract rather than concrete tests (Nunnally 1967). An abstract test measures something that is not directly observable. The 16 personality characteristics measured by the *Cattell Personality Questionnaire* (Cattell and Stice 1957) are abstract human traits that are neither readily apparent nor easily understood by an untrained professional. The number of basketball free throws made out of 100 tries, on the other hand, is a concrete measure of skill.

Construct validity is based on the scientific method. First, there is a hunch that a test or tests measure some abstract trait. Second, a theory is developed to explain both the construct and the tests that measure it. Finally, various statistical procedures are applied to confirm or reject the theory. An excellent example of this process is shown in the work of Kenyon (1968a, b), who developed valid scales (see chapter 12) for the measurement of attitude toward physical activity and the construct validation of distance run tests by Disch, Frankiewicz and Jackson (1975). Safrit (1977) provides a fine overview of the construct validation process.

Construct validity is determined by judging the extent to which theoretical and statistical information supports assumed constructs. The procedure gives physical education teachers and exercise specialists a way to evaluate their tests. For example, consider a swimming test administered to intermediate and varsity swimmers. Because the varsity swimmers are known to be better swimmers, we can demonstrate construct validity whenever the mean score of the varsity swimmers is superior to that of the intermediate swimmers. If the mean score of the varsity swimmers happened to be lower than that of the intermediate swimmers, the test would lack construct validity, indicating a need for reevaluation of the skill test.

Scientists may not consider this as a scientifically "true" example of the construct validation process, however, it does demonstrate that the process can be applied in the classroom. Whenever a superior performer does not achieve a score comparable to those of previously administered tests, the teacher must be alert to the possibility that the test lacks either reliability or validity.

Factor analysis is a statistical procedure that can be used to identify constructs and the valid tests of isolated constructs. In this context the isolated factor of the analysis is an abstract construct (Safrit 1975; Yates 1977).

Factors Affecting Validity

Selected Criterion Measure

The magnitude of a validity coefficient can be affected by several factors, among them the criterion measure selected. We have suggested several possible criterion measures (expert ratings, tournament standards, predetermined criteria) to use in estimating the validity of a test. It is reasonable to expect that each measure, when correlated with the same set of test scores, would yield a different validity coefficient. This is particularly true for a test of multicomponent skills.

Characteristics of the Individuals Tested

Characteristics of the individuals tested also play a part in determining validity. A test that is valid for 6-year-old children may not be valid for 15-year-old students; a test valid for males may not be valid for females; a test that is valid for beginners may not be valid for advanced students. We can assume that a test is valid only for individuals similar in age, gender, and experience to those on whom the test was validated. In fact, it is a good idea to determine validity for yourself the first time you use a test, even for like groups, because the individuals you are measuring cannot be exactly like those originally used to validate the test.

Reliability

As we have said, a test must be reliable to be valid. The validity coefficient is directly related to the reliability of both the test and the criterion measure. Ferguson (1981) suggests that the maximum validity coefficient possible between two tests can be computed with the following formula:

$$r_{x,y} = \sqrt{(r_{x,x})(r_{y,y})}$$

where $r_{x,y}$ is the correlation between Tests X and Y, $r_{x,x}$ is the reliability coefficient for Test X, and $r_{y,y}$ is the reliability coefficient for Test Y. For example, if the reliability of both Tests X and Y is .90, the maximum validity coefficient possible would be .90:

$$r_{x,y} = \sqrt{(.90)(.90)} = \sqrt{.81} = .90$$

If the reliability of Test X is .90 and that of Test Y is only .40, the maximum validity coefficient is much lower, only .60:

$$r_{x,y} = \sqrt{(.90)(.40)} = \sqrt{.36} = .60$$

Objectivity

Objectivity was defined as the agreement of two or more competent judges or scorers about the value of a measurement. Note that some people call objectivity rater reliability. If two judges or raters scoring the same individual on the same test cannot agree on a score, the test lacks objectivity and neither score is valid. Thus, a lack of objectivity reduces validity of a test.

Lengthened Tests

We know that the validity of a test is influenced by its reliability. We know, from the Spearman-Brown formula, that reliability increases as the number of test trials or the length of the test increases. Further, the more measures you obtain for each individual, the more valid an indication you have of his or her true ability. For example, a dribbling test and a shooting test are better indications of basketball-playing ability than a shooting test alone, but four measures of basketball-playing ability are preferable to two measures. It would seem, then, that by increasing the length of a test we would also increase its validity.

SELECTING A VALID CRITERION SCORE

A **criterion score** is the measure used to indicate a subject's ability. It is a better indicator when it is developed from more than one trial. Multiple-trial tests are common with jumping, throwing, and short running—skills whose performance is not adversely affected by fatigue. For a multiple-trial test, the criterion score can be either the person's best score or mean score. The best score is the optimal score a person receives on any one trial; the mean score is the mean of all the person's trial scores.

Much research has been done on the selection of a criterion score (Baumgartner 1974; Berger and Sweney 1965; Disch 1975; Henry 1967; Hetherington 1973; Johnson and Meeter 1977; Whitley and Smith 1963). The choice of best or mean score should be based on the amount of time available to obtain the criterion score and the use to be made of it. It is a much slower process to calculate a mean score than to list a best score for each subject. This is probably why standardized instructions for most multiple-trial tests suggest using the best score. Certainly when the criterion score is to be used as an indicator of maximum possible performance, the best score should be used. However, the best score from several trials may not be typical, in that it is unlikely to be achieved again for a long time and may be inflated by measurement error. The most reliable criterion score and the best indicator of true ability (typical performance), then, is the mean score. In theory, the sum of the errors of measurement is 0 when all of an individual's trial scores are added together. Because in most situations one wants an indication of status or typical performance, the mean score is the preferred criterion score for a multiple-trial test. And when scores are not stable, as may be true with special populations, the mean of the scores collected on several days may well be the only indicator of true ability.

The Role of Preparation

Preparation is an important determinant of the validity of a criterion score. A criterion score is a better indicator of true ability if individuals are measured only after they fully understand how to undertake a test. For example, suppose your instructor announces one day that he or she is going to measure your cardiorespiratory endurance by having you run a mile for time. If you have never done any distance running, you would not know how to pace yourself, how to run in a relaxed manner, how to avoid being boxed in by other runners, or how to run near the inside curve. Your score that day will not be a true indication of your cardiorespiratory endurance. If you were tested again the next day, your score would improve, not because your endurance had improved, but because you would have learned how to approach the test. And on a third day you might do better still.

Research indicates that people often need a day of practice before testing to familiarize themselves with a test, even if they have had experience with it (Baumgartner 1969b; Erickson et al. 1946). This practice allows a period of relearning and reinforcement necessary because skill retention is never perfect. Studies also show that a mean trial score for a multiple-trial test will be higher if several practice trials (called practice warm-up trials) are administered just before the test (Baumgartner and Jackson 1970).

SUMMARY

There are three characteristics essential to a sound measuring instrument: reliability, objectivity, and validity. Validity may be of four different types: content, concurrent, predictive, and construct. Content validity is a logically determined measure—the test must measure the stated instructional objectives. Both concurrent and predictive validity gauge a person's test scores against an established criterion, to determine that the test does correlate to the established criterion (concurrent validity) or does predict performance (predictive validity). Construct validity, which may be established through factor analysis, is the measure used with abstract rather than concrete tests.

Another major issue in testing is the selection of a criterion score, which can be either the person's best or mean score. A knowledge of how the criterion score is used is essential to intelligent selection and ultimately to the validity of the instrument itself.

FORMATIVE EVALUATION OF OBJECTIVES

Objective 1   Define validity, and outline the methods used to estimate it.

1. Important characteristics of all measurements are that they be reliable, objective, and valid. Describe the basic nature of validity.
2. Four types of test validity indicate the degree to which a test is capable of achieving certain aims: content validity, concurrent validity, predictive validity, and construct validity. Briefly describe these aims of testing and the four types of validity that parallel them.

3. Some authors refer to concurrent and predictive validity as criterion-related validity because validity is determined by the correlation between a test and criterion measure. Summarize the criterion measures especially suitable for physical education.

Objective 2   Describe the influence of test reliability on test validity.

1. A basic principle of measurement theory is that a test must first be reliable to be valid. Why is this so?
2. What effect does objectivity have on test validity?

Objective 3   Identify those factors that influence validity.

1. It is well established that test reliability is an essential factor of test validity. What other factors affect test validity?

Objective 4   Select a reliable, valid criterion score based on sound measurement theory.

1. Many psychomotor tests involve several trials. In multiple-trial tests either the best score or mean score is used as the criterion score. What can a teacher do to make sure that the criterion score is as reliable and valid as possible?
2. Why is the criterion score in athletic events the best score, while in a physical education class it is generally the mean score?

ADDITIONAL LEARNING ACTIVITIES

1. There are many tests commonly used in testing programs (runs, jumps, throws). Administer one of these tests and determine the validity of it.
2. Construct a new sport-skill test. Administer the test and decide how to calculate its validity.

BIBLIOGRAPHY

American Psychological Association, et al. 1966. *Standards for Educational and Psychological Tests and Manuals*. Washington, D.C.

Baumgartner, T. A. 1969. "Stability of Physical Performance Test Scores." *Research Quarterly* 40:257–61.

————. 1974. "Criterion Score for Multiple Trial Measures." *Research Quarterly* 45:193–98.

Baumgartner, T. A., and A. S. Jackson. 1970. "Measurement Schedules for Tests of Motor Performance." *Research Quarterly* 41:10–17.

Berger, R. A., and A. B. Sweney. 1965. "Variance and Correlation Coefficients." *Research Quarterly* 36:368–70.

Cattell, R. B., and G. F. Stice. 1957. *Handbook for the Sixteen Personality Factor Questionnaire*. Champaign, Ill.: Institute for Personality and Ability Testing.

Disch, J. 1975. "Considerations for Establishing a Reliable and Valid Criterion Measure for a Multiple Trial Motor Performance Test." In *Proceedings of the C.I.C. Symposium on Measurement and Evaluation in Physical Education*. T. A. Baumgartner, Ed. Indiana University.

Disch, J. R.; R. J. Frankiewicz; and A. Jackson. 1975. "Construct Validation of Distance Run Tests." *Research Quarterly* 46:169–76.

Erickson, L., et al. 1946. "The Energy Cost of Horizontal and Grade Walking on the Motor Drive Treadmill." *American Journal of Physiology* 145:391–401.

Ferguson, G. A. 1981. *Statistical Analysis in Psychology and Education.* 5th ed. New York: McGraw-Hill.

Henry, F. M. 1967. "Best Versus Average Individual Score." *Research Quarterly* 38:317–20.

Hetherington, R. 1973. "Within Subject Variation, Measurement Error, and Selection of a Criterion Score." *Research Quarterly* 44:113–17.

Johnson, R., and D. Meeter. 1977. "Estimation of Maximum Physical Performance." *Research Quarterly* 48:74–84.

Kenyon, G. A. 1968a. "A Conceptual Model for Characterized Physical Activity." *Research Quarterly* 39:96–105.

———. 1968b. "Six Scales for Assessing Attitude Toward Physical Activity." *Research Quarterly* 39:566–74.

Nunnally, J. C. 1967. *Psychometric Theory.* New York: McGraw-Hill.

Safrit, M. J. 1975. "Construct Validity: Applications in Physical Education." In *Proceedings of the C.I.C. Symposium on Measurement and Evaluation in Physical Education.* T. A. Baumgartner, Ed. Indiana University.

———. 1977. "Construct Validity." In *Proceedings of the Colorado Measurement Symposium.* D. Mood, Ed. University of Colorado.

Whitley, J. D., and L. E. Smith. 1963. "Larger Correlations Obtained by Using Average Rather than Best Strength Scores." *Research Quarterly* 34:248–49.

Yates, M. E. 1977. "Construct Validity—Points to Consider." *JOPER,* Vol. 48:2, 64–65.

Evaluating Student Achievement 5

Contents

Key Words

Objectives

In this chapter we discuss the differences between formative evaluation and summative evaluation, and the standards used with both methods. The attributes, issues, and techniques of grading show that the process is a complicated and often an emotional one. There is no universal agreement among physical education teachers and exercise specialists as to which attributes are important or which grading system works best. Each issue, each technique, has its supporters; and each has its advantages and disadvantages as well. Finally, we arrive at program evaluation—which should also be part of the teacher's measurement program.

After reading chapter 5 you should be able to:

1. Define and compare the terms evaluation, measurement, and grading.
2. Select the components for inclusion in a grading program and calculate grades using several methods.
3. Identify ways to make an evaluation system as quick and efficient as possible.
4. Outline the procedures used for evaluating programs.

INTRODUCTION

A teacher's primary function is to promote desirable changes in students. The type of change deemed important by the teacher and school system depends on two factors: the stated instructional objectives and the procedures used to evaluate their achievement. If the instructional process is to be meaningful, it is essential that (1) the instructional objectives be relevant, (2) the instruction be designed to achieve the objectives efficiently, and (3) the evaluation procedures reliably and validly assess student achievement.

We administer tests primarily to facilitate the achievement of instructional objectives. As noted in chapter 1, tests can be used for placement, diagnosis, evaluation of learning, prediction, program evaluation, and motivation. Every teacher must formally or informally evaluate every student. The assignment of students to appropriate groups, the diagnosis of factors that inhibit learning, and the prediction of future success are all essential to individualized instruction. The evaluation of student achievement is tantamount to the evaluation of the instructional process, and so it is a vital part of that process. A student's failure to achieve important instructional objectives can indicate that the instructional program itself has failed and needs revision.

Student evaluation is not a popular issue with some teachers and prospective teachers, primarily because they think of it synonymously with grading. But, evaluation is more than grading. In fact, it need not result in the assignment of grades. This does not mean that grading itself is not necessary. Grading continues to be an integral part of the educational system and thus one of the teacher's responsibilities. A teacher who passes all students without regard to their level of achievement is ignoring a professional responsibility. Grading is too often a system of rewards and punishments, reflecting the teacher's frustrations and biases, rather than a reliable, valid measure of student achievement.

EVALUATION

Evaluation often follows measurement, taking the form of a judgment about the quality of a performance. Suppose, for example, that the students in a class run a 50-yard dash, and their scores are recorded by the teacher. When the teacher classifies these measurements "excellent," "good," "poor," and so on, he or she is making an evaluation.

Evaluation can be subjective: the judge uses no set standards for each classification and/or evaluates during the performance without recording any measurements. The objectivity of evaluation increases when it is based on defined standards. Three common standards are (1) required levels of performance based on the teacher's experience and/or convictions; (2) the ranked performances of the rest of the class; and (3) existing standards, called norms.

Types of Evaluation

Formative evaluation, as noted in chapter 1, goes on during instruction to inform the students and the teacher of the students' status. This information allows the teacher to judge the effectiveness of the unit in progress and to make future plans. Students are motivated by knowing the extent to which they are meeting the stated objectives. Thus formative evaluation is both continuous throughout the teaching unit and related to the program's objectives.

Summative evaluation—the final measurement of student performance at the end of the teaching unit—is often used to assign grades. This type of evaluation is likely to involve comparisons among students rather than comparisons with a single level of achievement.

Standards for Evaluation

Criterion-Referenced Standards

Criterion-referenced standards represent the level of achievement that nearly all students should be able to reach given proper instruction and ample practice. These standards are valuable to the students because they specify the expected level of performance and to the teacher because they clearly define student status in relation to the standard.

Criterion-referenced standards must be used with explicit instructional objectives—objectives that ordinarily must be accomplished before broader objectives can be achieved. Thus criterion-referenced standards can be used in formative evaluation to diagnose weaknesses and to determine when students are ready to progress.

For example, the American Red Cross has developed a hierarchy of swimming skills that reflect criterion-referenced standards:

Beginner Skills

1. Breath holding—10 seconds
2. Rhythmic breathing—10 times
3. Prone glide
4. Back glide and recovery
5. Prone glide with kick
6. Back glide with kick
7. Beginner stroke or crawl stroke—15 yards
8. Combined stroke on back—15 yards

Swimming Skills

1. Sidestroke
2. Back crawl
3. Breaststroke
4. Crawl stroke
5. Surface dives—pike, tuck
6. Feet-first surface dive

Obviously these standards must be met if the student is to achieve a wanted level of competence in swimming. The inability to meet a specified standard indicates that additional instruction or learning activities are needed. On both levels, summative evaluation would focus on combinations of these skills: at the upper level, for example, the distance a student can swim in 10 minutes using the breaststroke, sidestroke, crawl, and backstroke.

For an instructional unit on physical fitness, the criterion-referenced standards for ninth-grade boys might be a run of 1¼ miles in 12 minutes, 35 bent-knee sit-ups in 2 minutes, and 3 pull-ups. Thus, criterion-referenced standards tend to be pass-fail. In this case, performance on all 3 tests (the sum of the T-scores) could be used to summatively evaluate the broader objective of total fitness.

Many different procedures are used to develop criterion-referenced standards. One method involves the following steps:

Step 1
Identify the specific behaviors that must be achieved to accomplish a broad instructional objective.

Step 2
Develop clearly defined instructional objectives that correspond to the specific behaviors.

Step 3
Develop standards that give evidence of successful achievement of the objective. These standards may be based on logic, expert opinion, research literature, and/ or an analysis of test scores.

Step 4
Try the system and evaluate the standards. Determine whether the standards must be altered and do so if necessary.

Bloom and his associates (1971) have experimented extensively with criterion-referenced standards in the formative evaluation of knowledge tests. They specified, as indications of mastery criterion, levels of 80 to 90%—high required levels of performance. But they also stated:

> . . . This is arbitrary, however, and individual teachers may want to set the score for mastery higher or lower. If the accuracy level is too high (95 to 100 percent), it is likely to be obtained by only a few students; and there will be little positive reinforcement for mastery for very many students. On the other hand, if the mastery level is too low (50 to 60 percent), then a large number of students may have the illusion that they have mastered the unit of learning when in fact they have made many errors.

Because physical education teachers and exercise specialists use a variety of testing instruments that apply different units of measurement, the importance to them of evaluating and readjusting criterion-referenced standards is evident.

Norm-Referenced Standards

Norm-referenced standards, that compare the performances of peers, are useful for determining the degree to which students have achieved a broad instructional objective. In developing norm-referenced standards, levels of performance that discriminate among ability groups are specified; that is, the standards are set so that some students are classified "high ability" and some "low ability."

The traditional grading system (A,B,C,D,F) is based on norm-referenced standards. Grading and the development of norm-referenced standards are so important that most of this chapter is devoted to these two topics.

GRADING

The improvement of grading practices has been an educational issue for the last 50 years. Although many suggestions for improvement have been made, changes have been few. Gronlund (1974) cites two reasons for this: (1) A single grading system that would satisfy students, parents, teachers, and school administrators may be impossible to find. (2) Efforts to improve grading have been directed more toward alternative symbols (satisfactory-unsatisfactory) for the traditional A-B-C-D-F system than toward basic issues. Also, considerable thought has been given to the value of a plus-minus system (A+, A, A−, etc.) over the traditional A to F system.

The grading process is twofold: (1) the selection of the measurements—either subjective or objective—that form the basis of the grade and (2) the actual calculation. Both steps can be undertaken in many different ways.

As described in the systematic model of evaluation (see chapter 1), the instructional process begins with the instructional objectives and culminates with evaluation. The instructional objectives, then, are the basis on which the factors used to grade students are selected. These objectives may be cognitive, affective, or psychomotor, but, whatever, the test must be suited to their nature and content. Clearly, using only a written test to grade students in a unit on physical fitness would be illogical and unfair.

Not only must grades be based on important instructional objectives, but the testing instruments must be both reliable and valid. If a test has no reliability, the scores by definition are due entirely to measurement error. Using such a test to calculate a student's grade is much like flipping a coin. Validity is a function of the instructional objectives: a test can be very reliable but unrelated to the objectives of the unit. Thus when selecting testing instruments for grading, the teacher must ask: (1) What are the instructional objectives? (2) Were the students taught in accordance with these objectives? (3) Does the test reliably and validly measure the achievement of these objectives?

Whether they approve of them or not, most teachers are required by their school system to assign grades. Most people can remember taking courses that were excellent in terms of content and presentation, but the system for assigning grades was so bad that overall the course was not rated highly. Therefore, it is essential for the teacher not only to develop a good grading system, but to assign grades with skill, accuracy, and fairness.

Attributes

The relative merits of various bases for grading have received much attention in professional books and journals. Such attributes as improvement, knowledge, sportsmanship, attitude, leadership, uniform, attendance, showering, squad ranking in competition, and the like have all been mentioned. Each of these suggested attributes should be judged by three criteria: (1) Is it a major objective of the physical education program? (2) Do all students have identical opportunities to demonstrate their ability relative to the attribute? (3) Can the attribute be reliably and validly measured?

Although evaluation is common before a unit is taught, grading of initial fitness or skill is not recommended because the teacher has yet to contribute to student ability. Determination of improvement, then—the change in student performance from the beginning to the end of a course or unit—would seem valuable, but the process has three limitations:

1. Improvement scores are very unreliable (see difference scores, chapter 3).
2. Students who perform well at the beginning of a unit have less opportunity for improvement than students who start the unit poorly.
3. Students may purposely perform poorly on an initial test in order to attain impressive improvement scores.

The second limitation—unequal opportunities for improvement—can be overcome by the use of either residual scores (Glass and Stanley 1970; Henry 1956) or a simple procedure developed by Hale and Hale (1972). The instructor who uses the Hale and Hale method converts the student's initial and final scores to T-scores, then converts the T-scores to what Hale and Hale call 'progression scores,' using tables provided by Hale and Hale. The difference between the two progression scores is the student's improvement score. East (1979) does not recommend using residual scores as a measure of improvement. He modified the formula that Hale and Hale used for developing their table. We recommend the Hale and Hale techniques and the East modification if improvement scores are to be used.

Although sportsmanship, attitude, and leadership are wanted outcomes of physical education programs, their measurement is often difficult. Observation is the only means of determining whether a student has exhibited these three characteristics in desired amounts. Furthermore, opportunities for leadership must be extended to all students if they are to be graded on this attribute. Temper control in competition is impossible to judge if a student has never been observed in a trying situation.

Grading on uniform, attendance, showering, and the like is not uncommon. It has been argued that basing grades on attendance is equivalent to rewarding the student for doing what is required by law. Certainly regular attendance, clean uniforms, and showering are desirable, but hardly major objectives of physical education.

Grades are sometimes based on squad rank in competition, with members of winning squads receiving higher grades than members of losing squads. This procedure operates to the advantage of those low-ability students who are on a squad with a number of high-ability students. However, the reverse is true for a high-ability student on a low-ability squad. It is unwise to allow a student's grade to be influenced by the performance of others.

Issues

A teacher's philosophy on certain issues directly influences the grading system. There is no one correct approach to most of these issues, but you should consider them before developing a grading system. Remember that teachers communicate their values in their grading procedures.

If grades are assigned, it is only fair to explain to the students at the start of the course how grades will be determined. Thus the teacher should plan the grading system before the course begins. Planning usually works, not only to lessen student complaints about assigned grades, but also to make it easier and faster to assign grades.

Grades should be based on a sufficient amount of evidence to be valid and reliable. One trial where multiple trials of a test were possible or one comprehensive exam at the end of the course is not likely to be sufficient evidence. The worst objective testing situation we can envision for a tests and measurement course is one test at the end of the course composed of one multiple-choice question. If the student answers the question correctly, the student receives a high grade; otherwise??

The distribution of grades in summative evaluation is a controversial issue. Should physical educators like teachers of classroom subjects use A-B-C-D-F grades? Low grades tend to discourage students from continuing with a given subject once basic requirements are fulfilled. In science programs, for example, the grades D and F are assigned to discourage low-ability students from continuing to take science courses. This means, by the senior year in high school, only a select group of students is still in the program. (Of course, because only the better students continue to take courses, a smaller percentage of low grades should be given in advanced courses. For example, more A's and B's should be assigned in a senior-level course than in a junior-level course.) Physical education programs are not developed along these discriminatory lines. In an effort to encourage all students—despite their ability—to continue in the program, many physical educators assign only grades A, B, and C.

Another consideration that relates to the distribution of grades is whether the general quality of the class, or differences among classes, should affect the assignment or distribution of grades. With ability-grouped classes, it seems unfair to assign grades A through F in each class because every student in a high-ability class would probably have received a C or better if ability grouping were not used. On the other hand, grading A through C in a high-ability class, B through D in a middle-ability class, and C through F in a low-ability class is unfair because it makes no allowance for the misclassification of students. A high-ability student could loaf and still receive a C, while a middle-ability overachiever could never earn an A.

A philosophy endorsed by many experienced teachers and most measurement specialists is that the grade a student receives should not depend on (1) the semester or year in which the class is taken; (2) the instructor (if several instructors teach the course); or (3) the other students in the course. Thus standards should not change from semester to semester or year to year unless the course itself has been changed or upgraded. For example, if 65 sit-ups earn an A for seventh graders this semester, they should earn an A next semester. Likewise, if 65 sit-ups earn an A from one instructor, they should earn an A from all instructors. Inherent in this philosophy is the principle that all students should earn the same grade if their ability is at a given level. Two examples may clarify this point:

1. An instructor teaches 5 ungrouped eleventh-grade classes, which are combined for grading purposes. The top 20% of the combined group receive A's, the next 30% receive B's, and the remaining students receive C's. If grades had been allotted in the same percentages but assigned by classes, a student's grade would depend on those of the other students in the class. Thus it would be possible for 2 students with identical scores to receive different grades if one were in a class with many good performers and the other in a class with many poor performers.
2. An instructor teaches 3 ability-grouped classes of eighth graders and 2 ability-grouped classes of ninth graders. The eighth-grade classes are composed of high, middle, and low achievers; the ninth-grade class, of low and middle achievers. Because of the age difference, higher grading standards are applied to the ninth graders than to the eighth graders, but the grading standards for each grade are applied consistently to all classes in that grade.

The teacher must decide whether a grade represents only achievement or student effort as well. The teacher must also decide what type of student achievement (fitness, skill, knowledge) should be considered and how each should be weighted in the grade.

Usually school policy governs certain issues, among them the type of grade assigned (A-B-C-D-F or pass-fail), although the teacher may have a choice. Letter grades are by far the most prevalent, but pass-fail grading is gaining popularity. This system reduces the competitive pressure of letter grading and encourages students to explore new subject areas. However, the system also provides less information about student ability.

If pass-fail grades are assigned, the teacher must decide whether, in reality, anyone will fail. It seems that in many classes, if students attend class regularly, they will not receive a failing grade. Also, the teacher must decide how much information is needed on each student to assign a grade of pass or fail. Possibly less information on each student is needed with a pass-fail system than with a letter-grade system. Finally, the teacher must decide on the standard for a passing grade. Is passing equivalent to a C or a D in a letter grade system?

Improvement

No matter how good the present grading practices are, in physical education, improvement is always possible and wanted. Gronlund (1974) devotes a chapter to the topic, and a number of his suggestions, despite their classroom orientation, have great implications for physical educators.

Gronlund maintains that improvement in grading will not occur until questions like the following are carefully considered: What is the function of grading and the reporting of grades? What should be included in a grade or a report of student achievement? What type of grading and reporting form should be used? He believes that grading and grade reporting serve instructional, informational, guidance-related, and administrative functions. From them students learn of their progress in achieving instructional objectives; parents are informed of this achievement; guidance counselors derive often-important information; and administrators determine promotion, admission, and scholarship decisions.

No matter what the educational level, subject, or school, Gronlund maintains that student reports should be in two parts: achievement-related and behavioral. The first is an achievement report that should indicate only the extent to which a student has achieved course objectives; it should not reflect behavior or effort. This report should be summarized with a letter grade, but could also include a checklist of objectives met to give a better indication of a student's strengths and weaknesses. The second report, on a separate form, should include the student's effort, personal and social characteristics, and work habits.

The grading and reporting form that Gronlund advocates, a sample of which appears in figure 5.1, is commonly used in the elementary grades and is becoming more popular at the secondary level. This type of form is obviously more informative and useful for students, parents, counselors, and administrators than is the traditional report card with a single letter grade.

Methods

Of the five methods discussed below, no single method of assigning grades is best for all situations or all teachers. Ordinarily, each method yields a unique distribution of grades. For example, a student who is on the borderline between an A and a B may receive an A with one grading method and a B with another. Thus it is vital that the teacher understand the advantages and disadvantages of each grading method in order to select the one best suited to the situation.

Natural Breaks

When scores are ordered by rank, gaps usually occur in their distribution. The teacher may make each such break a cut-off point between letter grades, as shown in table 5.1. This is a norm-referenced standard.

The other methods to be discussed require that the teacher decide what letter grades are possible (A to F or A to C, for example) and usually what percentage of the students should receive each letter grade. This is not required with the **natural breaks** method. In theory, if there were no breaks in the distribution of scores, all students would receive the same grade. For the teacher who does not believe in specifying the possible grades and percentages for these grades, this is a useful method. Thus, the method has some characteristics of a criterion-referenced standard.

Figure 5.1 Sample comprehensive grading and reporting form.

PROGRESS REPORT—PHYSICAL EDUCATION

1. *Achievement.* The grade circled below is an indication of how well the instructional objectives of the class were met.

A	Outstanding	D	Below average
B	Above average	F	Failing
C	Average		

2. *Effort.* The grade circled below is an indication of the amount of effort the teacher believes the student exerted to achieve up to his/her potential.

A	Large	D	Below average
B	Above average	F	Small
C	Average		

3. *Personal-social characteristics and work habits.*

+	Above average	✓	Average	−	Below average

_____ Punctual (starts and ends class on time)
_____ Follows instructions
_____ Courteous and respectful
_____ Self-control
_____ Cooperation
_____ Appearance
_____ Responsible
_____ Peer acceptance
_____ Perseverance

Although used by some teachers, this method is the poorest of the five listed here. It provides no semester-to-semester consistency, and makes each student's grade dependent on the performance of other students in the class. If in another year the breaks in the distribution occur in different places, the cut-off points between letter grades change, as is evident in the table.

Teacher's Standard

Some teachers base grades on their own perceptions of what is fair and appropriate, without analyzing any data. For example, a teacher's standard for a 100-point knowledge test might be A, 93–100; B, 88–92; C, 79–87; D, 70–78; F, 0–69. If the teacher uses the same standard year after year, the grades will be consistent. Furthermore, a student's grade does not depend on the performance of other students in the class: each student who scores 93 points or more receives an A. This is a fine method if the teacher's standards are realistic in terms of the students' abilities and if measurements are quite reliable and valid. First-year teachers, and teachers working with students younger than they are familiar with, tend to misuse this method by setting their standards too high.

Table 5.1
Two Sets of Grades Assigned by Natural Breaks.

FIRST SEMESTER			SECOND SEMESTER		
x	f		x	f	
98	1		92	1	
95	1	A	91	2	
93	2		90	1	A
92	3		89	2	
			88	2	
88	4		87	3	
87	5				
85	7	B	82	6	
84	7		80	8	B
83	6		79	7	
			78	11	
77	8				
76	14		73	12	
75	10	C	72	11	
72	5		71	14	C
			70	6	
65	2		68	1	
60	1	D			

The **teacher's standards** are norm referenced, but the procedure used to develop them is very similar to that of criterion-referenced standards, in that standards are set by the teacher with no thought to what percentage of the class receives a given grade. In theory, the entire class could receive A's or F's.

If teacher's standards were used in a pass-fail or competent-incompetent system, the standards would be criterion referenced. Again in theory the entire class could be judged competent. Many teachers have difficulty selecting the standard for competence; there are no guidelines. The teacher must choose a standard that he or she believes is fair. This standard often becomes one of minimum competence. For example, the teacher might decide that hitting 1 out of 5 shots from the free-throw line in basketball is minimum competence.

One way minimum competence might be determined is by deciding what grade in a letter system corresponds to competent or pass. The letter grade D is defined as a low pass or minimum competence by some educators; it is defined as a charity grade by others, who would assign a competent grade with a C or higher. In most colleges, the instructor does not know which students are taking a graded class on a pass-fail basis. He or she assigns a letter grade to each student, which is converted to a pass in the records office for letter grades of D or better.

Rank Order

Rank order is a straightforward, norm-referenced method of grading. The teacher decides what percentage of the class should receive each letter grade; the scores are then ordered, and grades are assigned.

Table 5.2
Rank-Ordered Scores.

x	f		x	f		x	f		x	f	
78	1		64	4		60	8		51	2	
70	2	A	62	5	B	59	6	C	48	1	D
66	4		61	5		58	5		41	1	
65	4					57	2				

For example, assume there are 50 students in a class, and the teacher decides to assign grades as follows: A's to 20% of the class, or 10 students [(.20)(50)]; B's to 30% of the class, or 15 students [(.30)(50)]; C's to 40% of the class, or 20 students [(.40)(50)]; and D's to 10% of the class, or 5 students [(.10)(50)]. Now look at the scores and frequency distribution in table 5.2. In the table, the first 10 scores were supposed to be A's, but a choice had to be made between 7 or 11 A's. It was decided to use 11 because that number was closer to the wanted number of A's. To make up for the extra A, only 14 B's were given. Then a choice had to be made between 19 or 21 C's. The reasons for giving 21 rather than 19 C's are twofold: (1) it is preferable to give the higher grade in borderline cases, and (2) a distinct natural break occurs below score 57.

Among the advantages of the rank-order method are that it is quick and easy to use and that it makes a student's grade dependent on his or her rank-order position rather than the instructor's feelings about the student. The system also allows grades to be distributed as wanted.

A disadvantage of the method is that a student's grade depends on the performance of other students in the class. A student with average ability will receive a higher grade in a class with low-ability students than in a class with high-ability students. Another disadvantage is that no allowance is made for the quality of the class: a certain proportion of students must get high grades and a certain proportion must get low grades. For large heterogeneous classes, in which all levels of ability are represented, this is probably not a bad method; however, it is not recommended for small or ability-grouped classes unless the teacher adjusts the percentages in light of the quality of each class. Teachers who use the rank-order method obtain grade standards that vary from semester to semester and year to year, depending on the quality of their class.

Normal Curve

This norm-referenced method assumes that the scores are normally distributed and that the normal curve (see chapter 2) can be used to determine cut-off points between letter grades.

Step 1
Decide on the percentage of students to receive each letter grade.

Step 2
Determine the cut-off points between letter grades, based on the normal-curve table (in chapter 2). Note that one less cut-off point is needed than the total number of grades to be assigned.

Step 3
Find the cut-off points in the test scores by multiplying each of the normal-curve values in Step 2 by the test standard deviation. Then add each of these values to the test mean and round off the cut-off values to the nearest unit of measurement.

Step 4
Assign grades, using the values in Step 3. Any student whose score is a cut-off value receives the higher of the 2 letter grades.

Problem 5.1   For a sit-up test, the mean is 66 and the standard deviation is 7.65. Using the normal-curve method, determine the cut-off points between grades.

Solution   Before we begin, you may want to review the discussion of the normal curve in chapter 2.

Step 1
Grades will be allotted as follows: A's to 10% of the class; B's, 30%; C's, 40%; D's, 20%.

Step 2
From Step 1 we know the percentage of the area under the normal curve that each grade represents. We know also, by definition, that the midpoint in the curve, point 0, is the mean: 50% of the grades lie to the left of this point and 50% to the right. In the drawing below, the center line represents the mean and the broken lines represent the grade distribution wanted:

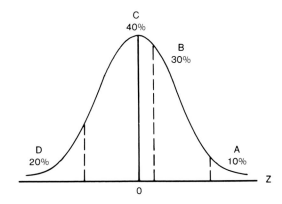

To determine the A cut-off, 10%, we deduct that amount from the total area to the right of the mean, 50%, leaving 40%. Going to the normal-curve table (in chapter 2), we find the closest point to 40% (39.97%) is where z is 1.28.

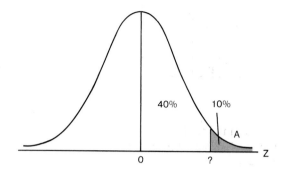

To determine the B cut-off, we add the B percentage (30) to the A percentage (10), giving a total of 40%. The cut-off point for grade B then is at 10%—50% less 40%. Checking the normal-curve table, we find the closest point to 10% (9.87%) is where z is .25.

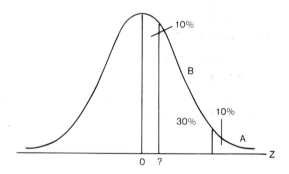

To determine the C cut-off, we add the C percentage (40) to the A and B percentage (40), giving a total of 80%. Because the maximum percentage to the right of the mean is 50%, the cut-off point for C must be at 30% to the left of the mean (80 − 50). Checking the table, the closest point to 30% (29.95) is where z is −.84. (The value is negative because it is to the left of the mean.)

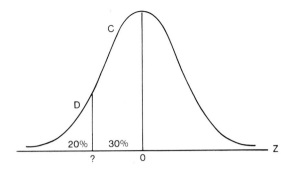

Notice that by determining the C cut-off point we have also determined the top cut-off of grade D. We could have determined D instead of C—the cut-off point would still be −.84.

Step 3
Now we multiply the normal-curve values by the standard deviation (7.65) and add the product to the test mean (66), rounding off the answers:

$$A = (1.28)(7.65) + 66$$
$$= 9.79 + 66 = 75.79 = 76$$
$$B = (.25)(7.65) + 66$$
$$= 1.91 + 66 = 67.91 = 68$$
$$C = (-.84)(7.65) + 66$$
$$= -6.43 + 66 = 59.57 = 60$$

Notice again that it is necessary to calculate the cut-off points for only 3 of the 4 grades; the cut-off for C tells us the maximum for D.

Step 4
Now we can assign grades using the cut-off values we have determined in Step 3:

A: 76→   C: 60–67
B: 68–75   D: 0–59

Notice that there is no upper limit on the A range because, in the abstract, a student could do an infinite number of sit-ups. If there were a finite number of points possible on the test, grade A would have an upper limit. Notice also that we assign the cut-off point itself to the higher grade: although 76 is the cut-off between A and B, it is considered an A, not a B.

Although a teacher can determine his or her own grading percentages, there are several sets of grading percentages and cut-off points that are sometimes used:

A: 7%, z = 1.5   A: 3.5%, z = 1.8
B: 24%, z = .5   B: 24%, z = .6
C: 38%, z = −.5   C: 45%, z= −.6
D: 24%, z = −1.5   D: 24%, z = −1.8
F: 7%   F: 3.5%

A: 16%, z = 1.0   A: 16%, z = 1.0
B: 68%, z = −1.0   B: 32%, z = .05
C: 16%   C: 48%, z = −1.75
                       D: 4%

The advantages and disadvantages of the normal-curve method are basically the same as those of the rank-order method, although the former is more time consuming. The wanted distribution of grades is approximated with this method, provided the scores are normally distributed and grades are not affected by the instructor's feelings about the student. Again, however, each student's grade depends on the performances of the other students in the class, because all scores contributed to the mean. Unless adjustments are made in the percentages from year to year, no allowance is made for the quality of the class.

The distinct difference between this method and the rank-order method is that the number of students who receive each letter grade is determined by the distribution of the scores, not arbitrarily by the teacher. Unless the scores are not at all normally distributed, however, the two methods yield similar results.

As we have said, the normal-curve grading method assumes that scores are normally distributed, not skewed (see chapter 2). To quickly determine whether a set of scores is markedly skewed, we subtract the median from the mean, and divide the answer by the standard deviation:

$$\text{Approximate skewness} = \frac{\text{mean} - \text{median}}{\text{standard deviation}}$$

If this value is small—say less than .10—the skewness is so slight that it will not markedly alter the wanted percentage of grades assigned by using the normal curve.

Norms
Norms are performance standards based on the analysis of data, not on a subjective standard chosen by a teacher. If norm-referenced standards are being used, norms are by far the best type of standard. Norms are developed by gathering scores for a large number of individuals of similar age, gender, ability, and other characteristics to the subjects with whom the norms will be used. These data are statistically analyzed, and performance standards are then constructed on the basis of the analysis. Norms have

many advantages over other types of standards. First, they are unaffected by the performance of the group or the class being evaluated. For example, if it is considered excellent to run the 50-yard dash in 6.15 seconds, all the students in the class can excel if they can run the dash within that time. Another advantage is that new performance standards need not be developed each year; once norms are developed, they usually can be used for 2 to 5 years. Also, because the same standards are used to evaluate several different groups or classes of students, the grades have a high degree of consistency—a given grade indicates the same degree of ability for each group.

There are many sources for norms. National norms are available for some tests, among them the AAHPER Youth Fitness Test (1976). Statewide tests often provide norms for that state; local norms for an entire school system are not uncommon; and teachers can develop norms using the scores of former students. Although norms should be developed using the scores of students similar to those on whom the norms will be used, this is unlikely to be true of national and state norms. Teacher-developed norms are probably fairest to the students.

The first step in developing norms is the administration of the same test each year under the same conditions as much as is possible for 2 to 5 years, until several hundred scores have been collected. These scores are then analyzed and used to develop norms that can be employed for the next 2 to 5 years. At the end of this time, several hundred more test scores have been collected, and the test is renormed. The advantages of this procedure are numerous. Because the norms are based on recent student performances, they are applicable to students currently in the class. When combined, scores collected in different years tend to cancel out any differences among years in terms of the quality of the students, and thus represent typical performance. (Norms developed on the scores of students from a single year are not representative if the students are not typical.) Because students and conditions change, norms should be revised every few years. And if major changes are made in the curriculum, norms may need to be revised.

Depending on the needs of the teacher, percentile-rank norms, T-score norms (see chapter 2), or letter-grade norms may be constructed. Probably because they are easier to explain to students and parents, percentile-rank norms are used more often than T-score norms. In deciding on a type of norm, determine how the norms will be used and then choose the type that best meets your needs. Percentile-rank norms are easily understood and indicate how a student's performance ranks relative to his or her peers. However, they should not be added together to obtain a composite score based on several measures. If you will eventually need a composite score, choose T-score norms. If students understand T-scores, they can determine their approximate class ranks for a single test. Furthermore, if several tests have been administered, they can easily determine from their T-score norms the test on which they performed best. For example, if on 3 different tests a student had T-scores of 55, 62, and 48 respectively, he or she could identify the second test as the best performance. Examples of percentile-rank and T-score norms are shown in tables 5.3 and 5.4.

Table 5.3
Sample Percentile-Rank Norms.

Percentile	PULL-UPS OR FLEXED-ARM HANG		SIT-UPS		SHUTTLE RUN	
	Boys	Girls	Boys	Girls	Boys	Girls
100th	15	64	100	50	8.5	9.0
95th	9	30	100	50	9.8	10.0
90th	7	23	100	50	10.0	10.2
85th	6	19	100	50	10.0	10.5
80th	5	15	100	50	10.2	10.8
75th	5	13	93	50	10.3	10.9
70th	4	11	75	50	10.5	11.0
65th	3	10	70	40	10.6	11.2
60th	3	8	59	39	10.7	11.3
55th	3	8	52	35	10.9	11.5
50th	2	6	50	32	11.0	11.6
45th	2	6	49	30	11.0	11.8
40th	1	5	42	26	11.1	11.9
35th	1	4	40	25	11.3	12.0
30th	1	3	35	22	11.5	12.1
25th	0	2	30	20	11.6	12.3
20th	0	1	28	18	11.9	12.5
15th	0	0	25	16	12.0	12.9
10th	0	0	20	13	12.4	13.2
5th	0	0	15	7	13.0	13.9
0	0	0	0	0	20.0	19.9

For grading purposes, letter-grade norms must be developed. The teacher's task is to determine the test scores that constitute each letter grade to be assigned. For example, the norms for a sit-up test might be A, 85–100; B, 60–84; C, 40–59; D, 20–39; F, 0–19. This grading standard is used each time the sit-up test is administered. Ideally these norms are developed on the basis of an analysis of the sit-up scores of students who have taken the test in the past.

A second example of the use of norms involves a physical fitness test with 7 items. For each of the 7 items, local T-score norms have been developed. When the test is administered, T-scores do not have to be calculated but can be assigned by using the norms. The sum of the T-scores for the 7 items in the test is the student's fitness score. Letter-grade norms corresponding to these fitness scores have been developed: A, 420→; B, 384–419; C, 315–384; D, 245–314; F, ←244.

Notice that any of the grading methods discussed here can be used to develop letter-grade norms. The teacher's standard is sometimes used, but the rank-order and normal-curve methods are more common.

Table 5.4
Sample T-Score Norms.

T-SCORE	SIT-UPS	CHINS	6-LAP RUN	T-SCORE	SIT-UPS	CHINS	6-LAP RUN
80	80	23	287	49	51		452
79	79		292	48			458
78		22	297	47	50	9	463
77	78		303	46	49		468
76	77	21	308	45	48	8	474
75	76		314	44	47		479
74	75		319	43	46		484
73	74	20	324	42	45	7	490
72	73		330	41	44		495
71	72	19	335	40	43	6	500
70	71		340	39	42		506
69	70	18	346	38	41		511
68	69		351	37	40	5	516
67	68		356	36			522
66	67	17	362	35	39	4	527
65	66		367	34	38		532
64	65	16	372	33	37	3	538
63			378	32	36		543
62	64		383	31	35		548
61	63	15	388	30	34	2	554
60	62		394	29	33		559
59	61	14	399	28	32	1	564
58	60		404	27	31		570
57	59	13	410	26	30		575
56	58		415	25	29	0	581
55	57		420	24	28		586
54	56	12	426	23	27		591
53	55		431	22			597
52	54	11	436	21	26		602
51	53		442	20	25		607
50	52	10	447				

Final Grades

At the end of a grading period a final grade must be assigned on the basis of all the information available on each student. There are many approaches to the assignment of this grade, some very simple, others more complex. The information available, the manner in which it is recorded, and the commitment of the teacher to fairly assign grades influence both the approach chosen and the time required for the procedure.

It is definitely to the teacher's advantage to adopt a simple, quick method of assigning final grades. Some teachers spend countless hours determining grades at the end of each grading period. To be fair to the students and to have a workable system, the teacher should choose a grading system before the course begins. Preplanning allows the teacher to announce the system at the beginning of the course, telling the students on what they will be measured and what standards they must meet. Preplanning is also to the teacher's advantage, allowing many time-consuming problems to be eliminated in advance.

The three common methods of assigning **final grades** are (1) the sum of the letter grades, (2) a point system, and (3) the sum of the T-scores.

Sum of the Letter Grades

This method is used when test scores reflect different units of measure that cannot be summed. The scores on each test are translated into letter grades, and the letter grades, in turn, are translated into points. The sum of these points is used to assign each student a final grade.

Many teachers believe this method is quicker than translating test scores into T-scores but, as we shall see, it is probably at best only slightly faster than calculating T-scores by the methods described in chapter 2.

If this method is selected, a plus-and-minus system should be used when assigning letter grades to each measure. If an A-B-C-D-F system is used for a given test, only 5 scores are possible (A is 4, B is 3, C is 2, D is 1, F is 0); a plus-and-minus system allows 15 possible scores (A+ is 14, A is 13, A− is 12, and so on, including F+ and F− values). (The final grades do not have to include pluses and minuses, which are seldom recorded on transcripts.)

To compute the final grade using the plus-and-minus system, we convert the student's letter grade on each test to points, add the points, and divide the sum by the total number of tests. This point value, the mean of the student's scores, is then converted back to a letter grade. For example, in table 5.5, the student's scores on 5 tests are changed from letter grades to points and then added. The total, 45, is then divided by the number of tests. The student's mean grade in points, 9, is then converted back into a letter grade, B−.

This process has several drawbacks. In the first place, it is a waste of time to calculate the mean. By multiplying each of the plus-and-minus values by the number of grades per student, we can express the final grade standards in terms of total points: A+ is 70 [(5)(14)], A is 65 [(5)(13)], and so on. In the second place, no allowance is made in the final grade for the regression effect—the tendency for individuals who score exceptionally high or low on one measure to score closer to the mean performance of the group on a second. Thus, a student who earns an A or an F on one test is likelier on the next to earn a grade closer to C than to repeat the first performance. The regression effect phenomenon always exists and must be allowed for in assigning final grades. Thus it would be unusual for a student to receive an A on each of 5 tests, although a superior student sometimes does. It is much more common to find the best student in the class receiving grades like those in table 5.6.

Table 5.5
Sample Grades and Points for Calculating a Final Grade.

TEST	GRADE	POINTS
Sit-ups	B+	11
Pull-ups	B	10
Distance run	C+	8
Volleyball	C−	6
Tumbling	B	10
		45

Table 5.6
Sample Grades and Points for the Best Student in the Class.

TEST	GRADE	POINTS
Sit-ups	A	13
Pull-ups	A−	12
Distance run	A−	12
Volleyball	B+	11
Tumbling	B+	11
	Sum =	59

Now, according to our standards, a student needs 60 points $[(12)(5)]$ to receive an A− in the course. If the teacher makes no allowance for the regression effect, the best student in the class (grades shown in table 5.6) will receive a B+, and no one in the class will get an A. In fact, if no allowance is made for the regression effect, very few final grades will be high or low; most students will receive grades in the middle of the possible range.

To allow for the regression effect, the teacher might decide to give the student with 59 points an A− because the student's total is closer to an A− than a B+. Another procedure is to lower the standards when assigning final grades. For example, the teacher might decide that any student who earns at least 3 A−'s and 2 B+'s will receive an A in the course. This means that 58 points are needed to earn an A when the final grade is based on 5 tests and an A+ is 14 points.

If such an arbitrary adjustment is made, it must be done for each letter grade. In the bottom half of the grading system, the adjustment must be up rather than down to allow for individuals below the mean regressing up toward the mean. But you must be careful in making arbitrary adjustments. If upward adjustments are made in the bottom half of the grading system, it is possible for a student to receive a final grade lower than any grade received on a test. Table 5.7 presents three arbitrary systems for adjusting final grades based on 5 tests.

Table 5.7

Three Arbitrary Grading Standards for Total Points Based on 5 Tests.

These standards are based on the sum of the letter-grade points for 5 tests. A+ = 14, A = 13, and so on.

Method One

Adjustment of points downward for all final grades, with the result that a very low final grade is highly improbable.

A: 58→(3 A−, 2 B+)
B: 43–57 (3 B−, 2 C+)
C: 28–42 (3C−, 2 D+)
D: 13–27 (3 D−, 2 F+)
F: ←12

Method Two

Adjustment of points downward for A and B and upward for D and F, with the result that a student who earns 5 C−'s receives a final grade of D.

A: 58→(3 A−, 2 B+)
B: 43–57 (3 B−, 2 C+)
C: 35–42 (5 C)
D: 20–34 (5 D)
F: ←19

Method Three

Adjustment of points downward for A and B, and upward for D and F, with the provision that a student's final grade can never be lower than his lowest test grade.

A: 58→(3 A−, 2 B+)
B: 45–57 (B, 3 B−, C+)
C: 30–44 (5 C−)
D: 15–29 (5 D−)
F: ←14

Rather than make arbitrary adjustments in the total number of points needed for each final grade, it might be better to calculate the total points earned by each student and use the rank-order, normal-curve, or norms method to assign final grades.

All tests need not be given equal weight in calculating a student's total points. If, using the grades in table 5.6, the instructor wants 30% of a student's final grade to represent fitness (scores on sit-ups, pull-ups, and the distance run) and the other 2 grades to represent 35% each, the following procedure can be used:

$$\text{Final grade} = .10 \text{ (sit-ups + pull-ups + distance run)}$$
$$+ .35 \text{ (volleyball + tumbling)}$$
$$= (.10)(13 + 12 + 12) + (.35)(11 + 11)$$
$$= (.10)(37) + (.35)(22)$$
$$= 3.7 + 7.7$$
$$= 11.4 \text{ (B+ or A−)}$$

The calculation of final grades with unequally weighted tests is very common, but it can also be time-consuming when there are a large number of tests and/or students to grade. To save time, the teacher can develop a chart like the one in table 5.8. The

Table 5.8
A Weighting Chart for Calculating Final Grades.*

Grade	Points	PERCENTAGE OF FINAL GRADE†							
		5	10	15	20	25	30	35	40
A+	14	.70	1.40	2.10	2.80	3.50	4.20	4.90	5.60
A	13	.65	1.30	1.95	2.60	3.25	3.90	4.55	5.20
A−	12	.60	1.20	1.80	2.40	3.00	3.60	4.20	4.80
B+	11	.55	1.10	1.65	2.20	2.75	3.30	3.85	4.40
B	10	.50	1.00	1.50	2.00	2.50	3.00	3.50	4.00
B−	9	.45	.90	1.35	1.80	2.25	2.70	3.15	3.60
C+	8	.40	.80	1.20	1.60	2.00	2.40	2.80	3.20
C	7	.35	.70	1.05	1.40	1.75	2.10	2.45	2.80
C−	6	.30	.60	.90	1.20	1.50	1.80	2.10	2.40
D+	5	.25	.50	.75	1.00	1.25	1.50	1.75	2.00
D	4	.20	.40	.60	.80	1.00	1.20	1.40	1.60
D−	3	.15	.30	.45	.60	.75	.90	1.05	1.20
F+	2	.10	.20	.30	.40	.50	.60	.70	.80
F	1	.05	.10	.15	.20	.25	.30	.35	.40
F−	0	.00	.00	.00	.00	.00	.00	.00	.00

* This type of chart is easy to develop because under any percentage numbers decrease by a constant amount; once all values for A+ and A have been calculated, the constant change can be used to work up the rest of the point values.

† The chart need only include the percentages you're actually using. For Problem 5.2, you'd only need four percentage columns: 5%, 10%, 20%, and 40%.

table lists the grades and their point values, and then a point value for each letter grade percentage of the final grade combination. For example, for grade A+, 5% of 14 is .70 [(.05)(14) = .70], 10% of 14 is 1.4, and so on.

Problem 5.2   At the end of a tennis unit you have assigned the following weights to the 6 grades that will make up the final grade: rally test, 20%; serve test, 20%; improvement, 5%; daily work, 10%; game observation, 5%; final exam, 40%. Use table 5.8 to calculate the final grade of a student whose scores on the items were C, B, A+, C+, C+, and C respectively.

Solution   For each measure, locate the intersection of the student's grade and the wanted percentage on the table, noting the amount in a column to the right of the grade. For this student's rally test the weighted score is 1.40 points (the intersection of grade C with 20%). When all the student's grades have been weighted, add them using a calculator. The total is the student's final grade:

	Percentage	Grade	Points
Rally test	20	C	1.40
Serve test	20	B	2.00
Improvement	5	A+	.70
Daily work	10	C+	.80
Game observation	5	C+	.40
Final exam	40	C	2.80
			8.10 = C+

The use of a calculator is even faster than using a chart to obtain a final grade when tests are unequally weighted. The points from each multiplication can be summed in memory as the multiplications take place. For example, using the grades in Problem 5.2 and the plus-and-minus point-values for them, you would begin:

Step 1
Rally test, 20% of C is .20 times 7 is 1.4.
Step 2
Put 1.4 in the calculator memory.
Step 3
Serve test, 20% of B is .20 times 10 is 2.
Step 4
Add 2 to the calculator memory. (There is now 3.4 [1.4 + 2] in memory.)

The process would continue for each grade and its weight, the final 3 steps as follows:

Step 11
Final exam, 40% of C is .40 times 7 is 2.8.
Step 12
Add 2.8 to the calculator memory.
Step 13
Display the sum in memory, which is 8.10 in this example.

Point Systems

Point systems are often used by classroom teachers, so that all test scores are in the same unit of measure and can be easily combined. In physical education activity classes, point systems require a great deal of planning and the development of norms. A sample point system is shown in table 5.9. To construct this system, the total number of points was chosen, points were allotted to the various activities, and standards were developed for each activity—that is, how many sit-ups earn 8 points, 7 points, and so on.

An instructor using the point system in the table would have 3 fitness scores, 3 volleyball scores, a tumbling score, a knowledge score, and a subjective score in the record book. Thus 9 scores must be summed before assigning a final grade, a procedure made easier if certain scores are combined before the calculation of final grades. For example, at the end of the fitness unit, the 3 fitness scores could be combined to form a single score. If the same thing is done at the end of the volleyball unit, only 5 scores have to be summed to calculate the final grade.

Sum of the T-Scores

When the units of measurement on a series of tests differ, some teachers translate the test scores into letter grades and the letter grades into points, and then sum the points. Another alternative is to change the test scores to T-scores and sum the T-scores, as discussed in chapter 2. Obviously it is possible to weight each test differently in summing the T-scores by using the procedures outlined for weighting letter-grade points.

Table 5.9
Sample Point System for an Activity Course.

I. Physical ability		70 points
A. Fitness	24 points	
1. sit-ups	8 points	
2. pull-ups	8 points	
3. distance run	8 points	
B. Volleyball	24 points	
1. serving test	8 points	
2. set or spike test	8 points	
3. game play	8 points	
C. Tumbling	22 points	
1. 11 stunts	2 points each	
II. Knowledge		20 points
40 questions	½ point each	
III. Subjective		10 points
Instructor's assessment of effort, improvement, attitude, attendance, and the like.		

Letter Grades versus T-Scores

In deciding between letter grades and T-scores, keep two criteria in mind: precision and speed. The sum of T-scores is more precise than the sum of letter grades because a better score means a higher T-score. For example, 2 students who perform 75 and 85 sit-ups respectively might both receive A's with the letter-grade system, while the latter would receive a higher T-score.

Although it is generally believed that the letter-grade system is quicker to use than the T-score system, the time difference is so slight that the loss of precision is not worth the time gain. We can compare the time involved in the two methods with an example.

Assume 40 students are tested on each of 7 items in a fitness test, and a fitness grade is wanted for each student. Assume also that norms or standards applicable to these students are unavailable. To sum the letter grades, a 5-step process is used: (1) develop letter-grade standards for each test; (2) assign each student a grade on each of the 7 tests, and translate this grade into points; (3) sum the points for each student; (4) develop final letter-grade standards based on the sums of the points; and (5) assign final grades.

To sum the T-scores, again 5 steps are used: (1) develop T-score norms for each test using the procedures outlined in chapter 2; (2) assign each student a T-score for each of the 7 tests; (3) sum the T-scores for each student; (4) develop final letter-grade standards; and (5) assign final grades. Notice that only the first step differs. If the rank-order method is used to develop letter-grade standards for each test, a simple frequency distribution will have to be constructed and standards developed for each test. About 1 hour per test should be allowed to develop grade standards. The development of T-score standards should also take about 1 hour per test.

If all 5 steps must be followed, both the letter-grade and T-score systems are going to take up too much time, assuming you have 200 or more students, each with 7 scores. Even if the first step could be eliminated because standards are available, both systems would still be time-consuming. Of course, we could reduce the number of tests on which the final grade is based, but in this day of accountability it might be hard to explain how 2 or 3 test scores are a valid indication of a student's achievement over a semester. Obviously, the solution is to use the computer in assigning final grades. We recommend the use of T-scores and the TSCORE program presented in chapter 2.

Incomplete Grades

Inevitably, some students do not take all the tests. This can pose a real problem in trying to obtain a total score on which to base a final grade. There is usually a valid reason why students do not take certain tests—injury, disability, or late enrollment, for example—and in such cases it would be unfair to penalize them. One possible solution is to estimate the score the student would have received had he or she taken the test. If the teacher feels unqualified to make this decision, the best procedure is to substitute the student's mean performance on the tests taken for each missing score. An estimated total score can thus be obtained, and a final grade assigned. For example, assume a student's scores on 5 of 7 items on a fitness test were as follows:

Item	Score	T-Score
Sit-ups	100.0	56.45
Pull-ups		
Shuttle run	11.3	45.94
Long jump		
Ball throw	135.0	55.13
600-yard run	128.0	44.22
50-yard dash	8.6	41.48

Notice there are no scores for the pull-up and long jump tests. The mean T-score for the 5 tests is 48.64:

$$\frac{243.22}{5} = 48.64$$

The estimated sum of the T-scores for the 7 tests, then, is 340.48:

$$(7)(48.64) = 340.48$$

PROGRAM EVALUATION

The **program evaluation** of instructional physical education programs has focused on their physical characteristics. Score cards (Bookwalter 1962; LaPorte 1955a, b) have been used to determine whether the learning environment—the facilities, professional staff, curriculum, equipment, and supplies—meets specified criteria. Evaluation specialists (Wittrock and Wiley 1970), however, view the learning environment as one of the least important factors in evaluating an instructional program: a school system may have excellent facilities and equipment, trained faculty, and a published curriculum guide, and still produce little teaching or learning.

The success of an instructional program depends less on its physical characteristics than on the manner in which they are used in the instructional process. Thus student performance offers the most valid index of the success of a program. The most crucial question is: Are students achieving important instructional objectives? If they are not, there is a need for change. Both formative and summative procedures can be used to judge program effectiveness.

Formative Evaluation

Evaluation is the process of judging performance with reference to an established standard. The qualities and levels of performance that a physical education program is designed to produce are reflected in its stated instructional objectives and criterion-referenced standards. Let us assume that one of a program's instructional objectives is the development of physical fitness, and more specifically that the program is designed to develop (1) muscular strength and endurance of the arms, (2) muscular strength and endurance of the abdominal muscles, and (3) cardiorespiratory endurance. The tests and criterion-referenced standards for seventh-grade boys are 3 chin-ups, 25 bent-knee sit-ups, and a run of 1½ miles in 12 minutes.

The formative evaluation of a program is the determination of the extent to which the stated standards are being achieved. The program developers may establish as a criterion that 80% of all students should achieve these goals. Progress toward the goal is easily determined by calculating the percentage of students who achieved the criterion-referenced standard for each fitness test. For example, assume that the percentage of students who achieved these criterion-referenced standards is as listed in table 5.10.

The program goal of 80% achievement was not reached in 1984 with the 12-minute run, which indicates that the instructional program failed in this aspect. The teachers must analyze this failure and make an instructional decision. Several interpretations are possible. First, more aerobic conditioning activities may be needed. Second, it may be that the 1½ mile criterion is an unrealistic standard for seventh-grade boys; perhaps it should be lowered to 1¼ miles. Third, the value of the instructional objective may be questioned, and the objective retained or dropped.

Table 5.10

Percentage of Seventh-Grade Boys Who Achieved Criterion-Referenced Standards for Physical Fitness.

TEST	1984	1985	1986
Chin-up	80	79	83
Bent-knee sit-up	90	93	91
12-minute run	40	75	84

The success of formative program evaluation depends directly on the selection of important, well-defined instructional objectives and the establishment of realistic standards. The failure to achieve a stated standard is thus a reliable indication that something is wrong. The value of formative program evaluation is that it signals that something is wrong while action can still be taken. In this sense, evaluation is a continuous process.

Summative Evaluation

The success of an instructional program is reflected in the degree of achievement of its broad objectives. Such success can usually be judged by comparing student performance to some norm. For this type of evaluation, published national, statewide, or local norms can serve as the basis for comparison.

It is common to compare a school's performance with national or statewide norms. For example, the average performance of students from a given school or district might be compared to the national norms that accompany the AAHPER Youth Fitness Test (1976). Although this procedure does stimulate interest, it also has several disadvantages. First, tests with national or statewide norms may not reflect the true objectives of the school district. For example, if the general objectives of a school were directed primarily toward motor-skill development, the Youth Fitness Test norms would not validly apply. A second disadvantage arises from the geographic and environmental factors that affect performance. Often, the testing conditions used by a school district are not similar to those used to develop national norms.

We agree with Safrit (1981) that local norms offer the most realistic basis for summative program evaluation. Although it is quite likely that all schools in a given system will be above the national norms, several of them may score considerably lower than others, indicating a need for program improvement.

Table 5.11 presents the means and standard deviations for an instructional unit on weight training. The local norm sample represents the performance of over 500 students; the Fall 1985 sample represents the performance of a group of students being compared to the established norms. As you can see, the average performance of the Fall 1985 group exceeded that of the norm group, indicating that the program is functioning properly in light of these objectives. If a school's means are considerably lower than the local norms, action can be taken to identify and correct the difficulty. If the means become progressively larger over succeeding years, this may be objective evidence that the program is improving.

Program Improvement

Evaluation is a decision-making process that works toward program improvement. The adoption of appropriate standards is essential for program evaluation and improvement. Bloom and his associates (1971) report that formative evaluation leads to higher-level achievement of objectives, evaluated summatively. Furthermore, the use of criterion- and norm-referenced standards helps the students to determine expected levels

Table 5.11
Summative Evaluation of Weight Training.

TEST	NORM SAMPLE		FALL 1985 SAMPLE	
	Mean	Standard Deviation	Mean	Standard Deviation
1. Dips	17.30	6.65	19.40	6.91
2. Sit-ups	24.71	8.17	25.09	7.70
3. Lat pull	27.33	9.47	34.09	12.70
4. Arm curl	23.45	9.89	28.02	9.77
5. Bench press	17.85	8.34	23.39	8.69

of performance. Students tend to strive to exceed standards. The use of explicit, realistic, and important standards, then, is necessary, not only for program evaluation, but also for motivation. A primary objective of program developers should be improved student performance over time.

SUMMARY

The method and rationale for student evaluation should be determined by the instructional objectives and content of the course. It is crucial that evaluation be based on reliable, valid information and that the process be carefully planned and explained to the students.

Before evaluating a class, the teacher must decide whether formative or summative evaluation is wanted. For summative evaluation, one of the grading methods described in the chapter—or a combination of several—can be used. We cannot stress enough the importance of deciding in advance how final grades will be determined.

Regular measurement and analysis of scores are essential to the ongoing process of evaluating the physical education program.

FORMATIVE EVALUATION OF OBJECTIVES

Objective 1   Define and compare the terms evaluation, measurement, and grading.

1. In discussing the broad topic of evaluation the terms measurement, grading, and summative and formative evaluation often are mentioned. In your own words, discuss how these terms are related to the broad topic of evaluation.
2. Many people feel strongly that grades should be eliminated. Is it possible that they are frustrated with the faulty techniques used to assign grades rather than the idea of grades? Explain your answer.

Table 5.12
Grading Standards.

Grades	Points	SIT-UPS Score	f	PULL-UPS Score	f	SHUTTLE RUN Score	f
A+	12	100	27	16	1	9.7	1
A	11			11	2	10.1–10.2	2
A−	10	75	1	10	1	10.3	1
B+	9			9	1	10.4	2
B	8			6–7	6	10.5–10.6	7
B−	7	70	2	4	6	10.7–10.8	4
C+	6	60	1	3	6	11.0–11.1	6
C	5			2	3	11.2–11.5	10
C−	4	40–52	5	1	7	11.7–11.9	4
D+	3	32	1	0	6	12.2	1
D	2	25–30	2			12.4	2
D−	1	22	1				

LONG JUMP Score	f	BALL THROW Score	f	600-YARD RUN Score	f	50-YARD DASH Score	f
		170	1				
84	1	168	1	95–98	3	6.8–7.0	3
81	3	163	1	101	1	7.1	1
78	2	148–153	3	102–107	4	7.3	2
72–75	5	138–145	6	108–111	5	7.5–7.6	7
69	6	135	3	112	3	7.7–7.8	3
66	8	125–133	5	113–115	5	7.9–8.0	6
63	7	108–123	10	116–129	10	8.1–8.3	9
60	2	93–106	6	130–140	5	8.4–8.6	6
54	1	90	1	146	2	9.1	1
51	2	86	1	151	1	9.7	1
48	2	54–63	2	156	1	10.3	1

Objective 2 Select the components for inclusion in a grading program and calculate grades using several methods.

1. There are certain attributes commonly used for determining grades in physical education. Also, as suggested in the text, grading programs themselves have desired characteristics. There are several different methods that can be used to assign grades. Considering these three points, outline the grading procedure you would like to use as a teacher.
2. Whatever method you select for assigning grades, it is important that you apply it accurately. Below are three situations to give you practice in using the various grading methods discussed in the text.
   a. Using first the rank-order and then the normal-curve method, assign letter grades for the first-semester scores in table 5.1, assuming A's, 20%; B's, 30%; C's, 45%; and D's, 5%.

b. Using the percentages in part (a) and the norms in table 5.3, what are the scores for an A, B, C, and D for girls on the shuttle-run test?

c. Using the plus-and-minus values listed in table 5.8, what final grade would you assign a student based on the tests and percentages below?

Test	Percentage of Final Grade	Student's Grade
1	15%	C−
2	25	B−
3	35	B
4	25	B+

3. Some teachers prefer to assign final grades by using the sum of the letter grades; others prefer to use, and we recommend, the sum of the T-scores. This exercise was designed to show you that the grades of some students change as you change from one method to the other, as well as that the assignment of final grades is a time-consuming process.

a. Using the standards in table 5.12 and the scores in table 2.12 (page 79), obtain the sum of the letter grade points for each student. Then, using the rank-order method, assign final grades based on these sums. Try to assign 1 A+, A−, D+, and D−; 2 A's and D's; 3 B+'s and B−'s; 6 B's; 5 C+'s and C−'s; and 10 C's.

b. Using rank-order grading, assign final grades based on the T-score sums in figure 2.11 (page 80), to assign 1 A+, A−, D+, and D−; 3 B+'s and B−'s; 6 B's; 5 C+'s and C−'s; and 10 C's. Round the T-score sums to whole numbers before assigning the grades. Keep in mind that 2 students could differ by 7 points on the sums but they could be quite close in score if mean T-scores were calculated.

c. Compare the results of parts (a) and (b) to determine how many students' grades changed.

Objective 3 Identify ways to make an evaluation system as quick and efficient as possible.

1. A common reason for not using an extensive evaluation system is lack of time. It is true that physical educators have large classes and that it does take time to combine scores from different tests and to grade knowledge tests, but with good planning the time involved in administering an evaluation system could be minimized. List at least 5 ways to make an evaluation system as quick and efficient to administer as possible.

2. Which 3 procedures in question 1 do you think would be easiest to implement? Defend your choices.

Objective 4 Outline the procedures used for evaluating programs.

1. Evaluation of the instructional program is an important part of the total measurement. In your own words, indicate the importance of both formative and summative evaluation.

ADDITIONAL LEARNING ACTIVITY

1. Interview faculty members at your school and in the local school system. Determine what attributes they consider in their grading systems, what methods they use for assigning grades, and what grading system (A-B-C-D-F, pass-fail) they use.

BIBLIOGRAPHY

AAHPER. 1976. *Youth Fitness Test Manual.* Washington, D.C.

Bloom, B. S., et al. 1971. *Handbook on Formative and Summative Evaluation of Student Learning.* New York: McGraw-Hill, 129.

Bookwalter, K. W. 1962. *A Score Card for Evaluating Undergraduate Professional Programs in Physical Education.* C. Bookwalter and R. Dollgener, Eds. Bloomington, Ind.: Indiana University.

East, W. B. 1979. "Mathematical Techniques for Estimating Motor Performance Improvement." Ed.D. dissertation, University of Georgia.

Glass, G. V., and J. C. Stanley. 1970. *Statistical Methods in Education and Psychology.* Englewood Cliffs, N.J.: Prentice-Hall.

Gronlund, N. E. 1974. *Improving Marking and Reporting in Classroom Instruction.* New York: Macmillan.

Hale, P. W., and R. M. Hale. 1972. "Comparison of Student Improvement by Exponential Modification of Test-Retest Scores." *Research Quarterly* 43:113–20.

Henry, F. M. 1956. "Evaluation of Motor Learning When Performance Levels Are Heterogeneous." *Research Quarterly* 27:176–81.

LaPorte, W. D. 1955a. *Health and Physical Education Score Card No. I for Elementary Schools.* Los Angeles, Calif.: University of Southern California.

———. 1955b. *Health and Physical Education Score Card No. II for Junior and Senior High Schools and for Four Year High Schools.* Los Angeles, Calif.: University of Southern California.

Safrit, M. J. 1981. *Evaluation in Physical Education.* 2d ed. Englewood Cliffs, N.J.: Prentice-Hall.

Wittrock, M. C., and D. E. Wiley, Eds. 1970. *The Evaluation of Instruction: Issues and Problems.* New York: Holt, Rinehart and Winston.

Performance Testing

Part 3

The Nature of Tests and Their Administration

6

Contents

Key Words

Mass Testability
Posttest Procedures
Pretest Planning
Useful Score

Objectives

In the first part of this chapter we will discuss those attributes that make up a sound measuring instrument. These include not only reliability, objectivity, and validity, but also other content-related, subject-related, and administration-related characteristics as well.

Pretest procedures, giving the test, and posttest procedures are also important aspects of testing. Pretest planning, in particular, is the key to a successful measurement procedure, providing the basis for all testing decisions and processes.

After reading chapter 6 you should be able to:

1. Identify the important characteristics of a test.
2. Plan the administration of a test.

INTRODUCTION

Many existing measurement programs are neither effective nor efficient while others produce invalid scores because the teacher, researcher, or exercise specialist has been careless in selecting tests or in planning their administrative procedures. The first level of planning in a good measurement program focuses on the selection or construction of a test. The second level involves the administration of the test.

TEST CHARACTERISTICS

Knowing the important characteristics of a test allows the teacher, researcher, or exercise specialist, not only to construct effective, efficient instruments, but also to recognize essential features in tests constructed by others. The characteristics themselves concern the test content, the individuals tested, and the administrative procedures, and, above all, reliability, objectivity, and validity.

Reliability, Objectivity, and Validity

The three most important characteristics of a test are reliability, objectivity, and validity (see chapters 3 and 4). If a test does not fulfill these requirements, you need not consider it further. Yet there are no rigid standards for acceptable levels of these characteristics. Acceptability is determined both by the testing situation itself and the values others have obtained in their measurement programs. This is not to say that no standards exist. In general, the test-retest reliability of most physical measures is between .85 and .93. Objectivity coefficients of between .85 and .93 also are usually expected. Acceptable validity varies from .80 or higher for a well-constructed, properly administered physical fitness test to between .70 and .85 for a sport-skill test. Remember, though, that a validity coefficient depends greatly on the criterion used, and that when construct validity is used there may be no coefficient at all.

Content-Related Attributes

These characteristics relate to the nature of the test content—what it measures and how it does so.

Important Attributes

To avoid spending more than 10% of the class time in testing, only the most important skills and abilities covered in a unit should be measured. These skills and abilities are those listed in the educational objectives for the unit.

Discrimination

A test should discriminate among different ability groups throughout the total range of ability. Ideally, there should be many different scores and the distribution of the scores basically normal or at least not markedly skewed. Also, it is important to select a test difficult enough so that nobody receives a perfect score, but easy enough so that nobody receives a 0. Consider the problem of two individuals' receiving the minimum or maximum score. How would you determine who is better? Although two individuals who receive a 0 on a pull-up test are both weak, they are probably not equal in strength per pound of body weight. Remember, however, that the fact that nobody receives a perfect score or a 0 is no guarantee that a test discriminates satisfactorily; conversely the fact that someone does receive a perfect score or a 0 is no guarantee that the test is a poor one.

Resemblance to the Activity

A test, particularly a sport-skill test, must require the subject to use good form, follow the rules of the activity, and perform acts characteristic of the activity. For example, a badminton short-serve test that does not require the serve to be low over the net is not requiring good form. And a basketball test that asks a student to run with the ball, rather than dribble it, or to dribble backward the length of the court, rather than forward, is neither following the rules of the game nor demanding a performance characteristic of it. The validity of a test should be questioned if the test does not resemble the activity.

Specificity

When a test measures a single attribute, it is possible to determine from it why a person is performing poorly; when a test measures a skill that has several components, it is more difficult to determine why a person is performing at a given level. For example, consider a basketball test of 10 shots at the basket. If the test asks the student to stand 3 feet away from the basket to shoot and the student misses all 10 shots, it is easy to determine that the student is a poor shot. If, however, the student were standing 40 feet away from the basket and missed the 10 shots, it would be difficult to determine whether the student simply shoots poorly or lacks strength.

Sometimes it is impossible not to measure several attributes at once; at other times your reason for testing is to measure how well a person combines several attributes. In either case, the test should be as specific as possible for whatever is being measured.

Unrelated Measures

Often a single measure is inadequate to describe fitness or a sport skill, so you will use a battery composed of several tests. The measures in a battery should be unrelated—that is, the correlation between the tests should be low—both to save testing time and to be fair to the individuals being tested. Of course, all tests in a battery should correlate highly with the criterion used to determine validity.

When 2 tests are highly correlated, they are probably measuring the same ability. This not only wastes time, but also gives the measured ability double weight in the battery, a practice unfair to individuals weak in the ability. If 2 tests in a battery are highly correlated, keep the better of the 2 and drop the other.

Student Concerns

Appropriateness to Students

Performance is influenced by the students' maturity, gender, and experience. For example, older students and boys generally score better on strength tests (push-ups, distance jumps) than do younger students and girls. The strength tests are usually acceptable for a variety of ages and both genders, but performance standards should be based on age and gender. Skill tests, on the other hand, are not universally applicable: they must apply to the age, gender, skill level, strength, and other capacities of the students. Again, tests that work well with junior high students may not work at all well with elementary or high school students; and tests that work well with females may not work at all well with males.

Performance is also influenced by the age and handicaps of the students. Physical performance tests (fitness tests in particular) for high school and college students are often not appropriate for adults over 30 years old and seldom appropriate for adults older than age 60. Handicapped students often do not score as well as nonhandicapped students. Strength and skill tests for normal students are not necessarily acceptable for handicapped students.

Individual Scores

A student's test scores should not be affected by another student's performance. That is, a test should not require student interaction and then score individuals on the basis of that interaction. For example, consider a basketball lay-up shot test, in which student 1 runs toward the basket and student 2 throws the ball to him to make the shot. If student 2 makes a poor or late throw, even the best student is going to look bad.

Enjoyability

When individuals enjoy taking a test and understand why they are being tested, they are motivated to do well and their scores ordinarily represent their maximum capacity. To be enjoyable, a test should be interesting and challenging, within reason. People are more likely to enjoy a test when they have a reasonable chance to achieve an acceptable score. Testing comfort is also an aspect of enjoyment. Although certain cardiorespiratory endurance tests and other maximum-effort tests can be uncomfortable, avoid any test so painful that few people can do it well.

Safety

Obviously, you should not use tests that endanger the students. Examine each test's procedures to see whether students might overextend themselves or make mistakes that could cause injury. The use of spotters in gymnastic tests, soft nonbreakable marking devices for obstacle runs, and nonslip surfaces and large areas for running and throwing events is always necessary.

Administrative Concerns

Mass Testability

For public school teachers, researchers, or exercise specialists who have a large number of people to test in a short period of time, **mass testability** can be a vital test characteristic. The longer it takes to administer each test, the fewer tests are likely to be administered. With large groups it is essential that people be measured quickly, either successively or simultaneously. For example, a standing long jump test can be mass testable when students jump successively, every 10 to 15 seconds. A sit-up test can be mass testable when half the group is tested while the other half helps with the administration. Remember too that short tests or tests that keep most of the subjects active at once help prevent the discipline problems that often result from student inactivity and reduce dissatisfaction of participants in research or fitness programs.

The teacher, researcher, or exercise specialist can become so concerned about mass testing that validity and reliability of the data suffers. With careful thought and planning this need not be true.

Minimal Practice
Subjects must be familiar with a test and allowed to practice before testing. Familiarity, either through previous testing, the exercise program, regular class instruction, or practice sessions prior to the testing day, lessens both explanation and practice time. Even when a test is unfamiliar, if it is easy to understand, little time need be spent to explain it. Avoid tests that require elaborate directions or considerable practice.

Minimal Equipment and Personnel
Tests that require a lot of equipment and/or administrative personnel are often impractical. Equipment is usually expensive to purchase and maintain, and can be time-consuming to assemble. In the same way, when several people are needed to administer a test, time must be spent finding and training them. Even when you plan to use members of the class or exercise group, you must expect to spend time training them.

Ease of Preparation
Always select a test that is easy to set up over one that takes more time, provided the first does the job as well. Tests that use complex equipment or several pieces of equipment placed at specific spots, or that require a large number of boundary or dimension marks on floors and walls, are usually neither easily nor quickly set up.

Adequate Directions
When you construct a test, you must develop a set of directions for it. When you use a test constructed by others, you must make sure that complete directions accompany it. Directions should specify how the test is set up, subject preparation, and administration and scoring procedures.

Norms
When the norms provided with a test are both recent and appropriate, they can save the time necessary to develop local norms, or at least offer temporary standards until local norms can be developed. Unhappily, provided norms are usually so old that they are no longer valid, or are based on a group of different gender, age, or experience, they are not appropriate to the individuals being tested.

Useful Scores
Especially when the test group is large, a test should yield **useful scores.** These are scores that can be used at once or inserted into a formula with little effort. Most physical measures—push-up, pull-up, sit-up, and dash scores, for instance—can be used immediately after a measurement session. If scores must be placed in a formula before they can be used, the formula should be sufficiently simple so that calculations can be done quickly. For example,

$$Y = 2X + 5$$

where Y is the calculated score and X is the score collected is a simple enough formula that a test requiring it could be considered. However, a test that requires the following calculation:

$$Y = .6754 \sqrt{X} + .2156X^2 - 3.14$$

would be very time consuming if a Y score had to be calculated by hand for each of several hundred people. With computer support, the computer program would have the formula for Y in it and only the X score for each person would have to be input to the computer.

ADMINISTRATION

The key to good testing is the planning before the test is given, and then the follow-up to that planning during and after the administration.

Pretest Procedures

We plan before giving a test to be sure that our preparation is adequate and that the actual administration will proceed smoothly. **Pretest planning** is all of the preparation that occurs before test administration. It involves a number of tasks: knowing the test, developing test procedures, developing directions, preparing the subjects, planning warm-up and test trials, securing equipment and preparing the testing facility, making scoring sheets, estimating time needed, and giving the test.

Knowing the Test
Whenever you plan to administer a test for the first time, read the directions or test manual several times, thinking about the test as you read. This is the only way to avoid overlooking small details about procedures, dimensions, and the like.

Developing Test Procedures
Once you are familiar with the test, start to develop procedures for administering it. These include selecting the most efficient testing procedure, deciding whether to test all the subjects together or in groups, and determining whether one person will do all the testing or pairs of subjects will test each other.

If you plan to administer several tests on the same day, order them so that fatigue is minimized. Do not give consecutive tests that tire the same muscle groups. Also, plan to administer very fatiguing events, such as distance runs, last.

The next step is the identification of exact scoring requirements and units of measurement. For example, in a sit-up test, you would require the subject to start in a supine position with both shoulder blades on the floor, then to sit up with hands interlaced behind the head, to lean forward until both elbows touch the thighs, and to return to the starting position, all to score one sit-up. Here too, when necessary, the unit of measurement with which you will score must be selected. For example, do you want to express distance in feet or inches or both; time in minutes or seconds or both? To obtain a score that can immediately be analyzed mathematically, only one unit of measurement—usually the smaller one—is used.

At this point you should also decide what to do if a subject makes a mistake during the test. By anticipating possible situations and rulings, you will be able to deal fairly with all subjects. For example, what do you do if a subject fails to go all the way down on a sit-up? Whether you disregard the mistake, warn the subject and count the sit-up, or discount it, you must follow the same policy for all subjects.

Finally, safety procedures are essential. Always plan to use spotters in tumbling and gymnastics tests. Consider your marking devices as well. In obstacle runs they should be soft, unbreakable, and tall enough so that subjects cannot step over them. Use marking cones instead of chairs, soda bottles, or volleyball standards. Think too about the testing area. Hold dashes, agility runs, and similar running events in a large enough area that subjects do not run into obstacles. Plan for organization of subjects waiting to be tested, so that participants do not run into them.

If you have never administered a specific test before, try one or two practice administrations before the actual test. This is a good way, not only to see what changes in and additions to the procedures must be made, but also to train administrative personnel.

Developing Directions

After you have determined procedures, it is necessary to develop exact directions. It is perfectly acceptable to read these directions to a group before administering the test to them. The directions should be easy to understand and should specify the following:

1. Administration procedures
2. Instructions on performance
3. Scoring procedure and the policy on incorrect performance
4. Hints on techniques to improve scores

Preparing the Students

Announce the test well in advance so that students can practice if they think it will improve their scores. When the class is unfamiliar with a test, spend some time before the day of the test explaining it and the techniques that will improve test scores, and supervising pretest practice.

Even when students have had exposure to a test, they may need some time to re-learn the necessary techniques. Girardi (1971) familiarized a group of high school boys with a jump-and-reach test and a 12-minute-run test, and then tested them. Eight weeks later, he retested the students without review, and found that a number of them, particularly the poorly skilled, had forgotten the necessary techniques.

With the exception of a few research situations (learning research for example), students should know well in advance that they are going to be tested, what is the test, and what the test involves. This allows the subject to be psychologically and physiologically ready to be tested and score up to his or her potential. This is vital when important things like grades, admission to or release from programs, or health-fitness ratings are involved.

Planning Warm-Up and Test Trials

We saw in chapter 3 that reliability improves with pretest warm-up. The amount and nature of this warm-up must be planned. Ideally, warm-up should be specific to the skill being tested (that is, practice rather than calisthenics). It has been shown too that supervised warm-up, in which the tester tells the subjects what to do and ensures that all subjects receive the same amount of practice, is better than unsupervised warm-up. In some situations it is acceptable to administer multiple trials of a test and to consider the first few trials as warm-up, making each subject's score the sum or mean of the latter test trials.

Securing Equipment and Preparing the Testing Facility

You should have all equipment on hand and the facility prepared before the day of the test. Having all equipment available and all boundary lines and other markings positioned correctly when the subjects arrive to be tested saves time and avoids the problems that inevitably arise when subjects are kept waiting while the test is set up.

Making Scoring Sheets

At some point before the test, locate or prepare either a master scoring sheet for the entire group or individual scorecards. Enter the subjects' names on the sheets or cards before they arrive to be tested.

There are many advantages to using individual scorecards over a master score sheet. Scorecards allow subjects to rotate among testing stations and to quickly record scores when they have tested one another. Even when one person is testing and recording the scores of the entire group, time can be saved by gathering the scorecards in order after the subjects are in line rather than having the subjects get in line in the same order they are listed on the scoring sheet.

Estimating the Time Needed

When a test will not take an entire class period, or when half the class will be tested on each day, you must plan some activity to fill the extra time or to occupy the rest of the class. If testing will occur during an agency or corporate fitness program, similar planning is necessary. Estimating the time needed to administer a test both minimizes confusion and maximizes the use of available time.

Giving the Test

If you have planned properly, the testing should go smoothly. Although your primary concern on the day of the test is the administration of the test itself, you should also be concerned with subject preparation, motivation, and safety. If, after you have administered the test, you can say, "The subjects were prepared and the test was administered in a way that I would have liked if I were being tested," the testing session was undoubtedly a success.

Preparation

The subjects should already know what the test is and why it is being given, so your first concern is the warm-up or practice. Next, explain the test instructions and procedures, even demonstrating the test for them if possible. Ask for questions both before and after the demonstration. When the skill or procedures are particularly complicated, let the subjects run through a practice trial of the test.

Motivation

Give all subjects the same degree of motivation and encouragement. Although we all tend to encourage poor performers and compliment superior ones, in fairness all or none of the subjects should receive a comment. Whenever possible, indicate to a subject his or her score immediately after the test trial. This can motivate subjects to perform better on a second or third trial. However, the reporting of the score should not embarrass the subject.

Safety

During a testing session, watch for safety problems. Subjects often perform unsafely when they are not following instructions. Try to anticipate these or other unsafe situations.

Posttest Procedures

The rationale for testing is to collect information about the subjects and in education, the instructional program. Only after the test is given can the information be used. Surprisingly, many teachers and exercise specialists fail to do enough or even any posttest analysis. Barrow and McGee (1979) note that the sooner the results of tests are returned to the students, the more meaningful they will be in the educational process. **Posttest procedures** include the analyzing, reporting, and recording of test scores.

Analyzing Test Scores

Shortly after a test, the scores must be analyzed using the appropriate techniques from chapter 2. Analysis serves, not only to reveal characteristics that could influence the teaching procedures or program conduct, but also to provide information for the group tested and prepare the data for grading or other evaluation purposes. Students are usually interested in their scores, their relative standings in the class, and their degree of improvement or decline since the last test. Reporting test results to subjects is an effective motivational device.

Recording Test Scores

The recording of scores is usually nothing more than placing the scoring sheets and your analysis of them in an appropriate file. The information makes possible interclass comparisons within and between school years, program evaluation over years, as well as the development of norms. Notice that these are group or class standards rather than individual standards, based solely on the scores and your analysis. Often it is not even necessary to identify the scores, particularly in situations where a permanent record card for each student or program participant is kept. It is from this card, that follows the student from grade to grade or the program participant from year to year, that you can trace individual improvement over time.

SUMMARY

Whether you develop your own test or select a preconstructed test, which is certainly easier, you will require certain attributes in the instrument. It is these characteristics that make the measurement procedure both efficient and meaningful.

Although the successful administration of a test depends on many factors, the key to success is good planning in the pretest stage and attention to the details of that planning during and after the testing procedure.

FORMATIVE EVALUATION OF OBJECTIVES

Objective 1   Identify the important characteristics of a test.

1. The text discusses many important attributes of a test. In addition to reliability, objectivity, and validity, what are several of these attributes?
2. Certain characteristics listed in the text relate to the subjects taking the tests, while others act simply to make the procedure more efficient. What are the subject-related attributes?

Objective 2   Plan the administration of a test.

1. The success of a testing program depends on how well the pretest planning is carried out. What type of planning and procedures would you use to administer the following tests?
   a. A timed bent-knee sit-up test
   b. A pull-up test
   c. A mile-run test or some other cardiovascular test

ADDITIONAL LEARNING ACTIVITIES

1. From the material in this book and other physical education measurement texts, develop a summary of test characteristics and a checklist of pretest planning procedures.
2. Select a test with which you are unfamiliar and administer it following the pretest, administrative, and posttest procedures outlined in the text.

BIBLIOGRAPHY

Barrow, H. M., and R. McGee. 1979. *A Practical Approach to Measurement in Physical Education.* 3d ed. Philadelphia, Pa.: Lea & Febiger.
Girardi, G. 1971. "A Comparison of Isokinetic Exercises with Isometric and Isotonic Exercises in the Development of Strength and Endurance." P.E.D. dissertation, Indiana University.

Measuring Physical Abilities

7

Contents

Key Words

Objectives

Physical educators have long accepted the concept of generality, but recent research has questions about the concept, although the theory and measurement procedures used to evaluate generality are still important. General motor ability and motor educability tests have been traditionally used to measure generality, but they have not proven to be valid. The theory of basic physical abilities does provide a sound measurement model. This chapter provides a discussion of the theory and practical procedures for measuring basic physical abilities. This text lists many tests and the procedures and norms for administering them.

After reading chapter 7 you should be able to:

1. Describe the tests historically used to measure generality.
2. Define and differentiate between basic physical abilities and a motor skill.
3. Apply the theory of basic physical abilities to the evaluation of athletes.
4. Identify basic physical abilities and tests for their valid measurement.
5. Construct a test battery that can be used to evaluate athletes.

INTRODUCTION

The assumption of the concept of generality is that the performance of many different motor tasks can be predicted from a single or limited number of test items. The principle of generality can be traced to the work of Sargent (1921), who first reported a test of generality. The Sargent Physical Test of Man simply measures the height of a vertical jump, on the assumption that a single test is sufficient to measure motor ability. This assumption paralleled the concept of generality accepted by psychologists, who felt a g-factor, or general factor of intelligence, is adequate to represent human intellectual ability.

The interest in developing physical tests of generality peaked between 1930 and 1960. During this period, several batteries of general motor ability, and motor educability were published. Research published from the discipline of motor learning cast doubt on the principle of general motor ability and the validity of these tests. This research suggested that learning motor skills was very task-specific and interest in using the general tests lessened.

More recently, psychologists interested in measuring intelligence recognized that a single g-factor of intellectual ability was not adequate; rather several abilities are needed to validly represent this domain. For example, both verbal and quantitative sections are used to measure intellectual aptitudes on college entrance examinations. Each is important for predicting different types of intellectual performance. Edwin Fleishman (1964), an industrial psychologist, has extended this multi-ability theory to the physical domain. His research has shown that several different basic physical abilities exist and various abilities are important for predicting motor-skill performance.

Common physical abilities include strength, endurance, power, agility, balance, flexibility, and basic movement patterns that involve sprinting, jumping, and throwing. Tests of these abilities are included in motor fitness batteries (see chapter 9). Two important uses of basic physical ability tests are for evaluating athletes and preemployment testing for physically demanding jobs. This chapter examines the historical development of generality testing and provides methods for measuring important physical abilities.

HISTORY OF GENERALITY TESTING

The purpose of generality tests was to provide a method by which it would be possible to predict an individual's performance on a wide range of motor activities from a simple test battery. Several types of tests have been used by physical educators to measure generality, but their validity has not been established. A brief summary of methods used to test generality follow.

Age-Height-Weight Classification Index

Generally, students who differ in age, height, and weight will differ in their ability to perform motor tasks. McCloy (1932) was the first to propose a system for classifying students into homogeneous groups for instruction on these age and size dimensions.

The Neilson-Cozens **classification index** (CI) was used as a basis for developing norms on the AAHPERD Youth Fitness test prior to the 1976 revision. The equation was:

$$CI = 20(age) + 5.5(height) + 1.1(weight).$$

The CI score would be higher for the older and larger child, and these children were supposedly more physically capable than children with a lower CI. Age, height, and weight are correlated. As children become older, they become taller, heavier, and stronger. For this reason, age alone has been shown (Espenchade 1963; Gross and Casciani 1962) as useful for classifying students as the entire CI. Today, age and gender are the variables used most when making norms for evaluating motor performance. Information about height and weight does not improve the ability to evaluate student performance on motor fitness tests.

General Motor Ability

According to Larson and Yocom (1951), **general motor ability** is the "present acquired and innate ability to perform motor skills of a general or fundamental nature, exclusive of highly specialized sports or gymnastic techniques." Numerous general motor ability batteries have been published and examples of two popular tests (Barrow 1954; Scott 1939) are shown in figure 7.1. The batteries typically consist of sprinting, jumping, throwing, and agility tests.

General motor batteries are highly reliable because the individual test items that comprise the battery are very reliable. But the purpose of general motor ability tests is to measure a wide range of motor skills with a few easily administered tests, and in this sense the tests are not valid. Cumbee and Harris (1953) showed that the batteries were measuring a single factor rather than the seven or eight proposed by the test makers. A student's test score on a general motor ability test is not predictive of performance on a wide range of motor skills. Rather it represents a student's speed, jumping, and throwing abilities.

Figure 7.1 Test items of general motor ability batteries.

SCOTT MOTOR ABILITY TEST
1. Basketball throw for distance
2. Standing long jump
3. Wall pass
4. Dash (4 seconds)

BARROW MOTOR ABILITY TEST
1. Standing long jump
2. Zigzag run
3. Softball distance throw
4. Wall pass
5. Medicine ball put
6. 60-yard dash

Motor Educability

Motor educability is defined as "the ability to learn motor skills easily and well" (McCloy and Young 1954). Motor educability tests were gymnastic "stunt-like" tasks. The successful completion of these unfamiliar motor tasks was supposedly an indication of how rapidly one could learn a motor skill. Several different batteries were published (Brace 1927; Carpenter 1942; Johnson 1932; McCloy and Young 1954; Metheny 1938).

The validity of motor educability tests—their ability to predict motor-skill learning aptitude—has not been established. The reported correlations between motor-skill acquisition and motor educability are low (Gire and Espenschade 1942; Gross et al. 1956). Additionally, the correlation between different types of motor educability tests is low (.20 or less), which suggests they are not measuring the same thing (Gire and Espenschade 1942).

Specificity of Motor Skill

In the late 1950s, Franklin Henry advanced the memory-drum theory of neuromotor reaction, claiming that motor ability is specific to a task rather than general to many tasks. In other words, a student's performance on one **motor skill** is of little or no value in predicting performance on a different task. On the basis of his theory, Henry claims that there is no such thing as general motor ability; rather each individual possesses many specific motor abilities. A student who scores well on a general motor test is gifted with several specific abilities, whereas, a student who scores poorly has only a few neural patterns stored on his or her memory drum (Henry 1956; 1958). The theory of specificity cast doubt on the validity of general motor ability and motor educability tests and is largely responsible for the demise of these tests.

Certainly physical education teachers and exercise specialists must acknowledge the theory of specificity; however, complete acceptance of the theory would signal the need to measure all the specifics that enter into the complex domain of motor skills. Obviously this is not feasible given the limited testing time available to most teachers. In fact, the practice of using physical abilities tests is on the rise. Testing programs for athletes is becoming common practice at public school, college, and professional levels. Physical abilities tests are now used to screen applicants for physically demanding jobs such as a fire fighter and coal miner.

THEORY OF BASIC PHYSICAL ABILITIES

The theory of **basic physical abilities** was developed by Edwin Fleishman (1964) and is especially useful for generality testing because individual performance of a specific motor skill is explained in terms of a relatively small number of psychomotor abilities. His theory is based on research conducted for the U.S. Air Force, in which tests of psychomotor abilities were found valid for predicting the subsequent performance of various air crew members (1956).

Fleishman distinguishes between psychomotor skills and psychomotor abilities, but considers both essential and complementary. A psychomotor skill is one's level of proficiency on a specific task or limited group of tasks. Dribbling a basketball, catching a softball, swimming the sidestroke, and playing the piano are examples of very different psychomotor skills. Learning a psychomotor skill involves acquiring the sequence of responses that results in a coordinated performance of the task. A psychomotor ability is a more general trait that may be common to many psychomotor tasks. For example, running speed has been found to be important to several different specific motor skills, such as football and the running long jump.

Fleishman describes the relationship between basic physical abilities and motor skills as follows:

> The assumption is that the skills involved in complex activities can be described in terms of the more basic physical abilities. For example, the level of performance a man can attain on a turret lathe may depend on his basic physical abilities of manual dexterity and motor coordination. However, these same basic physical abilities may be important to proficiency in other skills as well. Thus, manual dexterity is needed in assembling electrical components, and motor coordination is needed to fly an airplane.
>
> Implicit in the previous analysis is the relation between abilities and learning. Thus, individuals with high manual dexterity may more readily learn the specific skill of lathe operation (1964).

Basic physical abilities are measured with many types of tests, and individuals differ in the extent to which they possess an ability (e.g., some people run faster than others). An individual with many highly developed basic physical abilities can become proficient at a wide variety of specific motor skills. For example, the all-around athlete is a boy or girl who has many highly developed basic physical abilities important to many different sports. Then, too, certain basic physical abilities are more generalized than others. For example, in our culture verbal abilities are important in a greater variety of tasks than are many other abilities. Certainly speed, jumping ability, and muscular strength are important basic physical abilities related to athletic success.

According to Fleishman (1964), both the rate of learning and the final level of skill achieved depend on an individual's level of achievement in the more basic physical abilities. In this sense a test that measures basic physical abilities (construct validity) may also demonstrate concurrent and/or predictive validity. Remember, however, that the importance of a basic physical ability varies from skill to skill, which is the crucial difference between the theory of generality and that of basic physical abilities. General motor ability combines all test scores into a single score that supposedly is highly related to many different motor skills. In contrast, basic physical ability tests are themselves combined for each skill, and their relative importance varies for each skill. For example, the basic physical abilities for learning how to swim are different from those for learning how to pass a football; but the same basic physical abilities can be important to the performance of several different gross motor skills. Muscular strength is an important ability of many sports skills.

The development of basic physical abilities is a product of both genetic and environmental influences, with the genetic factor the limiting condition. Consider, for example, the basic physical ability, muscular strength. By participating in weight training programs, we can greatly influence the development of muscular strength; but the limit of that development (the maximum strength) depends on our hereditary conditions. Basic physical abilities develop during childhood and adolescence, reaching a fairly stable level in adulthood.

Fleishman reports that both the rate of learning and the final level achieved by an individual on specific motor skills are limited by basic physical abilities. Because an ability is a lasting, stable pattern of behavior, individual differences in basic physical abilities make it possible to predict the subsequent performance of specific skills. For example, the SAT measures verbal and quantitative abilities. Using a student's score on the quantitative ability section would be predictive of success in programs such as engineering, where math skills are very important, but not predictive of success in nonmathematical majors such as English. In this same way, running speed is an important factor in the running long jump; on the basis of a student's speed, we could judge better how well he or she will do on the long jump. Coaches maintain that the major reason that the world's premiere long jumper Carl Lewis is in a class of his own can be traced to his world class sprinting speed.

Basic physical abilities tests have at least two important applications. First, for evaluating athletes, and second, for use as preemployment tests in physically demanding jobs. These applications are illustrated next.

Application 1: Evaluating Athletes

The testing of athletes has become accepted procedure. Before the 1976 Olympics, sport scientists studied the psychological, physiological, biomechanical, and medical characteristics of 20 world-class distance runners (Pollock et al. 1978). The East German Olympic team, which has been very successful in Olympic competition, has initiated an extensive testing program for its athletes. Several years before its 1978 Super Bowl victory, the Dallas Cowboys team had developed a scientific program for evaluating and training its football players. Today, most university and professional teams hire a full-time strength coach who is responsible for testing and training athletes.

The United States Olympic Committee has developed a central facility for testing athletes in Colorado Springs, Colorado. This facility is fully staffed with exercise scientists who provide comprehensive testing of athletes. These data are given to the athlete and coach and used to improve training and performance.

The important concern is to find the physical abilities that are most relevant to the demands placed on an athlete. The more specific the test, the more valid it will be. At the U.S. Olympic testing site for example, different exercise modes are used to measure $\dot{V}O_2$ Max. For distance runners, a treadmill-running protocol is followed; in contrast, specially devised bicycle-ergometer protocols are used to evaluate cyclists.

Figure 7.2 Types of tests commonly used to evaluate athletes.

1. Maximal oxygen uptake ($\dot{V}O_2$ Max)
2. Percent body fat
3. Muscular strength
4. 40 or 50 yard sprint
5. Vertical or standing long jump
6. Agility run test

Although evaluative batteries of different sports and varying degrees of skill have not been scientifically validated, many different physical ability tests appear to have logical relevance. These are summarized in figure 7.2. We would suggest following 6 steps when developing a battery for evaluating athletes.

1. Consider the sport and the basic qualities it demands of the athlete. For example, jumping ability would be especially important for volleyball and basketball players.
2. Select tests that measure these defined traits. The tests may be found in chapters 7, 8, and 9.
3. Administer the tests to as many athletes as possible.
4. From their scores, develop percentile-rank norms using the procedures furnished in chapter 2.
5. Use these norms to evaluate your athletes. The criterion for comparison here can also be earlier data on outstanding athletes, allowing you to evaluate your athletes with both the norm and outstanding players.
6. Reevaluate your selection of tests to be sure you are measuring the abilities most relevant to the sport. You should see a tendency for the best athletes to achieve the highest scores.

Provided in tables 7.1 and 7.2 are sample test batteries used for college football players and female volleyball players. A profile for an athlete can be obtained by simply plotting his or her score on the table. In this way an athlete's strengths and weaknesses become apparent. The performance expectations of defined groups of football players are different, so profiles for defined subgroups of players are also provided on the team norms. The subgroup profile is the mean of all players in that subgroup. Thus, an athlete's profile can be compared to the entire team and any subgroup. The University of Houston players who have gone on to play professional football have all been faster, stronger, and leaner than the average for their respective subgroup. This lends credence to the system.

Notice that we have used percentile-rank norms rather than composite T-score norms in the evaluations. By using T-scores and transforming individual test results into a single score, we would lose in the composite the unique strengths and weaknesses of the athletes. Percentile-rank norms allow us to plot the athletes' test scores individually in a profile that we can then examine to determine whether an athlete shows a performance level compatible to that needed for a given sport. The profile is more than

Table 7.1

Percentile-Rank Norms for High School and College Female Volleyball Players.

Percentile	HIGH SCHOOL PLAYERS				COLLEGE PLAYERS				Percentage Fat*
	Height	Vertical Jump	20-Yard Dash	Basketball Throw	Height	Vertical Jump	20-Yard Dash	Basketball Throw	
99	74.0	22.0	2.87	70.8	77.0	24.0	2.83	82.3	11.2
95	71.0	18.5	3.04	64.5	72.0	20.5	3.00	68.5	12.3
90	70.0	17.8	3.12	60.0	71.0	19.8	3.07	66.8	12.6
85	69.0	16.5	3.17	57.0	70.0	19.0	3.12	64.0	13.2
80	68.0	16.0	3.20	55.0	69.5	18.5	3.16	61.2	13.5
75	67.5	15.7	3.23	52.8	69.0	18.0	3.17	59.4	14.0
70	67.0	15.3	3.26	51.5	68.5	17.5	3.20	58.3	14.4
65	66.5	15.0	3.28	50.5	68.5	17.0	3.27	57.6	14.6
60	66.0	14.5	3.32	49.0	68.0	16.8	3.30	56.6	15.1
55	65.5	14.2	3.34	48.4	67.5	16.5	3.33	56.1	15.5
50	65.5	14.0	3.37	47.2	67.5	16.0	3.37	55.0	16.0
45	65.5	13.7	3.42	46.0	67.0	15.8	3.40	53.9	16.5
40	65.0	13.5	3.46	44.5	67.0	15.5	3.42	52.3	17.5
35	65.0	13.3	3.47	43.5	66.0	15.0	3.44	51.1	18.2
30	64.0	13.0	3.50	42.0	66.0	14.7	3.50	51.0	18.8
25	64.0	12.5	3.53	40.8	65.5	14.0	3.53	50.1	20.5
20	63.0	12.3	3.57	39.2	65.0	13.5	3.60	48.7	21.5
15	62.5	12.0	3.60	37.8	64.0	12.7	3.67	46.6	22.9
10	62.0	11.5	3.67	36.4	63.5	11.5	3.73	45.8	26.0
5	61.5	11.0	3.80	33.5	62.5	10.5	3.83	41.2	31.3

Source: Data used with the permission of Dr. James G. Disch, Associate Professor of Physical Education, Rice University, Houston, Texas.
*Percentage fat was not determined for high school players. See Chapter 7 for methods and norms appropriate for high school girls, as provided with the AAHPERD Health Related Physical Fitness Test (1980).

an evaluative technique; by identifying a variation from the general profile it becomes a training aid as well. For example, assume a profile shows an athlete with a higher level of body fat than average. With this information, the coach can initiate an individualized diet and exercise program for the athlete.

An athlete's test profile will reflect relative strengths and weaknesses, which can be used for several purposes. Many of the abilities can be altered with training; thus, the profile provides both the coach and the athlete an objective means of designing an individualized training program and motivating the athlete. Plotting retests can be used to gauge progress. And finally, the profile may give a coach insight into an athlete's potential.

Table 7.2
Percentile-Rank Norms for University Football Players.

PERCENTILE	0–5 YARDS	20–40 YARDS	0–40 YARDS	PERCENTAGE FAT	BENCH PRESS	LEG PRESS	
99	0.985	1.933	4.412	4.1	422	778	
95	1.029	1.995	4.626	6.5	389	726	
90	1.052	2.028	4.737	7.7	376	707	
85	1.067	2.049	4.812	8.7	360	681	
80	1.080	2.067	4.903	9.2	350	666	Line-
75	1.091	2.083	4.926	9.8	342	653	men
70	1.101	2.096	4.973	10.3	335	642	
65	1.109	2.108	5.013	10.7	329	632	
60	1.118	2.121	5.057	11.3	322	622	
55	1.126	2.131	5.094	11.6	316	613	LB-TE
50	1.134	2.143	5.134	12.0	310	603	
45	1.142	2.155	5.174	12.3	304	593	
40	1.150	2.166	5.212	12.7	298	584	
35	1.159	2.178	5.255	13.2	291	574	Backs
30	1.167	2.190	5.295	13.6	285	564	
25	1.177	2.203	5.342	14.1	278	553	
20	1.188	2.219	5.394	14.6	270	540	
15	1.201	2.237	5.456	15.1	260	525	
10	1.216	2.258	5.531	15.9	244	500	
5	1.239	2.291	5.642	16.9	231	480	
1	1.283	2.353	5.856	18.8	198	428	
Mean	1.134	2.143	5.134	12.0	310	603	
S.D.	0.064	0.090	0.310	3.1			

Source: Data used with the permission of William F. Yeoman, Head Football Coach, University of Houston, Houston, Texas.

Application 2: Preemployment Testing

Many different types of tests are used for hiring purposes. Federal law requires that the tests be valid for the tasks demanded by the specific job. Physical test batteries are being used for hiring into physically demanding occupations. One example is the physical abilities required to be hired as a fire fighter. Most major cities require applicants to pass fire fighter job-related physical abilities test. These tests have been developed by professionals who have conducted an extensive analysis of the tasks demanded of fire fighters, and then developed tests to measure these abilities. Illustrated in figure 7.3 is the test required of fire fighter applicants for the city of Houston, Texas.

Figure 7.3 Physical abilities tests and body composition standards for firefighter applicants for Houston, Texas. An applicant must pass all tests and meet the body composition standard in order to be considered for employment.

PHYSICAL ABILITIES TESTS
1. 100-pound Dummy Carry
2. Charged line drag (Must pull a hose that is full of water and under pressure.)
3. Ladder Reach (Must reach up and remove a ladder from a rack and set the ladder on the ground in a controlled manner.)
4. Bent-leg sit-up (Must complete 25 in 90 seconds.)
5. 300-yard shuttle run (Must complete in 70 seconds.)

BODY COMPOSITION—PERCENT BODY FAT
Men—below 24%
Women—below 34%

Table 7.3

Correlations Between Isometric Strength* and Simulated Work Tasks.

WORK TASK	CORRELATION
Shoveling rate	0.71
50-pound bag carry	0.63
70-pound block carry	0.87
One-arm push force	0.91
Pushing force	0.86
Pulling force	0.78
Lifting force	0.93
Valve turning endurance	0.83

*Sum of grip, arm lift, and back lift isometric strength. (From Jackson 1985a; 1985b; Jackson and Osburn 1983; Laughery and Jackson 1984).

The logic of preemployment testing is to determine if an applicant has the physical ability to be a productive and safe worker. The energy industry has several physically demanding jobs that have typically been held by males. Several energy companies have sponsored studies (Jackson 1985a, b; Jackson and Osburn 1983; Laughery and Jackson 1984) to develop a preemployment physical ability test that validly hires workers on the basis of physical ability rather than gender. Isometric strength has been found to be a useful method of determining if an applicant has sufficient strength to be a successful employee. Provided in table 7.3 are the correlations between isometric strength and simulated job performance demanded of coal miners, and workers on oil production and drilling facilities. This research has established that performance of these physically demanding tasks is related to muscular strength.

A major industrial problem in physically demanding occupations is back injuries. A great deal of effort has been devoted to identify the levels of strength needed to safely lift weight loads (Snook and Ciriello 1974; Snook et al. 1970). It has been shown that the closer the load lifted is near a worker's maximal strength level, the more likely the worker will sustain a musculoskeletal injury. These data lead Keyserling et al. (1980a; 1980b) to recommend the use of isometric strength tests for preemployment screening.

Table 7.4

Basic Abilities of the Motor Performance Domain.

Muscular strength
    1. Upper-body strength
    2. Leg strength

Muscular power
    1. Arm power
    2. Leg power

Endurance
    1. Arm and shoulder girdle muscle endurance
    2. Abdominal muscle endurance
    3. Cardiorespiratory endurance

Basic movement patterns
    1. Running speed
    2. Running agility
    3. Jumping ability
    4. Throwing ability

Flexibility

Balance

MEASUREMENT OF BASIC PHYSICAL ABILITIES

Provided in this section are basic physical abilities and tests that can be used to measure the ability. The system for classifying basic physical abilities shown in table 7.4 is empirical, or measurement-oriented. It rests on the findings of several factor analysis studies (Baumgartner and Zuidema 1972; Disch 1973; Fleishman 1964; Harris and Liba 1965; Liba 1967; Jackson 1971; Jackson and Frankiewicz 1975; Safrit 1966; Zuidema and Baumgartner 1974). The tests listed as measures of the same ability are highly correlated with that ability; the correlations between tests of different basic physical abilities tend to be lower, closer to 0. This system allows you to develop test batteries that reliably measure different abilities. For each ability we've included at least one test.

Muscular Strength

Muscular strength is the maximum force that a muscle group can exert over a brief period of time. Muscular strength can be measured with a maximum static contraction, isometric strength, or maximal dynamic contractions that include isotonic and isokinetic strength. Additionally, it has been shown that absolute endurance is highly correlated with strength (deVries 1980). A brief discussion of each measurement method follows.

Figure 7.4 Isometric testing equipment for the test grip strength.

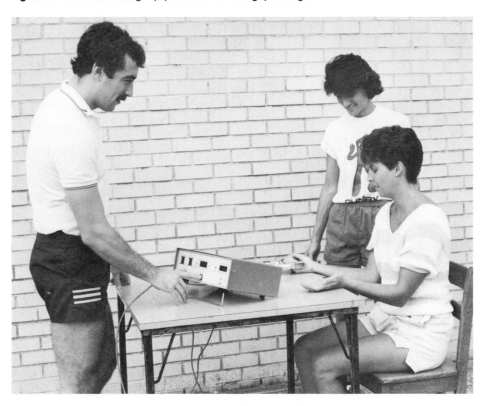

Isometric Strength. This is measured by having a subject exert maximal force in a standardized test position. The exerted force is measured on a recording instrument. Mechanical instruments such as a cable tensiometer or dynamometer have been used to record exerted force. The more modern method is to use a load cell with an electronic recording unit. Such a unit[1] records the exerted force in pounds and can standardize the time that force is recorded (see figure 7.4).

The isometric strength tests commonly used are the cable tension strength tests developed by Clarke (1948). In a cable tension strength test, the student is secured in a standardized position on a table with a special strap, link chain, and stainless-steel, flexible aircraft cable. As the student applies maximum force against the secured cable, with either arm or leg, the tensiometer measures the tension created (see figure 7.5). Isometric cable tension tests measure strength at a single joint angle. The cable tensiometer can be replaced with the electronic load cell. This will enhance test administration and improve accuracy.

1. The isometric system (Model 32528) is manufactured by the Lafayette Instrument Company, Lafayette, Indiana. The equipment was developed for preemployment testing for physically demanding jobs for the Shell Oil Company, Houston, Texas.

Figure 7.5 Cable tension tests for strength of (a) arm, and (b) leg.

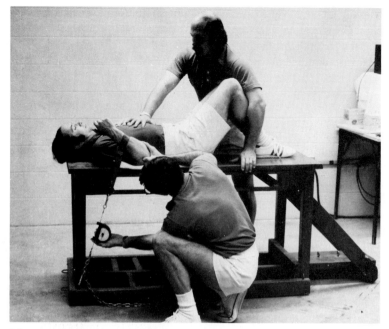

(a)

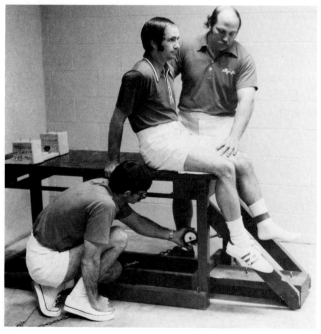

(b)

Isotonic Strength. A popular strength test is to measure the maximal force one can lift for one repetition (1-RM test). The most difficult part of the test is to find the subject's maximal load. Several different weights will need to be tried to find the proper 1-RM weight. This test can be administered with standard bar bells, but we recommend strength development machines common to most facilities (e.g., Universal gymnasium). Because equipment varies in design, 1-RM tests need to be specific to the muscle group tested. The maximal weight lifted will be higher for progressive resistance equipment (e.g., Nautilus) because the resistance changes during the exercise.

Isokinetic Strength. The sound way to measure strength is with isokinetic equipment. This is the method used at the U.S. Olympic Training Center to measure the strength of our Olympic athletes and by NASA scientists to measure astronauts' loss of strength during extended space missions. The speed of resistance is set at a constant rate, while the subject exerts maximal force through the entire range of motion. The exerted force is recorded on graph paper, allowing the test to be scored by measuring: (1) the force output achieved at a specified joint angle; (2) the peak force output; and (3) the total work applied through the range of motion which is the area under the curve. A test position is shown in figure 7.6. The major disadvantage of the isokinetic method is cost. The equipment is expensive and for this reason is usually only used at well-equipped testing centers such as NASA and the U.S. Olympic Center.

Absolute Endurance. Muscular strength and absolute endurance are highly correlated. In an absolute endurance test, a weight load is repeatedly lifted until exhaustion is reached and the same weight is used for all subjects tested. Examples of absolute endurance tests are the strength tests recommended by the YMCA. These are provided in chapter 8.

DeVries (1980) has reported that the correlations between strength and absolute endurance tests are high (at least .90). The reason for the high relation between strength and absolute endurance is that subjects are lifting at different percentages of maximal strength. For example, assume the maximal bench press strengths of two people are 120 and 125 pounds. If the weight load for the test is 110 pounds, the weaker person would be lifting at 92% of maximal while the stronger person would be lifting at 73% of maximal strength.

Measuring Upper-Body Strength

Tests of upper-body strength measure the maximum force that can be generated with the arms and back and can be static or dynamic contractions. Because muscular strength is related to the cross-sectional size of a muscle group, there is a positive correlation between body weight and performance on these tests. All other factors being equal, heavier students tend to generate higher force outputs. Provided next are sample isotonic and isometric strength tests.

Bench Press, Curls, and Lat. Pull Tests (Jackson and Smith 1974)

Objective: To measure 1-RM strength or absolute endurance.

Validity: Construct validity of muscular strength of the arms.

Equipment: A Universal gymnasium or similar weight-training machine.

Figure 7.6 Cybex equipment for testing isokinetic strength. This equipment is used by NASA to evaluate the expected loss of strength as a result of extended space flight; (a) testing equipment, (b) device for testing arm strength, and (c) device for testing leg strength. (Photos courtesy of Cybex.)

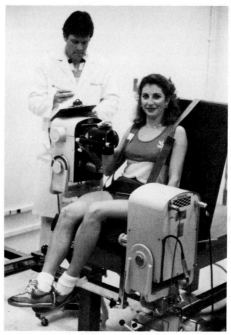

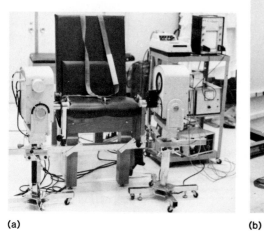

(a)

(b)

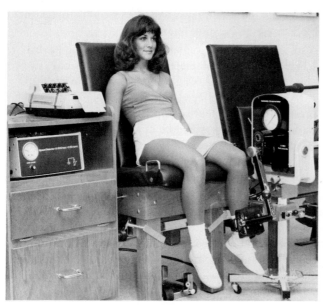

(c)

Figure 7.7 Bench press with free weights.

Besides serving as a teaching station for weight-training instruction, this type of equipment is excellent for measuring arm strength. Free weights can also be used with proper spotting. In fact, the YMCA (Golding, Meyers and Sinning 1982: see chapter 8) recommends the bench press with free weights to measure arm strength. The bench press test is shown in figure 7.7.

Procedures: If the 1-RM test is to be used, students will need to practice in order to find their 1-RM. This should be completed prior to the test day. If absolute endurance is to be the test, select a weight load appropriate for the group being tested. For a group of male college freshmen the following weight loads were used: bench press, 110 pounds; curls, 50 pounds; lat. pull, 100 pounds. For different groups other weights would be appropriate. You need to select a weight load that every student can execute with at least one repetition. For the YMCA two-arm curl test, the weights are 25 pounds for women and 40 pounds for men. For the bench press, 80 and 35 pound barbells are used for men and women respectively.

Each repetition is done on the regulated cadence of a 3-second count. Each repetition must be completed in the 3-second limit, and each new repetition cannot begin until a new 3-second interval begins. Each effort must begin from the original starting position. The students should not drop or slam the weights.

   1. **Bench press.** The student can assume any width grasp outside the shoulders. Feet must be on the floor, the back straight. At the end of each repetition the weights must be brought back to touch the weights beneath them.

2. **Curls.** The student stands with head, shoulders, and buttocks against a wall, feet bracing his or her back, and feet some 12 to 15 inches away from the wall. Place a sheet of paper behind the buttocks. The student must keep the paper pinned against the wall during the exercise, which both forces the student to use the elbow flexors and prevents a rocking motion. Stop the count when the paper falls. Position the machine so that when the student holds the weight with arms fully extended the exercise weight is suspended slightly above the remaining weight. A complete repetition is when the arms are fully flexed and the bar touches the chin. Be sure the student remains against the wall and fully extends the arms at the end of each repetition.

3. **Lat pull.** The student grasps the bar on the handle grips and kneels on the floor. The bar is pulled down behind the head to touch at the juncture of the neck and shoulders, just below the hairline. The weight should be brought back to the starting position without jerking or lifting the student off the floor.

Scoring: For the 1-RM test a student's score is the maximal weight lifted and for absolute endurance it is the number of repetitions completed. Stop the count whenever a student fails to complete a repetition correctly or to maintain the 3-second cadence.

Norms: Percentile-rank norms developed on college men who have completed a 16-week weight-training program are listed in table 7.5. The norms have been adjusted for body weight. Additional norms for adults are provided with the

Table 7.5

The 25th, 50th, and 75th Percentiles for Arm Strength of Men (Adjusted for Body Weight).

BODY WEIGHT	BENCH PRESS			CURLS			LAT. PULL		
	P_{25}	P_{50}	P_{75}	P_{25}	P_{50}	P_{75}	P_{25}	P_{50}	P_{75}
100–109	6	11	16	10	17	23	12	18	24
110–119	7	12	17	11	18	24	13	19	24
120–129	8	13	18	13	19	25	14	20	25
130–139	9	14	20	14	20	26	15	20	26
140–149	10	16	21	15	21	28	16	21	27
150–159	12	17	22	16	22	29	16	22	28
160–169	13	18	23	17	24	30	17	23	28
170–179	14	19	24	19	25	31	18	24	29
180–189	15	20	26	20	26	32	19	24	30
190–199	16	22	27	21	27	33	20	25	31
200–209	18	23	28	22	28	35	20	26	32
210–219	19	24	29	23	29	36	21	27	32
220–229	20	25	30	24	31	37	22	28	33
230–239	21	26	31	26	32	38	23	28	34
240–249	23	28	33	27	33	39	24	29	35

Source: Department of HPER, University of Houston, Houston, Texas.

Table 7.6
**Percentile Norms for College Women for 1-RM
Bench Press Strength for Selected Body Weights.**

BODY WEIGHT	PERCENTILE*				
	95	75	50	25	5
90	93	73	65	55	43
100	97	77	69	59	47
110	101	81	73	63	51
120	105	85	77	67	55
130	109	89	81	71	59
140	113	93	85	75	63
150	117	97	89	79	67
160	121	101	93	83	71
170	126	106	98	88	76
180	130	110	102	92	80
190	134	114	106	96	84
200	138	118	110	100	88

*Data from 202 college women using the Universal Gym Spartacus (Jackson and Gibson 1984).

YMCA test in chapter 8. The YMCA test uses barbells for their curl and bench press test. 1-RM bench press test norms for University football players are provided in table 7.2. Bench press norms for college women adjusted for body weight are presented in table 7.6.

Isometric Strength Test Battery

Objective: To measure the maximal force for selected muscle groups.

Validity: Isometric tests have been recognized as a valid method for measuring strength. The isometric strength tests have been shown to be highly correlated with simulated work tasks of physically demanding occupations (see table 7.3).

Reliability: The reliability estimates exceed 0.90 for each test.

Equipment: The tests are administered on equipment manufactured by Lafayette Instrument Company (Model 32528) and consist of a grip strength apparatus, an arm and back lift apparatus, and a load cell and digital recorder. The equipment is calibrated in pounds by hanging a known weight from it and measuring the weight.

Procedures: Once the subject is in the test position, the tester pushes the "start" button. A "beep" will sound and 3 seconds later a second "beep" will be heard. The subject is instructed to exert force on this first "beep" and stop on the second "beep." The equipment allows you to set the length of the trial. A 3-second trial is used during which force is recorded only for the last 2 seconds. Typically, subjects will jerk at the start of the trial. By not measuring this first second, the jerk is not reflected in the strength score, which is the average force exerted during the final two seconds. A warm-up trial at 50% effort is administered first, followed by two trials for score.

Figure 7.8 Arm-lift test.

1. **Grip.** The grip strength is tested with the load cell attached to the grip apparatus. The subject is seated at a table with the free hand on the table. The apparatus is gripped with the palm up. Maximal force is exerted in this position (see figure 7.4).

2. **Arm Lift.** The arm lift apparatus is used to measure lifting strength. The load cell is attached and equipment is adjusted so the elbows are at 90° flexion. The legs should be straight and the subject is not allowed to lean back. Maximal lifting force is exerted in this position (see figure 7.8).

Figure 7.9 Arm press.  **Figure 7.10** Back-lift test.

3. **Arm Press.** The subject sits on a chair, keeping the back straight. The apparatus is set so the bar is even with the bottom of the chin. The palms are forward and the arms should be under the bar allowing for a push upward. Maximal lifting force is exerted in this position (see figure 7.9).

4. **Back Lift.** The apparatus is adjusted so the bar is 17 inches from the base of the platform. The subject uses a reverse grip (palms facing the rear) and keeps the legs straight. From this position, the subject lifts. Extra warm-up trials are given for this test (see figure 7.10).

Scoring: The average of two trials are used for score. Descriptive data for male and female physically fit college students and male coal miners are furnished in table 7.7.

Table 7.7
**Means and Standard Deviations of Isometric Strength Tests
for Physically Fit College Students and Coal Miners.**

TEST	FEMALES		MALES		MINERS	
	X̄	SD	X̄	SD	X̄	SD
Grip strength	56.3	12.2	88.3	26.6	124.5	16.9
Arm lift	49.8	13.4	88.5	18.3	95.9	14.3
Back lift	125.3	34.7	204.4	63.1	252.4	54.7
Arm press					134.1	36.2

Source: (Jackson 1985a; Jackson 1985b; Jackson and Osburn 1983; Laughery and Jackson 1984; Laughery et al. 1985). The unit of measurement is in pounds of force and the tests are shown in Figures 7.4, 7.8, 7.9, and 7.10.

Measuring Leg Strength

Research shows that muscular strength is comprised of more than a single component. Three studies (Jackson 1971; Jackson and Frankiewicz 1975; Start et al. 1966) have identified separate abilities in the arms and legs. Isometric and isokinetic strength testing equipment can be used to measure leg strength, but the availability of weight training equipment make 1-RM leg strength tests a realistic option. The tests listed in this section are designed to measure the maximal force capacity of the leg muscles.

1-RM Leg Strength Test

Objective: To determine the greatest weight one can lift with the legs during one repetition.

Validity: Construct validity of leg strength.

Equipment: A Universal gymnasium or similar weight-training machine. Free weights are not recommended because the need for heavy weight increases the chance of injury.

Procedures: Start with a weight that can be lifted comfortably, continuing to add weight until the individual's maximum value is found. The appropriate weight is easy to identify with experienced weightlifters; trial and error method have to be used with inexperienced lifters. The Universal gymnasium allows you to measure leg press and leg extension strength.

1. **Leg press.** The subject sits in the provided chair, fully extends the legs, and executes a maximal repetition. The starting position is shown in figure 7.11. The seat should be adjusted to standardize the knee angle at approximately 120°.

2. **Leg extension.** The subject is in a sitting position and the test is to extend the knee from 90° to 180°. The test position is shown in figure 7.12.

Scoring: The subject's score is the maximum weight lifted during one repetition. The procedure of using the number of repetitions with a constant weight load is not recommended: some subjects are so strong they will achieve an excessive number of repetitions, creating positively skewed distributions.

Figure 7.11 Using the Universal Gym to test leg strength.

Norms: Wilmore (1976) provides optimal leg press strength values for males and females in table 7.8. Furnished in table 7.9 are leg extension norms for college women adjusted for body weight.

Muscular Power

Muscular power has traditionally been defined as maximum force released in the shortest possible time. Power movement, then, is the movement of one's body mass in the shortest possible time. The vertical jump, standing long jump, and shot put have been the recommended measures of power (McCloy 1932). However, studies (Barlow 1970; Considine 1970; Glencross 1966; Gray 1962) have challenged this definition of power and shown that jumping tests are not highly correlated with power when measured mechanically.

Muscular strength and work are essential in demonstrating power, as is clear from the following formula:

$$W = F \times D$$

where W is work, F is force, and D is the distance the force moves.

Figure 7.12 Leg extensions. An individual with knee extended (a) 90°, and (b) 180°.

(a)

(b)

Table 7.8

Optimal 1-RM Leg Press Standards.

BODY WEIGHT	MALES	FEMALES
80	160	112
100	200	140
120	240	168
140	280	296
160	320	224
180	360	252
200	400	280
220	440	308
240	480	336

Data from Dr. Jack H. Wilmore, Department of Physical Education, University of Arizona, Tucson, Arizona.

Table 7.9

Percentile Norms for College Women for 1-RM Leg Extension Strength for Selected Body Weights.

| BODY WEIGHT | PERCENTILE | | | | |
	95	75	50	25	5
90	104	84	65	45	23
100	112	92	73	53	31
110	120	100	81	61	39
120	128	108	89	69	47
130	136	116	97	77	55
140	144	124	105	85	63
150	152	132	113	93	71
160	160	140	121	101	79
170	168	148	129	109	87
180	176	156	137	117	95
190	184	164	145	125	103
200	192	172	153	133	111

Data from 202 college women using the Universal Gym Spartacus (Jackson and Gibson 1984).

Power is defined as the rate at which work is performed, and is calculated with the following formula:

$$P = \frac{W}{T}$$

where P is power, W is work, and T is the time required to perform the work.

Two studies (Glencross 1966; Jackson and Frankiewicz 1975) have reported that arm and leg power have different components, which means that motor tasks requiring leg power differ from those that require arm power. Leg power tests generally measure the work required to move a weight load equal to one's body weight. Tests of arm power, on the other hand, involve moving a weight load that remains constant for different individuals. Examples are putting a shot and throwing a ball.

We can use the work and power formulas above, to illustrate the characteristics of human arm and leg power outputs. For example, if, using the bench press, a boy moves a 70-pound weight load a vertical height of 1.5 feet, the work is 105 foot-pounds:

$$W = (70)(1.5) = 105 \text{ foot-pounds}$$

Assuming the weight was moving as fast as possible and that the boy took .15 second to move the weight load 1.5 feet, his power output is 700 foot-pounds per second:

$$P = \frac{(70)(1.5)}{.15} = 700 \text{ foot-pounds per second}$$

Let's look at another example. Assume that the same boy, who weighs 180 pounds, sprints up a 15-foot hill. The work performed equals 2700 foot-pounds:

$$W = (180)(15) = 2700 \text{ foot-pounds}$$

If the sprint took 2 seconds, the boy's power output is 1350 foot-pounds per second:

$$P = \frac{(180)(15)}{2} = 1350 \text{ foot-pounds per second}$$

Measuring Arm Power

Arm power is characterized by an explosive contraction of the muscle groups of the arms and shoulder girdle. As we've said, arm power is measured by applying force to a weight load that is relatively heavy and constant for all subjects.

Researchers have measured arm power with specially developed power levers and electronic timing devices, neither of which is feasible for mass testing. Although not verified by research, putting the shot and medicine ball for distance are traditionally accepted tests of arm power (McCloy and Young 1954). Body weight has been shown to be moderately correlated with arm power.

Shot Put or Medicine Ball Put Test

Objective: To put a weighted object for distance with a maximal effort of the arms

Validity: Construct validity of muscular power of the arms.

Equipment: A 100-foot tape measure to measure the puts. A shot put that weighs from 4 to 12 pounds, or a 6 or 9 pound medicine ball may be used. The size of the weighted object depends on the age, gender, and strength of the participants. With an indoor shot put or medicine ball the test can be administered in a gymnasium.

Procedure: The student assumes a position behind a restraining line with the shoulders in line with the test course; the side opposite the throwing arm should be facing the direction of the throw. The shot put or medicine ball should be tucked under the chin. From a standing position the student dips back, without moving the feet, to gather momentum and puts the object down the test course. In track and field terminology this is referred to as putting from the reverse position. A run is not recommended.

Alternative Procedures: The test can be administered with the student sitting in a chair or on the ground.

Scoring: The student's score is the distance of the put measured to the last half-foot. Concentric circles drawn 1 foot apart are recommended for scoring the test, eliminating the need to measure each throw. In most situations measurements accurate to the last foot are precise enough to produce reliable data.

Other Considerations: The shot put is recommended over the medicine ball because many students have difficulty controlling the medicine ball. It's important that the students be allowed to practice this test before taking it. This test can be very time consuming to administer to a large class. Taking the necessary precautions of setting up the test course so that each throw does not need to be measured, one person can easily administer three or four trials to a class in 45 minutes. By measuring to the last foot rather than the last half-foot, some precision is lost, but efficiency is gained.

Measuring Leg Power

Leg power is characterized by the explosive movement of the entire body. Leg power, or anaerobic power, is the power generated by the legs when moving the body. Because body weight is the mass moved, the mass varies among subjects.

Margaria and his associates (1966) were the first to publish a leg power test, which has been revised as shown in figure 7.13 (Mathews and Fox 1971). The subject begins 6 meters from the bottom stair and runs up the stairs as fast as possible, taking three steps at a time. Switch mats are placed on the third and ninth steps. By stepping on the third stair, the subject activates a clock accurate to one-hundredth of a second; when the subject steps on the ninth stair, the clock is stopped. The time recorded by the clock represents the time required to move the body a height of 1.05 meters. Power is calculated using the following formula:

$$\text{Power} = \frac{(W \times 1.05)}{T}$$

where, W is the subject's weight in kilograms, 1.05 is the height in meters, and T is elapsed time.

Chaloupha (Mathews 1978) revised this test for boys, grades 2 through 6, placing the switch mats on the second and sixth steps. It was reported that this variation represents a more valid procedure for classifying boys for age-group football teams. Margaria and his associates (1966) report that athletes have higher levels of leg power than nonathletes. Leg power appears to be useful for predicting athletic success in a power-related sport such as football.

Figure 7.13 Margaria-Kalamen leg power test. (From D. K. Matthews and E. L. Fox, *The Physiological Basis of Physical Education and Athletics,* second edition. Philadelphia, Pa.: W. B. Saunders, 1976, p. 501. Reprinted by permission of Holt, Rinehart and Winston.)

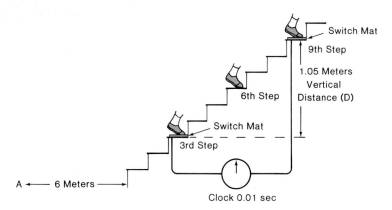

Endurance

Muscular endurance is the ability to persist in physical activity or to resist muscular fatigue (deVries 1980). Endurance tests can measure absolute endurance where the weight load moved to exhaustion is the same for all subjects tested or relative endurance where the weight moved varies among the subjects tested. The muscular endurance abilities described here involve moving or maintaining one's own body weight to exhaustion. Since body weights among subjects will vary, these are tests of relative endurance. Three basic endurance abilities have been identified: (1) muscular endurance of the arms and shoulder girdle, (2) muscular endurance of the abdominal muscles, and (3) cardiorespiratory endurance. Tests used to measure these endurance abilities are included in motor fitness and health-related fitness tests (see chapters 8 and 9).

Measuring Arm and Shoulder Girdle Endurance

Tests of this ability require the subject to move or support the body weight against the pull of gravity, and may involve either isometric or isotonic contractions of the muscles executed to exhaustion. It's been claimed that tests of this ability measure both strength and endurance. Dynamic strength, arm and shoulder girdle strength, and muscular endurance are the terms used by physical educators to describe this ability. There is a negative correlation between body weight and this basic physical ability, and the correlation is even higher between percent of body fat and this basic ability.

When preparing to measure this ability, it's important to select a test of appropriate difficulty for the group being tested. There is a tendency for the distributions of these tests to be positively skewed. Many students (for example, junior high girls) have difficulty maintaining or moving their body weight against gravity.

The tests most often recommended for motor fitness or physical fitness batteries are pull-ups or chin-ups, and the flexed-arm hang. The AAHPERD Youth Fitness test (1976) includes pull-ups for boys and the flexed-arm hang for girls. On both tests, the student is required to use the forward grip, palms facing away from the body. These tests can also be administered with the reverse grip, palms facing the body. Wells (1971) maintains that the reverse grip is the most favorable position for the biceps. With the forward grip, the function of the biceps is greatly diminished because the tendon is wrapped around the radius and the effective lever arm is reduced.

Testing procedures for the AAHPERD pull-up and flexed arm hang tests are provided in chapter 9. Provided with the test instructions are norms. Remember, the AAHPERD test uses a forward grip.

Modified Pull-Up Test (Baumgartner 1978)

Objective: To measure the arm and shoulder girdle strength and/or endurance.

Validity and Reliability: The test involves moving the body weight with the arms to exhaustion, so it logically measures arm and shoulder girdle strength and/or endurance. Intraclass reliability estimates exceeding .90 have been reported.

Equipment: The pull-up board itself is constructed of two 8-foot-long 2 × 12's fastened together, side by side, with three 2 × 4's. The pull-up bar is constructed of 3/4-inch iron plumbing pipe and right-angle fittings connected to the top of the board with floor plates. The scooter board is a 18 × 36 inch piece of 1/2-inch plywood. The four wheels for the scooter board and track for the wheels are those for a garage door. Several steps of 2 × 4's are nailed to the bottom of the pull-up board. The pull-up board is positioned at a 30° angle with the floor by placing it on a doorway pull-up or wall bracket positioned 4 feet above the floor.

Some of the equipment descriptions are modifications of those in the original sources. Commercially developed equipment is available and this is shown in figure 7.14.

Procedure: The student lies on the scooter board with the top of the board at the bottom of the sternum. The student pushes, or is pushed, to the top of the pull-up board. The student grasps the pull-up bar located at the top end of the pull-up board with an overhanded grip, hands about a shoulder-width apart. The student then assumes a straight-arm hanging position, pulls up the inclined board until the chin is over the bar, and returns to a straight-arm hanging position. This action is repeated as many times as possible.

Scoring: The score is the number of completed repetitions.

Norms: Norms for most ages 6 through college and both genders are reported by Baumgartner et al. (1984) and Jackson et al. (1982). Almost without exception scores range from 3 to 50.

Other Considerations: This test was developed to discriminate better among students with low strength and endurance. The test has been used successfully with students ranging from elementary to college age. Baumgartner and Wood (1984) used the modified pull-up equipment to develop strength in elementary school children.

Figure 7.14 (a) Testing position for the modified pull-up. (b) Testing equipment. From Gene Turner, University of Georgia.

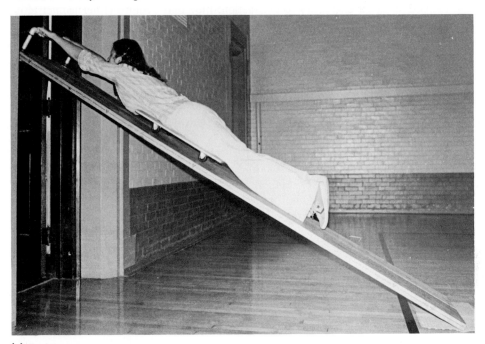

(a)

(b)

Measuring Abdominal Muscle Endurance

Tests of this ability require the subject to use the abdominal muscles to move or maintain the body's upper extremity to exhaustion; they may require either isometric or isotonic contractions of these muscles. Tests that measure this ability have been called measures of abdominal muscle strength or endurance.

Sit-ups are generally recommended on physical or motor fitness batteries. Prior to the 1976 revision of the AAHPERD Youth Fitness test, the straight-leg sit-up was used. When executing a straight-leg sit-up, the hip flexors are in position for their most forceful contraction. This is due to the strong hip flexor, the iliopsoas group, shown in figure 7.15. With a straight-leg sit-up there is a tendency to arch or hyperextend the lumbar spine during its execution. When this occurs, it indicates that the abdominal muscles do not have enough strength to prevent the hip flexors from increasing the pelvic tilt. Kendall (1965) reports that the hyperextension of the lumbar spine may result in injury to the lower back. Hyperextension of the lower back can result in ligamentous strains, muscle or tendon ruptures, and even intervertebral disc ruptures.

The hyperextended lower back may be eliminated by substituting the hook-lying (that is, flexed knee and hip joints) or bent-knee sit-up for the straight-leg sit-up. In these positions, the hip flexors are not stretched, and the abdominal muscles (flexors of the lumbar spine) assume the major responsibility for movement. It is for this reason that the flexed-leg sit-up is the recommended test.

The 1-minute, flexed-leg sit-up is the recommended test of the AAHPERD Youth Fitness battery (1976). In the newer Health Related Physical Fitness battery (AAHPERD 1980), the sit-up has been modified by moving the hands from behind the head and placing them on the chest. Testing procedures and norms for both tests are provided in chapter 9.

Measuring Cardiorespiratory Endurance

Maximal oxygen uptake ($\dot{V}O_2$ Max) is considered by exercise scientists to be the best index of cardiorespiratory endurance. The most valid method of measuring $\dot{V}O_2$ Max is in the laboratory using sophisticated gas analysis equipment and motor driven treadmills. A less accurate but easier method is to measure submaximal heart rate response to exercise. The method most appropriate for use in the public schools is with distance runs either at least one mile in length or at least nine minutes in duration. The laboratory methods are fully discussed in chapter 8 and the distance runs tests and norms for the AAHPERD Health Related (1980) and Texas tests (1973; 1986) are furnished in chapter 9.

Basic Movement Patterns

The importance of basic movement patterns—running, jumping, and throwing—is recognized by physical educators, and tests of these abilities are included in published general motor ability and motor fitness batteries. These abilities are especially important for evaluating athletes.

Figure 7.15 Anterior view of the iliopsoas group. (From K. F. Wells and K. Luttgens, *Kinesiology: Scientific Basis of Human Emotion,* page 151. Copyright © 1976 by W. B. Saunders. Reprinted by permission of Holt, Rinehart and Winston.)

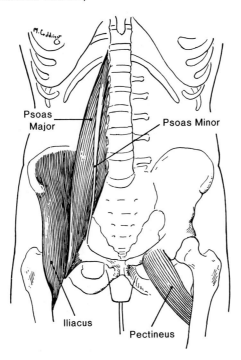

Measuring Running Speed

Tests of running **speed** require the subject to run at maximum speed in a straight path. The basic physical ability is measured by the elapsed time required to run a specified distance (usually 10 to 60 yards) or the distance the student can run during a specified time period (usually 4 to 8 seconds).

This basic physical ability is normally represented on motor ability and motor fitness test batteries by a sprinting test ranging from 40 to 60 yards in length. Several investigators (Disch 1973; Fleishman 1964; Jackson 1971) report that sprints as short as 20 yards reliably measure this basic physical ability; however, longer sprints, 40 or 50 yards, are more reliable (Jackson and Baumgartner 1969). Most motor ability or motor fitness batteries recommend 50-yard sprints, while 40-yard sprints are universally accepted by football coaches. Testing procedures and norms for the 50-yard dash (AAHPERD 1976) are provided in chapter 9.

Measuring Running Agility

Agility is the ability to change the direction of the body or body parts rapidly. This ability is measured with running tests that require the subject to turn or start and stop. Such tests appear in most published general motor ability and motor fitness batteries. Running speed tends to be related to agility.

Research indicates (Jackson and Baumgartner 1970) that the tests used to measure running agility present a common measurement problem: students learn to perform these tests with practice. It was found that when five trials were administered, the best scores for the group were achieved on trials 4 and 5. These tests are time consuming, so it would not normally be feasible to allow five trials, but you should give students an opportunity to practice before the test or while other students are being tested. Proper traction is another problem posed by these tests. It's essential that students wear proper shoes and that the test be administered on a suitable surface; a tile floor or a dirty floor may be too slippery.

Many tests of running agility have been published. The shuttle run requires the subject to run back and forth between two parallel lines. In the AAHPERD Youth Fitness Test (1976), the lines are 30 feet apart and the student must run across four times; the score is the elapsed time required to run the 120 feet. Test procedures and norms for the AAHPERD shuttle run are provided in chapter 9.

A second type of running agility test requires the student to run a test course that calls for constant turning. The zigzag run is an example.

Zigzag Run Test (Texas Test 1973)

Objective: To run a test course that requires turning as fast and efficiently as possible.

Validity: Construct validity of running agility.

Equipment: A test course of appropriate size, a stopwatch accurate to a tenth of a second, and five markers to outline the test course. (See figure 7.16.)
Although the instructions for several agility tests recommend the use of chairs, volleyball standards, or wooden clubs for outlining the test course, we strongly recommend that you not use these objects because of possible injury to students. Rubber pylons are ideal for outlining the course safely.

Procedures: At the signal the student begins from behind the starting line and runs the outlined course one time as fast as possible.

Scoring: The student's score is the elapsed time accurate to the nearest tenth of a second. Give three trials. The first should be at three-quarter speed to familiarize the student with the procedure and to serve as a specific warm-up. The score is the mean of the last two trials.

Norms: Norms for boys and girls ages 10 through 17 are provided in table 7.10.

Other Considerations: Although some authorities recommend that the test consist of three circuits through the course, it's been found that high reliability can be achieved by using several trials of just one circuit. With ample rest between each trial fatigue is not a factor. The test is time consuming because each trial must be administered individually, but several test courses can be used to administer the test to a large group.

Figure 7.16 Test course for zigzag run.

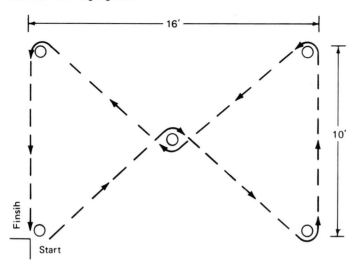

Table 7.10
Percentile-Rank Norms for Boys and Girls on the Zigzag Run.

| PERCENTILE | BOYS—AGE TO THE LAST YEAR | | | | | | | |
	10	11	12	13	14	15	16	17
95	7.5	7.4	7.2	7.0	6.8	6.7	6.5	6.3
75	8.3	8.2	8.0	7.8	7.6	7.5	7.3	7.1
50	8.9	8.8	8.6	8.4	8.2	8.1	7.9	7.7
25	9.5	9.4	9.2	9.0	8.8	8.7	8.5	8.3
5	10.3	10.2	10.0	9.8	9.6	9.5	9.3	8.7

| PERCENTILE | GIRLS—AGE TO THE LAST YEAR | | | | | | | |
	10	11	12	13	14	15	16	17
95	7.2	7.0	6.8	6.7	6.5	6.3	6.3	6.3
75	8.4	8.2	8.0	7.9	7.7	7.5	7.5	7.5
50	9.2	9.0	8.8	8.7	8.5	8.3	8.3	8.3
25	9.6	9.4	9.2	9.1	8.9	8.7	8.7	8.7
5	11.2	11.0	10.8	10.7	10.5	10.3	10.3	10.3

Source: (Texas Test 1973).

Measuring Jumping Ability

Tests of this factor measure the ability to expend maximum energy in one explosive act, projecting the body through space. The vertical jump, chalk jump, Sargent jump, and standing long jump (the easiest to administer) are the most frequently used tests of the ability.

Jumping tests have been described as tests of power (McCloy and Young 1954) and of explosive strength (Fleishman 1964). Although physical educators generally refer to these tests as measures of power, research (Barlow 1970; Considine 1970) has reported low correlations between jumping tests and mechanical measures of power.

The need for leg strength in jumping is self-evident; body weight, however, is negatively correlated with jumping ability. The negative relation can be largely traced to body fatness. More force, or greater muscular strength, is needed to propel a heavier individual through space. Jumping ability, then, depends on individual differences in leg strength and body composition. If two individuals are capable of generating the same amount of force, the leanest person, all other things being equal would jump highest.

The standing long jump is very easy to administer and is the recommended test of the AAHPERD (1976) Youth Fitness battery. The test and norms are fully presented in chapter 9. The vertical jump is used by many coaches to test athletes, and test procedures and norms from the Texas test (1973) are provided next.

Vertical Jump Test (Texas test 1973)

Objective: Using a double-foot take off, to jump vertically as high as possible with maximim effort.

Validity: Construct validity of jumping ability.

Equipment: A smooth wall of sufficient height, a yardstick, and chalk.

Procedure: Secure the student's standing height by having him or her stand with heels together on the floor and the side of his or her dominant hand, holding a piece of chalk, next to the wall. From this position the student reaches upward as high as possible and marks on the wall. To execute the jump, the student squats next to the wall, jumps as high as possible, and marks the wall. Once in the starting position the student should not move his or her feet (that is, to walk in or step into the jump).

Scoring: The height of the jump is the measured distance between the standing and jumping heights. Measurements accurate to the last inch are precise enough for reliable results. Give three trials, the first at three-quarter speed to familiarize the student with the procedure and to serve as a specific warm-up. The score is the mean of the last two trials to the nearest half inch.

Norms: Norms for boys and girls ages 10 through 17 are listed in table 7.11.

Table 7.11

Percentile-Rank Norms for Boys and Girls on the Vertical Jump.

| PERCENTILE | BOYS—AGE TO THE LAST YEAR | | | | | | | |
	10	11	12	13	14	15	16	17
95	15.5	16.5	17.5	19.0	20.5	21.5	22.5	24.0
75	12.5	13.5	14.5	16.0	17.5	18.5	19.5	21.0
50	11.0	12.0	13.0	14.5	16.0	17.0	18.0	19.5
25	9.0	10.0	11.0	12.5	14.0	15.0	16.0	17.5
5	6.0	7.0	7.0	8.5	10.0	11.0	12.0	13.5

| PERCENTILE | GIRLS—AGE TO THE LAST YEAR | | | | | | | |
	10	11	12	13	14	15	16	17
95	14.0	14.5	15.0	15.5	16.0	17.0	17.0	17.0
75	11.5	12.0	12.5	13.0	13.5	14.5	14.5	14.5
50	10.0	10.5	11.0	11.5	12.0	13.0	13.0	13.0
25	8.5	9.0	9.5	10.0	10.5	11.5	11.5	11.5
5	6.0	6.5	7.0	7.5	8.0	9.0	9.0	9.0

Source: (Texas Test 1973).

Measuring Throwing Ability

Test of this ability required the subject to throw a relatively light ball (baseball, soft-ball, or basketball) overarm for distance. These tests have been reported to measure arm and shoulder girdle strength and/or coordination. Eckert (1965) reports a high correlation between muscular strength and speed of movement when the mass of the ball is high relative to the strength of the muscle groups involved. Obviously strength is necessary to throw a ball for distance; however, the weight of the ball relative to the strength of the thrower must be considered. For example, if young and relatively weak children are required to throw a basketball, muscular arm strength or power may be the dominant factor measured; if a Little League baseball is used, throwing ability is more likely to be measured. With older and stronger students, the ability to throw a basketball for distance may be only slightly affected by individual differences in arm strength. Given adequate strength, the basic physical ability measured is the execution of a coordinated overarm pattern with maximal speed.

Orthopedic surgeons have questioned the advisability of having younger children throw with maximal effort. "Little League elbow" is a common injury among preteen athletes. The softball throw for distance, once an item in the AAHPERD Youth Fitness battery, was dropped with the 1975 revision.

For any throw for distance, it's recommended that the students be conditioned and warmed up before testing. Do not allow the students who complain of sore arms to take the test.

Basketball Throw for Distance Test (Disch et al. 1977)

Objective: To throw a basketball as far as possible.

Validity and Reliability: The test has been shown to discriminate among levels of performance of female volleyball players. The intraclass reliability estimates with samples of females have ranged from .85 to .97.

Equipment: Two basketballs and a 100-foot tape measure.

Procedure: The throws are made with both feet parallel to the restraining line. The subject may not take a step to throw, but may follow through by stepping over the line after the throw, minimizing the action of the lower body. In this way the throw more closely represents the overarm pattern used when spiking or serving a volleyball. Each subject is awarded five throws.

Scoring: The student's score is the distance thrown to the nearest half foot. This test was shown to have a warm-up effect, thus the best score achieved is the recommended score.

Norms: Norms for female volleyball players are listed in table 7.1.

Flexibility

Flexibility is the range of movement about a joint. Individual differences in flexibility depend on physiological characteristics that influence the extensibility of the muscles and ligaments surrounding a joint. Physical educators agree that certain levels and types of flexibility are wanted, but the degree of flexibility desired is yet to be determined.

Leighton (1955) has published the most comprehensive battery of flexibility tests using a specially developed instrument, the Leighton Flexometer, to measure the flexibility of a joint. Physical therapists use a protractor-like instrument called a goniometer to measure joint flexibility; and in research laboratories, electronic and slow-motion photographic methods are used to measure flexibility. Although these are reliable methods for measuring flexibility, the investment of time and money prohibit their use out of the laboratory setting.

Flexibility is often regarded as a single general factor or ability. Clarke (1967) represents flexibility as a component of general motor ability. Harris (1969) conducted a factor analysis study to determine whether flexibility is a single general factor. Two types of flexibility tests were used in her study: (1) tests that measure the movement of a limb involving only one joint action; and (2) composite measures of movements that require more than one joint or more than one type of action within a single joint. The analysis revealed many of the intercorrelations to be near 0, which implies specificity rather than generality. A factor analysis of these data revealed 13 different factors of flexibility. Harris concluded, then, that there is no evidence that flexibility is a single general factor.

Harris's finding indicates that we must think in terms of several types of flexibilities. We can easily recognize the importance of different types of flexibility in different motor skills. Figure 7.17 shows the types of flexibility needed by the modern dancer and the football punter. These specific types of flexibility are developed over time with

Figure 7.17 Different types of flexibility.

special stretching exercises and practice in the given skill. The specificity of flexibility, then, means that we cannot use a single test to measure the various types of flexibility necessary to the execution of different motor skills.

Fleishman (1964) has identified a factor, called dynamic flexibility, involving the ability to change direction with the body parts rapidly and efficiently. Physical educators (McCloy and Young 1954) call this factor "agility that does not involve running." The squat thrust test is reported to measure the factor and is included in some motor fitness batteries as a measure of agility. Harris (1969) identified the same factor. The tests used to measure the factor are difficult to standardize and thus tend to lack reliability and are of questionable value. Fleishman (1964) offers a full description and norms for this test.

Kraus and Raab (1961) maintain that a degree of flexibility in the back and hamstring muscle groups is essential for the prevention of lower back disorders. Kraus and Hirschland (1954) have published a battery of minimum muscular fitness tests, the Kraus-Weber Tests, developed in a posture clinic for the diagnosis and treatment of patients with low-back pain. When these ten tests were administered to several thousand European and American school children, the American failure rate was considerably higher than the European rate. The test, scored on a pass-fail basis, is described below:

> The subject stands erect in stockings or bare feet, hands at the sides, feet together. The test is for the subject to lean down slowly and touch the floor with the finger tips and hold the position for three seconds. The knees should be held straight and bouncing is not permitted.

The value of flexibility for a healthy lower back is recognized by physicians, physical therapists, and physical educators. It is for this reason that the sit-and-reach test is a recommended test of the AAHPERD Health Related Fitness (1980) and Texas Youth Fitness (1986) tests. Test procedures and norms for these tests are provided in chapter 9.

A high degree of specific types of flexibility is needed to be a skilled athlete or dancer. The unique types of flexibility needed can serve as a basis for developing specific flexibility tests.

Balance

Balance is the ability to maintain body position, which is obviously essential to the successful execution of motor skills. Two general types of balance are commonly recognized: static balance is the ability to maintain total body equilibrium while standing in one spot. Dynamic balance is the ability to maintain equilibrium while moving from one point to another. These two types of balance were first reported by Bass (1939), who stated that static balance depends on the ability to coordinate stimuli from the three semicircular canals; proprioceptive receptors located in the muscles, tendons, and joints; and visual perception. Dynamic balance depends on similar but more complex stimuli.

Singer (1968) argued against the assumption that there are only two general types of balance, claiming instead that different motor skills require different types of balance. The balance needed by the tennis player differs from that needed by the swimmer. Furthermore, he points out that different tests of balance do not correlate highly with each other. Fleishman (1964) suggests the existence of several factors in balance. He reported two factors in static balance, one measured with the eyes closed and the other with the eyes open. Because dynamic balance is more complex, it's likely to be composed of more than four factors.

Due to the specificity of balance, the value of balance tests in the instructional process is yet to be determined. Balance tasks are often used by motor learning researchers because significant improvements can be noted in a relatively short time. This learning effect, inherent in balance tests, indicates that they are not reliable in terms of stability. Thus, the tests do not offer stable measurements for purposes of placement, diagnosis, or prediction. By contrast, many gymnastic and tumbling stunts—among them, the head stand—involve learning a specific type of balance. Because the performance of such balance stunts is an instructional objective of a tumbling or gymnastics unit, the value of measuring these specific types of balance is easily defended. Provided next are the static balance tests most commonly used.

> The static balance was first recommended by Bass (1939) and the test was revised by Fleishman (1964). Wooden sticks (1 inch by 1 inch by 12 inches) are taped to the floor. At the word "Ready," the subject places the supporting foot lengthwise on the stick. At the command "Go," the subject raises the free foot and holds this position as long as possible for a maximum of 60 seconds. The test is terminated if: 1) either foot touches the floor; or 2) balance is maintained for 60 seconds. The subject is given three practice trials, and the subjects score is the sum of six trials of the test. Fleishman (1964) administered the test with the eyes open and closed and found they measured different factors.

Kinesthetic Perception

Kinesthesis, or kinesthetic perception, is the ability to perceive the body's position in space and the relationship of its parts (Singer 1968). The proprioceptors, highly developed sense organs located in the muscles, tendons, and joints, compose a highly sensitive system of kinesthetic perception. They provide the brain with information about what the parts of the body are doing when executing a skill.

The need for and importance of kinesthesis for skill learning is universally acknowledged, and several physical educators (Roloff 1953; Scott 1955; Wiebe 1954; Young 1945) have tried to develop kinesthesis tests. These tests tend to have very low reliabilities and their value for general testing is questionable. Kinesthesis is an ability that is central to the execution of motor skill, but one that cannot be measured with accuracy.

SUMMARY

Physical educators have traditionally accepted the notion of generality and believe that a test or group of tests are predictive of a wide range of motor skills. The theory of specificity of motor skill acquisition was largely responsible for showing that motor ability and motor educability tests lacked validity. The age-height-weight classification indexes were found to have limited value because the addition of height and weight to age fails to improve prediction power. The theory of basic physical abilities does provide a theoretically sound base for generality testing. This theory is especially useful for use with athletes and preemployment testing.

Researchers have identified three basic motor performance abilities—muscular strength, muscular power, and endurance—and three basic movement patterns—running, jumping, and throwing. Several different tests are available to measure each ability. Although tests can be used for general evaluation, they are especially useful for identifying students with athletic potential.

The assessment of flexibility, balance, and kinesthesis is a difficult problem. Flexibility is not a general factor; rather it is task-specific, and different types are needed to perform different motor tasks. Balance has been thought to consist of two basic types: dynamic and static. However, research suggests that several additional types of balance also exist. Kinesthesis is the ability to perceive the body's position in space and the relationship of its parts. The reliability of kinesthetic tests tend to be low, making this trait difficult to measure.

FORMATIVE EVALUATION OF OBJECTIVES

Objective 1   Describe the tests historically used to measure generality.

1. Summarize the traditional procedures used to measure the generality of motor performance.
2. Describe the differences between motor educability and general motor ability.
3. What effect did Henry's memory-drum theory have on the generality concept?

Objective 2   Define and differentiate between basic physical abilities and a motor skill.

1. Using Fleishman's definition, distinguish between a basic ability and motor skill.
2. The terms *ability* and *skill* are often used interchangeably. Describe the essential difference between the two.
3. Could a basic ability be considered a measure of generality?

Objective 3   Apply the theory of basic physical abilities to the evaluation of athletes.

1. In evaluating different groups of athletes (for example, gymnasts and basketball players), would you use the same basic abilities?
2. Outline the steps a teacher or coach could follow to develop a test for athletes.

Objective 4 Identify basic physical abilities and tests for their valid measurement.

The text provides a system for classifying basic abilities and tests that measure each ability. Summarize the general characteristics of each basic ability and list one test that measures each.

Objective 5 Construct a test battery that can be used to evaluate athletes.

Develop a five-item motor performance battery that includes tests of different basic abilities. Use tests that are feasible for mass testing.

ADDITIONAL LEARNING ACTIVITIES

1. Summarize the research supporting the specificity of motor skill learning. Pay close attention to the procedures used by the researcher to conclude specificity or generality.

2. Select a sport and identify the basic abilities demanded by it. Using Fleishman's theory of basic abilities, develop a test battery that could be used to evaluate athletes.

3. A test can be made more reliable, valid, and feasible for mass use by improving the procedures used to administer it. For example, some have constructed inexpensive devices to measure balance, vertical jumping, and push-ups. Try to develop equipment that would improve the testing of some basic ability.

4. Are absolute endurance and 1-RM really highly correlated? If you have access to weight lifting equipment, devise tests that measure both. Administer the tests to a group of students and determine if the 1-RM score is correlated with the absolute endurance score.

5. Gain testing experience by using some of the tests listed in this chapter and administer the tests to a group of students. Determine how reliable your testing methods are.

BIBLIOGRAPHY

AAHPERD. 1976. *Youth Fitness Test Manual.* Washington, D.C.

AAHPERD. 1980. *Health Related Physical Fitness Manual.* Washington, D.C.

Barlow, D. A. 1970. "Relation Between Power and Selected Variables in the Vertical Jump." In *Selected Topics on Biomechanics,* ed. J. M. Cooper, 233–41. Chicago, Ill.: Athletic Institute.

Barrow, H. M. 1954. "Test of Motor Ability for College Men." *Research Quarterly* 25: 253–60.

Baumgartner, T. A. 1978. "Modified Pull-up Test." *Research Quarterly* 49:80–84.

Baumgartner, T. A. et al. 1984. "Equipment Improvements and Additional Norms for the Modified Pull-Up Test." *Research Quarterly for Exercise and Sport* 55:64–68.

Baumgartner, T. A., and A. S. Jackson. 1970. "Measurement Schedules for Tests of Motor Performance." *Research Quarterly* 41:10–14.

Baumgartner, T. A., and S. Wood. 1984. "Development of Shoulder-Girdle Strength-Endurance in Elementary Children." *Research Quarterly for Exercise and Sport* 55:169–171.

Baumgartner, T. A., and M. A. Zuidema. 1972. "Factor Analysis of Physical Fitness Tests." *Research Quarterly* 43:443–50.

Bass, R. I. 1939. "An Analysis of the Components of Tests of Semicircular Canal Function and Static and Dynamic Balance." *Research Quarterly* 2:33–52.

Brace, D. K. 1927. *Measuring Motor Ability.* New York: Barnes.

Carpenter, A. 1942. "The Measurements of General Motor Capacity and General Motor Ability in the First Three Grades." *Research Quarterly* 13:444–46.

Clarke, H. H. 1967. *Application of Measurement to Health and Physical Education.* 4th ed. Englewood Cliffs, N.J.: Prentice-Hall.

Clarke, H. H. 1948. "Objective Strength Tests of Affected Muscle Groups Involved in Orthopedic Disabilities." *Research Quarterly* 19:118–47.

Considine, W. J. 1970. "A Validity Analysis of Selected Leg Power Tests Utilizing a Force Platform." In *Selected Topics on Biomechanics,* ed. J. M. Cooper, 243–50. Chicago, Ill.: Athletic Institute.

Cumbee, F. Z., and C. W. Harris. 1953. "The Composite Criterion and Its Relation to Factor Analysis." *Research Quarterly* 24:127–34.

deVries, H. A. 1980. *Physiology of Exercise for Physical Education and Athletics.* Dubuque, Iowa: W. C. Brown.

Disch, J. 1973. "A Factor Analysis of Selected Test for Speed of Body Movement." P.E.D. dissertation, Indiana University.

Disch, J. G. et al. 1977. "The Construction and Analysis of a Test Related to Volleyball Playing Capacity in Females." Mimeographed. Houston, Tx.: Rice University.

Eckert, H. M. 1965. "A Concept of Force-Energy in Human Movement." *Journal of American Physical Therapy Association* 45:213–18.

Espenschade, A. S. 1963. "Restudy of Relationships Between Physical Performances of School Children and Age, Height, and Weight." *Research Quarterly* 34:144–53.

Fleishman, E. A. 1956. "Psychomotor Selection Tests: Research and Application in the U.S. Air Force." *Personnel Psychology* 9:449–67.

Fleishman, E. A. 1964. *The Structure and Measurement of Physical Fitness.* Englewood Cliffs, N.J.: Prentice-Hall.

Gire, E., and A. Espenschade. 1942. "The Relationship Between Measure of Motor Educability and Learning of Specific Motor Skills." *Research Quarterly* 13:43–56.

Glencross, D. J. 1966. "The Nature of the Vertical Jump Test and the Standing Broad Jump Test." *Research Quarterly* 37:353–59.

Golding, L. A., C. R. Meyers, and W. E. Sinning. 1982. *The Y's Way to Physical Fitness.* 2d ed. Chicago, Ill.: National Board of YMCA.

Gray, R. K. 1962. "Relationship Between Leg Speed and Leg Power." *Research Quarterly* 33:395–400.

Gross, E., and J. A. Casciani. 1962. "Value of Age, Height and Weight as a Classification Device for Secondary School Students in the Seven AAHPER Youth Fitness Test." *Research Quarterly* 33:51–58.

Gross, E. et al. 1956. "Relationship Between Two Motor Educability Tests, A Strength Test, and Wrestling Ability After Eight Weeks' Instruction." *Research Quarterly* 27:395–402.

Harris, C. W., and M. R. Liba. 1965. *Component, Image and Factor Analysis of Tests of Intellect and of Motor Performance.* U.S. Department of Health Education and Welfare, Office of Education Cooperative Research Project No. S–192–64.

Harris, M. L. 1969. "A Factor Analytic Study of Flexibility." *Research Quarterly* 40:62–70.

Henry, F. M. 1956. "Coordination and Motor Learning." In 59th *Proceedings* Annual College Physical Education Association, 68–75.

Henry, F. M. 1958. "Specificity vs. Generality in Learning Motor Skills." In 61st Annual *Proceedings* College Physical Education Association, 126–28.

Jackson, Allen et al. 1982. "Baumgartner's Modified Pull-Up Test for Male and Female Elementary School Aged Children." *Research Quarterly for Exercise and Sport* 53:163–64.

Jackson, Allen W., and D. J. Gibson. 1984. "The Measurement of Bench Press and Leg Extension Strength in College Age Females: Controlling for Individual Difference in Body Weight." Paper presented at 1984 AAHPERD Convention, Anaheim, Calif.

Jackson, A. S. 1971. "Factor Analysis of Selected Muscular Strength and Motor Performance Test." *Research Quarterly* 42:164–72.

Jackson, A. S. 1985a. "Validity of Isometric Strength Tests for Predicting Performance in Production and Drilling Facilities." Employment Services, Shell Oil Company, Houston, Tx.

Jackson, A. S. 1985b. "Validity of Isometric Strength Tests for Predicting Performance of Valve Turning Endurance." Employment Services, Shell Oil Company, Houston, Tx.

Jackson, A. S., and T. A. Baumgartner. 1969. "Measurement Schedules of Sprint Running." *Research Quarterly* 40:708–11.

Jackson, A. S., and R. J. Frankiewicz. 1975. "Factorial Expressions of Muscular Strength." *Research Quarterly* 46:206–17.

Jackson, A. S., and H. G. Osburn. 1983. "Validity of Isometric Strength Tests for Predicting Performance in Underground Coal Mining Tasks." Employment Services, Shell Oil Company, Houston, Tx.

Jackson, A. S., and L. Smith. 1974. "The Validation of an Evaluation System for Weight Training." Paper presented at AAHPER Convention, Anaheim, Calif.

Johnson, G. B. 1932. "Physical Skill Tests for Sectioning Classes into Homogeneous Units." *Research Quarterly* 3:128–34.

Kendall, F. P. 1965. "A Criticism of Current Tests and Exercises for Physical Fitness." *Journal of American Physical Therapy Association* 45:187–97.

Keyserling, W. M. et al. 1980(a). "Isometric Strength Testing as a Means of Controlling Medical Incidents on Strenuous Jobs." *Journal of Occupational Medicine* 22:332–36.

Keyserling, W. M. et al. 1980(b). "Establishing an Industrial Strength Testing Program," *American Industrial Hygiene Association Journal* 41:730–36.

Kraus, H., and R. P. Hirschland. 1954. "Minimum Muscular Fitness Tests in School Children." *Research Quarterly* 125:178–88.

Kraus, H., and W. Raab. 1961. *Hypokinetic Disease.* Springfield, Ill.: Thomas.

Laughery, K. R. et al. 1985. "Physical Abilities and Performance Tests for Coal Miner Jobs." From the Center of Applied Psychological Services, Rice University, Houston, Tx.

Laughery, K. R., and A. S. Jackson. 1984. "Pre-Employment Physical Test Development for Roustabout Jobs on Offshore Production Facilities." Kerr McGee Corp., Lafayette, La.

Larson, L. A., and R. D. Yocom. 1951. *Measurement and Evaluation in Physical, Health, and Recreation Education.* St. Louis, Mo.: Mosby.

Leighton, J. 1955. "An Instrument and Technique for the Measurement of Range of Joint Motion." *Archives of Physical Medicine* 36:571–78.

Liba, M. R. 1967. "Factor Analysis of Strength Variables." *Research Quarterly* 38:649–62.

Margaria, R., et al. 1966. "Measurement of Muscular Power (Anaerobic) in Man." *Journal of Applied Physiology* 21:1662–64.

Mathews, D. K. 1978. *Measurement in Physical Education.* 3d ed. Philadelphia, Pa.: Saunders.

Mathews, D. K., and E. L. Fox 1971. *The Physiological Basis of Physical Education and Athletics.* Philadelphia, Pa.: Saunders.

McCloy, C. H. 1932. *The Measurement of Athletic Power.* New York: Barnes.

McCloy, C. H., and N. D. Young. 1954. *Test and Measurements in Health and Physical Education.* New York: Appleton-Century-Crofts.

Metheny, E. 1938. "Studies of the Johnson Test as a Test of Motor Educability." *Research Quarterly* 9:105–14.

Pollock, M. L., et al. 1978. "Characteristics of Elite Class Distance Runners." *Annals of New York Academy of Sciences* 301:278–410.

Roloff, L. L. 1953. "Kinesthesis in Relation to the Learning of Selected Motor Skills." *Research Quarterly* 24:210–17.

Safrit, M. J. 1966. *The Structure of Gross Motor Skill Patterns.* U.S. Department of Health, Education and Welfare, Office of Education Cooperative Research Project No. S–397.

Sargent, D. A. 1921. "The Physical Test of Man." *American Physical Education Review* 26 (April):188–94.

Scott, M. G. 1939. "The Assessment of Motor Abilities of College Women, Through Objective Test." *Research Quarterly* 10:63–89.

Scott, M. G. 1955. "Test of Kinesthesis." *Research Quarterly* 26:324–41.

Singer, R. N. 1968. *Motor Learning and Human Performance.* New York: Macmillan.

Snook, S. H., and V. M. Ciriello. "Maximum Weights and Work Loads Acceptable to Female Workers." *Journal of Occupational Medicine* 16:527–34.

Snook, S. H. et al. 1970. "Maximum Weights and Work Loads Acceptable to Male Industrial Workers." *American Industrial Hygiene Association Journal* 31:579–86.

Start, K. B. et al. 1966. "A Factorial Investigation of Power, Speed, Isometric Strength, and Anthropometric Measures in the Lower Limb." *Research Quarterly* 37:553–58.

Texas Governor's Commission on Physical Fitness. 1986. *Texas Youth Fitness Test.* Austin, Tx.

Texas Governor's Commission on Physical Fitness. 1973. *Physical Fitness-Motor Ability Test.* Austin, Tx.

Wells, K. F. 1971. *Kinesiology.* 5th ed. Philadelphia, Pa.: Saunders.

Wiebe, V. R. 1954. "A Study of Test of Kinesthesis." *Research Quarterly* 25:222–27.

Wilmore, J. H. 1976. *Athletic Training and Physical Fitness.* Boston, Mass.: Allyn and Bacon.

Young, O. G. 1945. "A Study of Kinesthesis in Relation to Selected Movements." *Research Quarterly* 16:277–87.

Zuidema, M. A., and T. A. Baumgartner. 1974. "Second Factor Analysis Study of Physical Fitness Test." *Research Quarterly* 45:247–56.

Evaluating Adult Fitness

8

Contents

Key Words

Objectives

The methods used to evaluate adult and youth fitness differ. The focus of this chapter is adult fitness. The methods for measuring physical fitness of public school children are covered in chapter 9. Adult exercise testing takes place in a variety of places including medical or university laboratories, YMCA's, and private or corporate fitness centers. Cardiorespiratory endurance or aerobic fitness and body composition are the primary components of adult fitness. Aerobic exercise is the recommended exercise mode for health promotion. Aerobic endurance and body composition measurements are used to prescribe scientifically sound individualized exercise programs and these tests are used to gauge progress and adjust an exercise program. Exercise specialists typically assume responsibility for the testing and exercise prescription.

The purpose of this chapter is to outline the tests used to evaluate adult fitness. This requires an integration of measurement theory with exercise physiology. To fully achieve the objectives of this chapter, you should have a sound understanding of exercise physiology.

After reading chapter 8, you should be able to:

1. Identify the maximal and submaximal tests that are used to measure $\dot{V}O_2$ Max.
2. Calculate $\dot{V}O_2$ Max from: (A) maximal treadmill time; and (B) submaximal work using the single and multi-stage models.
3. Identify maximal and submaximal treadmill protocols.
4. Identify bicycle ergometer submaximal protocols.
5. Identify the methods used to measure body composition.
6. Calculate body density and percent body fat from generalized skinfold equations.
7. Calculate desired weight for various levels of desired percent body fat.
8. Identify the items of the YMCA test.
9. Identify computer methods that can be used to evaluate adult fitness.

INTRODUCTION

Data presented in chapter 1 shows that sedentary living and obesity are related to cardiovascular health. Aerobic exercise is the most efficient form of exercise for developing cardiorespiratory fitness and controlling body weight. In this chapter we discuss the general measurement procedures used to measure cardiorespiratory endurance and body composition of adults.

CARDIORESPIRATORY ENDURANCE

Cardiorespiratory endurance depends on several factors: efficient lungs, heart, and blood vessels; the quality and quantity of blood (red blood count, volume); and the cellular components that help the body utilize oxygen during exercise. Because an individual's ability to utilize oxygen during exhaustive work depends on these factors, maximal oxygen uptake $\dot{V}O_2$ Max—the maximal rate at which oxygen can be used—is an accepted test of cardiorespiratory endurance and an indicator of subsequent exercise ability (ACSM 1980).[1] In fact, Åstrand and Rodahl (1970) consider it to be the best index of physical fitness:

> During prolonged heavy physical work, the individual's performance capacity depends largely upon his ability to take up, transport, and deliver oxygen to working muscle. Subsequently, the maximal oxygen uptake is probably the best laboratory measure of a person's physical fitness, providing the definition of physical fitness is restricted to the capacity of the individual for prolonged heavy work (1970, p. 314).

$\dot{V}O_2$ Max can be determined from either maximal or submaximal work. At maximal work, $\dot{V}O_2$ is measured directly from expired gases or estimated from work intensity. $\dot{V}O_2$ Max can be estimated from submaximal treadmill and cycle ergometer

---

1. The terms maximal aerobic power, maximal aerobic capacity, maximal oxygen uptake or consumption, and $\dot{V}O_2$ Max are used interchangeably.

work and heart rate response to the exercise. This chapter outlines methods of measuring $\dot{V}O_2$ Max from maximal and submaximal exercise on a treadmill and bicycle ergometer.

Essential Definitions

$\dot{V}O_2$ **Max** is the maximal volume of oxygen one can consume during exhausting work and is measured by slowly and systematically increasing work intensity until exhaustion is reached. Åstrand and Rodahl (1970) report a linear increase in oxygen uptake with a linear increase in the workload. As the workload increases the exercising muscle requires more oxygen. You can see this easily when you walk up a hill; as the hill gets steeper (increased workload), your heart rate and breathing rates increase (increased oxygen uptake)—your body needs and uses more oxygen. The workload is increased gradually (for example, the treadmill slope may incline an additional degree per minute) until the individual is unable to continue. The tester collects and analyzes the oxygen utilized at various workloads. $\dot{V}O_2$ Max is that point at which the increased workload is not associated with increased oxygen uptake, as shown in figure 8.1.

Oxygen uptake is measured in liters per minute ($1 \cdot min^{-1}$) or milliliters per min ($ml \cdot min^{-1}$). Because heavier people normally have more muscle mass for oxygen utilization, oxygen uptake is divided by body weight in kilograms (kg) and expressed in milliliters per kilogram body weight per minute ($ml \cdot kg^{-1} \cdot min^{-1}$). Another method of scoring maximal oxygen uptake is in **METs,** defined as the amount of oxygen used when at rest. For a human, one MET is defined as a $\dot{V}O_2$ of $3.5\ ml \cdot kg^{-1} \cdot min^{-1}$. Thus, one just needs to divide $\dot{V}O_2$ ($ml \cdot kg^{-1} \cdot min^{-1}$) by 3.5 to obtain METs.

To illustrate, assume a 160 pound person was tested and the $\dot{V}O_2$ Max was 2.375 $1 \cdot min^{-1}$. First, let's convert to $ml \cdot min^{-1}$. This is accomplished by multiplying $1 \cdot min^{-1}$ by 1000.

$$\dot{V}O_2 \text{ Max } (ml \cdot min^{-1}) = 2.375 \times 1000 = 2375$$

Next, convert weight in pounds to kilograms (kg). This is accomplished by multiplying weight (lb) by 0.4536.

$$\text{Weight} = 160 \times 0.4536 = 72.6 \text{ kg}$$

To obtain $\dot{V}O_2$ Max ($ml \cdot kg^{-1} \cdot min^{-1}$) divide $\dot{V}O_2$ $ml \cdot min^{-1}$ by weight (kg).

$$\dot{V}O_2 \text{ Max } (ml \cdot kg^{-1} \cdot min^{-1}) = \frac{2375}{72.6} = 32.7.$$

To calculate METs, divide by 3.5.

$$\text{METs} = \frac{32.7}{3.5} = 9.34.$$

Figure 8.1 Relationship of oxygen uptake to workload. $\dot{V}O_2$ Max is the point where an increase in workload does not produce an increase in the volume of oxygen used. This is the point of physical exhaustion. (Graph by MacASJ)

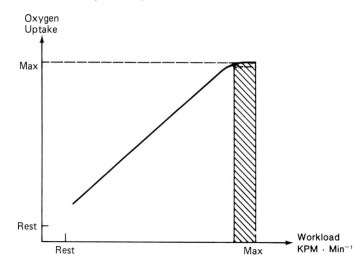

Evaluating Cardiorespiratory Endurance

$\dot{V}O_2$ Max is used to assess the physical working capacity of athletes and individuals engaged in fitness programs. The standards used for athletes would not be suitable for evaluating the fitness level of nonathletic adults. Provided in figure 8.3 are average oxygen uptake values for elite runners and average men of different ages. High level endurance athletes (e.g., cross-country skiers, and long distance runners) have the highest, exceeding $70 \ ml \cdot kg^{-1} \cdot min^{-1}$.

Most of us have neither the ability nor the motivation to become world class endurance athletes, but a suitable level of cardiorespiratory endurance is needed for health and fitness. $\dot{V}O_2$ Max is related to age, steadily increasing during childhood, reaching a peak at about age 20, after which it slowly declines. The aerobic capacity of females is about 10% to 20% less than males (Åstrand and Rodahl 1977). For these reasons, the standards for evaluating $\dot{V}O_2$ Max of healthy adults (table 8.1) need to be adjusted for age and gender.

Measuring $\dot{V}O_2$ Max

Cardiorespiratory endurance may be measured by several methods, but each method involves: (1) standardizing work intensity; and (2) measuring the individual's physiological response to the work. Motor-driven treadmills and bicycle ergometers (see figure 8.2) are the most common and accepted methods of standardizing work. $\dot{V}O_2$ Max can be measured from either maximal or submaximal work.

Figure 8.2 Treadmill and bicycle ergometer. (a) Measuring maximal oxygen uptake on a motor-driven treadmill. Dr. W. Squires, exercise physiologist at the Cardiopulmonary Laboratory at NASA's Johnson Space Center, supervises the stress test of NASA scientist Dr. Stan Fink. The computerized system determines the amount of oxygen uptake from the expired air. (b) Bicycle ergometer test.

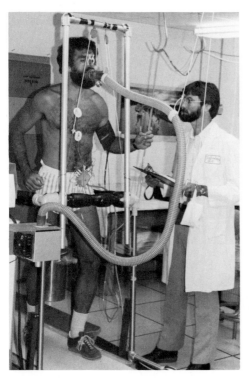

(a)   (b)

Treadmill Exercise

The work intensity of a treadmill is intensified by: (1) increasing treadmill speed; (2) increasing the grade of the treadmill; or (3) increasing both the speed and grade. Several test protocols have been developed to standardize work intensity.

Treadmill Protocols.   Provided in figure 8.4 is a graphic representation of the speed and elevation for the two most common treadmill protocols. Of all treadmill tests administered in the United States, it has been estimated that about 71% follow the Bruce protocol and about 10% use the Balke (Pollock, Wilmore and Fox 1984). It has been shown with men and women (Pollock, Bohannon, Cooper et al. 1976) that these protocols produce similar $\dot{V}O_2$ Max values, but the rate or time required to reach maximum will vary. This is shown in figure 8.5. It takes longer to reach $\dot{V}O_2$ Max with the Balke protocol than with the Bruce.

Table 8.1
Standards for Evaluating Cardiorespiratory Fitness.

| AGE | LOW | $\dot{V}O_2$ MAX (ml·kg^{-1}·min^{-1}) | | GOOD | HIGH |
		FAIR	AVERAGE		
		Women			
20–29	<24	24–30	31–37	38–48	≥49
30–39	<20	20–27	28–33	34–44	≥45
40–49	<17	17–23	24–30	31–41	≥42
50–59	<15	15–20	21–27	28–37	≥38
60–69	<13	13–17	18–23	24–34	≥35
		Men			
20–29	<25	25–33	34–42	43–52	≥53
30–39	<23	23–30	31–38	39–48	≥49
40–49	<20	20–26	27–35	36–44	≥45
50–59	<18	18–24	25–33	34–42	≥43
60–69	<16	16–22	23–30	31–40	≥41

Table developed from data from the Preventive Medicine Center, Palo Alto, California and from a survey of published sources (AHA 1972).

Figure 8.3 Average values of elite male distance runners by age group, and normative averages for the age groups. (The data for the runners taken from Pollock, M. L. 1977. "Submaximal and Maximal Working Capacity of Elite Distance Runners-Part 1: Cardiorespiratory Aspects." *Annals of New York Academy of Science* 301:310–322 and Pollock, M. L., C. Foster, K. Knapp, et al. "Effect of Age, Training and Competition on Aerobic Capacity and Body Composition of Master's Athletes." Submitted for publication. Graph by MacASJ)

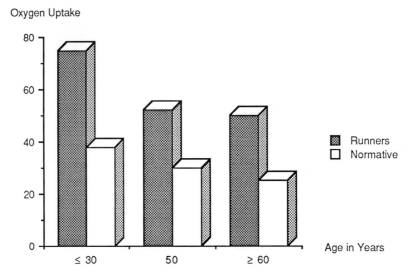

Figure 8.4 The Bruce and Balke Treadmill protocols are most often used to measure VO_2 Max. (Figure adapted from Pollock, M. L., D. H. Schmidt, A. S. Jackson, 1980. "Measurement of Cardiorespiratory Fitness and Body Composition in the Clinical Setting." *Comprehensive Therapy.* 6:12–24. Graphics by MacASJ)

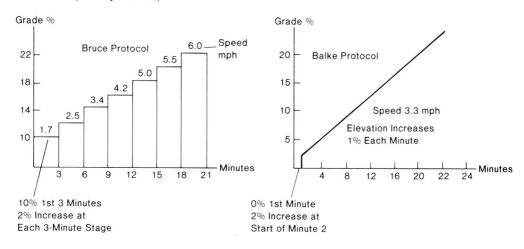

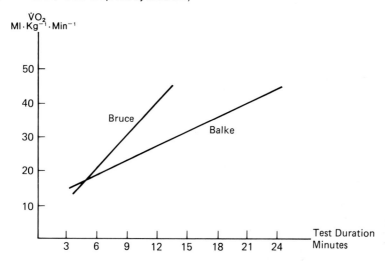

Figure 8.5 Rate of increase in oxygen uptake for the Bruce and Balke treadmill protocols. Graph is adapted from data for 51 men, aged 25 to 55 years of age. (Pollock, M. L., R. L. Bohannon, K. H. Cooper, et al., 1976. "A Comparative Analysis of Four Protocols for Maximal Treadmill Stress Testing." *American Heart Journal* 92:39–46.) Similar trends have been found for women. (Pollock, M. L. et al., 1982. Graphics by MacASJ)

The Balke protocol (Balke 1963) is at a constant speed of 3.4 mph and work is increased by raising grade 1% every minute. A major disadvantage of this protocol is that one minute is not long enough for the subject to reach a submaximal steady state. Typically, one must exercise at a constant submaximal work intensity for about three minutes in order to reach a steady state. This is a major requirement for estimating $\dot{V}O_2$ Max from submaximal work, which is illustrated later in this chapter.

Energy Cost of Submaximal Treadmill Work. The calculation of work intensity for submaximal treadmill exercise is based on treadmill speed and elevation. Equations (ACSM 1980; Pandolf, Givoni and Goldman 1977; Ross and Jackson 1986) have been published to quantify exercise for walking and jogging at various speeds and elevations. The ACSM (1980) and total work (TW) equations (Ross and Jackson 1986) are provided in table 8.2. The energy expenditure for submaximal walking or jogging speed is used to estimate $\dot{V}O_2$ Max from submaximal exercise and this is shown in a later section of this chapter.

The accuracy of several walking equations was evaluated with a large sample of men (Ross and Jackson 1986). All equations were accurate, but the TW model was slightly more accurate and much easier to use. The TW model is illustrated next. Assume one walks on a treadmill at 3.5 mph at 8% grade. The exercise intensity would be:

$$\dot{V}O_2 = [75 + (6 \times 8)] \times \left[\frac{3.5}{60}\right] \times 3.5$$
$$= (75 + 48) \times (0.0583 \times 3.5)$$
$$= 123 \times 0.0583 \times 3.5 = 25.1 \ (\text{ml} \cdot \text{kg}^{-1} \cdot \text{min}^{-1})$$

More energy is needed to jog one mile than to walk a mile. For this reason, the walking equations are not appropriate for treadmill speeds that require jogging, for example after minute 9 of the Bruce protocol. Presented in table 8.2 is the equation published by ACSM (1980) which can be used to estimate the energy cost for jogging on the treadmill at a submaximal steady state. To illustrate, assume you jog at 6 mph at 5% grade. First jogging speed in meters per minute ($\text{m} \cdot \text{min}^{-1}$) must be found. Jogging at 6 mph is equal to jogging at a speed of 160.9 $\text{m} \cdot \text{min}^{-1}$. The intensity is:

$$\dot{V}O_2 = [(160.9 \times 0.2) + 3.5] + (160.9 \times 1.8 \times 0.05)$$
$$= (35.68 + 14.48) = 50.1 \ (\text{ml} \cdot \text{kg}^{-1} \cdot \text{min}^{-1})$$

Bicycle Ergometer Exercise

Mechanical and electronically braked **bicycle ergometers** are used to measure $\dot{V}O_2$ Max. Work intensity on the mechanically braked bike is increased by: (1) placing more resistance on the flywheel; (2) increasing pedaling speed; or (3) both. The most common method is to have the subject pedal at a constant rate (e.g., 50 rpm) and increase work by placing more resistance on the flywheel. Several different ergometers are available for testing, and methods for calculating work varies among bikes. NASA scientists used an electronically braked computer controlled bike on extended space flights (see figure 8.6). The bike adjusted the resistance to account for changes in pedaling rate and heart rate.

Table 8.2

Submaximal $\dot{V}O_2$ (ml·kg^{-1}·min^{-1}) for Walking and Jogging at Various Speeds and Elevations.

MODEL	MODE	EQUATION
ACSM	Walking	$\dot{V}O_2 = (S_w \times 0.1) + \left(1.8 \times S_w \times \left(\dfrac{\%}{100}\right)\right)$
Total work	Walking	$\dot{V}O_2 = \left((75 + (6 \times \%)) \times \left(\dfrac{mph}{60}\right)\right) \times 3.5$
ACSM	Jogging	$\dot{V}O_2 = (S_J \times 0.2) + \left(1.8 \times S_J \times \left(\dfrac{\%}{100}\right)\right)$

Key: S_w walking speed in meters per minute. S_J jogging speed in meters per minute. % is percent elevation. mph is speed in miles per hour.

Figure 8.6 Bicycle ergometer used by NASA to evaluate the aerobic capacity of astronauts. This ergometer, computer-controlled to regulate the work load, was used on Skylab missions to evaluate cardiorespiratory functions and to provide exercise for astronauts during long space flights: (a) the ergometer, and (b) the bicycle in use.

(a)

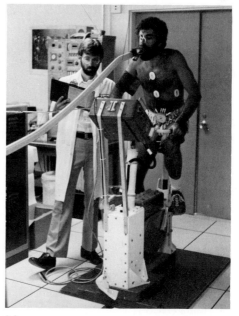

(b)

Quantifying Cycle Exercise. Mechanical work on a bicycle ergometer is regulated by the resistance placed on the flywheel and pedaling rate per minute (rpm). **Kiloponds (kp)**[2] is the unit used to quantify the resistance. A kilopond is another term for kilogram (i.e., 2.2 pounds) and is the amount of resistance placed on the flywheel. For some ergometers, such as a Monarch, resistance is regulated by a weight. For the Schwinn Biodyne as a second example, resistance is regulated with a braking system. The Monarch and Schwinn ergometers have been shown to accurately quantify work and are suitable for testing (Wilmore, Constable, Stanforth et al. 1982).

The number of revolutions completed per minute (rpm) is the second factor used to calculate work intensity. Each turn of the flywheel represents a distance traveled. Work intensity on a bicycle ergometer is quantified by **kpm·min^{-1} (kilopound meters per minute)** or Watts. The basic formula is:

$$\textbf{kpm}\cdot\textbf{min}^{-1} = \text{kp} \times \text{D} \times \text{rpm},$$

where, kp is the resistance on the flywheel in kilograms, D is the distance traveled with each revolution of the pedals, and rpm is the number of revolutions completed per minute.

Some ergometers express work in Watts. One **Watt** is equal to 6 kpm·min^{-1} [3]; thus, one may easily make conversions by:

$$\text{kpm}\cdot\text{min}^{-1} = 6 \times \text{Watts}$$
$$\text{Watts} = \frac{\text{kpm}\cdot\text{min}^{-1}}{6}$$

The Monarch bicycle ergometer is one of the most popular testing ergometers. Work in kp is regulated with a calibrated weight. A distance of 6 meters is traveled with each revolution of the pedal. To illustrate the calculation of work in kpm·min^{-1}, assume a subject pedals at 50 revolutions per minute at a setting of 3 kp. The work intensity would be:

$$\text{kpm}\cdot\text{min}^{-1} = 3 \times 6 \times 50 = 900$$
$$\text{Watts} = \frac{900}{6} = 150$$

The Schwinn Biodyne ergometer, another popular testing cycle, automatically calculates kpm·min^{-1} from pedaling rate and the resistance placed on the flywheel by the braking system. A gauge mounted on the handle bars provides a scale for calculating work (kpm·min^{-1}) for selected pedaling rates (rpm).

Once work is quantified in kpm·min^{-1}, $\dot{V}O_2$ (ml·min^{-1}) can be determined. The formula (ACSM 1980) is:

$$\dot{V}O_2 \text{ (ml}\cdot\text{min}^{-1}) = (2 \times \text{kpm}\cdot\text{min}^{-1}) + 300,$$

---

2. A kilopond is equal to 2.2 pounds or a kilogram. Both terms have been used. For consistency the term kilopond will be used in this book.
3. The true conversion is 6.12 Watts (Åstrand and Rodahl 1977), but in common practice 6 is used.

Figure 8.7 The graph shows the linear relation between bicycle ergometer exercise in Watts, or kpm/min and $\dot{V}O_2$ (ml/min). $\dot{V}O_2 = (2 \times \text{kpm/min}) + 300$. (Graph by MacASJ)

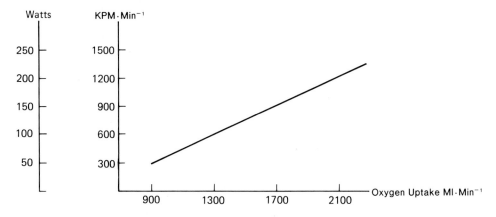

where 300 ml·min^{-1} of oxygen is used at rest and oxygen uptake increases by 2 ml·min^{-1} with each kpm·min^{-1} increase in exercise. To illustrate, assume one exercises at the workloads of 300 kpm·min^{-1} (50 Watts) and 900 kpm·min^{-1} (150 Watts). The oxygen uptake would be (see figure 8.7):

$$\dot{V}O_2 \ (\text{ml·min}^{-1}) = (2 \times 300) + 300 = 900$$
$$\dot{V}O_2 \ (\text{ml·min}^{-1}) = (2 \times 900) + 300 = 2100$$

Maintaining a steady pedaling rate is essential for bicycle ergometer tests. An electronic metronome can be used to regulate pedaling rate. A common rate is 50 rpm, but research has shown that power output efficiency varies little for rates between 50 and 80 rpm (Pollock, Wilmore and Fox 1984). Provided in table 8.3 is work intensity (kpm·min^{-1}, and $\dot{V}O_2$ ml·min^{-1}) for common pedaling rates and kp levels.

Table 8.3
Bicycle Ergometer Work Intensity in kpm·min^{-1} and $\dot{V}O_2$ ml·min^{-1} for Selected Resistance Levels and Pedaling Rates 50, 60, 70, and 80 Revolutions Per Minute.

	kpm·min^{-1}				$\dot{V}O_2$ ml·min^{-1*}			
kp	50	60	70	80	50	60	70	80
0.5	150	180	210	240	600	660	720	780
1.0	300	360	420	480	900	1020	1140	1260
1.5	450	540	630	720	1200	1380	1560	1740
2.0	600	720	840	960	1500	1740	1980	2220
2.5	750	900	1050	1200	1800	2100	2400	2700
3.0	900	1080	1260	1440	2100	2460	2820	3180
3.5	1050	1260	1470	1680	2400	2820	3240	3660
4.0	1200	1440	1680	1920	2700	3180	3660	4140
4.5	1350	1620	1890	2160	3000	3540	4080	4620
5.0	1500	1800	2100		3300	3900	4500	
5.5	1650	1980			3600	4260		
6.0	1800				3900			

*$\dot{V}O_2$ mm·min^{-1} = (2 × kpm·min^{-1}) + 300 (ACSM 1980)

Bicycle Ergometer Protocols. Unlike a treadmill, a standard method of increasing work intensity (e.g., the Bruce treadmill protocol) is not appropriate for general bicycle ergometer testing because people vary in leg strength and fitness level that affect heart rate response to ergometer exercise. For this reason, different initial work loads are recommended for men and women, and work intensity is increased at different rates based on the person's heart rate response. The procedures suggested by the YMCA (Golding, Meyers and Sinning 1982) are shown in figures 8.8 and 8.9. The suggested starting intensity is 150 kpm·min^{-1} (25 Watts) for women and 300 kpm·min^{-1} (50 Watts) for men. Åstrand and Rodahl (1977) suggest starting intensities of 450 to 600 kpm·min^{-1} (75 to 100 Watts) for women and 600 to 900 kpm·min^{-1} (100 to 150 Watts) for men; however, the level may need to be altered depending on the fitness level and leg strength of the subject being tested.

Treadmill vs. Bicycle Ergometer

The major advantages of a bicycle ergometer over a treadmill is that it is portable and less expensive. Additionally, upper body movement is minimal, making it easier to measure exercise heart rate and blood pressure. The major disadvantage of the cycle ergometer is that most Americans are not accustomed to bicycle riding and fail to reach their true maximum. Lower heart rate and $\dot{V}O_2$ values ranging from 5% to 25%, have been reported (Pollock, Wilmore and Fox 1984). For this reason, maximal cycle ergometer tests are not normally used if accurate estimates of $\dot{V}O_2$ Max or heart rate are needed.

Task specificity is an important criterion to consider when selecting a testing mode. For example, at the United States Olympic Training Center in Colorado Springs, special cycle ergometers and test protocols are used to measure $\dot{V}O_2$ Max of olympic cyclists. Specially constructed electronic ergometers were flown on NASA Skylab missions (see figure 8.6). Astronauts trained on the ergometer on earth and tested their aerobic capacity in space at zero gravity.

Methods of Measuring $\dot{V}O_2$ Max

$\dot{V}O_2$ Max can be determined from either maximal or submaximal work. At maximal work, it can be either measured directly from expired gases or estimated from treadmill workload. At submaximal work, the heart rate response to the given level of treadmill and cycle ergometer exercise is used to estimate $\dot{V}O_2$ Max. Single and multi-stage models can be used to estimate $\dot{V}O_2$ Max from submaximal work.

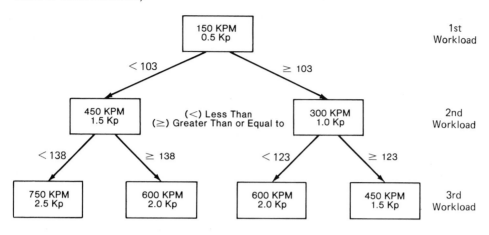

Figure 8.8 Guide to setting workloads for females on the bicycle ergometer. (Data from Golding, L. A., C. R. Meyers, W. E. Sinning, 1982. *The Y's Way to Physical Fitness.* Chicago, Ill.: National Board of YMCA 2d edition.)

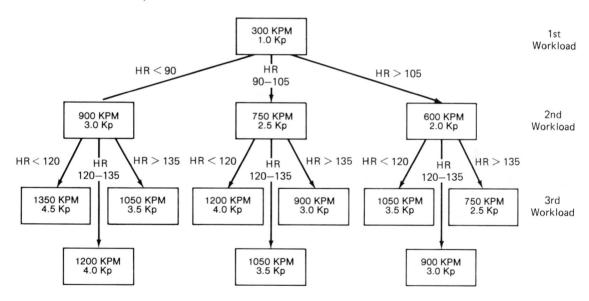

Figure 8.9 Guide to setting workloads for males on the bicycle ergometer. (Data from Golding, L. A., C. R. Meyers, W. E. Sinning, 1982. *The Y's Way to Physical Fitness.* Chicago, Ill.: National Board of YMCA 2d edition.)

Maximal Exercise Tests

The objective of a maximal test is to systematically increase work intensity until the subject reaches exhaustion. The most accurate method of measuring $\dot{V}O_2$ Max is the direct measurement of expired gases. At submaximal work loads, $\dot{V}O_2$ consumption increases at a linear rate with work intensity. $\dot{V}O_2$ Max is the point at which increases in work do not produce changes in $\dot{V}O_2$ consumption, or the point of physical exhaustion (see figure 8.1).

Measurement of Expired Gases. The most valid way to measure $\dot{V}O_2$ Max is the direct analysis of expired gases. Oxygen and carbon dioxide concentrations of room and expired air, and volume of air expired per minute are needed to measure $\dot{V}O_2$ Max. Standard methods are available for calculating $\dot{V}O_2$ consumption (Jones and Campbell 1982). The direct measurement of $\dot{V}O_2$ Max is expensive in terms of needed equipment and personnel; thus, this method is normally used just for research. However, with the advancement in microcomputer technology, several commercial systems are now available to expedite these measurements, as shown in chapter 1. For example, at NASA/Johnson Space Center in Houston, $\dot{V}O_2$ is measured when astronauts are tested. It is important to know an astronaut's true working capacity.

Estimating $\dot{V}O_2$ Max from Treadmill Time. $\dot{V}O_2$ Max can be measured from maximal treadmill or cycle ergometer work. Many people are not accustomed to riding a bicycle ergometer and find it difficult to reach their maximum; their legs fatigue prior to reaching maximal exercise. For this reason, maximum tests are more often administered on a treadmill.

Work systematically increases by time in a treadmill protocol; thus, the time it takes one to reach exhaustion is an index of maximum work capacity. The workloads for the Balke and Bruce protocols are shown in figure 8.4. Several valid regression equations have been published (Bruce, Kusumi and Hosmer 1973; Pollock, Bohannon, Cooper et al. 1976; Foster, Jackson, Pollock et al. 1984) that estimate $\dot{V}O_2$ Max ($ml \cdot kg^{-1} \cdot min^{-1}$) from maximal treadmill time. Since each treadmill protocol increases work at different rates, unique equations are needed for different protocols. The reported correlations between $\dot{V}O_2$ Max measure directly and maximal treadmill exercise is high, ranging from 0.88 to 0.97. The standard error of prediction is about $3\ ml \cdot kg^{-1} \cdot min^{-1}$. Table 8.4 lists $\dot{V}O_2$ Max from treadmill time for the Balke and Bruce protocols. It has been shown with the Bruce protocol that the $\dot{V}O_2$ Max of cardiac patients is slightly lower than healthy adults for the same max work treadmill time (Foster, Jackson, Pollock et al. 1984); therefore, different $\dot{V}O_2$ Max estimates are provided for these groups.

Submaximal Exercise Tests

Measuring $\dot{V}O_2$ Max from maximal work is physically exhausting and can be dangerous for individuals with cardiovascular disease. For these reasons, $\dot{V}O_2$ Max is often estimated from submaximal work. Either treadmill or cycle ergometer tests may be used.

Oxygen uptake at rest and exercise is defined as follows:

$$\dot{V}O_2 = \text{Cardiac Output} \times \text{A} \cdot \text{V Oxygen difference}$$

Table 8.4

Prediction of $\dot{V}O_2$ Max ($ml \cdot kg^{-1} \cdot min^{-1}$) from Treadmill Time for the Balke and Bruce Protocols.

TIME IN MINUTES	BALKE PROTOCOL	BRUCE PROTOCOL CARDIAC	BRUCE PROTOCOL NORMAL
2		13.8	18.0
3	19.3	14.9	19.1
4	20.8	16.4	20.6
5	22.2	18.3	22.5
6	23.7	20.5	24.7
7	25.1	23.1	27.3
8	26.5	26.0	30.3
9	28.0	29.1	33.3
10	29.4	32.3	36.5
11	30.9	35.7	39.9
12	32.3	39.2	43.4
13	33.8	42.7	46.9
14	35.2	46.7	50.4
15	36.7	49.6	53.8
16	38.1	53.0	57.2
17	39.5	56.2	60.4
18	41.0	59.2	63.4
19	42.4	62.1	66.3
20	43.9	64.5	68.7
21	45.3	66.7	70.9
22	46.8		
23	48.2		
24	49.6		
25	51.1		
26	52.5		
27	54.0		
28	55.4		
29	56.9		
30	58.3		

Source: Balke-Pollock, Bohannon, Cooper, et. al 1976. Bruce-Foster, Jackson, Pollock, et. al 1984.

where, cardiac output is the product of heart rate and stroke volume and A·V is the difference in oxygen concentration of arterial and venous blood (Åstrand and Rodahl 1977; Froelicher 1983; Jones and Campbell 1982). From rest to exercise, stroke volume and A-V difference increase slightly, whereas heart rate increases substantially. Therefore, the increase in oxygen uptake from rest to exercise is mainly due to the increase in heart rate that increases at a linear rate with work.

The measurement objective of submaximal tests is to define the slope of an individual's heart rate response to exercise and use the slope to estimate $\dot{V}O_2$ Max from submaximal readings. A less fit person's slope is steeper than for a fit person. This is shown in figure 8.10. $\dot{V}O_2$ Max may be estimated from several submaximal heart rates (multi-stage model) or a single reading (single stage model). Steady state heart rates between about 115 and 150 b·min should be reached (Golding, Meyers and Sinning 1982; Åstrand and Rodahl 1977).

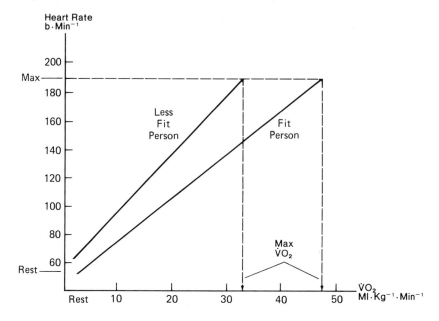

Figure 8.10 Slope in the rise in exercise heart rate with the increase in exercise. It is assumed that both have a Max heart rate of 190 b/min. Note the different slope in the heart rate-$\dot{V}O_2$ line. (Graph by MacASJ)

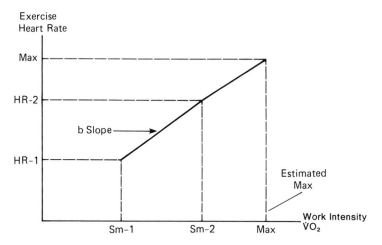

Figure 8.11 The multi-stage model estimates $\dot{V}O_2$ Max by measuring heart rate response to exercise at two or more submaximal levels. Based on the assumption that submaximal heart rate and $\dot{V}O_2$ are linearly related, $\dot{V}O_2$ Max is estimated by extending the line to maximal heart rate and projecting to $\dot{V}O_2$ Max. (Graph by MacASJ)

Multi-stage Model. The **multi-stage** model requires that heart rate and work be measured at two or more submaximal levels (Golding, Meyers and Sinning 1982). These data points are then used to project to maximal heart rate which is used to estimate $\dot{V}O_2$ Max. Submaximal heart rates between 115 and 150 b·min are recommended. This is shown in figure 8.11. The formula for the multi-stage model is:

$$\dot{V}O_2 \text{ Max} = SM\text{-}2 + b(\text{Max HR} - HR\text{-}2), \text{ where}$$
$$b = \left[\frac{(SM\text{-}2 - SM\text{-}1)}{(HR\text{-}2 - HR\text{-}1)}\right]$$

SM-1 and SM-2 are submaximal work ($\dot{V}O_2$) and may be expressed ml·min^{-1}, 1·min^{-1}, ml·kg^{-1}·min^{-1} or METs. For bicycle ergometer tests, $\dot{V}O_2$ is often expressed as 1·min^{-1} or ml·min^{-1}; whereas, for treadmills $\dot{V}O_2$ is expressed in METs or ml·kg^{-1}·min^{-1}. The factor "b" represents the slope of the line and is the change in $\dot{V}O_2$ per change in heart rate. Maximal heart rate can be either: (1) true maximal heart rate if known; or (2) estimated maximal heart rate. In practice, maximal heart rate is estimated by:

$$\text{Max HR} = 220 - \text{Age in years.}$$

The use of the multi-stage model can be illustrated by example. Assume, the heart rate responses at two levels of bicycle ergometer work were: 300 kpm·min^{-1}, 118 b·min^{-1}; and 900 kpm·min^{-1}, 145 b·min^{-1}. The $\dot{V}O_2$ for these two work levels is estimated to be 0.9 1·min^{-1} and 2.1 1·min^{-1} (ACSM 1980). The first step is to solve for "b."

$$b = \left[\frac{(2.1 - 0.9)}{(145 - 118)}\right] = \left(\frac{1.2}{27}\right) = 0.0444$$

The factor "b" is the slope and defines the rise in $\dot{V}O_2$ per change in heart rate. With each increased beat in heart rate, oxygen intake increases by 0.0444 1·min^{-1}. Assume, the person's age is 35 years and maximal heart rate is not known. $\dot{V}O_2$ Max (1·min^{-1}) would be estimated to be:

$$\dot{V}O_2 \text{ Max } (1\cdot\text{min}^{-1}) = 2.1 + [0.0444 \times (220 - 35 - 145)]$$
$$= 2.1 + 0.0444 \times 40$$
$$= 2.1 + 1.776$$
$$= 3.876$$

If the person's weight was 70 kg, $\dot{V}O_2$ Max (ml·kg^{-1}·min^{-1} and METs) would be:

$$\dot{V}O_2 \text{ } (\text{ml}\cdot\text{kg}^{-1}\cdot\text{min}^{-1}) = \left[\frac{(3.876 \times 1000)}{70}\right] = 55.37$$
$$\text{METs} = \frac{55.37}{3.5} = 15.82$$

The aerobic fitness for a 35-year-old male would be judged to be high (from table 8.1).

Single Stage Model. The **single stage** model uses one heart rate at a submaximal work load to estimate $\dot{V}O_2$ Max, and is based on the principle of a linear change in heart rate associated with increased work. This is the basis for the popular Åstrand-Rhyming nomogram (Åstrand and Rodahl 1977). The single stage model is not only easier to use, but it has also been shown to be as accurate as the double stage model (Mahar, Jackson, Ross et al. 1985). $\dot{V}O_2$ Max for males and females is calculated as follows (Shephard 1972):[4]

$$\text{Men:} \qquad \dot{V}O_2 \text{ Max} = \dot{V}O_{2(SM)} \times \left[\frac{(\text{Max HR} - 61)}{(\text{SM-HR} - 61)} \right],$$

$$\text{Women:} \quad \dot{V}O_2 \text{ Max} = \dot{V}O_{2(SM)} \times \left[\frac{(\text{Max HR} - 72)}{(\text{SM-HR} - 72)} \right],$$

where, SM-HR is the submaximal heart rate at the submaximal work load ($\dot{V}O_{2(SM)}$) which may be expressed in $ml \cdot min^{-1}$, $1 \cdot min^{-1}$, $ml \cdot kg^{-1} \cdot min^{-1}$ or METs.

If maximal heart rate is known, it should be used. Åstrand originally assumed that maximal heart rate was 195 $b \cdot min^{-1}$, but later published a method to correct the estimated $\dot{V}O_2$ Max to adjust for aging (Åstrand and Rodahl 1977). Recent research (Mahar, Jackson, Ross et al. 1985) showed that the standard formula of estimating maximal heart rate (Max HR $= 220 -$ age) was more accurate than the method recommended by Åstrand and Rodahl (1977).

Let's illustrate the single stage model by example. Assume a man and woman were tested on the Bruce treadmill protocol. At minute 6, the heart rate of a 38 year old woman was 135. At minute 3, the exercise heart rate of a 42 year old man was 148. $\dot{V}O_2$ Max (METs) for each will be calculated.

First, the TW model (table 8.2) is used to estimate the submaximal work load for minutes 3 (1.7 mph, 10% grade) and 6 (2.5 mph, 12% grade) of the Bruce protocol.

$$\text{Man:} \qquad \dot{V}O_2 = [(75 + (6 \times 10)] \times \left[\left(\frac{1.7}{60} \right) \right] \times 3.5$$
$$= 135 \times 0.0283 \times 3.5$$
$$= 13.4 \text{ ml} \cdot kg^{-1} \cdot min^{-1}$$

$$\text{Woman:} \quad \dot{V}O_2 = [(75 + (6 \times 12)] \times \left[\left(\frac{2.5}{60} \right) \right] \times 3.5$$
$$= 147 \times 0.0417 \times 3.5$$
$$= 21.4 \text{ ml} \cdot kg^{-1} \cdot min^{-1}$$

Next, the exercise intensity for submaximal work is used with the single stage model to estimate $\dot{V}O_2$ Max. For the man, with a submaximal heart rate of 148 $b \cdot min^{-1}$ after minute 3 on the Bruce protocol, $\dot{V}O_2$ Max is:

$$\dot{V}O_2 \text{ Max} = \frac{[13.4 \times (220 - 42 - 61)]}{(148 - 61)}$$
$$= 13.4 \times 1.344$$
$$= 18.0 \text{ ml} \cdot kg^{-1} \cdot min^{-1}$$

---

4. The basic equations were developed by R. J. Shepard by fitting the data from the Åstrand-Rhyming Nomogram. Personal communication by A. Jackson and R. J. Shepard at the 1986 ASCM Annual Meeting.

Next, for a woman with a heart rate of 135 b·min^{-1} after 6 minutes of the Bruce protocol, $\dot{V}O_2$ Max is:

$$\dot{V}O_2 \text{ Max} = \frac{[21.4 \times (220 - 38 - 72)]}{(135 - 72)}$$
$$= 21.4 \times 1.746$$
$$= 37.4 \text{ ml·kg}^{-1}\text{·min}^{-1}$$

Using table 8.1, the woman's fitness level would be judged to be good and the man's level would be low. If a bicycle ergometer was used, $\dot{V}O_2$ Max would have been calculated from submaximal heart rate and $\dot{V}O_2$ expressed as 1·min^{-1} or ml·min^{-1}.

Bicycle Ergometer Test Methods

The basic procedures to follow when administering bicycle ergometer tests are provided next. These are a summary of the procedures recommended for the YMCA fitness test (Golding, Meyers and Sinning 1982).

1. Adjust the seat height on the ergometer so that the knee is relatively straight on the downward stroke. The pedaling should be comfortable for the subject.
2. Use a metronome to help standardize the work. The recommended pedaling rates are between 50 to 80 rpm, with 50 rpm being the rate most often used.
3. The submaximal multi-stage YMCA Test provides excellent guidelines for increasing work to reach the desired heart rate zone in a safe, comfortable manner. These protocols are furnished in figures 8.8 and 8.9. The recommendation is to start men at a workload of 300 kpm (1 kp at 50 rpm) and women at 150 kpm (0.5 kp at 50 rpm). Each work stage lasts for three minutes and the increase in work for the next stage depends on the heart rate reached by a person at a given workload. The total length of the test is nine minutes.
4. The submaximal, single stage Åstrand protocol is 6 minutes in duration with the goal of reaching a steady state heart rate between 130 and 150 b·min^{-1}. If after 6 minutes, heart rate is between 130 and 150 b·min^{-1}, the test is ended, but if the pulse rate is below 130 b·min^{-1}, 300 kpm·min^{-1} should be added and the test continued for another 4 to 6 minutes (Åstrand and Rodahl 1977). The recommended starting load is 450 to 600 kpm·min^{-1} for women and 600 to 900 kpm·min^{-1} for men.
5. Heart rate is measured during the final 15 seconds of each minute. If possible, heart rate should be measured with electronic equipment; however, with trained technicians heart rate for bicycle ergometer exercise can be measured with reasonable accuracy by the palpitation method (see figure 8.12).
6. With a mechanically braked bike, the tension tends to slip and will need constant attention and proper adjustment.

Figure 8.12 Measuring heart rate.

Performance testing

Treadmill Submaximal Test Methods

Single and double stage models may be used to estimate $\dot{V}O_2$ Max from submaximal treadmill exercise. A submaximal test requires the subject to reach a steady state heart rate for a given work level; therefore, the submaximal work stages need to be at least three minutes in duration. The objective of the protocol is to reach a steady state heart rate between 110 and 150 b·min^{-1} for the multi-stage model and 130 to 150 b·min^{-1} for the single stage model. The following test procedures are suggested:

1. Select a suitable test protocol. Two treadmill protocols are suggested for general use: (1) modified Bruce; and (2) Modified Balke treadmill test (Ross 1984). Provided in table 8.5 is a description of each protocol and the steady state energy cost for the submaximal work intensities.

   a. Modified Bruce Protocol. The first three stages of the Bruce protocol can be used for submaximal testing (figure 8.4). The fourth stage of the protocol is not recommended because the speed is 4.2 mph which requires some to jog and others walk. The modified Bruce is better for the single stage model than it is for the double stage model (Mahar, Jackson, Ross et al. 1985).

Table 8.5

Submaximal Treadmill Test Protocols and the Estimated Steady State Energy Cost for the Last Minute of Each Stage.

STAGE	MINUTES	mph	% GRADE	ENERGY COST*	
				$\dot{V}O_2$ (ml·kg^{-1}·min^{-1})	METs
Bruce Protocol					
I	1–3	1.7	10	13.4	3.82
II	4–6	2.5	12	21.4	6.12
III	7–9	3.4	14	31.5	9.01
Ross Submaximal Protocol—Women					
I	1–3	3.4**	0	14.9	4.25
II	4–6	3.4	3	18.4	5.27
III	7–9	3.4	6	22.0	6.29
IV	10–12	3.4	9	25.6	7.31
V	13–15	3.4	12	29.2	8.33
Ross Submaximal Protocol—Men					
I	1–3	3.4**	0	14.9	4.25
II	4–6	3.4	4	19.6	5.61
III	7–9	3.4	8	24.4	6.97
IV	10–12	3.4	12	29.2	8.33
V	13–15	3.4	16	33.9	9.09

*$\dot{V}O_2$ (ml·kg^{-1}·min^{-1}) $= \left((75 + (6 \times \%)) \times \left(\dfrac{mph}{60} \right) \right) \times 3.5$.

**We have discovered that a speed of 3.0 mph can be used and is especially useful for someone not accustomed to treadmill walking. The energy cost for the first stage would be 3.75 METs.

b. Modified Balke Submaximal Protocol. Ross (1984) modified the Balke treadmill protocol for submaximal treadmill testing. The speed is constant, a comfortable walk at 3.4 mph. Every three minutes the elevation of the treadmill is increased. For men, the change is 4% per stage and the change is slightly lower for women, 3% per stage. The various stages are shown in table 8.5.

2. Submaximal heart rate should be measured during the last 15 seconds of every minute. Electronic equipment (see figure 8.13) needs to be used to measure exercise heart rate for treadmill tests. The movement produced by walking on a treadmill makes it very difficult to measure heart rate by the palpitation method.

3. Because of differences in fitness, individuals will vary in their heart rate response to the work. The submaximal heart rate at any stage should not exceed about 150 to 155 $b \cdot min^{-1}$. The following guidelines are offered to insure that submaximal work is achieved.

   a. Bruce Protocol. Do not go to the next stage if the subject's heart rate exceeds 135 $b \cdot min^{-1}$. For most healthy adults, a heart rate between 135 and 150 will be reached in the first 6 minutes at the treadmill test.

   b. Modified Balke (Ross) Submaximal Protocol. Do not proceed to stage two if the heart rate exceeds 140 at stage one; this person would be very unfit. Stages IV and V should only be used for individuals under age 50. Never go to the next stage if the heart rate exceeds 145 $b \cdot min^{-1}$. The Ross modification of the Balke protocol is better than the modified Bruce for the multi-stage model because work is increased at a slower rate (see table 8.5).

4. Submaximal $\dot{V}O_2$ in $ml \cdot kg^{-1} \cdot min^{-1}$ and METs for each stage of the submaximal tests is furnished in table 8.5. These submaximal work values and their associated heart rates can be used with either the single or multi-stage models to estimate $\dot{V}O_2$ Max.

Final Considerations

$\dot{V}O_2$ Max can be used for designing individualized exercise programs and documenting fitness changes produced through exercise. Several methods are available to measure $\dot{V}O_2$ Max. The method selected depends on the degree of accuracy desired as contrasted with ease in testing. An important concern when testing adults is to recognize the need for medical supervision.

Which Method Should Be Used?

The direct measurement of expired gases is the most accurate but least practical method for measuring $\dot{V}O_2$ Max. This method requires expensive equipment and highly trained technicians. For this reason, the direct measurement of $\dot{V}O_2$ from expired gases is usually reserved for research.

Figure 8.13A Dr. Michael Pollock monitoring an exercise stress test for diagnosis of heart disease.

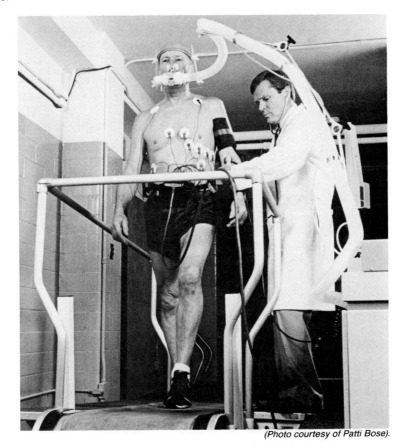

(Photo courtesy of Patti Bose).

Figure 8.13b EKG tracing.

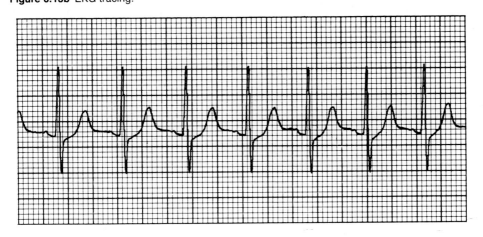

Figure 8.14 Standard errors for various methods used to measure V̇O₂ Max. About 50% of the prediction errors for V̇O₂ estimated from submaximal work can be traced to errors associated with maximal tests.

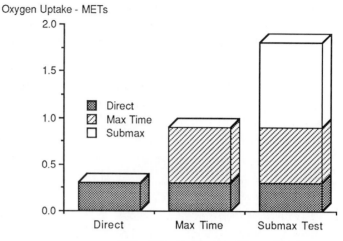

Oxygen Uptake - METs

Legend:
- Direct
- Max Time
- Submax

Method Used to Measure Oxygen Uptake

Estimating V̇O₂ Max from maximal treadmill time (see table 8.4) is the next most accurate method. A major disadvantage is the subject must reach exhaustion and many do not enjoy the experience. The least accurate, but most feasible method for general use is the submaximal test. The correlations between V̇O₂ Max measured and estimated from submaximal work tends to range between 0.70 and 0.80 (Pollock, Wilmore and Fox 1984).

Figure 8.14 compares the accuracy of the various methods and illustrates the additional amount of measurement error introduced by each method. The standard error for the direct measurement of V̇O₂ Max represents the random error associated with measuring oxygen uptake and was estimated to be 0.3 METs (Mahar, Jackson, Ross et al. 1985). The reported standard errors for estimating V̇O₂ from maximum treadmill time is about 0.9 METs (Pollock, Bohannon, Cooper et al. 1976; Foster, Jackson, Pollock et al. 1984). The standard error for estimating V̇O₂ Max from submaximal work was 1.8 METs (Mahar, Jackson, Ross et al. 1985). About 50% of the submaximal error can be traced to the other two methods.

Stress vs. Exercise Test

Treadmill and bicycle ergometer tests provide two types of information, medical and fitness data. A stress test is a medical test. The physician monitors exercise blood pressure, electrocardiogram (EKG) measurements, and physical symptoms (e.g., angina or chest pain) during the test to identify patients who may have cardiovascular disease. The objective of a stress test is the medical diagnosis of heart disease.

The goal of an exercise test is to determine one's $\dot{V}O_2$ Max and is often administered by an exercise specialist or exercise physiologist. With proper medical supervision, an exercise test can be used to assess both cardiovascular and aerobic capabilities. For example, at NASA/Johnson Space Center (Houston, Texas) astronauts are tested annually to evaluate their cardiovascular health and ability to perform the work necessary for extended space flights. The objective of an astronaut's test is to obtain both fitness and cardiovascular data.

Exercise tests can be safely administered without medical supervision on subjects at low risk from cardiovascular diseases. This would include younger subjects (age $\leq$ 40) who do not have significant cardiovascular disease risk factors. Subjects at high risk of cardiovascular diseases need to be tested under medical supervision. Proper procedures are outlined in other sources (ACSM 1980; AHA 1972; AHA 1975; Ellestad 1980; Jones and Campbell 1982).

The Borg RPE Scale

Psychophysical scales are useful for estimating exercise intensity, and RPE scales are often used when administering exercise tests (Borg 1977; Pollock, Jackson and Foster In Press). During the test, the subject is asked to rate exercise intensity during the last 15 seconds of each minute of the test. RPE ratings are useful for determining when the subject is reaching his or her max. The scales and directions are fully provided in chapter 10.

$\dot{V}O_2$ Max Computer Program

The calculating $\dot{V}O_2$ Max by the various methods presented in this chapter is cumbersome to complete by hand, but an easy task for a computer. The equations in this chapter can be used to develop an SPSS computer program by using COMPUTE statements. Let us show this by example. Assume a submaximal treadmill test was used to estimate $\dot{V}O_2$ Max by the single stage model for a man. The following data are needed: (1) treadmill speed (MPH) and elevation (EL) for the submaximal exercise; (2) submaximal heart rate for submaximal exercise (SMHR); and (3) age. The total work model is used to estimate the oxygen uptake for the submaximal exercise (SMVO). The compute statements to calculate $\dot{V}O_2$ Max (VOMAX) are:

```
COMPUTE   SMVO = ((75 + (6 * EL)) * (MPH/60)
COMPUTE   MAXHR = 220 − AGE
COMPUTE   VOMAX = SMVO * ((MAXHR-61)/(SMHR-61))
```

The publishers of this text provide a microcomputer disc. Side two of this disc developed by Morrow, Pivarnik, and Jackson, 1987, is a program designed to calculate $\dot{V}O_2$ Max from metabolic data and from all estimation models presented in this chapter. The program is designed to run on Apple and IBM compatible microcomputers and it is very user-friendly. The outline of the program is furnished in figure 8.15.

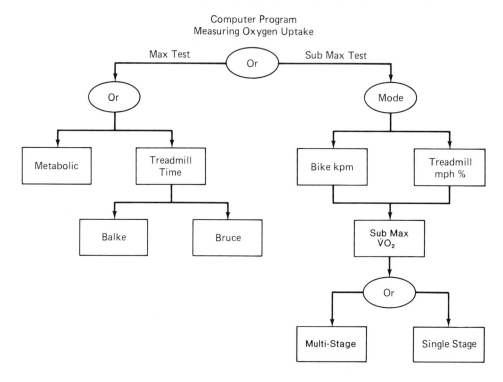

Figure 8.15 Flow chart for microcomputer program to calculate VO_2 Max. The program is designed for Apple and IBM compatible microcomputers. The program can be obtained from the publisher of this text. (Source: Morrow, Pivarnik, and Jackson, 1987)

BODY COMPOSITION

With the growing supply of literature supporting the value of regular physical activity for health and fitness, the evaluation of body composition has become an important aspect of adult fitness and medically supervised rehabilitation programs. A major goal of adult fitness and rehabilitation programs is to control body weight and fat with regular exercise and proper nutrition. Therefore, accurate measurements of body composition are needed to develop sound weight reduction and preventive health programs. Being overweight has been shown to be associated with hypertension, diabetes, and heart disease (Hubert, Feinleib, McNamara et al. 1983; Pollock, Wilmore and Fox 1984). Suitable body composition is important not only for general health but also for athletes interested in maximizing their performance. Athletes must move their body mass quickly and efficiently in most sports. Excessive accumulation of body fat decreases jumping ability, reduces running speed, and lowers endurance.

Essential Definitions

In very simple terms, body weight is made up of fat weight and **lean body weight,** or fat-free weight. **Percent body fat** is simply the proportion of total weight that is fat weight. It is possible for two individuals of the same height and body weight to differ substantially in percent body fat, which is why we use it as the standard for evaluating body composition. If percent body fat and body weight are known, it becomes possible to calculate fat weight and fat-free weight.

Although the terms overweight and obesity are often used interchangeably, there are important differences between them. **Overweight** is weight that exceeds the "normal" weight defined for an individual on the basis of sex, height, and frame size. These values are based on norms compiled by insurance companies. **Obesity** is the excessive accumulation of fat weight and is expressed as percent body fat.

Evaluating Body Composition

What is a desirable level of body fatness? This is difficult to say with certainty, but normative data have provided some guidelines. Although some have suggested more stringent guidelines for general health, Lohman (1982) considered that levels of 10% to 22% fat content in men and 20% to 32% fat content in women were suitable. As a general rule, men should stay under 20% fat, preferably at 15%; women should try to stay below 25%. The standards published for the YMCA adult fitness program (Golding, Meyers and Sinning 1982) are 16% and 23% body fat for men and women respectively.

The body fat values for average adults would be too high for athletes. Wilmore (1982; 1983) has published comprehensive descriptive data on athletes. The average levels are about 12% for men and 18% for women. For events that emphasize efficient body movement (distance running, cross-country skiing, gymnastics, etc.), the averages are lower ranging from 4% to 10% for men and 13% to 18% for women. For more precise data on specific athlete groups, you are directed to other sources (Pollock, Wilmore and Fox 1984; Wilmore 1982; 1983). Presented in figure 8.16 are typical average values for various groups.

Scientific evidence supporting precise standards for athletes and health promotion are not presently available. There is evidence, however, showing a health risk is associated with the "creeping obesity" of middle-aged Americans. Recent data from the Framingham heart study (Hubert, Feinleib and McNamara 1983) showed that increased weight resulted in increased risk of coronary heart disease. This was true for both men and women. Losing excess weight reduced risk. Medical authorities now consider obesity to be a public health problem of the same magnitude as smoking. About 35% of adults in developed countries are obese and the prevalence is increasing (Craddock 1978). The typical American gains about 50 pounds of fat weight during early adult lifetime.

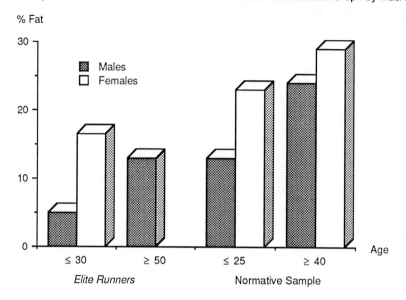

Figure 8.16 Average hydrostatically determined percent body fat values for elite distance runners (Pollock, Foster, Knapp, et al. In press. Pollock, Gettman, Jackson et al., 1977; Wilmore, 1982 and normative samples. Data for elite female master's runners are not available. Graph by MacASJ)

Measurement Methods

Several methods are available for measuring body composition (Behnke and Wilmore, 1974). The methods most often used are laboratory techniques, of which hydrostatic weighing is the most popular, and anthropometric techniques, that include height-weight indexes, skinfold fat, body circumferences, and bone diameters. The laboratory methods are accurate but expensive in terms of time, equipment, and need for trained technicians. For these reasons, the hydrostatic method is not usually used in the clinical setting or for mass testing. Various height-weight ratios have been used most often to evaluate body fatness. However, research has shown that skinfold and body circumference variables provide more accurate estimates of hydrostatically measured body density than height-weight ratios (Lohman 1982; Pollock, Schmidt and Jackson 1980). A popular method is to use a regression equation and predict body density from various combinations of anthropometric variables.

Underwater Weighing

Done correctly, underwater weighing is one of the most valid measurements of body composition. The method is based on Archimedes' principle for measuring the density of an object. An object placed in water must be buoyed upon by a counterforce that equals the weight of the water it displaces. The density of bone and muscle tissue are higher than water (1.2 to 3.0), while fat is less dense than water (.90). Therefore, a person with more bone and muscle mass will weigh heavier in water and have a higher body density and lower percentage of fat (Pollock, Wilmore and Fox 1984).

Figure 8.17 Method of determining body density by underwater weighing. (Photos courtesy Dr. M. L. Pollock, Mt. Sinai Medical Center, Milwaukee, Wisc.)

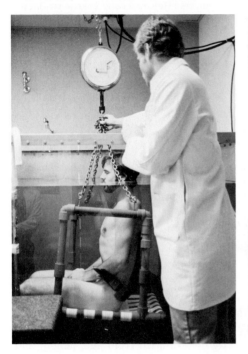 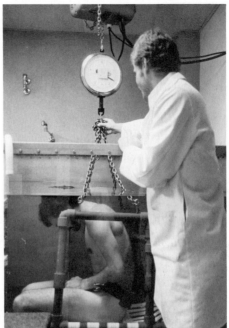

The values needed to calculate body density are body weight on land, body weight in water (see figure 8.17), and **residual lung volume,** which is needed to adjust for air left in the lungs. We can calculate body density (BD) using the following formula:

$$BD = \frac{W_a}{\dfrac{W_a - W_w}{D_w} - (RV + 100 \text{ ml})}$$

where W_a is the individual's weight in air, W_w is the individual's weight in water, D_w is the density of the water corresponding to water temperature, and RV is residual lung volume. The 100-ml value is added to residual lung volume to adjust for gas bubbles in the gastrointestinal tract (Behnke and Wilmore 1974).

Once hydrostatic body density (BD) is determined, we can calculate the percentage body fat using the method recommended by Siri (1961) or that of Brožek and his associates (1963).

$$\text{Percent fat}_{(Siri)} = \left(\frac{495}{BD}\right) - 450$$

$$\text{Percent fat}_{(Bro\check{z}ek)} = \left(\frac{457}{BD}\right) - 414$$

These two formulas yield nearly identical percent fat values through the human range of body fatness.

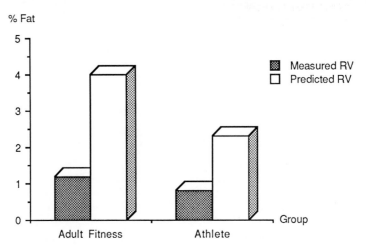

Figure 8.18 Standard errors of measurement for hydrostatically determined percent body fat when residual lung volume was measured and predicted. (Data by Morrow, J. R., A. S. Jackson, P. W. Bradley, et al., 1985. "Function of Measured and Predicted Residual Lung Volume on Body Density Measurement Errors." *Medicine and Science in Sports and Exercise.* 17:204. Graph by MacASJ)

The sources of measurement error for measuring body density by the underwater weighing method include: (1) land weight, (2) underwater weight, (3) density of water, and (4) residual lung volume, measured directly or estimated from age, height, and gender. Research (Morrow, Jackson, Bradley et al. 1985) has shown that residual lung volume is the largest source of body density measurement error. The standard error is increased by over 300% when residual lung volume is estimated rather than measured directly. Provided in figure 8.18 are the estimated standard errors for percent body fat measured for adult fitness and Olympic athlete samples when residual lung volume was measured and estimated. If the underwater method is to be used, it is important to measure residual lung volume rather than predict it.

It has been shown that hydrostatically determined body density can be accurately measured (Jackson, Pollock, Graves 1986). The reliability of hydrostatically determined body density was high, 0.977. The standard error of measurement was 1.2 percent body fat.

Predicting Body Density

Many people have published regression equations with functions to predict hydrostatically measured body density from various combinations of anthropometric variables. More than 100 equations appear in the literature. The results of these studies are provided in table 8.6.

Early researchers developed equations for relatively homogeneous populations termed "population specific equations." The more recent trend is to use what is termed "generalized equations," equations that can be validly used with heterogeneous samples. Population specific equations were developed on relatively small, homogeneous

Table 8.6
Means and Standard Deviations of Hydrostatically Determined Body Density and Concurrent Validity of Regression Equations for Males and Females.

SOURCE	SAMPLE Age*	n	BODY DENSITY $\bar{x}$	s	REGRESSION ANALYSIS R	SE
Males						
Brožek and Keys (1951)	20.3	133	1.077	.014	.88	.007
	45–55	122	1.055	.012	.74	.009
Cureton et al. (1975)	8–11	49	1.053	.013	.77	.008
Durnin and Rahaman (1967)	18–33	60	1.068	.013	.84	.007
	12–15	48	1.063	.012	.76	.008
Durnin and Wormsley (1974)	17–19	24	1.066	.016	†	.007
	20–29	92	1.064	.016	†	.008
	30–39	34	1.046	.012	†	.009
	40–49	35	1.043	.015	†	.008
	50–68	24	1.036	.018	†	.009
Forsyth and Sinning (1973)	19–29	50	1.072	.010	.84	.006
Haisman (1970)	22–26	55	1.070	.010	.78	.006
Harsha et al. (1978)	6–16	79‡	1.046	.018	.84	.010
	6–16	49§	1.055	.020	.90	.009
Jackson and Pollock (1978)	18–61	308	1.059	.018	.92	.007
Katch and McArdle (1973)	19.3	53	1.065	.014	.89	.007
Katch and Michael (1969)	17.0	40	1.076	.013	.89	.006
Parizkova (1961)	9–12	57	†	†	.92	.011
Pascale et al. (1956)	22.1	88	1.068	.012	.86	.006
Pollock et al. (1976)	18–22	95	1.068	.014	.87	.007
	40–55	84	1.043	.013	.84	.007
Sloan (1967)	18–26	50	1.075	.015	.85	.008
Wilmore and Behnke (1969)	16–36	133	1.066	.013	.87	.006
Wright and Wilmore (1974)	27.8	297	1.061	.014	.86	.007
Females						
Durnin and Rahaman (1967)	18–29	45	1.044	.014	.78	.010
	13–16	38	1.045	.011	.78	.008
Durnin and Wormsley (1974)	16–19	29	1.040	.017	†	.009
	20–29	100	1.034	.021	†	.011
	30–39	58	1.025	.020	†	.013
	40–49	48	1.020	.016	†	.011
	50–68	37	1.013	.016	†	.008
Harsha et al. (1978)	6–16	52‡	1.033	.016	.85	.008
	6–16	39§	1.041	.019	.90	.008
Jackson et al. (1980)	18–55	249	1.044	.016	.87	.008
Katch and McArdle (1973)	20.3	69	1.039	.015	.84	.009
Katch and Michael (1968)	19–23	64	1.049	.011	.70	.008
Parizkova (1961)	9–12	56	†	†	.81	.012
	13–16	62	†	†	.82	.010
Pollock et al. (1975)	18–22	83	1.043	.014	.84	.008
	33–50	60	1.032	.015	.89	.007
Sinning (1978)	17–23	44	1.064	.010	.81	.006
Sloan et al. (1962)	20.2	50	1.047	.012	.74	.008
Wilmore and Behnke (1970)	21.4	128	1.041	.010	.76	.007
Young (1964)	53.0	62	1.020	.014	.84	.008
Young et al. (1962)	17–27	94	1.034	.009	.69	.007

*Age is expressed as the mean or range.   †Data not provided.   ‡White.   §Black.

Figure 8.19 Scattergram showing the nonlinear relationship between hydrostatically determined body density and the sum of seven skinfold tests. (Jackson and Pollock, 1978)

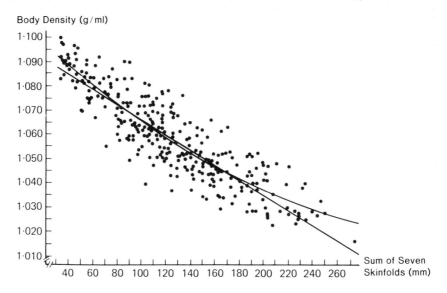

samples, and their application is limited to that sample. The generalized equations (Durnin and Wormsley 1974; Jackson and Pollock 1978; Jackson, Pollock and Ward 1980; Hodgdon and Beckett 1984a, 1984b) were developed on large heterogeneous samples using models that accounted for the nonlinear relationship between skinfold fat and body density (figure 8.19). Age was found to be an important variable for generalized equations (Durnin and Wormsley 1974; Jackson and Pollock 1978; Jackson, Pollock and Ward 1980). The main advantage of the generalized approach is that one equation replaces several without a loss in prediction accuracy. A detailed discussion of population-specific and generalized equations can be found in other sources (Cureton 1984; Jackson 1984; Jackson and Pollock 1982; Lohman 1982).

Generalized Skinfold Equations

Skinfold measurements are highly correlated with underwater determined body density. The correlations for individual skinfolds and the sum of seven and various combinations of the sum of three are presented in table 8.7. Multiple regression models were used to develop generalized skinfold equations for men (Jackson and Pollock 1978) and women (Jackson, Pollock and Ward 1980). Several equations are presented in tables 8.8 and 8.9. Separate equations are provided for men and women to account for sex differences. A quadratic component is used to adjust for the nonlinearity (see figure 8.19), and age is an independent variable to account for aging. The sum of three and seven skinfolds are highly correlated ($r \geq 0.97$), which demonstrates that different

Table 8.7

Linear Correlations between Body Density and Anthropometric Variables for Adults (Jackson and Pollock 1978; Jackson, Pollock and Ward 1980).

VARIABLES	MEN (N = 402)	WOMEN (N = 283)
General characteristics		
Height	−0.03	−0.06
Weight	−0.63	−0.63
Body mass index*	−0.69	−0.70
Skinfolds		
Chest	−0.85	−0.64
Axilla	−0.82	−0.73
Triceps	−0.79	−0.77
Subscapula	−0.77	−0.67
Abdomen	−0.83	−0.75
Suprailium	−0.76	−0.76
Thigh	−0.78	−0.74
Sum of Seven	−0.88	−0.83
Circumferences		
Waist	−0.80	−0.71
Gluteal	−0.69	−0.74
Thigh	−0.64	−0.68
Biceps	−0.51	−0.63
Forearm	−0.35	−0.41

*$\dfrac{Wt}{ht^2}$, where weight is in kg and height is in meters.

Table 8.8

Generalized Regression Equations for Predicting Body Density of Adult Men from the Sum of Skinfold Fat and Age.

REGRESSION EQUATION	R	STANDARD ERROR g·cc⁻¹	% fat
BD(M-1) = 1.112000 − 0.00043499(X_1) + 0.00000055(X_1)^2 − 0.00028826(X_4)	0.90	0.008	3.4
BD(M-2) = 1.1093800 − 0.0008267(X_2) + 0.0000016(X_2)^2 − 0.0002574(X_4)	0.91	0.008	3.4
BD(M-3) = 1.1125025 − 0.0013125(X_3) + 0.0000055(X_3)^2 − 0.0002440(X_4)	0.89	0.008	3.6

Key: X_1 = sum of seven skinfolds; X_2 = sum of chest, abdomen and thigh skinfolds; X_3 = sum of chest, triceps and subscapular skinfolds. X_4 = age in years.

Table 8.9

Generalized Regression Equations for Predicting Body Density of Adult Women from the Sum of Skinfold Fat and Age.

REGRESSION EQUATION	R	STANDARD ERROR $g \cdot cc^{-1}$	% fat
$BD(F\text{-}1) = 1.0970 - 0.00046971(X_1) + 0.00000056(X_1)^2 - 0.00012828(X_4)$	0.85	0.008	3.8
$BD(F\text{-}2) = 1.099421 - 0.0009929\,(X_2) + 0.0000023(X_2)^2 - 0.0001392(X_4)$	0.84	0.009	4.0
$BD(F\text{-}3) = 1.089733 - 0.0009245(X_3) + 0.0000025(X_3)^2 - 0.0000979(X_4)$	0.83	0.009	4.0

Key: X_1 = sum of seven skinfolds (see Table); X_2 = sum of triceps, thigh, and suprailium skinfolds; X_3 = sum of triceps, suprailium and abdominal skinfolds; X_4 = age in years.

combinations of the sum of skinfolds can be used with minimal loss of accuracy. The use of the sum of three instead of seven enhances feasibility. The logic used to develop the generalized equations is fully presented in another source (Jackson 1984).

In our experience abdominal skinfold in men and thigh skinfold for women are difficult for some technicians to measure. Additionally, the best sum of the three skinfold equations, shown as BD(M-2) and BD(F-2) in tables 8.8 and 8.9, requires the removal of clothing, which can be awkward in some testing situations. For these reasons equations BD(M-3) and BD(F-3) were developed.

The multiple correlations and standard errors of measurement for the generalized equations are well within the range reported for population specific-equations (see table 8.8). These findings demonstrate that a generalized equation can be used to replace several different population-specific equations and are valid for adults varying greatly in age and body fatness. However, an important caution should be raised when using the generalized equations: They were developed on men and women ranging from 18–61 years of age, so the accuracy of the equations outside this age range is not known. For this reason, the equations should be used cautiously with subjects outside this age range. For these extreme age-groups, body water and bone density vary, which could affect an equation's accuracy (Lohman 1981). Another concern should be raised with extremely obese individuals.

Reliability of Skinfold Fat Predictions. With properly trained testers, percent body fat estimated from skinfolds can be reliably measured. Using three testers who varied in experience, but practiced together, the reliability was found to exceed 0.99 for the sum of seven and three skinfolds. The standard error of measurement was about 1.0 percent body fat (Jackson, Pollock and Gettman 1978).

In a more comprehensive study (Jackson, Pollock and Graves 1986), both day-to-day and tester-to-tester measurement error was examined. These results are furnished in table 8.10. All reliability estimates were high, with standard errors of measurement about 1.0 percent body fat. This showed that percent body fat estimated from generalized skinfold equations is not only internally consistent, but also quite stable.

Table 8.10

Reliability Estimates and Standard Errors of Measurement for Estimating Body Density for Generalized Skinfold Equations.*

| SAMPLE | N | Σ 7 SKINFOLDS | | | Σ 3 SKINFOLDS | | |
| | | R_{xx} | Standard Error | | R_{xx} | Standard Error | |
			$g \cdot cc^{-1}$	% Fat		$g \cdot cc^{-1}$	% Fat
Total	68	0.989	0.0020	0.90	0.980	0.0027	1.21
Males	24	0.978	0.0019	0.85	0.968	0.0024	1.08
Females	44	0.988	0.0021	0.94	0.977	0.0029	1.30

*Data taken from Jackson, Pollock, Graves et al. (1986). The reliability estimates and standard errors are for a measurement schedule testing a subject on any day by a reasonably trained testor. The estimates reflect both among day and among tester measurement error.

Cross Validation of Generalized Skinfold Equations. The best evidence supporting an equation's validity is established through cross validation research. Presented in table 8.11 is a summary of the studies that have cross validated the generalized skinfold equations. The cross validation correlations were somewhat lower than found in the original study (see tables 8.8 and 8.9), but this can be traced to the variability of the samples studied. Correlations are higher with heterogeneous sample. The standard error of measurement is the more important statistic and the cross validation values agree closely with the validation data. The standard errors of prediction ranged from about 0.006 to 0.009 grams per cubic centimeter ($g \cdot cc^{-1}$).

The cross validation research supports the generalizability of the equations to athletes. The data published by Thorland and associates (1984) showed that the equations could be used with high school-aged athletes while Sinning and associates (1984;1985) showed the equations were accurate for college-aged athletes.

Measuring Skinfold Fat

The accuracy of body composition estimates from regression equations depends on securing accurate measures of skinfold fat. Accuracy is enhanced by using a suitable caliper and having a trained technician measure skinfold fat at the proper locations. Improper site selection is probably the most common reason for error in measuring skinfold fat (Lohman 1982; Pollock and Jackson 1984).

Several acceptable calipers are available for measuring skinfold fat. A skinfold caliper that conforms to specifications established by the committee of Food and Nutrition Board of the National Research Council of the United States should be used. The Lange, Harpenden, and Lafayette[5] calipers meet these criteria. The Harpenden caliper tends to produce measurements about 1 or 2 mm lower than the Lange and Lafayette calipers.

5. The Lange caliper is manufactured by Cambridge Scientific Industries, Cambridge, Maryland. The Harpenden caliper is manufactured by British Indicators LTD., St. Albans, Herts, England and distributed in the United States by Quinton Equipment, Seattle, Washington. Lafayette Instrument Company, Lafayette, Indiana manufactures the Lafayette caliper.

Table 8.11

Sample Description and Statistics for the Cross Validation of Generalized Skinfold Equations.

SOURCE	EQUATION	SAMPLE Age	SAMPLE N	PERCENT FAT[1] M	PERCENT FAT[1] S	CROSS VALIDATION $r_{yy'}$	CROSS VALIDATION SE[2]
Females							
Thorland et al. (1984)	$\Sigma 3$	16.5	133	14.5	4.3	0.82	0.007
Bulbulion (1984)	$\Sigma 3$	26.1	27	36.6	7.3	0.83	0.009
	$\Sigma 3$	20.9	35	20.9	5.1	0.72	0.008
	$\Sigma 3$	19.9	30	16.9	3.4	0.57	0.009
Sinning et al. (1984)	$\Sigma 3$	19.8	71	20.1	5.3	0.80	0.007
	$\Sigma 4$	19.8	71	20.1	5.3	0.81	0.007
Males							
Thorland et al. (1984)	$\Sigma 3$	17.4	141	9.1	3.8	0.76	0.006
	$\Sigma 7$	17.4	141	9.1	3.8	0.81	0.007
Sinning et al. (1985)	$\Sigma 7$	20.3	265	9.2	4.4	0.84	0.005
	$\Sigma 3$	20.3	265	9.2	4.4	0.83	0.006
Smith et al. (1984)	$\Sigma 3$	19.8	68	12.8	4.3	0.76	0.009
	$\Sigma 7$	19.8	68	12.8	4.3	0.73	0.008

[1]Percent body fat measured by the underwater weighing method.

[2]$SE = \sqrt{\dfrac{\Sigma(Y - Y')^2}{N}}$. The standard error is often termed "total error" because it considers not only the error associated with the lack of correlation between predicted (Y') and measured (Y) body density, but also the difference in intercepts.

The skinfold sites and methods are listed here. All measurements were taken on the right side of the body. Figures 8.20 through 8.26 illustrate the measurement methods.

1. *Chest:* a diagonal fold taken half of the distance between the anterior axillary line and nipple for men and one third of the distance from the anterior axillary line to the nipple for women (figure 8.20).
2. *Axilla:* a vertical fold on the midaxillary line at the level of the xlphoid process of the sternum (figure 8.21).
3. *Triceps:* a vertical fold on the posterior midline of the upper arm (over the triceps muscle), halfway between the acromion and olecranon processes; the elbow should be extended and relaxed (figure 8.22).
4. *Subscapular:* a fold taken on a diagonal line coming from the vertebral border to 1–2 cm from the inferior angle of the scapula (figure 8.23).
5. *Abdominal:* a vertical fold taken at a lateral distance of approximately 2 cm from the umbilicus (figure 8.24).
6. *Suprailium:* a diagonal fold above the crest of the ilium at the spot where an imaginary line would come down from the anterior axillary line (figure 8.25).
7. *Thigh:* a vertical fold on the anterior aspect of the thigh midway between hip and knee joints (figure 8.26).

Grasp the skinfold firmly by the thumb and index finger. The caliper is perpendicular to the fold at approximately 1 cm (0.25 in.) from the thumb and forefinger.

Figure 8.20 (a) and (b) Skinfold test sites for men and women; (c) placement of calipers for chest skinfold test. (*The Physician and Sports Medicine.* Vol. 13, No 5, May 1985.)

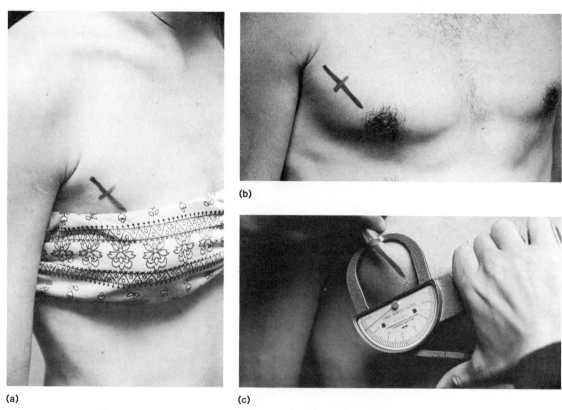

(a)   (c)

(Photos courtesy of Pollock, M. L., Schmidt, D. H., and Jackson, A. S., Measurement of Cardiorespiratory Fitness and Body Composition in the Clinical Setting, Comprehensive Therapy, Vol. 6; 9: 12–27, 1980 published with permission of the Laux Company, Inc. Harvard, MA.)

Figure 8.21 Test site and placement of calipers for axilla skinfold. The axilla skinfold site is shown in relation to the men's chest site. (Source: *The Physician and Sports Medicine.* Vol. 13, No. 5, May 1985.)

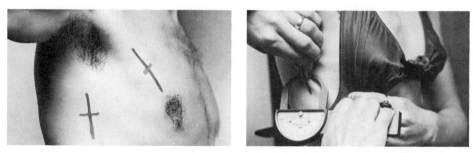

(Photos courtesy of Pollock, M. L., Schmidt, D. H., and Jackson, A. S., Measurement of Cardiorespiratory Fitness and Body Composition in the Clinical Setting, Comprehensive Therapy, Vol. 6; 9: 12–27, 1980 published with permission of the Laux Company, Inc. Harvard, MA.)

Figure 8.22 Test site and placement of calipers for triceps skinfold. The triceps skinfold site is shown in relation to the subscapular skinfold site. (Source: *The Physician and Sports Medicine.* Vol. 13, No. 5, May 1985.)

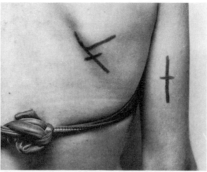 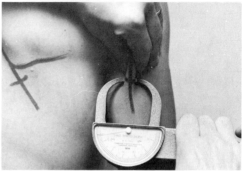

(Photos courtesy of Pollock, M. L., Schmidt, D. H., and Jackson, A. S., Measurement of Cardiorespiratory Fitness and Body Composition in the Clinical Setting, Comprehensive Therapy, Vol. 6; 9: 12–27, 1980 published with permission of the Laux Company, Inc. Harvard, MA.)

Figure 8.23 Placement of calipers for subscapular skinfold. The proper site location is shown in figure 8.21. (Source: *The Physician and Sports Medicine.* Vol. 13, No. 5, May 1985.)

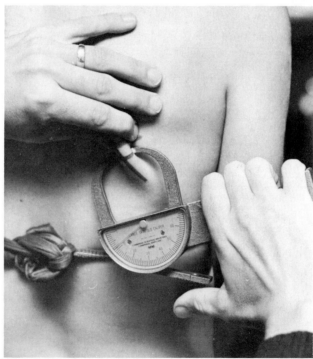

(Photos courtesy of Pollock, M. L., Schmidt, D. H., and Jackson, A. S., Measurement of Cardiorespiratory Fitness and Body Composition in the Clinical Setting, Comprehensive Therapy, Vol. 6; 9: 12–27, 1980 published with permission of the Laux Company, Inc. Harvard, MA.)

Figure 8.24 Test site and placement of calipers for abdominal skinfold. The abdominal site is shown in relation to the suprailium site. (Source: *The Physician and Sports Medicine.* Vol. 13, No. 5, May 1985.)

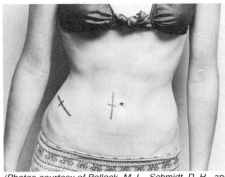
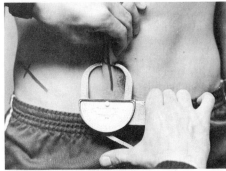

(Photos courtesy of Pollock, M. L., Schmidt, D. H., and Jackson, A. S., Measurement of Cardiorespiratory Fitness and Body Composition in the Clinical Setting, Comprehensive Therapy, Vol. 6; 9: 12–27, 1980 published with permission of the Laux Company, Inc. Harvard, MA.)

Figure 8.25 Caliper placement for suprailium skinfold. The proper site location is shown in figure 8.23. (Source: *The Physician and Sports Medicine* Vol. 13, No. 5, May 1985.)

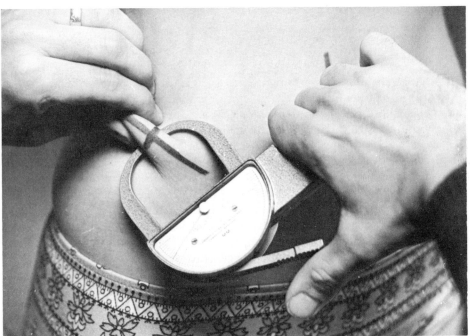

(Photos courtesy of Pollock, M. L., Schmidt, D. H., and Jackson, A. S., Measurement of Cardiorespiratory Fitness and Body Composition in the Clinical Setting, Comprehensive Therapy, Vol. 6; 9: 12–27, 1980 published with permission of the Laux Company, Inc. Harvard, MA.)

Figure 8.26 Caliper placement for thigh skinfold. (Source: *The Physician and Sports Medicine.* Vol. 13, No. 5, May 1985.)

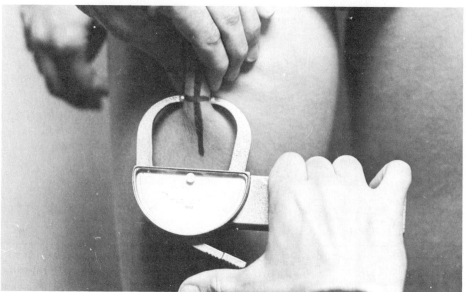

(Photos courtesy of Pollock, M. L., Schmidt, D. H., and Jackson, A. S., Measurement of Cardiorespiratory Fitness and Body Composition in the Clinical Setting, Comprehensive Therapy, Vol. 6; 9: 12–27, 1980 published with permission of the Laux Company, Inc. Harvard, MA.)

Then release the caliper grip so that full tension is exerted on the skinfold. Use the pads at the tip of thumb and finger to grasp the skinfold. (Testers may need to trim their nails.) Read the dial to the nearest 0.5 mm approximately one to two seconds after the grip has been released. A minimum of two measurements should be taken. If they vary by more than 1 mm, a third should be taken.

If consecutive fat measurements become smaller and smaller, the fat is being compressed; this occurs mainly with 'fleshy' people. The tester should go on to the next site and return to the trouble spot after finishing the other measurements; the final value will be the average of the two that seem to best represent the skinfold fat site. Typically, the tester should complete a measurement at one site before moving to another. It is better to make measurements when the skin is dry, because when the skin is moist or wet the tester may grasp extra skin (fat) and get larger values. Measurements should not be taken immediately after exercise or when a subject is overheated, because the shift of body fluid to the skin will increase skinfold size. Practice is necessary to grasp the same size of skinfold consistently at the same location every time. Consistency can be ensured by having several technicians take the same measurements and comparing results. Proficiency in measuring skinfolds may take practice sessions with up to 50 to 100 subjects. Descriptive statistics for skinfold fat are presented in table 8.12.

Proper training and practice are needed to insure the accurate measurement of skinfold fat (Pollock and Jackson 1984). The detailed instructions and pictures (figures 8.20 to 8.26) are provided to standardize testing procedures.

Table 8.12
Descriptive Statistics of Sample Used to Develop Generalized Body Density Prediction Equations.

VARIABLES	MEN (N = 402)		WOMEN (N = 283)	
	MEAN	SD	MEAN	SD
General characteristics				
Age (yr)	32.8	11.0	31.8	11.5
Height (cm)	179.0	6.4	168.6	5.8
Weight (kg)	78.2	11.7	57.5	7.4
Body mass index*	24.4	3.2	20.2	2.2
Laboratory determined				
Body density (g·cc⁻¹)	1.058	0.018	1.044	0.016
Percent fat (%)	17.9	8.0	24.4	7.2
Lean weight (kg)	63.5	7.3	43.1	4.2
Fat weight (kg)	14.6	7.9	14.3	5.7
Skinfolds (mm)				
Chest	15.2	8.0	12.6	4.8
Axilla	17.3	8.7	13.0	6.1
Triceps	14.2	6.1	18.2	5.9
Subscapula	16.0	7.0	14.2	6.4
Abdomen	25.1	10.8	24.2	9.6
Suprailium	16.2	8.9	14.0	7.1
Thigh	18.9	7.7	29.5	8.0
Sum of skinfolds (mm)				
All seven	122.9	52.0	125.6	42.0
Chest, Abdomen, Thigh	59.2	24.5		
Triceps, Chest, Subscapula	45.3	19.6		
Triceps, Suprailium, Thigh			61.6	19.0
Triceps, Suprailium, Abdomen			56.3	21.0

*Body mass index is Weight (kg) divided by Height in meters squared (kg/m²).

Computing Body Density and Percent Body Fat

In many situations, the calculation of percent body fat is wanted. Tables 8.13 and 8.14 should speed your calculations of percent body fat from the quadratic sum of three skinfolds and age. In the tables we have used the sum of the chest, abdomen, and thigh skinfolds for men, and the sum of the triceps, suprailium, and thigh skinfolds for women—each sum having proved the most valid for each sex. Similar tables based on other equations have been published (Jackson and Pollock 1985; Golding, Meyers and Sinning 1982).

To use tables 8.13 and 8.14, first select the appropriate skinfold sites and measure them following the recommended measurement procedures. Using the sum of three skinfolds and age, find the percentage fat value from the appropriate table. For example, if the sum of the triceps, suprailium, and thigh skinfolds for a 21-year-old woman was 82 millimeters, her estimated percent fat would be 30.1.

Table 8.13

Estimates of Percentage of Fat for Women;
Sum of Triceps, Suprailium, and Thigh Skinfolds.

SUM OF SKINFOLDS (MM)		AGE TO THE LAST YEAR							
	Under 22	23 to 27	28 to 32	33 to 37	38 to 42	43 to 47	48 to 52	53 to 57	Over 58
23–25	9.7	9.9	10.2	10.4	10.7	10.9	11.2	11.4	11.7
26–28	11.0	11.2	11.5	11.7	12.0	12.3	12.5	12.7	13.0
29–31	12.3	12.5	12.8	13.0	13.3	13.5	13.8	14.0	14.3
32–34	13.6	13.8	14.0	14.3	14.5	14.8	15.0	15.3	15.5
35–37	14.8	15.0	15.3	15.5	15.8	16.0	16.3	16.5	16.8
38–40	16.0	16.3	16.5	16.7	17.0	17.2	17.5	17.7	18.0
41–43	17.2	17.4	17.7	17.9	18.2	18.4	18.7	18.9	19.2
44–46	18.3	18.6	18.8	19.1	19.3	19.6	19.8	20.1	20.3
47–49	19.5	19.7	20.0	20.2	20.5	20.7	21.0	21.2	21.5
50–52	20.6	20.8	21.2	21.3	21.6	21.8	22.1	22.3	22.6
53–55	21.7	21.9	22.1	22.4	22.6	22.9	23.1	23.4	23.6
56–58	22.7	23.0	23.2	23.4	23.7	23.9	24.2	24.4	24.7
59–61	23.7	24.0	24.2	24.5	24.7	25.0	25.2	25.5	25.7
62–64	24.7	25.0	25.2	25.5	25.7	26.0	26.7	26.4	26.7
65–67	25.7	25.9	26.2	26.4	26.7	26.9	27.2	27.4	27.7
68–70	26.6	26.9	27.1	27.4	27.6	27.9	28.1	28.4	28.6
71–73	27.5	27.8	28.0	28.3	28.5	28.8	28.0	29.3	29.5
74–76	28.4	28.7	28.9	29.2	29.4	29.7	29.9	30.2	30.4
77–79	29.3	29.5	29.8	30.0	30.3	30.5	30.8	31.0	31.3
80–82	30.1	30.4	30.6	30.9	31.1	31.4	31.6	31.9	32.1
83–85	30.9	31.2	31.4	31.7	31.9	32.2	32.4	32.7	32.9
86–88	31.7	32.0	32.2	32.5	32.7	32.9	33.2	33.4	33.7
89–91	32.5	32.7	33.0	33.2	33.5	33.7	33.9	34.2	34.4
92–94	33.2	33.4	33.7	33.9	34.2	34.4	34.7	34.9	35.2
95–97	33.9	34.1	34.4	34.6	34.9	35.1	35.4	35.6	35.9
98–100	34.6	34.8	35.1	35.3	35.5	35.8	36.0	36.3	36.5
101–103	35.3	35.4	35.7	35.9	36.2	36.4	36.7	36.9	37.2
104–106	35.8	36.1	36.3	36.6	36.8	37.1	37.3	37.5	37.8
107–109	36.4	36.7	36.9	37.1	37.4	37.6	37.9	38.1	38.4
110–112	37.0	37.2	37.5	37.7	38.0	38.2	38.5	38.7	38.9
113–115	37.5	37.8	38.0	38.2	38.5	38.7	39.0	39.2	39.5
116–118	38.0	38.3	38.5	38.8	39.0	39.3	39.5	39.7	40.0
119–121	38.5	38.7	39.0	39.2	39.5	39.7	40.0	40.2	40.5
122–124	39.0	39.2	39.4	39.7	39.9	40.2	40.4	40.7	40.9
125–127	39.4	39.6	39.9	40.1	40.4	40.6	40.9	41.1	41.4
128–130	39.8	40.0	40.3	40.5	40.8	41.0	41.3	41.5	41.8

Table 8.14

Estimates of Percentage of Fat for Men;
Sum of Chest, Abdominal, and Thigh Skinfolds.

SUM OF SKINFOLDS (MM)	AGE TO THE LAST YEAR								
	Under 22	23 to 27	28 to 32	33 to 37	38 to 42	43 to 47	48 to 52	53 to 57	Over 58
8–10	1.3	1.8	2.3	2.9	3.4	3.9	4.5	5.0	5.5
11–13	2.2	2.8	3.3	3.9	4.4	4.9	5.5	6.0	6.5
14–16	3.2	3.8	4.3	4.8	5.4	5.9	6.4	7.0	7.5
17–19	4.2	4.7	5.3	5.8	6.3	6.9	7.4	8.0	8.5
20–22	5.1	5.7	6.2	6.8	7.3	7.9	8.4	8.9	9.5
23–25	6.1	6.6	7.2	7.7	8.3	8.8	9.4	9.9	10.5
26–28	7.0	7.6	8.1	8.7	9.2	9.8	10.3	10.9	11.4
29–31	8.0	8.5	9.1	9.6	10.2	10.7	11.3	11.8	12.4
32–34	8.9	9.4	10.0	10.5	11.1	11.6	12.2	12.8	13.3
35–37	9.8	10.4	10.9	11.5	12.0	12.6	13.1	13.7	14.3
38–40	10.7	11.3	11.8	12.4	12.9	13.5	14.1	14.6	15.2
41–43	11.6	12.2	12.7	13.3	13.8	14.4	15.0	15.5	16.1
44–46	12.5	13.1	13.6	14.2	14.7	15.3	15.9	16.4	17.0
47–49	13.4	13.9	14.5	15.1	15.6	16.2	16.8	17.3	17.9
50–52	14.3	14.8	15.4	15.9	16.5	17.1	17.6	18.2	18.8
53–55	15.1	15.7	16.2	16.8	17.4	17.9	18.5	19.1	19.7
56–58	16.0	16.5	17.1	17.7	18.2	18.8	19.4	20.0	20.5
59–61	16.9	17.4	17.9	18.5	19.1	19.7	20.2	20.8	21.4
62–64	17.6	18.2	18.8	19.4	19.9	20.5	21.1	21.7	22.2
65–67	18.5	19.0	19.6	20.2	20.8	21.3	21.9	22.5	23.1
68–70	19.3	19.9	20.4	21.0	21.6	22.2	22.7	23.3	23.9
71–73	20.1	20.7	21.2	21.8	22.4	23.0	23.6	24.1	24.7
74–76	20.9	21.5	22.0	22.6	23.2	23.8	24.4	25.0	25.5
77–79	21.7	22.2	22.8	23.4	24.0	24.6	25.2	25.8	26.3
80–82	22.4	23.0	23.6	24.2	24.8	25.4	25.9	26.5	27.1
83–85	23.2	23.8	24.4	25.0	25.5	26.1	26.7	27.3	27.9
86–88	24.0	24.5	25.1	25.7	26.3	26.9	27.5	28.1	28.7
89–91	24.7	25.3	25.9	25.5	27.1	27.6	28.2	28.8	29.4
92–94	25.4	26.0	26.6	27.2	27.8	28.4	29.0	29.6	30.2
95–97	26.1	26.7	27.3	27.9	28.5	29.1	29.7	30.3	30.9
98–100	26.9	27.4	28.0	28.6	29.2	29.8	30.4	31.0	31.6
101–103	27.5	28.1	28.7	29.3	29.9	30.5	31.1	31.7	32.3
104–106	28.2	28.8	29.4	30.0	30.6	31.2	31.8	32.4	33.0
107–109	28.9	29.5	30.1	30.7	31.3	31.9	32.5	33.1	33.7
110–112	29.6	30.2	30.8	31.4	32.0	32.6	33.2	33.8	34.4
113–115	30.2	30.8	31.4	32.0	32.6	33.2	33.8	34.5	35.1
116–118	30.9	31.5	32.1	32.7	33.3	33.9	34.5	35.1	35.7
119–121	31.5	32.1	32.7	33.3	33.9	34.5	35.1	35.7	36.4
122–124	32.1	32.7	33.3	33.9	34.5	35.1	35.8	36.4	37.0
125–127	32.7	33.3	33.9	34.5	35.1	35.8	36.4	37.0	37.6

Body composition values are easy to calculate by computer. The COMPUTE statements for SPSS[x] can be used to devise a simple program for the mainframe computer. Let us illustrate. Assume you want to develop a program to calculate body density (BD), percent body fat (PFAT), lean body weight (LBW) and fat weight (FWT) for women. The necessary entry data are: triceps (TRS), suprailium (SPS) and thigh skinfolds (THS); age, and weight (WT). The program would be as follows:

$$\text{COMPUTE} \quad \text{SUM} = \text{TRS} + \text{SPS} + \text{THS}$$
$$\text{COMPUTE} \quad \text{BD} = 1.0994921 - (0.0009929*\text{SUM})$$
$$+ (0.0000023*(\text{SUM}*\text{SUM})) -$$
$$(0.0002574*\text{AGE})$$
$$\text{COMPUTE} \quad \text{PFAT} = (495/\text{BD}) - 450$$
$$\text{COMPUTE} \quad \text{FWT} = (\text{PFAT}/100) * \text{WT}$$
$$\text{COMPUTE} \quad \text{LBW} = \text{WT} - \text{FWT}$$

A program (Jackson, Morrow, and Pivarnik, 1987) has been written to run on Apple and IBM compatible microcomputers. The program is available from the publisher of this text (see page 241) and the flowchart is provided in figure 8.27.

Generalized Circumference Equations
In 1981, the United States Navy changed from using height and weight standards to percent body fat for making weight control decisions. In order to develop the testing methods, two studies (Hodgdon and Beckett 1984a; 1984b) were completed to develop equations for estimating body density from body circumferences. The studies were conducted on large samples of men ($N = 602$) and women ($N = 214$) who varied in age and body density, and generalized equations were developed. Navy equations are provided in table 8.15.

The variables used for the Navy equations and testing instructions are presented next.

1. Height. Standing height is measured to the nearest 0.25 inch without shoes.
2. Abdomen Circumference (1). At the level of minimal abdominal width, approximately midway between the xlphoid and the umbilicus (Beckett and Hodgdon 1984c).
3. Abdomen Circumference (2). The measurement is taken at the level of the umbilicus (Beckett and Hodgdon 1984c).
4. Hip Circumference. The measurement is taken in the horizontal plane at the largest circumference around the hips (Beckett and Hodgdon 1984c).
5. Neck Circumference. The measurement is taken just inferior to the larynx with the tape sloping slightly downward to the front (Beckett and Hodgdon 1984c).

The body circumference measurements are made with the subject standing relaxed and using a calibrated, fiberglass reinforced measuring tape. All measurements are recorded to the nearest 1.0 mm. The abdominal circumferences are measured at the end of a normal expiration.

Figure 8.27 Flow chart for body composition computer program. The program can be obtained from the publisher and is designed to run on Apple and IBM compatible microcomputers. (Source: Morrow, Pivarnik, and Jackson, 1987.)

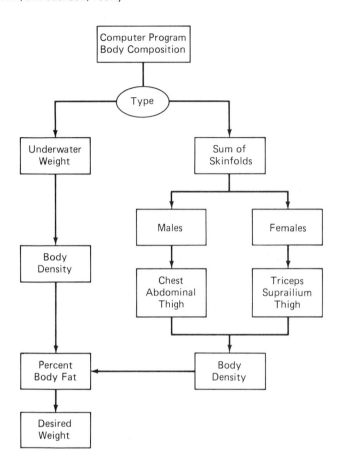

Table 8.15

Regression Equations for Predicting Body Density of Adults from Body Circumferences and Height.

REGRESSION EQUATION	R	SE$_{(\% \text{ Fat})}$
Adult women		
BD$_{(W)}$ = 1.29579 − 0.35004(X$_1$) + 0.22100(X$_3$)	0.85	3.72
Adult men		
BD$_{(M)}$ = 1.0324 − 0.19077(X$_2$) + 0.15456(X$_3$)	0.90	3.52

Key: X1 = LOG$_{10}$(Abdomen(1) + Hip − Neck);
    X2 = LOG$_{10}$(Abdomen(2) − Neck);
    X3 = LOG$_{10}$(Height)

Statistical analyses showed that the relationship between measured and estimated body fat was not linear. Log transformations were used to correct for the nonlinearity. The equations were cross-validated on a second sample of men (N = 100) and women (N = 80). The cross validation correlations were 0.90 and 0.87 for the men and women respectively and the cross validation standard errors of prediction were 2.7% fat for men and 4.0% for the women. The Navy equations have not been cross-validated in other laboratories.

Determining Desired Weight

Once percent fat is known, the weight of an individual for desired percent body fat level can be calculated. This can help an individual establish a weight reduction goal or a suitable weight. **Desired weight** is calculated from lean weight. The calculation methods are:

$$\text{Lean Weight} = \text{Weight} - \left(\text{Weight} \times \left(\frac{\% \text{ fat}}{100}\right)\right)$$

$$\text{Desired Weight} = \text{Lean Weight}/\left(1 - \left(\frac{\% \text{ fat}_D}{100}\right)\right)$$

where, % fat is measured percent body fat and % fat$_D$ is desired percent body fat.

We recommend using a range of desirable weight to account for the measurement error associated with estimating body density. For adult fitness, we recommend that 15% to 22% for men and 23% to 28% for women be used for weight reduction goals. To illustrate, assume a 200 pound man was found to be 28% fat. The desired weight range (15% to 22%) would be 169 to 185 pounds.

$$\text{Lean Weight} = 200 - \left(200 \times \left(\frac{28}{100}\right)\right) = 200 - 56 = 144$$

$$\text{DW } (15\%) = 144/(1 - (15/100)) = \frac{144}{0.85} = 169.4$$

$$\text{DW } (20\%) = 144/(1 - (22/100)) = \frac{144}{0.78} = 184.6$$

For use with athletes, lowered desired percent body fat levels would be used and the levels would depend on an athlete's gender and event. A weight reduction program that combines exercise with diet can result in a lean weight gain and a fat weight loss. It's not uncommon to find a reduction in percentage fat without weight loss. When a program uses only diet, both lean and fat weight may be lost, possibly leaving the percent fat unchanged while total weight is lost. It's important to monitor both body weight and percentage fat during a weight reduction program to be sure that the participant's body composition is being altered in the wanted direction. Consult another source (Pollock and Jackson 1977) for a detailed discussion of this subject.

Desired weights can be easily calculated by computer. An option of the micro-computer program that accompanies this test is the calculation of desired weight for any percent body fat. The only variables needed are lean body weight (LBW) and body weight (WT). Using the previous SPSS example, let's determine the desired weight (DWT) for the values of 22% and 28% body fat. The COMPUTE statements would be:

$$\text{COMPUTE} \quad \text{DWT22} = \text{LBW}/(1 - 0.22)$$
$$\text{COMPUTE} \quad \text{DWT28} = \text{LBW}/(1 - 0.28)$$

YMCA TEST

The YMCA test (Golding, Meyers and Sinning 1982) has developed a health-related physical fitness program and test for adults to provide a scientifically sound plan for developing and maintaining physical fitness. The test and program was developed by leaders in the field of adult fitness, exercise physiology, and measurement. The program requires a medical examination before exercise can begin; the tests are used to evaluate current physical fitness, providing the basis on which physical activity is prescribed.

Cardiorespiratory endurance and body composition are major components of the YMCA battery. In addition, flexibility, strength, and endurance are evaluated. The YMCA standards for these components are published in tables 8.16 and 8.17.

Body Composition

The percentage body fat is estimated from the data used to develop generalized body composition equations on women and on men (Jackson, Pollock and Ward 1980) and men (Jackson and Pollock 1978). The YMCA test uses several different combinations of skinfolds and tables are published in the book to speed the calculation of percent body fat from the sum of skinfolds.

Flexibility

Trunk flexibility is the test used to measure flexibility. Sitting on the floor with the heels 10 to 12 inches apart, the person slowly reaches with both hands as far forward as possible. A 15-inch mark rests on the near edge of the heel line. The score, in inches, is the most distant point reached on a yardstick.

Table 8.16

Physical Fitness Evaulation Standards for the YMCA Fitness Test for Adult Males.*

RATING	PERCENTILE RANKING	TRUNK FLEXION	BENCH PRESS	1-MIN SIT UPS
Males ≤ 35 years				
Excellent	95	21	35	45
Good	85	19	29	41
Above Av	75	17	24	37
Average	50	15	20	33
Below Av	30	12	15	28
Fair	15	9	11	23
Poor	5	7	7	18
Males 35 to 46 years				
Excellent	95	22	30	42
Good	85	19	24	38
Above Av	75	16	19	32
Average	50	14	17	27
Below Av	30	12	14	21
Fair	15	10	10	18
Poor	5	5	3	11
Males ≥ 46 years				
Excellent	95	20	28	38
Good	85	17	22	33
Above Av	75	15	19	26
Average	50	13	16	21
Below Av	30	11	12	18
Fair	15	8	8	15
Poor	5	5	3	10

*Tables adopted from *The Y's Way to Physical Fitness* (Golding, Meyers and Sinning 1982). Norms were developed for the YMCA test by A. Jackson, University of Houston.

Muscular Strength and Endurance

Three tests are used to evaluate these components of physical fitness:

1. *Two-arm curl test.* This test measures the number of times an individual can repeatedly move a barbell. A 25-pound load is used with women; a 40-pound barbell with men. The individual stands against a wall to standardize the movement. A metronome, set at 44 beats per minute, regulates the rate of movement. Each click of the metronome signals a movement—up, down, up, down, and so on. The score is the number of repetitions.

2. *Bench-press test.* This test is similar to the two-arm curl test except that the bench-press position is used. The weight load is 35 pounds for women, 80 pounds for men.

3. *One-minute timed sit-ups.* This is the typical bent-knee sit-up test. The participant performs as many correct sit-ups as possible within a 1-minute period.

Table 8.17

Physical Fitness Evaluation Standards for the YMCA Fitness Test for Adult Females.*

RATING	PERCENTILE RANKING	TRUNK FLEXION	BENCH PRESS	1-MIN SIT UPS
Females ≤ 35 years				
Excellent	95	23	30	39
Good	85	21	24	34
Above Av	75	20	20	30
Average	50	18	16	25
Below Av	30	15	13	20
Fair	15	14	10	15
Poor	5	11	5	10
Females 35 to 46 years				
Excellent	95	23	29	39
Good	85	21	21	29
Above Av	75	19	18	22
Average	50	17	15	18
Below Av	30	14	11	12
Fair	15	12	7	9
Poor	5	10	4	4
Females ≥ 46 years				
Excellent	95	22	30	24
Good	85	19	22	20
Above Av	75	18	18	17
Average	50	15	14	14
Below Av	30	14	9	11
Fair	15	11	5	7
Poor	5	9	2	2

*Tables adopted from *The Y's Way to Physical Fitness* (Golding, Meyers and Sinning 1982). Norms were developed for the YMCA test by A. Jackson, University of Houston.

Cardiorespiratory Endurance

The bicycle ergometer is used to evaluate this component. Maximal oxygen uptake is predicted from the participant's response to a submaximal workload. The double stage model is used to estimate $\dot{V}O_2$ Max from submaximal heart rate response to work. The suggested test protocols for men and women are presented in figures 8.8 and 8.9. The YMCA provides a graph to calculate $\dot{V}O_2$ Max by hand. This would be somewhat less accurate than using the multi-stage formula.

COMPUTER EXAMPLE—GENERAL FITNESS ASSESSMENT

A sample output of the GENERAL FITNESS ASSESSMENT (GFA)® is furnished in figure 8.28. This is from a commercially developed program written for use on a microcomputer. Once the exercise test data are entered, the program has the capacity to make selected calculations that include: estimating percent body fat from skinfolds; estimating ideal body weight for a selected percent body fat level; estimating $\dot{V}O_2$ Max from any submaximal bike or treadmill test; and evaluating respiratory function.

Figure 8.28 Sample computer output used with the permission of Cardio-Stress Inc., Houston, Texas. (Source: Jackson, A. S. and R. M. Ross. *Understanding Exercise for Health and Fitness.* MacJ-R Publishing Co., Houston, Texas 1986.)

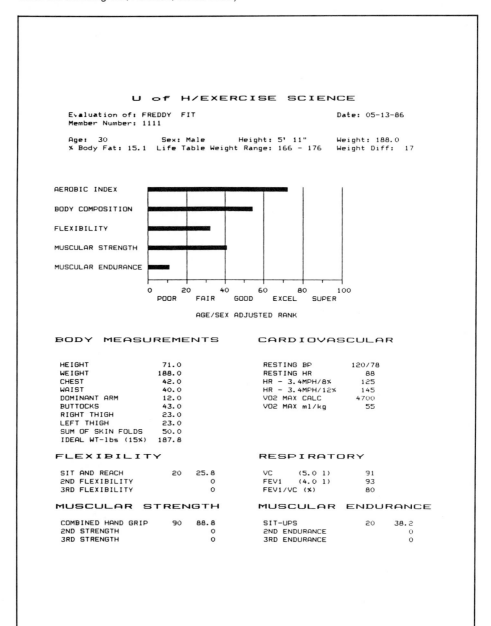

U of H/EXERCISE SCIENCE

Evaluation of: FREDDY FIT   Date: 05-13-86
Member Number: 1111

Age: 30   Sex: Male   Height: 5' 11"   Weight: 188.0
% Body Fat: 15.1 Life Table Weight Range: 166 - 176 Weight Diff: 17

AEROBIC INDEX

BODY COMPOSITION

FLEXIBILITY

MUSCULAR STRENGTH

MUSCULAR ENDURANCE

         0   20   40   60   80   100
        POOR FAIR GOOD EXCEL SUPER

              AGE/SEX ADJUSTED RANK

BODY MEASUREMENTS   **CARDIOVASCULAR**

HEIGHT   71.0   RESTING BP   120/78
WEIGHT   188.0   RESTING HR   88
CHEST   42.0   HR - 3.4MPH/8%   125
WAIST   40.0   HR - 3.4MPH/12%   145
DOMINANT ARM   12.0   VO2 MAX CALC   4700
BUTTOCKS   43.0   VO2 MAX ml/kg   55
RIGHT THIGH   23.0
LEFT THIGH   23.0
SUM OF SKIN FOLDS   50.0
IDEAL WT-lbs (15%) 187.8

FLEXIBILITY   **RESPIRATORY**

SIT AND REACH   20 25.8   VC   (5.0 l)   91
2ND FLEXIBILITY   0   FEV1 (4.0 l)   93
3RD FLEXIBILITY   0   FEV1/VC (%)   80

MUSCULAR STRENGTH   **MUSCULAR ENDURANCE**

COMBINED HAND GRIP 90 88.8   SIT-UPS   20 38.2
2ND STRENGTH   0   2ND ENDURANCE   0
3RD STRENGTH   0   3RD ENDURANCE   0

If available, measured $\dot{V}O_2$ Max (ml·min^{-1}) and percent body fat will override the estimated values. For this example, percent body fat was estimated, but $\dot{V}O_2$ Max was measured. In addition, several different flexibility, strength and endurance scores and various body measurements can be entered.

The program has the capacity to evaluate the individual's fitness for his or her age and sex, graphically shown on the sample output. An excellent feature of the program is the capacity to individualize norms. The graphic output is then adjusted to account for unique sample characteristics and permits the use of many different types of fitness tests. A powerful feature of microcomputers is the capacity to store and recall data. A feature of the GFA is the ability to store test results and provide a comparison of two different fitness tests. Periodically, descriptive statistics for all tests administered can be obtained, providing the capacity for updating norms.

SUMMARY

Adult physical fitness is important for maintaining health. There is a growing body of evidence supporting the value of regular vigorous exercise on health. Physical activity has been shown to reduce the risk of heart attack and obesity is related to major diseases such as diabetes mellitus, and cardiovascular diseases. Many universities, YMCA's, private corporations, and commercial organizations are providing adults with health-related fitness programs.

Cardiorespiratory endurance ($\dot{V}O_2$ Max) is a major component of fitness. It may be measured by either maximal or submaximal tests. The most valid method is a maximal test where $\dot{V}O_2$ Max is measured directly from expired gases. Typically, this method is reserved for research purposes. A second maximal method is to estimate $\dot{V}O_2$ Max for treadmill time with regression equations. Submaximal tests are more realistic for mass use. $\dot{V}O_2$ Max is estimated from submaximal work load and exercise heart rate response to the work. Single and multi-stage models are available for estimating $\dot{V}O_2$ Max. They have similar accuracy, with the standard error of prediction about 1.8 METs.

Another major component of adult fitness is body composition. Hydrostatically determined body density is the most valid laboratory measure of body composition. Once body density is known, an individual's percent body fat can be calculated easily with a standard formula. Skinfold measurements provide a valid field test of body composition, and multiple regression equations are available for estimating laboratory-determined body density from the sum of skinfold fat and age. The generalized equations have been shown to be valid for men and women varying greatly in age and body fatness. The YMCA has published a comprehensive adult fitness testing and exercise program. The program was developed by leaders in the field of adult fitness. The components of fitness measured include: (1) cardiorespiratory endurance; (2) body composition; (3) flexibility; (4) muscular strength; and (5) muscular endurance.

FORMATIVE EVALUATION OF OBJECTIVES

Objective 1   Identify the maximal and submaximal tests that are used to measure $\dot{V}O_2$ Max.

1. The most valid tests of $\dot{V}O_2$ Max are termed "maximal" tests. Describe the two methods you can use to measure $\dot{V}O_2$ Max with maximal tests.
2. $\dot{V}O_2$ Max can be estimated from submaximal work. Describe the steps followed for the single and multi-stage models.

Objective 2   Calculate $\dot{V}O_2$ Max from: (A) maximal treadmill time; and (B) submaximal work using the single and multi-stage models.

1. What is $\dot{V}O_2$ Max for the following treadmill times and protocols:
   a. 10 minutes for: (1) Bruce; (2) Balke?
   b. 18 minutes for: (1) Bruce; (2) Balke?
   c. Would you expect someone to last 25 minutes on the Bruce or Balke? Why or why not?
2. Calculate $\dot{V}O_2$ Max from the following:
   a. Female with a maximal heart rate of 187, and submaximal values: $\dot{V}O_2$ of 6 METs, and heart rate 145 b·min^{-1}.
   b. Male, age 37 years. Submaximal work on a bike 900 kpm·min^{-1} and heart rate 140 b·min^{-1}.
   c. A 28-year-old person had the following submaximal treadmill data: (1) speed 2.9 mph, grade 3%, heart rate 110 b·min^{-1}; (2) 3.4 mph, grade 6%, heart rate 148 b·min^{-1}.

Objective 3   Identify maximal and submaximal treadmill protocols.

1. Define the speeds and elevations for the Balke and Bruce treadmill protocols.
2. Define the speeds and elevations for the Ross and Bruce submaximal treadmill protocols.

Objective 4   Identify bicycle ergometer submaximal protocols.

1. List the work loads you would follow to test a typical woman.
2. List the work loads you would follow to test a typical man.
3. What would be the work load differences for a: (a) single-stage model; and (b) multi-stage model?

Objective 5   Identify the methods used to measure body composition.

1. Outline the steps you would follow to measure percent body fat by the hydrostatic weighing method.
2. Outline the steps you would follow to measure percent body fat using the generalized skinfold equations.

Objective 6   Calculate body density and percent body fat from generalized skinfold equations.

1. A 42-year-old woman has a sum of 7 skinfolds of 130 mm. What is body density and percent body fat? What would these values be if she had a sum of three of 64 mm?
2. A 38-year-old man had the following skinfold values: sum of seven of 142 mm and sum of three of 65 mm. What would be his estimated body density and percent body fat?

Objective 7   Calculate desired weight for various levels of percent body fat.

1. Assume a 165 pound woman's percent body fat is 35%. What would her weight be if she was 23%? How about 28%?
2. Assume a football player's body weight is 245 pounds and his measured percent body fat is 23%. If a coach would like his body composition to be between 10% and 15%, what would his weight range be?

Objective 8   Identify the items of the YMCA test.

1. List the test items of the YMCA fitness test.
2. Describe the method used to measure $\dot{V}O_2$ Max.
3. Describe the method used to measure body composition.

Objective 9   Identify computer methods that can be used to evaluate adult fitness.

ADDITIONAL LEARNING ACTIVITIES

1. A true understanding of $\dot{V}O_2$ Max is best obtained by measuring it. Find a partner and measure your own $\dot{V}O_2$ Max. If your college or university has metabolic equipment, try this method and compare the results you get by maximal treadmill time and the submaximal models.
2. Measure the skinfold thickness on several individuals. The secret to obtaining accurate percent body fat estimates from the generalized skinfold equations is to correctly measure skinfold thickness. Work with a partner and compare your results. Follow the instructions and pictures provided in this chapter.
3. Have your body composition determined by the underwater weighing method. This is the most valid method of measuring body composition. Be certain they measure your residual lung volume.
4. Use the computer at your college or university and calculate $\dot{V}O_2$ Max and body composition with SPSS. Use the sample programs provided in this chapter.
5. Many of you may have your own microcomputer, or have access to a microcomputer, and will have taken a course on their use. Develop a microcomputer program that will calculate $\dot{V}O_2$ Max or body composition. If you know a basic programming language, it is not difficult. Use the SPSS examples provided in this chapter as a guide. If you have not taken a microcomputer course, consider doing so. You will find it very useful.

BIBLIOGRAPHY

ACSM. 1978. "Position Statement on the Recommended Quantity and Quality of Exercise for Developing and Maintaining Fitness in Healthy Adults." *Medicine and Science in Sports* 10:vii.

ACSM. 1980. *Guidelines for Graded Exercise Testing and Exercise Prescription.* Philadelphia, Pa.: Lea & Febiger.

ACSM. 1983. "Position Statement on Proper and Improper Weight Loss Programs." *Medicine and Science in Sports and Exercise.* 15:ix–xiii.

AHA. 1972. *Exercise Testing and Training of Apparently Healthy Individuals: A Handbook for Physicians.* The Committee on Exercise, American Heart Association.

AHA. 1975. *Exercise Testing and Training of Individuals with Heart Disease or at High Risk for its Development: A Handbook for Physicians.* The Committee on Exercise, American Heart Association.

Åstrand, P., and I. Rhyming. 1954. "A Nomogram for Calculation of Aerobic Capacity (Physical Fitness) for Pulse Rate During Submaximal Work." *Journal of Applied Physiology* 7:218–221.

Åstrand, P., and K. Rodahl. 1970. *Textbook of Work Physiology.* New York: McGraw-Hill.

Åstrand, P., and K. Rodahl. 1977. *Textbook of Work Physiology.* 2d ed. New York: McGraw-Hill.

Balke, B. 1963. "A Simple Field Test for the Assessment of Physical Fitness." CARI Report. Oklahoma City, Okla.: Civil Aeromedical Research Institute, Aviation Agency.

Behnke, A. R., and J. H. Wilmore. 1974. *Evaluation and Regulation of Body Build and Composition.* Englewood Cliffs, N.J.: Prentice-Hall.

Borg, G. 1977. *Physical Work and Effort.* (Proceedings of the First International Symposium, Wenner-Gren Center, Stockholm, Sweden) Pergamon Press: Oxford, England.

Brožek, J., and A. Keys. 1951. "The Evaluation of Leanness-Fatness in Man: Norms and Intercorrelations." *British Journal of Nutrition* 5:194–206.

Brožek, J., F. Grande, J. T. Anderson et al. 1963. "Densitometric Analysis of Body Composition: Revision of Some Quantitative Assumptions." *Annals of New York Academy of Science* 110:113–40.

Bruce, R. A., F. Kusumi, and D. Hosmer. 1973. "Maximal Oxygen Intake and Nomographic Assessment of Functional Aerobic Impairment in Cardiovascular Disease." *American Heart Journal* 85:546–62.

Bulbulion, R. 1984. "The Influence of Somatotype on the Anthropometric Prediction of Body Composition in Young Women." *Medicine and Science in Sports and Exercise* 16:387–89.

Craddock, D. 1978. *Obesity and its Management.* 3d ed. New York: Churchill Livingston.

Cureton, K. J. 1984. "A Reaction to the Manuscript of Jackson." *Medicine and Science in Sports and Exercise.* 16:621–22.

Cureton, K. J., R. A. Boileau, and T. G. Lohman. 1975. "A Comparison of Densitometric, Potassium-40, and Skinfold Estimates of Body Composition in Prepubescent Boys." *Human Biology* 47:321–36.

deVries, H. A. 1966. *Physiology of Exercise.* Dubuque, Iowa: Wm. C. Brown.

Durnin, J. V. G. A., and M. M. Rahaman. 1967. "The Assessment of the Amount of Fat in the Human Body from Measurements of Skinfold Thickness." *British Journal of Nutrition* 21:681–89.

Durnin, J. V. G. A., and J. Wormsley. 1974. "Body Fat Assessed from Total Body Density and its Estimation from Skinfold Thickness: Measurements on 481 Men and Women Aged from 16 to 72 Years." *British Journal of Nutrition* 32:77–92.

Edwards, D. A. W. 1951. Differences in the distributions of subcutaneous fat with sex and maturity. *Clinical Science.* 10:305–315.

Ellestad, M. H. 1980. *Stress Testing: Principles and Practice.* 2d ed. Philadelphia, Pa.: F. A. Davis Co.

Forsyth, H. L., and W. E. Sinning. 1973. "The Anthropometric Estimation of Body Density and Lean Body Weight of Male Athletes." *Medicine and Science in Sports* 5:174–80.

Foster, C., A. S. Jackson, M. L. Pollock et al. 1984. "Generalized Equations for Predicting Functional Capacity from Treadmill Performance." *American Heart Journal* 107:1229–34.

Froelicher, V. F. 1983. *Exercise Testing and Training.* New York: LeJacq Publishing.

Golding, L. A., C. R. Meyers, W. E. Sinning. 1982. *The Y's Way to Physical Fitness.* 2d ed. Chicago, Ill.: National Board of YMCA.

Haisman, M. F. 1970. "The Assessment of Body Fat Content in Young Men from Measurements of Body Density and Skinfold Thickness." *Human Biology* 42:679–88.

Harsha, D. W., R. R. Fredrichs, and G. S. Berenson. 1978. "Densitometry and Anthropometry of Black and White Children." *Human Biology* 50:261–80.

Hodgdon, J. A., and M. B. Beckett. 1984a. *Prediction of Percent Body Fat for U.S. Navy Men from Body Circumferences and Height.* Report No. 84-11, Naval Health Research Center, San Diego, Calif.

Hodgdon, J. A., and M. B. Beckett. 1984b. *Prediction of Percent Body Fat for U.S. Navy Women from Body Circumferences and Height.* Report No. 84-29, Naval Health Research Center, San Diego, Calif.

Hodgdon, J. A., and M. B. Beckett. 1984c. *Technique for Measuring Body Circumferences and Skinfold Thicknesses.* Report No. 84-39, Naval Health Research Center, San Diego, Calif.

Hubert, H. B., M. Feinleib, P. M. McNamara et al. 1983. "Obesity as an Independent Risk Factor for Cardiovascular Disease: a 26-Year Follow-Up of Participants in the Framingham Heart Study." *Circulation.* 67:968–77.

Jackson, A. S. 1984. "Research Design and Analysis of Data Procedures for Predicting Body Density." *Medicine and Science in Sports and Exercise.* 16:616–20.

Jackson, A. S., and M. L. Pollock. 1976. "Factor Analysis and Multivariate Scaling of Anthropometric Variables for the Assessment of Body Composition." *Medicine and Science in Sports* 8:196–203.

Jackson, A. S., and M. L. Pollock. 1978. "Generalized Equations for Predicting Body Density of Men." *British Journal of Nutrition* 40:497–504.

Jackson, A. S., and M. L. Pollock. 1985. "Practical Assessment of Body Composition." *The Physician and Sportsmedicine* 13:76–90.

Jackson, A. S., and M. L. Pollock. 1977. "Prediction Accuracy of Body Density, Lean Weight, and Total Body Volume Equations." *Medicine and Science in Sports* 9:197–201.

Jackson, A. S., and M. L. Pollock. 1982. "Steps Toward the Development of Generalized Equations for Predicting Body Composition of Adults." *Canadian Journal of Applied Sport Science.* 7:187–96.

Jackson, A. S., M. L. Pollock, and L. R. Gettman. 1978. "Intertester Reliability of Selected Skinfold and Circumference Measurements and Percent Fat Estimates." *Research Quarterly* 49:546–51.

Jackson, A. S., M. L. Pollock, and J. Graves, 1986. "Effect of Inter and Intra Tester Error Predicting Body Density Skin Fold." *Medicine and Science in Sports and Exercise.* 18: s.31.

Jackson, A. S., M. L. Pollock, and A. Ward. 1980. "Generalized Equations for Predicting Body Density of Women." *Medicine and Science in Sports.* 12:175–82.

Jackson, A. S. and R. M. Ross. 1986. *Understanding Exercise for Health and Fitness.* Houston, Texas: MacJ–R. 107–9.

Jones, N. L., and E. J. M. Campbell. 1982. *Clinical Exercise Testing.* Philadelphia, Pa.: W. B. Saunders Company.

Katch, F. I., and W. D. McArdle. 1973. "Prediction of Body Density from Simple Anthropometric Measurements in College Age Women and Men." *Human Biology* 45:445–54.

Katch, F. I., and W. D. McArdle. 1977. *Nutrition, Weight Control, and Exercise.* Boston, Mass.: Houghton Mifflin.

Katch, F. I., and E. D. Michael. 1968. "Prediction of Body Density from Skinfold and Girth Measurements of College Females." *Journal of Applied Physiology* 25:92–94.

Katch, F. I., and E. D. Michael. 1969. "Densitometric Validation of Six Skinfold Formulas to Predict Body Density and Percent Fat of 17-Year-Old Boys." *Research Quarterly* 40:712–16.

Keys, A. 1956. "Recommendations concerning Body Measurements for the Characterization of Nutritional Status." *Human Biology* 28:111–23.

Lohman, T. G. 1982. "Body Composition Methodology in Sports Medicine." *Physician and Sports Medicine.* 10:46–58.

Lohman, T. G. 1981. "Skinfolds and Body Density and Their Relation to Body Fatness: a Review." *Human Biology.* 53:181–225.

Lohman, T. G., and M. L. Pollock. 1981. "Which Caliper? How Much Training?" *JOPER.* 52:27–29.

Lohman, T. G., M. L. Pollock, M. H. Slaughter et al. 1984. "Methodological Factors and the Prediction of Body Fat in Female Athletes." *Medicine and Science in Sports and Exercise.* 16:92–96.

Mahar, M., A. S. Jackson, R. L. Ross et al. 1985. "Predictive Accuracy of Single and Double Stage Sub Max Treadmill Work for Estimating Aerobic Capacity." *Medicine and Science in Sports and Exercise.* 17:206–7.

Morrow, J. R., A. S. Jackson, P. W. Bradley et al. 1985. "Function of Measured and Predicted Residual Lung Volume on Body Density Measurement Errors." *Medicine and Science in Sports and Exercise.* 17:204.

Morrow, J. R., J. Pivarnik, and A. S. Jackson. 1987. *Microcomputer Program for Calculating $\dot{V}O_2$ Max and Body Composition.* Dubuque, Ia.: Wm. C. Brown.

Pandolf, K. B., B. Givoni, and R. Goldman. 1977. "Predicting Energy Expenditure with Loads While Standing or Walking Very Slowly." *Journal of Applied Physiology* 43:577–81.

Parizkova, J. 1961. "Total Body Fat and Skinfold Thickness in Children." *Metabolism* 10:794–807.

Pascale, L., et al. 1956. "Correlations between Thickness of Skinfolds and Body Density in 88 Soldiers." *Human Biology* 28:165–76.

Pollock, M. L. 1977. "Submaximal and Maximal Working Capacity of Elite Distance Runners—Part I: Cardiorespiratory Aspects." *Annals of New York Academy of Science* 301:310–22.

Pollock, M. L., R. L. Bohannon, K. H. Cooper et al. 1976. "A Comparative Analysis of Four Protocols for Maximal Treadmill Stress Testing." *American Heart Journal* 92:39–46.

Pollock, M. L., C. Foster, D. Knapp et al. "Effect of Age, Training and Competition on Aerobic Capacity and Body Composition of Master's Athletes." Submitted for Publication.

Pollock, M. L., C. Foster, D. H. Schmidt et al. 1982. "Comparative Analysis of Physiologic Responses to Three Different Maximal Graded Exercise Test Protocols in Healthy Women." *American Heart Journal* 103:363–73.

Pollock, M. L., L. R. Gettman, A. S. Jackson et al. 1977. "Body Composition of Elite Class Distance Runners." *Annals of New York Academy of Sciences.* 301:361–70.

Pollock, M. L., T. Hickman, Z. Kendrick et al. 1976. "Prediction of Body Density in Young and Middle-aged Men." *Journal of Applied Physiology.* 40:300–304.

Pollock, M. L., and A. S. Jackson. 1977. "Body Composition: Measurement and Changes Resulting from Physical Training." *Proceedings,* 1977 Annual Meeting of NCPEAM and NCPEAW, Orlando, Fla.

Pollock, M. L., and A. S. Jackson, 1984. "Research Progress in Validation of Clinical Methods of Measuring Body Composition." *Medicine and Science in Sports and Exercise.* 18:606–13.

Pollock, M. L., E. Laughridge, E. Coleman et al. 1978. "Prediction of Body Density in Young and Middle-aged Women." *Journal of Applied Physiology.* 38:745–49.

Pollock, M. L., D. H. Schmidt, and A. S. Jackson. 1980. "Measurement of Cardiorespiratory Fitness and Body Composition in the Clinical Setting. *Comprehensive Therapy* 6:12–27.

Pollock, M. L.; J. H. Wilmore, and S. M. Fox, III. 1984. *Exercise in Health and Disease.* Philadelphia, Pa.: W. B. Saunders.

Pollock, M. L., J. H. Wilmore, and S. M. Fox, III. 1978. *Health and Fitness Through Physical Activity.* New York: Wiley.

Ross, R. M. 1984. *Understand Exercise.* Houston, Tx.: Cardio-Stress Inc.

Ross, R. M. and A. S. Jackson. 1986. "Development and Validation of Total Work Equations for Estimating the Energy Cost of Walking." *Journal of Cardiopulmonary Rehabilitation.* 6:182–92.

Shephard, R. J. 1972. Alive Man: *The Physiology of Physical Activity.* Springfield, Ill.: Charles C. Thomas.

Sinning, W. E. 1978. "Anthropometric Estimation of Body Density, Fat and Lean Body Weight in Women Gymnasts." *Medicine and Science in Sports* 10:234–49.

Sinning, W. E., D. G. Dolny, K. D. Little et al. 1985. "Validity of 'Generalized' Equations for Body Composition in Male Athletes." *Medicine and Science in Sports and Exercise* 17:124–30.

Sinning, W. E. and J. R. Wilson. 1984. "Validity of 'Generalized' Equations for Body Composition Analysis in Women Athletes." *Research Quarterly for Exercise and Sport.* 55:153–60.

Siri, W. E. 1961. "Body Composition from Fluid Space and Density." In *Techniques for Measuring Body Composition,* Ed. J. Brožek and A. Hanschel, 233–34. Washington, D.C.: National Academy of Science.

Sloan, A. W. 1967. "Estimation of Body Fat in Young Men." *Journal of Applied Physiology* 23:311–15.

Sloan, A. W., J. J. Burt, and C. S. Blyth. 1962. "Estimation of Body Fat in Young Women." *Journal of Applied Physiology* 17:967–70.

Smith, J. F. and E. R. Mansfield. 1984. "Body Composition Prediction in University Football Players." *Medicine and Science in Sports and Exercise.* 16:398–405.

Thorland, W. G., G. O. Johnson, G. D. Tharp et al. 1984. "Validity of Anthropometric Equations for the Estimation of Body Density in Adolescent Athletes." *Medicine and Science in Sports and Exercise.* 16:77–81.

Wilmore, J. H. 1983. "Body Composition in Sport and Exercise: Directions for Future Research." *Medicine and Science in Sports and Exercise* 15:21–31.

Wilmore, J. H. 1982. *Training for Sport and Activity: The Physiological Basis of the Conditioning Process.* 2d ed. Boston, Mass.: Allyn and Bacon.

Wilmore, J. H., and A. R. Behnke. 1969. "An Anthropometric Estimation of Body's Density and Lean Body Weight in Young Men." *Journal of Applied Physiology* 27:25–31.

Wilmore, J. H., S. H. Constable, P. R. Stanforth et al. 1982. "Mechanical and Physiological Calibration of Four Cycle Ergometers." *Medicine and Science in Sports and Exercise* 14:322–25.

Wilmore, J. H., and A. R. Behnke. 1970. "An Anthropometric Estimation of Body Density and Lean Body Weight in Young Women." *American Journal of Clinical Nutrition* 23:267–74.

Wright, H. F., and J. H. Wilmore. 1974. "Estimation of Relative Body Fat and Lean Body Weight in a United States Marine Corps Population." *Aerospace Medicine* 45:301–06.

Young, C. M. 1964. "Prediction of Specific Gravity and Body Fatness in Older Women." *Journal of American Dietetic Association* 45:333–38.

Young, C. M., M. Martin, W. R. Tensuan et al. 1962. "Predicting Specific Gravity and Body Fatness in Young Women." *Journal of American Dietetic Association* 40:102–07.

Evaluating Youth Fitness

9

Contents

Key Words

AAHPERD YFT
AAHPERD HRFT
Aerobic Fitness
Agility
Body Composition
Cardiorespiratory Function
Circulatory-Respiratory Endurance
Distance Runs
Flexibility
Health-Related Physical Fitness
Motor Fitness
Muscular Endurance
Muscular Power
Muscular Strength
Presidential Physical Fitness Award
Skinfold Fat
Speed
Steady State Run
Texas Youth Fitness Test
$\dot{V}O_2$ Max

Objectives

One important goal of physical education programs is to develop physical fitness. The two methods used to evaluate youth fitness are motor fitness and health-related fitness tests. Here we present tests and norms for evaluating youth fitness. The procedures used to measure adult fitness (chapter 8) require the use of equipment, such as motor-driven treadmill or bicycle ergometer, and are not practical for mass testing. Instead we include valid tests that are feasible for administering in a field setting. These types of tests are used in public school physical education programs.

    After reading chapter 9, you should be able to:

1. Identify the general tests that comprise a motor fitness battery.
2. Identify the general tests that comprise health-related fitness batteries.
3. Differentiate between motor fitness and health-related fitness batteries.
4. Analyze the validity of tests used to evaluate youth fitness.
5. Identify the changes in youth fitness that have occurred in the United States.
6. Understand the use of computers for the evaluation of youth fitness.

INTRODUCTION

Although the development of an acceptable level of physical fitness is a universal goal of physical education programs, a definition of physical fitness is less widely accepted. The President's Council on Physical Fitness and Sports defines it as follows:

> . . . the ability to carry out daily tasks with vigor and alertness, without undue fatigue, and with ample energy to enjoy leisure-time pursuits and to meet unforeseen emergencies. Thus, physical fitness is the ability to last, to bear up, to withstand stress, and to persevere under difficult circumstances where an unfit person would quit. It is the opposite to becoming fatigued from ordinary efforts, to lacking energy to enter zestfully into life's activities, and to becoming exhausted from unexpected, demanding physical exertion.
>
> The definition given implies that physical fitness is more than "not being sick" or merely "being well." It is different from immunity to disease. It is a positive quality extending on a scale from death to abundant life. All living individuals, thus, have some degree of physical fitness, which is minimal in the severely ill and maximal in the highly trained athletes; it varies considerably in different people and in the same person from time to time (Clarke 1971).

Recent research has shown that physical inactivity is associated with higher levels of hypertension, heart disease, diabetes, and low back problems. This link between exercise and disease has led to a health-related view of physical fitness (Jackson et al. 1976) that is the foundation of the newer health-related batteries. The definition that provided the direction for the development of the AAHPERD Health-Related Fitness Test (AAHPERD 1980) is:

> Physical fitness testing, and programs for developing fitness, should emphasize the relationship between health and physical activity. Physical fitness is a multifaceted continuum that is affected by physical activity, and ranges from death at one end to the other extreme of optimal functional abilities in all aspects of life. Between the two extremes are severely limiting diseases related to physical inactivity and low to high levels of different physical fitnesses.
>
> Since physical fitness can be operationally defined by the tests used for its evaluation, specific criteria were needed for choosing the tests. The criteria selected were as follows:
>
> 1. A physical fitness test should measure an area which extends from severely limited dysfunction to high levels of functional capacity.
> 2. It should measure capacities that can be improved with appropriate physical activity.
> 3. It should accurately reflect an individual's physical fitness status as well as changes in functional capacity by corresponding test scores and changes in these scores.
>
> The areas of physiological function which are related to positive health, are of national concern, and appear to meet the above criteria are:
>
> 1. Cardiorespiratory function
> 2. Body composition (leanness/fatness)
> 3. Abdominal and low back-hamstring musculoskeletal function

Since the concern for positive health extends to all ages, it is recommended that all persons be tested periodically on health related fitness components. Periodic testing places emphases on the importance of an active life style to achieve and maintain low amounts of fat, high levels of cardiorespiratory function, and sufficient muscular strength, muscular endurance, and flexibility in the lower trunk and posterior thigh areas for healthy low back function (AAHPERD 1980).

In the past, physical fitness has been defined in broad terms, and tests have measured either an aspect of physiological function or selected aspects of motor performance. This type of test has been termed motor fitness and includes not only strength and endurance components, but also factors of speed, power, and agility (Clarke 1971). Motor fitness tests are more indicative of potential for athletic excellence than fitness for health promotion. As the concept of physical fitness has moved away from athletic participation toward health, the components have changed to include cardiorespiratory function, body composition (leanness/fatness), strength, endurance, and lower-back flexibility, traits shown by medical and exercise scientists to promote health and reduce the risk of disease.

In the text we discuss both motor fitness and health-related fitness batteries. The AAHPERD Youth Fitness Tests (YFT) is presented in its entirety. Selected percentile rank norms and the standards needed to qualify for the Presidential Youth Fitness Award are provided. In addition, two health-related fitness batteries are furnished. First, the AAHPERD Health Related Physical Fitness Test (HRFT) with norms appears in full. Second, the new Texas Youth Fitness Test is provided. The Texas test is a dramatic departure from traditional fitness testing by defining criterion levels of fitness for health promotion. The validity of fitness tests is discussed and sample computer programs for evaluating youth fitness are provided. The final section explores recent youth fitness trends.

MOTOR FITNESS

The terms physical fitness and motor fitness are often used interchangeably, but **motor fitness** is actually broader and less definitive in scope. It includes both physical fitness and motor ability factors. The seven components that define motor fitness (Clarke 1971) and tests often used to measure a component are:

1. **Muscular strength** is characterized by the contraction power of the muscles. This capacity involves the amount of force a muscle can exert (see chapter 7). Pull-ups, flexed-arm hangs, or push-ups are normally included in motor fitness batteries and said to measure strength, but one can question if these items are measuring strength or endurance.
2. **Muscular endurance** is characterized by the ability to perform work. The capacity involves performing a task to exhaustion. The bent-knee sit-up is commonly used to measure this trait.

3. **Circulatory-respiratory endurance** is characterized by moderate contractions of large muscle groups over long periods of time. Examples are running long distances.

4. **Muscular power** is the ability to release maximum muscular force in the shortest possible time, as in executing a standing long jump.

5. **Agility** is the ability to change body position or direction rapidly and is often tested with a shuttle run test.

6. **Speed** is the rapidity of movement and can be tested with the 50-yard dash.

7. **Flexibility** is the range of movement in a joint or joints and tests are usually not included in motor fitness batteries.

Many different motor fitness tests have been published and are reported in older editions of measurement texts. The AAHPERD Youth Fitness Test (1976) has proved to be a popular test and is provided next.

AAHPERD Youth Fitness Test (YFT)

The original **AAHPERD YFT** was published in 1958 and revised in 1975 and 1976. The test was developed in response to a study (Kraus and Hirschland 1954) that reported that European children scored higher on the Kraus-Weber tests of minimum muscular fitness than did American children. The Kraus-Weber tests were designed to identify adults who were likely to have low back problems.

The AAHPERD YFT was developed by a group of physical educators who met and selected tests on the basis of logic. The YFT was not developed through test validation research. In 1975, major changes were made. The straight-leg sit-up was replaced with the flexed-leg sit-up from the Texas test (1973) and the softball throw was dropped. It was thought that the straight-leg sit-up and throw-for-distance might cause musculoskeletal injuries. In addition, the longer distance runs of the Texas test (1973) were offered as options.

In 1976, a national normative survey was completed and national norms for the YFT were revised (AAHPERD 1976). The only distance run included in the normative survey was the 600-yard run. The six tests in the current battery with national normative data are:

1. Pull-up (boys) or flexed-arm hang (girls)
2. Sit-up (flexed leg, 60-second time limit)
3. Shuttle run
4. Standing long jump
5. 50-yard dash
6. 600-yard run

The test instructions for each item of the AAHPERD Youth Fitness Test are provided next. Selected percentile ranks are furnished in tables 9.1 through 9.6. Complete norms are available in the original source (AAHPERD 1976).

Table 9.1

Percentile Rank Norms from the AAHPER Test for Pull-Ups.

	AGE							
PERCENTILE	*10	11	12	13	14	15	16	17+
95	9	8	9	10	12	15	14	15
75	3	4	4	5	7	9	10	10
50	1	2	2	3	4	6	7	7
25	0	0	0	1	2	3	4	4
5	0	0	0	0	0	0	1	0

Percentile Rank Norms for Girls on the AAHPER Flexed-Arm Hang Test (In Seconds).

	AGE							
PERCENTILE	9–10	11	12	13	14	15	16	17+
95	42	39	33	34	35	36	31	34
75	18	20	18	16	21	18	15	17
50	9	10	9	8	9	9	7	8
25	3	3	3	3	3	4	3	3
5	0	0	0	0	0	0	0	0

Source: Adapted from *Youth Fitness Test Manual* (Washington, D.C.: AAHPER, 1976), p. 38. Used by permission.

Pull-Up Test

Equipment: A horizontal bar positioned at a height that allows the student to hang without touching the ground.

Procedure: The bar should be adjusted to a height that permits the student to hang free from the floor. From the hanging position with an overhand grip (palms forward), the body is then pulled upward until the chin rests over the bar, and then is lowered until the arms are straight. This movement should be repeated to exhaustion. The student is not allowed to kick, jerk, or use a "kip" movement.

Scoring: The student's score is the number of correctly executed chins. Selected norms are provided in table 9.1.

Flexed-Arm Hang Test

Equipment: A horizontal bar positioned at a height that allows the student to hang without touching the ground, and a stopwatch.

Procedure: The student uses the overhand grasp (palms forward). With the assistance of two spotters, one in front and one in back, the pupil raises the body off the floor to a position where the chin is above the bar, the elbows are flexed, and the chest is close to the bar. Start the stopwatch when the student reaches the hanging position. Stop the watch when: (1) the student's chin touches the bar; (2) the student's head tilts backward to keep the chin above the bar; or (3) the student's chin falls below the level of the bar.

Scoring: The score is the number of seconds measured to the nearest second that the student maintained the hanging position. Selected AAHPERD norms are listed in table 9.1.

Sit-Up (Flexed leg-60 seconds)

Equipment: A clean surface and a stopwatch is needed for test administration.

Procedure: The student lies on his or her back with the knees bent, feet on the floor, and heels no more than 12 inches from the buttocks. The angle at the knees should be less than 90 degrees. The student's hands should be on the back of the neck with fingers clasped and elbows touching the surface. By tightening the abdominal muscles, the student brings the head and elbows forward, as he or she curls up, to touch their elbows to their knees. This action constitutes one sit-up. The student must return to the starting position before executing another sit-up. The student begins on the command "Go," and stops on the command "Stop."

Scoring: The student's score is the number of correctly executed sit-ups performed in 60 seconds. Selected AAHPERD norms for girls and boys are listed in table 9.2.

Table 9.2
Percentile Norms for Girls for Sit-Ups.*

AGE	5	6	7	8	9	10	11	12	13	14	15	16	17+
Percentile													
95	28	35	40	44	44	47	50	52	51	51	56	54	54
75	24	28	31	35	35	39	40	41	41	42	43	42	44
50	19	22	25	29	29	32	34	36	35	35	37	33	37
25	12	14	20	22	23	25	28	30	29	30	30	29	31
5	2	6	10	12	14	15	19	19	18	20	20	20	19

*The complete table is available in *AAHPERD Manual* (AAHPERD, 1980).

Percentile Norms for Boys for Sit-Ups.*

AGE	5	6	7	8	9	10	11	12	13	14	15	16	17+
Percentile													
95	30	36	42	48	47	50	51	56	58	59	59	61	62
75	23	26	33	37	38	40	41	46	48	49	49	51	52
50	18	20	26	30	32	34	37	39	41	42	44	45	46
25	11	15	19	25	25	27	30	31	35	36	38	38	38
5	2	6	10	15	15	15	17	19	25	27	28	28	25

*The complete table is available in *AAHPERD Manual* (AAHPERD, 1980).

50-Yard Dash

Equipment: A stopwatch accurate to one-tenth second per runner, or a stopwatch accurate to one-tenth second with a split timer, and a test course of suitable length to ensure safe stopping after the sprint.

Procedure: Have two students run at the same time for competition. The students assume a starting position behind the starting line. The starter uses the commands "Are you ready?" and "Go!" On "Go," the starter makes a downward sweep of the arm, giving a visual signal to the timer to start the watch. The timer, standing at the finish line, stops the watch when the runner crosses the line.

Scoring: The student's score is the elapsed time between the starter's signal and the instant the pupil crosses the finish line. Scores are recorded to the nearest tenth of a second. Selected AAHPERD norms for girls and boys are listed in table 9.3.

Other considerations: Allow students to take one or two warm-up trials before they are timed for score.

Shuttle Run

Equipment: Floor space sufficiently large to allow acceptable traction, stopwatches accurate to a tenth of a second, and two wooden blocks (2″×2″×4″) per test station.

Procedure: The test course is comprised of two parallel lines placed on the floor 30 feet apart. The student starts from behind the first line and, after the

Table 9.3
Percentile Rank Norms for Girls and Boys on the 50-Yard Dash (In Seconds and Tenths of Seconds).

Percentile	GIRLS Age							
	9–10	11	12	13	14	15	16	17+
95	7.4	7.3	7.0	6.9	6.8	6.9	7.0	6.8
75	8.0	7.9	7.6	7.4	7.3	7.4	7.5	7.4
50	8.6	8.3	8.1	8.0	7.8	7.8	7.9	7.9
25	9.1	9.0	8.7	8.5	8.3	8.2	8.3	8.4
5	10.3	10.0	10.0	10.0	9.6	9.2	9.3	9.5
	BOYS							
95	7.3	7.1	6.8	6.5	6.2	6.0	6.0	5.9
75	7.8	7.6	7.4	7.0	6.8	6.5	6.5	6.3
50	8.2	8.0	7.8	7.5	7.2	6.9	6.7	6.6
25	8.9	8.6	8.3	8.0	7.7	7.3	7.0	7.0
5	9.9	9.5	9.5	9.0	8.8	8.0	7.7	7.9

Source: Adapted from *Youth Fitness Test Manual* (Washington, D.C.: AAHPER, 1976), pp. 42 and 50. Used by permission.

Table 9.4

Percentile Rank Norms for Boys and Girls on the Shuttle Run (in Seconds and Tenths).

	BOYS Age							
Percentile	9–10	11	12	13	14	15	16	17+
95	10.0	9.7	9.6	9.3	8.9	8.9	8.6	8.6
75	10.6	10.4	10.2	10.0	9.6	9.4	9.3	9.2
50	11.2	10.9	10.7	10.4	10.1	9.9	9.9	9.8
25	12.0	11.5	11.4	11.0	10.7	10.4	10.5	10.4
5	13.1	12.9	12.4	12.4	11.9	11.7	11.9	11.7
	GIRLS							
95	10.2	10.0	9.9	9.9	9.7	9.9	10.0	9.6
75	11.1	10.8	10.8	10.5	10.3	10.4	10.6	10.4
50	11.8	11.5	11.4	11.2	11.0	11.0	11.2	11.1
25	12.5	12.1	12.0	12.0	12.0	11.8	12.0	12.0
5	14.3	14.0	13.3	13.2	13.1	13.3	13.7	14.0

Source: Adapted from *Youth Fitness Test Manual* (Washington, D.C.: AAHPER, 1976). Used by permission.

starting command, runs to the second line, picks up one wooden block, runs back to the first line, and places the wooden block behind the line. The student then runs back and picks up the second block, carrying it back across the first line.

Scoring: The score is the elapsed time accurate to the nearest tenth of a second. Each student is allowed two trials and the best score is selected. The watch is started on the signal "Go," and stopped when the second block is carried across the line. Students who fall or slip significantly should be given another trial. Norms for boys and girls are listed in table 9.4.

Other considerations: This test is time consuming because the trials must be administered individually. You can save time by setting up several test courses and having a sufficient number of scorers. Efficiency can also be improved when two students run the course at the same time, in which case the tester needs two stopwatches or one with a split-second timer.

Standing Long Jump

Equipment: A tape measure at least 10 feet long and masking tape. You can construct the test station by attaching the tape measure to the floor with the starting line at 0 inches. We have found the gym floor to be a suitable surface, although mats can also be used.

Procedure: The student should straddle the tape measure, with feet parallel, about a shoulder-width apart, and toes behind the starting line. From this position, the student should squat and then jump horizontally as far as possible. The student should land straddling the tape measure.

Table 9.5

Percentile Rank Norms for Boys and Girls on the Standing Long Jump (in Feet and Inches).

| Percentile | BOYS Age | | | | | | | |
	9–10	11	12	13	14	15	16	17+
95	6'0"	6'2"	6'6"	7'1"	7'6"	8'0"	8'2"	8'5"
75	5'4"	5'7"	5'11"	6'3"	6'8"	7'2"	7'6"	7'9"
50	4'11"	5'2"	5'5"	5'9"	6'2"	6'8"	7'0"	7'2"
25	4'6"	4'8"	5'0"	5'2"	5'6"	6'1"	6'6"	6'6"
5	3'10"	4'0"	4'2"	4'4"	4'8"	5'2"	5'5"	5'3"
	GIRLS							
95	5'10"	6'0"	6'2"	6'5"	6'8"	6'7"	6'6"	6'9"
75	5'2"	5'4"	5'6"	5'9"	5'11"	5'10"	5'9"	6'0"
50	4'8"	4'11"	5'0"	5'3"	5'4"	5'5"	5'3"	5'5"
25	4'1"	4'4"	4'6"	4'9"	4'10"	4'11"	4'9"	4'11"
5	3'5"	3'8"	3'10"	4'0"	4'0"	4'2"	4'0"	4'1"

Source: Adapted from *Youth Fitness Test Manual* (Washington, D.C.: AAHPER, 1976). Used by permission.

Scoring: The recommended procedure is to administer three trials and award the student the best of the three trials. The test is scored in feet and inches to the nearest inch. Norms for boys and girls are listed in table 9.5.

Other considerations: Because the test must be administered individually, it's suggested that several test stations be used. It is important that students be allowed to practice the specific test because a learning effect has been shown to exist.

600-Yard Run

Equipment: The test can be administered on a track or a running course with the following dimensions: a 50 yard by 50 yard square; or a 30 yard by 120 yard rectangle. A stopwatch is needed to measure elapsed time.

Procedures: At the signal "Ready? Go." the student starts running the 600-yard distance. Walking is permitted, but the object is to cover the distance in the shortest time. It is possible to have a dozen students run at one time by having the students pair off before the start of the run and the partner serves as the runner's scorer. The scorer listens for the runners time when crossing the finish line when the timer calls out the times as the runners cross the finish line.

Scoring: The time of the run is recorded in minutes and seconds. Selected norms are presented in table 9.6.

Other considerations: Optional longer distance run tests are available. These include: ages 10 to 12 years, 1-mile or 9-minute run; and ages 13 years or older, 1.5-mile or 12-minute run. The norms are from the Texas Test (1973) and are presented in tables 9.7 and 9.8.

Table 9.6

Percentile Rank Norms on the AAHPERD 600-Yard Run Test.

	GIRLS Age							
Percentile	≤10	11	12	13	14	15	16	≥17
95	2'20"	2'14"	2'6"	2'4"	2'2"	2'0"	2'8"	2'2"
75	2'39"	2'35"	2'26"	2'23"	2'19"	2'22"	2'26"	2'24"
50	2'56"	2'53"	2'47"	2'41"	2'40"	2'37"	2'43"	2'41"
25	3'11"	3'16"	3'13"	3'6"	3'1"	3'0"	3'3"	3'2"
5	4'0"	4'15"	3'59"	3'49"	3'49"	3'28"	3'49"	3'45"
	BOYS							
95	2'5"	2'2"	1'52"	1'45"	1'39"	1'36"	1'34"	1'32"
75	2'17"	2'15"	2'6"	1'59"	1'52"	1'46"	1'44"	1'43"
50	2'33"	2'27"	2'19"	2'10"	2'3"	1'56"	1'52"	1'52"
25	2'53"	2'47"	2'37"	2'27"	2'16"	2'8"	2'1"	2'2"
5	3'22"	3'29"	3'6"	3'0"	2'51"	2'30"	2'31"	2'38"

From *AAHPERD Youth Fitness Test Manual* (1976).

Table 9.7

The Optional AAHPERD Youth Fitness Distance Run Tests for Males and Females, Ages 10 to 12 Years.*

	9-MINUTE RUN (YARDS)			1-MILE RUN (MIN:SEC)		
Percentile	10	11	12	10	11	12
	Females					
95	1969	1992	2015	7:28	6:57	6:23
75	1702	1725	1748	9:16	8:45	8:11
50	1514	1537	1560	10:29	9:58	9:24
25	1326	1349	1372	11:42	11:11	10:37
5	1059	1082	1105	13:30	12:59	12:24
	Males					
95	2294	2356	2418	5:55	5:32	5:09
75	1952	2014	2076	7:49	7:26	7:03
50	1717	1779	1841	9:07	8:44	8:21
25	1482	1544	1606	10:02	10:02	9:39
5	1140	1202	1264	12:19	11:56	11:33

*Normative data from Texas Test (1973).

Table 9.8
Optional Distance Run Tests for Boys and Girls, Age 13 and Older.

Percentile	12-MINUTE RUN (YARDS)		1.5 MILE RUN (MIN:SEC)	
	Boys	Girls	Boys	Girls
95	3297	2448	8:37	12:17
75	2879	2100	10:19	15:03
50	2592	1861	11:29	16:57
25	2305	1622	12:39	18:50
5	1888	1274	14:20	21:36

Normative data from Texas Test (1973).

Presidential Youth Fitness Award

The AAHPERD fitness battery is used by the President's Council on Physical Fitness and Sports to evaluate the achievement of physical fitness. The Council offers the **Presidential Physical Fitness Award** to any child who achieves at or above the 85th percentile for his or her age and sex on all tests. The standards that qualify a student for the Presidential award are furnished in tables 9.9 and 9.10.

The Presidential Award is quite difficult to achieve because a student must score at or above the 85th percentile on all six tests. Failure on just one test results in a failure to qualify for the award. Far less than 15% of the students should be expected to qualify for an award.

HEALTH-RELATED PHYSICAL FITNESS

The development of **health-related physical fitness** tests represents a major innovation in fitness testing. These tests were developed in response to both the growing dissatisfaction with traditional motor fitness batteries and the growing body of evidence supporting the value of regular, vigorous exercise for health promotion.

Health-Related Batteries

Texas Test
The Texas Governor's Commission on Physical Fitness published a test in 1973 because many felt the AAHPERD YFT was too time consuming to administer and did not measure true components of physical fitness. The Texas Test was a motor fitness test, but the battery was split into physical fitness components and motor ability components. Both types of abilities were measured, but the award for achievement applies only to the fitness tests. The major contribution of the Texas test in advancing the health related concept was the publication of true aerobic distance run tests.

Table 9.9

Standards of Performance for Boys to Qualify for the Presidential Youth Fitness Award.

TEST ITEM*				AGE IN YEARS				
	≤10	11	12	13	14	15	16	17
Pull-ups	5	5	6	7	9	11	11	12
Sit-ups	42	43	45	48	50	50	50	49
Shuttle run	10.4	10.1	10.0	9.7	9.3	9.2	9.1	9.0
Standing long jump	68	70	73	80	83	89	93	96
50-yard dash	7.7	7.4	7.1	6.9	6.5	6.3	6.3	6.1
600-yard run	135	132	124	117	110	105	102	101

*The units of measurement are: number of pull-ups, and sit-ups; long jump in inches; and shuttle run, 50-yard dash and 600-yard dash in total seconds.

Table 9.10

Standards of Performance for Girls to Qualify for the Presidential Youth Fitness Award.

TEST ITEM*				AGE IN YEARS				
	≤10	11	12	13	14	15	16	17
Flexed arm hang	24	24	23	21	26	25	20	22
Sit-up	38	38	38	40	41	40	38	40
Shuttle run	10.9	10.5	10.5	10.2	10.1	10.2	10.4	10.1
Standing long jump	65	67	69	72	75	73	72	75
50-yard dash	7.8	7.5	7.4	7.2	7.1	7.1	7.3	7.1
600-yard run	150	145	141	136	131	134	139	134

*The units of measurement are: number of sit-ups; long jump in inches; and flexed arm hang, shuttle run, 50-yard dash and 600-yard dash in total seconds.

A feature of the Texas battery is that alternate tests are provided for each component. Many of these tests and test instructions are provided in chapter 7. The components and items of the Texas test are as follows.

1. Physical fitness components
   a. Muscular strength and endurance of the arms and shoulder girdle: pull-ups, dips, flexed-arm hang (90 seconds).
   b. Muscular strength and endurance of the abdominal region: bent-leg sit-ups (2 minutes).
   c. Cardiorespiratory endurance in distance running: 1.5 mile and 12 minute walk/run for distance (grades 7 to 12); 9-minute walk/run for time, 1 mile walk/run for time (grades 4 to 6).
2. Motor ability components
   a. Running speed: 50-yard timed sprint, 8-second run for distance.
   b. Running agility: shuttle run for distance (15 seconds), zig-zag run.
   c. Explosive movement: vertical jump, standing long jump.

South Carolina Test

Using the AAHPERD position paper on physical fitness (Jackson et al. 1976) as a guide, South Carolina published a health-related fitness test and statewide norms (Pate 1978). One unique feature of the test is its inclusion of both criterion and norm-referenced standards. The battery includes the following components and recommended test:

1. Cardiorespiratory function. One mile run or 9 minute run for distance.
2. Body composition. The sum of triceps and abdominal skinfolds.
3. Abdominal and low-back musculoskeletal function. Bent-knee sit-ups in 1 minute, and sit and reach.

The test provides norms for boys and girls ages 9 to 16. Criterion-referenced standards are also included to evaluate the physical fitness status of teachers, encouraging teachers to demonstrate the importance of fitness through participation.

Manitoba Physical Fitness Performance Test

The Manitoba Department of Education (1977) in Canada offers a health-related fitness test designed for boys and girls ages 5 to 19. The test includes fitness standards for teachers as well. The components of the test are as follows:

1. Cardiovascular endurance. 800-meter run (ages 5 to 9); 1600-meter run (ages 10 to 12); 2400-meter run (ages 13 to 60).
2. Flexibility. Sit and reach.
3. Muscular endurance. One minute speed bent-knee sit-ups and flexed arm hang.
4. Body composition. Percentage fat estimated from biceps, triceps, subscapular, and suprailium skinfolds.

The test also included an agility run, which many consider more of a motor ability component than a health-related battery. The prediction of body composition with the Manitoba equation is not recommended. The New Texas Test does provide a valid estimate from the sum of calf and triceps skinfolds.

AAHPERD Health-Related Physical Fitness Test (HRFT)

After five years of development, the AAHPERD (1980) published the health-related physical fitness battery. The components and test items are:

1. Cardiorespiratory function. 1-mile run or 9-minute run for all students. The Texas 1.5-mile or 12-minute run/walk tests are optional for students 13 years or older.
2. Body composition (leanness/fatness). Sum of triceps and subscapular skinfolds or triceps skinfold if only one site is used.
3. Abdominal and low back hamstring musculoskeletal function. Modified, timed (60 seconds), bent-knee sit-ups, and sit and reach tests.

The **AAHPERD HRFT** was developed by a joint committee representing the Measurement and Evaluation, Physical Fitness, and Research Councils of AAHPERD. The test manual (AAHPERD 1980) includes the test items and norms, and a chapter on the general principles of exercise prescription. This allows the teacher to diagnose student weaknesses and to provide a scientifically sound, individualized physical fitness program. A major advantage of the AAHPERD HRFT is it can be used with children in grades 1 through 12; whereas, the range for the AAHPERD YFT is only grades 5 to 12. Provided next are the test's administrative instructions. Selected normative data are furnished in tables 9.11 through 9.22. A more detailed discussion on the normative data can be found in the technical manual (AAHPERD 1984).

Distance Runs

Objective: To measure the maximal functional capacity and endurance of the cardiovascular system.

Validity and reliability: The 1-mile and 9-minute runs are valid field tests of cardiorespiratory function and performance because they are related to maximal oxygen uptake, along with other physiological parameters of cardiorespiratory function, and provide an index of the participant's ability to run distances. Also the proposed runs give essentially the same information as those of longer distance. The 1.5-mile and 12-minute run alternatives are offered mainly because of their current widespread use. Distance runs have acceptable reliability when administered carefully to properly prepared students. The test user should note that other factors (body fatness, running efficiency, maturity, motivation) also affect distance run time.

Equipment: Either of the two distance-run tests can be administered on a 440-yard or 400-meter track, or on any other flat measured area (the 110-yard or 100-meter straight-away, other outside fields, an indoor-court area). Sample test courses are shown in figure 9.1.

Procedures: Standardized procedures and norms are provided for two distance run tests: the 1-mile run for time and the 9-minute run for distance. In deciding which of the tests to administer, consider your facilities, equipment, time limitations, administrative problems, and personal preference.

1. **1-mile run** Instruct students to run 1 mile in the fastest possible time. This should begin on the signal "Ready, start!" As they cross the finish line, call out elapsed time to the participants (or their partners). Walking is allowed, but the objective is to cover the distance in the shortest possible time.

2. **9-minute run** Instruct students to run as far as possible in 9 minutes. They should begin on the signal "Ready, start!" and continue to run until a whistle is blown, at 9 minutes. Walking is allowed, but the objective is to cover as much distance as possible during the 9 minutes.

Alternate Tests: For students 13 and older, the 1.5-mile run for time or the 12-minute run for distance can be used as the distance run item. The administrative procedures for these tests are the same as for the 1-mile and 9-minute runs.

Figure 9.1 Test courses for administering the distance run tests of the AAHPERD Health-Related Physical Fitness Test.

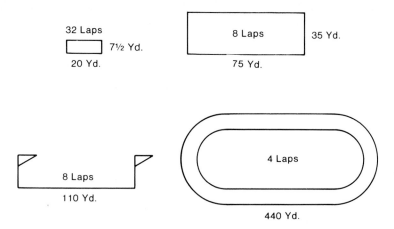

Scoring: The 1-mile and 1.5-mile runs are scored to the nearest second; the 9-minute and 12-minute runs are scored to the nearest 10 yards. Record performances on a score card.

Norms: Norms were established from data collected on over 10,000 students throughout the United States and appear in tables 9.11 through 9.14. The norms for the optional 1.5-mile and 12-minute run tests are in table 9.8.

Criterion-referenced standards: Give special attention to those students who score below the 25th percentile for their sex and age, and strongly encourage them to improve their **aerobic fitness.** Urge students who score below the 50th percentile for their sex and age to try to perform up to the 50th percentile as a minimum level of **cardiorespiratory function.** Improvements in aerobic fitness will only come through sound training programs.

Interpretation: Use the norms here, in the Technical Manual, or locally developed norms to compare students with persons of the same age and sex. Remember, however, that the results of a running test are not entirely determined by cardiorespiratory function; heredity, body composition, running efficiency, maturity, and effort also contribute to test results.

One way to interpret a student's progress (or lack of progress), then, is to follow his or her distance run time longitudinally. Heredity will not cause changes in distance run performance, and relative leanness and skill normally change less than cardiorespiratory function. And we can account for maturity by comparing results with different age norms. Thus, assuming consistent motivation, the change in distance run performance primarily reflects change in cardiorespiratory fitness and endurance.

Table 9.11

Percentile Norms for Boys for the 1-Mile Run (in Minutes and Seconds).*

AGE	5	6	7	8	9	10	11
Percentile							
95	9:02	9:06	8:06	7:58	7:17	6:56	6:50
75	11:32	10:55	9:37	9:14	8:36	8:10	8:00
50	13:46	12:29	11:25	11:00	9:56	9:19	9:06
25	16:05	15:10	14:02	13:29	12:00	11:05	11:31
5	18:25	17:38	17:17	16:19	15:44	14:28	15:25

AGE	12	13	14	15	16	17+
Percentile						
95	6:27	6:11	5:51	6:01	5:48	6:01
75	7:24	6:52	6:36	6:35	6:28	6:36
50	8:20	7:27	7:10	7:14	7:11	7:25
25	10:00	8:35	8:02	8:04	8:07	8:26
5	13:41	10:23	10:32	10:37	10:40	10:56

*The complete table is available in *AAHPERD Manual* (AAHPERD, 1980).

Table 9.12

Percentile Norms for Girls for the 1-Mile Run (in Minutes and Seconds).*

AGE	5	6	7	8	9	10	11
Percentile							
95	9:45	9:18	8:48	8:45	8:24	7:59	7:46
75	13:09	11:24	10:55	10:35	9:58	9:30	9:12
50	15:08	13:48	12:30	12:00	11:12	11:06	10:27
25	17:59	15:27	14:30	14:16	13:18	12:54	12:10
5	19:00	18:50	17:44	16:58	16:42	17:00	16:56

AGE	12	13	14	15	16	17+
Percentile						
95	7:26	7:10	7:18	7:39	7:07	7:26
75	8:36	8:18	8:13	8:42	9:00	9:03
50	9:47	9:27	9:35	10:05	10:45	9:47
25	11:34	10:56	11:43	12:21	13:00	11:28
5	14:46	14:55	16:59	16:22	15:30	15:24

*The complete table is available in *AAHPERD Manual* (AAHPERD, 1980).

Other considerations: In order to obtain valid, reliable results, adequately prepare the students for the test. First, be sure that all the students are medically able to take the test. Second, allow the students to practice distance running, emphasizing the concept of pace. Most uninstructed children run too fast early in the test and are then forced to walk during the last stages. Results are usually better when a child maintains a constant pace during most of the run, walking for short periods of time only when necessary and perhaps using a

Table 9.13
Percentile Norms for Boys for the 9-Minute Run (in Yards).*

AGE	5	6	7	8	9	10	11
Percentile							
95	1760	1750	2020	2200	2175	2250	2250
75	1320	1469	1683	1810	1835	1910	1925
50	1170	1280	1440	1595	1660	1690	1725
25	990	1090	1243	1380	1440	1487	1540
5	600	816	990	1053	1104	1110	1170

AGE	12	13	14	15	16	17+
Percentile						
95	2400	2402	2473	2544	2615	2615
75	1975	2096	2167	2238	2309	2380
50	1760	1885	1956	2027	2098	2169
25	1500	1674	1745	1816	1887	1958
5	1000	1368	1439	1510	1581	1652

*The complete table is available in *AAHPERD Manual* (AAHPERD, 1980).

Table 9.14
Percentile Norms for Girls for the 9-Minute Run (in Yards).*

AGE	5	6	7	8	9	10	11
Percentile							
95	1540	1700	1900	1860	2050	2067	2000
75	1300	1440	1540	1540	1650	1650	1723
50	1140	1208	1344	1358	1425	1460	1480
25	950	1017	1150	1225	1243	1250	1345
5	700	750	860	970	960	940	904

AGE	12	13	14	15	16	17+
Percentile						
95	2175	2085	2123	2161	2199	2237
75	1760	1785	1823	1861	1899	1937
50	1590	1577	1615	1653	1691	1729
25	1356	1369	1407	1445	1483	1521
5	1000	1069	1107	1145	1183	1221

*The complete table is available in *AAHPERD Manual* (AAHPERD, 1980).

strong closing effort. Third, motivate the students. This test, like many other physical tests, is only as good as the effort provided by the participants. One form of motivation is understanding: fully explain the purpose of the test to the students. Fourth, properly train students for aerobic exercise. Finally, encourage both warm-up and cool-down activities that involve slow stretching, walking, and slow jogging.

Sum of Skinfold Fat

Objective: To evaluate the level of fatness in school age boys and girls.

Validity and Reliability: Hydrostatic weighing is an accepted, valid method used by scientists to measure the degree of body fatness. The correlations (validity coefficients) between skinfolds and hydrostatically determined body fatness have ranged consistently from 0.70 to 0.90 in both children and adults. The test-retest reliability of skinfold fat measure has exceeded 0.95 with experienced testers. Objectivity among investigators has also been high when instruction in the same technique and site location procedures has been given.

Equipment: Use skinfold calipers that have an accurate calibration capability and a constant pressure of 10 g/mm^2 throughout the range of skinfold thickness. Be sure that the instrument is properly calibrated and that when it's closed it registers "0".

Procedures: In several parts of the body, the adipose (fat) tissue can be lifted with the fingers to form a skinfold. The **skinfold fat** measure consists of a double layer of subcutaneous fat and skin, the thickness of which can be measured with skinfold fat calipers (see figure 9.2). The test uses two skinfold fat sites, the triceps and the subscapular, because they are easy to measure and correlate highly with total body fat. The triceps skinfold is measured over the triceps muscle of the right arm. The subscapular site, also on the right side of the body, is 1 centimeter (slightly less than 0.5 inch) below the inferior angle of the scapula, in line with the natural cleavage line of the skin (see figures 9.3 and 9.4).

The recommended testing procedure is as follows:

1. Firmly grasp the skinfold between the thumb and forefinger, and lift up.
2. Place the contact surfaces of the calipers 1 centimeter (0.5 inch) above or below your finger.
3. Slowly release the grip on the calipers, so that they exert their full tension of the skinfold.
4. Read the skinfold to the nearest half millimeter after the needle stops (1 to 2 seconds after you have released your grip on the calipers).

It is easier to measure the subscapular skinfold of a female if she is wearing a loose fitting T-shirt. Raise the shirt in back for access to the skinfold site. If the subject is wearing a bra, push it upward 2 to 3 inches. It may be best to ask female subjects to wear a two-piece swimsuit and it is best to have a female teacher test female students.

Scoring: The skinfold measurement registers on the dial of the calipers. Take each measurement three consecutive times, recording only the median (middle) of the three scores. For example, if the three values were 18, 15, and 16 millimeters, you would record score 16. Each reading should be recorded to the nearest half millimeter. The recommended scoring procedure is to use the sum of the two skinfolds. If it is possible to secure just one skinfold, use the triceps site.

Figure 9.2 Measurement of skinfold fat.

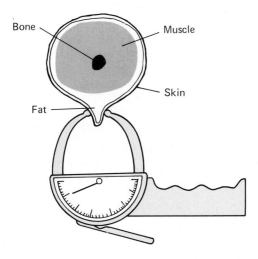

Figure 9.3 Anatomical landmarks for measuring subscapular (left) and triceps (right) skinfolds.

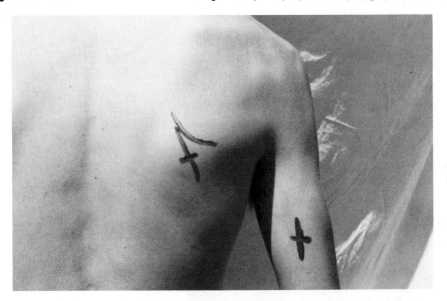

Figure 9.4 Procedures for testing subscapular (a) and tricep (b) skinfolds.

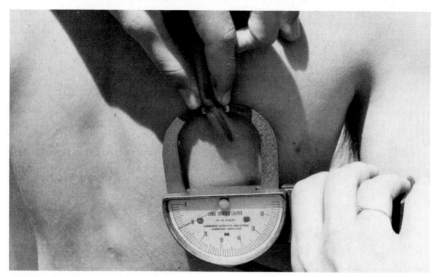

(a)

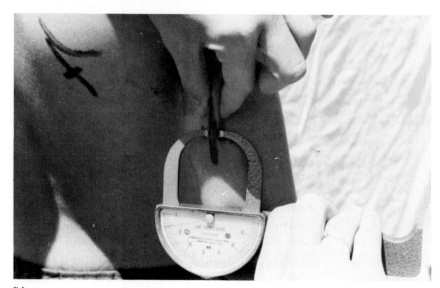

(b)

Table 9.15

Percentile Norms for Boys for Sum of Triceps Plus Subscapular Skinfolds (in Millimeters).

AGE	6	7	8	9	10	11	12	13	14	15	16	17*
Percentile												
95	8	9	9	9	9	9	9	9	9	9	9	9
75	11	11	11	11	12	12	11	12	11	12	12	12
50	12	12	13	14	14	16	15	15	14	14	14	15
25	14	15	17	18	19	22	21	22	20	20	20	21
5	20	24	28	34	33	38	44	46	37	40	37	38

*The norms for age 17 can be used for age 18.

Source: From F. E. Johnson et al., *Skinfold Thickness of Children 6–11 Years* and *Skinfold Thickness of Youth 12–17 Years* (Washington, D.C.: U.S. National Center for Health Statistics, 1972, 1974). Also presented in full in the *AAHPERD Manual,* 1980.

Table 9.16

Percentile Norms for Girls for Sum of Triceps Plus Subscapular Skinfolds (in Millimeters).

AGE	6	7	8	9	10	11	12	13	14	15	16	17*
Percentile												
95	9	10	10	10	10	11	11	12	13	14	14	15
75	12	12	13	14	14	15	15	16	18	20	20	20
50	14	15	16	17	18	19	19	20	24	25	25	27
25	17	19	21	24	25	25	27	30	32	34	34	36
5	26	28	36	40	41	42	48	51	52	56	57	58

*The norms for age 17 can be used for age 18.

Source: From F. E. Johnson et al., *Skinfold Thickness of Children 6–11 Years* and *Skinfold Thickness of Youth 12–17 Years* (Washington, D.C.: U.S. National Center for Health Statistics, 1972, 1974). Also presented in full in the *AAHPERD Manual,* 1980.

Norms: Percentile norms for boys and girls appear in tables 9.15 through 9.18. The norms were developed on a national sample of over 13,000 children ages 6 to 17 (Johnson et al. 1972, 1974). Notice that tables 9.17 and 9.18 list norms for the triceps skinfold only.

The percentile value reflects the percentage of boys or girls in the national sample who had or exceeded that skinfold thickness. For example, for a 15-year-old girl, the 25th percentile for the sum of triceps and subscapular skinfolds is 34 millimeters (table 9.16). This means that the sum of skinfolds was 34 millimeters or more in 25% of girls age 15. If we look at the tables, we can see that the higher the skinfold reading, the lower the percentile. Thus lower percentile ranking reflects a higher degree of fatness.

Table 9.17

Percentile Norms, Sample Sizes, Means, and Standard Deviations for Triceps Skinfold Thickness (in Millimeters) for Boys.

AGE	PERCENTILES					n	$\overline{X}$	s
	5th	25th	50th	75th	95th			
6	13	9	8	6	5	575	8.1	2.8
7	14	10	8	6	4	632	8.4	3.2
8	17	11	8	6	4	618	9.0	3.8
9	20	12	8	7	5	603	10.0	5.0
10	20	12	9	7	5	576	10.1	4.4
11	22	14	10	7	5	628	11.0	5.3
12	23	13	9	7	5	643	10.7	5.8
13	23	13	9	7	4	626	10.5	5.9
14	21	12	8	6	4	617	9.5	5.6
15	21	11	8	6	4	613	9.0	5.1
16	20	11	8	6	4	555	8.9	4.9
17*	20	11	8	6	4	489	9.0	5.4

*The norms for age 17 can be used for boys age 18.

Source: From F. E. Johnson et al., *Skinfold Thickness of Children 6–11 Years* and *Skinfold Thickness of Youth 12–17 Years* (Washington, D.C.: U.S. National Center for Health Statistics, 1972, 1974). Also presented in full in *AAHPERD Manual,* 1980.

Table 9.18

Percentile Norms, Sample Sizes, Means, and Standard Deviations for Triceps Skinfold Thickness (in Millimeters) for Girls.

AGE	PERCENTILES					n	$\overline{X}$	s
	5th	25th	50th	75th	95th			
6	16	11	9	7	6	536	9.7	3.4
7	17	12	10	8	6	609	10.4	3.6
8	20	14	10	8	6	613	11.4	4.4
9	22	14	11	9	6	581	12.3	4.8
10	23	15	12	9	6	584	12.6	5.1
11	23	15	12	9	6	564	12.6	5.2
12	25	16	12	9	6	547	12.9	5.8
13	26	17	12	9	6	582	13.6	6.1
14	27	18	14	11	7	586	14.8	6.1
15	29	20	15	12	7	502	15.8	6.6
16	30	21	16	12	8	535	16.5	6.9
17*	29	20	16	12	8	468	16.5	6.2

*The norms for age 17 can be used for girls age 18.

Source: From F. E. Johnson et al., *Skinfold Thickness of Children 6–11 Years* and *Skinfold Thickness of Youth 12–17 Years* (Washington, D.C.: U.S. National Center for Health Statistics, 1972, 1974). Also presented in full in the *AAHPERD Manual,* 1980.

Interpretation: The relation of triceps and subscapular skinfold fat to the percent body fat in children has yet to be fully validated. Although we know skinfolds are related to body fatness in children, we cannot determine the absolute percentage of body fat with certainty.

Criterion-referenced standards: Today, national percentile norms are the best frame of reference for interpreting skinfold fat results. The criterion for the degree of fatness wanted in children is above the 50th percentile. Children between the 50th and 25th percentile should maintain their weight at that level for the current year. Those below the 25th percentile should be strongly encouraged to reduce their weight until their skinfold fat measurement reaches a more acceptable level (closer to the 50th percentile). Usually an increase in daily physical activity, together with a reduction in food intake, both control weight and reduce fat.

Children whose measurements fall above the 90th percentile are exceptionally lean. At this level, a reduction in weight could involve muscle tissue or other no-fat tissue, creating both short and long range problems for health, performance, and growth. Do not encourage weight reduction in children who are already at or above the 90th percentile.

Other considerations when taking the skinfold: Lift the skin by grasping the fold between your thumb and forefinger. Use a firm grasp, but don't hurt the student. Do not put the calipers at the base of the skinfold. A reading there does not reflect the true thickness; it will be too large. The correct distance from the crest is that point on the fold where true double thickness exists: this is approximately midway between the crest and the base of the skinfold. Place the calipers about one centimeter from the point where the skinfold is held. See figures 9.3 and 9.4 for proper caliper placement. You should practice with several students before measuring for score. When your repeated measurements are consistently within 1 to 2 millimeters, you can begin actual evaluations. With obese children, consecutive measurements may differ by more than 2 millimeters, even with experienced testers. In this case, take an additional set of three measurements and record the average of the two middle scores.

To avoid embarrassing a child, measure each student separately, without comment or reaction. Your interpretation of the measurements should also be given individually. Remember that each student has the right to share or withhold the results of the test.

Modified Sit-Ups

Objective: To evaluate abdominal muscular strength and endurance.

Validity and Reliability: You can improve the validity and reliability of the test by giving students sufficient instruction and practice in the correct sit-up procedure before testing. The validity of the sit-up test has been determined logically. Studies show that abdominal muscles are being used in the performance of a sit-up. The reliability of the test has been satisfactory, with test-retest reliability coefficients ranging from 0.68 to 0.94.

Figure 9.5 Positions for the modified sit-up test of the AAHPERD Health-Related Physical Fitness Test (a) on the back and (b) in the up position.

(a)

(b)

Equipment: Use mats or other comfortable surfaces for the students. A stopwatch, or watch or clock with a sweep-second hand, can be used for timing.

Procedure: To start, the student lies on the back with knees flexed and feet on the floor, heels 12 to 18 inches from the buttocks. Arms are crossed on the chest, with hands on opposite shoulders. The feet should be held down by a partner to keep them on the testing surface. The student, by tightening his or her abdominal muscles, curls to the sitting position, touching elbows to thighs. Arms must remain on the chest, as should the chin (figure 9.5). To complete the sit-up, the student returns to the down position, until the mid-back touches the testing surface.

The timer gives the signal "Ready, Go." The student starts on the word "Go" and must stop on the word "Stop." The student should know before the test begins that rest between sit-ups is allowed, but that the objective is to perform as many correctly executed sit-ups as possible in a 60-second period.

Scoring: Record the number of correctly executed sit-ups completed in 60 seconds.

Norms: Tables 9.19 and 9.20 list norms for the test. These are based on data secured from over 10,000 school-aged children throughout the United States in 1979.

Criterion-referenced standards: Weak abdominal muscles contribute to the development of lower back pain and other related problems. Encourage students who score below the 50th percentile on this test to improve their abdominal strength and endurance, as well as their lower back, hip, and posterior thigh flexibility. This is especially critical for students who score below the 25th percentile, for whom an individualized, remedial program is warranted.

Other considerations: The heels must be a proper distance (12 to 18 inches) from the buttocks. To ensure that this distance is maintained, you may want to use a measuring stick. Also, the student's feet must be in contact with the testing surface, a simple matter when a partner holds the student's feet, ankles, or calves. Although partners can count and record each other's score, the supervising tester should be sure that the sit-ups are being done correctly.

Table 9.19
Percentile Norms for Boys for Sit-Ups.*

AGE	5	6	7	8	9	10	11	12	13	14	15	16	17+
Percentile													
95	30	36	42	48	47	50	51	56	58	59	59	61	62
75	23	26	33	37	38	40	41	46	48	49	49	51	52
50	18	20	26	30	32	34	37	39	41	42	44	45	46
25	11	15	19	25	25	27	30	31	35	36	38	38	38
5	2	6	10	15	15	15	17	19	25	27	28	28	25

*The complete table is available in *AAHPERD Manual* (AAHPERD, 1980).

Table 9.20
Percentile Norms for Girls for Sit-Ups.*

AGE	5	6	7	8	9	10	11	12	13	14	15	16	17+
Percentile													
95	28	35	40	44	44	47	50	52	51	51	56	54	54
75	24	28	31	35	35	39	40	41	41	42	43	42	44
50	19	22	25	29	29	32	34	36	35	35	37	33	37
25	12	14	20	22	23	25	28	30	29	30	30	29	31
5	2	6	10	12	14	15	19	19	18	20	20	20	19

*The complete table is available in *AAHPERD Manual* (AAHPERD, 1980).

Sit and Reach

Objective: To evaluate the flexibility of the lower back and posterior thighs.

Validity and Reliability: You can improve the validity and reliability of the test by giving students sufficient instruction and warm-up. Warm-up should include slow, sustained, static stretching of the lower back and posterior thighs. The test has been validated against several other flexibility tests. The validity coefficients have ranged between 0.80 and 0.90. The measure also has logical validity, in that a student must have good flexibility in the lower back, hips, and posterior thighs in order to score well. Reliability coefficients for this test have been high, ranging above 0.70.

Equipment: The test apparatus consists of a specially constructed box (12 inches by 12 inches by 21 inches) with a measuring scale where 23 centimeters is at the level of the feet. The box is shown in figure 9.6. Plans for building it can be found in the test manual (AAHPERD 1980).

Procedure: To start, have the student remove his or her shoes and sit down at the test apparatus with knees fully extended and feet shoulder width apart. The feet should be flat against the end board. To perform the test, the student extends the arms forward, with hands placed on top of each other as shown in figure 9.6. The pupil reaches directly forward, palms down, along the measuring scale four times, and holds the position of maximum reach on the fourth trial. This position must be held for one second.

Figure 9.6 Testing position for the sit-and-reach test from the AAHPERD Health-Related Physical Fitness Test. (Note the specially constructed box used to standardize the testing procedure.)

Scoring: The score is the farthest point reached, measured to the nearest centimeter, on the fourth trial. The administrator should remain close to the scale and note the most distant line touched by the fingertips of both hands. If the hands reach unevenly, re-administer the test.

Norms: Tables 9.21 and 9.22 list the norms for the sit and reach test. These are based on data secured from over 10,000 school-age children throughout the United States.

Criterion-referenced standard: A score above the 50th percentile on this test item reflects suitable flexibility; a score below the 50th percentile reflects poor flexibility in at least one of the following areas: posterior thighs, lower back, posterior hips. Poor flexibility in these areas can contribute to the development of musculoskeletal problems. Students who score below the 25th percentile have a critical lack of flexibility. Provide these students the remedial program of exercises offered in the test manual.

Table 9.21
Percentile Norms for Boys for Sit and Reach (in Centimeters*).

AGE	5	6	7	8	9	10	11	12	13	14	15	16	17+
Percentile													
95	32	34	33	34	34	33	34	35	36	39	41	42	45
75	29	29	28	29	29	28	29	29	30	33	34	36	40
50	25	26	25	25	25	25	25	26	26	28	30	30	34
25	22	22	22	22	22	20	21	21	20	23	24	25	28
5	17	16	16	16	16	12	12	13	12	15	13	11	15

*The complete table is available in *AAHPERD Manual* (AAHPERD, 1980).

Table 9.22
Percentile Norms for Girls for Sit and Reach (in Centimeters*).

AGE	5	6	7	8	9	10	11	12	13	14	15	16	17+
Percentile													
95	34	34	34	36	35	35	37	40	43	44	46	46	44
75	30	30	31	31	31	31	32	34	36	38	41	39	40
50	27	27	27	28	28	28	29	30	31	33	36	34	35
25	23	23	24	23	23	24	24	25	24	28	31	30	31
5	18	18	16	17	17	16	16	15	17	18	19	14	22

*The complete table is available in *AAHPERD Manual* (AAHPERD, 1980).

Remember that it's normal for many boys and girls not to reach the 23-centimeter level during the pre-adolescent and adolescent growth spurt (ages 10 to 14). This is because the legs become proportionately longer in relation to the trunk during this period.

Other considerations: Repeat the test trial if (1) the student's hands reach out unevenly or (2) the knees are flexed during the trial. You can prevent the knees from flexing by keeping your hand, or a monitor's hand, lightly on the knees. To prevent the apparatus from sliding away from the student, place it against a wall or a similar immovable object.

Texas Youth Fitness Test

In 1973, the Texas Governor's Commission on Physical Fitness published the Texas Physical Fitness and Motor Ability battery. In 1985 and 1986, the health-related portion of the test was under revision. The revision was through the combined efforts of public school physical educators and leading medical, fitness, health, and measurement specialists. The test was reviewed by national fitness and medical experts. The unique nature of the revised Texas test warrants its inclusion in this revision. In 1986 and 1987, the test was scheduled for extensive pilot research.

A basic assumption of the Texas Youth Fitness Test was that there is a desirable level of fitness that every child should and can achieve for health promotion. If one can achieve this desired level, and maintain it throughout life, it will significantly impact the person's functional health and well-being. The test was designed to achieve two general purposes:

1. To provide a method of evaluating physical fitness performance.
2. To provide a means of educating and conditioning students for a lifetime of fitness and healthy living.

The emphasis is not on maximum performance as compared to other classmates (i.e., norm-referenced standards), but rather a level of fitness considered to be desirable for all students of a given gender and grade (i.e., criterion-referenced standards). In order to facilitate test administration, scoring, and reporting of results, scores are reported by grade and sex rather than by age and sex; thus, a single set of standards exists for boys and girls for each grade level. All students are not the same age within a grade, but typical normative values change little from one age to the next; thus, the slight loss in normative accuracy is off-set by administrative feasibility.

The four tests of the Texas Youth Fitness battery are:

1. Steady State Run
2. Curl-Up
3. Sit and Reach
4. Body Composition

Table 9.23

Criterion Distances for the Texas Steady State Test in Miles for and the Speed of the Run in Miles Per Hour, Minutes to Cover One Mile, and Energy Cost of the Jog in METs.*

GRADE	DISTANCE (miles)	DISTANCE (yards)	SPEED (mph)	MINUTES (per mile)	METs
Males-30 Minutes					
4	2.50	4,400	5.0	12.0	8.3
5	2.75	4,840	5.5	10.9	9.2
6	3.00	5,280	6.0	10.0	10.0
7–12	3.50	5,720	7.0	8.6	11.7
Females-30 Minutes					
4	2.20	3,960	4.4	13.6	7.3
5	2.40	4,400	4.8	12.5	8.0
6	2.60	4,840	5.2	11.5	8.7
7–12	3.00	5,280	6.0	10.0	10.0
Males-20 Minutes					
4	1.70	2,990	5.1	11.8	8.5
5	1.85	3,260	5.5	10.8	9.2
6	2.00	3,520	6.0	10.0	10.0
Females-20 Minutes					
4	1.50	2,640	4.5	13.3	7.5
5	1.60	2,820	4.8	12.5	8.0
6	1.85	3,260	5.5	10.8	9.2

*The provided distances were the initial recommendations. These may change when the test is in its final form. For further information, contact the Governor's Commission for Physical Fitness, Austin, Texas.

Steady State Run Test

The **steady state run** test is the most dramatic departure from traditional fitness testing. The test is to travel a specified distance in 30 minutes. The proposed distances to be covered are furnished in table 9.23. For grades 4, 5, and 6 an optional 20-minute test is provided. The 30-minute test is recommended for all students, but time constraints at some Texas elementary schools do not permit a 30-minute test.

The steady state run is designed to assess aerobic fitness by measuring a student's ability to perform prolonged aerobic exercise. The steady state run differs in philosophy from the maximal distance run tests of the AAHPERD (1976; 1980) and Texas (1973) tests. The shorter maximal run tests (e.g., 1 mile run/walk) are valid measures of $\dot{V}O_2$ **Max,** but also include an anaerobic component because an all-out effort is required. The steady state run is a submaximal aerobic test consistent with generally accepted recommendations for the amount of exercise needed to develop and maintain aerobic fitness. The American College of Sports Medicine guidelines (1978) specify submaximal, continuous aerobic exercise for approximately 30 minutes per day for at least three days per week.

A major limitation in using the 1 mile run/walk test is students often are not trained prior to taking the test and the distance is short enough that students can complete the mile. In contrast, the successful achievement of the criterion-referenced standard on the steady state run requires not only an adequate $\dot{V}O_2$ Max, but also habitual aerobic training consistent with generally accepted exercise guidelines (ACSM 1978).

The rules for administering the steady state run are:

1. The test is designed to be administered at the end of proper instruction. This would be typically at the end of a semester or marking period. The test is *not to be used for pre-assessments*.

2. Students should not be tested until they have been properly aerobically trained. The Governor's Commission also published a pilot aerobic conditioning program to properly condition students. The test should not be administered until students have been aerobically trained for a *minimum of eight weeks*. Jogging should be part of the training program.

3. The goal is to have students jog the entire time period. In order to maximize performance, they need to pace themselves properly. Prior to testing, students should learn to run at a comfortable steady pace that they can maintain over the entire test.

The steady state run test can be administered on the test courses described for the AAHPERD HRFT (see figure 9.1), but an excellent option is to use a measured jogging trail. The test is simply to jog for the 20- or 30-minute time period and cover a specified distance. Walking should be discouraged, but it is allowed. Students should be trained and encouraged to jog for the full time. Following completion of the test, students should engage in cool-down activities such as slow to moderate paced walking for three to five minutes. The test should not be administered during adverse weather conditions. Avoid administering the test on hot, humid days, during high winds and storms, and excessively cold days. The test is scored as "Pass or Fail" by judging the student's performance against the criterion-referenced standards provided in table 9.23.

Curl-Up Test

The test is a 2-minute, bent-knee, arms-crossed-at-the-chest, curl-up. This is the same test recommended for the AAHPERD HRFT sit-up test with the exception that the time limit is 2 minutes rather than 60 seconds. The test instructions have been previously presented in this chapter. The task is to achieve the criterion-referenced standard number of curl-ups for a given grade and gender. The recommended standards are provided in table 9.24. Students may rest, but should be encouraged to continue at a steady pace throughout the two minutes.

Table 9.24

Criterion Referenced Standards for the Curl-up and Body Composition Tests of the Texas Youth Fitness Test.[1]

| | SIT-UPS | | TRICEPS AND CALF[2] M | | TRICEPS AND CALF F | |
GRADE	M	F	THE SUM	% FAT	THE SUM	% FAT
4	34	32	23	19	32	26
5	36	33	26	21	32	26
6	38	34	29	23	33	27
7	40	35	29	23	35	29
8	40	35	29	23	37	30
9	40	35	27	22	37	30
10	40	35	25	20	37	30
11	40	35	23	19	37	30
12	50	35	23	19	37	30

1. The provided values were the initial recommendations. These may change when the test is in its final form. For further information, contact the Governor's Commission for Physical Fitness, Austin, Texas.

2. The body composition standards were developed from the data provided by Dr. T. Lohman, University of Arizona. Conversion to % fat is: boys % fat = $(0.709 X) + 2.7$: and girls % fat = $(0.709 X) + 3.7$ where X is equal to the sum of triceps and calf skinfold.

Sit-and-Reach Test

The test is administered like the AAHPERD HRFT sit-and-reach-test previously described. The scale of the box (see figure 9.6) is to the 0.5 inch rather than in centimeters (the AAHPERD HRFT uses centimeters). The nine-inch line must be exactly in line with the vertical plane against which the student's feet are placed. The student sits on the floor in stocking feet with the legs extended and feet flat against the test apparatus. The hands are placed one on top of the other. On a signal, the student gradually reaches forward as far as possible and holds the position. The student is permitted three additional consecutive attempts to stretch further. The fully extended position must be held for at least one second and the student's legs must be straight.

The recommended criterion-referenced standard for this test is that the student reaches the point of the toes. This point is located at the nine-inch mark of the testing apparatus.

Body Composition Test

Body composition is measured with the calf and tricep skinfolds. The tricep test procedures used for the AAHPERD HRFT (1980) are followed. To measure the vertical calf skinfold, the subject places his right foot on a bench or chair, and the measurement is taken on the inside of the calf at the largest circumference. The recommended criterion-referenced standards are provided in table 9.24.

VALIDITY OF YOUTH FITNESS TESTS

There is a growing trend among physical educators and exercise physiologists to more precisely define physical fitness. Central to this process is to examine the validity of purported fitness tests. With the growing body of evidence supporting the role of exercise on health, the validation process has been expanded to consider not only traditional methods such as concurrent validity, but also long-term health effects from medical science.

AAHPERD Youth Fitness Test (YFT)

The six items of the AAHPERD YFT have proved on many occasions to be reliable and the tests have traditionally been used with motor fitness and motor-ability batteries. The correlations among the tests were assumed to be low because each measures a different basic ability, but this is not always the case. With youth, moderate correlations have been reported between the sprinting, jumping, and agility tests. Additionally, 50-yard dash time is substantially correlated with 600-yard run/walk time.

Aerobic fitness or $\dot{V}O_2$ Max is considered to be the most valid index of physical fitness (Åstrand and Rodahl 1977). A major limitation of the Youth Fitness Test is that most items measure anaerobic endurance, which is more important for athletic excellence than health promotion. Using the optional distance runs improves the validity of the Youth Fitness Test because longer distance runs are more highly correlated with $\dot{V}O_2$ Max, but many public school teachers still insist on using the less valid 600-yard test.

Distance Runs

Distance runs are the most common means of evaluating aerobic fitness of youth. The 600-yard run is included in the AAHPERD YFT (1976) as a test of endurance. However, exercise physiologists maintain that 600 yards is more anaerobic than aerobic. Balke (1963) suggested that the distance covered during 15 minutes of running or walking is a valid indicator of $\dot{V}O_2$ Max. Cooper (1968), whose study intensified efforts to establish the concurrent validity of distance runs, reported a correlation of 0.90 between $\dot{V}O_2$ Max and the distance covered during a 12-minute run/walk.

Factor analysis studies (Burke 1976; Disch et al. 1975; Jackson and Coleman 1976) have shown that distance runs normally measure two factors: (1) speed, represented in distances less than 440 yards; and (2) endurance, represented in longer distances (one mile in length or longer) or 9 minutes or longer in duration. Intermediate distances and duration (from 600 to 800 yards and 3 to 6 minutes) have been found to measure both speed and endurance. These studies have also shown that runs of 1 mile and 9 minutes in duration or longer measure the same basic component.

The most widely used laboratory test of aerobic fitness is $\dot{V}O_2$ Max and a detailed discussion of this method can be found in chapter 8. Distance run tests have been shown to have moderate to high correlations with $\dot{V}O_2$ Max when the runs are 1 mile or longer and 9 minutes or more in duration. The concurrent validity coefficients for running tests are listed in table 9.25.

Table 9.25
**Means and Standard Deviations of Maximal Oxygen Uptake
and Concurrent Validity of Distance Run Tests.**

SOURCE	SAMPLE	RUN	MAX $\dot{V}O_2$ (ML/KG·MIN)		r_{XY}*
			$\overline{X}$	s	
Burke (1976)	44 college men	12 minutes	52.8	6.1	.90
		1 mile			.74
Burris (1970)	30 college women	12 minutes	†		.74
Cooper (1968)	115 men, age 17–52	12 minutes	†		.90
Cureton et al. (1977)	140 boys, age 10	1 mile	48.0	6.7	−.66
	56 girls, age 10	1 mile	45.4	5.9	−.66
Doolittle and Bigbee (1968)	9 boys, grade 9	12 minutes	†		.90
Getchell et al. (1977)	21 college women	12 minutes	46.2	5.9	.91
Gutin et al. (1976)	15 boys and girls, age 11	1800 yards	47.5	5.8	−.76
		1200 yards			−.81
		12 minutes			.75
Gutin et al. (1978)	33 girls, age 11–12	1120 yards	37.0	5.9	−.70
Jackson and Coleman (1976)	22 boys, grades 1–6	9 minutes	44.5	4.6	.82
		12 minutes			.82
	25 girls, grades 1–6	9 minutes	40.6	4.1	.71
		12 minutes			.71
Katch (1970)	50 college women	12 minutes	†		.54
Katch et al. (1973a)	36 college women	12 minutes	38.9	4.6	.67
Kitagawa et al. (1977)	39 college men	2400 meters	51.8	6.6	−.63
	33 college women	2400 meters	50.0	3.9	−.42
Krahenbuhl et al. (1977)	20 boys, age 8	¾ mile	47.6	7.1	−.64
		1 mile			−.71
	18 girls, age 8	¾ mile	42.9	5.7	−.22
		1 mile			−.26

*Correlation between Max $\dot{V}O_2$ and distance run.
†Values not reported.

Table 9.25, continued.

| SOURCE | SAMPLE | RUN | MAX $\dot{V}O_2$ (ML/KG·MIN) | | r_{XY}* |
			$\bar{X}$	s	
Maksud and Coutts (1971)	17 boys, ages 11–14	12 minutes	47.4	4.0	.65
Maksud et al. (1976)	26 college women	12 minutes	41.0	3.8	.70
Mayhew and Andrew (1975)	24 college men	1½ miles	55.5	7.9	−.74
Ribisl and Kachadarian (1969)	24 middle-age men	2 miles	48.6	5.4	−.86
	11 college men	1 mile 2 miles	57.4	3.6	−.79 −.85
Shaver (1975)	30 college men	1 mile 2 miles 3 miles	53.5	5.6	−.43 −.76 −.82
Vodak and Wilmore (1975)	69 boys, ages 9–12	6 minutes	53.6	5.6	.50
Wiley and Shaver (1972)	35 college men	1 mile 2 miles 3 miles	52.6	6.3	−.29 −.47 −.43

Prior to 1973, the longer distance runs were not considered acceptable tests for public school children. We can now see that these tests are considered suitable for school-aged children. As an additional guide for evaluating distance run tests, the sample characteristics, means, and standard deviations of many different populations are listed in table 9.26.

Sum of Skinfolds

The sum of triceps and subscapular skinfolds is the recommended test of the AAH-PERD HRFT and Texas Youth Fitness tests. In adults, skinfolds have been found to be highly correlated with laboratory-measured body composition and these data are summarized in chapter 8. Triceps and subscapular skinfolds of youth are also highly correlated with laboratory-determined body density summarized in table 9.27.

Table 9.26
Descriptive Statistics for Distance Run Tests.

SOURCE	SAMPLE	TEST*	$\bar{X}$	s
Cooper et al. (1975)	778 boys and girls (exp.), grades 9–12	*12-min run/walk	2235† 2640‡	475† *563‡
	437 boys and girls (cont.), grades 9–12	12-min run/walk	2358† *2340‡	510† 545‡
Disch (1970)	50 male students after 14 weeks of basic aerobic conditioning	12-min run/walk	3126	334
Doolittle et al. (1969)	100 girls, grades 9–10	12-min run/walk	2022	§
	45 girls, grade 9	12-min run/walk	2296	§
Gutin et al. (1976)	15 boys and girls, ages 10–12	12-min run/walk	2320	400
Jackson and Coleman (1976)	25 boys, grades 1–6	12-min run/walk	2560	314
	25 girls, grades 1–6	12-min run/walk	2255	284
Katch et al. (1973a)	12 women, college athletes	12-min run/walk	2489	264
	14 women, college students	12-min run/walk	1929	229
	10 female phys. ed. majors	12-min run/walk	2019	331
Maksud and Coutts (1971)	44 boys, ages 11–12	12-min run/walk	2308	357
	36 boys, ages 13–14	12-min run/walk	2507	371
Maksud et al. (1976)	26 women, college athletes	12-min run/walk	2381	270
Texas Test (1973)	662 girls, grades 4–6	9-min run/walk	1536	277
	556 boys, grades 4–6	9-min run/walk	1778	355
	375 girls, grades 4–6	1-mile run/walk	10:09	1:54
	312 boys, grades 4–6	1-mile run/walk	8:54	1:59
	1397 girls, grades 7–12	12-min run/walk	1862	357
	1234 boys, grades 7–12	12-min run/walk	2543	428
	471 girls, grades 7–12	1½-mile run	16:11	2:36
	745 boys, grades 7–12	1½-mile run	11:29	1:44

*Timed tests are scored in minutes and seconds; distance runs, in yards.
†Pretest   ‡Posttest   §Values not reported.

Table 9.27

Range of Correlations between Skinfolds and Laboratory-Determined Percent Fat for Males and Females, Ages 8 to 17 Years.

SKINFOLD SITE	MALES	FEMALES
Triceps	0.76 to 0.93	0.58 to 0.82
Subscapular	0.64 to 0.89	0.52 to 0.80
Both Sites	0.78 to 0.85	0.81 to 0.82

Correlations summarized from Table 4 of Technical Manual: Health Related Physical Fitness Test (AAHPERD 1984).

Health-Related Evidence

During the past 20 years a great deal of evidence has been reported in the medical literature supporting the value of regular vigorous exercise for health promotion. These studies support the development and maintenance of the components measured by the health-related tests and are briefly summarized next.

Aerobic Fitness

Epidemiologists have reported that individuals who spend a lifetime employed in physically demanding occupations have a lower heart disease mortality than those who work in less demanding jobs. It was first reported (Morris 1953) in England that the conductors on London double-decker buses had a lower incidence of heart disease than the drivers. It was suspected that the lower death rate could be traced to the worker's activity patterns. The conductors walked and climbed stairs while the drivers sat and drove. Similar results have been reported in the United States with railroad workers (Taylor 1960). The heart disease mortality of the construction workers who maintained the tracks was lower than their more sedentary coworkers who were switchmen and clerks. Of interest, the most sedentary group, clerks, had the highest level of cardiac deaths.

Paffenbarger and his associates (1977; 1980; 1984) provide the strongest evidence linking aerobic exercise with cardiac death. They studied the work habits of longshoremen and recreational habits of Harvard alumni. The researchers developed methods to estimate the number of calories expended for the longshoremen's work and alumni's recreation and were able to show that caloric expenditure was related in a curvilinear manner with the risk of cardiac mortality. The individuals with the lowest level of caloric expenditure were at the highest risk of sudden cardiac death. Increased energy expenditure was associated with reduced heart disease risk and with the alumni leveled off at about 2,000 kilocalories per week. The total energy expenditure of the alumni included both recreation, such as playing vigorous sports, and daily tasks like walking or climbing stairs. It was estimated that the risk of sudden death would be reduced by 33 percent if all reached these energy expenditure levels.

A recent study (Gordon et al. 1981) was designed to examine the influence of diet on heart disease in three different populations. Much to the surprise of the researchers, they found with all three groups that those who consumed the greatest number of calories were at the lowest risk of heart disease. The opposite was expected. Scientists have discovered that caloric consumption and energy expended through exercise are related. This led the researchers to conclude that their findings were due to higher levels of physical activity of those who eat more.

An adequate level of caloric expenditure is a key factor for improving aerobic fitness and enhancing health with exercise. Most of our calories are expended through aerobic metabolism. High levels of caloric expenditure are achieved by exercising aerobically at a high intensity (e.g., 75% of $\dot{V}O_2$ Max) for a long duration. Having a higher $\dot{V}O_2$ Max allows one to exercise more intensely for longer durations resulting in a high caloric expenditure. The development and maintenance of aerobic fitness not only increases our caloric expenditure capabilities, but also shows evidence that endurance training increases the HDL-cholesterol component in our blood (Hartung et al. 1980). The higher your HDL component, the lower your heart disease risk.

Aerobic fitness is developed and maintained through aerobic exercise consisting of: (1) an intensity between 50 and 85 percent of $\dot{V}O_2$ Max; (2) a duration between 15 to 30 minutes per day; and (3) for a minimum frequency of three days per week (ACSM 1978). An adult life of habitual exercise at this level coupled with normal daily physical tasks is likely to reach the caloric expenditure levels shown by Paffenbarger and associates (1984) to reduce the risk of adult cardiac death and increase longevity (1986). A major goal of the steady state run of the Texas Youth Fitness Test (i.e., aerobically exercise for 30 minutes) is to teach and reinforce the important role of energy expenditure on cardiovascular health.

Body Composition

The following is well documented in the medical research. First, it is estimated that from 10 to 50 million adult Americans are overweight to the point that it affects their health. About 2.8 million men and 4.5 million women are severely obese. Second, about 85 percent of all adulthood obesity can be traced to childhood obesity. And finally, the success rate of treating adulthood obesity is very low (Pollock, Wilmore and Fox 1984). Many medical experts believe that the best way to reduce the incidence of obesity in the United States is through prevention.

In 1983, results from the famous Framingham Heart study (Huber et al. 1983) showed that being overweight for a long period of time (about 14 years or longer) was a potent, independent cardiovascular disease risk factor. This study provides strong proof that weight control is an important health behavior. Weight control is achieved through proper aerobic exercise and diet. Skinfold measurements are not only useful for evaluating body composition, repeated testing reinforces the concept of maintaining a desirable weight for health promotion.

Sit-Ups and Sit and Reach

Many practitioners believe that maintenance of minimal levels of trunk and hip strength, and endurance and flexibility in the lower back and leg regions are important for the prevention and alleviation of low back pain and tension. It has been estimated that 25 to 30 million Americans (about 16%) suffer from low back problems. Low back problems are a major reason people miss work and it is estimated that from 12% to 38% of all reported industrial injury claims are for back problems (AAHPERD 1984).

Many fitness experts, physical therapists, and orthopedic surgeons link the incidence of low back problems to the lack of exercise, but it must be remembered that low back problems are complex and that exercise is only one factor. The logic is that weak muscles are easily fatigued and cannot support the spine in proper alignment. Weak abdominal and inflexible posterior thigh muscles allow the pelvis to tilt forward causing an abnormal arch in the lower back, increasing the stress on the vertebral column. The sit-up and sit-and-reach tests measure the fitness of these components.

Controlled experimental research has not focused on the relationship between exercise habits and low back pain. It has been shown that sedentary workers who lift boxes on the job sustained more low back injuries than comparable workers who engage in daily exercise training (Chaffin and Park 1973). Workers who were required to work at levels closer to their maximal strength were most likely to injure their back (Keyserling, Herrin and Chaffin 1980). Finally, it was shown, with a YMCA exercise program for low back pain, that better than 82% of the 312 people who completed the course reported a reduction or elimination of pain (Kraus, Glover and Melleby 1976).

CHANGES IN YOUTH FITNESS

The AAHPERD HRFT norms published in 1980 were based on over 12,000 boys and girls. A cluster sample representing several geographic regions was followed. In 1985, results of National Children and Youth Fitness Study (NCYFS) was published in the January issue of *Journal of Physical Education, Recreation and Dance*. Over 8,500 boys and girls in grades 5 through 12 were administered health-related and motor-fitness tests. This represented a national probability sample. A comparison of the median performance of selected tests is presented in figures 9.7 through 9.10.

With few exceptions for selected age groups, the children that comprised the 1980 HRFT sample were more fit than the 1985 NCYFS sample. A similar study (Morrow et al. 1984) with over 6,000 Texas school children produced similar results. These changes present physical educators with an interesting paradox; medical research has shown that regular, vigorous exercise is an important health habit, yet the fitness of American youth is declining.

COMPUTERS AND YOUTH FITNESS TESTING

Both micro and mainframe computer programs are available to provide students with test results, store results, make comparisons, and calculate local norms. This service may be contracted, or microcomputer programs can be purchased. An example of each is provided next.

Figure 9.7 Median mile run performance for boys and girls of various ages. (Data from the AAHPERD HRFT [1980] and National Children and Youth Fitness Study [NCYFS 1985]. Graph by MacASJ)

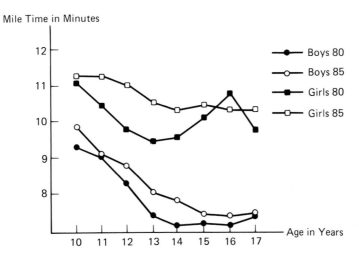

Figure 9.8 Median sum of triceps and subscapular skinfolds for boys and girls of various ages. (Data from the AAHPERD HRFT [1980] and National Children and Youth Fitness Study [NCYFS 1985]. Graph by MacASJ)

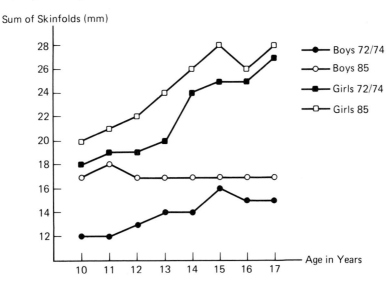

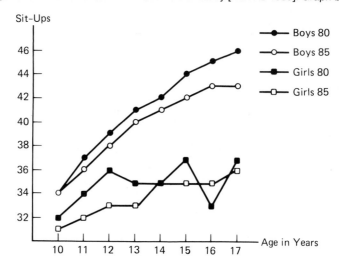

Figure 9.9 Median number of sit-ups for boys and girls of various ages. (Data from the AAHPERD HRFT [1980] and National Children and Youth Fitness Study [NCYFS 1985]. Graph by MacASJ)

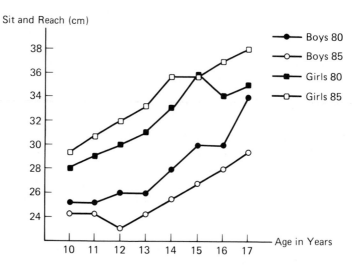

Figure 9.10 Median sit-and-reach performances for boys and girls of various ages. (Data from the AAHPERD HRFT [1980] and National Children and Youth Fitness Study [NCYFS 1985]. Graph by MacASJ)

Figure 9.11 Sample graphic and data output for the FITNESSGRAM®. Features of the FITNESSGRAM® include a summary of data, an exercise prescription, and a message to parents. (Source: Courtesy of the Institute for Aerobic Research, Dallas, Tx.)

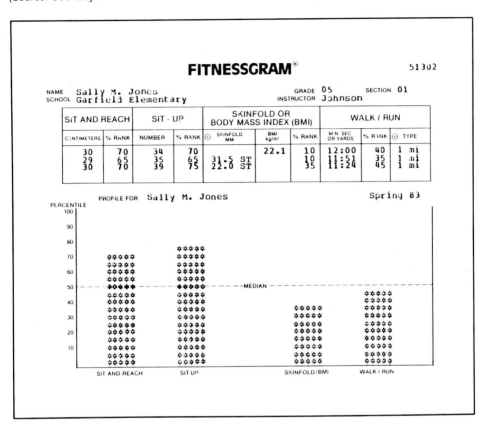

The FITNESSGRAM® is a national program developed by the Institute for Aerobic Research, Dallas, Texas and sponsored by the Campbell Soup Company. The Institute is the "research arm" of the clinic founded by Dr. Kenneth Cooper (1985). The FITNESSGRAM® is the output of a service that scores and reports fitness test results. Both the AAHPERD YFT and HRFT can be used and the data of well over a million students have been processed.[1]

A sample computer output of the FITNESSGRAM® for the AAHPERD HRFT is provided in figure 9.11. The FITNESSGRAM® includes both the test raw data and percentile ranks. The graphic output offers students a visual picture of their fitness status. The program provides results of previous tests that can be used to make comparisons. Another advantage of the computer is that it can easily make difficult calculations. The body mass index (BMI) is provided as additional information. The BMI is weight (kilograms) divided by height (meters) squared $\left(BMI = \dfrac{kg}{m^2} \right)$. Finally, the program provides each student with a personalized message on how to improve fitness.

1. For enrollment information write: Youth Fitness, Institute for Aerobic Research, 12200 Preston Road, Dallas, Texas 75230.

Figure 9.11 Continued.

TOTAL PHYSICAL FITNESS SCORE	
EXCELLENT	234 +
ABOVE AVERAGE	211-233
AVERAGE	191-210
BELOW AVERAGE	167-190
WELL BELOW AVERAGE	0-166

DATE	HEIGHT	WEIGHT	TOTAL FITNESS SCORE
SEM - YR	FT IN	LBS	
Sp 82	4-04	85	195
Fa 82	4-05	89	193
Sp 83	4-06	90	210

These activities are recommended:

To improve your cardiorespiratory endurance: walking, jogging, swimming, cycling and rope jumping.

To improve your body composition: Extend the length of time each day that you walk, jog, swim, cycle or jump rope and do strength development activities.

① SKINFOLD TYPES	② WALK/RUN TYPES
T = TRICEP	1 mi = 1 MILE (M:N SEC)
ST = SUBSCAPULAR	1.5 = 1.5 MILE (M:N SEC)
+ TRICEP	9 = 9 MINUTE (YARDS)
	12 = 12 MINUTE (YARDS)

Dear Parent:
We are pleased to send you this FITNESSGRAM* to provide information on your child's level of physical fitness as indicated by his/her performance in the AAHPERD Health Related Physical Fitness Test recently administered in our school. This test was developed by the American Alliance for Health, Physical Education, Recreation and Dance.

Your child participates in the test at least once a year. The FITNESSGRAM* will show you any progress in his/her growth and development over the school years.

The FITNESSGRAM* provides the following information:

1. A total physical fitness score for your child based on assessments of
    • low-back hamstring flexibility—measured by sit-and-reach test;
    • abdominal strength and endurance-1 minute sit-up test;
    • body composition — indicated by one of the following tests:
      a) measurement of triceps skinfold (back of upper arm) plus subscapular (below shoulder blade) or triceps skinfold only
      b) ratio of weight to height as indicated by Body Mass Index (weight in kilograms divided by height in meters squared)
      Please note, it is not recommended that children already in the 90th percentile attempt to lose more weight;
    • cardiovascular fitness-1-mile, 1.5-mile, 9-minute, or 12-minute walk/run.

2. A percentile rank (% RANK) for each test item is computed based on a norm developed for your child's age and sex. You can see both your child's score and the average (50%) of other students who have taken this test.

3. An exciting feature of the FITNESSGRAM* is the recommendation for activities which can help improve your child's individual scores.

4. The FITNESSGRAM* reflects past performances which will allow the monitoring of improvement from test date to test date!

We hope you will find the FITNESSGRAM* a useful tool to assess your child's fitness level, height and weight development—and to encourage your entire family to enjoy the benefits of an active lifestyle.

Mr. Frederick Johnson
Physical Education Instructor
Garfield Elementary

A second program has been developed by University of Houston professors[2] to run on the Apple computer. The program is user friendly and designed to be used by physical education teachers at their schools. The program can store test results and provide students with feedback of their fitness. A feature of the program is the ability to make local norms. Test batteries available include the AAHPERD YFT, HRFT, and 1973 Texas tests. A sample output is provided in figure 9.12. The program with just the AAHPERD YFT and HRFT batteries can also be purchased from AAHPERD.

SUMMARY

The development of physical fitness is a recognized objective of physical education programs and measured with motor fitness or health-related test batteries. The AAHPERD YFT is a popular motor fitness test. Recently, the validity of motor fitness as an index of physical fitness has been questioned and health-related fitness tests have been published. These tests are based on the growing body of medical research that

2. The program was developed by Drs. James Morrow and Janice Wendt, Department of Physical Education, University of Houston, Texas, 77004, and may be purchased directly from Dr. Morrow. Additionally, the program is marketed by AAHPERD under the title of *Computer Application of the Health Related Physical Fitness Test*.

Figure 9.12 Sample data output for the AAHPERD Health-Related Physical Fitness Test. The program is designed to be used by the teacher at school. (Source: Courtesy of Dr. J. Morrow and J. Wendt, University of Houston, Houston, Tx.)

```
                       A A H P E R D

       LIFETIME HEALTH RELATED PHYSICAL FITNESS TEST

Name: Jane Doe                 Date: Dec 1985

Age: 13 Years                  School: Jones
Sex: Girl                      Teacher: Smith
                               Grade: 8




        Test           Score  Percentile       Evaluation

9 Minute Run (Yds)     1550       45        Average
1 Mile Run Time        8:55       60        Average
Skinfold Sum (MM)        17       70        Above Average
Sit-Ups (1 Min)          50       90        Excellent
Sit and Reach            45       95        Excellent

Cardiorespiratory Function
      Your Cardiorespiratory Test Indicates That Your Fitness Level
      Needs Improvement. A Sound Aerobic Exercise Program is
      Necessary to Improve Cardiorespiratory Function. Activities to
      Include Are: Running, Walking, Swimming, Bicycling, Etc.



              * * * * * * * * * * * * * * * * * * * * * * * * * * * *
              * All-American Fitness Award *
              * * * * * * * * * * * * * * * * * * * * * * * * * * * *


For Information On Improving Your Results in Any Area, Please
Contact Your Physical Education Teacher.
```

Courtesy of Dr. J. Morrow and J. Wendt, University of Houston, Houston, Texas.

supports the value to health of regular, vigorous exercise. Health-related batteries normally include tests of cardiorespiratory function, body composition, and abdominal and low-back function. The AAHPERD HRFT and Texas Youth Fitness Test measure these components.

Even though research supports the value of exercise for health promotion, evidence shows that the health-related fitness of American youth is on the decline. A comparison of the norms of the AAHPERD HRFT and 1985 youth fitness national survey showed that the median values of the national survey were lower than the HRFT norms. This was true almost without exception for boys and girls of all ages.

Computer programs are available for providing students with their fitness results. This service can be commercially contracted or programs are available for microcomputer use in the public schools. The programs ease the work of record keeping and improve student feedback.

Evaluating youth fitness **317**

FORMATIVE EVALUATION OF OBJECTIVES

Objective 1   Identify the general tests that comprise a motor fitness battery.

1. The most popular motor fitness test is the AAHPERD YFT. List the tests that comprise this battery.
2. What does a student need to do to qualify for a Presidential Youth Fitness Award?

Objective 2   Identify the general tests that comprise health-related fitness batteries.

1. What are the test items of the AAHPERD HRFT and Texas Youth Fitness Test?
2. What are the general differences between the AAHPERD HRFT and Texas Youth Fitness Test?

Objective 3   Differentiate between motor fitness and health-related fitness batteries.

1. Motor fitness and health-related fitness batteries each evolved from different philosophies of fitness. Explain these philosophies.
2. Health-related fitness tests can be used to teach students the value of exercise for health promotion. For what can motor fitness tests be used?

Objective 4   Analyze the validity of tests used to evaluate youth fitness.

1. Aerobic fitness is considered important for health purposes. Does the AAHPERD YFT measure aerobic fitness? Why or why not?
2. If a distance run test is to be used, what should the distance be to validly measure $\dot{V}O_2$ Max?
3. Are skinfolds valid for use with public school children?
4. Medical research has shown that vigorous exercise is important for health purposes. How is this related to the following: (1) aerobic fitness; (2) body composition; (3) sit-ups and sit-and-reach?

Objective 5   Identify the changes in youth fitness that have occurred in the United States.

1. Describe the general fitness trends of American youth.
2. Average and age-trend differences are present normative fitness data of boys and girls. Describe these differences.

Objective 6   Understand the use of computers for the evaluation of youth fitness.

1. Describe the computer programs that can be used with youth fitness tests.

ADDITIONAL LEARNING ACTIVITIES

1. Gain experience in youth fitness testing. Go to the public schools and help a teacher administer fitness tests.

2. Learn how to take skinfold measurements accurately. With one or more of your classmates, take triceps, subscapular, and calf skinfolds on a group of students. Compare your results with your classmates. If your scores do not agree, determine what you are doing differently. The intraclass reliability method can be used to analyze tester differences. Check the procedures and pictures in this chapter to standardize your testing methods.

3. Examine the validity of the steady state run. We can offer two suggestions. First, with a group of students correlate steady state run performance with another index of aerobic capacity such as a maximal distance run. Second, if you have $\dot{V}O_2$ equipment and a treadmill, determine the energy cost ($\dot{V}O_2$ ml·kg^{-1}min^{-1}) of steady state running for various speeds.

4. If you have some basic computer skills, try to develop a program that can be used for youth fitness tests. Good luck.

BIBLIOGRAPHY

AAHPERD. 1976. *Youth Fitness Test Manual.* Washington, D.C.

AAHPERD. 1980. *Health Related Physical Fitness Manual.* Washington, D.C.: AAHPERD.

AAHPERD. 1984. *Technical Manual: Health Related Physical Fitness.* Washington, D.C.: AAHPERD.

American College of Sports Medicine. 1978. "Position Statement on the Recommended Quantity and Quality of Exercise for Developing and Maintaining Fitness in Healthy Adults." *Medicine and Science in Sports* 10:vii.

Åstrand, P., and K. Rodahl. 1977. *Textbook of Work Physiology.* 2d ed. New York: McGraw-Hill.

Balke, B. 1963. "A Simple Test for the Assessment of Physical Fitness" *CARI Report,* Oklahoma City, Okla.: Civil Aeromedical Research Institute.

Burke, E. 1976. "Validity of Selected Laboratory and Field Tests of Physical Working Capacity." *Research Quarterly* 47:95–104.

Burris, B. 1970. "Reliability and Validity of the Twelve Minute Run Test for College Women." Paper read at AAHPER Convention, Seattle, Washington.

Chafin, D. B., and K. S. Park. 1973. "A Longitudinal Study of Low Back Pain as Associated with Occupational Weight Lifting Factors." *American Indian Hygiene Association Journal* 34:513–25.

Clarke, H. H., ed. 1971. "Basic Understanding of Physical Fitness." *Physical Fitness Research Digest.* Washington, D.C.: President's Council on Physical Fitness and Sport.

Cooper, K. H. 1968. "A Means of Assessing Maximal Oxygen Intake." *JAMA* 203:201–04.

Cooper, K. H. 1985. *Running Without Fear.* New York: M. Evans and Co.

Cureton, K. J. 1977. "Determinants of Distance Running Performance in Children: Analysis of a Path Model." *Research Quarterly* 48:270–79.

Disch, J., R. Frankiewicz, and A. Jackson. 1975. "Construct Validation of Distance Run Tests." *Research Quarterly* 46:169–76.

Doolittle, R. L., and R. Bigbee. 1968. "The Twelve-Minute Run-Walk: A Test of Cardiorespiratory Fitness of Adolescent Boys." *Research Quarterly* 39:491–95.

Getchell, L. et al. 1977. "Prediction of Maximal Oxygen Uptake in Young Adult Women Joggers." *Research Quarterly* 49:44–52.

Gordon, T. et al. 1981. "Diet and Its Relation to Coronary Heart Disease and Death in Three Populations." *Circulation* 63:500–14.

Gutin, B. et al. 1976. "Relationship Among Submaximal Heart Rate, Aerobic Power, and Running Performance in Children." *Research Quarterly* 47:536–39.

Hartung, G. H. et al. 1980. "Relation of Diet to High-Density Lipoprotein Cholesterol in Middle-Aged Marathon Runners, Joggers and Inactive Men." *New England Journal of Medicine* 302:357–61.

Hubert, H. B. et al. 1983. "Obesity as an Independent Risk Factor for Cardiovascular Disease: A 26-Year Follow-Up of Participants in the Framingham Heart Study." *Circulation* 67:968–77.

Jackson, A. S. et al. 1976. "A Position Paper on Physical Fitness." Position paper of a joint committee representing the Measurement and Evaluation, Physical Fitness, and Research Councils of the AAHPER, Washington, D.C.

Jackson, A. S., and A. E. Coleman. 1976. "Validation of Distance Run Tests for Elementary School Children." *Research Quarterly* 47:86–94.

Johnson, F. E. et al. 1972. Skinfold Thickness of Children 6-11 Years. Series 11, No. 120. Washington, D.C.: U.S. National Center for Health Statistics, U.S. Department of HEW.

Johnson, F. E. et al. 1974. Skinfold Thickness of Youth 12-17 Years. Series 11, No. 132. Washington, D.C.: U.S. National Center for Health Statistics, U.S. Department of HEW.

Katch, F. I. et al. 1973. "Maximal Oxygen Intake, Endurance Running Performance and Body Composition in College Women." *Research Quarterly* 44:301–12.

Katch, V. L. 1970. "The Role of Maximal Oxygen Intake in Endurance Performance." Paper read at AAHPER Convention, Seattle, Washington.

Keyserling, W. M., L. D. Herrin, and A. D. Chaffin. 1980. "Isometric Strength Testing as a Means of Controlling Medical Incidents in Strenuous Jobs." *Journal of Occupational Medicine.* Vol. 22:332–36.

Kitagawa, K., M. Miyashita, and K. Yamamoto. 1977. "Maximal Oxygen Uptake, Body Composition, and Running Performance in Young Japanese Adults of Both Sexes." *Japanese Journal of Physical Education* 21:335–40.

Krahenbuhl, G. et al. 1977. "Field Estimation of $\dot{V}O_2$ Max in Children Eight Years of Age." *Medicine and Science in Sports* 9:37–40.

Kraus, H., R. Glover, and A. Melleby. 1976. "The Y's Way to a Healthy Back." *Journal of Physical Education.* Summer:190–91.

Kraus, H., and R. P. Hirschland. 1954. "Minimum Muscular Fitness Test in School Children." *Research Quarterly* 25:177–88.

Maksud, M. G., C. Connistra, and D. Dublinski. 1976. "Energy Expenditure and $\dot{V}O_2$ Max of Female Athletes During Treadmill Exercise." *Research Quarterly* 47:692–97.

Maksud, M. G., and K. Coutts. 1971. "Application of the Cooper Twelve Minute Run-Walk Test to Young Males." *Research Quarterly* 42:54–59.

Manitoba Department of Education. 1977. *Manitoba Physical Fitness Performance Test Manual and Fitness Objectives.* Manitoba, Canada.

Mayhew, J. L., and J. Andrew. 1975. "Assessment of Running Performance in College Males from Aerobic Capacity Percentage Utilization Coefficients." *Journal of Sports Medicine* 15:342–46.

Morris, J. N. et al. 1953. "Coronary Heart Disease and Physical Activity or Work." *Lancet* 2:1053–63.

Morrow, J. R. et al. 1984. *Texas Youth Fitness Study*. Austin: TAHPER.

NCYFS. 1985. Summary of Findings from National Children and Youth Fitness Study. *JOPERD*. 56:43–90.

Paffenbarger, R. S. et al. 1986. "Physical Activity, All-Cause Mortality, and Longevity of College Alumni." *New England Journal of Medicine*. 314:605–13.

Paffenbarger, R. S. et al. 1984. "A Natural History of Athleticism and Cardiovascular Health." *JAMA* 252:491–95.

Paffenbarger, R. S. et al. 1980. "Exercise as Protection Against Heart Attack." *New England Journal of Medicine* 302:1025–27.

Paffenbarger, R. S. et al. 1977. "Work-Energy Level, Personal Characteristics and Fatal Heart Attack: A Birth-Cohort Effect." *American Journal of Epidemiology* 108:161–75.

Pate, R. R. (ed.) 1978. *South Carolina Physical Fitness Test Manual*. Columbia, S.C.: Governor's Council on Physical Fitness.

Pollock, M. L., J. H. Wilmore, and S. M. Fox III. 1984. *Exercise in Health and Disease*. Philadelphia, Pa.: W. B. Saunders Co.

Public Health Service. 1985. "Summary of Finding from National Children and Youth Fitness Study." *JOPERD* 56:43–90.

Ribisl, P. M., and W. A. Kachadarian. 1969. "Maximal Oxygen Intake Prediction in Young and Middle-aged Males." *Journal of Sports Medicine and Physical Fitness* 9:17–22.

Siri, W. E. 1961. "Body Composition from Fluid Space and Density." In *Techniques for Measuring Body Composition,* J. Brožek and A. Hanschel (ed.) Washington, D.C.: National Academy of Science, 223–24.

Shaver, L. G. 1975. "Maximum Aerobic Power and Anaerobic Work Capacity Prediction from Various Running Performances of Untrained College Men." *Journal of Sports Medicine* 15:147–50.

Taylor, H. L. 1960. "Chapter 3: The Mortality and Morbidity of Coronary Heart Disease of Men in Sedentary and Physically Active Occupations." *Exercise and Fitness*. The Athletic Institute: Chicago, Ill.: 20–39.

Texas Governor's Commission on Physical Fitness. 1973. Physical Fitness-Motor Ability Test. Austin, Tx.

Texas Governor's Commission on Physical Fitness. 1986. *Texas Youth Fitness Test*. Austin, Tx. (Final Working Draft)

Vodak, P., and J. H. Wilmore. 1975. "Validity of the 6-Minute Jog-Walk and 600-Yard Run-Walk in Estimating Endurance Capacity in Boys, 9–12 Years of Age." *Research Quarterly* 46:230–34.

Wiley, J. F., and L. G. Shaver. 1972. "Prediction of Max $\dot{V}O_2$ Intake from Running Performances of Untrained Young Men." *Research Quarterly* 43:89–93.

Evaluating Skill Achievement 10

Contents

Key Words

Accuracy Tests
Objective Evaluation
Rating Scales
Skill Tests
Subjective Evaluation
Wall Volley Tests

Objectives

The achievement of psychomotor skills can be measured by three general means: skill tests, rating scales, and performance itself. Skill tests are an objective, often-used means of evaluating a variety of psychomotor objectives. These tests can be standardized or developed individually. Rating scales are instruments that standardize and define a performance that will be subjectively evaluated by a teacher. Finally, in some instances the performance itself can be used to evaluate achievement.

After reading chapter 10, you should be able to:

1. Identify the four general types of sport skill tests.
2. Evaluate the four general types of sport skill tests using the criteria reliability, validity, and feasibility for mass testing.
3. Evaluate the weaknesses and strengths of rating scales.
4. Identify motor skills that are best evaluated by performance.
5. Outline methods that could be used to develop reliable, valid, and feasible measurement procedures for evaluating motor skill achievement.

INTRODUCTION

A universal goal of physical education programs is to produce permanent, measurable changes in student psychomotor behavior, in skills ranging from touch football, to modern dance, volleyball, or scuba diving. For the achievement of psychomotor objectives to be evaluated, the measurement procedures—tests, rating scales, or other instruments—must parallel the instructional objectives. Today the trend is away from standardized evaluation methods, whose objectives often vary from instructional ones (Klein 1971). Instead, it is the teacher—the person who has developed the instructional objectives—who must develop the procedures for evaluating them.

Sport skill tests are an objective method for evaluating motor skill achievement, and several of these tests are outlined in the chapter. From them, and the extensive bibliography of tests in the Appendix, you should be able to develop your own reliable, valid skill tests.

Rating scales are a subjective but systematic method for evaluating those skills that do not lend themselves to objective evaluation. The subjectivity of the method presents numerous problems, but there are procedures for constructing reliable, valid scales discussed in the text.

Finally, for certain skills (golf, bowling, archery) performance can provide an objective score for skill evaluation. The advantages and limitations of performance-derived evaluation are presented here as well.

SPORT SKILL TESTS

Skill tests require an environment similar to the game environment and standardized procedures for administration. The validity of skill tests is judged to some extent on the consistency between testing and performing environments. This does not mean you must recreate exactly the playing environment; it does mean that the movements and the activity must correspond to those of the actual sport. For example, you can use repeated volleying of a volleyball against a wall to measure achievement in the skill of volleyball passing; however, the student must be standing in the proper position.

The virtue of skill tests is a subject of ongoing debate. Many skill tests offer an objective, reliable, and valid method for evaluating motor skill objectives, while others are a waste of time. Do not use a skill test that does not meet your evaluation needs or the important criteria of reliability, validity, and feasibility for mass testing. Also, be sure to adopt tests that were developed on students of the same sex, age, and experience level as your students. You can also modify an existing test to meet your needs. Collins and Hodges (1978) describe many skill tests that might be adopted or modified for use in your testing program. Barrow and McGee (1979) and Johnson and Nelson (1979) are also good sources of skill tests.

Although skill tests are most useful for the evaluation of learning, they can also be used for (1) placement, (2) diagnosis, (3) prediction, (4) comparative evaluation, and (5) motivation. The tests used to evaluate achievement can be placed into four groups: (1) accuracy tests, (2) wall volley tests, (3) total bodily movement tests, and (4) throws, kicks, or strokes for power or distance. A few tests have aspects of several groups and so are combination tests.

Accuracy Tests

Accuracy tests involve throwing, striking, or kicking an object toward a target for accuracy. Basketball free throws, badminton short serves, and volleyball serves are common accuracy tests.

Basketball Passing Test for Accuracy (AAHPER 1966a)

Objective: To measure the accuracy with which a player can make a two-hand-push pass at a target.

Equipment: Standard inflated basketballs; a target painted or drawn on a wall or mat, or on a piece of canvas hung on a smooth wall; chalk; and a measuring tape. The floor should be properly measured and marked as shown in figure 10.1.

Procedure: The player stands behind a line 25 feet from and parallel to the target. Using a two-hand push pass (chest pass), the player tries to hit the center of the target with the basketball. Passes must be made with both feet behind the passing line, and the two-hand-push pass must be used. After a practice pass, each student takes 10 passes.

Scoring: Award 3 points for hitting the center circle, 2 points for the next circle, and 1 point for the outer circle. Score hits on a line as though they had struck the higher of the two adjacent circles (figure 10.1, part b). Record points as they are made, the total being the score. The maximum possible score is 30 points.

Other considerations: The basic disadvantage of accuracy tests is that the scoring system does not allow discrimination among skill levels. For example, it would be meaningless to use a single basketball pass as an index of passing skill because the score could range from only 0 to 3. This lack of variability reduces reliability. Two general procedures, however, can improve the reliability of accuracy tests. The first increases the variability of the target. A target with a range from 0 to 1 (figure 10.1, part a) is less reliable than the recommended target, whose range is from 0 to 3 (part b). Given 10 passes, the range of scores on the first target would be from 0 to 10; on the second, from 0 to 30, a more precise measure. The second procedure increases the number of trials. Obviously 20 trials yield more reliable results than do 5 or 10. Ideally, then, 15 to 30 trials should be administered for most accuracy tests. Of course, too many trials can make a test unfeasible for mass testing.

Figure 10.1 Two procedures for scoring an accuracy test. (Adapted from AAHPER, *Basketball Skills Test Manual for Boys,* 1966; reprinted by permission of the American Alliance for Health, Physical Education, Recreation and Dance, 1900 Association Drive, Reston, Virginia 22091.)

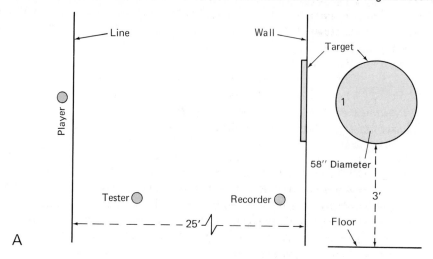

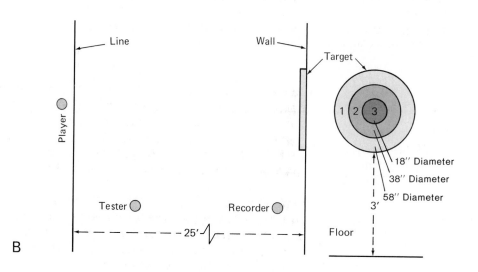

Wall Volley Tests

Wall volley tests require the subject to repeatedly stroke, pass, throw, or kick an object at a wall over a specified period of time with the number of successful trials the unit of measurement, or for a specified number of successful trials with time as the unit of measurement.

Basketball Passing Test (AAHPER 1966a)

Objective: To measure the speed with which the subject can continue to pass and catch a ball.

Equipment: A level floor or ground; a smooth, solid wall; a stopwatch; and standard inflated basketballs.

Procedure: The player stands behind a line on the floor parallel to and 9 feet from the wall. At the signal "Go," the player passes the ball against the wall, about head high, catches the rebound, and continues passing against the wall as rapidly as possible until ten passes have been completed. Any method of passing can be used, but the push pass is fastest. A practice trial is allowed. All passes must be made from behind the line. The ball must be caught and passed, not batted. The ball can hit the wall at any height. If the ball is dropped, the subject must recover it and continue from behind the line until the ball has hit the wall ten times. Two complete trials are allowed.

Scoring: The test is timed from the instant the first pass hits the wall until the tenth pass hits the wall. (Although the player begins at the signal "Go," the watch is not started until the ball hits the wall.) Record the time in seconds and tenths of seconds. Record two complete trials, using the better score of the two.

Other considerations: In general wall volley tests tend to be reliable, but because the testing and playing environments can differ considerably, validity poses a problem. Does repeatedly passing a ball against a wall truly measure a student's basketball passing skill? The original Dyer Tennis Wall Volley Test

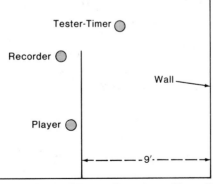

(Dyer 1935) required the student to volley a tennis ball against a wall repeatedly for 30 seconds. The restraining line was only 5 feet from the wall, and students tended to tap rather than stroke the ball. In a revision of the test (Hewitt 1965), the restraining line was moved back sufficiently to require the subject to use appropriate ground strokes. Because the wall volley test environment differs from the game environment, it's especially important that students be allowed to practice the test. Then too, wall volleying can be a useful way to practice a skill, allowing the student both practice in the skill and greater familiarity with the testing environment.

Notice in the example basketball passing test the number of passes against the wall was set (10) and the score was the amount of time it took to complete the ten passes. An alternative procedure and scoring system for wall volley tests is to count the number of hits on the wall in a set length of time, usually 15 to 60 seconds. The Dyer Tennis Wall Volley Test just cited is an example. The advantage of the alternative procedure is that only one timer is needed and several students may take the test at the same time if sufficient wall space is available. The student's partner counts the number of hits, and watches for correct form.

Tests of Total Bodily Movement

These tests require the subject to run a standardized test course using movements characteristic of the sport.

Basketball Control Dribble Test (AAHPERD, 1984)

Objective: To measure skill in handling the ball that a player is moving.

Equipment: Standard inflated basketballs, a stopwatch, and six obstacles arranged as shown.

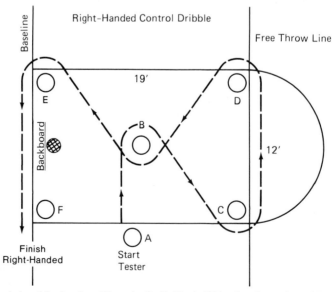

Reprinted by permission of the American Alliance for Health, Physical Education, Recreation and Dance, Reston, Virginia.

Procedure: The player stands on his or her nondominant hand side of cone A with a ball in hand. At the signal "Go," the player begins dribbling with the nondominant hand to the nondominant hand side of cone B and continues to dribble through the course using the preferred hand, changing hands when desired until he or she crosses the finish line. The ball may be dribbled with either hand, but legal dribbles must be used. Each player is allowed three trials.

Scoring: The score in seconds and tenths of seconds is the time required to dribble the entire course. The last two trials are timed and recorded; and the sum of the two is the player's score on the test.

Other considerations: In general these tests are reliable. Their value is determined by the extent to which they relate to the objectives being taught. Allow students to practice on the test course. They will learn how to travel it more efficiently with each practice or trial. These types of tests, like most skill tests, can also be used as skill practice.

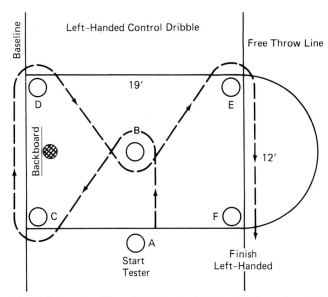

Reprinted by permission of the American Alliance for Health, Physical Education, Recreation and Dance, Reston, Virginia.

Throws, Kicks, or Strokes for Power or Distance

These tests, among the more common types of skill tests, measure the student's ability to throw, kick, or strike an object forcefully. Obvious examples are the football pass for distance, the football punt for distance, and the softball throw for distance. Two less obvious tests are given below.

Badminton Drive for Distance

Objective: To drive a badminton shuttlecock for distance using an underhand stroke.

Equipment: A test station with two lines at right angles to each other, such as the sideline and center court line of a basketball court; and a 50-foot tape measure.

Procedure: Standing at the T formed by the two lines, the student drives an indoor shuttlecock as far as possible. The long service stroke is used. Ten trials are given each student. Trials in which the student obviously misses the shuttlecock are repeated.

Scoring: Each trial is measured to the last half foot. The score is the sum of the ten trials. To facilitate scoring, the measurement is taken at the point where the shuttlecock comes to rest, not where it first hits the floor.

Cornish Handball Power Test (Cornish 1949)

Objective: To measure the power of the handball drive.

Equipment: The test course and scoring system are shown in figure 10.2.

Procedure: Standing behind the service zone, the subject throws the ball against the front wall. Letting the ball hit the floor, the subject drives the ball into the wall as hard as possible, trying to make it rebound as far back as possible. The ball must strike the wall below the 6-foot line, and the subject must strike the ball from behind the front service line. A retrial is allowed if the ball hits the front wall above the 6-foot line or if the subject hits the ball in front of the service line.

Scoring: The score is the value of the scoring zone in which each trial first touches the floor.

Other considerations: Normally such tests are reliable because the distance the object travels can be accurately measured. Attention must be paid, however, to each test's relevance to the instructional objectives.

Combination Tests

These tests are a combination of several of the four groupings just mentioned; usually speed and accuracy.

Speed Spot Shooting (AAHPERD, 1984)

Objective: To measure skill in rapidly shooting from specified positions.

Equipment: Standard inflated basketball, standard goal, stopwatch, marking tape.

Figure 10.2 Scoring zones for Cornish handball drive test. (From C. Cornish, "A Study of Measurement of Ability in Handball." *Research Quarterly,* 20:215–222, 1949; reprinted by permission of the American Alliance for Health, Physical Education, Recreation and Dance, 1900 Association Drive, Reston, Virginia 22091.)

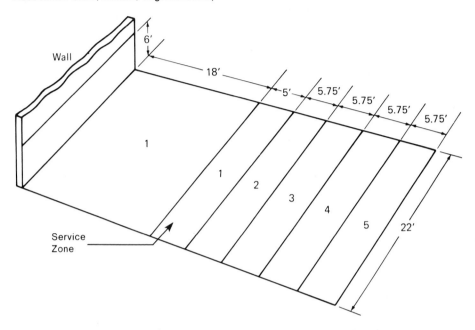

Procedure: Grades 5 and 6 shoot from 9 feet; grades 7, 8, and 9 shoot from 12 feet; grades 10, 11, 12, and college shoot from 15 feet (figure 10.3). Three 60-second trials are administered, with the first trial considered practice and the last two scored. During each trial a student must shoot at least once from each of the five spots (A–E) and may shoot a maximum of four lay-up shots, but not two in succession.

Scoring: Two points are awarded for each shot made and one point is awarded for each unsuccessful shot that hits the rim. The final score is the total of the last two trial points.

Test: Passing (Johnson and Nelson, 1979; AAHPERD 1984)

Objective: To measure skill in passing and recovering the ball while moving.

Equipment: Standard inflated basketball, stopwatch, smooth wall surface, marking tape.

Procedure: Six squares are marked on the wall and a restraining line is marked on the floor 8 feet from the wall (figure 10.4). Three 30-second trials are administered, with the first trial considered practice and the last two timed. The player, holding a ball, stands behind the restraining line and faces target A. On the command "Go," the player chest passes at target A, recovers the rebound

Figure 10.3 Speed Shot Shooting Test. (Source: AAHPERD, 1984. *Basketball Skills Test Manual for Boys and Girls,* Reston, Va.)

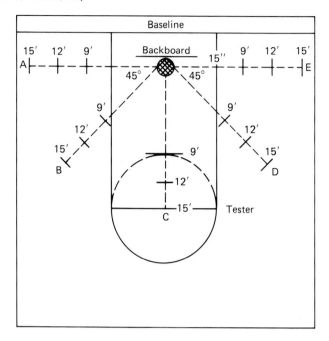

Figure 10.4 Basketball Passing Test. (From Johnson, B. L., and J.K. Nelson, *Practical Measurements for Evaluation in Physical Education.* Minneapolis, Minn.: Burgess Publishing Company, 1979 and AAHPERD, *Basketball Skills Test Manual for Boys and Girls,* 1984.)

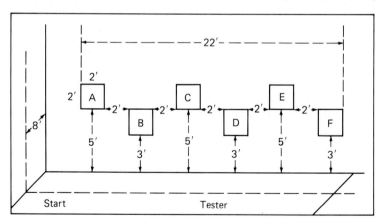

and moves opposite target B. From behind the restraining line the player chest passes at target B. This pattern continues until target F, where two chest passes are executed. Then the player moves to the left, passes at target E, and continues to move left passing at each target in turn.

Scoring: Each pass that hits the desired target counts two points. Each pass hitting the wall but missing the target counts one point. The sum of the last two trial points is the final score.

RATING SCALES

Rating scales are useful for evaluating qualities that can not be measured objectively, or at least not easily and efficiently. This section focuses on procedures for constructing and using rating scales, particularly to evaluate skill achievement.

Subjective or Objective Evaluation?

Most of the measurement techniques discussed to this point have had good objectivity, for the simple reason that most of the measurements conducted in physical education are objective rather than subjective. With **objective evaluation,** the test has a clearly defined scoring system, so the scorer does not affect the final score. Examples of objective tests are a 50-yard dash measured with a stopwatch, a standing long jump measured with a tape, a one minute sit-up measured in number of executions, or a basketball free throw test. If a student makes seven free throws out of ten shots, two scorers would have little difficulty arriving at the same score. Remember, objectivity is the degree of agreement between two or more competent scorers. With subjective evaluation, a qualified person or persons judge the quality of a performance and assign a score, so the scorer can and does affect the final score. A subjective evaluation may be based on a defined scoring system, as in the scoring of gymnastics events in competition, or the evaluation may be just the impressions of each scorer. In the latter case, agreement between the scorers would probably not be high and objectivity would be low. Rating scales are designed to help objectify subjective evaluation, by defining the scoring system just as a tape measure defines the system of scoring the distance a person jumps.

Some people do not think highly of subjective evaluations, but it must be remembered that **subjective evaluations** are often used to determine the validity of objective tests. Judges' ratings are among the most widely-used criteria for validating skill tests for team sports. Although it is true that anything that exists can be measured, the system for measuring it may not be an objective test. Certainly, wherever feasible, objective evaluation should be used. But many important instructional objectives cannot be measured objectively. In fact objective skill tests are not even available for gymnastics, folk dancing, fencing, and teamwork. For a number of the more complex team sports, it would be almost impossible to develop a test or test battery to validly measure total playing ability, for two reasons: (1) the difficulty of identifying or measuring in a short period of time all the skill components that make up a given sport, and (2) the difficulty of measuring objectively the interaction among the skill components of a given sport, making the sum of the measurable components less than descriptive of the whole sport.

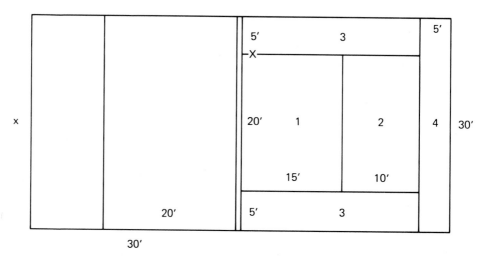

Figure 10.5 Volleyball serving test. (From AAHPER, *Volleyball Skills Test Manual*, 1969, p. 20; reprinted by permission of the American Alliance for Health, Physical Education, Recreation and Dance, 1900 Association Drive, Reston, Virginia 22091.)

Subjective evaluation may also be more efficient than objective testing. Certain subjective scoring can be carried out while the students are practicing or competing, making it unnecessary to set aside special testing periods. Also, the number of trials required in certain tests for objective evaluation can make those tests unfeasible for mass testing. For example, assume that a teacher wants to evaluate student skills in serving and passing a volleyball for a class of 60. The two recommended objective tests (AAHPER 1969) described in figures 10.5 and 10.6 would require a total of 600 serves and 1200 passes to reliably evaluate these skills. Certainly a more efficient use of time would be to develop a rating scale and evaluate the students while they play the game.

Problems with Subjective Evaluation

Subjective evaluation must be not only valid, reliable, and efficient, but also as objective as possible. We can satisfy these four criteria if the procedure is well planned.

The first stage in the planning process is the determination of which skills are going to be evaluated and how much each skill is going to affect the final score. Consider, for example, a teacher who at the end of a volleyball unit has not planned what to evaluate or how to weigh what has been evaluated. This teacher may have neglected not only to observe the same skills in each student, but also to weigh each equally in the final score. Serving skill may account for 35% of one student's final score and only 20% of another's.

Figure 10.6 Volleyball passing test. (Adapted from AAHPER, *Volleyball Skills Test Manual,* 1969, p. 23; reprinted by permission of the American Alliance for Health, Physical Education, Recreation and Dance, 1900 Association Drive, Reston, Virginia 22091.)

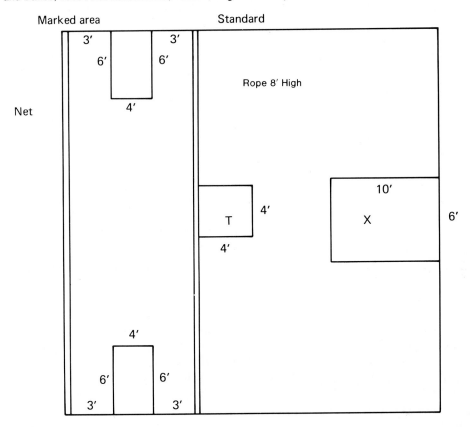

The second stage in the planning process is the formulation of performance standards. Suppose that a teacher, having decided which skills to evaluate and their weight, begins to evaluate the students' serves without formulating performance standards. If the teacher expected well-placed, hard-to-return services and the first few students do not serve well, the teacher may unconsciously lower his or her standards, applying different criteria to the next students. These sliding standards would give two students of equal ability different scores.

The third stage in the planning process is a system for immediate recorded scoring. Even when a teacher knows what to evaluate, the weight of each evaluation and the performance standards, and, unless the scores are recorded immediately, the evaluation will probably be neither reliable nor valid. Scores are too easily interchanged if the teacher tries to remember the score of each student and record it later.

In a sense, a rating scale reflects the careful planning procedure required to give reliability, validity, and objectivity to subjective evaluation. The scale lists the traits to be evaluated, reflects the teacher-determined importance of each trait, describes the performance standards, and provides a format for immediate recorded scoring.

Constructing a Rating Scale

The process of constructing a rating scale is threefold: (1) determining the purpose of the subjective evaluation, (2) identifying the basic components of the trait being evaluated, and (3) selecting the levels of ability for each component.

Purpose

The purpose of a rating scale determines the degree to which subjective evaluations must discriminate among ability groups. The more they must discriminate, the greater the number of classifications of ability. If, for example, posture is subjectively evaluated, only two classifications (acceptable-unacceptable) or three classifications (excellent-average-poor) may be needed. For grading purposes 3 to 5 classifications are usually adequate; occasionally 7 to 10 are used in competition.

Basic Components

The trait being rated is almost always evaluated in parts or components, which must themselves be identified. The importance of each component and subcomponent must be defined so that points reflecting their relative value can be assigned. In table 10.1, for example, three components are identified and three subcomponents are listed under each. These components and subcomponents reflect the instructional objectives of the activity.

Levels of Ability

The third step in the process is the decision of how many levels of ability should be assigned to each component. Two levels—pass-fail—are usually considered too crude an evaluation procedure. When three levels of ability are sufficient, a student can be rated above average, average, or below average on each subcomponent. A 5-level scoring system is probably the most common: each student is rated superior, above average, average, below average, or inferior on each subcomponent. Systems beyond five levels require that the teacher be knowledgeable enough about the characteristics being evaluated to identify small differences in ability or status. If a teacher creates more ability levels than he or she can identify, the reliability of the evaluations will be low. Remember that reliability and objectivity are improved when the rating scale lists exactly what is looked for in each subcomponent.

Using the Scale

No rating scale, however well prepared, works unless it is used. You should have a copy of the scale for each subject and record the ratings on it immediately after the evaluation. There are also several ways to improve the effectiveness of a rating scale; increasing the number of qualified raters, retesting on several occasions, allowing sufficient time for both the test and the evaluation, preparing the students, and developing your own scale where possible.

Table 10.1

Sample Volleyball Rating Scale.

Each of the three components of volleyball-playing ability has a point value of 15, and is scored on a 5-4-3-2-1 basis:

5 points—Exceptional ability, near perfect for the age and sex of the participant.
4 points—Above average ability, not perfect but quite skillful for the age and sex of the participant.
3 points—Average ability, typical for the age and sex of the participant.
2 points—Below average ability, characterized by more mistakes than is typical performance for the age and sex of the participant.
1 point—Inferior ability, far below typical performance for the age and sex of the participant.

For each subheading, circle the appropriate score.

I. Serve						
A. Height above net	5	4	3	2	1
B. Accuracy of placement	5	4	3	2	1
C. Difficulty of return	5	4	3	2	1
II. Setting or Spiking—choose one						
A. Setting						
1. Height above net	5	4	3	2	1
2. Accuracy of placement	5	4	3	2	1
3. Coordination with spiker	5	4	3	2	1
B. Spiking						
1. Accuracy of placement	5	4	3	2	1
2. Difficulty of return	5	4	3	2	1
3. Coordination with setter	5	4	3	2	1
III. General team play						
A. Hustle	5	4	3	2	1
B. Alertness—saves and play of difficult shots	5	4	3	2	1
C. Teamwork	5	4	3	2	1

Total Score _____

Number of Raters

The reliability and validity of subjective evaluations increase as the number of raters increases, as predicted by the Spearman-Brown prophecy formula and the validity prediction formula (chapters 3 and 4), provided of course that the raters are qualified. One well-qualified rater is preferable to several poorly qualified raters. When there are several raters, objectivity improves if they decide before the rating what they are looking for and what standards to use. For example, assume there are four judges in a gymnastics meet—two college coaches and two high school coaches—and that each rates performers on a 10-point system. The college coaches may expect more of the performers than do the high school coaches. Thus, if the participants are junior high boys, the judges must decide whether a perfect score indicates perfect performance, or the best that can be expected of this age group.

Number of Trials

Rating each student on several occasions within a short period—three days, for example—and using the average of the ratings as a score usually improves the score's reliability and validity. The justification and advantages of rating each person several times are the same as the reasons for using multiple trials on a physical performance test. By rating each person on several different days we minimize the chances of a student receiving a poor rating because of an off day, or a high score due to luck.

If you are able to rate a student on several different occasions, do not look at the student's previous ratings, which are bound to influence your evaluation. For example, if you know that a student was rated below average on the first performance, there is little chance that you will rate the student above average on a subsequent performance, even if the student deserves it. This preconceived idea of ability is a problem common to all forms of subjectivity evaluation.

Testing Time

Allow enough time to rate an individual completely and to record the ratings immediately. It is better to rate only 10 people each hour and to do a good job than to try to rate 30 people in an hour and to obtain invalid ratings.

Student Preparation

As with objective tests, the students should know what is expected of them and what you will be looking for when you evaluate them. Let the students know that you plan to evaluate them in the near future so that they can prepare themselves if they want to. This makes the evaluation a type of formative evaluation and communicates to the students their weaknesses. Finally, students should be informed that they are being evaluated the day that ratings are made.

Teacher-Prepared Scales

We believe that a teacher should construct his or her own rating scales. The objectives of the course, the manner in which it is taught, the types of students, and their prior experiences are all variables that affect what is evaluated and how. Only a teacher-made rating scale can meet the evaluation needs of a specific situation. In preparing your own scales, you can look to others, like those shown in tables 10.2 and 10.3, for help.

THE PERFORMANCE

For many motor skills, performance is a reliable means of evaluating instructional objectives. Some authors refer to such measures as skill tests or rating scales, which in a sense they are. However, it is important to remember that in this context the performance environment is also the evaluation environment. The instructional objectives and the performance may thus be identical, and content validity more readily assured. For example, a tumbling objective might be to execute a forward roll; when the student does so, the objective has been evaluated.

Table 10.2
Badminton Rating Scale.

The four areas of badminton-playing ability may all be rated during competition. However, the first two areas may be rated in a noncompetitive situation, if so desired, by asking the student to demonstrate the various serves and strokes.

Each subarea is scored on a 3-2-1 basis:

3 points—Above average ability, considerably more skillful than the performance typical of the student's age and sex.
2 points—Average ability, typical performance for age and sex.
1 point—Below average ability, far inferior to typical performance for age and sex.

For each subarea, circle the appropriate score.

I. Serve
   A. Position of shuttlecock upon contact—racket head strikes shuttlecock below waist level.   3   2   3
   B. Position of racket at end of serve—if short serve, racket head does not rise above chest; if long serve, racket head stops between shoulders and top of head at end of serve.   3   2   1
   C. Placement of serve—well-placed relative to type of serve and position of opponent.   3   2   1
   D. Height of serve relative to type of serve—short serve is low over net; drive serve is low over net and deep; clear serve is high and deep.   3   2   1
II. Strokes—consider placement and quality of each stroke.
   A. Clear—high and deep.   3   2   1
   B. Smash—hit from position above head and in front of body; path of bird is down.   3   2   1
   C. Drive—sharp and low over net; hit from position about shoulder height; can be deep or midcourt, but not short.   3   2   1
   D. Drop—hit from position waist- to shoulder-height; low over net; a hairpin-type shot.   3   2   1
III. Strategy
   A. Places shots all over court.   3   2   1
   B. Executes a variety of shots at the most opportune moments.   3   2   1
   C. Takes advantage of opponent's weaknesses (for example, poor backhand, strength problem in back court, poor net play).   3   2   1
   D. Uses own best shots.   3   2   1
IV. Footwork and Position
   A. Near center court position so flexible to play any type of shot.   3   2   1
   B. Has control of body at all times during play.   3   2   1
   C. Body is in correct position when making each shot (usually determined by the feet).   3   2   1
   D. Racket is shoulder- to head-height and ready for use (wrist cocked) at all times; eyes are on the shuttlecock at all times.   3   2   1

Total Score _____

Suggested by Bill Landin, Indiana University.

Table 10.3
Swimming Rating Scale for Elementary Backstroke.

The arm stroke, leg kick, complete stroke, and stroke efficiency are rated on a three-point scale. Complete stroke and stroke efficiency are double-weighted so as to be twice as influential as arm stroke and leg kick in the total rating.

Circle the appropriate score for each area.

A. Arm stroke

3 points—Arms do not break water or rise above top of head; elbows are kept at sides and fingers move up midline of body; stroke is powerful and smoothly coordinated.

2 points—Arms do not break water or rise above top of head; elbows are usually kept at sides and fingers move up midline of body; stroke is reasonably powerful and reasonably well-coordinated.

1 point—Arms break water and/or rise above top of head; elbows are not kept at sides and fingers do not move up midline of body; stroke is not powerful and/or poorly coordinated.

B. Leg Kick

3 points—Legs drop at knees for whip kick; toes are outside of heels as feet spread; kick is powerful and smoothly coordinated.

2 points—Legs drop at knees for whip kick but some flexation occurs at hips; toes are not outside of heels as feet spread, causing knees to spread; kick is reasonably powerful and reasonably well-coordinated.

1 point—Legs do not drop at knees for whip kick, but are brought toward stomach by flexing at the hips; knees spread too wide; no power in kick; kick is poorly coordinated.

C. Complete Stroke

6 points—Arms and legs are coordinated during stroke; arms are at sides, trunk and legs straight, and toes pointed during glide position.

4 points—Minor deviations from the standard for 6 points occur.

2 points—Arms and legs are not coordinated during stroke; glide position is poor with reference to arm-trunk-leg-toe position.

D. Stroke Efficiency

6 points—Long distance is covered in glide; body is relaxed in water; swims in straight line; hips on surface.

4 points—Average distance is covered in glide; body is relaxed in water; does not swim in straight line; hips slightly below surface.

2 points—Little distance is covered in glide; body is not relaxed in water; does not swim in straight line; hips are well below surface (swimmer is sitting in water rather than lying on top of it).

Total Score _____

When performance is evaluated, it is usually in terms of achievement, but it could be in terms of developmental or biomechanical instructional objectives. Among the skills where performance can serve as a means of evaluation are the following:

Archery. Archery achievement is validly determined by measuring the student's accuracy in shooting a standardized target from specified distance.

Bowling. The bowling average achieved under standardized conditions is an objective measure of bowling skill. Subjectively evaluating bowling form would certainly be possible.

Golf. If the school has access to a golf course, the student's score on several rounds can serve as an objective index of golf skill. This criterion is well accepted by touring professionals.

Swimming. The number of breaststrokes required to swim 25 yards is an objective measure of breaststroke ability. Stroke mechanics and/or form are commonly evaluated.

PROCEDURES FOR EVALUATING SKILL ACHIEVEMENT

We recognize that teachers are not researchers with unlimited computer facilities at their disposal. The procedures below for the development of skill test batteries represent the application of scientific test construction principles to the public school teacher's situation. They also represent several years' work. Do not expect high-quality evaluation of psychomotor objectives to be instantly performed.

1. *Define what is to be measured.* This is one of the most important steps in the test construction process: if it is not carried out correctly, subsequent procedures will also be incorrect. Use your instructional objectives as the source of what is to be measured. These objectives describe the skills that should be achieved during an instructional phase, so they also define what needs to be measured.

2. *Select a measuring instrument.* Choose tests or rating scales that measure the achievement of the instructional objectives. In most instances the process of matching objectives and measuring instruments is based on logic. Remember that the skill learned during instruction must also be the skill used during the test. That is, individual differences in scores on a basketball dribble test must be due to individual differences in dribbling skill, not to unrelated factors.

   In selecting a measuring instrument, you can choose from among published skill tests, construct a rating scale, or use the performance itself. It may be necessary to alter an instrument to fit your instructional objectives. In constructing a skill test battery, skill tests and rating scales can be used together to evaluate the different motor skill components of an activity. For example, you can use a serving test to evaluate the achievement of volleyball serving skill and a rating scale to evaluate spiking skill. When it is impossible to evaluate all the skills you have taught, as it usually is, select those that are most important.

3. *Pretest the instrument.* Before you administer a test or rating scale to a class, try it out on a group of 5 to 15 students. No matter how explicit test instructions appear, you will truly understand the test and its procedures only after you have administered it. Several important questions must be answered: Does the test seem to be valid? Does it measure the stated instructional objective? Does it seem to be reliable? Are the directions clear? What is the best way to standardize its administration? How long does it take to test one student? If the test is too long, you may have to set up several test stations, and recruit and train additional testing personnel. At this point you should also develop standardized procedures for administering the test.

4. *Revise the test and testing procedures.* On the basis of your findings from the pretest, you may want to revise, delete, or add tests to the battery. If the changes are numerous, you should administer the revised test to another small group.

5. *Administer the instrument.* At the end of the instructional phase, administer the selected test to the class.

6. *Evaluate the administered test.* After you administer the battery, examine the reliability, validity, and feasibility of each test.

    a. Reliability. Because testing procedures and the variability of the group can affect reliability, it is important that you estimate each test's reliablity for your testing procedures and students. If a test lacks reliability, it may be necessary to use additional trials, alter your testing procedures, or search for a better test.

    b. Validity. Once you have determined reliability, you must determine validity. In most instances, you can do so logically: if the test obviously measures an instructional objective, you can assume content validity. For example, a test that requires a student to swim 25 yards in as few strokes as possible using the sidestroke is a valid test of sidestroke skill. If validity cannot be determined logically, you could compare the scores achieved by the best and poorest students in the class. If the achieved scores do not confirm your observations, the test is suspect. Or, you could compare the test scores with tournament standings. If the tests are valid, the two sets of scores should be related.

    c. Feasibility. Tests can be both reliable and valid, yet simply impractical for mass testing. If you can not revise the testing procedures to make them applicable for mass testing, you must select or develop a new battery.

7. *Revise the final battery.* The final battery should consist of reliable, valid instruments that measure important instructional objectives. A battery normally consists of from 3 to 5 individual tests. Two criteria for compiling the final battery are (1) that the selected tests be reliable, valid, and feasible for mass testing, and (2) that the correlation among the final items be low. If the correlation between two tests in the final battery is high, one should be eliminated.

8. *Develop norms.* Once you have finalized the content of the battery, you must develop norms. T-score and percentile norms (see chapters 2 and 5) are especially useful. T-score norms have the advantage of allowing you to sum the test items and calculate a total score for the entire battery. Many published tests provide national norms; however, you should try to develop your own norms because testing procedures and climatic conditions vary.

SAMPLE SPORT SKILL TESTS

AAHPER Sport Skill Test Series

The Research Council of the AAHPERD (formerly the AAHPER) has published several sport skill tests that were developed from the combined efforts of researchers, city directors of physical education, and public school teachers. Currently, test manuals are available for the archery, football, softball (boys and girls), and volleyball tests. The manuals list administration procedures as well as percentile norms for boys and girls ages 10 to 18. They are available at nominal cost from the AAHPERD.

The following criteria were used in developing the tests:

Validity. Each test should measure the student's ability to perform a skill basic to the sport.

Reliability. Accuracy tests should have reliability above .70; the other tests should have reliability above .80.

Test environment. Preference was given to tests that were also a method of practicing the skill.

Scoring. Preference was given to tests that could be scored objectively.

Degree of difficulty. Each test should differentiate among the various skill levels at each grade level.

Variability. The distribution of scores for each age level should be normal.

The report (Morris 1977) of a committee that evaluated the AAHPER series concluded that the procedures for the test items are vague; that the items should be studied in typical physical education situations and the results reported; that a task analysis of the sport skills should be conducted if logical validity is to be used for the selection and retention of items; that some of the items fail to meet the criterion of reliability; and that, although the test items are supposed to measure skill achievement, some of them actually predict potential achievement. This last is of special concern, in that many of the tests include basic ability items (speed, jumping, agility) that predict, rather than indicate, skill ability. Another common criticism, although not presented by Morris, is that the various batteries each contain eight or nine items, which often take a good deal of time to administer or overlap in terms of skill tested.

The Measurement and Evaluation Council of the AAHPERD formed a task force in 1979 to revise and expand the AAHPER sport skill test series. The basketball skills committee revised the 1966 basketball test and AAHPERD published the revision in 1984. Presently, tennis, volleyball, soccer, and softball skills committees are at work.

The AAHPERD sport skill tests presently available are not without merit. With the exception of the basketball test, a person should probably select 2 to 4 items from a test battery to administer to a class, keeping in mind the concerns of Morris (1977). A brief discussion of each battery follows, for your reference. Individuals planning to use these tests should obtain the test manuals from AAHPERD in order to have the complete administrative procedures and norms.

Archery

The archery test (AAHPER 1967a) requires the student to shoot two ends (12 arrows) at a 48-inch target from distances of 10 to 30 yards. Girls shoot from 10 and 20 yards; boys shoot from 10, 20, and 30 yards. The target has five zones, scored 9-7-5-3-1. Misses are scored 0.

Basketball

The basketball battery (AAHPERD 1984) consists of four tests recommended for both boys and girls, with minor changes for gender differences.

> *Speed Spot Shooting.* This test was presented earlier in the chapter (see pages 330 and 331).
>
> *Passing.* This test was presented earlier in the chapter (see pages 327 and 328).
>
> *Control dribble.* This test was presented earlier in the chapter (see page 328).
>
> *Defensive Movement.* The purpose of this test is to measure basic defensive movement. A course of six cones is set up on the free throw lane of the court. Three timed trials of side-stepping (slide-step) through the course are administered. The final score is the sum of the last two trial times.

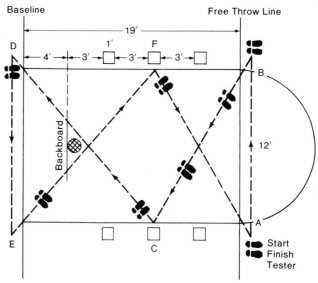

In a factor analysis study (Hopkins 1977) of basketball skill tests, 21 items were administered to 70 male subjects. Four factors were identified: (1) shooting, (2) passing, (3) jumping, and (4) moving with or without the ball. A similar study (Gaunt 1979), using 20 variables administered to 167 female subjects, also identified four factors: (1) lay-up shooting, (2) passing, (3) explosive leg strength, and (4) dribbling. These findings influenced the selection of tests in this battery.

Football

The football battery (AAHPER 1966b) was developed for use with boys. It consists of the following ten tests.

Forward Pass for Distance. The test involves passing a football as far as possible. Distance is measured to the last foot, at right angles to the throwing line. A restraining line is six feet behind the throwing line to define the throwing zone. The best of three throws is scored.

50-Yard Dash with Football. The test involves sprinting 50 yards while carrying a football. The score is the elapsed time accurate to a tenth of a second for the better of two trials.

Blocking. The test course is an obstacle course consisting of three blocking bags. The boy must cross-body block each of the three bags to the ground. The score is the elapsed time required to run the test course, accurate to a tenth of a second for the better of two trials.

Football Pass for Accuracy. The test involves passing a football at a circular target with diameters of 2, 4, and 6 feet. The target is placed so the bottom of the largest circle is three feet from the ground. Each boy tries ten passes from behind a 15-yard throwing line. Each pass is scored from 0 to 3 points.

Football Punt for Distance. The test involves punting a football as far as possible. The kicking zone, and administration and scoring of the test are the same as for the forward pass for distance.

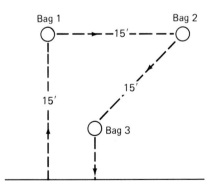

From Johnson, B. L. and J. K. Nelson, *Practical Measurements for Evaluation in Physical Education*, 3d ed. Minneapolis, MN: Burgess Publishing Company, 1979.

Ball-Changing Zigzag Run. While running an obstacle test course, the student must change the ball from hand to hand (see diagram). This is a timed test scored to a tenth of a second. The better of the two trials is the subject's score.

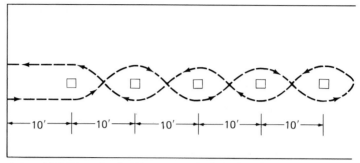

From Johnson, B. L. and J. K. Nelson, *Practical Measurements for Evaluation in Physical Education, 3d ed.* Minneapolis, MN: Burgess Publishing Company, 1979.

Catching the Forward Pass. The student starts on the scrimmage line nine feet to the left of the center (a player), runs 30 feet straight down field, and turns at a right angle to the left. A passer standing 15 feet behind the center passes the ball to the student as he runs. The student is thrown ten passes. The same thing is done with the student nine feet to the right of the center and turning to the right. One point is awarded for each pass caught. The score is the sum of the 20 passes caught.

Pull-out. On the command "Go," the student pulls out, runs around a goalpost that is 9 feet, 3 inches, from the starting position, and sprints straight down field 30 feet. This is a timed test accurate to a tenth of a second. The better of the two trials is recorded as the subject's score.

Kickoff. The student is tested for the distance that he can place-kick a football off of a kicking tee. The player may take as long a run as desired to kick the ball. Three trials are given. The scoring is the same as for the forward pass for distance.

Dodging run. The student runs an obstacle test course while carrying a football. Two complete runs through the course are a trial and two trials are given. This timed test is scored to a tenth of a second. The better of the two trials is recorded as the subject's score.

Softball

Separate test manuals (AAHPER 1967b,c) have been published for boys and girls. Each battery consists of eight tests, described here.

Throw for Distance. The same test is used for boys and girls. As in the football forward pass for distance, the throwing zone, and administration and scoring of the test are the same.

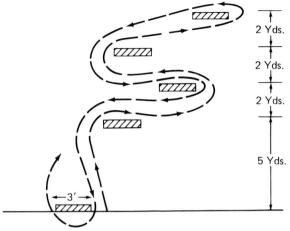

2 Yds.

2 Yds.

2 Yds.

5 Yds.

←3'→

From Johnson, B. L. and J. K. Nelson, *Practical Measurements for Evaluation in Physical Education, 3d ed.* Minneapolis, MN: Burgess Publishing Company, 1979.

Overhand Throw for Accuracy. The test involves throwing a softball at a circular target. The target, its placement, the number of trials, and scoring are the same as the football pass for accuracy. Boys throw from behind a 65-foot restraining line; girls, from behind a 40-foot restraining line.

Underhand Pitching. Each student is allowed 15 underhand pitches. The ball is pitched at a rectangular target with two scoring zones: the inner rectangle is 17 inches by 30 inches: the outer is 29 inches by 42 inches. Boys pitch from a 46-foot restraining line; girls, from a 38-foot restraining line. Each pitch is scored from 0 (missing target) to 2 points (hitting inner rectangle).

Speed Throw. The same test is used for boys and girls. From behind a 9-foot restraining line the student repeatedly throws a ball into a smooth wall and catches the rebound. This wall volley test is scored by the time, accurate to a tenth of a second, required to hit the wall 15 times. The stopwatch is started when the first ball hits the wall and is stopped when the fifteenth ball hits the wall.

Fungo Hitting. The student tosses the ball in the air and tries to hit a fly ball into the outfield, alternately hitting the ball to right and left field. For fly balls that land beyond the baseline, 2 points are awarded; 1 point is awarded for balls that cross the baseline on the ground. Each student is allowed 20 hits, 10 to each side. Two entirely missed balls in succession count as a trial, and any ball hit counts as a trial.

Base Running. The same test is used for boys and girls. A player standing in the batter's box swings a bat on the command "Hit," and then runs the bases. The score is the elapsed time from the command to the instant the player touches home plate. All bases must be touched.

Fielding Ground Balls. A tester throws a ball on a smooth ground surface, and the student tries to field the ball cleanly. The ball must travel at least 25 feet before it is fielded. A total of 20 trials are allowed, and the balls are thrown at 5-second intervals. The score is the number of balls cleanly fielded out of the 20 attempts.

Catching Fly Balls. For girls: Standing in a 60-foot square with second base as the middle of the square, a tester throws fly balls from behind home plate. The girl's score is the number of balls caught out of 20 tries. For boys: The test involves catching balls tossed through a second-story window of a building. The boy's score is the number of balls caught out of 20 tries.

Volleyball

The volleyball battery (AAHPER 1969) consists of four tests recommended for both boys and girls.

Volleying. This is a wall volley test that involves volleying a ball above a 5-foot long line 11 feet above the floor. The score is the number of legal volleys during a 60-second period.

Serving. The court is divided into scoring zones that range from 1 to 4 points. Each student is awarded ten serves. For children younger than 12 the serving line should be located 20 feet from the net.

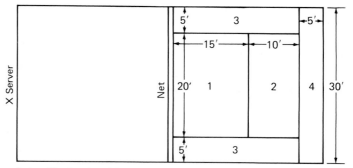

Reprinted by permission of the American Alliance for Health, Physical Education, Recreation and Dance, Reston, Virginia.

Passing. From the rear of the court the student must pass a volleyball above an 8-foot rope into a 6 × 4 foot target outlined on the floor. The ball is tossed to the student, who must pass the ball to either the right or left side of the court. A total of 20 passes, 10 to each side, is allowed; 1 point is scored for each pass that goes over the rope and lands in the proper target.

Set-up. From the middle of the front court a student receives a pass from a thrower in the back court. The student must set up the volleyball by passing the ball over a rope (10 feet high for boys, 9 feet for girls) and into a 4 × 6 foot target outlined on the floor at the corner of the court next to the net. Each student is allowed 20 trials, 10 set to the right and 10 to the left. The sum of the 20 trials that go over the rope and land within the target is the student's score.

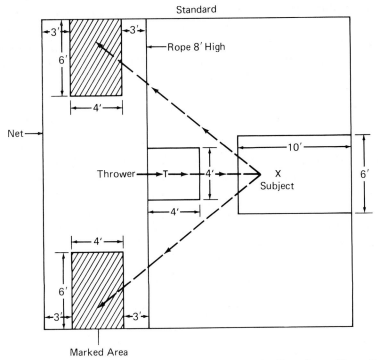

Reprinted by permission of the American Alliance for Health, Physical Education, Recreation and Dance, Reston, Virginia.

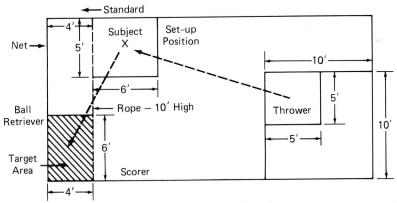

Reprinted by permission of the American Alliance for Health, Physical Education, Recreation and Dance, Reston, Virginia.

Other Sport Skill Tests

Presented below are numerous other sport skill tests as examples of the types of tests that have been used in the past. If these tests meet your needs, use them. However, we hope that many physical education teachers will use these tests as examples and construct their own sport skill tests.

Badminton

Sebolt Short Service Test (Sebolt 1968)

Objective: To measure the achievement of the badminton short service.

Validity and reliability: Because the ability to serve the shuttlecock close to the net and into the front middle corner of the opponent's service court is an important badminton skill, content validity is assumed. With college students the correlation between performance on a ladder tournament and the service test was .61. The intraclass reliability for the students was estimated at .72 and .79.

Equipment: The test is administered on a standard court, with scoring zones as shown in figure 10.7. A string is stretched 16 inches directly above and parallel to the net. A badminton racket and ample supply of new indoor shuttle cocks are needed.

Procedure: Each student is given a 5-minute warm-up period on a practice court before being tested. The test consists of 20 legal serves from the right service court. The bird must be served between the net and the string into the target area. Shuttlecocks served above the string are scored 0. If the shuttlecock hits the string, another serve is allowed. Shuttlecocks that hit the net are scored in the same manner as birds that clear the net.

Scoring: A scorer is needed for each test station. The student's score is the sum of the 20 serves. The scoring zones are shown in figure 10.7. A shuttlecock that hits on the line is awarded the higher value.

Other considerations: An objective of the short serve is to serve the shuttlecock near the net and have it land near or on the short service line. The 3-inch band outside the service court, an important feature of the test, encourages the student to serve for the line. In the game situation a shuttlecock landing just outside the service court should be hit because the player cannot be certain if the bird is in or short. If several test stations are available, the test is feasible for mass use.

Scott and Fox Long Service (Scott and French 1959)

Objective: To measure the accuracy of the badminton long service.

Validity and reliability: Because the ability to serve the shuttlecock deep into the opponent's backcourt is an important skill for singles, content validity is assumed. A correlation of .54 was reported between the service scores and the subjective rating made by three judges during play. The internal-consistency reliability estimates with college women were .77 and .68.

Figure 10.7 Scoring zones for the Sebolt short service test. (Reprinted by permission of Don Sebolt, Virginia Polytechnic Institute, Blacksburg, Virginia.)

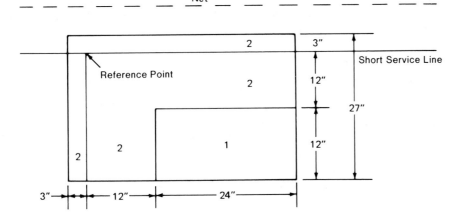

Equipment: The test is administered on a standard court, with scoring zones marked as shown in figure 10.8. A restraining rope at a height of 8 feet is placed parallel to and 14 feet from the net. The student needs a suitable racket and an ample supply of new indoor shuttlecocks.

Procedure: Before the test the student should be given sufficient opportunity for practice. Each student is allowed 20 trials, that can be administered in groups of 5 to 10. The student tries to serve the shuttlecock in a legal manner over the rope into the highest scoring zone. Serves that hit the rope are taken over.

Scoring: A scorer is needed for each test station. The student's score is the sum of 20 serves. The scoring zones are shown in figure 10.8. A 0 is awarded for serves that fail to land in the service court or that go under the restraining rope. Any shuttlecock that lands on a line dividing two scoring areas is awarded the higher value.

Other considerations: A weakness of the scoring system is that the student receives a 0 when a shuttlecock misses the back line by 1 or 2 inches. In the game situation a serve up to about 6 inches long may be good because the opponent may be forced to play the shot. Generally, for a long serve used in singles, the server wants to aim for the deep back line near the center T. We recommend scoring zones be used that encourage the student to aim for the back line. An alternate scoring zone is offered in figure 10.8.

Figure 10.8 Scoring zones for the badminton long service test. (Adapted from M. G. Scott and E. French. *Measurement and Evaluation in Physical Education,* Dubuque, Iowa, Wm. C. Brown, 1959, p. 145. Reprinted by permission of M. Gladys Scott.)

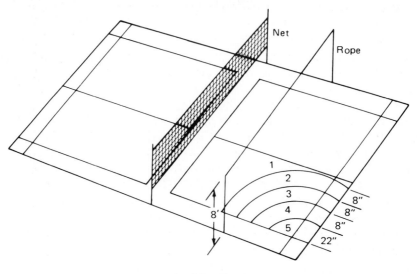

Scott-Fox Scoring

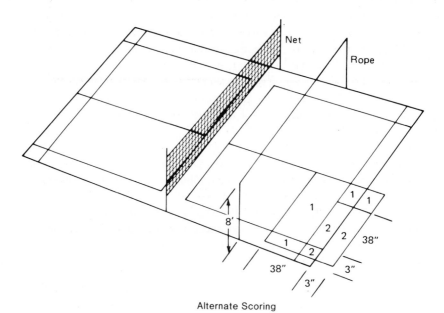

Alternate Scoring

West-Thorpe Eight-Iron Approach Test (West and Thorpe 1968)

Objective: To measure the accuracy of a golf approach shot.

Validity and reliability: The authors reported that accuracy is a function of three independent components of ball flight: (1) the vertical angle of projection, (2) the lateral angle of projection, and (3) velocity. Content validity is assumed because the test scoring considers both an accuracy score and a vertical angle of projection score. The scores of the beginning golfers were compared to an experienced group of ten women golfers with handicaps of 20 or less. The experienced group's mean score was significantly higher than the beginning group's mean score. Thus construct validity can be claimed. A sample of 424 college women enrolled in beginning golf classes was used to estimate the reliability of 12 trials administered on two different days. The intraclass reliability estimate of 24 trials over two days was .75.

Equipment: The target should be marked on a level grassy area approximately 72 feet square. A pin designating the center of the target is surrounded by six concentric circles. The inner circle has a radius of 1½ yards; the remaining circles have radii of 1½-yard increments, so that the outermost is 18 yards in diameter. A restraining line is placed 12 yards from the pin. Each golfer needs 12 balls and an eight-iron.

Procedure: The entire test consists of 24 trials, 12 of which are administered on each of two days. Using the eight-iron, the student must contact the ball while remaining entirely behind the restraining line.

Scoring: Two scorers are needed: one to rate the vertical angle of projection; the second to observe for accuracy. The score for each trial is the accuracy score (the point at which the ball comes to rest in the target) multiplied by the ball flight score. The innermost circle is scored 7, the next 6, and so on. The ball flight is scored by the observer as follows: a topped ball is scored 1; a low angle of projection (under 29 degrees) is 2; and a high angle of projection (over 29 degrees) is 3. A maximum score of 21 is possible on each trial. A swing and miss is scored 0 on both accuracy and ball flight.

Other considerations: The difficulty of this test is in rating ball flight. Using two trained observers, a .95 product-moment correlation was obtained between their observations. When the observers disagreed, the difference was never more than 1 point. When the subjects are familiar with the procedure, about 30 students can be tested in a 35-minute period.

Gymnastics Skills Test for College Women (Ellenbrand 1973)

The 16-item battery consists of the following events: balance beam (5 items), floor exercise (4 items), uneven parallel bars (5 items), and vaulting (2 items). The items were selected using the following criteria: contribution to the category in which they were placed, extent to which they were considered basic skills (as opposed to a variation of some skill), progression within the category, and similarity to a gymnastics performance.

Objective: To measure achievement of gymnastics skills.

Validity and reliability: Concurrent validity was estimated by correlating the scores of three judges of varied experience (an experienced gymnastics teacher, a college teacher with limited gymnastics teaching experience, a student majoring in physical education with a single basic course in gymnastics) with the ratings of two experienced gymnastics judges. The correlations were balance beam, .93; floor exercise, .97; uneven parallel bars, .99; vaulting, .88; and total test, .97. The intercorrelations among the four events ranged from .44 to .70, low enough to warrant the inclusion of all four. The reliability for each event and for the total test was investigated again using the three judges of varied experience. In addition the test was administered on a second day by one teacher. The intraclass reliability estimates were as follows:

Event	*Among Teachers*	*Between Days*
Balance beam	.99	.98
Floor exercise	.97	.99
Uneven parallel bars	.99	.94
Vaulting	.97	.99
Total tests	.98	.99

Procedure: The skills for each item were ordered from simple to difficult. The difficulty ratings were logically assigned. The student selects one skill under each item that demonstrates her achievement in that area. She should have an opportunity to practice. Deduct points for falls, but give students the opportunity to repeat stunts.

We present here the test items and difficulty ratings for the floor exercises only. For the floor exercise event, skills are performed on the length of mats provided. A return trip can be used if necessary. Connecting skills can be added if needed for preparation of a selected skill (for example, a round-off to prepare for a back handspring). However, extra steps and runs should be avoided because they detract from the execution rating.

Test item: Tumbling skills (rolls)

Difficulty	Skills
.5	a. Forward roll to stand
.5	b. Backward roll to knees
1.0	c. Back roll to stand
2.0	d. Pike forward or back roll
2.0	e. Straddle roll (forward or back)
3.0	f. Dive forward roll (pike)
4.0	g. Handstand forward roll
4.0	h. Back roll to headstand
4.5	i. Back extension
5.0	j. Dive forward roll (layout)
6.0	k. Back tuck somersault (aerial)
6.5	l. Back pike somersault
6.5	m. Forward tuck somersault
7.0	n. Back layout somersault
8.0	o. Somersault with a twist

Test item: Tumbling skills (springs)

Difficulty	Skills
1.0	a. Handstand snap-down
2.0	b. Round-off
2.5	c. Neck spring (kip)
3.0	d. Head spring
3.5	e. Front handspring to squat
4.0	f. Front handspring arch to stand
4.5	g. Front handspring walk-out
5.0	h. Back handspring
5.0	i. Front handspring on one hand or with a change of legs
5.5	j. Series of front handsprings
6.0	k. Series of back handsprings
6.5	l. Back handspring to kip (cradle)
6.5	m. Back handspring with twist

Test item: Acrobatic skills

Difficulty	Skills
1.0	a. Mule kick (three-quarter handstand)
1.0	b. Bridge (back arch position)
2.0	c. Handstand
2.0	d. Cartwheel
2.5	e. Backbend from standing
3.0	f. Front limber
3.0	g. One-handed cartwheel
4.0	h. Walk-overs (forward and back)
4.0	i. Dive cartwheel
4.0	j. Tinsica
4.5	k. Dive walk-over
5.0	l. Handstand with half turn or straddle-down to a sit
5.0	m. One-handed walk-overs
6.0	n. Butterfly (side aerial)
7.0	o. Aerial cartwheel or walk-over

Test item: Dance skills

Difficulty	Skills
1.0	a. Half turn (one foot), run, leap
2.0	b. Half turn, step, hitch kick forward, step, leap
3.0	c. Half turn, slide, tour jeté, hitch kick
4.0	d. Full turn (one foot), step, leap, step, leap
5.0	e. Full turn, tour jeté, cabriole (beat kick forward)
6.0	f. One and one-half turns, step, leap, step, leap with a change of legs

Scoring: The score is the product of the skill difficulty and the execution rating. The following scale is used for the execution rating:

3 points: Correct performance; proper mechanics; execution in good form; balance, control, and amplitude in movements.

2 points: Average performance; errors evident in either mechanics or form; some lack of balance, control, or amplitude in movement.

1 point: Poor performance; errors in both mechanics and form; little balance, control, or amplitude in movements.

0 points: Improper or no performance; incorrect mechanics or complete lack of form; no display of balance, control, or amplitude in movements.

Other considerations: This test is designed to evaluate the instructional objectives of gymnastics for college women only; it should not be used for other students. However, the same logic could be applied to develop a test for any gymnastics or tumbling class.

Figure 10.9 Scoring zones for the handball skill test. (Adapted from G. G. Pennington et al., "A Measurement of Handball Ability," *Research Quarterly* 38:247–253, 1967; reprinted by permission of the American Alliance for Health, Physical Education, Recreation and Dance, 1900 Association Drive, Reston, Virginia 22091.)

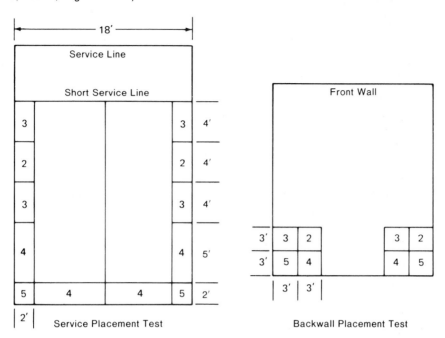

Handball

Handball Test Battery (Pennington et al. 1967)

Objective: To measure status and achievement of handball skills.

Validity and reliability: Using the criterion of the average score per game in which the server or the server's opponent could score during a round-robin tournament, the following product-moment correlation coefficients were reported: .711 for service placement, .663 for total wall volley, and .384 for back-wall placement. No reliability was reported.

Equipment: The court should be marked as shown in figure 10.9.

Procedures: The authors recommend the following three-item battery:

1. *Service placement.* The scoring zones are shown in figure 10.9. The student is given ten tries to place serves into the area having the highest numerical value.

2. *Total wall volley.* The total wall volley consists of two 30-second volleys, both administered in the same way: one with the dominant hand, the second with the nondominant hand. The student stands at the center of the court behind the short service line, drops the ball to the floor, and strokes it against the front wall repeatedly for 30 seconds. He

or she is allowed to step ahead of the line for one return, but the next must be played behind the line. If the student violates this rule or loses control, he or she must recover the ball and begin a new series in the same way.

3. *Back-wall placement.* The front wall is divided into different areas and assigned numerical values, as shown in the figure. The subject throws the ball high and hard against the front wall and, after it hits the floor and rebounds off the back wall, tries to stroke it into the high scoring areas of the front wall. The subject is allowed five trials with the right hand off the right back wall and five trials with the left hand off the left back wall.

Scoring: A scorer is needed for each test. The score for the service placement is the sum of the ten trials. The score for the wall volley is the sum of wall hits for the dominant and nondominant volleys. The score for back-wall placement is the sum of the five right-hand and the five left-hand placements.

Other considerations: This test was developed on a smaller than regulation handball court, and the ball was larger than the regulation handball. The authors published both the standard score and regression equations for their test. However, these equations would not be valid for a regulation-sized court and ball. For this reason the equations are not recommended. It is suspected, however, that these tests could be used with a regulation-sized court and ball.

Racquetball

Racquetball Battery (Poteat 1983)[1]

Objective: To measure basic racquetball playing ability of beginning players.

Validity and reliability: Twelve collegiate and professional racquetball instructors evaluated the skills test battery as to its content validity and all 12 agreed that the test battery items measured skills necessary for beginning racquetball players. Further, correlations between test items and expert ratings of the skill involved in the test item varied from .62 to .76.

Stability reliability coefficients for the items varied from .75 to .84. Internal consistency reliability coefficients varied from .85 to .91.

Equipment: A regulation racquetball court with official markings is necessary. Also, a racquetball racquet, stopwatch, measuring tape, and four racquetballs and marking tape are needed.

Procedures: The original battery consisted of forehand and backhand passing shot, service placement, forehand and backhand wall play, and wall volley tests. Because of high correlations between comparable passing and wall play items, the author suggests dropping the passing shot item but changing the wall play item so it has the same target area and scoring procedure as the passing shot and service placement items. The three suggested test items in their original form are presented here.

1. Reprinted by permission of Charles Poteat.

Figure 10.10 Court markings for the service placement and examples of good serves. (Reprinted by permission of Charles Poteat, Lincoln Memorial University, Harrogate, TN.)

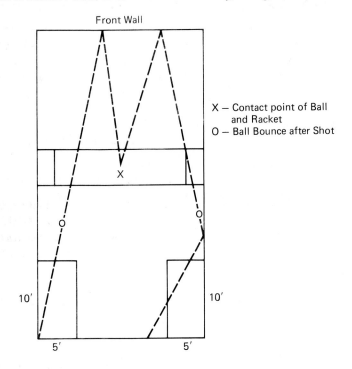

Front Wall

X — Contact point of Ball and Racket
O — Ball Bounce after Shot

10′   10′

5′   5′

1. Service placement. The court markings for this test item are shown in figure 10.10. The student stands in the center of the service area, bounces the ball, and hits it to the front wall so that it will rebound and hit in or pass through the 10 × 5 foot target area. The ball is served to the student's backhand. The student is allowed 10 attempts per trial and 2 trials. No points are awarded if the ball is an illegal serve or contacts the front wall higher than 5 feet above the floor. One point is awarded if the ball bounces in the target area or passes through the target area. The ball may contact the side wall if the above criteria are met. Each successful serve is awarded one point. The maximum total is 20.

2. Back wall play. The court markings for this test item are shown in figure 10.11. The student stands about 5 feet from the back wall and 10 feet from the side wall. He or she throws the ball to the back wall so that it bounces to the side wall, and then bounces on the floor. The player then returns the ball to the front wall so that the ball does not contact the side wall on the way to the front wall. The ball must contact the front wall at a height of five feet or less above the floor. The student is allowed 2 trials of 10 attempts per trial with the forehand stroke, and 2 trials of 10 attempts per trial with the backhand stroke.

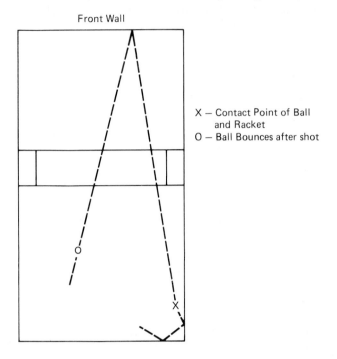

Front Wall

X — Contact Point of Ball and Racket
O — Ball Bounces after shot

No points are awarded if the above criteria are not met. The score is recorded as the total number of successful attempts for both trials.

3. Wall volley. The student, holding two balls, begins the test from the service line 15 feet from the front wall. The student drops one of the balls and hits it to the front wall, then continues to rally the ball for 30 seconds. The ball may bounce any number of times on the return to the subject or the ball may be volleyed. The subject may not cross the service line to contact the ball, but may cross the line to retrieve a ball. Any stroke may be used to rally the ball. If the ball passes the player, he/she may put the second ball in play. Additional balls may be obtained from the test administrator. Two 30-second trials are given. One point is awarded for each legal hit to the front wall. The total score is the total number of successful attempts.

Other considerations: Poteat (1983) reports T-scores for scores on each test and percentile ranks for sum of the T-scores. He states that all items in his test battery have sufficient range to discriminate among students with varying ability. The test battery takes 15–18 minutes to administer to each student.

If a single item is administered it probably should be a wall volley (Hensley, East and Stillwell 1979). Their wall volley test and most tests of this type allow the student to use either a forehand or backhand stroke. Karpman and Isaacs (1979) maintain there should be one of each.

Soccer

Soccer Battery (Yeagley 1972)

Objective: To measure basic soccer skills of beginning players.

Validity and reliability: The validity of each of the four test items was examined with two different criteria: (1) the ratings of four judges on the soccer juggling skill and (2) the composite standard score of the four tests. The concurrent validity coefficients were as follows:

	Judges' Ratings	Composite Standard Score
1. Dribble	−.66	−.80
2. Wall volley	.54	.81
3. Juggling	.69	.74
4. Heading	.38	.61

A multiple correlation of .76 was reported between the criterion (the judges' ratings) and the dribble and juggling tests. The addition of the wall volley and heading tests increased the multiple correlation to only .78; thus we recommend that dribble and juggling be used if a short form is wanted. With a sample of male physical education majors who were beginning soccer players, the following internal-consistency coefficients were reported: dribble, .91; wall volley, .90; juggling, .95; and heading, .64.

Equipment: The test was designed to be administered in a standard gym with the basketball floor markings used to outline the various test stations. Nine soccer balls inflated to 10 pounds and stopwatches accurate to a tenth of a second are needed. Two assistants are needed for each test.

Procedures: The four tests are described below.

1. *Dribble.* The course for the dribble test is on half a basketball court, as shown in figure 10.12. On the signal "Go," the student dribbles around the obstacles following the course. The test is scored by the time measured to the nearest second from the signal until the student dribbles the ball across the finish line between the four line markings and brings the ball to a halt using only the feet. It's legal to touch, knock down, or move any obstacle with the ball or the feet so long as the course outline is followed. Two trials are given, and the best time is used.

Figure 10.12 Test course for the Yeagley soccer battery test. (Reprinted by permission of J. L. Yeagley, Indiana University, Bloomington, IN.)

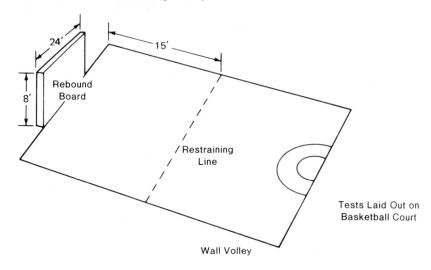

24'

Rebound
Board

8'

15'

Restraining
Line

Tests Laid Out on
Basketball Court

Wall Volley

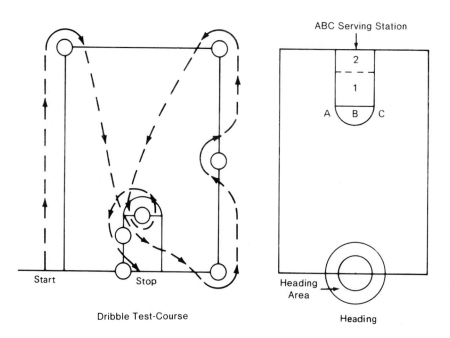

Start

Stop

Dribble Test-Course

ABC Serving Station

2

1

A B C

Heading
Area

Heading

2. *Wall volley.* The test course for the wall volley consists of an unobstructed wall 8 × 24 feet, and a restraining line 15 feet from the wall (figure 10.12). On the signal "Go," the student begins kicking the ball from behind the restraining line and continues kicking the rebounded ball to the kickboard area as many times as possible in 30 seconds. Any type of kick and any legal trapping method is permissible; however, to score a legal volley, the nonkicking foot must be behind the restraining line. Additional balls should be available in case the student loses control of the volleyed ball. The score is the number of legal volleys during the 30-second period. Two trials are given, and the best score is used.

3. *Juggling.* This test also uses half a basketball court as the testing area. The student starts at any point in the area, holding one soccer ball. On the signal "Go," the subject bounces the ball to the floor and then tries to juggle or tap the ball into the air with his or her other body parts as many times as possible in 30 seconds. All parts of the body excluding the arms and hands can be used to continue juggling the ball. (The primary parts used for juggling are the feet, thighs, and head; but the shoulders, chest, and other parts are also legal.) The ball is allowed to bounce on the floor any number of times between touches, although it does not have to bounce at all. It is to the student's advantage to keep the ball in the air for a series of rapidly controlled juggles. The student's score is the number of legal juggles completed in the 30-second period. Juggles outside the half court boundary are not counted. Each time the student controls the ball with the hands or arms 1 point is deducted. Two trials are given, and the best score is used.

4. *Heading.* The course for the heading test is also shown in figure 10.12. The student stands at any point in the heading area, which is the far half of the center circle. The center line of the basketball court is the restraining line, behind which one foot must be placed when the ball is headed. The ball is thrown by the tester from the three spots designed in the figure. The throw should be soft, ideally at the same arc on each trial, and no higher than 15 feet. A total of three tosses are administered from spots A and C, four tosses from B. The student being tested can refuse a poorly tossed ball. The student tries to head the tossed ball in the specified scoring zone. Ten trials are administered, and the total points of these trials constitute the subject's score. Balls landing on the line receive the higher value.

Other considerations: One advantage of this battery is that it can be administered in a gym. This not only controls for environmental conditions, but also allows the teacher to proceed with skill testing, even in bad weather. A test of total soccer skill ability is not available. Yeagley reported that the juggling test is used as an instructional technique for developing ball sensitivity "touch," very important in performing basic soccer skills. The juggling test was selected by the American Professional Soccer League for a national youth soccer skill test. Coaches and teachers in European countries have used ball juggling as the primary test item in national youth soccer skill contests for the past several years.

If four testing stations are available (two basketball courts), the test could be administered to a class of 30 students during a 50-minute class period.

The reliability of the heading test is somewhat low. For a total of 20 trials the estimated reliability is .78.

Swimming

Swimming Achievement for Intermediate Swimmers (Jackson and Pettinger 1969)

Objective: To measure achievement of swimmers defined at an intermediate level—that is, those who can swim one length of the pool with the front and back crawl, sidestroke, elementary backstroke, and breaststroke.

Validity and reliability: These swimming tests have been examined for content and concurrent validity with college women, and for content, concurrent, and construct validity with college men.

1. *Content validity.* The objectives of the intermediate swimming course were defined in terms of stroke efficiency, mechanics, speed, and endurance. Tests were selected that logically measure these objectives.

2. *Concurrent validity.* The criterion for rating stroke efficiency and mechanics was the independent ratings of three judges over the five strokes. The criterion for speed and endurance was a 5-lap medley swim for time in which the swimmer was required to use each of the five strokes for one lap. The product-moment correlation between each of the tests and these criteria are listed in table 10.4. Because most of the tests are intercorrelated, combinations of them could be used.

   a. Men. To measure speed and endurance, the multiple correlation between the criterion and a combination of a 2-length medley and a 15-minute swim was .94.

   b. Men. To measure stroke efficiency and mechanics, the multiple correlation between the criterion and a combination of a 15-minute swim and the breaststroke was .91.

Table 10.4

Concurrent Validity Coefficients for Swimming Stroke Efficiency and Mechanics.

TEST	MEN	WOMEN	SPEED AND ENDURANCE FOR MEN
1. 15-minute swim	.85	.61	.86
2. 2-length medley	.78	.04	.93
3. Front crawl	.61	.63	.53
4. Back crawl	.57	.79	.49
5. Sidestroke	.64	.72	.54
6. Elementary backstroke	.65	.72	.54
7. Breaststroke	.76	.64	.61

c. Women. To measure stroke efficiency and mechanics, the multiple correlation between the criterion and a combination of back crawl, 15-minute swim, 2-length medley, elementary backstroke, and breaststroke was .90.

3. *Construct validity.* The performances of three groups of varying ability were compared: intermediate male swimmers; certified water safety instructors; and the Indiana University varsity swimmers, who qualified for the 1968 Olympic swimming tryouts. For every test the means for the intermediates were the lowest and those for the varsity swimmers were the highest.

The reliability coefficients for each of the subtests were not calculated, but the concurrent validity coefficients indicated that the tests were reliable. In another study with college students the reliability estimates of two 25-yard trials of the breaststroke and elementary backstroke administered on two days (a total of four 25-yard trials) were high, .93.

Equipment: A timer (with stopwatch) is needed for the 2-length medley. For the other tests a scorer must count strokes or laps for each swimmer. Because this is a relatively simple procedure, other students can be used as scorers.

Procedures: The procedures for the seven tests in the battery are as follows:

1. *15-minute swim for distance.* On the starting signal each subject dives into the water and swims as many laps as possible in the 15-minute period. Counters should record the distance. This test can be administered either lengthwise or widthwise in the pool; the score is the number of lengths or widths swum during the 15 minutes. Some pools have distances marked on the side, or tape can be placed at 1-yard intervals on the pool deck. In this way the test can be scored to the last yard.

2. *2-lap timed medley.* Either a 10-pound diving brick or hockey is placed on the pool bottom at the halfway mark; sometimes a hockey puck is used. Subjects start in the water. On "Go," they front crawl to the halfway line, surface dive, and retrieve the object to the surface. Using the sidestroke, they continue forward with the brick or puck to the far end, deposit it onto the pool deck, push off on their backs, and swim toward the starting end using the elementary backstroke. At the halfway mark, indicated by a line of pennants easily visible from the back position, they turn over and swim using the front crawl to the finish line. The score is the elapsed time measured to the last tenth of a second.

3. *The number of strokes to complete the length of the pool for each of five strokes.* For each of these tests the student starts in the water, pushes off, and swims 1 length. Because the efficiency of the push off is related to overall efficiency, it should be counted as the first stroke. The student should swim at a moderate pace—not a sprint, but not too slow.

Strokes are counted until the swimmer touches the opposite end.
Strokes and counting methods are as follows:

    a. Front crawl. Strokes are counted by noting the number of hand recoveries.

    b. Back crawl. Same as the front crawl.

    c. Sidestroke. Each power phase—that is, each complete arm-leg cycle—is counted as a stroke.

    d. Elementary backstroke. Same as the sidestroke.

    e. Breaststroke. Same as the sidestroke.

Other considerations: With the exception of the 2-length medley, these tests are feasible for mass testing. Using other students for scorers, it is possible to simultaneously test as many swimmers as the size of the pool allows. If the pool width is used, half the class can be tested while the remaining half serves as scorers.

The 15 minutes for the distance swim may be too long for younger students, and this should be altered accordingly. If widths are used for the stroke count tests, we recommend that the sum of four widths be used to ensure reliable measures.

Red Cross Swimming Skills

The American Red Cross has identified basic swimming skills for various swimming classification groups. The skills are subjectively rated on a pass-fail basis. The ratings can be used for the formative evaluation of swimming achievement.

A. Beginner skills
1. Water adjustment skills
2. Hold breath—10 sec.
3. Rhythmic breathing—10 times
4. Prone float and recovery
5. Prone glide
6. Back glide and recovery
7. Survival float

B. Advanced beginner skills
1. Bobbing—deep water
2. Rhythmic breathing to side
3. Survival float—2 min.
4. Crawl stroke
5. Elementary backstroke
6. Survival stroke
7. Treading water—30–45 sec.

Tennis

Kemp-Vincent Rally Test (Kemp and Vincent 1968)

Objective: To measure the ability to rally a tennis ball under game conditions.

Validity and reliability: Two types of concurrent validity were reported: (1) the rank difference correlation between this test and the rank in a round-robin tournament was .84 for beginners and .93 for intermediate players; (2) the product-moment correlation between this test and the Iowa modification of the Dyer test was .80 for all players. The mean score for the intermediate group was 64.47; the mean for the beginning group was only 31.42. Thus construct validity is assumed. The test-retest reliability estimates were .86 for college students judged as beginners and .90 for those judged as intermediate players.

Equipment: Each student should have a good tennis racket and four balls. The test is administered on a regulation tennis court, and a stopwatch is needed.

Procedure: Two players of similar ability take positions on opposite sides of the net on a singles court, with each player having two tennis balls on his or her side of the court. Both players are tested simultaneously. On the command "Ready, go," one player drops a ball so that it bounces behind the baseline and with a courtesy stroke puts the ball into play. The two players keep the ball in play, or rally, as long as possible within the 3-minute test period. When a ball is hit into the net or out of bounds so that it is not playable, either player starts another ball into play with a courtesy stroke from behind the baseline. Any stroke can be used during the rally. Players are responsible for retrieving their own balls to continue the test after the four original balls have been used. It is recommended that the test be administered after the students have had a trial, so that the procedure and scoring are understood. A 1-minute warm-up period should be provided immediately before the test.

Scoring: Use three counters on each court: one to count the combined hits, defined as contacts of the ball and racket of both players; the other two to count the errors committed by each player. For the 3-minute period the combined total number of hits (contacts of ball and racket) for the two players are counted, regardless of whether an error is made on a hit. The courtesy stroke to put a ball in play counts as a hit. Next, the errors committed by each individual player are counted. From the combined total number of hits for both players each individual player subtracts the number of his or her errors, arriving at a final rally score for each of the players. The errors are defined as (1) the failure to get the ball over the net on the courtesy stroke or during the rally, (2) the failure to start a new ball from behind the baseline, (3) the failure to keep the ball in the singles court areas and (4) the failure to hit a ball before the second bounce. A player can play a ball on which the partner has scored an error if he or she believes it is advantageous to keep the ball in play.

Table 10.5
Norms for the Hewitt Tennis Achievement Test.

GRADE	SERVICE PLACEMENTS	SERVICE SPEED	FOREHAND PLACEMENTS	BACKHAND PLACEMENTS
	Junior varsity and varsity tennis			
F	20–24	20–22	25–28	20–23
D	25–29	23–25	29–32	24–27
C	30–39	26–32	33–39	28–34
B	40–45	33–36	40–45	35–40
A	46–50	37–40	46–50	41–47
	Advanced tennis			
F	11–14	8– 9	24–25	22–26
D	15–19	11–13	26–29	27–30
C	20–30	14–21	30–39	31–37
B	31–37	22–25	40–44	38–42
A	38–44	26–30	45–48	43–46
	Beginning tennis			
F	1– 2	1– 3	1– 3	1– 2
D	3– 6	4– 7	4– 8	3– 7
C	7–16	8–13	9–21	8–19
B	17–21	14–17	22–28	20–26
A	22–26	18–21	29–36	27–34

Other considerations: An obvious weakness of the test is that a student's score is affected by the performance of another student. It is very important that players of similar ability be paired. When the instructional phase of the class includes a round-robin or ladder tournament, the results can provide an objective pairing procedure. A rating scale could also be used. This test is feasible for mass use because it takes only about 5 minutes to test two students on one court.

Hewitt Service Placement Test (Hewitt 1966)

Objective: To measure the accuracy of a student's tennis service.

Validity and reliability: Players of various ability levels were ranked on the basis of a round-robin tournament. The concurrent validity of the placement serve scores and the ranks were .93 for varsity/junior varsity players, .63 for advanced players, and .72 for beginning players. Hewitt's norms, appearing in table 10.5, indicate that better players achieve higher scores. Thus construct validity can be claimed. Because service accuracy is obviously an important tennis skill, content validity can be assumed. With college students who ranged in ability from beginning to varsity players, the test-retest reliability was .94.

Equipment: The right service court is used, marked as shown in figure 10.13. A ¼-inch rope is stretched over the net at a height of 7 feet. A good racket and at least ten good tennis balls are needed.

Figure 10.13 Test station for the Hewitt service-placement and speed-of-service tests. (Adapted from Jack E. Hewitt, "Hewitt's Tennis Achievement Test," *Research Quarterly,* 37:231–237, 1966; reprinted by permission of the American Alliance for Health, Physical Education, Recreation and Dance, 1900 Association Drive, Reston, Virginia 22091.)

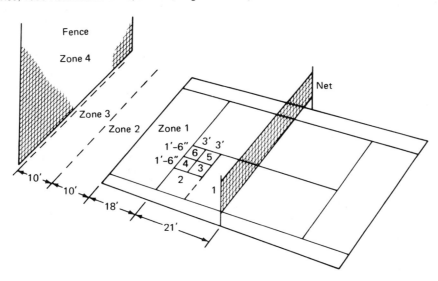

Procedure: After a demonstration of the test, the student is given a 10-minute warm-up on a different court. Each student has ten tries to serve the ball accurately into the marked-off service court, keeping the service under the 7-foot-high rope. (These same ten serves are used for Hewitt's Speed-of-Service Test.)

Scoring: A scorer is needed at each test station. Each of the ten serves is scored from 0 to 6. Served balls going over the 7-foot-high rope, wide or long of the service court, are scored 0. Scores of 1 to 6 are awarded according to the scoring zone in which the ball lands. Net balls are repeated; higher values are given when balls land on the line.

Hewitt Speed-of-Service Test (Hewitt 1966)

Objective: To measure the speed of a served tennis ball.

Validity and reliability: After much experimentation with a stopwatch, Hewitt discovered that the distance the ball bounces after it hits the service court is a good indicator of the server's speed. Thus, content validity is assumed. Players of various ability levels were ranked on the basis of a round-robin tournament. The concurrent validity of the speed-of-service scores was .89 for beginning players, .72 for advanced players, and .86 for varsity/junior varsity players. Hewitt's norms, listed in table 10.5, indicate that better players achieve higher scores. Thus construct validity can be assumed. With college students who ranged in ability from beginning to varsity level, the test-retest reliability was .84.

Evaluating skill achievement   **369**

Equipment: Because the Speed-of-Service and Service Placement Tests are administered together, the same court is used. The former is scored with the four 10-foot zones linked off behind the service court, as shown in figure 10.13.

Procedure: The procedures are the same as those of the Hewitt Service Placement Test, except the speed of the service is measured.

Scoring: A scorer is needed at each test station. Each of the ten good serve placements are scored for speed. The score is the distance the ball bounces on the second bounce (the first landing in the service court). A good serve is one that is served between the net and the 7-foot-high rope and lands in the right service court. The number of the zone represents the speed score for the served ball. The total of the ten serves is the student's score. Net balls are repeated.

Other considerations: This test, in combination with the Service Placement Test, allows both speed and accuracy scores to be secured during the same administration. To do so, however, two scorers are needed at each test station. If several courts and ample scorers are available, the test is feasible for mass use. The procedure used to score this test can be altered to fit unique facilities. The zones could be marked off with other distances (every yard or every 5 feet). Using smaller scoring zones could improve the reliability for beginning players, who rarely hit the ball into Zone 4.

Modified Timmer Forehand and Backhand Drive Test (Timmer 1965; Hensley 1979)

Timmer (1965) developed this test using a ball-boy to project balls to the student. Hensley modified this test by having the instructor hit tennis balls with a tennis racket to the student.

Objective: To measure the ability to volley a ball deep into the backcourt with a forehand or backhand stroke.

Validity and reliability: Timmer correlated test performance with tournament standings and obtained validity coefficients that ranged from .75 to .86 (Hensley 1979). Hensley did not find a significant difference among the trial means, but did find a large spread in total scores (3–36), so that good internal consistency reliability was assured.

Equipment: The tennis court should be marked as shown in figure 10.14. Two tennis rackets and two dozen tennis balls are needed.

Procedures: The student taking the test stands in a three foot square area just behind the net in the ready position. The instructor hits tennis balls with a racket to the forehand side of the student who attempts to return the ball with a volley. The student is instructed to hit the first ball and all following odd numbered balls "down-the-line" of the court. The second ball and all succeeding even numbered balls are hit "cross-court." Each student receives ten trials to the forehand side. After sufficient rest, the same procedures are followed with the tennis ball hit to the backhand of the student.

Figure 10.14 Court markings for Timmer forehand and backhand drive test. (Reprinted by permission of L. D. Hensley, University of Northern Iowa, Cedar Falls, Iowa.)

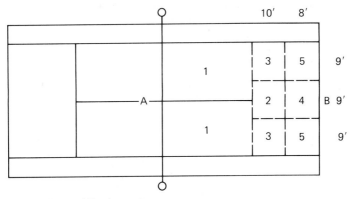

A = Student and B = Instructor

Scoring: Each of the ten forehand and backhand trials are scored according to the zone in which they land—5,4,3,2,1 (see figure 10.14). If a student returns the ball to the wrong side of the court and beyond the service line but within the boundaries, only two points are awarded. Balls going into the net, over the baseline, or wide of the singles sideline are scored as zero. The total score is the sum of ten trials.

Other considerations: A problem with this test is the difficulty for the instructor of hitting the ball in a standardized manner to all the students. If available, a ball-throwing machine can be used. Teachers may find it easier to throw, rather than stroke, the ball to the students, especially if several different instructors administer the test. These tests are very time consuming to administer to large classes. Because the wall volley test involves the forehand and backhand and yields high validity coefficients (.87 to .73), it may be preferred for large classes.

Hewitt Revision of the Dyer Backboard Test (Hewitt 1965)

Objective: To repeatedly volley a tennis ball against a wall with the forehand and/or backhand ground stroke.

Validity and reliability: On the basis of performance in a round-robin tournament, students were ranked from highest to lowest. Using Spearman's Rho, the concurrent validity ranged from .68 to .73 for beginning classes and from .84 to .89 for advanced classes. The means of the advanced players were higher than the means of the beginning players, which supports the test's construct validity. The following test-retest reliability estimates were reported: .82 with college students judged as beginning players and .93 with college students judged as advanced players.

Equipment: A smooth wall 20 feet high and 20 feet wide is needed. Each test station should have a good tennis racket, a stopwatch or wristwatch with a sweep second hand, and a basket with at least a dozen new tennis balls. The station is marked off with inch-wide tape. One 20-foot line is placed on the wall at a height of 3 feet; this line simulates the net. A 20-foot restraining line is placed parallel to and 20 feet from the wall. The person with the watch serves as the timer and scorer. Students waiting to be tested can retrieve missed balls.

Procedure: The student starts the test behind the 20-foot restraining line with two balls. One ball is served against the wall, and then the student tries to continuously volley it using any type of stroke. The ball can be hit on the fly or on any bounce. The student should continue to rally the ball even when it hits below the 3-foot line. If a ball should get away from the student, a new one is secured from the basket and the test is restarted with a serve. The volley continues for 30 seconds.

Scoring: For each ball that hits above the 3-foot line, 1 point is scored. Points are not awarded when the subject steps over the 20-foot restraining line to stroke the ball. Balls that hit the 3-foot net line are good. Start the watch when the served ball hits above the net line on the wall. Three 30-second trials are administered, and the mean of the three trials is used on the score.

Other considerations: Many beginning students find it easier to start the test by bouncing the ball off the court. Either this procedure or the serve can be used, but the starting procedure selected must be standardized for all students. (Hewitt does not recommend the bounce procedure.) The student taking the test should be the only person responsible for getting additional balls if the ball gets away. The basket of balls must be placed in a standard spot for all students. If several test stations are used this test can easily be administered in one class period. To facilitate the procedure, the person with the watch can simultaneously start and stop several test stations, thus eliminating the need for a stopwatch at each one. An advantage of this test is that it can be administered either indoors or outdoors. The Scott-French Backboard Test (Scott & French 1959) is the same as the Dyer test except they use a 27.5 foot restraining line.

Hensley (1979) conducted a factor analysis of tennis skill tests. Fourteen tennis tests were administered to 80 male and female college students. Three factors were identified: (1) stroking—ground strokes with a forehand or backhand motion as measured by the Kemp-Vincent Rally Test, (2) serving—as measured by the Hewitt Serve Placement or Hewitt Speed-of-Service tests, and (3) volleying—as measured by the Modified Timmer Forehand or Backhand Drive tests. The factors are listed in order of importance, with factor one by far the most important one.

SUMMARY

The achievement of psychomotor objectives is a universal goal of physical education programs. We can measure the achievement of psychomotor skills with three general procedures: skill tests, rating scales, and the performance itself.

Skill tests require the creation of an environment similar to the game environment and the standardization of procedures for administration. The validity of skill tests can be judged in part by the extent to which the testing environment duplicates the playing environment. There are four general types of skill tests:

1. Accuracy tests. Accuracy tests require the subject to throw, strike, or kick an object at a target for accuracy. Examples are the basketball free throw, the badminton short serve, and the volleyball serve.
2. Wall volley tests. Wall volley tests require the subject to repeatedly stroke, pass, throw, or kick an object at a wall. The score may be the number of successful volleys completed during a specified time period or the time required to execute a specified number of volleys.
3. Tests of total bodily movement. These tests require the subject to run a standardized test course using movements typical of the sport. Dribbling a basketball through an obstacle course is one example.
4. Throws, kicks, or strokes for power or distance. These tests require the subject to throw, kick, or strike an object (a football, a shuttlecock, etc.) for distance.

Rating scales are a device for evaluating skill achievement subjectively. They are used for evaluating qualities that cannot be efficiently measured by objective means. In a sense these scales add a measure of objectivity to subjective measurement, and can yield reliable, valid measurements of skill achievement if they are properly constructed and used.

For some motor skills, the performance itself is a reliable, valid method of evaluating achievement. This type of evaluation tends to be content-valid because the performance environment is also the evaluation environment. Archery, bowling, golf, and swimming are skills that can be evaluated by performance.

The steps in the development of reliable, valid procedures for evaluating skill objectives are as follows:

1. Define what is to be measured.
2. Select a measuring instrument.
3. Pretest the instrument.
4. Revise the test and testing procedures.
5. Administer the instrument.
6. Evaluate the administered test.
7. Revise the final battery.
8. Develop norms.

FORMATIVE EVALUATION OF OBJECTIVES

Objective 1   Identify the four general types of sport skill tests.

1. Skills tests involve creating an environment similar to the game situation and standardizing testing procedures. Numerous skill tests have been published for a variety of sport skills. Skill tests can be categorized under one of four general groups. Summarize the characteristics of each group.
   a. Accuracy tests
   b. Wall volley tests
   c. Tests of total bodily movement
   d. Throws, kicks, or strokes for power or distance

Objective 2   Evaluate the four general types of sport skill tests using the criteria reliability, validity, and feasibility for mass testing.

1. In order for a test to be valid it must first be reliable. However, a test may be both reliable and valid but still not be feasible for mass use. In order to evaluate the achievement of motor skill objectives, the teacher must select skill tests that meet acceptable levels of reliability and validity and that can be administered in the public school. Each of the four general categories of skill tests has inherent weaknesses and strengths. Identify the basic weakness associated with each category, and summarize the actions you could take to improve its effectiveness.
   a. Accuracy tests
   b. Wall volley tests
   c. Tests of total bodily movement
   d. Throws, kicks, or strokes for power or distance

Objective 3   Evaluate the weaknesses and strengths of rating scales.

1. In many evaluation situations it is neither feasible nor possible to measure motor skill achievement with an objective sport skill test. In these situations a rating scale is used. A rating scale is a subjective measurement procedure. Differentiate between the terms objective and subjective as applied to the evaluation of motor skill achievement.
2. List the weaknesses and strengths of rating scales.
3. Like all forms of measuring instruments, rating scales must be reliable. Certain procedures in the development and use of rating scales help guard against measurement error and ensure objectivity. Outline the procedures you should follow when constructing and using this type of measurement instrument.

Objective 4   Identify motor skills that are best evaluated by performance.

1. For many motor skills the actual performance may be used to evaluate skill achievement. List the basic advantage of using performance as a criterion for skill evaluation.
2. The text offers several illustrations in which skill achievement can be evaluated by performance. Identify an additional motor skill that could be evaluated in this way. Using your example, outline the specific procedures you would follow to evaluate achievement in the skill.

Objective 5   Outline methods that could be used to develop reliable, valid, and feasible measurement procedures for evaluating motor skill achievement.

1. The text lists systematic procedures for evaluating skill achievement. Briefly outline these procedures.

ADDITIONAL LEARNING ACTIVITIES

1. Many studies published in *Research Quarterly* have attempted to develop sport skill tests. References for several of these studies are in Appendix C. Select three or four articles and review them. Pay close attention to the methods used to establish the reliability and validity of the tests and the procedures used to develop the battery. Would you use the tests for your physical education class?

2. Often a published skill test does not fit the specific needs of a teacher, who must either revise the published tests or develop a new one. Select a sport skill and develop a test to evaluate it. You might alter an existing test, develop an alternate scoring system, or develop a new test. Administer the test to a group of students and calculate its reliability. Is your test feasible for mass use? Do the most highly skilled students achieve the best test scores?

3. A test can be valid for one group of students but not for another. Select a published sport skill test and determine the concurrent validity of the test with a group of students. In order to accomplish this you must select a criterion measure. (You may want to review chapter 4 before you begin.)

4. Select a skill that cannot be evaluated with an objective skill test, and construct a rating scale for it. With a classmate, independently rate the performances of a group of students and then calculate the correlation between your two ratings. How reliable were your ratings? Remember that reliability can be improved by properly training raters.

5. For some skills, performance provides an objective score for evaluating their achievement. Using a skill such as archery, bowling, or golf, estimate the stability reliability of the performance scores. Remember that for stability reliability you must have the performance scores of the same group of students for two different days.

BIBLIOGRAPHY

A more complete bibliography of sport skill tests, listed by sport, can be found in the Appendix.

AAHPER. 1966a. Basketball Skills Test Manual for Boys. Washington, D.C.
————. 1966b. *Football Skills Test Manual.* Washington, D.C.
————. 1967a. *Archery Skills Test Manual.* Washington, D.C.
————. 1967b. *Softball Skills Test Manual for Boys.* Washington, D.C.
————. 1967c. *Softball Skills Test Manual for Girls.* Washington, D.C.
————. 1969. *Volleyball Skills Test Manual.* Washington, D.C.
AAHPERD. 1984. *Basketball Skills Test Manual for Boys and Girls.* Reston, VA.

Barrow, H. M., and R. McGee. 1979. *A Practical Approach to Measurement in Physical Education.* 3d ed. Philadelphia, Pa.: Lea and Febiger.

Collins, D. R., and P. B. Hodges. 1978. *A Comprehensive Guide to Sports Skills Tests and Measurements.* Springfield, Ill.: Thomas.

Cornish, C. 1949. "A Study of Measurement of Ability in Handball." *Research Quarterly* 20:215–22.

Dyer, J. T. 1935. "The Backboard Test of Tennis Ability." *Research Quarterly* 6 (supp.):63–74.

Ellenbrand, D. A. 1973. "Gymnastics Skills Tests for College Women." Master's thesis, Indiana University, Bloomington, Ind.

Gaunt, S. 1979. "Factor Structure of Basketball Playing Ability." P.E.D. dissertation, Indiana University, Bloomington, Ind.

Hensley, L. 1979. "A Factor Analysis of Selected Tennis Skill Tests." Ed.D dissertation, University of Georgia, Athens, Ga.

Hensley, L., W. East, and J. Stillwell. 1979. "A Racquetball Skills Test." *Research Quarterly* 50:114–18.

Hewitt, J. E. 1965. "Revision of the Dyer Backboard Tennis Test." *Research Quarterly* 36:153–57.
———. 1966. "Hewitt's Tennis Achievement Test." *Research Quarterly* 37:231–37.

Hopkins, D. R. 1977. "Factor Analysis of Selected Basketball Skill Tests." *Research Quarterly* 48:535–40.

Jackson, A. S., and J. Pettinger. 1969. "The Development and Discriminant Analysis of Swimming Profiles of College Men." *Proceedings of 72d Annual Meeting, National College Physical Education Association for Men* 104–10.

Johnson, B. L., and J. K. Nelson. 1979. *Practical Measurements for Evaluation in Physical Education.* 3d ed. Minneapolis, Minn.: Burgess.

Karpman, M., and L. Isaacs. 1979. "An Improved Racquetball Skills Test." *Research Quarterly* 50:526–27.

Kemp, J., and M. F. Vincent. 1968. "Kemp-Vincent Rally Test of Tennis Skill." *Research Quarterly* 39:1000–04.

Klein, S. P. 1971. "The Uses and Limitations of Standardized Tests in Meeting the Demands for Accountability." *UCLA Evaluation Comment* vol. 2, no. 4 (January 1971), 1–7.

Morris, H. H. 1977. "A Critique of the AAHPER Skill Test Series." Paper presented to the Measurement and Evaluation Council, AAHPER National Convention, Seattle, Wash.

Pennington, G. G. et al. 1967. "A Measure of Handball Ability." *Research Quarterly* 38:247–53.

Poteat, C. 1983. "A Skill Test Battery to Measure Overall Racquetball Playing Ability." Ed.D. dissertation, University of Georgia, Athens, Ga.

Scott, M. G., and E. French. 1959. *Measurement and Evaluation in Physical Education.* Dubuque, Iowa: Wm. C. Brown.

Sebolt, D. R. 1968. "Badminton Skills Tests." Unpublished paper, Virginia Polytechnic Institute and State University.

Timmer, K. 1965. "A Tennis Skill Test to Determine Accuracy in Playing Ability." Master's thesis, Springfield College, Springfield, Mass.

West, C., and J. Thorpe. 1968. "Construction and Validation of an Eight-Iron Approach Test." *Research Quarterly* 49:1115–20.

Yeagley, J. 1972. "Soccer Skills Test." Unpublished paper, Indiana University, Bloomington, Ind.

Cognitive and Affective Testing

Part 4

Evaluating Knowledge

11

Contents

Key Words

Completion Item
Discrimination Index
Discrimination Test
Essay Test
Item
Item Analysis
Item Difficulty
Knowledge Test
Mastery Test
Matching Item
Multiple-Choice Item
Objective Test
Short-Answer Item
True–False Item

Objectives

The process of evaluating knowledge is threefold: (1) constructing a knowledge test, (2) administering it, and (3) analyzing it. Before the actual construction, the type of test and the test items must be selected, to be sure that the content is correct and the items themselves are well constructed. In addition, it's important to administer and score the test so that all students have the same opportunity to do well, and so that the scores themselves are valid. Finally, it's vital to analyze the test to determine the quality of each item and the test as a whole. This analysis indicates, not only the quality of the test, but also how it might be revised.

After reading chapter 11, you should be able to:

1. Differentiate among various types of knowledge tests.
2. Define the levels of knowledge most applicable to physical education.
3. Outline the basic procedures used for constructing, administering, and grading a knowledge test.
4. Evaluate knowledge test items.
5. Analyze knowledge tests in terms of test reliability and item analysis.

INTRODUCTION

Why do we give knowledge tests in physical education if our work involves physical rather than mental skills? Knowledge is one of the stated objectives of most physical education programs. Teachers want their students to know the rules, etiquette, terminology, procedures, and strategy of various sports and physical activities. And, as a result of physical education training, students should understand the importance of physical fitness, how to stay fit, and something of personal health. The extent to which these objectives are met can best and sometimes exclusively be determined by knowledge tests.

Many physical education teachers and exercise specialists administer knowledge tests so that students whose physical performance is mediocre can demonstrate their learning. The justification for this is that it is important for students to acquire knowledge about physical education even when their physical skills are unexceptional. It is also true that skill alone does not create a talented student. Knowledge is a vital tool as well.

Knowledge is often retained longer than physical skill and fitness. Obviously people lose a degree of skill and fitness as soon as they stop participating in sports, but they can continue to enjoy sports as spectators if they have acquired sufficient knowledge. Then, too, as health-related physical fitness programs become more popular, greater emphasis is being placed on the cognitive aspects of physical fitness and health. Knowledge, then, is a wanted objective of physical education programs and should be one of the first areas of attention in any measurement procedure.

LEVELS OF KNOWLEDGE

Unfortunately many physical education teachers and exercise specialists, in developing knowledge tests, fail to recognize that there are different levels or degrees of knowledge. This is apparent whenever a group of students is tested: student understanding of a given topic can range from superficial to thorough.

Bloom's taxonomy of educational objectives (1956) proposes six levels of behavior arranged in ascending order of complexity: knowledge, comprehension, application, analysis, synthesis, and evaluation. Each level corresponds to a level of knowledge. Bloom then divides the levels of behavior and provides illustrative questions for each subdivision. Table 11.1 lists Bloom's six levels and their subdivisions. Because the two highest levels are quite complex and usually exceed the educational objectives of a typical physical education activity course, only the first four levels of knowledge in the taxonomy are presented, defined, and illustrated with a test question in table 11.2. The educational objectives of most courses do exceed Bloom's first level because teachers want students to acquire more than a superficial knowledge of the topics covered in class.

Table 11.1

Bloom's Taxonomy of Educational Objectives.

1.00 Knowledge
  1.10 Knowledge of specifics
  1.20 Knowledge of ways and means of dealing with specifics
  1.30 Knowledge of the universals and abstractions in a field

2.00 Comprehension
  2.10 Translation
  2.20 Interpretation
  2.30 Extrapolation

3.00 Application

4.00 Analysis
  4.10 Analysis of elements
  4.20 Analysis of relationships
  4.30 Analysis of organizational principles

5.00 Synthesis
  5.10 Production of an unique communication
  5.20 Production of a plan for operations
  5.30 Derivation of a set of abstract relations

6.00 Evaluation
  6.10 Judgments in terms of internal evidence
  6.20 Judgments in terms of external evidence

Although the majority of questions on many physical education knowledge tests require the student only to remember facts, some questions should draw on higher levels of knowledge. And certainly, as the class becomes more advanced, the number of knowledge questions should be smaller, and the number of questions from the higher levels of the taxonomy should be larger.

TYPES OF KNOWLEDGE TESTS

Knowledge tests are either essay or objective tests and either mastery or discrimination tests. Each question on a knowledge test, whether stated as a question or not, is called an **item.** Teachers must choose the type of test they want before they can begin to construct it.

Essay Versus Objective

An **essay test** is any test on which students answer each item with whatever information they choose and write their answers in sentences. The answer to an essay item may be short or long, depending on how much the student knows and how full an answer the item requires. **Objective tests**—true–false, multiple choice, matching, and the like— have potential answers provided with each test item. After reading an item, the student selects one of the provided answers. For example, T or F on a true–false item.

Table 11.2
The First Four Levels of Bloom's Taxonomy.

LEVEL	DEFINITION	SAMPLE QUESTION FOR GOLF TEST
I. Knowledge	Recall of ideas, terms, facts, etc.	What is a slice?
II. Comprehension	The use of translation, interpretation, or extrapolation to understand certain ideas, terms, facts, etc.	What causes a slice?
III. Application	The use of general ideas, rules of procedure, or generalized methods in particular and concrete situations.	The following scores were recorded by four golfers on 9 holes. In what order should the golfers tee off on the 8th tee?
IV. Analysis	The separation of a phenomenon into its constituents so that its nature, composition, and organizational principles may be determined.	A golf ball is located on a hill above the cup, and the shot will be made downhill onto a very fast green. The ball is best played with what kind of grip and stroke, and off what part of the club face?

For the Application row, the sample question includes:

Player	1 2 3 4 5 6 7 8 9	Total
A	3 6 3 4 3 4 7 3 6	39
B	4 5 4 4 4 5 4 3 4	37
C	6 6 5 3 3 3 3 3 3	35
D	3 3 4 4 2 4 5 7 3	35

The question of which test to use—essay or objective—raises both philosophical and economic issues. Some educators believe that objective tests encourage students to memorize facts rather than to put the fact together into a total understanding of the material. These people use essay tests on the theory that the students must have a total understanding to answer essay questions. Other educators maintain that essay tests allow students to write everything they know about the subject, while objective tests determine if they know only what has been asked. Students frequently complain after objective tests that the teacher didn't ask any of the things they knew. We can think of the items on an objective test as a sample from an infinite number of items that could have been used.

Economically, objective tests are time consuming to construct but quick to grade, while essay tests are the reverse. It does not take long to construct three to five general essay-type items, but it takes considerable time to properly read and grade each one.

Whenever tests are to be used with many students, either in one testing session or over numerous sessions, objective tests are more economical than essays in terms of total time involvement. Once the objective test is developed, it's easy and fast to use. This is probably the major reason why objective tests are used more than essay tests.

Mastery Versus Discrimination

A **mastery test**—a kind of formative evaluation with criterion-referenced standards— is used to determine whether the students have mastered the material. Items on the test pertain to information the teacher expects the majority of students to know. Many of these items are easy, and often the entire class answers them correctly. However, the performance standards for mastery tests tend to be high. Bloom and his associates (1971; 1981) recommend that the criterion for passing a knowledge test be 80% to 90% correct answers. This means a mastery test should be graded pass-fail.

The purpose of a **discrimination test**—a form of summative evaluation with norm-referenced standards—is to differentiate among students in terms of knowledge. Each test item is written to discriminate among ability groups. Thus, discrimination tests include a larger number of difficult items than do mastery tests. They also often do not elicit basic information because it does not discriminate sufficiently. As a result of using a discrimination-type test, a few excellent students will have high scores on the test while the rest of the students will have lower scores.

Mastery tests tend to include items from the knowledge, comprehension, and application levels of Bloom's taxonomy (1956); discrimination tests tend to include items from the higher levels. Because discrimination tests are more difficult than mastery tests, their performance standards must be lower. For example, on a 100-point test, an A might start at 80 points, B at 70 points, C at 55 points, and D at 45 points (A: 80–100, B: 70–79, C: 55–69, D: 45–54, F: below 45).

The decision about which test to use—mastery or discrimination—should depend on how the test scores will be used. For a formative evaluation of student achievement, a mastery test should be used. For a summative evaluation of student achievement, a discrimination test should be used. Formative evaluation is graded on a pass-fail basis; summative evaluation allows the teacher to identify individual differences in achievement by assigning letter grades.

For years teachers have used mastery tests to make summative evaluations, a serious mistake. The reliability of letter grades based on scores of mastery tests is almost always low because most of the items are too easy to discriminate well. To achieve high reliability, test items must discriminate sufficiently so that the students' scores are spread out. Later in the chapter we discuss that the larger the standard deviation, the higher the Kuder-Richardson reliability. Low reliability means, in turn, that the standard error of measurement (see chapter 3) is similar in value to the standard deviation for the test.

An example should clarify these points. It's very common in first aid classes to administer a mastery test and assign letter grades based on the test scores. Suppose that the grading standard for a 100-point test is A: 93–100, B: 87–92, C: 78–86, D: 70–77, and F: below 69. If the standard deviation is 8 and the reliability of the test .44, the standard error of measurement for the test is 6. Thus the probability is .68 that a student who scored 88 will score between 82 and 94 (88 ± 6) if retested. Notice that 82 is a C and 94 is an A; the assigned grade is not reliable. If formative standards are used and a score of 80 or above is considered passing, the large standard error of measurement poses no problem because the student passes whether the score is 82 or 94.

Similarly, assume that the instructional objectives for a physical education unit pertain to knowledge of the rules of a sport. The best policy in this situation is probably to give a mastery test for formative evaluation. If a student can correctly answer 80% of the items on the test, the teacher can assume that the student has enough knowledge to play the sport. The mastery test is designed essentially to measure knowledge of basic rules.

Of course mere knowledge of the rules is not sufficient for playing a sport. The rules must be applied and several different rules may have to be considered to resolve a situation. To interpret rules the higher levels of the cognitive domain must be used. The teacher might use a discrimination test for summative evaluation of the students' ability to apply, analyze, and synthesize the rules in a game situation. Although students may know all the basic rules, they are likely to differ in their ability to understand, apply, and interpret them.

CONSTRUCTION

Whenever possible, the teacher should develop his or her own knowledge tests. A major advantage of teacher-made tests is that they tend to cover the material stressed in the unit in terminology the students understand. Thus, teacher-made tests tend to have content validity (see chapter 4). Another person's test not only may omit important material and include irrelevant material, but also may confuse students with the use of unfamiliar terminology.

Procedure

There is a great deal more to constructing a good knowledge test than just writing down items, typing the test, and administering it. If you are seriously interested in test construction, read Ebel's comprehensive book (1979) on knowledge testing since such coverage is beyond the scope of this test. Typically, there are four general procedural steps to follow in constructing a good knowledge test:

Step 1. Construct a table of specifications.
Step 2. Decide the nature of the test.
Step 3. Construct the test items.
Step 4. Determine the test format and administrative details.

Table 11.3
Sample Table of Specifications for a Basketball Test.

	TYPE OF TEST ITEMS		
Subject Topic	**Knowledge**	**Comprehension**	**Application**
Rules	15%	5%	0%
Player duties	20%	10%	0%
Offensive plays	10%	10%	10%
Defenses	5%	5%	0%
Strategy	0%	0%	10%

A table of specifications is an outline for the test construction. It lists the areas and levels of knowledge to be tested, as shown in table 11.3. By adhering to a table of specifications, the test developer ensures that all the material on it is covered and that the correct weight is given to each area.

In deciding which type of test to give, consider the advantages and disadvantages of essay and objective tests, and then, if an objective test is chosen, of true–false, multiple-choice, or other types of items. This choice should depend on the type of test that best fulfills the educational objectives for the material. There is a tendency among physical education teachers and exercise specialists to select either true–false or multiple-choice items for their tests, but there are times when neither is the best choice. There is no reason why a test must be composed of a single type of item, although all items of the same type should be grouped together. Tests that include both true–false and multiple-choice items, or some objective and some essay items, are not uncommon.

The third step is writing the test items. Begin this task well in advance of the testing session. It's important to allow enough time to develop items that are carefully conceptualized and constructed. Tests constructed at the last minute can be very frustrating to take; they usually fail to cover the unit fully and often are poorly worded, ambiguous, and hard to understand. In fact, after constructing the items, the constructor should read them, correct them, and then put them aside for at least a day before reading them again. A fresh look may pinpoint other errors and ambiguities.

Finally the test format is chosen. One important consideration is the directions, which should appear at the top of the test. The instructions themselves depend on the type of test, the age of the students, the type of test items, the use of an answer sheet, the scoring procedure, and so on. Another consideration is the presentation of the items. They should be typed neatly with enough space to make them easy to read. When several items pertain to information supplied on the test (for example, a diagram), the information and the items should be on the same page.

Table 11.4, an example of a test with a poor format, reveals a number of errors and poor procedures. First there's the absence of directions, a definite disadvantage for the students. Typing strike-overs is inexcusable, and the failure to space between words is simply sloppy proofreading. The crowding of the last few items and the lack of consistent spacing of the second lines in items are also hard on the students.

Table 11.4

Example of a Test with a Poor Format.

HANDBALL

1. Studentw name _____

2. Time and days the class meets. _____

3. T.F.   Theshort line divides the court into half.   (if number
          3 if false indicate location of the sort line) _____

4. T.F.   The service line is 5 feet in front of the short line.

5. T.F.   The Ballis indicated as black in the official rules.

6. T.F.   Gloves may or not be used.

7. Name the three types of player combinations used to play the
   game.
   1. _____ 2. _____ 3. _____

8. Who can score points? _____

9. T.F.   The ball must hot the floor once before being played.

10. T.F.   After the service the ball need not strike the front
           wall first.

11. T.F.   The server must be within the service zone while
           serving.

12. T.F.   It is the duty of the players to get out of the way of the person playing
    X   the ball.

13. T.F.   A player entirely missing the ball has another opportunity to play
           it except on the serve.

14. T.F.   To play the ball and miss it on the serve ɸs considered
                   as a   point for the side serving.

15. T.F.   A player playing and missing a short service has a
           point scored against him.

16. T.F.   In doubles both partners have the opportunity to play
           the ball.

17. T.F.   The tact that "the ball was killed" does not preclude
           calling a hinder.

18. T.F.   In doubles only one man serves th the first half of the
           first inning.

19. R.F.   It is illegal to turn around to watch an opponent play
           the ball.

Types of Test Items

True–False

A **true–false item** consists of a short, factual statement. If the statement appears to be true, the student marks True or T; otherwise the student marks False, or F. This type of item is quite popular.

Advantages and Disadvantages: The advantages of true–false items are as follows:

1. The rapidity with which students can answer these items makes it possible to include many items on the test.
2. It's easier and quicker to construct true–false items than other types of objective items.
3. Test items can be graded quickly.
4. Factual information is easily tested.
5. Standardized answer sheets can be used.

The disadvantages are these:

1. Probably only the first level of Bloom's taxonomy (1956), knowledge, can be tested by a true–false test.
2. Students have a 50 percent chance of guessing the correct answer.
3. It's easy for a student to cheat by glancing at another student's paper.
4. This type of item can encourage memorization rather than understanding of facts.
5. This type of item is often ambiguous, in that the students and the teacher may not interpret an item in the same way.
6. True–false items often test trivial information.
7. To ensure reliability, a true–false test requires more items than does a multiple-choice test.

Construction Procedures: Many people believe that true–false test items are easy to construct. Unfortunately this is not entirely the case. Although they are easier to construct than some other types of objective items, true–false items must be constructed with care, using the following rules:

1. Keep the statement short. If it's long, the student may have to read it several times, which means that fewer items can be asked.
2. Use only a single concept in any one statement. This way, if a student answers incorrectly, you can identify the concept he or she does not know.
3. Keep the vocabulary simple.
4. Don't reproduce statements exactly from the text unless your objective is for the student to identify the passage.
5. Whenever possible, state the items positively rather than negatively.
6. Avoid using words like "always," "never," "all," and "none." Absolute statements are almost always false, and many students know this.
7. Don't allow more than 60% of the items to have the same answer. Students expect approximately half the items to be true, which influences their thinking as they take a test.
8. Avoid long strings of items with the same answers.

9. Avoid patterns in the answers like true, false, true, false, etc.
10. Don't give clues in one item to the answer of another. For example, don't let the statement in item 1 help answer item 14.
11. Avoid interdependent items. They put the student who misses the first item in double jeopardy.

Examples of Poor True–False Items: Most of the items in table 11.4 are poor because they deal with trivial information and their answers are obvious to anyone who has played handball. Ebel (1979) provides many examples of poor true–false items, but a sampling of poor items and the reasons why follow:

1. T (F) In soccer, the hands cannot touch the ball except when the ball is thrown in or when the player is the goalie.
   Explanation. The key word "legally" has been omitted. Also, two questions are being asked: (1) Can the hands be used to throw the ball in? (2) Can the goalie touch the ball with his or her hands?
2. T (F) Never go swimming just after you've eaten.
   Explanation. An absolute like "never" should not be used. A better item would be "It's not recommended that a person go swimming immediately after eating."
3. T (F) Physical fitness is important because a sound body and a sound mind usually go hand in hand, and, further, the physically fit person does not tire as easily as the unfit person and, thus, is usually more productive, but the fit person does not necessarily live longer than the less fit person.
   Explanation. The statement is too long and includes multiple concepts.
4. T (F) A shuttle run may be used to test cardiorespiratory endurance.
   Explanation. The statement is ambiguous because the distance of the shuttle run isn't stated.

Multiple Choice

A **multiple-choice item** is composed of a short complete or incomplete question or statement followed by three to five potential answers. The first part of the item, the question or statement, is called the stem; the answers are called responses. After reading the stem, the student selects the correct response. Complete stems are preferred over incomplete stems. Multiple-choice items are the most popular type of item with professional testmakers, and are commonly used by all people who construct knowledge tests.

Advantages and Disadvantages: Among the advantages of this type of item are the following:

1. Because students can answer each multiple-choice item quickly, many items can be included in the test.
2. Test items can be graded quickly.
3. All levels of knowledge in Bloom's taxonomy can be tested with multiple-choice items.
4. The chances of a student guessing correctly are slimmer than for true–false items, and decrease as the number of responses (plausible answers) increases.
5. Standardized answer sheets can be used.

Among the disadvantages of multiple-choice items are these:

1. Fewer items can be asked than with true–false items.
2. Considerable time is needed to think of enough plausible responses to each item.
3. There is a certain danger of cheating on multiple-choice items.
4. To some degree, multiple-choice items encourage memorization of facts without regard to their implications. This is more of a problem with items at the lower end of Bloom's taxonomy, and is generally less of a problem than it is with true–false items.
5. Students are unable to demonstrate the extent of their knowledge; they can respond only to the items as the instructor has constructed it. Of course this is a legitimate criticism of all objective test questions.

Constructive Procedures: Multiple-choice items are not easy to construct. The development of items with good stems and responses takes time, and it can be difficult to think of enough responses for an item. It's not uncommon to spend 15–30 minutes constructing a single item. However, if the following few rules are followed, you should end up with an acceptable test.

1. Keep both stems and responses short and explicit.
2. Make all responses approximately the same length. Beginning test constructors have a tendency to include more information in the correct responses than in the incorrect responses, a fact the students quickly pick up.
3. Use apparently acceptable answers for all responses. There is no excuse for writing sloppy or obviously incorrect responses.
4. If possible, use five responses for each item. This keeps the guess factors acceptably low (.20), and it's usually hard to think of more. All multiple choice items on a test do not have to have the same number of responses, but it is desirable.
5. If the stem is an incomplete sentence or question, make each response complete the stem.
6. Don't give away the correct answer with English usage. If the stem is singular, all responses should be singular. Words beginning with a vowel must be preceded by "an."
7. Don't give away the answer to one item in the content of another.
8. Don't allow the answer to one item to depend on the answer to another. If students answer the first incorrectly they'll answer the second incorrectly as well.
9. Don't construct the stem in such a way that you solicit the students' opinion. For example, don't begin questions with "What should be done?" or "What would you do?"
10. If the items are numbered, use letters (a,b,c,d,e) to enumerate the responses. Students tend to confuse response numbers with item numbers if the responses are numbered, particularly when standardized answer sheets are used.

11. Try to use each letter as the correct answer approximately the same number of times in the test. If the constructor is not careful, (c) may be the correct response more often than any other, which could help students guess the correct answer.

12. State the stem in positive rather than negative terms.

Examples of Poor Multiple-Choice Items: Again see Ebel (1979) for additional examples.

1. What should you do if the right front wheel of your car goes off the pavement as you are driving?
    a. Brake sharply.
    b. Cut the front wheels sharply to the left.
    c. Brake sharply and cut the wheels sharply to the left.
    d. Brake sharply and turn the wheels gradually to the left.
    *e. Brake gradually, maintaining control of the car by driving along the shoulder of the road if necessary. Then pull gently back onto the pavement when speed is reduced.

    Explanation. (1) The stem asks for the students' opinion; (2) it's understood, but should be stated in the stem, that the right front wheel went off the right side of the pavement; (3) the longest response is the correct answer; (4) responses c, d, and e make it clear that responses a and b are not true.

2. A switch in wrestling is countered with a
    *a. reswitch   b. inside step-over
    c. elbow roll   d. snap down
    e. scissors

    Explanation. Responses b and c can be eliminated because the stem ends in "a" and they both begin with vowels. The best solution is to end the stem at "with" and to add "a" or "an" to each response.

3. What is the worst position in wrestling?
    a. on both knees   b. flat-footed
    c. leaning forward   d. weight all on one leg
    *e. none of the above

    Explanation. It's not clear from the question what's wanted and whether the wrestlers are standing or prone. In truth, the most disadvantageous position is on the back because the wrestler is in danger of being pinned.

4. Pick the incorrect statement from the following:
    a. Only the serving team can score in volleyball.
    *b. In badminton, a person can't score unless he or she has the serve.
    c. In tennis, a set has not been won if the score is 40–30.
    d. In tennis, volleyball, and badminton, a net serve is served again.
    e. In tennis and badminton, a player cannot reach over the net to contact the ball or shuttlecock.

    Explanation. (1) When an incorrect response is to be identified, all responses should be stated positively so as not to confuse the students. (2) In response e, it would be preferable to say "it is illegal for a player to reach. . . ."

Table 11.5
A Sample Matching Test.

VOLLEYBALL

For each item on the left-hand side of the page, find an answer on the right-hand side. Place the letter of the correct answer in the space provided at the left of each item. Each answer can be used only once.

Items

_____ 1. The official height of the net in feet

_____ 2. The number of players on an official team

_____ 3. The number of points needed to win a game

_____ 4. Loss of the serve

_____ 5. Loss of a point

_____ 6. Illegal play

a. 6
b. 8
c. 12
d. 15
e. 18
f. 21
g. Net serve that goes over
h. More than 3 hits by receiving team
i. Reaching over the net to spike the ball
j. Stepping on a side boundary line
k. Serving team carries the ball

GOLF

In items 7–10, determine which of the four clubs listed on the right is best suited for the shot described on the left. Each answer can be used more than once.

Items

_____ 7. Tee shot on a 90-yard hole

_____ 8. 100-yard approach to the green

_____ 9. Fairway shot 140 yards from the green

_____ 10. 200-yard shot from the rough

l. Three-wood
m. Two-iron
n. Five-iron
o. Nine-iron

Matching

In a **matching item** test, a number of short questions or statements are listed on the left of the page and the answers are listed in order on the right. Matching items are a logical extension of multiple-choice items in that both provide the students with several answers from which to choose. Matching items are used less often than true–false or multiple-choice items, but they are very helpful in situations in which the same answers can be used with several test items. A sample matching test is shown in table 11.5.

Advantages and Disadvantages: Among the advantages of matching items are the following:

1. You can save space by giving the same potential answers for several questions.
2. The odds of guessing the right answer are theoretically quite low because there are so many answers to choose from. In actuality, students will probably be able to detect that no more than five to eight answers apply to any given question.
3. These items are quicker to construct than are multiple-choice questions.

The disadvantages of matching items are these:

1. Matching items usually test only factual information (the lowest level in Bloom's taxonomy).
2. Matching items are not particularly versatile, and a multiple-choice item often serves just as well.
3. Standardized answer sheets usually cannot be used with these items.

Construction Procedures: To develop a fair test, carefully plan the format and directions using the following rules:

1. State the items and potential answers clearly; neither should be more than two lines long.
2. Number the items and identify the potential answers with letters.
3. Allow a space at the left of each item for the correct answer.
4. Keep all items and answers on the same page.
5. Make all items similar in content. It's preferable to construct several sets of matching items rather than to mix content.
6. Arrange potential answers in logical groupings—all numerical answers together, all dates together, and so on. This saves students the time necessary to scan all the answers before responding.
7. Provide more answers than items to prevent students from deducing answers by elimination.
8. Tell the students in the directions whether an answer can be used more than once.
9. Have several potential answers for each item.

Completion

In a **completion item,** one word or several words are omitted from a sentence, and the student is asked to supply the missing information. This type of item has limited usefulness and application, and is less satisfactory than a multiple-choice item. In fact, none of the better textbooks (Ahmann and Glock 1981; Barrow and McGee 1979; Ebel 1979; Gronlund 1982, 1985; Scott and French 1959; Sheehan 1971; Thorndike and Hagen 1977) discuss this type of item in detail. Unless completion items are stated carefully, students may be uncertain what information the teacher wants. For example, consider the following item:

Three playing combinations in handball are _____ , _____ , and _____ .

Some students will answer singles, doubles, and cutthroat, while others, thinking about doubles play, will respond side-by-side, front-and-back, and rotation. Dizney (1971), suggests that acceptable answers to the item "$.02 and $.03 are _____ ?" must include "$.05," "5," "a nickel," "5 pennies," and "money." Obviously true–false or multiple-choice items could do the job with less ambiguity.

Short Answer and Essay

Short-answer and **essay** items are appropriate when the teacher wants to determine the students' depth of knowledge and their capacity to assemble and organize facts. For each item students answer with whatever facts and in whatever manner they think appropriate.

Advantages and Disadvantages: The advantages of essay items are the following:

1. Students are free to answer essay items in the way that seems best to them.
2. These items allow students to demonstrate the depth of their knowledge.
3. These items encourage students to relate all the material to a total concept rather than just to learn facts.
4. The items are easy and quick to construct.
5. All levels of Bloom's taxonomy can be tested with essay items.

Their disadvantages are these:

1. Essay items are time consuming to grade.
2. The objectivity of test scores is often low.
3. The reliability of test scores is often low.
4. Essay items require some skill in self-expression; if this skill is not an instructional objective, the item lacks validity.
5. Penmanship and neatness affect grades, which again lowers the item's validity.

Construction Procedures: Most teachers can construct reasonably good short-answer or essay items. However, if an item is hastily constructed, the students may not respond in the manner wanted. The biggest disadvantage of this type of item may be its grading. Teachers must key an item carefully to identify the characteristics wanted in the answer and to determine how partial credit points are assigned. Without an answer sheet, the reliability of scores is often low. For example, if a test item is worth 20 points and 5 specific facts should be mentioned in the answer, each fact is worth 4 points. If only 3 of the 5 facts are included, the student receives 12 points. Thus if the teacher should grade the item again, the student is likely again to receive 12 points. Research that required an instructor to grade a set of essay tests twice has found the test-retest reliability is usually low. The objectivity of essay test grades has also been investigated by assigning two qualified teachers to grade a set of essays independently. The objectivity has seldom been high.

If the following rules for constructing short-answer and essay items are followed, the items should be satisfactory:

1. State the item as clearly and concisely as possible.
2. Note on the test the approximate time students should spend on each item.
3. Note on the test the point value for each item.
4. Carefully key the test before administration. This is the only way to identify ambiguous items.

Sample Tests

Ideally teachers should construct their own knowledge tests. Those constructed by others often do not have the terminology or material emphasis needed for every teacher and class. If, for example, two teachers do not use the same technique, the correct answer to a question about that technique will not be the same for both instructors. The content and emphasis of a knowledge test also are influenced considerably by the age, sex, and ability level of the students. Knowledge tests can quickly become outdated as ideas, techniques, and rules change.

There are several sources of knowledge tests. Some have been published in research journals, and most books and manuals about specific sports and skills include sample knowledge tests. Unpublished knowledge tests (theses, dissertations, tests constructed by teachers in your school system) are also available.

Several sample knowledge test items are included here.

Badminton

Part I. True–False   If the answer is true, put a plus ($+$) to the left of the item number. If the answer is false, put a minus ($-$) to the left of the item number. Please respond to each item.

_____   1. In singles play it's tactically poor to return your opponent's drop with another drop unless your opponent is completely out of position in the back court.

_____   2. Proper position of the feet is more important in the execution of strokes made from a point near the rear boundary line than from a point near the net.

_____   3. Players A-1 and A-2, a two-person team, are trailing in their game 5–3. They have just broken the serve of Team B, so A-1 will start the serve in the right service court for Team A.

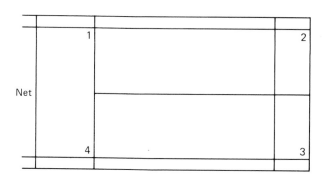

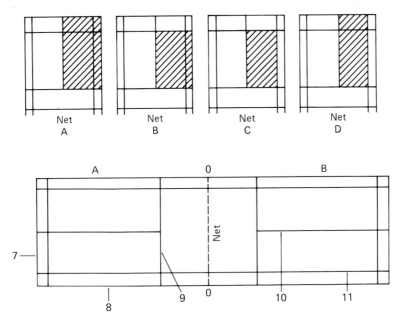

Part II. Multiple Choice   To the left of the item number put the letter of the answer that is most correct. Please respond to each item.

_____ 4. During the execution of a stroke the arm is straightened
   a. at no particular time
   b. just prior to contact between racket and bird
   c. at the moment of contact between racket and bird
   d. just after contact is made between racket and bird

_____ 5. If your opponent is in the back left-hand corner of his or her court when you play the bird, what number in the diagram represents your best target?
   a. 1
   b. 2
   c. 3
   d. 4

_____ 6. In which diagram does the shaded portion represent the singles service court?
   a. a
   b. b
   c. c
   d. d

Part III. Identification   Give the official names of the lines of the court that are numbered in the diagram, placing the name next to the number.

Volleyball

Read the instructions that precede each section of the test before you answer any of the items in that section.

Part I. True–False   If the statement is true, blacken the a on the answer sheet. If the statement is false, blacken b on the answer sheet for that numbered statement.

1. To start the game, Team A serves. Team B's first server will be the player who started the game as the right forward.
2. If the spiker is left-handed, the "ideal" set-up will be on his or her right side.
3. The blocker's jump is begun just before the spiker's jump.
4. If two opposing players contact the ball simultaneously directly above the net, either may play the ball on the next hit.
5. If the net is driven under the blocker's fingers by a ball spiked into the net, the referee rules the blocker fouled.

Part II. Multiple Choice   On the answer sheet, blacken the letter of the response that best answers the item.

6. What is the maximum number of players who can legally block?
   a. 3
   b. 4
   c. 5
   d. No limit
7. In a 4–2 offense with the setter in the right forward position, which two players exchange positions?
   a. the right forward and the center forward
   b. the right forward and the right back
   c. the left forward and the left back
   d. the left forward and the center forward
8. In trying to recover the ball, players from both teams touch the net simultaneously. The referee calls
   a. "point"
   b. "reservice"
   c. "side out"
   d. "rotate"
9. A player on Team A serves out of turn and scores 2 points, but the error is not discovered until after the opponents have served. The decision of the official is that
   a. the score stands as played and Team A returns to proper rotation order
   b. A loses the points and play continues
   c. A loses the points and Team B rotates
10. With a 6–9 score, Team A serves to Team B. B lets the serve go and it hits on the back line. What is the score now?
    a. 9–6, B serving
    b. 9–7, A serving
    c. 6–10, B serving
    d. 7–9, A serving

Part III. Matching   Read each numbered statement and choose the best answer from the five responses. Then, on the answer sheet, blacken the letter of the correct response for that numbered statement. Use the same five responses for items 11 through 15.

a. Point for Team A
b. Point for Team B
c. Loss of serve
d. Legal, play continues
e. Reserve or serve over

11. During the return of Team A's serve, a member of Team B spikes the ball. Team A has used a two-person block and the spike hits both people. The blocked ball bounds up in the air; A's left back sets to A's right forward, who spikes the ball. The ball hits a member of Team B on the shoulder and goes out of bounds.
12. While Team B is serving, a player on Team A tries to play the ball, but it bounces off his or her shoulder and a teammate successfully spikes the ball over the net where it strikes the floor in bounds.
13. During the return of B's serve a player on Team A spikes the ball, which lands in bounds on B's side of the net.
14. Team A serves. Team B sets the ball for its spiker, while Team A sets up a two-person block. During the spike-block play, Spiker B lands over the center line; however, one of A's blockers' hands goes over the net.
15. Team B serves. Team A sets the ball for the spiker, while Team B sets up a two-person block. Player A spikes the ball into Blocker B's hands and the ball bounds over Team A's end line.

Wrestling Knowledge Test (Kraft 1971)

(This test has good directions, diagrams, and so on.) Instructions to be read by the test examiner:

1. This test consists of 50 multiple-choice questions. Read each question carefully. Select the most appropriate answer and using the pencil provided mark your answer on the separate answer sheet. Do not mark on the test booklet. Scratch paper has been provided for use in any computations.
2. There are a number of questions on the test that refer to illustrations of wrestling maneuvers.
3. Make a heavy black line in the box on the answer sheet. Be sure that the number on the answer sheet corresponds to the number in the test booklet. Do not make stray marks and erase carefully any answer you want to change. Questions with more than one answer will be marked incorrect. Do not fold, bend, or tear the answer sheet.
4. Mark only one answer for each question, but answer all questions. When you do not know an answer, make an intelligent guess. Your score will be the number of right responses.

5. When you finish the test, place your answer sheet face down in the front of your test booklet and close the booklet.

6. You may leave the room quietly through the door nearest your seat.

7. Remember, follow all directions carefully, and be sure the number on the answer sheet corresponds with that in the test booklet.

8. Are there any questions?

9. You have approximately 45 minutes to complete the test.

10. Please turn the page and begin.

1. In the maneuver illustrated on page 399, which of the following moves by Contestant B will counter A?
   a. Keeping the center of gravity high and staying above A
   b. Keeping the feet apart and maintaining a solid base
   c. Keeping the right elbow close to the body
   d. Keeping the weight forward
   e. Maintaining a firm hold on A's triceps

2. What is the maneuver illustrated on page 399 called?
   a. arm drag
   b. duck under (head drag)
   c. go behind
   d. snap down
   e. switch

3. Listed below are the five steps necessary to successfully execute the maneuver illustrated on page 399.
   1. Get B's right elbow away from his body
   2. Snap head back and jerk B's neck with right hand
   3. Snap the head down and under B's right armpit
   4. Swing behind
   5. Tie-up

   In what order are these steps executed?
   a. 1,5,3,2,4
   b. 2,5,1,4,3
   c. 5,1,2,3,4
   d. 5,1,3,2,4
   e. 5,2,1,3,4

4. If the final score of a match is A5 and B4, how many team points are earned by each wrestler?
   a. A0, B3
   b. A3, B0
   c. A5, B0
   d. B5, A0
   e. None of the above

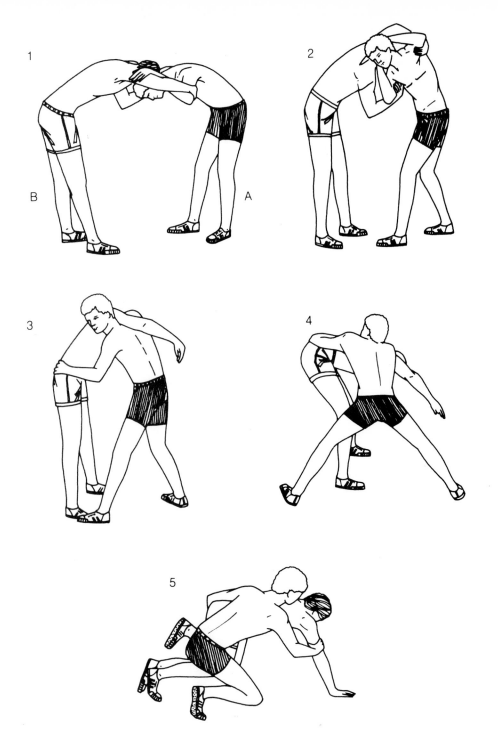

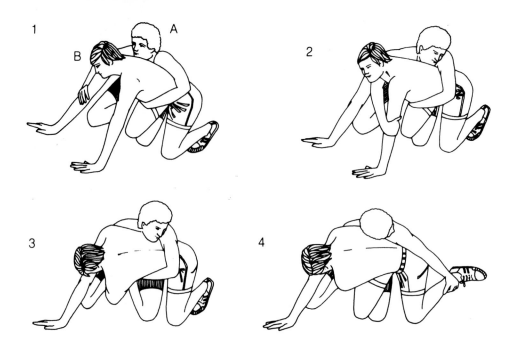

5. How many points are awarded Contestant A for successful execution of the maneuver illustrated?
   a. 0
   b. 1
   c. 1 or 2
   d. 2
   e. None of the above

6. Contestant A switches B. In the move, B's shoulder is injured and he cannot continue. What is the correct decision?
   a. A wins by default
   b. A wins by forfeit
   c. B wins by default
   d. B wins by disqualification
   e. None of the above

ADMINISTRATION AND GRADING

Administration Procedures

A test setting should be quiet, well lighted, properly heated, odor-free, spacious, and comfortable. The failure to furnish a comfortable and distraction-free testing site places students at a disadvantage. Physical education teachers and exercise specialists often are not careful about the testing atmosphere and setting: the practice of instructing students to lie on the gym floor to take a test while other students participate in another part of the gym leaves much to be desired.

The teacher must also consider test security. During a test, students should all face the same direction. They should be sitting close enough to allow the teacher to see everyone, but far enough apart to preclude cheating and whispering. In a classroom, you may assign a student to every other seat or, better still, to every other seat of every other row. Encourage students to keep their eyes on their own papers and their papers covered. Sometimes alternate test forms with the same items arranged on each form in a different order, are used. Also a procedure for collecting the papers is essential. If students stand around the teacher waiting to turn in their tests, they can exchange answers while they wait; and, students still taking the test can exchange answers while the teacher is busy collecting other students' tests.

If you plan to use the same test with several classes, you must ensure that students who have taken the test do not give the test items and answers to those yet to take it. If only two consecutive classes are to take the test, security poses no problem. However, if even as much as an hour elapses between the two administrations, the test's contents will probably be known to the second class. The best approach, then, is to use several forms of the test. Of course each form must test the same material. A common procedure with multiple-choice tests is to construct parallel items. For example, all forms of the test include an item dealing with the volleyball serve. With true–false tests, a common procedure is to reword some of the items on the second form so that the answer changes.

Grading Procedures

On an essay test, grade each student's answer to a single item before going on to the next item. This procedure, and the use of a key, increase the likelihood that the same standards will be applied to all answers. Reliability suffers when an essay test is graded in a hurry. This is one reason why essay tests take so much time to grade.

The grading of true–false and multiple-choice items, although usually less time consuming than essay questions, can be tedious. Consider a 50-item true–false test administered to 180 students in a public school. Grading a test paper by referring alternately to the answer key and each student's answers takes at least 2 minutes per test—6 hours for the entire group. Few teachers want to spend this amount of time grading.

Figure 11.1 Standardized commercial answer sheet.

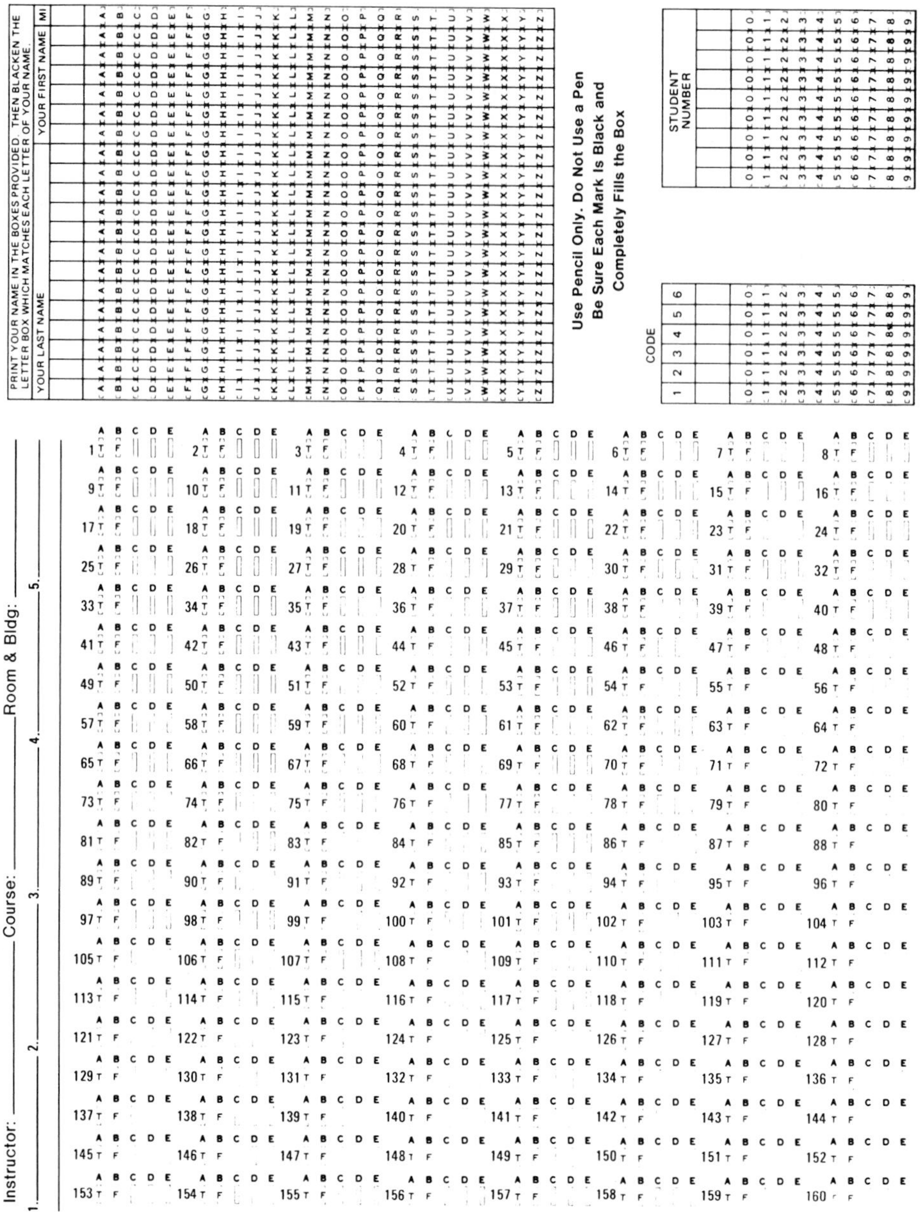

Cognitive and affective testing

Standardized answer sheets can speed up the grading of true–false and multiple-choice tests. These answer sheets can be constructed by the teacher or purchased commercially. A sample of a commercial, standardized answer sheet is shown in figure 11.1. These standardized answer sheets have the advantage of being machine-scorable, thus eliminating the time needed to score the tests by hand. Machines to score tests vary from the large and expensive ones used by scoring services and universities to the small and inexpensive desktop models used by individual public or private schools. In addition, the use of standardized answer sheets makes it possible to reuse test booklets.

A layover answer key—a standardized answer sheet on which the correct answers are cut or punched out—is used to grade standardized tests by hand. (Special hand punches are available for cutting answer keys, so that razor blades do not have to be used.) To use a layover answer key, first scan the student's answer sheet to make sure there are no multiple responses to any of the test items. Then the layover answer key is placed on top of the answer sheet, and the number of visible pencil marks is the student's score. A 50-question true–false or multiple-choice test can be graded in 20 to 30 seconds using a layover answer key. A sample layover answer key for a teacher-made answer sheet is shown in figure 11.2.

To score commercial answer sheets by machine, the students must use a pencil to mark the answer sheets. Many colleges and school districts offer free scoring services to their personnel. The answer key and answer sheets are fed into a machine that grades the tests and stamps a score on each answer sheet.

ANALYSIS AND REVISION

Most teachers use an objective test more than once. After an objective test has been administered and graded, the teacher should examine certain of its characteristics to determine the merits of the test and of particular questions, and to identify those items that should be revised or deleted before the test is used again. The failure to analyze a knowledge test after its first administration not only lowers the reliability and validity of the test scores, but also can raise the question of fairness.

After administering and grading a test, the teacher should examine the following characteristics:

1. Overall difficulty
2. Variability in test scores
3. Reliability
4. The difficulty of each item
5. The discrimination, or validity, of each item
6. Quality of each response in a multiple-choice item.

Figure 11.2 Sample layover answer key for a teacher-made answer sheet.

Name _____ Score _____ _____ _____
          Last   First   Initial   Right — Wrong Omitted

Date _____ Class _____ Test Number _____

	A B C D E		A B C D E		A B C D E		A B C D E
1	■ (A)	26		51		76	
2	■ (D)	27		52		77	
3	■ (D)	28		53		78	
4	■ (B)	29		54		79	
5	■ (E)	30		55		80	
6	■ (C)	31		56		81	
7	■ (A)	32		57		82	
8	■ (B)	33		58		83	
9	■ (E)	34		59		84	
10	■ (C)	35		60		85	
11		36		61		86	
12		37		62		87	
13		38		63		88	
14		39		64		89	
15		40		65		90	
16		41		66		91	
17		42		67		92	
18		43		68		93	
19		44		69		94	
20		45		70		95	
21		46		71		96	
22		47		72		97	
23		48		73		98	
24		49		74		99	
25		50		75		100	

Analyzing the Test

Difficulty and Variability

The overall difficulty of a test is determined by calculating the mean performance for the class and dividing by the number of test questions. The higher the mean, the easier the test. The variability in test scores is determined by calculating the standard deviation. The larger the standard deviation, the more the test discriminates among ability groups.

Reliability

The reliability of a knowledge test is usually estimated using either the split-half or the Kuder-Richardson method. (The test-retest method discussed in chapter 3 is inappropriate because students would be expected to do better the second day due to a carryover of knowledge and an exchange of information about the test.)

Split-Half Method.   The split-half reliability method was described in chapter 3. To estimate the reliability of a test, we divide it in half and obtain a score for each student on each half. Note that a test can be split in half in a large number of ways: first half—second half; odd numbered items—even numbered items; etc. For a knowledge test, usually the odd-even system is used. Once the number of items correctly answered in each half is determined for each student, we can determine the correlation between the two halves. This correlation (Pearson product moment) is the internal-consistency reliability for half of the whole test. To estimate the internal-consistency reliability for the whole test (the number of items correctly answered), we use the following formula:

$$r_{1,1} = \frac{2\, r_{1/2,1/2}}{1 + r_{1/2,1/2}}$$

where $r_{1,1}$ is the reliability of the whole test and $r_{1/2,1/2}$ is the Pearson correlation between the two halves of the test.

The reliability coefficient for the whole test ($r_{1,1}$) is interpreted as the correlation coefficient that would be obtained if the whole test were correlated with itself or with another whole test composed of the same number of items.

Problem 11.1   Use the information in table 11.6 to calculate the split-half reliability coefficient of the test.

Table 11.6
Split-Half Scores.

STUDENT	NUMBER OF ODD ITEMS CORRECT	NUMBER OF EVEN ITEMS CORRECT
A	32	35
B	43	41
C	36	38
D	26	25
E	24	26

Solution   Where $r_{1/2,1/2}$ is .96, the split-half reliability coefficient $r_{1,1}$ is .98:

$$r_{1,1} = \frac{(2)(.96)}{1 + .96} \quad \frac{1.92}{1.96} = .98$$

NOTE: Using the Pearson product-moment formula, substituting the odd-items for X and the even items for Y, where n is 5, ΣXY is 5525, ΣX is 161, ΣY is 165, ΣX^2 is 5421, and ΣY^2 is 5651, r (or $r_{1/2,1/2}$) is .96:

$$r = \frac{n\Sigma XY - (\Sigma X)(\Sigma Y)}{\sqrt{[n\Sigma X^2 - (\Sigma X)^2][n\Sigma Y^2 - (\Sigma Y)^2]}}$$

$$= \frac{(5)(5525) - (161)(165)}{\sqrt{[(5)(5421) - 161^2][(5)(5651) - 165^2]}}$$

$$= \frac{27625 - 26565}{\sqrt{(27105 - 25921)(28255 - 27225)}} = \frac{1060}{\sqrt{(1184)(1030)}}$$

$$= \frac{1060}{\sqrt{1219520}}$$

$$= \frac{1060}{1104} = .96$$

Kuder-Richardson Method.   The Kuder-Richardson formula 20 reliability coefficient is the average of all possible split-half reliability coefficients that could be calculated by splitting a test in different ways (Ferguson 1981). Nunnally (1978) states that with dichotomous items (items scored as either right or wrong) formula 20's reliability coefficient is the same as coefficient alpha. (In chapter 3 we noted coefficient alpha.) Formula 20 is time consuming to use because the percentage of the class answering each item correctly must be determined. On the assumption that all test items are equally difficult, the formula can be simplified to the Kuder-Richardson formula 21, which is even easier to use than the split-half method. Although formula 21 is commonly used, Ebel (1979) notes that it underestimates the reliability coefficient when test items vary in difficulty, which they usually do. The Kuder-Richardson formula 21 is as follows:

$$r_{21} = \frac{k(s^2) - \overline{X}(k - \overline{X})}{(k - 1)(s^2)}$$

where k is the number of test questions, s^2 is the test's standard deviation squared, and $\overline{X}$ is the test mean.

Problem 11.2   Use the information in table 11.7 to calculate the Kuder-Richardson formula 21 reliability coefficient of the test.

Solution   Where k is 10, s^2 is 2.96, and $\overline{X}$ is 6.2, the reliability coefficient r using formula 21 is .23:

$$r = \frac{(10)(2.96) - (6.2)(10 - 6.2)}{(10 - 1)(2.96)}$$

$$= \frac{2.96 - (6.2)(3.8)}{(9)(2.96)} = \frac{29.6 - 23.56}{26.64}$$

$$= \frac{6.04}{26.64} = .23$$

Table 11.7

Kuder-Richardson Formula Scores.

					ITEM						
Student	1	2	3	4	5	6	7	8	9	10	X
A	1	1	1	1	0	1	1	1	1	1	9
B	1	0	0	0	0	1	1	0	1	1	5
C	0	1	0	0	0	0	1	1	0	1	4
D	1	1	0	0	0	1	0	1	1	1	6
E	1	1	0	0	0	1	1	1	1	1	7

$\overline{X} = 6.2$

$s^2 = 2.96$

Formula 20 yields a correlation coefficient of .63, which as Ebel suggested is a higher value than the .23 yielded by formula 21.

NOTE: The Kuder-Richardson formula 20 is as follows:

$$r_{20} = \left(\frac{k}{k-1}\right)\left[\frac{(s_x)^2 - \Sigma pq}{(s_x)^2}\right]$$

where k is the number of test items, $(s_x)^2$ is the variance of the test scores $[\Sigma X^2/n - (\Sigma X)^2/n^2]$, p is the percentage answering an item correctly, q is $1 - p$, and Σpq is the sum of the pq products for all k items. Using the figures in table 11.7, we can calculate the following percentages (p) for the ten items:

Item	1	2	3	4	5	6	7	8	9	10
p	.8	.8	.2	.2	.0	.8	.8	.8	.8	1.0
q	.2	.2	.8	.8	1.0	.2	.2	.2	.2	.0

Where k is 10, $(s_x)^2$ is 2.96, and Σpq is 1.28, r is .63:

$$r = \left(\frac{10}{10-1}\right)\left(\frac{2.96 - 1.28}{2.96}\right)$$

$$= \left(\frac{10}{9}\right)\left(\frac{1.68}{2.96}\right) = (1.11)(.568) = .63$$

Remember that—all other factors being equal—the larger the standard deviation, the higher the reliability coefficient. If in Problem 11.2 the scores had been 9,8,7,5, and 4; $\overline{X}$ was 6.6; and s^2 was 3.44, the reliability coefficient r using formula 21 would have been .39. Thus high reliability is harder to obtain with homogeneous groups than it is with heterogeneous ones.

Item Analysis

The last two relevant characteristics of a test—the difficulty and validity of the items and the efficiency of responses—can be determined by an item analysis—a procedure that is important but tedious to do by hand. This analysis should be conducted whenever a test is used the first time.

For the results of an item analysis to be reliable and valid, a large number of students (over 100) must have taken the test. There are several reasons why a large number is essential, one being that all ability levels are apt to be represented in a big group. Also, some estimates of correlation coefficients are used in the item analysis procedure, and coefficients based on small groups are often uncommonly high or low and thus untrustworthy.

The first step in an item analysis is to identify from the total test scores a top and bottom group. We will use the top and bottom 27% of the scores. Use only the tests of students in these ranges in the analysis. The next step is to make a chart on which to record the answer each student in the top and bottom groups chose for each item. Figure 11.3 shows a sample chart using the test papers of the top and bottom 16 students in a class of 60. You can see that 12 students in the top group and 5 students in the bottom group answered Item 1 correctly. By using only the top and bottom 27% of the test papers in the analysis, we minimize the work of constructing the chart and can also determine how well each item discriminates between the best and worst students. With the information in the chart, it's possible to determine the difficulty and validity of each test item, and whether all responses functioned.

Item Difficulty

Because each student answers each item correctly or incorrectly, we can calculate the percentage of students who chose the right answer. This percentage, called the **item difficulty** (D), is large when the test item is easy, and small when it's hard. We use the following formula to determine item difficulty:

$$D = \frac{\text{number right in top group} + \text{number right in bottom group}}{\text{number in top group} + \text{number in bottom group}}$$

Problem 11.3   Determine the difficulty of item 1 in figure 11.3.

Solution   Where the number right in the top group is 12, the number right in the bottom group is 5, and the number of students in each of the groups is 16, the item difficulty, D, is .53:

$$D = \frac{12 + 5}{16 + 16} \quad \frac{17}{32} = .53$$

Discrimination Index

Item validity, or item discrimination, indicates how well a test item discriminates between those who performed well on the test and those who did poorly. If, as is wanted, an item is answered correctly by more of the better students than the worse students, it discriminates positively; if more of the worse students answer the item correctly than

ITEM	CORRECT ANSWER		RESPONSE						OMIT
			a	b	c	d	e		
1	b	top		𝚃𝙷𝙻 𝚃𝙷𝙻 //	///	/			
		bottom	//	𝚃𝙷𝙻	𝚃𝙷𝙻	//	//		
2	e	top	//	//	/	///	𝚃𝙷𝙻 ///		
		bottom	//	///	//	𝚃𝙷𝙻	////		
3	c	top			𝚃𝙷𝙻 𝚃𝙷𝙻 𝚃𝙷𝙻 /				
		bottom		///	𝚃𝙷𝙻 𝚃𝙷𝙻 ///				
4	a	top	𝚃𝙷𝙻	𝚃𝙷𝙻 ///	///				
		bottom	𝚃𝙷𝙻 𝚃𝙷𝙻 //	////					

do the better students, the item is a poor one and discriminates negatively. The first time a test is used, it's not uncommon to find that a few items discriminate negatively. These items should be revised or rejected before the test is used again.

The discrimination index (r) is essentially a correlation coefficient between scores on one question and scores on the whole test. Thus its value ranges from $+1$ to -1; $+1$ corresponding to the best possible positive discrimination. The calculation of the correlation between scores on each question and on the total test is too time consuming, but we can estimate it, using the top and bottom 27% of the class, with the following formula (Scott and French 1959; Sheehan 1971):

$$r = \frac{\text{number right in top group} - \text{number right in bottom group}}{\text{number in each group}}$$

Problem 11.4   Determine the discrimination index of Item 1 in figure 11.3.

Solution   Where the number right in the top group is 12, the number right in the bottom group is 5, and the number of students in each group is 16, the discrimination, or validity, index r is .44:

$$r = \frac{12 - 5}{16} = \frac{7}{16} = .44$$

The discrimination index is quite easy to compute with a calculator; it can be tedious if done by hand.

It's apparent from the discrimination index formula that a positive value is obtained when more people in the top group than in the bottom group answer an item correctly; a zero value is obtained when the same number of students in both groups answer correctly.

We assume in determining item validity that the total test score is a valid measure of knowledge. Therefore, total test validity must be determined, usually by examining the content validity, before the item analysis. Item validity has no meaning if the total test is not valid. Also, as noted earlier, all other factors being equal, the larger the standard deviation, the more reliable the test. The more a test discriminates, the larger the standard deviation tends to be.

It's worth noting as well that the difficulty of a test item affects the maximum attainable discrimination index. If, for example, the difficulty of an item is .50, a discrimination index of 1.0 is obtained if all students in the top group and none in the bottom groups answer the item correctly. If, however, the difficulty of a test item is .60, the best possible discrimination (.80) is obtained when 100% of the top group and 20% of the bottom group respond to the item correctly. The maximum possible discrimination if item difficulty is .40 is also .80. As item difficulties go up or down from .50, the maximum possible **discrimination index** decreases. For this reason teachers who want to develop discrimination tests, rather than mastery tests, try to write as many test items whose difficulty is approximately .50 as possible—a difficult task.

Response Quality

Ideally, at least some of the students whose test papers are analyzed should select each response of a multiple-choice item. The instructor can use the chart developed to do the item analysis to determine whether all responses were indeed selected. Figure 11.3 shows that all responses were selected in Item 1, but only responses b and c were selected for Item 3. Thus Item 3 might as well have been a true–false item.

Two Quick-Item Analysis Methods

The **item analysis** just presented is time consuming to do by hand. Rather than forgo the procedure entirely when time is limited, it's possible to obtain at least a general idea of the difficulty and discrimination of each test item. Two fast methods are available. The first (Educational Testing Service 1964) substitutes the following procedures for an item analysis:

Step 1
Determine the median score for the group tested.

Step 2
Return the test papers to the class and ask students with scores above the median to move to one side of the room; the rest of the class should move to the other side.

Step 3

Announce the correct answer to Item 1 and ask those students with the correct answer to raise their hands.

a. On the basis of the approximate percentage of the class that answered correctly, classify the item as either easy, moderate, or hard.

b. If many more hands are raised in the above-median group than in the below-median group, the item discriminates positively. If the number of hands is approximately the same in both groups, its discrimination is 0. If many more hands are raised in the below-median group, the item discriminates negatively.

Step 4

Record the item's difficulty and discrimination.

Step 5

Repeat Steps 3 and 4 for each item.

This method can be used to identify poor test items and an item analysis could be conducted on those items only.

Educational Testing Service (1964) suggests that if an item discriminates well the difference between the number of students in the top and bottom 50% of the class who answer it correctly should be 10% of the class. For example, if 80 students take a test, at least 8 more top than bottom students should answer a test item correctly if the item discriminates well.

The second method utilizes the computer (mainframe or micro) and is feasible when standardized answer sheets are used. As noted previously, many schools offer machine scoring. As each answer sheet is scored, the machine can record the student's name, test score, and response to each item. This information for the entire group is then submitted to the computer for item analysis. Computer analysis is more complete than the item analysis undertaken by hand because all the students' scores are used; the top group becomes the upper 50% of those tested. The *Statistics with Finesse* package (Bolding 1985) of microcomputer programs has a test analysis feature that provides item difficulty, item discrimination, Kuder-Richardson reliability, etc. On many college and university campuses the item analysis service is free.

A sample of the data from a computer printout of an item analysis appears in table 11.8. The test was administered to 15 students and was composed of 24 multiple-choice items. Notice that much useful information accompanies the analysis. Having the frequency distribution, mean, standard deviation, percentile ranks, T-scores, and two estimates of the test's reliability (under the item analysis) immediately available can save the teacher a lot of calculating.

In the item analysis section of the printout, D represents the item difficulty and r represents its discrimination. Because all calculations are done so quickly by the computer, difficulty and discrimination can be calculated for each response. For each item, the starred response is the correct answer. The sample test used only four responses.

Table 11.8
Sample Item Analysis Printout.

FREQUENCY DISTRIBUTION

Raw Score	Frequency	Cumulative Frequency
20	1	15
19	1	14
18	2	13
17	2	11
16	2	9
15	1	7
12	2	6
11	2	4
7	1	2
5	1	1

Mean = 14.27
Standard deviation = 4.431

ROSTER OF CLASS

Name	Raw Score	Percentile Rank	T-score
A	15	46	51.65
B	20	99	62.94
C	17	73	56.17
D	16	59	53.91
E	5	6	29.09
F	17	73	56.17
G	7	13	33.60
H	16	59	53.91
I	18	86	58.42
J	12	39	44.89
K	11	26	42.63
L	12	39	44.89
M	19	93	60.68
N	18	86	58.42
O	11	26	42.63

ITEM ANALYSIS

Item Number	a	b	c	d	e	Blank
1	$r = -.02$	$r = 0.00$	$r = -.56$	$r = .37^*$	$r = 0.00$	
	$D = 13.33$	$D = 0.00$	$D = 6.67$	$D = 80.00$	$D = 0.00$	0
2	$r = .63^*$	$r = .16$	$r = 0.00$	$r = -.70$	$r = 0.00$	
	$D = 40.00$	$D = 6.67$	$D = 0.00$	$D = 53.33$	$D = 0.00$	0
3	$r = .66^*$	$r = -.51$	$r = -.33$	$r = -.04$	$r = 0.00$	
	$D = 40.00$	$D = 13.33$	$D = 20.00$	$D = 26.67$	$D = 0.00$	0
.						
.						
.						
24	$r = .05$	$r = -.56$	$r = 0.00$	$r = .42^*$	$r = 0.00$	
	$D = 20.00$	$D = 20.00$	$D = 0.00$	$D = 60.00$	$D = 0.00$	0

Kuder-Richardson reliability = .79
Standard error = 2.03
Spearman-Brown reliability = .74
Standard error = 2.25

Table 11.9
Standards for Evaluating a Discrimination Type Multiple-Choice Test.

1. The total test
   a. The validity of the test is acceptable.
   b. The reliability of the test is acceptable.
   c. The mean performance of the class approximates that wanted by the teacher.
   d. At least 90% of the class finished the test (not applicable to speed tests).
2. Each test item
   a. Difficulty: No more than 5% of the test items have difficulty indexes above .90, and no more than 5% are below .10.
   b. Discrimination:
      (1) More than 25% of the test items have discrimination indexes above .40.
      (2) More than 25% of the test items have discrimination indexes between .21 and .39.
      (3) More than 15% of the test items have discrimination indexes between 0 and .20.
      (4) Less than 5% of the test items have zero or negative discrimination indexes.
   c. Responses: On each test item, each response was selected by at least 5% of the students whose test papers were used in the item analysis.

The difficulty value for Item 1, response d is 80, which means that 80% of the group answered the question correctly. Although it's an easy item, Item 1 is also a good item: three of the four responses functioned even with the small group, the difficulty and discrimination of the correct responses are acceptable, and the discrimination of the incorrect answers is negative.

Revising the Test

After calculating the difficulty of and discrimination index for each item, the overall quality of the test and of each item must be determined so the test can be revised as necessary. A set of standards for evaluating discrimination type multiple-choice tests appears in table 11.9.

Using these standards, we can evaluate the four items in figure 11.3:

Item 1. D is .53; r is .44. All responses functioned; a good item.

Item 2. D is .38; r is .25. All responses functioned; an acceptable but difficult item.

Item 3. D is .91; r is .19. Only two responses functioned; essentially an easy true–false item. Revision might improve the responses. If left as is, it should be changed to a true–false item.

Item 4. D is .47; r is −.31. Three responses functioned. Revise or reject the item. Either the item itself or response b misled many of the top group. If this problem is corrected by revision, most students will probably answer correctly because ten of the bottom group did so this time. However, because it's unlikely that the item will ever discriminate and because two responses do not function, the item probably should be rejected.

SUMMARY

Knowledge testing should be a component of most measurement programs. Before trying to construct a knowledge test, you must be aware of the types of knowledge tests and items, the advantages and disadvantages of each, and the construction process.

Certain techniques are necessary in administering a knowledge test, and their use can help you obtain reliable, valid scores. It's also important to be aware of the different techniques that can be used in grading a knowledge test after it's administered.

Finally, you should understand the importance of analyzing a knowledge test after it's been administered and should master the techniques used in item analysis. Improving the quality of knowledge tests through item analysis should be every teacher's goal.

FORMATIVE EVALUATION OF OBJECTIVES

Objective 1 Differentiate among various types of knowledge tests.

1. Knowledge tests can be classified as either essay or objective tests. Differentiate between these two basic test types.
2. Knowledge tests can also be classified as either mastery or discrimination tests. Differentiate between these two categories in terms of the difficulty and the objectives of the tests.

Objective 2 Define the levels of knowledge most applicable to physical education.

1. The taxonomy for educational objectives lists six classes, or levels, of knowledge. Ranging from low to high, the levels are knowledge, comprehension, application, analysis, synthesis, and evaluation. Define the first four of these levels and write a test item for each.

Objective 3 Outline the basic procedures used for constructing, administering, and grading a knowledge test.

1. Listed below are basic steps that a teacher can follow in constructing a knowledge test. Summarize the major decisions made at each step.
   a. Construct a table of specifications.
   b. Decide what type of test to give.
   c. Construct the test items.
   d. Determine the test format and administrative details.
2. The teachers must consider the basic problems and procedures of test administration.
   a. What types of considerations should be given to the testing environment and test security?
   b. Is it advantageous to have alternate forms of the same test on hand?
3. Differentiate between the procedures used to grade an essay test and those for an objective test.
4. Listed in the text are basic rules that professional testmakers follow in constructing various types of test items. Briefly summarize these basic procedures, being sure to list the key points.

Objective 4 Evaluate knowledge test items.

1. In constructing a test you can choose from several types of items. Each type has its advantages and disadvantages, as discussed in the text. Briefly summarize these advantages and disadvantages for each type of item listed below.
   a. true–false
   b. multiple choice
   c. matching
   d. completion
   e. short answer and essay
2. What's wrong with the following items on the handball test in Table 11.4?
   a. Item 5   b. Item 6   c. Item 11
3. What's wrong with the following two multiple-choice items?
   a. The score of a student on a multiple-choice test is the number of correct answers minus some fraction of the number wrong. On a 50-item, 5 response test a student had 30 items correct and omitted 5. The student's score should be (1) 26; (2) 27; (3) 28; (4) 29; (5) 30.
   b. When executing a setup in volleyball, contacting the ball with the palms is (1) illegal; (2) legal; (3) poor technique; (4) seldom done; (5) not encouraged.
4. What's wrong with the following two multiple-choice items that were together on an archery test?
   a. What is the term that designates a bow made of several pieces of wood and/or other materials? (1) Self-bow; (2) Laminated bow; (3) Multiple bow; (4) Chrysal bow.
   b. Which of the following is the smoothest shooting wood for a self-bow? (1) Birch; (2) Lemonwood; (3) Hickory; (4) Yew.

Objective 5 Analyze knowledge tests in terms of test reliability and item analysis.

1. Test reliability is useful for evaluating knowledge tests. Assume that a 50-item multiple-choice test was administered to 225 students. Calculate the test reliability from the following.
   a. A test mean of 37 and a standard deviation of 3.5.
   b. A correlation of .20 between scores on halves of the test.
2. It's difficult to write a reliable knowledge test on the first try. A test's quality will improve if an item analysis is conducted after the first administration, and the test is revised accordingly. An item analysis consists of item difficulty and item discrimination.
   a. Define item difficulty and interpret the following item difficulties: (1) .68 and (2) .21.
   b. Define item discrimination and interpret the following discrimination indices: (1) .45, (2) .15, (3) .03, and (4) −.67.
3. Outline the basic procedures involved in an item analysis.

ADDITIONAL LEARNING ACTIVITIES

1. Several of the books referenced in the text offer complete discussions of knowledge test construction and analysis. Read some of them to increase your familiarity with the subject.

2. Construct a knowledge test composed of some true–false and some multiple-choice items. Administer the test and do an item analysis.

3. As noted in the text, an item analysis can be obtained by using a standardized answer sheet and a test-scoring service on campus. Determine the type of standardized answer sheet to use and the procedures to follow in using your school's service.

BIBLIOGRAPHY

Ahmann, J. S., and M. D. Glock. 1981. *Evaluating Student Progress: Principles of Tests and Measurements.* 6th ed. Boston, Mass.: Allyn and Bacon.

Barrow, H. M., and R. McGee. 1979. *A Practical Approach to Measurement in Physical Education.* 3d ed. Philadelphia, Pa.: Lea & Febiger.

Bloom, B. S., ed. 1956. *Taxonomy of Educational Objectives: Cognitive Domain.* New York: McKay.

Bloom, B. S. et al. 1971. *Handbook on Formative and Summative Evaluation of Student Learning.* New York: McGraw-Hill.

Bloom, B. S. et al. 1981. *Evaluation to Improve Learning.* New York: McGraw-Hill.

Bolding, James. 1985. Statistics with Finesse. Fayetteville, Ark.

Dizney, H. 1971. *Classroom Evaluation for Teachers.* Dubuque, Iowa: Wm. C. Brown.

Ebel, R. L. 1979. *Essentials of Educational Measurement.* 3d ed. Englewood Cliffs, N.J.: Prentice-Hall.

Educational Testing Service. 1964. *Short-Cut Statistics for Teacher-made Tests.* 2d ed. Evaluation and Advisory Series. Princeton, N.J.

Ferguson, G. A. 1981. *Statistical Analysis in Psychology and Education.* 5th ed. New York: McGraw-Hill.

Gronlund, N. E. 1985. *Measurement and Evaluation in Teaching.* 5th ed. New York: Macmillan.

————. 1982. *Constructing Achievement Tests.* 3d ed. Englewood Cliffs, N.J.: Prentice-Hall.

Kraft, G. C. 1971. "The Construction and Standardization of a Wrestling Knowledge Test for College Men." P.E.D. dissertation, Indiana University, Bloomington, Ind.

Nunnally, J. C. 1978. *Psychometric Theory.* 2d ed. New York: McGraw-Hill.

Scott, M. G., and E. French. 1959. *Measurement and Evaluation in Physical Education.* Dubuque, Iowa: Wm. C. Brown.

Sheehan, T. J. 1971. *An Introduction to the Evaluation of Measurement Data in Physical Education.* Reading, Mass.: Addison-Wesley.

Thorndike, R. L., and E. Hagen. 1977. *Measurement and Evaluation in Psychology and Education.* 4th ed. New York: Wiley.

Measuring Psychological Dimensions of Physical Education and Exercise

12

Contents

Key Words

Objectives

Measuring psychological dimensions is of interest to physical education teachers, exercise specialists, and researchers. A major problem is that psychological dimensions are difficult to measure in a reliable and valid manner. In this chapter we are concerned with the problems of measuring psychological dimensions. We outline valid methods that can be used to measure attitude toward physical activity. Valid scales are provided for adults and children. As discussed in chapter 1, regular, vigorous exercise has a positive influence on cardiovascular health, but many who start exercise programs will quit. It has been discovered that compliance to an exercise program is related to self-motivation. Body image or one's feeling toward his or her body can be measured and is related to physical reality. Finally, we provide the Borg perceived exertion scale used to assess exercise intensity. This psychophysical scale can be used for fitness testing and prescribing exercise.

After reading this chapter, you should be able to:

1. Evaluate the validity of physical education attitude scales.
2. Outline the procedures used to develop semantic differential scales.
3. Describe the nature of the Self-Motivation Inventory (SMI).
4. Describe the nature of body image scales.
5. Evaluate the validity and value of the psychophysical rating of perceived exertion scales.

INTRODUCTION

Affective goals—interests, attitudes, appreciations, values, and emotional sets or biases (Krathwohl et al. 1964)—are not a new development in education. Three of the seven traditional objectives of secondary education are affective: worthy home membership, citizenship, and ethical character. In physical education, too, affective goals such as interpretive cortical development and emotional development have played a part in the general objectives of the field. A major problem is that affective behavior is not only difficult to measure, but also difficult to teach. As Ebel (1972) has noted:

> Feelings . . . cannot be passed along from teacher to learner in the way information is transmitted. Nor can the learner acquire them by pursuing them directly as he might acquire understanding by study. Feelings are almost always the consequence of something—of success, of failure, of duty done or duty ignored, of danger encountered or danger escaped.

Physical education and exercise programs can affect one's attitude; however, these psychological dimensions also motivate behavior. For example, attitudes and feelings may be predictive of how someone will react in various types of exercise programs. Psychological measurements are not only useful for evaluating the outcomes of a program, they can be used to predict what is likely to happen.

Teachers often use affective criteria to evaluate students. Participation, attitude, attendance, sportsmanship, effort, and dress are commonly used in grading. Unfortunately these factors are difficult to define and measure. Moreover, using them in grading often reflects discipline and punishment, more so than evaluation. The measurement of psychological dimensions, then, is more appropriate for gaining an understanding of individuals and examining the effects of a program than assessing student achievement.

MEASURING ATTITUDES

Much of the physical education research in the **affective domain** has focused on attitudes and their measurement. "Attitudes concern feelings about particular social objects—physical objects, types of people, particular persons, social institutions, government policies" (Nunnally 1978). Attitudes are generally measured with scales that require a student to agree or disagree with a series of statements, worded both positively and negatively. Several types of scales are used to determine a respondent's degree of affect. The most common offer two alternatives (Disagree-Agree) or five alternatives (Strongly Disagree, Disagree, Undecided, Agree, Strongly Agree). A 7-step scale can be created by adding very strongly disagree and very strongly agree to the 5-step scale.

Nunnally (1978) recommends the use of a graphic scale demarcated with numbers, like that shown below, to clearly convey degrees of feeling. A graphic scale also allows greater flexibility in selecting the number of steps offered.

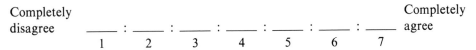

An attitude scale lists various statements that elicit one's feelings about the attitude object. The individual's attitude is determined by adding the scores of the statements. In scoring them, the positive statement scores are simply added as they appear; the point values for the negative statements, however, must be reversed by subtracting the score from the total number of levels plus 1. Using a 7-step scale like the one shown here, the marked score of a negative statement is subtracted from 8. For example, assume that a student marks a "2" next to the following statement: "If for any reason a few subjects must be dropped from the school program, physical education should be one of the subjects dropped." Notice that this is a negative statement in terms of an attitude toward physical education and that by scoring it with a low number the student is actually showing a positive attitude toward physical education. Using the 7-step scale, then, the marked negative score 2 becomes 6, correctly reflecting the student's positive attitude (i.e., $8 - 2 = 6$).

In contrast, assume that a student marks a 2 next to the following statement: "Participation in physical education activities establishes a more wholesome outlook on life." Because the statement is positive, a score of 2 on the 7-step scale indicates a negative attitude.

Validity of Attitude Scales

An **attitude** is a self-report measure and suffers from the weaknesses typical of this type of instrument. Its principal limitation is that it reflects only what individuals know and are willing to relate about their attitudes. Students who like a teacher tend to respond more favorably than their true attitudes may warrant; and often favorable responses on a self-report scale are accompanied by contrary behavior. For example, students may express a favorable attitude toward physical activity and fitness yet be inactive and unfit.

Because it is unrealistic to establish an attitude scale's concurrent validity with actual behavior, most scales claim face validity. This involves defining the content area to be measured and devising attitude statements that logically relate to it. Usually an individual's attitude toward the content area is represented by the total score on the scale. Unfortunately this has created a serious problem of validity on physical education attitude scales. If you sum all the scores on the scale, it is essential that all statements measure the same general attitude.

Kenyon (1968b) has demonstrated that attitude must be considered multidimensional. That is, there are several different types of attitudes toward an object and that the composite score must be split into several scores to validly measure each dimension. For example, assume that a scale measures two factors in a subject's attitude toward physical education: (1) the value of physical education for social development and (2) the value of physical education for health and fitness. By simply summing all the scores, two individuals with very different attitudes might receive the same total score. Yet, one may value physical education highly for social development; the other may consider it valueless for social development but important for health and fitness. Thus the total score is not a valid representation of the true feelings of either person.

Several physical education teachers and exercise specialists have published attitude scales. The targeted objects have included physical education (Adams 1963; Carr 1945; Edington 1968; Kappes 1954; Kneer 1971; Mercer 1971; O'Bryan and O'Bryan 1969; Penmon 1971; Seaman 1970; Wear 1951, 1955); athletic competition (Harris 1968; Lakie 1964; McCue 1953; McGee 1956; Scott 1953); creative dance (Allison 1976); and sportsmanship (Johnson 1969). These published scales report high reliability estimates (≥ 0.85), but their validity has not been established. In addition, the scales have not proved to be valuable to either the public school physical education teacher and exercise specialist or researcher. Many of these scales are fully published in other sources (Barrow and McGee 1971; Johnson and Nelson 1979; Neilson and Jensen 1972).

Attitude toward Physical Activity

Kenyon (1968a,b,c) developed a model by which attitudes toward physical activity (ATPA) could be measured. He used a model with six dimensions of physical activity as the foundation for the development of the scales. In the original study (1968c), semantic differential scales were used to measure attitude toward the six dimensions. (The semantic differential method is discussed later in this chapter.) That research showed that males and females responded differently on the six scales. Therefore, when the ATPA scales were constructed, different inventories were developed for men and women.

Kenyon's work is especially important. This was the first instrument that offered multidimensional scales. A considerable amount of construct validity research was conducted to define the six dimensions. A second major feature of the Kenyon scales was a departure from using physical education as the attitude object being measured. Instead, the scales measure the various ways and degrees that respondents value physical activity.

The ATPA scale for men consists of 59 items and the parallel scale for women consists of 54 items. Included next is a description of the six dimensions. The complete instrument with instructions is provided in other sources (Baumgartner and Jackson 1982; Kenyon 1968c; Safrit 1981). The six dimensions measured by the ATPA are:

Dimension 1. **Physical activity as a social experience.** Physical education teachers and exercise specialists maintain that physical activity meets certain social needs. Individuals who score high on this factor would value physical activities "whose primary purpose is to provide a medium for social intercourse, i.e., to meet new people and to perpetuate existing relationships." The internal consistency reliability estimates for this scale are about 0.70.

Dimension 2. **Physical activity for health and fitness.** The importance of physical activity for maintaining health and fitness is generally recognized. Individuals who score high on this factor would value physical activity for its "contribution to the improvement of one's health and fitness." The internal consistency reliability estimates are above 0.79.

Dimension 3. **Physical activity as the pursuit of vertigo.** The pursuit of vertigo is the search for excitement: "those physical experiences providing, at some risk to the participant, an element of thrill through the medium of speed, acceleration, sudden change of direction, exposure to dangerous situations, with the participant usually remaining in control." The internal consistency reliability estimates ranges are about 0.88 for men and 0.87 for women.

Dimension 4. **Physical activity as an aesthetic experience.** Many people believe that forms of physical activity have a certain beauty or artistry. People who score high on this factor perceive the aestheticism of physical activity. The internal consistency reliability estimates were 0.82 and 0.87 for men and women respectively.

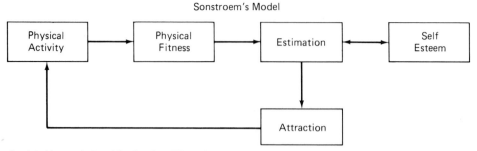

Figure 12.1 Sonstroem's 1975 psychological model for physical activity. (Source: Sonstroem, R. J. 1974. "Attitude Testing Examining Certain Psychological Correlates of Physical Activity." *Research Quarterly* 45:93–103.

Reprinted by permission of the American Alliance for Health, Physical Education, Recreation and Dance, Reston, Virginia.

Dimension 5. **Physical activity as catharsis.** Many believe that physical activity can provide a release from the frustrations of daily living. The validity of this factor has not been fully established. A negative relationship was reported between catharsis scores and preference for "physical activity for recreation and relaxation." The internal consistency reliability estimates were 0.77 and 0.79 for men and women respectively.

Dimension 6. **Physical activity as an ascetic experience.** Individuals who score high on this scale value the type of dedication involved in championship-level performance. Such activity demands long, strenuous, often painful training and competition, forcing a deferment of many of the gratifications of general physical activity. The internal consistency reliability estimates were 0.81 for men and ranged from 0.74 to 0.78 for women.

Physical Estimation and Attraction Scales

The Physical Estimation and Attraction Scales (PEAS) were developed by Sonstroem (1974, 1976, 1978). The PEAS is an attitude scale designed to explain motivation toward physical activity (see figure 12.1). It consists of 100 items to which the student responds either "True" or "False" as it pertains to him or her. Of the 100 items, 33 measure physical estimation; 56 measure physical attraction (including 2 items that pertain to the social aspects of physical activity); and 11 are neutral items that are not scored, but are included to hide the nature of the scale.

The *estimation* items ask students to affirm or deny their own physical characteristics, fitness, athletic ability, or potential in motor performance. Examples of items are as follows.

> I am stronger than a good many of my friends.
> It is difficult for me to catch a thrown ball.
> I am in better physical condition than most boys my age.
> Even with practice I doubt that I could learn to do a handstand well.

The *attraction* items ask students to affirm or deny their personal interests or likes for certain forms of physical activity. Sample items are:

Sports provide me with a welcome escape from present-day life.
I love to run.
Playing tennis appeals to me more than does golfing.
I enjoy the discipline of long and strenuous physical training.

Reliability and validity research has been conducted with boys in grades 8 through 12. Internal consistency reliability estimates of .87 and .89 and stability reliability estimates of .92 and .94 have been reported for the estimation and attraction scales, respectively (Sonstroem 1974, 1976).

A factor analysis of the PEAS isolated seven factors, but the estimation and attraction items were represented by a near-perfect separation from each other, allowing them to be combined into the two global scales (Sonstroem 1974). Physical attraction scores have been found to be correlated with self-report participation in sport-type activities (Neale et al. 1969; Sonstroem 1976). Both estimation and attraction scales were found to be correlated with height, weight, athletic experience, and various motor performance tests (Sonstroem 1974).

The estimation scale has also been found to relate to self-concept. Sonstroem (1976) showed a correlation between estimation scores and the Tennessee Self-Concept Scale, an important measure of mental health. This correlation allows the PEAS to be used to identify those students who have low self-esteem of their physical capabilities.

The research that led to the development of the PEAS was conducted with boys only. The 100-item scale is published in other sources (Baumgartner and Jackson 1982; Safrit 1981). More recently, Safrit, Wood and Dishman (1985) revised and shortened the scale for men and women. The scales, consisting of 23 items for men and 25 items for women, are provided in tables 12.1 and 12.2. The administrative and scoring methods of the adult form of the PEAS are:

The subject responds to the statements either "True" or "False." An answer key, provided with the scale, shows that response to each statement that reflects a positive attitude: True for a positive statement, False for a negative one. For every response consistent with the scoring key, the student receives 1 point. The score is the sum of all items, with a high total reflecting a positive attitude.

The PEAS is scored to obtain a separate point count for the estimation and attraction dimensions. Either of two methods can be used. Using the first method, the student's score in each classification is obtained by simply counting the number of correct responses, that is when the student responds "True" for a positive statement and "False" for a negative one. Using the second method, a 0 is awarded for each "False" response and a 1 for each "True" response. For negative statements keyed False, the obtained score is subtracted from 1 to determine the actual score (i.e., $0 - 1 = 1$).

Table 12.1
PEAS Attitude Questionnaire for Adult Males.

SCALE[1]	KEY[2]	PEAS ITEM
E	T	1. My body is strong and muscular compared to other men my age.
A	F	2. I like to be in sports that do not require a great amount of running.
E	F	3. I just do not have the coordination necessary to look like a graceful skier.
A	T	4. I would like to belong to some type of exercise group.
E	T	5. I am a good deal stronger than most of my friends.
E	F	6. Compared to other people I am somewhat clumsy.
E	T	7. I am stronger than a good many of my friends.
E	T	8. Most people I know think I have very good physical skills.
A	T	9. Sports provide me with a welcome escape from the pressures of life.
A	F	10. I prefer to watch an exciting basketball game to playing it myself.
A	T	11. I would enjoy participating in a vigorous weight-lifting program.
A	T	12. Long-distance running would seem to be an enjoyable activity.
A	F	13. When tensions are high, I prefer to lie down and rest rather than to absorb myself in physical activity.
E	T	14. I exhibit a fair amount of leadership in a sports situation.
E	F	15. I lack confidence in performing physical activities.
E	T	16. I'm a natural athlete.
A	T	17. I love to run.
A	T	18. Absorbing myself in a good sport activity provides an escape from the routine of a work day.
A	T	19. Exercise relieves me of emotional strain.
E	F	20. I often doubt my physical abilities.
E	F	21. I'm not very good at most physical skills.
E	F	22. Poor timing handicaps me in certain physical activities.
A	T	23. I enjoy the exhilarated feeling one gets after doing calisthenics.

[1]E is the physical estimation scale; A is the physical attraction scale.
[2]T when True is the correct response; F when False is the correct response.

The scale begins with an explanation of the procedure:

The statements below reflect certain attitudes and interests of persons. Read each statement and decide whether it is true or false as applied to you. Indicate your answer by blackening the appropriate space on the separate answer sheet. In some cases you may have difficulty deciding which response is best, but please make some decision and answer every item. Please do not make an attempt to be consistent in your answers during the test, but respond to each item individually. Even if an item asks about things you haven't experienced, answer it as best you can on the basis of what you have heard, seen, or read.

Table 12.2

PEAS Attitude Questionnaire for Adult Females.

SCALE[1]	KEY[2]	PEAS ITEM
E	T	1. My body is strong and muscular compared to other women my age.
A	F	2. I like to be in sports that do not require a great amount of running.
E	F	3. I just don't have the coordination necessary to look like a graceful skier.
E	T	4. I am a good deal stronger than most of my friends.
E	F	5. Compared to other people I am somewhat clumsy.
A	F	6. I like to engage in recreational exercise rather than in organized, competitive, athletics.
E	T	7. I am stronger than a good many of my friends.
E	T	8. Most people I know think I have very good physical skills.
A	F	9. I would rather walk than run through an open meadow or field.
A	T	10. Sports provide me with a welcome escape from the pressures of present-day life.
A	T	11. I like the rough and tumble of athletic competition.
A	T	12. I rather enjoy the physical risk involved when I play sports.
A	T	13. Long-distance running would seem to be an enjoyable activity.
A	F	14. I prefer not to participate in physical activities that involve risk of injury.
A	F	15. When tensions are high, I prefer to lie down and rest rather than to absorb myself in physical activity.
A	T	16. I would rather run in a track meet than play badminton.
E	T	17. I exhibit a fair amount of leadership in a sports situation.
E	F	18. I lack confidence in performing physical activities.
E	T	19. I'm a natural athlete.
A	T	20. I love to run.
A	T	21. Absorbing myself in a good sport activity provides an escape from the routine of a work day.
A	T	22. Exercise relieves me of emotional strain.
E	F	23. I often doubt my physical abilities.
E	F	24. I'm not very good at most physical skills.
E	F	25. Poor timing handicaps me in certain physical activities.

[1]E is the physical estimation scale; A is the physical attraction scale.
[2]T when True is the correct response; F when False is the correct response.

SEMANTIC DIFFERENTIAL SCALES

A flexible device for measuring attitude is the **semantic differential scale** (Osgood et al. 1957; Snider and Osgood 1969), which asks the subject to respond to bipolar adjectives. Because feelings about any experience (e.g., physical fitness) ordinarily are expressed with adjectives, the system uses logically opposing adjectives to measure attitude, as table 12.3 shows.

Table 12.3
Semantic Differential Scales Illustrated.*

PHYSICAL FITNESS		
(E) pleasant	____ : ____ : ____ : ____ : ____ : ____ : ____ : ____	unpleasant
(A) relaxed	____ : ____ : ____ : ____ : ____ : ____ : ____ : ____	tense
(A) passive	____ : ____ : ____ : ____ : ____ : ____ : ____ : ____	active
(E) unsuccessful	____ : ____ : ____ : ____ : ____ : ____ : ____ : ____	successful
(P) delicate	____ : ____ : ____ : ____ : ____ : ____ : ____ : ____	rugged
(A) fast	____ : ____ : ____ : ____ : ____ : ____ : ____ : ____	slow
(E) good	____ : ____ : ____ : ____ : ____ : ____ : ____ : ____	bad
(P) weak	____ : ____ : ____ : ____ : ____ : ____ : ____ : ____	strong
(A) lazy	____ : ____ : ____ : ____ : ____ : ____ : ____ : ____	busy
(P) heavy	____ : ____ : ____ : ____ : ____ : ____ : ____ : ____	light
(E) unfair	____ : ____ : ____ : ____ : ____ : ____ : ____ : ____	fair

*Note: Any concept may be used; the concept "Physical Fitness" is illustrated.

This approach is flexible in that many different concepts can be measured without revising the scale. In the table, for example, the object **"physical fitness"** could be replaced with **"swimming instruction," "physical education class," "teacher," "folk dancing," "interschool athletics,"** or some other concept, without revising the lists of adjectives.

Semantic Dimensions

Numerous studies using various concepts have concluded that three major factors are measured by the semantic differential technique: *evaluation, potency, and activity.* **Evaluation,** the most common factor, involves the degree of "goodness" the subject attributes to the concept in question. It is measured with the following types of bipolar adjectives:

good-bad valuable-worthless
new-old pleasant-unpleasant
healthy-unhealthy fair-unfair
beautiful-ugly successful-unsuccessful
fresh-stale honest-dishonest

The second factor, **potency,** involves the strength of the concept being rated. Among the bipolar adjectives that measure potency are the following:

deep-shallow	smooth-rough
heavy-light	dominant-submissive
strong-weak	hard-soft
full-empty	thick-thin
light-dark	rugged-delicate

The third factor, **activity,** is measured by adjective pairs that describe action, like the following:

excitable-calm	active-passive
stable-unstable	changeable-stable
happy-sad	lazy-busy
hot-cold	cheerful-sober
fast-slow	dynamic-static
tense-relaxed	

Construction of Semantic Differential Scales

The first step in constructing a semantic differential scale is the selection of concepts relevant to the general attitude being evaluated. The second step is the selection of appropriate adjective pairs. Two criteria determine the pairs: how well they represent the factor and their relevance to the concept in question.

Certain adjective pairs have proved valid for measuring the evaluation, potency, and activity factors. Because a minimum of three adjective pairs is suggested to measure a factor reliably, at least nine adjective pairs are needed to measure all three factors. Finally, the adjective pairs must be at the reading comprehension level of the students being evaluated and must relate logically to the concept in question.

The letters E, P, and A in table 12.3 identify the factor measured by the adjective pair. These letters would not appear on the instrument itself. The various adjective pairs are randomly ordered to prevent those relating to a single factor from being clustered. It is also essential that both negative and positive adjectives appear in each column.

Scoring and Interpretation

The respondent places a mark at that point between the two adjectives that best reflects his or her feeling about the concept. Adjective pairs in which the positive alternative appears on the left are scored by assigning the following values:

pleasant 7: 6: 5: 4: 3: 2: 1: unpleasant

In the opposite situation, the values are reversed:

unsuccessful 1: 2: 3: 4: 5: 6: 7: successful

The student's score on a factor is the sum for all bipolar adjectives that measure that factor. Thus if all three factors are measured, each scale yields three scores. Because these data can be analyzed statistically, it is possible to develop norms from them.

The semantic differential scale was designed to measure an individual's feelings about a given concept. Nunnally (1978) reports that the evaluation factor serves as a definition of attitude, so that responses to this factor's adjective pairs are excellent measures of verbalized attitudes. Often, just the evaluation factor is used. The potency and activity factors tend to be partly evaluative, but they also tend to reveal the respondent's interpretation of the concept's physical characteristics. Assume, for example, that two groups of students are administered a semantic differential scale for the concept "physical education class." One group is enrolled in a 12-week basic course in archery; the other, in a basic body-conditioning course that involves distance running and weight training. Although both groups might rate the physical education class "good" on the evaluation factor, their responses are likely to differ on the potency and activity factors. The archery students are apt to respond to the potency adjectives "delicate," and "weak." Students in the conditioning class are more likely to rate their class "strong" and "hard," and the activity adjectives "active," "fast," and "busy." Thus all three factors would be useful to determine how the students feel about the concept.

CHILDREN'S ATTITUDE TOWARD PHYSICAL ACTIVITY INVENTORY

The Children's Attitude Toward Physical Activity Inventory (CATPA-I) is a fine example of the use of semantic differential scales to measure attitude. The instrument was developed by Simon and Smoll (1974) to measure the six dimensions of physical activity (Kenyon 1968a,b) and has been expanded to seven dimensions. "Social Experience" was split in two dimensions: "Social Growth" and "Social Relations" (Schultz et al. 1985). The authors warn that the CATPA-I should not be used to evaluate individuals. Rather it is best used to assess groups and changes in group attitudes.

Administration and Scoring of CATPA-I

The CATPA-I dimensions are presented in figure 12.2. Two forms of the scale have been developed. One scale can be used with children in grades 7 through 11. A single-item scale using "happy faces" was developed for children in grade 3. Detailed scoring directions for both scales have been published (Schultz et al. 1985) and will not be duplicated here.

The scale format for grades 7 through 11, as shown in figure 12.3 presents the concept (dimension) being measured, followed by five semantic differential scales used by the student to evaluate the concept. It should be noted that word pairs 1, 4, and 5 are reverse ordered in comparison to word pairs 2 and 3. The value of "5" is assigned to the positive word. The score for each concept is the sum of the student's scores on the five scales. There is one exception; the health and fitness dimension is split into two scores. The word pairs "good-bad" and "of no use-useful" are summed to comprise

Figure 12.2 CATPA-1 inventory subdomain descriptions (Schultz, et al. 1985).

Physical activity for social growth
Taking part in physical activities that give you a chance to meet new people.

Physical activity to continue social relations
Taking part in physical activities that give you a chance to be with your friends.

Physical activity for health and fitness
Taking part in physical activities to make your health better and to get your body in better condition.

Physical activity as a thrill but involving some risk
Taking part in physical activities that could be dangerous because you move very fast and must change direction quickly.

Physical activity as the beauty in movement
Taking part in physical activities that have beautiful and graceful movements.

Physical activity for the release of tension
Taking part in physical activities to reduce stress or to get away from problems you might have.

Physical activity as long and hard training
Taking part in physical activities that have long and hard practices. To spend time in practice you need to give up other things you like to do.

Figure 12.3 Scale format for the Children's Attitude Toward Physical Activity Inventory (CATPA-1), grades 7 through 11. (Graphics by MacASJ)

How Do You Feel about the Idea Below?

Physical Activity for Social Growth
Taking Part in Physical Activities that Give You
a Chance to Meet New People

Always Think about the Idea in the Box

If You Do Not Understand This Idea, Mark This Box ☐
and Go to the Next Page.

1. Good					Bad
2. Of No Use					Useful
3. Not Pleasant					Pleasant
4. Nice					Awful
5. Happy					Sad

Figure 12.4 Grade 3 CATPA-1 Sample for the "Social Growth" dimension.

I Do Not Understand

the dimension "Health & Fitness: Value Dimension." This two-item sum is then multiplied by 2.5. The remaining three word pairs "not pleasant-pleasant," "nice-awful," "happy-sad" are summed to form the dimension "Health & Fitness: Enjoyment." This three-item sum is then multiplied by 1.67.

A form of the CATPA-I has been developed for children in grade 3. Because of reading difficulties, the concept being rated is read to the child who responds by marking the "happy faces" scale equivalent to the adjective pair "happy-sad." The sample scale is provided in figure 12.4. There is a single score for each dimension and it can range and "Ascetic" dimensions are not tested. Extensive research (Schultz et al. 1985) has been conducted to establish the normative data reproduced in table 12.4.

Reliability of CATPA-I

The internal consistency reliability estimates between 0.80 and 0.90 have been consistently found. Test-retest reliability calculated for each subdomain, separately by sex, ranged from 0.53 to 0.83 (median = 0.71) for a two-week interval and 0.46 to 0.78 (median = 0.67) for a nine-week interval. It is important to understand that we feel that the CATPA-I inventory has adequate reliability for evaluating group status and change and should not be used for individual assessment, especially with young children (Schultz et al. 1985).

The "Health & Fitness: Value" subdomain does have a reliability problem. The test-retest reliability for this dimension was only 0.20 and 0.52 for males and females respectively. This is because the mean is very close to the maximum possible value of 25 (see table 12.4). A factor analysis showed that the "Health & Fitness" subdomain needed to be divided into "Value" and "Enjoyment" dimensions, but this reduced the number of items for both. Additional research is needed to improve the reliability of this dimension. However, we do recommend including the scale item in its present form for use with normative comparative studies.

Table 12.4

Normative Data[1] for the CATPA-I.

SUBDOMAIN	GRADE 3		GRADE 7		GRADE 11	
	MALE	FEMALE	MALE	FEMALE	MALE	FEMALE
Social growth	4.7	4.8	21.4	22.1	21.4	22.6
	±0.6	±0.5	±3.0	±3.1	±3.0	±2.9
Social continuation	4.7	4.8	22.5	22.6	22.5	22.9
	±0.7	±0.4	±3.0	±3.3	±2.8	±2.9
Health & fitness: value[2]			23.9	24.2	24.0	24.2
			±2.2	±1.7	±2.1	±1.8
Health & fitness: enjoyment[3]	4.8	4.8	21.7	22.3	20.4	21.0
	±0.6	±0.5	±3.0	±2.8	±3.3	±3.7
Vertigo	3.5	3.2	18.9	17.6	20.1	16.6
	±1.2	±0.7	±5.4	±4.1	±5.5	±4.1
Aesthetic	3.9	4.6	18.0	20.8	16.4	20.1
	±1.2	±0.7	±5.4	±4.1	±5.5	±4.1
Catharsis			21.0	21.3	20.7	21.6
			±3.6	±3.7	±3.9	±3.5
Ascetic			18.9	18.4	16.9	15.8
			±4.4	±4.5	±4.5	±5.0
Number tested	576	515	517	498	430	434

[1]Means and standard deviations (±).
[2]Score equals the sum of (good-bad & of no use-useful) × 2.5.
[3]Score equals the sum of (not pleasant-pleasant, nice-awful & happy-sad) × 1.67.

Use with Adults

Kenyon (1968c) used semantic differential scales in his original research on the six dimensions of attitude toward physical activity. Schultz and Smoll (1974) administered their adult scale and the CATPA-I to 220 college students. They reported that the scales were equivalent, and that the CATPA-I could be used reliably with adults. One advantage of using the CATPA-I with adults is that the same instrument can be administered to both men and women and it takes less time to administer.

SELF-MOTIVATION AND ADHERENCE TO EXERCISE

Approximately 50% of adults who begin a health-related exercise program will quit within the first six months. There are several different factors that affect exercise adherence (Dishman 1984), but it has been shown that people who score high on a paper-and-pencil test of self-motivation (SMI) have consistently been observed to stay with exercise for a longer period of time than those who score low (Dishman 1984).

Dishman and Ickes (1981) developed a Self-Motivation Inventory (SMI) designed to measure potential exercise compliance. The 40-item scale consists of 19 positively keyed and 21 negatively keyed statements. The subject is instructed to read each item and select an alternative that best describes how characteristic the statement is when applied to the subject. The alternatives are:

1. Extremely uncharacteristic of me.
2. Somewhat uncharacteristic of me.
3. Neither characteristic nor uncharacteristic of me.
4. Somewhat characteristic of me.
5. Extremely characteristic of me.

This is a Likert-type scale scored with a value of "1" for alternative A to "5" for alternative E. The subject's score is the sum of all items after the negative statements have been corrected. The scale, item polarity, and scoring method are provided in table 12.5.

Using a sample of over 400 undergraduate men and women, the internal consistency reliability was estimated to be 0.91. Stability reliability has been found to be high, exceeding 0.86 (Dishman and Ickes 1981). The SMI was found to be the best psychological instrument for discriminating among those who would and would not adhere to exercise in athletic and adult fitness environments. A major finding in the adult fitness setting was that the decision to adhere or to drop out of a prescribed exercise program appears to be largely dependent upon body composition, and the behavioral disposition of self motivation (Dishman, Ickes and Morgan 1980). This suggests that both biological and psychological variables need to be considered when studying the complex problem of exercise adherence.

BODY IMAGE

Body image is both the attitude one has toward the body and the way in which one's own body is perceived. Psychologists have discovered that an individual's feelings about his or her body reflect anxieties and values.

Body image can be measured with projective tests and self-report inventories. Projective tests require a psychologist for scoring and interpretation, which makes them inappropriate for use by physical education teachers and exercise specialists. The most common self-report inventory used is the **Body Cathexis Scale** (Secord and Jourard 1953), which focuses on those aspects of body image related to an individual's satisfaction or dissatisfaction with different parts of the body and its functions. The scale assumes the following:

1. Feelings about the body are related to feelings about the self.
2. Negative feelings about the body are related to anxiety about pain, disease, or bodily injury.
3. Negative feelings about the body are associated with insecurity.

Table 12.5
Self-Motivation and Adherence to Exercise Inventory.

KEY[1]	SMI STATEMENT
−	1. I'm not very good at committing myself to do things.
−	2. Whenever I get bored with projects I start, I drop them to do something else.
+	3. I can persevere at stressful tasks, even when they are physically tiring or painful.
−	4. If something gets to be too much of an effort to do, I'm likely to just forget it.
+	5. I'm really concerned about developing and maintaining self-discipline.
+	6. I'm good at keeping promises, especially the ones I make to myself.
−	7. I don't work any harder than I have to.
−	8. I seldom work to my full capacity.
−	9. I'm just not the goal-setting type.
+	10. When I take on a difficult job, I make a point of sticking with it until it's completed.
+	11. I'm willing to work for things I want as long as it's not a big hassle for me.
+	12. I have a lot of self-motivation.
+	13. I'm good at making decisions and standing by them.
−	14. I generally take the path of least resistance.
−	15. I get discouraged easily.
+	16. If I tell somebody I'll do something, you can depend on it being done.
−	17. I don't like to overextend myself.
−	18. I'm basically lazy.
+	19. I have a very hard-driving, aggressive personality.
+	20. I work harder than most of my friends.
+	21. I can persist in spite of pain or discomfort.
+	22. I like to set goals and work toward them.
+	23. Sometimes I push myself harder than I should.
−	24. I tend to be overly apathetic.
+	25. I seldom if ever let myself down.
−	26. I'm not very reliable.
+	27. I like to take on jobs that challenge me.
−	28. I change my mind about things quite easily.
+	29. I have a lot of will power.
−	30. I'm not likely to put myself out if I don't have to.
−	31. Things just don't matter much to me.
−	32. I avoid stressful situations.
+	33. I often work to the point of exhaustion.
−	34. I don't impose much structure on my activities.
−	35. I never force myself to do things I don't feel like doing.
−	36. It takes a lot to get me going.
+	37. Whenever I reach a goal, I set a higher one.
+	38. I can persist in spite of failure.
+	39. I have a strong desire to achieve.
−	40. I don't have much self-discipline.

[1]Scoring: the point values for each response are: (1) extremely uncharacteristic of me; (2) somewhat uncharacteristic of me; (3) neither characteristic nor uncharacteristic of me; (4) somewhat characteristic of me; (5) extremely characteristic of me. Items negatively keyed are scored $6 - X$, where X is the assigned value (1 to 5). SMI score is the sum of the 40 items.

The Secord and Jourard Body Cathexis Scale consists of 46 words describing body parts (hair, hands, ankles) or functions (keenness of senses, digestion, sex drive). The respondent considers each body part or function and rates his or her feelings using the following scale:

1. Wish strongly a change could somehow be made.
2. Don't like, but can put up with.
3. Have no particular feelings one way or the other.
4. Am satisfied.
5. Consider myself fortunate.

The subject's score is the sum of the responses to each item. A high score represents a positive body image. Secord and Jourard (1953) estimated the internal consistency reliability of the scale at .88 and .92 for men and women respectively.

Langston (1979) administered the scale to three different groups of college women and factor analyzed each set of responses. She found a general factor related to perceived size and body weight, and several additional factors related to other body parts and functions. She also found that the body image factor related to perceived size and weight was significantly correlated (-0.47) with the percentage body fat measured with skinfolds (Jackson, Pollock and Ward 1980). This showed that women who had the highest levels of body fat were the most dissatisfied. Langston used ten items to measure body weight and size factors.

1. Figure
2. Waist
3. Size of abdomen
4. Thighs
5. Hips
6. Weight
7. Appetite
8. Shape of legs
9. Upper arms
10. Body build

All 46 items of the Secord-Jourard scale appear in the original source (1953). If you use the entire instrument, you will need the help of a psychologist for valid interpretation of the results. We recommend, instead, that a body image inventory be restricted to those items related to the size and weight factors.

A NOTE OF CAUTION

Paper-and-pencil psychological inventories are commercially available or readily obtainable from books. These tests are easy to administer and many can be scored objectively, even by someone with no professional education. This can pose a real threat of misuse, with potentially damaging results to the individual tested.

No measuring instruments are more threatening and potentially harmful than personality instruments administered and interpreted by untrained persons. Although standardized paper-and-pencil inventories are used by government, industry, and education, neither the purpose of nor the necessity for such evaluations has been clearly demonstrated. The use of psychological testing in general raises serious issues, some of which are discussed by Arthur Miller in *The Assault on Privacy:*

> Because of the intensely personal nature of many aptitude, intelligence and psychological tests, the entire subject is in the vortex of the current debate over the right of the citizen to be free from intrusion by any form of physical, mental or informational surveillance. . . .
>
> Psychological evaluation may be a valuable aide-de-camp for many purposes, especially in diagnosing and treating various mental disorders. But because of its propensity to extract highly personal information from people and encourage others to make decisions on the basis of data that are capable of interpretation only by specially trained professionals, without any real assurance that the resulting evaluations will be accurate, psychological testing requires special precautions (1971, pp. 90, 97–98).

Personality inventories and behavior rating scales are especially open for concern. You can clarify the legitimacy of using these psychological instruments by asking these two simple questions. (1) Do you have a need and right to secure such data? (2) Are you capable of validly interpreting and using the test results in a way that will help the student? The use of psychological data by untrained persons can lead to erroneous decisions. The problems associated with psychological instruments are not inherent to the instruments themselves; many reliable, valid instruments have been developed. The danger is in the way they are used. It is difficult to conceive any valid purpose for the use of personality inventories and behavior rating scales by public school physical education teachers and many exercise science researchers. You need to seek advice and direction from trained professionals.

PSYCHOPHYSICAL RATINGS

Individuals are able to perceive and rate strain during physical exercise. The **rating of perceived exertion** (RPE) is a valid and simple method for determining exercise intensity. The RPE scale was developed by the Swedish psychologist Gunnar Borg (1962, 1978, 1982) and is used extensively for exercise testing and exercise prescription. It is Borg's opinion (1982) that perceived exertion is the single best indicator of the degree of physical strain because the overall perception rating integrates many sources of information elicited from the peripheral working muscles and joints, central cardiovascular and respiratory functions, and central nervous system. "All these signals, perceptions and experiences are integrated into a configuration of a 'Gestalt' perceived exertion" (Borg 1982).

Borg has published two RPE scales. The first is a category scale with values ranging from 6 to 20 which assumes a linear relation between exercise heart rate and RPE rating (Borg 1962). The second scale was developed to be consistent with the non-linearity of psychophysical ratings (Borg 1978, 1982).

Borg's Category RPE Scale

The Borg category RPE scale increases linearly with exercise heart rate. The scale has been shown to correlate between 0.80 and 0.90 with heart rate, $\dot{V}O_2$, and lactic acid accumulation (Borg 1982). The scale values range from 6 to 20. This was proposed to denote heart rates ranging from 60 to 200 $b \cdot min^{-1}$. For example, a rating of 15 was meant to correspond with a heart rate of 150 $b \cdot min^{-1}$. Borg did not intend that the heart rate-RPE rating be taken literally, because many factors can affect exercise heart rate. Age, exercise mode, environment (e.g., heat, humidity), anxiety and drugs (e.g., beta blocker drugs that are used to control high blood pressure) all can affect exercise heart rate. The influence of aging on RPE is illustrated in figure 12.5.

The RPE scale (figure 12.6) is very popular and very easy to use. Research by Pollock, Jackson and Foster (In Press) shows that the scale provides an excellent estimate of exercise intensity and can be used to prescribe exercise and regulate exercise testing. RPE values of 12 and 13 represent exercise intensities at about 60% of heart rate reserve[1] and $\dot{V}O_2$ Max. Ratings of 16 and 17 correspond to about 90% of heart rate reserve and 85% of $\dot{V}O_2$ Max. These ranges have been valid for both leg and arm exercise and subjects on beta blocker drugs that lowered $\dot{V}O_2$ Max and maximal heart rate (Pollock, Jackson and Foster, In Press). The instructions used for the RPE scale during exercise testing are:[2]

> You are now going to take part in a graded exercise test. You will be walking or running on the treadmill while we are measuring various physiological functions. We also want you to try to estimate how hard you feel the work is; that is, we want you to rate the degree of perceived exertion you feel. By perceived exertion we mean the total amount of exertion and physical fatigue. Don't concern yourself with any one factor such as leg pain, shortness of breath, or work grade, but try to concentrate on your total, inner feeling of exertion. Try to estimate as honestly and objectively as possible. Don't underestimate the degree of exertion you feel, but don't overestimate it either. Just try to estimate as accurately as possible.

Borg's Category Scale with Ratio Properties

It has been shown that psychophysical ratings are not linear (Borg 1978). This has led to the development of a category scale with ratio properties (see figure 12.7). The new scale is not only suitable for rating exercise intensity, but other subjective symptoms such as breathing difficulties, aches, and pains (Borg 1982). The scale has also been found to be useful for judging the difficulty of work tasks, such as carrying 50-pound bags or shoveling coal (Jackson and Osburn 1983).

---

1. % Heart Rate Reserve = [X(Max HR − Rest HR)] + Rest HR, where X is the desired percentage and HR is heart rate (Pollock, Wilmore and Fox 1984).

2. Instructions developed by William Morgan Ed.D., University of Wisconsin, Madison, WI. Published with permission.

Figure 12.5 Graph shows the change in the heart rate and RPE ratings with the decrease in maximal heart rate associated with aging. RPE ratings ≥18 are typically an indication that maximal heart rate has been reached. (Graphics by MacASJ)

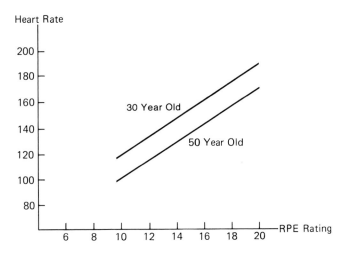

Figure 12.6 The 15-grade category scale for rating perceived exertion (RPE scale). (Source: Dr. G. Borg, Department of Psychology, University of Stockholm, Stockholm, Sweden.)

6	
7	Very, very light
8	
9	Very light
10	
11	Fairly light
12	
13	Somewhat hard
14	
15	Hard
16	
17	Very hard
18	
19	Very, very hard
20	

Figure 12.7 Borg's category scale with ratio properties (RPE). (Source: Dr. G. Borg, Department of Psychology, University of Stockholm, Stockholm, Sweden.)

0	Nothing at all	
0.5	Extremely weak	(just noticeable)
1	Very weak	
2	Weak	(light)
3	Moderate	
4	Somewhat strong	
5	Strong	(heavy)
6		
7	Very strong	
8		
9		
10	Extremely strong	(almost max)
•	Maximal	

The feature of the ratio RPE scale is that numbers anchor verbal expressions that are simple and understandable for use by most people. The expressions are placed in the correct position on the ratio scale where they belong according to their quantitative meaning. A simple range of 0 to 10 is used to anchor the verbal expressions. It is permissible to use fractional ratings (e.g., 2.5 or 3.8) and values above 10. The ratio RPE scale has been shown to correlate highly with both blood lactate and muscle lactate level, which are the biochemical markers of cardiorespiratory and muscle fatigue (Borg 1982).

The ratio properties of the new RPE scale result in non-linear scale. This is shown in figure 12.8. Ratings of between 4 and 7 are consistent with an exercise intensity window between 50 and 85% of $\dot{V}O_2$ Max. The instructions[3] for the ratio RPE scale are:

We would like you to estimate the exertion you feel by using this scale.

The scale starts with 0 **"Nothing at All"** and goes on to 10, **"Extremely strong"**—that is **"almost max"** you should say 10. For most people this corresponds to the hardest physical exercise they have ever done, as for example the exertion you feel when you run as fast as you can for several minutes till you are completely exhausted, or when you are lifting or carrying something which is so heavy that you nearly can't make it.—Maybe it is possible to imagine exertion or pain that is even stronger, and that is why the maximum value is somewhat over 10. If you feel the exertion or pain to be stronger than **"Extremely strong"** ("almost max") you can use a number that is over 10, for example 11, 13 or an even higher number.

3. Personal communication with Dr. Gunnar Borg, Department of Psychology, University of Stockholm, Stockholm, Sweden, November 1985.

Cognitive and affective testing

Figure 12.8 Relation between ratio RPE scale and exercise intensity (% $\dot{V}O_2$ Max). (Graphics by MacASJ)

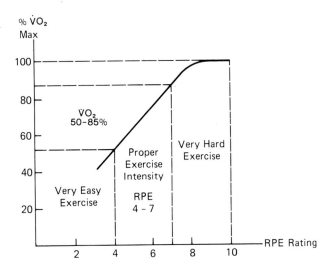

If the exertion is **"Very weak"** you should answer with the number 1. If it is only **"Moderate"** you say 3 and so on. Feel free to use any number you wish on the scale, as well as half values as for example 1.5 or decimals as 0.8, 1.7 or 2.3. It is important that you give the answer that you yourself feel to be right and not that which you think you ought to give. Answer as honestly as possible and try neither to overestimate nor underestimate the degree of exertion that you feel.

Uses of Psychophysical Ratings

Psychophysical ratings are used for many different purposes. Some of the more common uses are:

1. **Exercise testing.** The RPE scale is used to judge exercise intensity when administering a graded exercise test on a treadmill or cycle ergometer. The objective of an exercise test is to slowly and systematically increase the exercise intensity from submaximal levels to maximal. Often, percent of maximal heart rate is used to quantify exercise intensity. But, in most instances, maximal heart rate is not known and must be estimated from age (Max HR = 220 − age).

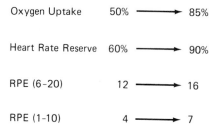

Oxygen Uptake	50% $\longrightarrow$ 85%
Heart Rate Reserve	60% $\longrightarrow$ 90%
RPE (6–20)	12 $\longrightarrow$ 16
RPE (1–10)	4 $\longrightarrow$ 7

However, there tend to be errors in this estimate (± 10 to 15 b·min^{-1}). The RPE ratings are used to determine when a subject is reaching his or her maximal tolerance (≥ 17 on the 6-20 RPE scale and ≥ 7 on the 1–10 RPE scale).

2. **Exercise prescription.** Percentage of $\dot{V}O_2$ Max is the most valid method of prescribing exercise, but this is typically not known. Therefore, percentage of maximal heart rate reserve is recommended. A difficulty with this method is that maximal heart rate must be known. It has been found that RPE ratings (see figure 12.9) are an excellent method of selecting the proper intensity for exercise and can be used to supplement heart rate estimates (Pollock, Jackson and Foster, In Press).

3. **Quantification of energy expenditure.** Many adult fitness programs seek to quantify energy expended through exercise which is often expressed in kilocalories. This can be done very accurately with aerobic exercise modes such as walking, jogging, or cycling, because external work can be quantified (see chapter 8). There are other popular aerobic exercise modes such as aerobic dancing or playing tennis where external work cannot be quantified. Individuals vary in the intensity to which they exercise. The computer logging system at the Tenneco Health and Fitness center and the CSI logging computer program (see chapter 1) both use psychophysical ratings to estimate exercise intensity when external work cannot be measured. To illustrate, more calories would be expended when playing tennis at an RPE rating of 7, Very strong, as compared to a rating of 3, Moderate.

SUMMARY

Most of the published physical education attitude scales were developed on the assumption that a single factor was being measured. Scales that gauge attitudes toward physical education report high reliability, but their construct validity—what factors are measured—is yet to be determined. The Kenyon and Sonstroem scales are multidimensional instruments that have established construct validity.

Semantic differential scales that use bipolar adjectives to measure feelings about concepts are a flexible technique for measuring attitude. The factors measured with these scales are evaluation, potency, and activity. The CATPA-I uses the semantic differential method to measure children's attitudes toward physical activity. Scales are available for very young children as well as older children, and it has been shown they can be used with adults.

Many adults who start exercise programs will quit. It has been shown that adherence to exercise is related to self-motivation as measured by the SMI. Body image scales measure attitude about the body. Research has shown one general factor (related to body size and weight) that itself relates to the subject's percentage body fat.

The psychophysical RPE scale has been shown to be useful for determining exercise intensity. Borg has developed two scales, either of which can be used for: (1) exercise testing; (2) exercise prescription; and (3) quantifying the energy expended through exercise.

Because of the technical and potentially damaging nature of many types of psychological measurement, personality data and behavior ratings should be used only when trained psychologists or competent school counselors participate in the evaluation effort.

FORMATIVE EVALUATION OF OBJECTIVES

Objective 1   Evaluate the validity of physical education attitude scales.

1. Attitude scales are self-report instruments designed to measure attitudes by the way one responds to statements. In terms of validity, what is the basic weakness of this type of measurement?
2. Kenyon's attitude scale offers a valid method of measuring attitudes toward physical activity. The scale measures six different types, or dimensions, of attitudes. Identify and briefly describe each.
3. The Physical Estimation and Attraction Scales were developed to explain motivation toward physical activity. Identify and briefly describe each scale.

Objective 2   Outline the procedures used to develop semantic differential scales.

1. Semantic differential scales provide a flexible method for evaluating attitudes. Research indicates that three basic factors are measured with these scales: evaluation, potency, and activity. Define these concepts and list three adjective pairs that measure each of them.
2. Outline the process you would follow to develop semantic differential scales.
3. Outline the procedure for scoring semantic differential scales that would calculate a score for each of the three factors.
4. What are the concepts being measured by the Children's Attitude Toward Physical Activity Inventory? What semantic dimensions are being used with the CATPA-I?

Objective 3 Describe the nature of the Self-Motivation Inventory (SMI).

1. What does the SMI predict?
2. How might one use the SMI?

Objective 4 Describe the nature of body image scales.

1. What is the definition of body image?
2. How is body image measured?
3. Is body image related to one's physical characteristics?

Objective 5 Evaluate the validity and value of the psychophysical rating of perceived exertion scales.

1. What are the similarities and differences between the two Borg RPE scales?
2. How can the RPE scales be used?
3. In order to improve aerobic fitness, one should exercise at what level on the RPE scales?

ADDITIONAL LEARNING ACTIVITIES

1. Several studies have sought to determine the correlation between attitude and physical fitness. Review the articles published in the *Research Quarterly* to determine whether a positive attitude is associated with a high level of physical fitness. How was attitude measured? How was physical fitness measured?

2. Select either the CATPA-I or the PEAS and administer it to a group of students. Can you develop a microcomputer or SPSS program to score the scale?

3. Select a concept (e.g., physical fitness, athletics, aerobic dance) of particular interest to you and develop semantic differential scales to measure attitude toward the concept. Administer the scales to various groups and determine whether the groups' means differ. You might use as your groups male and female physical education majors. You may want to consult a basic statistics text to determine whether the means between the groups are significantly different.

4. Administer the CATPA-I to a group of children. Be sure to read the proper instructions (Schultz et al. 1985) and administer either the scale for 3rd graders or the scale for older children.

5. What are the reasons adults do not continue exercise programs? Conduct a review of the exercise science literature to answer this question. A good place to start is to conduct a computer search for research published by R. K. Dishman.

6. Learn how to use either of the Borg RPE scales. This can be accomplished several ways. If you take a maximal exercise test, relate the submaximal ratings with percent of heart rate reserve, or $\dot{V}O_2$ Max. A second method is to exercise at an exercise intensity that will produce an aerobic training effect and rate this intensity by either the 6 to 20 or 1 to 10 scale.

BIBLIOGRAPHY

Adams, R. S. 1963. "Two Scales for Measuring Attitude Toward Physical Education." *Research Quarterly* 34:91–94.

Allison, P. R. 1976. "An Instrument to Measure Creative Dance Attitude of Grade Five Children." Ph.D. dissertation, University of Alabama. Tuscaloosa, Ala.

Barrow, H. M., and R. McGee. 1971. *A Practical Approach to Measurement in Physical Education.* 2d ed. Philadelphia, Pa.: Lea & Febiger.

Baumgartner, T. A., and A. S. Jackson. 1982. *Measurement for Evaluation in Physical Education.* 2d ed. Dubuque, Ia.: Wm. C. Brown.

Borg, G. 1962. *Physical Performance and Perceived Exertion.* Lund, Sweden: Gleerup.

Borg, G. 1977. *Physical Work and Effort.* (Proceedings of the First International Symposium, Wenner-Gren Center, Stockholm, Sweden) Perguman Press: Oxford.

Borg, G. 1978. "Subjective Effort in Relation to Physical Performance and Working Capacity." In *Psychology: From Research to Practice.* H. L. Pick Jr. (ed.). Plenum Publishing: New York, 333–61.

Borg, G. 1982. "Psychophysical Bases of Perceived Exertion." *Medicine and Science in Sports and Exercise.* 14:377–81.

Carr, M. G. 1945. "The Relationship Between Success in Physical Education and Selected Attitudes Expressed in High School Freshmen Girls." *Research Quarterly* 16:176–91.

Dishman, R. K. 1984. "Chapter 29: Motivation and Exercise Adherence." In J. Silva and R. Weinberg (eds.) *Psychological Foundations of Sport.* Champaign, Ill.: Human Kinetics.

Dishman, R. K., and W. Ickes. 1981. "Self-Motivation and Adherence to Therapeutic Exercise." *Journal of Behavioral Medicine.* 4:421–36.

Dishman, R. K., W. Ickes, and W. P. Morgan. 1980. "Self-Motivation and Adherence to Habitual Physical Activity." *Journal of Applied Social Psychology.* 10:115–32.

Ebel, R. L. 1972. "What are Schools For?" *Phi Delta Kappan* 54:3–7.

Edington, C. W. 1968. "Development of an Attitude Scale to Measure Attitudes of High School Freshmen Boys Toward Physical Education." *Research Quarterly* 39:505–12.

Harris, B. 1968. "Attitudes of Students Toward Women's Athletic Competition." *Research Quarterly* 39:278–84.

Jackson, A. S., and H. G. Osburn. 1983. "Validity of Isometric Strength Tests for Predicting Performance in Underground Coal Mining Tasks." Employment Services, Shell Oil Company, Houston, Tx.

Jackson, A. S., M. L. Pollock, and A. Ward. 1980. "Generalized Equations for Predicting Body Density of Women." *Medicine and Science in Sports.* 12:175–82.

Johnson, M. L. 1969. "Construction of Sportsmanship Attitude Scales." *Research Quarterly* 40:312–16.

Johnson, B. L., and J. K. Nelson. 1979. *Practical Measurements for Evaluation in Physical Education.* Minneapolis, Minn.: Burgess.

Kappes, E. E. 1954. "Inventory to Determine Attitudes of College Women Toward Physical Education and Student Services of the Physical Education Department." *Research Quarterly* 25:429–38.

Kenyon, G. S. 1968a. "A Conceptual Model for Characterizing Physical Activity." *Research Quarterly* 39:96–105.

Kenyon, G. S. 1968b. "Six Scales for Assessing Attitude Toward Physical Activity." *Research Quarterly* 39:566–74.

Kenyon, G. S. 1968c. "Values Held for Physical Activity by Selected Urban Secondary School Students in Canada, Australia, England, and the United States." Washington, D.C.: U.S. Office of Education.

Kneer, M. E. 1971. "Kneer Attitude Inventory and Diagnostic Statements." In *A Practical Approach to Measurement in Physical Education* H. M. Barrow and R. McGee (ed.), 435–39. Philadelphia, Pa.: Lea & Febiger.

Krathwohl, D. R. et al. 1964. *Taxonomy of Education Objectives: Handbook II: The Affective Domain.* New York: McKay.

Lakie, W. L. 1964. "Expressed Attitudes of Various Groups of Athletes Toward Athletic Competition." *Research Quarterly* 35:497–503.

Langston, K. F. 1979. "The Relationship Between Body Image and Body Composition of College Females." Ed.D. dissertation, University of Houston, Houston, Tx.

McCue, B. F. 1953. "Constructing an Instrument for Evaluating Attitudes Toward Intensive Competition in Team Games." *Research Quarterly* 24:205–10.

McGee, R. 1956. "Comparison of Attitudes Toward Intensive Competition for High School Girls." *Research Quarterly.* 27:60–73.

Mercer, E. L. 1971. "Mercer Attitude Scale." In *A Practical Approach to Measurement in Physical Education* H. M. Barrow and R. McGee. (ed.), 431–34. Philadelphia, Pa.: Lea & Febiger.

Neale, D. C., et al. 1969. "Physical Fitness, Self-Esteem and Attitudes Toward Physical Activity." *Research Quarterly* 40:743–49.

Neilson, N. P., and C. R. Jensen. 1972. *Measurement and Statistics in Physical Education* Belmont, Calif.: Wadsworth.

Nunnally, J. C. 1978. *Psychometric Theory.* New York: McGraw-Hill. 590.

Osgood, C. et al. 1957. *The Measurement of Meaning.* Urbana, Ill.: University of Illinois Press.

Penmon, M. M. 1971. "Penmon Physical Education Attitude Inventory for Inner-City Junior High School Girls." In *A Practical Approach to Measurement in Physical Education* H. M. Barrow and R. McGee (ed.), 445–47. Philadelphia, Pa.: Lea & Febiger.

Pollock, M. L., A. S. Jackson, and C. Foster. In Press. "The Use of the Perception Scale for Exercise Prescription." *Physical Work and Effort.* (Proceedings of the Second International Symposium, Wenner-Gren Center, Stockholm, Sweden, Editor. G. Borg.)

Pollock, M. L., J. H. Wilmore, and S. M. Fox III. 1984. *Exercise in Health and Disease.* W. B. Saunders: Philadelphia, Pa.

Safrit, M. J. 1981. *Evaluation in Physical Education.* Englewood Cliffs, N.J.: Prentice-Hall.

Safrit, M. J., T. M. Wood, and R. K. Dishman. 1985. "The Factorial Validity of the Physical Estimation and Attraction Scales for Adults." *Journal of Sport Psychology.* 7:166–90.

Schultz, R. W., F. L. Smoll, F. A. Carre, and R. E. Mosher. 1985. "Inventories and Norms for Children's Attitudes Toward Physical Activity." *Research Quarterly for Exercise and Sport.* 56:256–65.

Scott, P. M. 1953. "Attitudes Toward Athletic Competition in Elementary School." *Research Quarterly* 24:353–61.

Seaman, J. A. 1970. "Attitudes of Physically Handicapped Children Toward Physical Education." *Research Quarterly* 41:439–45.

Secord, P. F., and S. M. Jourard. 1953. "The Appraisal of Body Cathexis: Body Cathexis and the Self." *Journal of Consulting Psychology* 17:343–47.

Simon, J. A., and F. L. Smoll. 1974. "An Instrument for Assessing Children's Attitudes Toward Physical Education." *Research Quarterly* 45:407–15.

Snider, J. G., and C. E. Osgood (eds.), 1969. *Semantic Differential Technique: A Sourcebook.* Chicago, Ill.: Aldine.

Sonstroem, R. J. 1974. "Attitude Testing Examining Certain Psychological Correlates of Physical Activity." *Research Quarterly* 45:93–103.

Sonstroem, R. J., 1976. "The Validity of Self-Perceptions Regarding Physical and Athletic Ability." *Medicine and Science in Sports* 8:126–32.

Sonstroem, R. J., 1978. "Physical Estimation and Attraction Scales: Rationale and Research." *Medicine and Science in Sports* 10:97–102.

Wear, C. L. 1951. "The Evaluation of Attitude Toward Physical Activity as an Activity Course." *Research Quarterly* 22:114–126.

Wear, C. L., 1955. "Construction of Equivalent Forms of an Attitude Scale." *Research Quarterly* 26:113–19.

APPENDIX

References for Selected Sport Skill Tests

Most of the sources listed are available to public school teachers.

Archery

AAHPER. 1967. *Archery Skills Test Manual.* Washington, D.C.

Hyde, E. I. 1937. "An Achievement Scale in Archery." *Research Quarterly* 8:109–16.

Shifflett, B., and B. Schuman. 1982. "A Criterion-Referenced Test for Archery." *Research Quarterly* 53:330–35.

Zabick, R. M., and A. S. Jackson. 1969. "Reliability of Archery Achievement." *Research Quarterly* 40:254–55.

Badminton

French, E., and E. Stalter. 1949. "Study of Skill Tests in Badminton for College Women." *Research Quarterly* 20:257–72.

Lockhart, A., and F. A. McPherson. 1949. "The Development of a Test of Badminton Playing Ability." *Research Quarterly* 20:402–05.

Miller, F. A. 1951. "A Badminton Wall Volley Test." *Research Quarterly* 22:208–13.

Thorpe, J., and C. West. 1969. "A Test of Game Sense in Badminton." *Perceptual and Motor Skills* 27:159–69.

Basketball

AAHPERD. 1984. *Basketball Skills Test Manual for Boys and Girls.* Reston, VA.

Gaunt, S. 1979. "Factor Structure of Basketball Playing Ability." P.E.D. dissertation, Indiana University, Bloomington, Ind.

Hopkins, D. R. 1977. "Factor Analysis of Selected Basketball Skill Tests." *Research Quarterly* 48:535–40.

Knox, R. D. 1973. "Knox Basketball Test." In *Measurement in Physical Education* D. K. Mathews, ed. Philadelphia, Pa.: Saunders.

Lehsten, C. 1973. "Lehsten Basketball Test." In *Measurement in Physical Education* D. K. Mathews, ed. Philadelphia, Pa.: Saunders.

Miller, W. K. 1954. "Achievement Levels in Basketball Skills for Women Physical Education Majors." *Research Quarterly* 25:450–55.

Stroup, F. 1955. "Game Results as a Criterion for Validating Basketball Skill Tests." *Research Quarterly* 26:353–57.

Bowling

Martin, J. L. 1960. "Bowling Norms for College Men and Women." *Research Quarterly* 31:113–16.

Martin, J., and J. Keogh. 1964. "Bowling Norms for College Students in Elective Physical Education Classes." *Research Quarterly* 25:325–27.

Olson, J. K., and M. R. Liba. 1967. "A Device for Evaluating Spot Bowling Ability." *Research Quarterly* 38:193–210.

Phillips, M., and D. Summers. 1950. "Bowling Norms and Learning Curves for College Women." *Research Quarterly* 21:377–85.

Schunk, C. 1969. *Test Questions for Bowling.* Philadelphia, Pa.: Saunders.

Fencing

Cooper, C. K. 1979. "Cooper Fencing Rating Scale." In *A Practical Approach to Measurement in Physical Education* 3d ed. H. M. Barrow and R. McGee. Philadelphia, Pa.: Lea & Febiger.

Field Hockey

Chapman, N. 1982. "Chapman Ball Control Test-Field Hockey." *Research Quarterly* 53:239–42.

Friedel, J. E. 1979. "Friedel Field Hockey Test." In *A Practical Approach to Measurement in Physical Education* 3d ed. H. M. Barrow and R. McGee. Philadelphia, Pa.: Lea & Febiger.

Schmithals, M., and E. French. 1940. "Achievement Tests in Field Hockey for College Women." *Research Quarterly* 9:84–92.

Strait, C. J. 1979. "Strait's Field Hockey Rating Scale." In *A Practical Approach to Measurement in Physical Education* 3d ed. H. M. Barrow and R. McGee. Philadelphia, Pa.: Lea & Febiger.

Football

AAHPER. 1966. *Football Skills Test Manual.* Washington, D.C.

Borleske, S. E. 1979. "Borleske Touch Football Test." In *A Practical Approach to Measurement in Physical Education* 3d ed. H. M. Barrow and R. McGee. Philadelphia, Pa.: Lea & Febiger.

Golf

Brown, H. S. 1969. "A Test Battery for Evaluating Golf Skills." *Texas Association for Health, Physical Education and Recreation Journal* May, 4–5, 28–29.

Nelson, J. K. 1979. "The Nelson Pitching Test." In *Practical Measurement for Evaluation in Physical Education* 3d ed. B. L. Johnson and J. K. Nelson. Minneapolis, Minn.: Burgess.

Rowlands, D. J. 1979. "Rowlands Golf Skills Test Battery." In *A Practical Approach to Measurement in Physical Education* 3d ed. H. M. Barrow and R. McGee. Philadelphia, Pa.: Lea & Febiger.

Shick, J., and N. Berg. 1983. "Indoor Golf Skill Test for Junior High School Boys." *Research Quarterly* 54:75–78.

West, C., and J. Thorpe. 1968. "Construction and Validation of an Eight-Iron Approach Test." *Research Quarterly* 49:1115–20.

Gymnastics

Ellenbrand, D. A. 1973. "A Gymnastics Skills Test for College Women." Master's thesis, Indiana University, Bloomington, Ind.

Faulkner, J., and N. Loken. 1967. "Objectivity of Judging at the National Collegiate Athletic Association Gymnastic Meet: A Ten-Year Follow-Up Study." *Research Quarterly* 33:485–86.

Johnson, M. 1971. "Objectivity of Judging at the National Collegiate Athletic Association Gymnastic Meet: A Twenty-Year Follow-Up Study." *Research Quarterly* 42:454–55.

Sheer, J. 1973. "Effect of Placement in the Order of Competition on Scores of Nebraska High School Students." *Research Quarterly* 44:79–85.

Handball

Cornish, C. 1949. "A Study of Measurement of Ability in Handball." *Research Quarterly* 20:215–22.

Montoye, H. J., and J. Brotzmann. 1951. "An Investigation of the Validity of Using the Results of a Doubles Tournament as a Measure of Handball Ability." *Research Quarterly* 22:214–18.

Pennington, G. G. et al. 1967. "A Measure of Handball Ability." *Research Quarterly* 38:247–53.

Lacrosse

Ennis, C. D. 1979. "Ennis Multi-Skill Test in Lacrosse." In *A Practical Approach to Measurement in Physical Education* 3d ed. H. M. Barrow and R. McGee. Philadelphia, Pa.: Lea & Febiger.

Hodges, C. V. 1979. "Hodges Lacrosse Rating Scale." In *A Practical Approach to Measurement in Physical Education* 3d ed. H. M. Barrow and R. McGee. Philadelphia, Pa.: Lea & Febiger.

Racquetball

Hensley, L. et al. 1979. "A Racquetball Skills Test." *Research Quarterly* 50:114–18.

Karpman, M. and L. Isaacs. 1979. "An Improved Racquetball Skills Test." *Research Quarterly* 50:526–27.

Poteat, C. 1983. "A Skills Test Battery to Measure Overall Racquetball Playing Ability." Ed.D. dissertation, University of Georgia, Athens, Ga.

Soccer

Bailey, C. I., and F. L. Teller. 1969. *Test Questions for Soccer.* Philadelphia, Pa.: Saunders.

Johnson, J. R. 1979. "Johnson Soccer Test." In *Practical Measurements for Evaluation in Physical Education* 3d ed. B. L. Johnson and J. K. Nelson. Minneapolis, Minn.: Burgess.

McDonald, L. G. 1979. "McDonald Soccer Test." In *Practical Measurements for Evaluation in Physical Education* 3d ed. B. L. Johnson and J. K. Nelson. Minneapolis, Minn.: Burgess.

Mitchell, J. R. 1979. "Mitchell Modification of the McDonald Soccer Skill Test." In *A Practical Approach to Measurement in Physical Education* 3d ed. H. M. Barrow and R. McGee. Philadelphia, Pa.: Lea & Febiger.

Smith, G. 1979. "Smith Kick-up to Self Test." In *A Practical Approach to Measurement in Physical Education* 3d ed. H. M. Barrow and R. McGee. Philadelphia, Pa.: Lea & Febiger.

Tomlinson, R. 1964. "Soccer Skill Test." In *Soccer-Speedball Guide—July 1964–July 1966.* Washington, D.C.: AAHPER.

Warner, G. F. H. 1950. "Warner Soccer Test." *Newsletter of the National Soccer Coaches Association of America* 6:13–22.

Whitney, A. H., and H. Chapin. 1946. "Soccer Skill Testing for Girls." In *Soccer-Speedball Guide—July 1946–July 1948.* Washington, D.C.: AAHPER.

Yeagley, J. 1972. "Soccer Skills Test." Unpublished paper, Indiana University, Bloomington, Ind.

Softball

AAHPER. 1967a. *Softball Skills Test Manual for Boys.* Washington, D.C.

———. 1967b. *Softball Skills Test Manual for Girls.* Washington, D.C.

Broer, M. R. 1958. "Reliability of Certain Skill Tests for Junior High School Girls." *Research Quarterly* 29:139–43.

Central Association for Physical Education of College Women. 1959. "Fielding Test." In *Measurement and Evaluation in Physical Education* M. G. Scott and E. French. Dubuque, Iowa: Wm. C. Brown.

Davis, R. 1959. "The Development of an Objective Softball Batting Test for College Women." In *Measurement and Evaluation in Physical Education* M. G. Scott and E. French. Dubuque, Iowa: Wm. C. Brown.

Fox, M. G., and O. G. Young. 1954. "A Test of Softball Batting Ability." *Research Quarterly* 25:26–27.

Safrit, M. J., and A. Pavis. 1969. "Overarm Throw Skill Testing." In *Selected Softball Articles* J. Felshin and C. O'Brien (ed.), Washington, D.C.: AAHPER.

Scott, M. G., and E. French. 1959. "Softball Repeated Throws Test." In *Measurement and Evaluation in Physical Education* M. G. Scott and E. French. Dubuque, Iowa: Wm. C. Brown.

Shick, J. 1970. "Battery of Defensive Softball Skills Tests for College Women." *Research Quarterly* 41:82–87.

Swimming

Bennett, L. M. 1942. "A Test of Diving for Use in Beginning Classes." *Research Quarterly* 13:109–15.

Fox, M. G. 1957. "Swimming Power Test." *Research Quarterly* 28:233–37.

Hewitt, J. E. 1948. "Swimming Achievement Scales for College Men." *Research Quarterly* 19:282–89.

———. 1949. "Achievement Scale Scores for High School Swimming." *Research Quarterly* 20:170–79.

Jackson, A. S., and J. Pettinger. 1969. "The Development and Discriminant Analysis of Swimming Profiles of College Men." *Proceedings of 72d Annual Meeting* 104–10. National College Physical Education Association for Men.

Rosentswieg, J. 1968. "A Revision of the Power Swimming Test." *Research Quarterly* 39:818–19.

Tennis

Avery, C., P. Richardson, and A. Jackson. 1979. "A Practical Tennis Serve Test: Measurement of Skill Under Simulated Game Conditions." *Research Quarterly* 50:554–64.

Broer, M. R., and D. M. Miller. 1950. "Achievement Tests for Beginning and Intermediate Tennis." *Research Quarterly* 21:303–13.

Cobane, E. 1962. "Test for the Service." In *Tennis and Badminton Guide—June 1962–June 1964*. Washington, D.C.: AAHPER.

DiGennaro, J. 1969. "Construction of Forehand Drive, Backhand Drive, and Service Tennis Tests." *Research Quarterly* 40:496–501.

Dyer, J. T. 1935. "The Backboard Test of Tennis Ability." *Research Quarterly* 6(supp.):63–74.

———. 1938. "Revision of the Backboard Test of Tennis Ability." *Research Quarterly* 9:25–31.

Edwards, J. 1979. "Wisconsin Wall Test for Serve." In *A Practical Approach to Measurement in Physical Education* 3d ed. H. M. Barrow and R. McGee. Philadelphia, Pa.: Lea & Febiger.

Felshin, J., and E. Spencer. 1963. "Evaluation Procedures for Tennis." In *Selected Tennis and Badminton Articles* D. Davis (ed.), Washington, D.C.: AAHPER.

Hensley, L. 1979. "A Factor Analysis of Selected Tennis Skill Tests." Ed.D. dissertation, University of Georgia, Athens, Ga.

Hewitt, J. E. 1965. "Revision of the Dyer Backboard Tennis Test." *Research Quarterly* 36:153–57.

———. 1966. "Hewitt's Tennis Achievement Test." *Research Quarterly* 37:231–37.

———. 1968. "Classification Tests in Tennis." *Research Quarterly* 39:552–55.

Johnson, J. 1957. "Tennis Serve of Advanced Women Players." *Research Quarterly* 28:123–31.

———. 1963. "Tennis Knowledge Test." In *Selected Tennis and Badminton Articles* D. Davis (ed.), Washington, D.C.: AAHPER.

Kemp, J., and M. F. Vincent. 1968. "Kemp-Vincent Rally Test of Tennis Skill." *Research Quarterly* 39:1000–04.

Purcell, K. 1981. "A Tennis Forehand-Backhand Drive Skill Test Which Measures Ball Control and Stroke Firmness." *Research Quarterly* 52:238–45.

Scott, M. G., and E. French. 1959. "Scott-French Revision of the Dyer Wallboard Test." In *Measurement and Evaluation in Physical Education* M. G. Scott and E. French (ed.), 222–25. Dubuque, Iowa: Wm. C. Brown.

Shephard, G. J. 1972. "The Tennis Drive Skills Test." In *Tennis-Badminton-Squash Guide—1972–74*. Washington, D.C.: AAHPER Publications.

Timmer, K. L. 1965. "A Tennis Skill Test to Determine Accuracy in Playing Ability." Master's Thesis, Springfield College, Springfield, Mass.

Volleyball

AAHPER. 1967. Volleyball Skills Test Manual. Washington, D.C.

Broer, M. A. 1958. "Reliability of Certain Skill Tests for Junior High School Girls." *Research Quarterly* 29:139–45.

Clifton, M. 1962. "Single Hit Volley Test for Women's Volleyball." *Research Quarterly* 33:208–11.

Cunningham, P., and J. Garrison. 1968. "High Wall Volley Test for Women." *Research Quarterly* 39:486–90.

Kronquist, R. A., and W. B. Brumbach. 1968. "A Modification of the Brady Volleyball Skill Test for High School Boys." *Research Quarterly* 39:116–20.

Liba, M. R., and M. R. Stauff. 1963. "A Test for the Volleyball Pass." *Research Quarterly* 34:56–63.

Lopez, D. 1957. "Serve Test." In *Volleyball Guide—July 1957–July 1959*. Washington, D.C.: AAHPER.

Mohr, D. R., and M. J. Haverstick. 1955. "Repeated Volleys Tests for Women's Volleyball." *Research Quarterly* 26:179–84.

Petry, K. 1979. "Petry Volleyball Serve Test." In *A Practical Approach to Measurement in Physical Education* 3d ed. H. M. Barrow and R. McGee. Philadelphia, Pa.: Lea & Febiger.

Snavely, M. 1960. "Volleyball Skill Tests for Girls." In *Selected Volleyball Articles* A. Lockhart (ed.), Washington, D.C.: AAHPER.

Thorpe, J., and C. West. 1967. "A Volleyball Skills Chart with Attainment Levels for Selected Skills." In *Volleyball Guide—July 1967–July 1969*. Washington, D.C.: AAHPER.

Watkins, A. 1960. "Skill Testing for Large Groups." In *Selected Volleyball Articles* A. Lockhart (ed.), Washington, D.C.: AAHPER.

Wrestling

Sickels, W. L. 1979. "Sickels Amateur Wrestling Ability Rating Form." In *A Practical Approach to Measurement in Physical Education* 3d ed. H. M. Barrow and R. McGee. Philadelphia, Pa.: Lea & Febiger.

GLOSSARY

Absolute endurance test: An endurance test that uses a weight load constant for all subjects tested

Accuracy test: A test in which the student projects an object at a target for a score

Activity factor: A semantic differential factor that involves motion; measured by adjective pairs such as fast-slow and excitable-calm

Aerobic power: The amount of work one can perform; normally determined by the rate at which oxygen is utilized during exercise. At exhausting levels of work, maximal aerobic power and maximal oxygen uptake are interchangeable

Affective domain: A system used to categorize affective behavior to help teachers formulate affective objectives

Agility: The ability to change the direction of the body or body parts rapidly

Analysis of variance: A statistical technique for dividing total test variance into parts

Attitude: A feeling about a particular object, such as a physical object, a certain type of person, or a social institution

Balance: The ability to maintain body position

Basic physical ability: A trait, more general than a psychomotor skill, that provides the foundation for the successful execution of many different psychomotor skills; also called *psychomotor ability*

Bell-shaped curve: See *normal curve*

Bicycle ergometer: A machine that regulates the work performed while cycling; workload can be accurately altered by increasing or decreasing the resistance on the ergometer

Body Cathexis Scale: A self-report scale used to measure body image

Body composition: The classification of the body into fat weight and lean body weight

Body density: A value used to calculate percentage body fat; calculated with the underwater weighing method, it is determined by the following formula:

$$\text{Body density} = \frac{\text{weight}}{\text{volume}}$$

Body image: The attitude one has toward the body and the manner in which one's own body is perceived

Cardiorespiratory function: The ability to continue work; depends on efficient respiratory (lungs) and cardiovascular (heart and blood vessels) systems

Central tendency: The tendency of scores to be concentrated at certain points; measures of central tendency include the mode, median, and mean

Change score: See *difference score*

Classification index: A mathematical formula used to combine age, height, and weight to predict excellence in the ability to perform a wide variety of motor tasks

Completion item: A knowledge test item that asks students to complete or fill in the blanks in the item

Composite standard score criterion: The sum of standard scores of several different tests; used as a criterion for validating individual test items of general motor ability tests

Concurrent validity: The degree to which scores on a test correlate with scores on an accepted standard

Construct validity: The degree to which a test measures some part of a whole skill or an abstract trait

Content validity: A validity technique based on the subjectively established fact that the test measures the wanted content; also called *face validity*

Continuous scores: Scores with the potential for an infinite number of values

Correlation: A mathematical technique for determining the relationship between two sets of scores

Correlation coefficient: A value between −1.0 and 1.0 that indicates the degree of relationship between two sets of measures

Criterion-referenced standard: A standard that explicitly defines the task to be achieved

Criterion score: An individual's recorded score; the score used to represent a person's ability

Curvilinear relationship: A relationship between two measures that is best described by a curved line

Data: A set of scores

Desired weight: A body weight determined for a specified percent body fat

Difference score: The difference between the scores of a person at the beginning and end of a teaching unit; also called *change score* or *improvement score*

Discrete scores: Scores with the potential for a limited number of specific values

Discrimination index: A value indicating how well a knowledge test item differentiates between the high- and low-scoring students

Discrimination test: A test designed to identify different ability groups based on test scores

Distance run tests: Running tests used to evaluate cardiorespiratory function; normally of 1 mile or longer in distance, or 9 minutes or more in duration

Dynamic balance: The ability to maintain equilibrium while moving from one point to another

Dynamometer: An instrument used to measure strength by recording force exerted

Energy cost of exercise: The amount of energy expended for aerobic exercise. It is typically expressed as kilocalories per minute or some form of steady-state VO_2

Essay test: A test that asks students to respond to questions in writing

Evaluation: A decision-making process that involves (1) the collection of suitable data (measurement); (2) a judgment of the value of these data against a standard; and (3) a decision based on these data and standards

Evaluation factor: A semantic differential factor that involves a degree of "goodness;" measured by adjective pairs such as good-bad and beautiful-ugly

Face validity: See *content validity*

Fat weight: In measuring a person's body, the weight, in pounds, that is body fat

Final grade: The grade assigned at the end of a unit or grading period

Flexibility: The range of motion about a joint

Formative evaluation: The process of judging achievement at the formative stages of instruction, to determine the degree of mastery and to pinpoint that part of the task yet to be mastered; often used as a form of student feedback

Frequency polygon: A graph of a frequency distribution with scores along the horizontal axis and frequencies along the vertical axis

General motor ability: The theory that individuals who are highly skilled on one motor task will be highly skilled on other motor tasks

General objectives: Objectives that define educational concerns in global terms

Goniometer: An instrument used to measure the flexibility of a joint

Health-related physical fitness: A scientific body of knowledge that links the positive effects of regular, vigorous exercise with the prevention of degenerative disease

Heart rate: The number of times per minute that the heart beats or ejects blood. Heart rate increases with exercise or increased workload

Improvement score: See *difference score*

Instructional objectives: Objectives that make clear to both students and teacher what is to be accomplished, including: (1) the task to be learned; (2) the conditions under which the task will be performed; and (3) the criterion-referenced standard that will be used to evaluate the achievement

Internal consistency reliability coefficient: The degree to which an individual's scores are unchanged within a day

Interval scores: Scores that have a common unit of measure between consecutive scores but not a true zero point

Intraclass correlation coefficient: A correlation coefficient that estimates test reliability; derived with analysis of variance

Isokinetic strength: Strength that is measured by recording the force exerted through the entire range of motion

Isometric strength: Strength that is measured by recording the force exerted against an immovable object

Isotonic strength: Strength that involves moving an object through a defined range of motion; often measured with a 1-RM test, which is the maximum weight that can be lifted during 1 repetition

Item: A question or statement on a knowledge test; one of the tests in a battery of tests

Item analysis: An item-by-item analysis of a knowledge test to identify valid questions

Item difficulty: The difficulty of a knowledge test item; the percentage of a group that correctly answers an item

Kiloponds (kp): The unit of measurement used to quantify resistance on a bicycle ergometer; kp represents the unit of resistance in kilograms

Kinesthesis: The ability to perceive the body's position in space and the relationship of its parts

Knowledge test: A paper-and-pencil test that measures knowledge

kpm: The unit of measurement used to quantify the intensity of exercise on a bicycle ergometer. This is a product of the resistance in kp and the rpm. $VO_2(ml \cdot min^{-1})$ can be determined from kpm

Lean body weight: The weight of the body with the fat tissue removed; also called *fat-free weight*

Linear relationship: A relationship between two measures that is best described by a straight line

Mainframe computer: A large computer that is located at a central site such as a large company or university

Mass testability: The degree to which a large number of students can be tested in a short period of time

Mastery test: A test that determines how well students have mastered the material

Matching item: A knowledge test item that asks students to match columns of questions and answers

Maximal oxygen uptake ($\dot{V}O_2$ Max): The amount of oxygen one utilizes during exhausting work; the criterion for validating field tests of cardiorespiratory function

Maximal stress test: A diagnostic medical test that systematically increases exercise to determine physical working capacity and changes in exercise blood pressure and the exercise EKG. This is an initial screening test for cardiovascular disease

Mean: A measure of central tendency, or average; obtained by dividing the sum of the scores by the number of scores

Median: A measure of central tendency, or average; the score below which 50% of a group scored

MET: A unit used to quantify oxygen consumption. A MET equals a VO_2 of 3.5 $ml \cdot kg \cdot ^{-1}min^{-1}$ and is the oxygen uptake at rest

Mode: A measure of central tendency, or average; the most frequent score for a group of people

Motor-driven treadmill: A machine used to regulate work while running or walking; workload is increased by increasing its speed or elevation

Motor educability: The ability to learn motor skills easily and well

Motor fitness: A category of the psychomotor domain that is defined by the components strength, power, and endurance

Motor skill: The level of proficiency achieved on a specific motor task; also called *psychomotor skill*

Multiple-choice item: A knowledge test item that asks students to select an answer from three or more provided answers

Multiple correlation: The correlation between a criterion and two or more predictors that have been mathematically combined to maximize the correlation between the criterion and predictors

Multiple regression: The prediction of the value of one measure based on the performance of two or more other measures; also called *multiple prediction*

Multi-stage exercise test: A method used to estimate VO_2 Max from two or more submaximal workloads and heart rates

Muscular endurance: The ability to persist in physical activity or to resist muscular fatigue

Muscular power: Traditionally, the maximum force released in the shortest possible time; more appropriately, the rate at which work can be performed by involved muscle groups

Muscular strength: The maximum force a muscle group can exert during a brief period of time

Natural breaks: A grading technique that assigns grades by breaks in the distribution of scores

Nominal scores: Scores that cannot be ordered from best to worst

Normal curve: A symmetrical curve centered around a point that is the mean score; also called *bell-shaped curve*

Norm-referenced standard: A standard that judges a performance in relation to the performance of other members of a well-defined group

Norms: Performance standards based on the scores of a group of people

Obesity: The excessive accumulation of fat weight

Objective evaluation: A test in which the student's performance yields a score without a value judgment by the scorer (see *subjective measure*); also a test that asks students to respond to questions by selecting one of two or more provided answers

Objectivity: The degree to which multiple scorers agree on the magnitude of scores

Ordinal scores: Scores that can be ordered from best to worst but that do not have a common unit of measure

Overweight: That weight that exceeds the "normal" weight based on sex, height, and frame size

Percentage body fat: That proportion of total weight that is fat weight

Percentile: A score that has a specified percentage of scores below it

Percentile rank: A score value that indicates the percentage of scores below a given score

Personality: The general psychological construct that explains an individual's motives; can be measured by many different psychological instruments

Posttest procedures: The analysis and recording of test scores

Potency factor: A semantic differential factor that involves the strength of the concept; measured by adjective pairs such as strong-weak and smooth-rough

Power: The rate at which work is performed; calculated with the following formula:

$$\text{Power} = \frac{\text{work}}{\text{time}}$$

Prediction: The estimating of the value of one measure based on the value of one or more other measures; see also *multiple regression*

Predictive validity: The degree to which one measure can predict performance on a second measure

Pretest planning: The procedures that must be followed before a test is administered; includes knowing the test, developing test procedures and directions, and preparing the students and the testing facility

Program evaluation: Determination of the extent to which a program achieves the standards and objectives set forth for it

Psychomotor ability: See *basic ability*

Psychomotor skill: See *motor skill*

Psychophysical: A term used to describe scientific methods used to integrate psychological and physical parameters. An example of a psychophysical test is Borg's RPE scale

Range: A measure of the variability or heterogeneity in a set of scores; the difference between the largest and smallest scores

Rank-order grading: A grading technique that assigns grades after ordering the scores

Rating of perceived exertion scale (RPE): A scale developed by Dr. G. Borg of Stockholm, Sweden that is used to rate the intensity of exercise

Rating scale: A set of standards or a checklist for measuring performance subjectively

Ratio scores: Scores that have a common unit of measure between consecutive scores and a true zero point

Reliability: The degree of consistency with which a test measures what it measures

Residual lung volume: The amount of air remaining in the lungs after a full expiration. This measurement is used when estimating body density by the underwater weighing method

Semantic differential scales: A method of measuring attitude by having someone react toward an object or concept by responding to bipolar adjective pairs

Short-answer item: A knowledge test item that requires the student to write a short answer to the item

Simple frequency distribution: An ordered listing of a set of scores, complete with the frequency of each score

Simple prediction (regression): The prediction of the value of one measure using another measure

Single-stage exercise test: A method used to estimate VO_2 Max from one submaximal workload and heart rate

Skewed curve: A curve that is not symmetrical; see *normal curve*

Skill test: A test that measures physical skill, not fitness

Skinfold calipers: An instrument used to measure the thickness of subcutaneous fat tissue

Skinfold fat: The subcutaneous fat tissue that lies just below the skin

Specificity of motor skill: A theory, used to explain the learning of a motor skill, that one must acquire a specific neurological pattern to execute a motor skill efficiently

Speed: The ability to move rapidly

Split-half method: The procedure used to correlate two parts of a test administered within a day; used to establish internal consistency reliability

Stability reliability coefficient: The degree to which an individual's scores are unchanged from day to day

Standard deviation: A measure of the variability, or spread, of a set of scores around the mean

Standard error of measurement: The amount of error expected in a measured score

Standard error of prediction: A value indicating the amount of error to expect in a predicted score

Standard error of the mean: A value indicating the amount of variation to expect in the mean if subjects were tested again

Standard score: A test score calculated using the test mean and standard deviation; usually expressed as a z or T

Static balance: The ability to maintain total body equilibrium while standing in one spot

Step tests: Tests used to evaluate cardiorespiratory function by having the subject repeatedly step up and down from a bench at a prescribed cadence

Subjective evaluation: A test in which the scorer must make a value judgment before assigning the performer a score

Submaximal exercise test: A test used to evaluate cardiorespiratory function by measuring one's ability to perform work at submaximal workloads and then predicting VO_2 Max from submaximal heart rate

Summative evaluation: The process of judging achievement at the end of instruction

Taxonomy: A classification for parts of a system; the educational taxonomies for the cognitive, affective, and psychomotor domains are used to formulate educational objectives

Teacher's standards: A grading technique that compares students' scores to a standard developed by the teacher

Tensiometer: An instrument used to measure strength by recording the tension applied to a steel cable

Test-retest method: The procedure used to correlate the scores of a test administered on each of two days; used to establish stability reliability

True–false item: A knowledge test item that asks students to answer either True or False

T-score: A standard score with mean 50 and standard deviation 10

Underwater weighing: Determining a person's body weight in water; one method used to determine body density

Useful score: A test score that can be used immediately or inserted into a formula with little effort

Validity: The degree to which a test measures what it is supposed to measure

Variability: The degree of heterogeneity in a set of scores; measures include the range and the standard deviation

$\dot{V}O_2$ Max: See *maximal oxygen uptake*

Wall volley tests: Skill test that requires the student to repeatedly volley a ball against a wall

Watts: Units of measurement used to quantify work intensity on a bicycle ergometer

Work: The ability to apply force over distance; calculated with the following formula:

$$\text{Work} = (\text{force})(\text{distance})$$

Workload: In exercise tests, workload defines the intensity of work. The workload of a bicycle ergometer is increased by adding resistance to the flywheel, which makes the ergometer harder to pedal. The workload of a motor-driven treadmill is increased by increasing the speed and/or elevation of the treadmill

z score: A standard score with mean 0 and standard deviation 1

Author/Source Index

Subject Index

Graphing of scores, 36–40,
63–65
Grip strength test, 184, 191
Group position, measurement
of, 47–53
Gymnastics skill test, 354–56,
448
for college women, 354–56

H

Handball skill test, 357–58,
448
Handicapped student, 166
Heading test (soccer skill),
362–63
Health and fitness industry, 9
Health-related physical
fitness, 454
Health-related physical
fitness test, 20, 202,
285–305, 316
Heart rate, 219, 236, 435,
436–37, 454
Height, age-height-weight
classification index,
174–75
Help desk, computer center,
21
Hewitt Service Placement
Test, 368–69, 372
Hewitt Speed-of-Service Test,
369–70, 372
Hip circumference, 260

I

Improvement:
of grading, 136–37
of program, 156–57
Improvement score, *see*
Difference score
Incomplete grade, 154
Instructional objective, 454
Instructional program, *see*
Program
Instruments, *see*
Measurement
instruments
Interclass correlation
coefficient, 92
Internal-consistency
reliability, 91–92, 114,
405, 454
Interval score, 35, 454
Intraclass correlation
coefficient, 92–97,
100–12, 114, 454
Isokinetic strength, 186, 454
Isometric strength, 182, 184,
190–93, 454
Isotonic strength, 186, 454
Item, *see* Test item

J

Job-related physical abilities
test, 181–82
Juggling test (soccer skill),
363
Jumping ability, measurement
of, 206–7

K

Kemp-Vincent Rally Test
(tennis skill), 367–68,
372
Kick for power or distance
test, 330, 373
Kickoff test (football skill), 346
Kilopound, 226, 454
Kilopound meters per minute,
226, 454
Kinesthesis, 454
Kinesthetic perception,
measurement of,
211–12
Knowledge:
evaluation of, 379–414
levels of, 380–82
Knowledge test, 454
administration of, 401
analysis of, 403–13
construction of, 384–400
difficulty of, 405
discrimination, 383–84
essay, *see* Essay test
grading of, 401–3
mastery, 383–84
objective, *see* Objective
test
reliability of, 405–7
revision of, 413
types of, 387–93
variability of, 405
See also Specific sports
Kraus-Weber Test, 210, 278
Kuder-Richardson reliability,
383, 406–7

L

Lacrosse skill test, 448
Lat pull test, 186–90
Layover answer key, 403–4
Lean body weight, 243, 262,
454
Learning, master, 8
Leg extension test, 193, 195,
196
Leg power measurement of,
198–99
Leg press test, 193, 196
Leg strength, measurement
of, 185, 187, 193–95
Leighton Flexometer, 208
Leptokurtic curve, 39, 41
Letter-grade norms, 145–46

Letter grading, 136, 383–84
assignment of final grade,
148–54
Linear relationship, 68, 454
Line of best fit, 64
Little League elbow, 207
Low back problems, 287, 312

M

Mainframe computer, 21,
74–77, 454
Manitoba Physical Fitness
Performance Test, 287
Mass testability, 166–67, 454
Master learning, 8
Mastery test, 383–84, 454
Matching test, 381, 391, 454
Mean, 44–45, 51, 52, 60, 455
reliability of, 71–72
standard error of, 71, 457
Mean score, 125, 126
Measurement:
common units of, 35
definition of, 4, 5, 26
functions of, 6
of group position, 47–53
standard error of, 98
See also Evaluation
Measurement and Evaluation
Council (AAHPERD),
343–44
Measurement error, 88–89,
98, 111, 125, 133
Measurement instruments,
167, 170
bicycle ergometer, 220–21,
224–25, 452
cable tensiometer, 184, 185
Cybex equipment, 187
dynamometer, 184, 453
goniometer, 208, 454
Leighton Flexometer, 208
pretesting of, 342
selection of, 341
skinfold calipers, 251–56,
292–94, 297, 457
treadmill, 10, 220–21
Universal gymnasium, 186,
193, 194
valid, *see* Validity
Median, 41–44, 58, 455
Medicine ball put test, 197–98
Metropolitan Relative Weight,
16
METs, 219, 240, 455
Microcomputer, 21–23, 77–83
Mode, 41, 58, 455
Mortality rate, exercise and,
16–19
Motivation, 6, 171, 431–33
Motor ability, 177–78
general, 174, 175, 176, 453
measurement of, 286
specificity of, 176

Static balance, 210–11, 457
Statistics with Finesse, 53, 83, 411
Steady state run test, 303–4
Step test, 457
Strength, muscular, *see* Muscular strength
Stress test, 240–41
  maximal, 455
Stroke for power or distance test, 330, 373
Student:
  appropriateness of test to, 165–66
  characteristics of, and test validity, 124
  concerns in test, 165–66
  evaluation of achievement of, 129–57
  handicapped, 166
  motivation of, 171
  placement of, 6
  preparation for test, 126, 338
  See also Youth
Subjective evaluation, 333–35, 457
Subjective test, 4
Subscapular skinfold, 252, 254, 257, 292–97, 308, 310, 313
Summative evaluation, 8, 9, 27, 131, 132, 135, 156–57, 383–84, 457
Suprailium skinfold, 252, 255, 257, 258
Swimming achievement for intermediate swimmers test, 364–66
Swimming rating scale, 340
Swimming skill test, 341, 364–66, 449
System information, 74

T

Tau coefficient, 97
Taxonomy, 457
Teacher, 5
  education programs for, 9
  grading by standards of, 138–39
Tennessee Self-Concept Scale, 423
Tennis skill test, 367–72, 450
Tensiometer, 457
Test:
  abstract, 123–24
  administration of, 168–72
  administrative concerns in, 166–68
  of attitude, 419–25
  of balance, 210–11
  of basic movement patterns, 202–10
  in battery, 165

of cardiorespiratory endurance, 218–42
characteristics of, 164–65
directions for, 167, 169, 385
discrimination, 164
of endurance, 199–202
enjoyability of, 166
equipment for, 167, 170
facility for, 170
of flexibility, 208–10
format of, 385, 386
F-test, 104–12
of general motor ability, 175
of health-related physical fitness, 20, 285–305
items of, *see* Test item
of kinesthetic perception, 211–12
of knowledge, *see* Knowledge test
lengthened, 125
of motor educability, 176
multiple-trial, 125, 126
of muscular power, 194–99
of muscular strength, 183–94
objective, 4, 381–83, 385
personnel for administering, 167
posttest procedures, 171–72
practice for, 167, 169–70, 171
preemployment, 21, 181–82
preparation for, 167, 338
pretest procedures for, 168–70
psychological, 417–41
resemblance to activity, 165
safety of, 166, 169, 171
specificity of, 165
of sport skill, *see* Sport skill test
student concerns in, 165–66
subjective, 4
time required for, 170, 338
Test, standardized:
  AAHPERD Health-Related Fitness, 7, 210, 276–77, 287–302, 313–17
  AAHPERD sport skill, 343–49
  AAHPERD Youth Fitness, 78–82, 145, 156, 175, 199–200, 202, 204, 206, 207, 277–85, 306–12, 316
  Barrow Motor Ability, 175
  Body Cathexis Scale, 432–34, 452
  Children's Attitude Toward Physical Activity, 428–31

Health-Related Physical Fitness battery, 202
Kraus-Weber, 210, 278
Manitoba Physical Fitness Performance, 287
Physical Estimation and Attraction Scale, 422–25
Sargent Physical Test of Man, 174
Scott Motor Ability, 175
South Carolina, 287
Texas, 202, 204–7, 278, 283–84, 285–86, 309
Texas Youth Fitness, 210, 277, 302–5, 311, 317
YMCA Fitness, 235, 263–65
YMCA strength, 186, 188–90
Testability, mass, 166–67
Test item, 385, 454
  analysis of, 408–13, 454
  difficulty of, 408, 454
  discrimination index, 408–10
  response quality, 410
  validity of, 410
Test-retest method, 90–91, 92, 114, 405, 457
Test-retest reliability, 164
Test score-T-score conversion table, 56–57
Test trial, 170
Texas Test, 202, 204–7, 278, 283–86, 309
Texas Youth Fitness Test, 210, 277, 302–5, 311, 317
Thigh skinfold, 250, 252, 256, 257, 258, 259
Throw for distance test (softball skill), 346
Throw for power or distance test, 330, 373
Throwing ability, measurement of, 207–8
Timed medley test (swimming skill), 365
Time required for test, 170, 338
Timmer Forehand and Backhand Drive Test, modified, 370–72
Title IX (Civil Rights Act, 1966), 20
Tournament standing, 122
Treadmill, 10
  motor-driven, 220–21
Treadmill exercise, 221, 228, 267
  energy cost of submaximal work, 224, 225
  maximal, 230, 231, 240